German and American
Constitutional Thought

Germany and the United States of America
The Krefeld Historical Symposia
Volume I

German and American Constitutional Thought

Contexts, Interaction, and Historical Realities

Edited by
Hermann Wellenreuther
with the assistance of
Claudia Schnurmann *and*
Thomas Krueger

BERG

New York / Oxford / Munich

Distributed exclusively in the U.S. and Canada by
St. Martin's Press, New York

First published in 1990 by
Berg Publishers, Inc.
Editorial offices:
165 Taber Avenue, Providence, RI 02906, U.S.A.
150 Cowley Road, Oxford OX4 1JJ, UK
Westermühlstraße 26, 8000 München 5, FRG

Library of Congress Cataloging-in-Publication Data

German and American constitutional thought : contexts, interaction,
  and historical realities / edited by Hermann Wellenreuther with the
  assistance of Claudia Schnurmann and Thomas Krueger.
      p.   cm.   — (Germany and the United States of America; v. 1)
    Papers and commentary from the Second Krefeld Historical Symposium
  held in May 1987 in Krefeld, West Germany.
    Includes bibliographical references.
    ISBN 0–85496–294–8
    1. Germany (West)—Constitutional history—Congresses.   2. United
  States—Constitutional history—Congresses.   I. Wellenreuther,
  Hermann.   II. Schnurmann, Claudia.   III. Krueger, Thomas.
  IV. Krefeld Historical Symposium (2nd : 1987 : Krefeld, Germany)
  V. Series.
  K3161.A3   1987a
  342.43′029—dc20
  [344.30229]   89–17619

British Library Cataloguing in Publication Data

German and American constitutional thought : contexts,
  interaction and historical realities. – (Germany and
  the United States of America : the Krefeld symposia;
  1).
  1. Germany. Constitution, history   2. United States.
  Constitution, history
  I. Wellenreuther, Hermann   II. Series
  344.302′29

ISBN 0–85496–294–8

Published with the assistance of the City of Krefeld, the Fritz
Thyssen Stiftung, and the Foreign Office of the German Federal
Republic.

Printed in Great Britain by
Billing & Sons Ltd, Worcester

Contents

Contents

Contents

Preface

Planning a program and organizing and directing a scholarly symposium provide innumerable opportunities for calling on others for help and assistance. The debt accumulated in the end is enormous – and indeed, this is why I am only able to single out a few instead of naming the many who have been so generous with their advice, time, and assistance. Among those few I must begin with the City of Krefeld, without whose help and constant understanding cooperation – and in concrete terms this is true especially for the support extended by the Lord Mayor as well as for that provided by the Verkehrsverein – this conference would have never gotten beyond the planning stage. After the first Krefeld Historical Symposium in 1983, Mayor Dieter Pützhofen and the Verkehrsverein's present director, Dr. H. Eichmanns, asked whether I would be willing to organize such symposia on a regular three-year basis. The resulting discussions not only produced the Academic Advisory Council (with Dr. Eichmanns representing the Verkehrsverein, Dr. Reinhard Feinendegen and Dr. Eugen Gerritz the City Council, Dr. Guido Rotthoff the City Archive, and Professors Erich Angermann, Hartmut Lehmann, Hans-Jürgen Schröder, and myself the academic side) but also the ideas that led to this symposium.

The reason that the City of Krefeld took this important, as well as for the historians rare, initiative was simple and straightforward: as in 1983, the city desired to make a concrete and material contribution toward improvement of German-American intellectual relations. And as was the case in 1983, the city was as good as its word (signaling the difference between the City of Krefeld and some particularly important politicians of this world): the city not only helped in a very material way in the preparations – in fact it made all the local arrangements – but took over well over one-third of the costs of the symposium and the publication of the conference proceedings. Finally, by underwriting the cost of a concert and two public receptions as well as a special dinner for the participants, Krefeld created a friendly and cordial atmosphere and prevented us from becoming buried in the dust of nineteenth-century paragraphs and constitutions.

There was yet another aspect that distinguished this conference from other gatherings, the effort to convey the conference's concerns to the citizens of Krefeld. This was done on three separate occasions: Dr. Dieter Buhl from *Die Zeit* was invited to give a public lecture on the importance of the American constitution; second, a panel composed of the chairpersons, ably chaired by Klaus Jürgen Haller from the West German Broadcasting System, discussed important results of the sessions with citizens; and last, publication of the proceedings not only in English, the international vernacular of historians, but also in German makes it more readily accessible.

As in so many endeavors, money is a necessary means to achieve scholarly ends. In this case it was generously provided not only by the City of Krefeld but by the Fritz Thyssen Foundation and by the German Federal Government through the Cultural Department of the German Foreign Office – all three deserve high praise for their generosity. These are tangible expressions of a firm determination to contribute to the improvement of scholarly relations between the United States and the Federal Republic of Germany.

Yet all this help and cooperation would have been in vain had the participants not lived up to the challenge: their cooperation in general and their willingness to meet deadlines and to submit cheerfully to the rigors of a stiff and demanding program were most important in making this symposium a success. We all had more to do than simply prepare for a symposium; often we snatched the hours before or after midnight to read the papers – the participants did that and more. As organizer and participating colleague I am grateful to them.

And finally, not only this publication, but the conference too, is the result of dedicated efforts by my most competent assistants – indeed, the German word "Mitarbeiter" is so much more adequate than the English "collaborator" or "assistants" because it signals that we were not a command unit but a team working together depending on each other's cooperation and understanding help. To all of them – Hannelore Peters, Claudia Schnurmann, Thomas Krueger, Ralf Pröve, and Joachim Gebert – I am deeply grateful. Claudia Schnurmann and Thomas Krueger worked especially hard in getting this publication out as soon as possible. They deserve praise for the quality of the edition; I will accept any blame for its deficiencies.

Introduction
German-American Constitutional History – The Past and the Present

Hermann Wellenreuther

German and American Studies of Each Other's Historical Traditions

German and American scholarly interest in each other's countries has varied considerably. This is not surprising considering the roles the countries have played in each other's history. While in the nineteenth century, to quote Rush Welter, American interest in constitutional developments in European countries in general and in Germany in particular was largely confined to detecting trends imitating the course initiated by the American Revolution,[1] German interest was shaped not only by the fascination with constitutional upheaval ushered in by the American Revolution, but by the fact that in the United States solutions to fundamental constitutional problems had already been worked out and tested. These same questions needed to be settled in Germany if the demand for German unification was to become a political and constitutional reality.[2] While up to now there has been, rightly or wrongly, very little American discussion of German influence on American

1. Rush Welter, *The Mind of America, 1820–1860* (New York, 1975), 50–51. For American interest in German constitutional developments of 1848 see below, Jörg-Detlef Kühne, "Civil Rights and German Constitutional Thought, 1848–1871."
2. German reaction and discussion of the American Revolution is analyzed in Horst Dippel, *Germany and the American Revolution, 1770–1800: A Sociohistorical Investigation of Late Eighteenth-Century Political Thinking*, trans. B.A. Uhlendorf, foreword by R.R. Palmer (Chapel Hill, NC, 1977), originally published as *Deutschland und die amerikanische Revolution: Sozialgeschichtliche Untersuchung zum politischen Bewußtsein im ausgehenden 18. Jahrhundert*, Diss. phil., Cologne 1972; German discussion of American notions of federalism is inter alia analyzed in Michael Dreyer, *Föderalismus als ordnungspolitisches und normative Prinzip: Das föderative Denken der Deutschen im 19. Jahrhundert*, Europäische Hochschulschriften, Series XXXI: Political Science, 102 (Frankfurt/Main, 1987).

1

constitutional or legal thought – in fact the latest comprehensive bibliography lists only two titles which can be supplemented by some additional work on Pufendorf's influence on American legal and constitutional thought and two studies of the activities of German forty-eighters in America[3] – there is a small but growing body of literature discussing American influences on German constitutional thought and developments.[4] In addition, a small but quite weighty body of German works discuss important aspects of American constitutional developments.[5]

3. Kermit L. Hall, *A Comprehensive Bibliography of American Constitutional and Legal History, 1896–1979*, 5 vols. (Millwood, NY, 1984–); Walter P. Metzger, "The German Contribution to the American Theory of Academic Freedom," *AAUP Bulletin* 41 (1955): 214–30; Leo L. Rockwell, "Academic Freedom – German Origin and American Development," *AAUP Bulletin* 36 (1950): 225–36; Daniel Augat, *Die Aufnahme der Lehren Samuel von Pufendorfs, 1632–1694, in das Recht der Vereinigten Staaten von Amerika* (Darmstadt, 1985); Carl Wittke, *Refugees of Revolution: The German Forty-Eighters in America* (Philadelphia, PA, 1952); A.E. Zucker, ed., *The Forty-Eighters: Political Refugees of the German Revolution of 1848* (New York, 1950); Eitel Wolf Dobert, *Deutsche Demokraten in Amerika: Die Achtundvierziger und ihre Schriften* (Göttingen, 1958).

4. Eckhart G. Franz, *Das Amerikabild der Deutschen Revolution von 1848/49: Zum Problem der Übertragung gewachsener Verfassungsformen*, Beihefte zum Jahrbuch für Amerikastudien, 2 (Heidelberg, 1958); Erich Angermann, "Republikanismus: Amerikanisches Vorbild und soziale Frage, 1848," *Die Welt als Geschichte* 21 (1961): 185–93; Rudolf Ullner, *Die Idee des Föderalismus im Jahrzehnt der deutschen Einigungskriege dargestellt unter besonderer Berücksichtigung des Modells der amerikanischen Verfassung für das deutsche politische Denken*, Historische Studien, 393 (Lübeck, 1965); Günter Moltmann, *Atlantische Blockpolitik im 19. Jahrhundert: Die Vereinigten Staaten und der deutsche Liberalismus während der Revolution von 1848/49* (Düsseldorf, 1973). The work of Ernst Fraenkel stands in a class by itself; probably no other scholar did more after the Second World War than he did to bridge the gap between German and American constitutional development. Among his important works are: *USA – Weltmacht wider Willen* (Berlin, 1957); *Amerika im Spiegel des politischen Denkens: Äußerungen deutscher Staatsmänner und Staatslehrer über Staat und Gesellschaft in den Vereinigten Staaten von Amerika* (Cologne, 1959); *Deutschland und die westlichen Demokratien* (Stuttgart, [5]1973); *Das amerikanische Regierungssystem: Eine politische Analyse* (Opladen, [3]1976). Equal in rank is the work of Carl J. Friedrich, *Der Verfassungsstaat der Neuzeit*, Enzyklopädie der Rechts- und Staatswissenschaft, Abteilung Staatswissenschaft (Berlin, 1953), originally published as *Constitutional Government and Democracy* (New York, 1937), a work of unsurpassed scope. The latest summary of this work is in Ulrich Scheuner, "Constitutional Traditions in the United States and in Germany," in Wilhelm A. Kewenig, ed., *Deutsch-Amerikanisches Verfassungsrechtssymposium 1976/American – German Bicentennial Symposium on Constitutional Law*, Veröffentlichungen des Instituts für Internationales Recht an der Universität Kiel, 78 (Berlin, 1978), 11–36, 23–30.

5. Walter Jellinek, ed., *Georg Jellinek, Die Erklärung der Menschen- und Bürgerrechte: Ein Beitrag zur modernen Verfassungsgeschichte* (Munich, [3]1919); Otto Vossler, *Die amerikanischen Revolutionsideale in ihrem Verhältnis zu den europäischen: Untersucht an Thomas Jefferson* (Munich, 1929); Willi Paul Adams, *Republikanismus und die ersten*

If one moves away from the narrower confines of constitutional history, however, the case is quite different. Then the handful of German monographs on American nineteenth- and twentieth-century history is no match at all for the American scholarly work covering all aspects of German foreign[6] and home affairs,[7] of economic,[8] cultural and educational,[9] religious,[10] intellectual,[11] and

---

amerikanischen Einzelstaatsverfassungen: Zur ideengeschichtlichen und verfassungs-geschichtlichen Komponente der amerikanischen Revolution, 1775–1780, Diss. phil., Berlin, 1968, American ed., *The First American Constitutions: Republican Ideology and the Making of the State Constitutions in the Revolutionary Era*, trans. Rita and Robert Kimber (Chapel Hill, NC, 1980); Gerald Stourzh, *Alexander Hamilton and the Idea of Republican Government* (Stanford, CA, 1970); idem, *Benjamin Franklin and American Foreign Policy* (Chicago, IL, 1954); Jürgen Heideking, *Die Verfassung vor dem Richter-stuhl: Vorgeschichte und Ratifizierung der amerikanischen Verfassung, 1787–1791* (Berlin, 1988), to date the most incisive and complete analysis of the public debate on the American Constitution and the Bill of Rights in any language.

6. William E. Griffith, *The Ostpolitik of the Federal Republic of Germany*, Studies in Communism, Revisionism, and Revolution, 24 (Cambridge, MA, 1978); Hans W. Gatzke, *Germany and the United States: A "Special Relationship"?* (Cambridge, MA, 1980); Anthony Komjathy and Rebecca Stockwell, *German Minorities and the Third Reich: Ethnic Germans of East Central Europe between the Wars* (New York, 1980); William W. Hagen, *Germans, Poles, and Jews: The Nationality Conflict in the Prussian East, 1772–1914* (Chicago, IL, 1980).

7. Kenneth R. Calkins, *Hugo Haase: Democrat and Revolutionary* (Durham, NC, 1979); Lawrence J. Baack, *Christian Bernstorff and Prussia: Diplomacy and Reform Conservatism, 1818–1832* (New Brunswick, NJ, 1980); Paul R. Sweet, *Wilhelm von Humboldt: A Biography*, 2 vols. (Columbus, OH, 1978–80); Wayne C. Thompson, *In the Eye of the Storm: Kurt Riezler and the Crisis of Modern Germany* (Iowa City, IA, 1980); Lloyd E. Lee, *The Politics of Harmony: Civil Service, Liberalism, and Social Reform in Baden, 1800–1850* (Newark, DE, 1980); William Harvey Maehl, *August Bebel: Shadow Emperor of the German Workers*, Memoirs of the American Philosophical Society, 138 (Philadelphia , PA, 1980); Robert P. Grathwol, *Stresemann and the DNVP: Reconciliation or Revenge in German Foreign Policy, 1924–1928* (Lawrence, KS, 1980).

8. Lawrence Schofer, *The Formation of a Modern Labor Force: Upper Silesia, 1865–1914* (Berkeley, CA, 1975); Shulamit Volkov, *The Rise of Popular Antimodern-ism in Germany: The Urban Master Artisans, 1873–1896* (Princeton, NJ, 1978).

9. Charles E. McClelland, *State, Society, and University in Germany, 1700–1914* (New York, 1980); L.J. Rather, *The Dream of Self-Destruction: Wagner's Ring and the Modern World* (Baton Rouge, LA, 1979); David Gross, *The Writer and Society: Heinrich Mann and Literary Politics in Germany, 1890–1940* (Atlantic Highlands, NJ, 1980); Anthony J. La Vopa, *Prussian Schoolteachers: Profession and Office, 1763–1848* (Chapel Hill, NC, 1980).

10. Ernst Christian Helmreich, *The German Churches under Hitler: Background, Struggle, and Epilogue* (Detroit, MI, 1979).

11. Thomas E. Willey, *Back to Kant: The Revival of Kantianism in German Social and Historical Thought, 1860–1914* (Detroit, MI, 1978); Gary P. Steenson, *Karl Kautsky, 1854–1938: Marxism in the Classical Years* (Pittsburgh, PA, 1978); Warren B. Morris, Jr., *The Revisionist Historians and German War Guilt*, Studies in Revisionist Historiography

military[12] affairs, as well as anti-Semitic and racist[13] attitudes, urban[14] development, and social life,[15] all attested to by my sample of reviews in the *American Historical Review* for the years 1980 and 1981.

American coverage of German history (and my sample also demonstrates this) is in its scope rather uneven: compared with the twentieth century, the period before 1870 receives rather little attention. In a way, the work of those German historians like Hajo Holborn, Leonard Krieger, and Hans Rosenberg,[16] who had fled to the United States during the Third Reich – and whose activities mark the beginning and the renaissance of German historiography in the United States – still dominates American notions about the Old Empire and the early nineteenth century, although Karl Otmar Freiherr von Aretin's revisionist and on the whole positive picture of the Old Empire has recently been energetically endorsed by the American historian John G. Gagliardo.[17]

Yet let me quickly add that German scholarly work on the

(New York, 1977); Paul Gottfried, *Conservative Millenarians: The Romantic Experience in Bavaria* (New York, 1979); Michael Ermarth, *Wilhelm Dilthey: The Critique of Historical Reason* (Chicago, IL, 1978); Ronald Hayman, *Nietzsche: A Critical Life* (New York, 1980); Ilse N. Bulhof, *Wilhelm Dilthey: A Hermeneutic Approach to the Study of History and Culture*, Martinus Nijhoff Philosophy Library, 2 (Boston, MA, 1980); H.P. Rickman, *Wilhelm Dilthey: Pioneer of the Human Studies* (Berkeley, CA, 1979).

12. Edward W. Bennett, *German Rearmament and the West, 1932–1933* (Princeton, NJ, 1979); David Clay Large, *The Politics of Law and Order: A History of the Bavarian Einwohnerwehr, 1918–1921*, Transactions of the American Philosophical Society, 70, pt. 2 (Philadelphia, PA, 1980).

13. Christopher R. Browning, *The Final Solution and the German Foreign Office: A Study of Referat D III of Abteilung Deutschland, 1940–43* (New York, 1978); Sanford Ragins, *Jewish Responses to Anti-Semitism in Germany, 1870–1914: A Study in the History of Ideas* (Cincinnati, OH, 1980); Donald L. Niewyk, *The Jews in Weimar Germany* (Baton Rouge, LA, 1980).

14. David F. Crew, *Town in the Ruhr: A Social History of Bochum, 1860–1914* (New York, 1979); Jeffry M. Diefendorf, *Businessmen and Politics in the Rhineland, 1789–1834* (Princeton, NJ, 1980).

15. Marion A. Kaplan, *The Jewish Feminist Movement in Germany: The Campaigns of the Jüdischer Frauenbund, 1904–1938*, Contributions in Women's Studies, 8 (Westport, CT, 1979); Jean H. Quataert, *Reluctant Feminists in German Social Democracy, 1885–1917* (Princeton, NJ, 1979).

16. Hajo Holborn, *A History of Modern Germany: Deutsche Geschichte in der Neuzeit* (Stuttgart, 1960); Hans Rosenberg, *Bureaucracy, Aristocracy, Autocracy: The Prussian Experience, 1660–1815* (Cambridge, MA, 1958). Leonard Krieger, *The German Idea of Freedom: History of a Political Tradition* (Boston, MA, 1957).

17. John G. Gagliardo, *Reich and Nation: The Holy Roman Empire as Idea and Reality, 1763–1806* (Bloomington, IN, 1980), x–xi.

United States is also heavily focused on the twentieth century; except for two recent general surveys of American history[18] and those works on the revolutionary period cited above, only five monographs deal with the period before 1800,[19] while another three treat the first[20] and yet another three the latter part of the nineteenth century.[21] The larger part of the remainder – among them the important monographs by Knud Krakau on American foreign policy and the works of Reinhard R. Doerries, Klaus Schwabe, Hans-Jürgen Schröder, Detlev Junker, and Werner Link on German-American relations – belongs to this century.[22] Among

18. Hans R. Guggisberg, *Geschichte der USA*, 2 vols. (Stuttgart, [2]1979); Udo Sautter, *Geschichte der Vereinigten Staaten von Amerika* (Stuttgart, [3]1986).
19. Dietmar Rothermund, *The Layman's Progress: Religious and Political Experience in Colonial Pennsylvania, 1740–1770* (Philadelphia, PA, 1961); Hermann Wellenreuther, *Glaube und Politik in Pennsylvania, 1681–1776: Die Wandlungen der Obrigkeitsdoktrin und des Peace Testimony der Quäker*, Kölner Historische Abhandlungen, 20 (Cologne, 1972); Karl Tilmann Winkler, *Von der Sklaverei in den Kolonien: Eine Untersuchung des Zusammenhanges zwischen der Entfaltung überseeischer Territorien und der Sklaverei an Hand von Virginia im 18. Jahrhundert* (Ann Arbor, MI, 1977); Gerhard Kollmann, *Revolution und Kontinuität: Eine Untersuchung der Pläne und Ansätze zur Organisation der Gebiete zwischen Appallachen und Mississippi, 1774–1786*, Diss. phil., Cologne, 1976; Barbara Krüger, *Die amerikanischen Loyalisten: Eine Studie der Beziehungen zwischen England und Amerika von 1776–1802*, Europäische Hochschulschriften, Reihe III: Geschichte und ihre Hilfswissenschaften, 73 (Frankfurt/ Main, 1977).
20. Marie-Luise Frings, *Henry Clays American System und die sektionale Kontroverse in den Vereinigten Staaten von Amerika, 1815–1829*, Europäische Hochschulschriften, Reihe III: Geschichte und ihre Hilfswissenschaften, 117 (Frankfurt/Main, 1979); Harald Thomas, *Das zweite amerikanische Parteiensystem im sektionalen Spannungsfeld, 1840–1850*, Europäische Hochschulschriften, Reihe III: Geschichte und ihre Hilfswissenschaften, 245 (Frankfurt/Main, 1984); Norbert Finzsch, *Die Goldgräber Kaliforniens: Arbeitsbedingungen, Lebensstandard und politisches System um die Mitte des 19. Jahrhunderts*, Kritische Studien zur Geschichtswissenschaft, 53 (Göttingen, 1982).
21. Hans-Ulrich Wehler, *Der Aufstieg des amerikanischen Imperialismus: Studien zur Entwicklung des Imperium Americanum, 1865–1900*, Kritische Studien zur Geschichtswissenschaft, 10 (Göttingen, 1974); Elisabeth Glaser-Schmidt, *"Die Philippinen den Filipinos!": Die amerikanische Debatte über die Wirtschafts- und Verwaltungspolitik auf den Philippinen, 1898–1906*, Europäische Hochschulschriften, Reihe III: Geschichte und ihre Hilfswissenschaften, 311 (Frankfurt/Main, 1986); Ragnhild Fiebig-von Hase, *Lateinamerika als Konfliktherd der deutsch- amerikanischen Beziehungen, 1890–1903: Vom Beginn der Panamerikapolitik bis zur Venezuelakrise von 1902–03*, Schriftenreihe der Historischen Kommission bei der Bayerischen Akademie der Wissenschaften, 27, 2 pts. (Göttingen, 1986).
22. Knud Krakau, *Missionsbewußtsein und Völkerrechtsdoktrin in den Vereinigten Staaten von Amerika* (Frankfurt/Main, 1967); idem, *Die kubanische Revolution und die Monroe-Doktrin: Eine Herausforderung der Außenpolitik der Vereinigten Staaten* (Frankfurt/Main, 1968); Reinhard R. Doerries, *Washington – Berlin, 1908/1917: Die Tätigkeit des Botschafters Johann Heinrich Graf von Bernstorff in Washington vor dem*

various attempts at general surveys of U.S. history in the twentieth century only one stands out, that of Erich Angermann.[23] What are we to conclude from all this work? I think three points deserve to be made: first, it is clearly obvious that American historians and American society at large are much more interested in German history than vice versa.[24] As Wolfgang Helbich's survey documented, the reasons for this sorry state of affairs in Germany are to be found in the – again compared with American colleges and universities – tiny number of teaching and research positions related to American history.[25] Second, although there is a much larger body of work done by American scholars on earlier German periods, this work is to a considerable extent lost to the over-

---

Eintritt der Vereinigten Staaten von Amerika in den Ersten Weltkrieg (Düsseldorf, 1975); Klaus Schwabe, *Deutsche Revolution und Wilson-Friede: Die amerikanische und deutsche Friedensstrategie zwischen Ideologie und Machtpolitik 1918/19* (Düsseldorf, 1971); Werner Link, *Die amerikanische Stabilisierungspolitik in Deutschland, 1921–1932* (Düsseldorf, 1970); Hans-Jürgen Schröder, *Deutschland und die Vereinigten Staaten, 1933–1939: Wirtschaft und Politik in der Entwicklung des deutsch-amerikanischen Gegensatzes*, Veröffentlichungen des Instituts für Europäische Geschichte, 59 (Wiesbaden, 1970); Detlev Junker, *Der unteilbare Weltmarkt: Das ökonomische Interesse in der Außenpolitik der USA, 1933–1941* (Stuttgart, 1975); Klaus Kipphan, *Deutsche Propaganda in den Vereinigten Staaten, 1933–1941* (Heidelberg, 1971); Werner Link, *Deutsche und amerikanische Gewerkschaften und Geschäftsleute, 1945–1975: Eine Studie über transnationale Beziehungen* (Düsseldorf, 1978); Ernst-Otto Czempiel, *Das amerikanische Sicherheitssystem, 1945–1949: Studie zur Außenpolitik der bürgerlichen Gesellschaft* (Berlin, 1966).

23. Erich Angermann, *Die Vereinigten Staaten von Amerika seit 1917* (Munich, ⁶1978).

24. It is obvious that the large percentage of German immigrants in American society is directly related to the greater American interest in German history. It is, however, extremely difficult to go beyond this rather general statement. Related to this "ethnic" argument is the strong interest in the history of one's own family which has no counterpart in Europe, including Germany. German interest in the United States also profited from this "ethnic" factor. Before the Second World War it led to a considerable number of works dealing with "Auslandsdeutsche" and, more prominently, to a large body of journalistic descriptions of the United States. From the First World War on the focus on the "Auslandsdeutsche" coincided with the politically motivated renewed interest in the history of England and North America as enemy countries. I have described the mixture of both and the resulting scholarly work at Göttingen University in Hermann Wellenreuther, "Mutmaßungen über ein Defizit: Göttingens Geschichtswissenschaft und die angelsächsische Welt," in Hartmut Boockmann and Hermann Wellenreuther, eds., *Geschichtswissenschaft in Göttingen: Eine Vorlesungsreihe*, Göttinger Universitätsschriften, Serie A: Schriften, 2 (Göttingen, 1987), 261–86.

25. Wolfgang J. Helbich, "United States History in the Federal Republic of Germany: Teaching and Research," in Lewis Hanke, ed., *Guide to the Study of United States History outside the U.S., 1945–1980*, vol. 2 (White Plains, NY, 1985), 39–133.

whelming part of the American historical profession as a result of their much more sophisticated specialization; indeed, there seems to be preciously little cross-fertilization between American specialists in American history and those working in European or German history. This is certainly a bit less true for German historians who have to cover much larger periods in their lectures, thus forcing them more often into unfamiliar fields – American history sometimes being one of them. Only in conferences is the American specialist in German or American history likely to find himself confronted with the history of another country. Recognizing this provided the general rationale for the Krefeld German-American symposia; what prompted the theme of this symposium however, was the third conclusion, namely, that there is a the lamentable lack of scholarship on and knowledge of each other's constitutional developments over the last two hundred years.

The Methodology of Comparative History

Within the historical as well as the legal scholarly community widespread skepticism prevails about the possibility and profitability of comparative history. Indeed at the end of the second Krefeld Historical Symposium Clyde Summers aptly summarized these feelings. He said: "I have come to the conclusion that there is something much more difficult than comparative labor law and that is comparative history. And indeed, at the moment I am nearly persuaded that it may well be nearly impossible to the human mind to deal with comparative history except in a very fragmentary way. I can only say that I admire the boldness and courage of the historians who engage in this enterprise and I wish them well. I am not entirely convinced that they will not feel more frustrated than I am."[26]

This sober summary of one scholar's reactions to three days of relentless and often rather unsystematic efforts to compare complex historical processes echoes scholars' earlier expressions of frustration after similar experiences. Thus C. Vann Woodward, in his introduction to a collection of essays entitled *A Comparative Approach to American History*, noted not without irony that "when the historian combines the instincts of his guild with a conviction about

---

26. See Clyde W. Summers's comments, 499.

the distinctiveness and uniqueness of the national experience he studies, he is likely to be skeptical about experiments with comparative analysis."[27] Woodward's dry statement can be supplemented by similar reluctant assessments. The late Theodor Schieder warned against too much faith in comparative methods[28] – for he too considered the uniqueness of the historical process an insurmountable barrier to sensible comparisons. Woodward and Schieder share the skepticism of the common man against comparing apples with pears.

Comparing apples and pears lacks scholarly sophistication. Yet we cannot overlook that both belong to the same family. They are fruits that share certain common features: they grow on trees, are dependent on the careful grafting skills of the horticulturist, grow for similar reasons – the protection of the seeds they encapsule – and are cherished for their tastiness. In short, they are within limitation subject to some general laws of nature which can be formulated and proven. These laws do not necessarily negate the uniqueness of apples or pears, so some maintain, but serve to clarify and define their relation to other plants. Ocular proof and simple tasting – and both are practical ways of comparing – confirm our naive suspicion that apples and pears may have more in common with each other than with raspberries or cranberries. In an analogue to these tasty procedures, a recent scholar has summarized the received wisdom that observed general similarities of historical processes can only be validated and tested by subjecting them to tests employing intercultural comparisons;[29] he could have meant something like comparing berries with apples and pears.

If Woodward, Schieder, Frederickson,[30] and other scholars are right, then historians, probably largely prompted by the implications of their methodology, remain preoccupied with the unique-

27. Comer Vann Woodward, ed., *A Comparative Approach to American History*, Voice of America Forum Lectures (New York, 1968), 16.

28. Theodor Schieder, "Möglichkeiten und Grenzen vergleichender Methoden in der Geschichtswissenschaft," in Theodor Schieder, *Geschichte als Wissenschaft: Eine Einführung* (Munich, 1965), 187–211.

29. Josef Meran, *Theorien in der Geschichtswissenschaft: Die Diskussion über die Wissenschaftlichkeit der Geschichte*, Kritische Studien zur Geschichtswissenschaft, 66 (Göttingen, 1985), 135.

30. George M. Frederickson, "Comparative History," in Michael Kammen, ed., *The Past before Us: Contemporary Historical Writing in the United States* (Ithaca, NY, 1980), 457–73.

ness of the apple. While not denying the truism that "all history that aims at explanation or interpretation involves some type of explicit or implicit comparison,"[31] they shy away from comparing complex entities like nations, states, cities, ideologies, cultures, or concepts. Yet there are exceptions: Barrington Moore and C.E. Black on a large scale; George M. Frederickson, Carl Degler, and Herbert S. Klein, for instance, on a more circumscribed scale within the American profession; and Jürgen Kocka and Hans-Jürgen Puhle within the German profession readily come to mind.[32] There is a fundamental difference in approach between these historians which I think reflects some of the uneasiness of Clyde Summers's complaint: some like Moore, Black, Puhle, and Kocka employ a social science approach, start with a theory, and aim at large-scale explanatory models, while others refrain from model building and rigorous definition of variables and criteria and focus on complex historical phenomena and relationships which are more impressionistically rather than rigorously compared with each other over time. Thus they invite the frequently voiced complaint that they indulge in "an exercise much akin to a comparison between apples and pineapples or between horses and cows," as one reviewer described Frederickson's comparison of South Africa and American racial attitudes.[33]

Is there a via media between the two approaches? Or put differently,

31. Ibid., 457; see also Hans-Jürgen Puhle, "Theorien in der Praxis des vergleichenden Historikers," in Jürgen Kocka and Thomas Nipperdey, eds., *Theorie und Erzählung in der Geschichte*, Theorie der Geschichte: Beiträge zur Historik, 3 (Munich, 1979), 120: "Es ist schon immer verglichen worden, wenn auch oft eher implizit, naiv und (methoden-) unbewußt. Jede historische Begriffsbildung, die sich auf mehr als nur ein eng und exakt umgrenztes singuläres Phänomen bezieht (also fast jede historische Begriffsbildung) impliziert, bewußt oder unbewußt, vorausgegangenes Vergleichen. Jede im Ansatz idealtypische oder modellhafte Verallgemeinerung resultiert aus einem Vergleich."

32. Barrington Moore, *Social Origins of Dictatorship and Democracy: Lord and Peasant in the Making of the Modern World* (Boston, MA, 1966); C.E. Black, *The Dynamics of Modernization: A Study in Comparative History* (New York, 1966); George M. Frederickson, *White Supremacy: A Comparative Study in American and South African History* (New York, 1981); Carl N. Degler, *Neither Black nor White: Slavery and Race Relations in Brazil and the United States* (New York, 1971); Herbert S. Klein, *Slavery in the Americas: A Comparative Study of Cuba and Virginia* (Chicago, IL, 1967); Jürgen Kocka, *Angestellte zwischen Faschismus und Demokratie. Zur politischen Sozialgeschichte der Angestellten: USA 1890–1940 im internationalen Vergleich*, Kritische Studien zur Geschichtswissenschaft, 25 (Göttingen, 1977); Hans-Jürgen Puhle, *Politische Agrarbewegungen in kapitalistischen Industriegesellschaften* (Göttingen, 1975).

33. Review by Franklin W. Knight in *American Historical Review* 86 (1981): 1140.

9

can complex ideas and concepts of the type studied by Frederickson be reduced to clearly defined variables and factors that can be singled out and isolated from the other component parts of the whole construct? For this does seem to me to be the point at issue between the humanistic and social science approaches. Does such a rigorous process not destroy the wholeness of a concept and thus a necessary part of the quality of the individual part? The problems raised by these questions are of truely awesome dimensions: do we have instruments gauging the weight and substance of ideas? Do we have a way to separate ideas from concrete social units (individuals, groups, families, corporate beings, etc.)? Of course all this is possible, depending on the slice we are willing to cut away from the one or other piece in order to make it fit the norm established by the logic of comparability or on the amount we are willing to count as a loss in order to focus on the "comparable" part. Alternatively, we can make things fit by reducing phenomena to Max Weber's cherished *Idealtypus*, for instance. My skepticism may be evident by the way I am raising these questions.

While I am a firm believer in comparative history and in the usefulness of comparisons, I admit that I am extremely skeptical about the possibility of using rigorous comparative methods within the field of historical analysis. Complaining about this will not do, I believe, for the impossibility of using rigorous comparative methods is rooted in the nature of historical phenomena themselves. But if we conscientiously stick to the rules of our trade (which, for example, enjoin us to define clearly the thing we want to talk about), we *should* and indeed in this volume we *do* come up with new, exciting, and important results.

In a typical German fashion I have started out with the beginning of the creation and have discoursed about its fate over the centuries until I arrived at what I had planned to say in the beginning. Carl Degler's approach is somewhat more direct. In his presidential address he began by defining the purpose of history for the American people as providing answers to the question of "what there is about them that makes them Americans" and then forcefully and directly entered his eloquent plea for comparative history as a way of "finding out how we have differed from others."[34]

34. Carl N. Degler, "In Pursuit of an American History," *American Historical Review* 92 (1987): 6–7.

The papers published in this collection are based on a similar matter-of-fact approach. Since there simply is no consensus – and probably never will be – on methods for comparative history, the contributors were not asked to use a particular methodology. Theoretical problems aside, there was a practical reason for such restraint: to my knowledge there are very few scholars in either the United States or Germany whose scholarly expertise allows them to discuss any of the central issues of this conference in a comparative manner. This is less a matter of human failing but instead a reflection, first, of the extreme complexity of the state of scholarship with respect to the six core questions dealt with during the conference,[35] and second, of the degree of specialization as well as organizational structure of the historical and legal professions in both countries.[36]

Faced with methodological uncertainty and a high degree of professional specialization, exploration of the comparative dimension of the problems chosen for the conference was dealt with only in the discussion. The contributors, who were chosen for their scholarly expertise in their particular fields, were asked to examine essentially identical problems that agitated the two respective nations during particular periods. It will be obvious to the reader that the richness of details and the specificity of situations made streamlining the historical processes for rigorous comparison impossible and that more often the discussion resulted in underlining the uniqueness rather than the similarity of developments, attitudes, and reactions to basically similar phenomena. If anything, the lengthy discussions more often than not put into sharper focus "those traits or developments that were peculiar to Americans" as well as Germans, to quote Carl Degler once more.[37]

The Application of Comparative History

In order to illustrate my concluding remarks above, I will report on and discuss some of the results of the symposium. The conference

35. Ibid., 1. Degler indeed begins his address by stating that "American history has splintered."

36. Frederickson, "Comparative History" (see n. 30), 459. His remarks apply too, although to a lesser extent, to the German profession.

37. Degler, "In Pursuit" (see n. 34), 3.

11

began with a session focusing on the concept of federalism in Europe and in North America in the latter part of the eighteenth century. In his detailed analysis of the federal structure of the German Reich, Helmut Neuhaus argued that the imperial federal structure even in the second half of the eighteenth century retained vitality and real meaning. The American founding fathers' rather sharp critique of German federalism was, he concluded, somewhat out of touch with reality. Hans R. Guggisberg's comment supplemented Neuhaus's description with a brief analysis of the Swiss and Dutch Confederations in which individual members, at least in theory, enjoyed equal status. Peter Onuf's paper concentrated on the interplay of three ideas in defining the new constitutional reality of 1788: the notions of peaceful, federally controlled expansion, of a strong consolidated national government, and of a federally guaranteed order in the new territories within which acceptable economic concepts could freely develop.

Both papers were subjected to some criticism: Hartmut Lehmann shed doubts on Neuhaus's central argument about the vitality of formal federal structures. To his mind, in the eighteenth century informal power circles formed by the leading dynasties of the empire were of more importance than formal structures.[38] On the other hand, in my discussion of Onuf's paper I pointed to considerable criticism in the newly opened western territories as evidence of considerable dissatisfaction with the "colonial system" established by the Northwest Ordinance of 1787.[39] I did concede, however, that from a federal and long-term perspective these

38. In 1760/61, during the debate about the English-Prussian alliance, much of the argument focused on disagreement about the nature of the Reich. While Israel Mauduit based his argument on the assumption that the federal nature of the Reich was alive and well, concluding that therefore the war between Prussia and Habsburg was but a civil war within the Reich (see [Israel Mauduit], *Considerations on the Present German War* [London, 1760], his opponents maintained that the Reich was a fiction because the members enjoyed full sovereignty and were free to enter alliances with other powers and to declare war or conclude peace at their pleasure, and thus they viewed the war between Prussia and Habsburg as a normal military conflict between two independent states, cf. N.N., *A Full and Candid Answer to a Pamphlet Entitled Considerations on the Present German War* (London, 1760).

39. Cf. Hermann Wellenreuther, "'First Principles of Freedom' und die Vereinigten Staaten als Kolonialmacht, 1787–1803: Die Northwest Ordinance von 1787 und ihre Verwirklichung im Northwest Territory," in Erich Angermann, ed., "Revolution und Bewahrung: Untersuchungen zum Spannungsgefüge von revolutionärem Selbstverständnis und politischer Praxis in den Vereinigten Staaten von Amerika," *Historische Zeitschrift*, Beiheft, 5 (1979): 89–188.

grumblings should not be overrated.

In the discussion a number of additional avenues were explored. Taking up Onuf's argument about the acceptance of federalism as a constitutional framework for expansion, Robert Post raised the question of the citizens' identification with the Constitution. As a criterion for comparison this seemed, however, as Hartmut Lehmann pointed out, not to carry very far, since *Reichspatriotismus* was largely absent in eighteenth-century Germany. Subjects identified more with their individual territorial states than with the Reich. The question of whether it is possible to talk about at least incipient nationalism in North America remained unexplored; the answer would, I think, largely depend on whether it is possible to identify adherence to "revolution principles" with nationalism. Does this mean, Timothy Breen asked, that the common man was not affected by federalism? Should it not, on the contrary, be argued that federalism provided the frame as well as the possibility for furthering differing regional cultures – both in the Reich and in the young American republic? This argument could be and was extended into another area, giving rise to heated discussions in the Constitutional Convention. It was also a key factor for the power relations of member states of the Reich in the eighteenth century as well as later, in the middle of the nineteenth century, when according to Gerhard A. Ritter, it developed into one of the key issues during the debate on German unification – the concept of hegemonial federalism.

Onuf had shown the importance of the conflict between small landless and large land-rich states in the Constitutional Convention. This had been resolved by "federalizing" the western territory of states like Virginia or New York as well as by balancing interests in the bicameral system. For the time being the notion of a hegemony of the large states over the smaller ones seemed defeated. But, as later discussion was to make clear, that notion cropped up again in the preponderance of regions[40] – South, North, West – that endangered the precarious balance during much of the period before the outbreak of the Civil War. Indeed, efforts to institutionalize the hegemony of particular regions in the end required a military solution in much the same way that the Austrian-Prussian conflict in the mid-1860s only seemed solvable on the battleground.

---

40. Frings, *Henry Clays American System* (see n. 20), passim.

This discussion again led to another related issue, the relationship between federalism and expansion: Did Onuf's central argument about federalism providing a possibility for peaceful expansion, so Paul Finkelman asked, not point to stark contrasts in Europe where expansion within as well as without the Reich only seemed possible through conquest? Was Prussia's robbing Silesia from Habsburg – as Maria Theresa at least saw it – not a blatant case in point illustrating too, as Hartmut Lehmann had suggested, one more breakdown in federal and imperial mechanisms? Doubt was cast on this notion. Gerald Stourzh pointed out that expansion within the Reich was usually a peaceful process achieved through inheritance. Even when acquired in war, the new sovereign as a rule respected the internal constitutional setup of a conquered territory and especially the privileges of the *Stände* – something that could not be claimed for North American expansion, at least with respect to the American Indians' original ownership of the land. And as for imperial mechanisms, Grete Klingenstein added, these at least did not really match the new idea of the state as an orderly machine constructed to achieve maximum efficiency. There was no way that the Reich's somewhat archaic structures, steeped with notions and rights dating back to the Middle Ages, could be adapted to the idea of a state functioning as smoothly as a well greased clockwork.

The papers in Part 2 can be read on different levels: on the one level they describe the tensions between ideas, experiences, and reality: it was the exposure to reality, as Grete Klingenstein argued in her paper, that slowly transformed the American traveler William Stephen Smith's enlightened ideas about rule in Prussia and Austria; and in the same way it was the experience of rule during the colonial period that loomed large in the debates of the Constitutional Convention in Philadelphia in the summer of 1787, as Ralph Ketcham pointed out and Timothy Breen underlined. Conversely, of course, in thinking about rule German eighteenth-century enlightened minds were less concerned about reality than about governing as an activity guided by a supreme idea from which all practical political measures were to be deduced. Yet again, in a parallel to the debates in America, Germans drew on practical experiences and theoretical insights in the 1780s and also started to develop concepts aimed at circumscribing the power of rulers on the one hand while safeguarding fundamental rights on the other, as Diethelm Klippel showed.

The notion of the state as a machine in which each individual part was finely tuned to the needs of the other parts in order to guarantee efficiency, regularity, and the attainment of happiness (*Glückseligkeit*) escaped the American traveler on his way to Vienna – although he was quite familiar with the concept of the state as machine – as did the theoretical insights on which the enlightened notions of rule of jurists like Franz von Zeiller were based. For he and other enlightened Germans shared with their American counterparts, so Ketcham insisted and Hartmut Lehmann somewhat less enthusiastically agreed, a culture shaped by Aristotle and ancient political and philosophical thought as well as at least a passing knowledge of the "famous" Mr. Locke and Montesquieu.

American and German basic philosophical concepts were not so fundamentally different in the last decades of the eighteenth century as is often thought. What turned America into the "Freystaaten," as the young republic was called at first in Germany, was a radically different *reality*, as Timothy Breen demonstrated, premised on the reality of rule shared between the people as the *pouvoir constitutant* and the rulers. In Europe on the other hand the ruler retained the *potestas legibus soluta*, the sole competence to formulate and ordain laws – although at least in some member states of the Reich this competence was limited by the right of *Landtage* to participate in legislation.[41] Yet Diethelm Klippel added that after 1780 in Germany, too, writers bound rulers to natural and fundamental laws while even earlier – in fact going back to the sixteenth century[42] – German rulers had realized that rule without the cooperation of their subjects meant flirting with disaster.

The discussion focused on two related problems: first, on the means available for governing in Germany and on those provided for in the American Constitution and, second, on the experience of

41. This problem remained unexplored during the discussion – which to some extent reflects the deplorable lack of modern research into the function and importance of *Landtage* in the eighteenth and first part of the nineteenth centuries. For Hesse a scholar has recently pointed out that, even in the latter part of the eighteenth century, the *Landtagsausschuß* had a much larger and important part in framing and shaping legislation than hitherto believed, Charles W. Ingrao, *The Hessian Mercenary State: Ideas, Institutions, and Reform under Frederick II, 1760–1785* (Cambridge, 1987), 38.

42. Bernard Guenée, *L'Occident aux xiv et xv siècles* (Paris, ²1981); English ed., *States and Rulers in Later Medieval Europe*, trans. Juliet Vale (Oxford, 1985), has pointed out that rulers in the fifteenth century began to realize that effective government required their subjects' cooperation and acceptance of that rule.

rule. James Hutson, while conceding the founding fathers' belief in the necessity for a strong executive, queried whether the Constitution did in fact grant the necessary means for governing energetically. On a more general level Grete Klingenstein pointed out that in Europe the notion of active rule supplanting that of maintaining the status quo was quite new in the second half of the eighteenth century. "Activity" in this context meant two different things: constant traveling around, inspecting the conditions of the country – which of course was an old notion characteristic of rulers in the fifteenth and sixteenth centuries – and improving conditions by formulating new laws geared toward shaping a happier future. This latter concept indeed marked one of the dividing lines between the American (and English) notions of rule and its German version. The Constitution of 1787 defined the president's duty as one of "execut[ing] the laws," which according to Fred L. Morrison even implied the possibility of an impass – Ralph Ketcham thought the concept of *balance* more appropriate – between the legislative and the executive branches. Did "executing the law" – a notion surely not calling for energetic initiatives – mean that laws were applied with equal force to everyone? Did Germans, in other words, so William Wiecek queried, know the notion of "rule of law"? And were the rulers, too, *under* or *above* the law? Diethelm Klippel and Grete Klingenstein agreed that in theory rulers were thought to be *under* the law; yet the reality was probably, as Hartmut Lehmann pointed out, quite otherwise in Germany – and the same of course was true for American slaves. As to equality under the law – probably an especially fruitful field for comparison – I contrasted American and German experiences of rule from the early eighteenth to the nineteenth century and concluded that, while the possibility for citizen participation in rule increased during that period in America, it declined in Germany. Put differently, in North America citizens (a designation that of course excluded slaves) improved their chances to work for their own happiness while in Germany, as Gerhard A. Ritter pointed out, rulers increasingly monopolized the means necessary to provide *Glückseligkeit* for their subjects.

In turning to the problem of civil rights and constitutional thought, the papers as well as the discussion in Part 3 sharply modified the last results by raising the question of the reality of law enforcement and the availability of law for various social groups.

Both indeed loomed large in Harold Hyman's analysis of the changing interpretations of the Thirteenth and Fourteenth Amendments between the 1870s and the seminal decision in *Brown v. the Board of Education* in 1954. The causes for these changing interpretations remained unresolved, with Hyman blaming juridical positivism and Fred L. Morrison the teleological attitudes of the Supreme Court's majority. But, at least by implication, Morrison agreed that we need to know much more about the social function of law and the way laws and their application by courts touch the life of individual citizens.

Jörg-Detlef Kühne's analysis of German civil rights and constitutional thought between 1848 and 1871 represents an approach to legal and constitutional history dramatically different from that of Harold Hyman. While Hyman's approach linked legal and constitutional issues and concepts to political, social, and economic reality, modern German *Rechts-* und *Verfassungsgeschichte* focuses more narrowly on legal and constitutional questions, as Morrison rightly pointed out in his comment.[43] In discussing both papers from the vantage point of the session's general theme, "Civil Rights and National Unity," Robert Post argued that turning constitutional thought into reality in both countries implied substituting *one national* legal culture for separate *regional* or *state* cultures. According to him the catch lay less in the text than in the enforcement of a law or constitutional article. By the middle of the nineteenth century in the United States and in Germany sections or individual states, respectively, were not ready to apply the constitutional principles of the Thirteenth and Fourteenth Amendments or those of the Paulskirche Constitution to their own particular cultures. In both cases federalism may have exercised a significant retarding influence on the process for attaining national unity.

Diethelm Klippel introduced another issue: in his comment he criticized the widespread notion of a German *Sonderweg* in formulating civil rights by pointing to the impressive efforts to define and draw up specific civil rights catalogues in the last years of the eighteenth century. To him this clearly placed German constitutional thought within the mainstream of Western developments.

---

43. Representative of this German approach are Dieter Grimme, *Deutsche Verfassungsgeschichte, 1776–1866*, Neue Historische Bibliothek, 271 (Frankfurt/Main, 1988), and Michael Stolleis, *Reichspublizistik und Policeywissenschaft, 1600–1800*, Geschichte des öffentlichen Rechts in Deutschland, 1 (Munich, 1988).

Kühne did not really object but merely pointed out that most of these products of the late Enlightenment were not incorporated into the many constitutions granted by monarchs – probably precisely because they were granted and did not emanate from the *volonté général*, as Knud Krakau pointed out in the discussion.[44]

Much of the discussion concentrated on two related issues which require much more study: what is the relationship between concepts of civil rights and liberties in the writings of scholars and in constitutions and reality? For Germany, Erich Angermann and Diethelm Klippel insisted that nineteenth-century developments were shaped by libertarian and civil rights traditions while Kühne, and to some extent Knud Krakau, accepted the argument as valid on the level of nineteenth-century theoretical concepts, writings, and political debate (at least for some periods) but insisted that after 1849 they were rather irrelevant to the process of attaining unity or shaping constitutional reality.

The problem was not all that different in North America: while the Thirteenth and Fourteenth Amendments contained clear provisions authorizing Congress to pass enforcing legislation, both amendments remained to a large extent unenforced. Hyman suggested, as part of the answer, changes in the reporting style of laws; Stanley Katz and Robert Post pointed to a hostile regional culture as another reason although Katz reported that recent research into state supreme court files had turned up more decisions favorable to amendments than hitherto known. I suggested as another reason inadequate bureaucracies. Gerhard A. Ritter added that some of these differences resulted from different notions of government: in Germany governments and, after 1871, the empire accepted responsibility for individual rights such as the citizen's right to education and the right to work, which even today are considered anathema in the United States.

Many of these questions were carried over to Part 4, which continued the discussion about the role of federalism in mid-nineteenth-century constitutional debates in Germany and America. Paul Finkelman illustrated the states' rights problem through a detailed examination of interstate disputes over extradition requests, while Hans Boldt concluded his comparison of the Constitutions of 1848–49 and 1870–71 with a description of the unified

---

44. See also Grimme, *Deutsche Verfassungsgeschichte* (see n. 43), 129.

Second Empire as an expression of hegemonic federalism dominated by Prussia. This did not lead to frictions between Prussia and the other member states, however, but to disagreements between Prussian and imperial interests.

In his comment Michael Dreyer pointed out that for two reasons German constitutional debate was free of the states' rights issue – a problem whose legal and technical implications were further clarified in the discussion, especially with relation to the character of the individual state and the concept of citizenship – that held center place in North America: the one was the absence of slavery and the other the solution of the Prussian-Austrian conflict *before* 1870–71. In turning to Hans Boldt's paper, Dreyer agreed in principle to Boldt's thesis about the many direct connections between the Constitutions of 1848–49 and 1871 but added that these connections should not blur significant structural differences between the two, especially with respect to the *Bundesrat*, whose function as a clearinghouse for intrastate conflicts was stressed by Gerhard A. Ritter. Turning to the question of the influence of American federalist concepts on the German founding fathers, however, Dreyer disagreed with Boldt. According to Dreyer, references to American federalism were of more rhetorical than real importance in part because American federal concepts stressing the idea of equality between states were poorly understood in Germany and unacceptable to the larger states.

The discussion concentrated on a number of issues, among them the problem of regional systems within a federation. There were no formal systems in the antebellum South, Paul Finkelman pointed out, yet informal regional systems, for example, churches, fulfilled similar functions both in America, said Timothy Breen, and in Germany, Jörg-Detlef Kühne added. More generally, Hartmut Lehmann pointed to the importance of Christianity in undermining federalism: blending Prussian and Christian values into a new kind of German Teutonism[45] prompted Germans to shift their allegiance from individual states to the German nation in a way similar to how concepts like "manifest destiny" fostered a new national consciousness in North America. For these reasons federalism, concluded Ralph Ketcham, was probably a failure: it failed to solve

---

45. For a comparative analysis see Hartmut Lehmann, *Martin Luther in the American Imagination*, American Studies: A Monographic Series, 63 (Munich, 1988).

the problem of slavery in America as well as the Prussian-Austrian conflict in Germany. In both cases these failures led to different forms of hegemonies: that of the North over the South in America, that of Prussia over the other member states in the Second German Empire.

While Part 4 continued earlier discussions about the function of federalism, Part 5 again took up the fate of civil rights as it was joined to the concept of *judicial review* in the latter part of the nineteenth and the earlier part of the twentieth century. In his analysis of the critique of the Supreme Court's attitude toward civil rights in general and new issues generated by industrialization and trade unionism in particular, William Wiecek found a certain circularity in arguments, which according to Knud Krakau were, depending on time and context, usable by liberals as well as conservatives. Gertrude Lübbe-Wolff, on the other hand, focused on the reasons for the late acquisition of judicial review by the *Reichsgericht*. When that court finally did exercise judicial review after 1919 it was largely prompted by antipathy and mistrust of a Parliament elected by the people at large.

The reasons for this time lag in the adoption of the principle of judicial review in America (where the principle was proclaimed in 1803 by Chief Justice John Marshall in *Marbury v. Madison*) and in Germany are to be found in the fact that in Germany civil rights were not considered as preexistent core features of fundamental rights but were granted in the Constitution. While the notion of fundamental or higher law was central to North America, it was unknown (despite its wide currency at the turn from the eighteenth to the nineteenth century, as Diethelm Klippel had shown) to Germans after 1871.

Both traditions proved mixed blessings, as the discussion was to make clear: in America the notion of higher or fundamental law served as a ready reference point to fight rights claimed by the people represented in Congress. Put differently, in a way the Constitution as the expression of a sovereign people clashed with the notion of civil and basic rights in the Constitution as expressions of preexistent fundamental rights. This of course offered the Supreme Court an alternative; it could reject laws passed by Congress not only for direct infringement of constitutional articles but, beyond that, by claiming that they violated some fundamental law. In the latter case, however, the Supreme Court exposed itself to charges of subverting the democratic legislative process. And that charge of course fueled those efforts to subjugate the Supreme Court to the people's will, however conceived, as William Wiecek demonstrated. From that vantage point, the recent and ongoing discussion about "original intent" may be just another variation of the same argument: since historians agree that it is impossible to reconstruct the original intention of the people and/or the founding fathers,[46] the notion turns out to be another means to divest particular constitutional ideas from current expressions of the people's will by tying them to mythical historically elusive prior attitudes.

In Germany, of course, the Constitution's position within society was different. Indeed, Bismarck viewed the Constitution of 1871 as a compact between states (Gerhard A. Ritter), although the Constitution had also been ratified by the parliaments of the individual states; whichever balance one prefers, it is clear that the Constitution of 1871 did not emanate from the people, but was granted to the people. The Constitution did convey to the people represented in Reichstag the right to change the constitution by simple majority (*Verfassungsdurchbrechungsklausel*), but reserved the decisive consecutive vote to the *Bundesrat* by stipulating that a change in the Constitution was impossible if fourteen votes were cast against it in the *Bundesrat*. In that system two fundamental concepts collided: that of the absolute sovereignty of Parliament copied from the English Constitution, as Gerhard A. Ritter pointed out, and that of hegemonic federalism on the other hand, with the latter retaining the upper hand up to 1918. While it is true that German constitutional thought did not differentiate between the role of the people as *pouvoir constituant* and the people as represented in Parliament (which in America had led to a radically different mode for adopting constitutional amendments), the Weimar Constitution did adopt the English idea of an absolute sovereign Parliament that had the right to change the Constitution by simple majority.

A large part of the discussion concentrated on the supposed or real legislative function of supreme courts by invoking its judicial review privilege. Ernst Benda considers judicial review necessary because a democracy needs the constitutional courts as umpires. He

---

46. Cf. James H. Hutson, "The Creation of the Constitution: The Integrity of the Documentary Record," *Texas Law Review* 65 (1986/87): 1–39.

dismissed the danger of a permanent collision between constitutional courts and democratically elected Parliaments because both were subject to the influence of the time. Others, including Ralph Ketcham, were more skeptical, however, arguing, as did Clyde Summers, for the necessity of judicial restraint. That much of the debate both in North America and in Germany was conducted in similar terms and with similar arguments may, as Post and Wiecek suggested, be the consequence of the fact that constitutional courts, legislatures, and debates were subject to the same ideological and generally contextual influences.

Part 6 focused on the relationship between changing social and economic conditions and the nature of constitutions, a subject which in a way continued the previous session's debate about the contrast between real or supposedly fixed or eternal or higher values as incorporated in constitutions on the one hand and changing social conditions on the other. As basis for the discussion Clyde Summers had offered a rather gloomy picture of the American Supreme Court's attitude toward labor legislation in general and unionism in particular. Ingwer Ebsen ended his analysis of the *Bundesverfassungsgericht*'s decisions in economic and social disputes with the conclusion that on the whole the court's attitude was rather cautious and, in contrast to the Supreme Court's decisions, geared toward furthering integrative tendencies in the divisive field of management-labor relations.

In her comments Laura Kalman wondered whether Summers, by blaming the courts, had not painted too rosy a picture of trade unions; were the trade unions not equally guilty, so she asked, because they had at least partially sacrificed their ideals for the improvement of wages and at the expense of improvement of structural relations between workers and management; she concluded with a plea for a much more thorough analysis of trade union behavior. In his comment Ernst Benda broadly sketched the development of *Sozialpolitik* from the beginning of the nineteenth century to the present time. By implication, he also illustrated one important aspect of the much more active functioning of the German government, which he briefly contrasted with the much less active functioning of the American government. Thus, in a way, the discussion returned again to the key issues that had been debated in the first two sessions and underlined principal philosophical and functional differences in North American and German constitutional developments and their concrete historical manifestations. In the past these differences shaped the structure of the dialogue between both countries, as they do today. Prevalent past and present tendencies to ignore these fundamental differences (as well as overlooking important similarities) continue to burden German-American partnership.

What the reader awaits in the following pages illustrates the old saying that things are usually more difficult than they seem to be. That is true enough. But more should be added: the intensive debates illustrated the complexity of exchanges between both countries. Contrasting constitutional development on only a legal and constitutional level, and that I take to be one of the most important results of the conference, will not do: one has to include the political, social, economic, and cultural developments to arrive at something more closely ressembling reality. Indeed, the really thorny questions, where we all agree much further study is required, related to the problems of enforcing laws; of how laws affected subjects and citizens; and how, conversely, social, political, and cultural developments not only affected the meaning of constitutions and laws, but more directly their interpretations (if meaning and interpretation can be separated in the way implied here).

Let me give an example. Recent research has clearly demonstrated that in the latter part of the eighteenth century German was not that far removed from American constitutional thought. What we now will have to find out is, how this new knowledge affected the people. Did it, indeed, affect them at all in Germany? And if so, how does it tie in with the considerably older notion of the German ruler as a much more active agent than what is called for in the American concept of government? Is the more energetic interventionist character of German government a product of the competing proximity of states and nations within Europe? Why did American notions develop in different directions? One could argue that this was because they were allowed to develop outside a system defined by power relations between states. Yet how does this square with the permanent anxieties about possible aggression from the French or Spanish colonies? Seventeenth-century New England governments certainly were as interventionist as German rulers of those days – they, the Puritans, that is, certainly did not foreshadow these developments.

Another important area which will require further work relates to the consequences of federalism. During the discussion we occasionally came close to suggesting that federalism may have been responsible (a) for retarding the evolution of a more benevolent legal culture in the South, (b) for checking the progress of unhealthy nationalist sentiments at least for a while, (c) for providing a legal framework for regionalism, and finally, (d) for fostering and improving notions of equality between states. Clearly some of these results are contradictory. But it may well be important to know more about the reasons why federalism failed to fulfill some of these enumerated positive functions.

Our discussions showed, finally, and this I think the exchange on federalism demonstrated with particular force, the usefulness and necessity of a more intensive dialogue between historians and legal scholars. No one should underrate the serious difficulties associated with such a dialogue. The gulf between history and the law occasionally seemed much wider than the Atlantic which separates North America from Europe. But the effort is richly repaid by many new insights from which both sides did and will continue to profit.

As is usual in such conferences, discussions did not follow the laws of logic; and that failing probably occasionally seriously impaired the conference's chances to explore additional new avenues of difference or similarity between North America and Germany. However, the papers, the comments, and the extracts from the discussion will, I hope, easily convince the reader that there was no lack of questions and problems. Indeed, if the success of a symposium is to be measured by the number of important new questions asked, then this symposium was, thanks to the exertions of all the participants, a worthwhile effort.

Part 1
Federalism in the Eighteenth Century

1

The Federal Principle and the Holy Roman Empire

Helmut Neuhaus

As far as I can see, the *Federalist Papers*, whose importance for American constitutional thought can hardly be overestimated, mention the Holy Roman Empire in seven out of eighty-five essays.[1] Essay no. 19 from December 8th, 1787, probably written by James Madison,[2] discusses it in great detail and, together with essays nos. 18 and 20, seeks to draw attention to problems connected with various federal state systems or political systems in an early phase of state development.[3] The ancient Greek republics, associated under the Amphictyonic Council (Amphictyonies were leagues of tribes connected with temples and the maintenance of their cults), the Achaen League, the Swiss Confederation, Poland, the United Netherlands, and the Holy Roman Empire serve as historical and contemporary examples. In 1786 Madison for the first time took a strong interest in these confederacies when he systematically perused books Thomas Jefferson had sent to him in two trunks from Europe. The results of his research are contained in his *Notes on Ancient and Modern Confederacies*, which he probably prepared in the spring or summer of 1786 after he was appointed a

---

1. I would like to express my gratitude to Erika Benn of Cologne for the translation of this study. Jacob E. Cooke, ed., *The Federalist* (Middletown, CT, 1961) no.12, 74; no. 14, 86; no. 19, 117–22; no. 21, 132; no. 42, 284; no. 43, 292; no. 80, 536–37.
2. Gerald Stourzh, *Alexander Hamilton and the Idea of Republican Government* (Stanford, CA, 1970), 160. See also Frederick Mosteller and David L. Wallace, *Inference and Disputed Authorship: The Federalist* (Reading, MA, 1964), 2–15, 263–64. The *Federalist*, no. 19, is also printed in Robert A. Rutland et al., eds., *The Papers of James Madison*, 15 vols. to date (Chicago, IL, 1962–), 10: 305–9. Harold C. Syrett et al., eds., *The Papers of Alexander Hamilton*, 27 vols. (New York, 1962–87), 4: 384–90, give The *Federalist*, no. 19, written "by James Madison with the Assistance of Alexander Hamilton."
3. Cooke, ed., *Federalist* (see n. 1), no. 18, 110–17; no. 19, 117–23; no. 20, 124–29.

delegate to the Philadelphia Constitutional Convention scheduled for May 1787.[4]

The main object of references to ancient and modern confederacies was, in Madison's notes as well as in essay no. 19 of the *Federalist Papers*, to draw attention – in a warning manner – to the political consequences of such confederations, which lacked inner coherence and effective central power. Alexander Hamilton, to cite another example, pursued the same object in his "Speech on a Plan of Government" to the Constitutional Convention in Philadelphia on June 18, 1787:

> Let us examine the federal institution of Germany. It was instituted upon the laudable principle of securing the independency of the several states of which it was composed, and to protect them against foreign invasions. Has it answered these good intensions? Do we not see that their councils are weak and distracted, and that it cannot prevent the wars and confusions which the respective electors carry on against each other? The Swiss cantons, or the Helvetic union, are equally inefficient. Such are the lessons which the experience of others afford us, and from whence results the evident conclusions that all federal governments are weak and distracted.[5]

The fact that the examples quoted were depicted in a particularly gloomy light is due to the *Federalist Papers*' propagandistic and journalistic function in connection with the violent disputes over the ratification of the federal Constitution accepted in Philadelphia on September 17, 1787.

It is in the nature of such texts that the authors do not always describe either historical or contemporary events true to fact. Representations of the whole, descriptions of detail, problem-oriented issues are subordinate to political objectives. With respect to the Holy Roman Empire this is done in manifold ways through incorrect generalization and exemplification. Approximately in the middle of the passage devoted to the Holy Roman Empire the following comments appear:

> The history of Germany is a history of wars between the Emperor and the Princes and States; of wars among the Princes and States themselves;

---

4. Rutland et al., eds., *Papers of James Madison* (see n. 2), 9: 3–24.
5. Syrett et al., eds., *Papers of Alexander Hamilton* (see n. 2), 4: 197–98 (Robert Yate's version of the speech, 195–202); see also Hamilton's notes (178–87), 182, and James Madison's version of the speech (187–95), 188, 190, 194.

of the licenciousness of the strong, and the oppression of the weak; of foreign intrusions, and foreign intrigues; of requisitions of men and money disregarded, or partially complied with; of attempts to enforce them, altogether abortive, or attended with slaughter and desolation, involving the innocent with the guilty; of general imbecility, confusion and misery.[6]

This, however, does not hold true for the Holy Roman Empire's late medieval and early modern history and in particular for the eighteenth century. Settling conflicts by means of law since the sixteenth century prevented many a passage at arms and upheld imperial peace. Frederick II, the Great, who had been dead for just over a year when the *Federalist Papers* were first published in various New York newspapers by Alexander Hamilton, John Jay, and James Madison, did not wage several wars against the emperor, but against Maria Theresa as archduchess of Austria and queen of Bohemia and Hungary. Not until the imperial execution (*Reichsexe-kution*) during the Seven Years' War did her consort, Emperor Francis I, become the Prussian king's enemy. Neither Charles VII nor Joseph II – as emperors – were involved in military conflicts with Frederick. Furthermore it is incorrect to speak of a "small body of national troops" in peacetime,[7] for at no time in its history did the Holy Roman Empire have a standing army at its disposal, nor were there "national Diets"[8] in the Old Empire. In addition, the Imperial Diet (Reichstag) of the late seventeenth and eighteenth centuries differed from the assembly of emperor and Imperial Estates (Reichsstände) which had been in existence since the end of the fifteenth century, and it was something totally different from medieval diets. If it is pointed out that the emperor had "a negative on the decrees of the Diet"[9] then at the same time it must not be omitted that consent between emperor and Imperial Estates was a *conditio sine qua non* for every imperial decision. Moreover, the Imperial Diet was neither "a representation" nor were the Imperial Estates "representatives" of the Holy Roman Empire,[10] and the

6. Cooke, ed., *Federalist* (see n. 1), no. 19, 119–20.
7. Ibid., 120.
8. Ibid., 118.
9. Ibid., 118.
10. Ibid., 119.

Old Empire was neither a "nation"[11] nor was it a "community of sovereigns."[12]

Summing up, one can say that the authors of the *Federalist Papers* had a very superficial, and partly incorrect, idea of the Holy Roman Empire and its history. They assume later phenomena existing in earlier times and vice versa. On account of their own political interests they try to explain the totally different world of the Holy Roman Empire, within the meaning of Otto Brunner, as an old European (*alteuropäisch*) state by using concepts of modern constitutional thought. As a result, however, the Holy Roman Empire's highly complex history disappears, the whole variety and singularity of its phenomena are buried.

When James Madison regarded the organization of the United States as a variant of the Holy Roman Empire – as he wrote to Thomas Jefferson on October 24, 1787[13] – then he and Alexander Hamilton at the same time realized the problems of such a comparison as well as the concept of the Old Empire as a "confederacy" or "federal system." In no. 17 of the *Federalist Papers* he says, "Though the ancient feudal systems were not, strictly speaking, confederacies, yet they partook of the nature of that species of association."[14] Nevertheless Madison, in his letter to Jefferson quoted above, speaks of the "federal Diet"[15] and in the *Federalist Papers* maintains that the "powers" of the Holy Roman Empire – besides those of the emperor – "are vested in a Diet representing the component members of the confederacy."[16] Before he had stated that,"Out of this feudal system, which has itself many of the important features of a confederacy, has grown the federal system, which constitutes the Germanic empire."[17]

With such a conception of the Holy Roman Empire, the *Federalist Papers* follows an old tradition. In 1661 Hofrat Ludolph Hugo (approx. 1630–1704), who was in the service of the duke of Brunswick-Lüneburg and was an envoy at the Regensburg Im-

---

11. Ibid., 120.
12. Ibid., 119.
13. Julian P. Boyd et al., eds., *The Papers of Thomas Jefferson*, 22 vols. (Princeton, NJ, 1950–86), 12: 274. See also Rutland et al., eds., *Papers of James Madison* (see n. 2), 10: 210.
14. Cooke, ed., *Federalist* (see n. 1), no. 17, 108.
15. Boyd, et al., eds., *Papers of Thomas Jefferson* (see n. 13), 12: 274.
16. Cooke, ed., *Federalist* (see n. 1) no. 19, 118.
17. Ibid.

perial Diet, had introduced the definition of a federal state into the discussion on the state organization of the Old Empire with his *Dissertatio de statu regionum Germaniae*, reprinted time and time again until 1736.[18] For him, the Holy Roman Empire meant a *civitas composita*, a state consisting of several states different both from an individual state and from a confederation whose members were not subjected to a supreme power applied to everyone and defined, for example, in accordance with state or feudal law. In the federal state the state power was divided between the state as a whole and the individual states.

Samuel Pufendorf (1632–94), who taught at Heidelberg University in the 1660s, disagreed with this view in his *De statu imperii Germanici* published in 1667 because, in accordance with Jean Bodin (1529/30–96) and Thomas Hobbes (1588–1679), he conceived undivided (and not divided as the "federal system" wanted to have it) sovereignty as an indispensable quality of a state.[19] Since the Holy Roman Empire was neither an individual state nor a confederation and could not be assigned to any of the classical types of state organization, Pufendorf characterized it as an irregular political body, as a monster;[20] this definition is also used in the *Federalist Papers*, probably with reference to Pufendorf, to characterize – incorrectly, in my opinion – the imperial circles (*Reichskreise*) of the Old Empire in the following manner: "Each circle is the miniature picture of the deformities of this political monster."[21] Only by neglecting the Holy Roman Empire's immense deficiencies, which made it a "monster," was it possible for Pufendorf to speak of a

---

18. *Ludolphi Hugonis Dissertatio de statu regionum Germaniae et regimine principum summae imperii rei publicae aemulo, nec non de usu et auctoritate iuris civilis privati, quam in hac parte iuris publice obtinet* (Helmstedt, 1661). Cf. Rüdiger Freiherr von Schönberg, *Das Recht der Reichslehen im 18. Jahrhundert: Zugleich ein Beitrag zu den Grundlagen der bundesstaatlichen Ordnung*, Studien und Quellen zur Geschichte des deutschen Verfassungsrechts, Reihe A: Studien, 10 (Heidelberg, 1977), 53–57.

19. Fritz Salomon, ed., *Severinus de Monzambano (Samuel von Pufendorf), De Statu Imperii Germanici: Nach dem ersten Druck mit Berücksichtigung der Ausgabe letzter Hand*, Quellen und Studien zur Verfassungsgeschichte des Deutschen Reiches in Mittelalter und Neuzeit, 3, 4 (Weimar, 1910). Cf. Horst Denzer, ed., *Samuel Pufendorf: Die Verfassung des Deutschen Reiches* (Stuttgart, 1976), 190–201. Harry Breßlau, ed., *Severinus von Monzambano (Samuel von Pufendorf): Über die Verfassung des Deutschen Reiches*, Klassiker der Politik, 3 (Berlin, 1922), 7*–53*.

20. Salomon, ed., *De Statu Imperii Germanici* (see n. 19), cap. VI, §9, 126: "Irregulare aliquod corpus et monstro simile."

21. Cooke, ed., *Federalist* (see n. 1), no. 19, 121.

federation of confederates with unequal rights, where the Imperial Estates depended on the emperor as head of state. In this respect he thought the condition of the Holy Roman Empire had come very close to a union of several states.[22]

The Göttingen professor and constitutional lawyer Johann Stephan Pütter (1725–1807) dealt with the Holy Roman Empire in a less theoretical and rather more historically pragmatic way. Unlike Pufendorf, he was not interested in assigning the Old Empire to one of the classical types of state organization but, without referring directly to Hugo, was nevertheless concerned with the same issue, that it was a composite state. Pütter, who published his *Beyträge zum Teutschen Staats- und Fürstenrechte*[23] a decade earlier than the *Federalist Papers*, regarded the division of the Holy Roman Empire into many individual, not altogether sovereign, states as a result of the feudal system. The Holy Roman Empire, with the emperor as its supreme – although not unlimited – power, was different from Switzerland or the Netherlands: that means, according to Pütter, that Germany is an empire divided into several individual states that are, however, united under a common supreme power in the shape of a composite political body.[24]

Even if Pufendorf's ideas of the Holy Roman Empire's irregularity and monstrosity still played a part in the thinking of Pütter's famous colleagues Johann Jacob Moser[25] (1701–85) and Christian August Beck[26] (1720–84), his conception of the Old Empire largely gained ground until the end of the eighteenth century. Germany is a composite state; it consists of small states whose princes are

22. Salomon, ed., *De Statu Imperii Germanici* (see n. 19), cap. VI, §9, 127: "ad foederatorum aliquod systema ultro vergit."

23. Johann Stephan Pütter, *Beyträge zum Teutschen Staats- und Fürstenrechte*, 1. Theil (Göttingen, 1777). Cf. Ulrich Schlie, *Johann Stephan Pütters Reichsbegriff*, Göttinger rechtswissenschaftliche Studien, 38 (Göttingen, 1961), 33–55.

24. Pütter, *Beyträge zum Teutschen Staats- und Fürstenrechte* (see n. 23), 38: "Das heißt, Teutschland ist ein Reich, das in lauter besondere Staaten eingetheilet ist, die jedoch alle noch unter einer gemeinsamen höchsten Gewalt in der Gestalt eines zusammengesetzten Körpers vereinigt sind."

25. See, e.g., Johann Jacob Moser, "Von Teutschland und dessen Staats-Verfassung überhaupt." in idem, *Neues teutsches Staatsrecht*, vol. 1 (Stuttgart, 1766), cap. 27, §8, 550–51.

26. Hermann Conrad, ed., *Recht und Verfassung des Reiches in der Zeit Maria Theresias: Die Vorträge zum Unterricht des Erzherzogs Joseph im Natur- und Völkerrecht sowie im Deutschen Staats- und Lehnrecht*, Wissenschaftliche Abhandlungen der Arbeitsgemeinschaft für Forschung des Landes Nordrhein-Westfalen, 28 (Cologne, 1964), cap. II, 1, 8, §1, 430.

entitled to territorial sovereignty[27] – this statement was made by Franz von Zeiller (1751–1828) in his lectures while tutoring the Austrian archduke Anton Victor (1779–1835), Emperor Leopold II's eighth son, from 1794 to 1797. Similarly, several handbooks on political law of the Old Empire set out from his conception of a state consisting of several states[28] because this came very close to reality. Even before Pütter, Montesquieu spoke of Germany as a confederate republic consisting of princes and free cities. In his opinion, the Holy Roman Empire only survived because there was a chief who was in a way both a public servant and the monarch of the confederacy.[29] Montesquieu also greatly influenced the constitutional thinking of the authors of the *Federalist Papers* in conceptual and argumentative ways.[30]

The Holy Roman Empire as a state consisting of states[31] was part of eighteenth century empirical knowledge. This empire was perceivable in its supreme constitutional institutions, the Imperial Diet, which since the 1660s had developed into an almost permanent assembly gathering in Regensburg. As his *Notes on Ancient and Modern Confederacies* from 1786 demonstrates, Madison was very well informed of this "Eternal Diet" as the most important institution of and the crucial point in the Constitution of the Holy Roman Empire.[32] In his lectures on German political law Christian

---

27. Wolfgang Wagner, ed., *Das Staatsrecht des Heiligen Römischen Reiches Deutscher Nation: Eine Darstellung der Reichsverfassung gegen Ende des 18. Jahrhunderts nach einer Handschrift der Wiener Nationalbibliothek*, Studien und Quellen zur Geschichte des deutschen Verfassungsrechts, Reihe B: Quellen, 1 (Karlsruhe, 1968), §122, 76: 'Deutschland ist ein zusammengesetzter Staat; es besteht aus kleinen Staaten, deren Regenten die Landeshoheit zusteht.''

28. See, e.g., Karl Friedrich Häberlin, *Handbuch des Teutschen Staatsrechts nach dem System des Herrn Geheimen Justizrath Pütter: Zum gemeinnützigen Gebrauch der gebildeten Stände in Teutschland, mit Rücksicht auf die neuesten merkwürdigsten Ereignisse*, vol. 1 (Berlin, 1797), 125–55, 367–417. Justus Christoph Leist, *Lehrbuch des Teutschen Staatsrechts* (Göttingen, 1803), 41–46.

29. Jean Brethe de la Gressaye, ed., *Montesquieu, De l'esprit des loix*, 2 (Paris, 1955), IX, 2, 8: "la république fédérative d'Allemagne, composée des princes et des villes libres, subsiste parce qu'elle a un chef, qui est en quelque façon le magistrat de l'union, et en quelque façon le monarque."

30. See, e.g., Cooke, ed., *Federalist* (see n. 1), no. 43, 292: "'As the confederate republic of Germany,' says Montesquieu, 'consists of free cities and petty states subject to different Princes, experience shews us that it is more imperfect than that of Holland and Switzerland.'"

31. Siegfried Brie, *Der Bundesstaat* (Leipzig, 1874), 28–29: "ein aus Staaten zusammengesetzter Staat."

32. Rutland et al., eds., *Papers of James Madison* (see n. 2), 18–19.

August Beck, coming from Thuringia's small state world, exemplified its characteristics and functioning in great detail to the young Austrian archduke Joseph, who later became Emperor Joseph II.[33] In particular the estates of the Holy Roman Empire (Reichsstände) were enumerated; they, together with the emperor, formed and were entitled to take part in the Imperial Diet. Altogether there were 279 members of the Imperial Estates, 9 of whom were electors, 3 ecclesiastical and 6 secular; 37 ecclesiastical princes (*geistliche Reichsfürsten*), including the bishops of Osnabrück and Lübeck; 59 secular princes (*weltliche Reichsfürsten*); 39 imperial prelates (*Reichsprälaten*), 20 of whom formed the Suabian and 19 the Rhenish bench, 84 imperial counts (*Reichsgrafen*) who formed a Suabian (20), a Wetterau (14), a Franconian (16), and a Westphalian (34) bench; and 51 imperial cities (*Reichsstädte*) divided into a Rhenish (15) and a Suabian bench (36).[34] Even if the figures quoted by Beck for the years from 1755 to 1760 are not always quite exact, the proportions are correct.

As is shown in a list of the estates of the Holy Roman Empire compiled in 1792 following the works of Johann Stephan Pütter, this situation remained more or less unchanged till the end of the eighteenth century. Apart from the fact that, after the Munich line of the House of Wittelsbach became extinct at the end of 1777,

---

33. Conrad, ed., *Recht und Verfassung des Reiches in der Zeit Maria Theresias* (see n. 26), 525–46. Cf. Friedrich Hermann Schubert, *Die deutschen Reichstage in der Staatslehre der frühen Neuzeit*, Schriftenreihe der Historischen Kommission bei der Bayerischen Akademie der Wissenschaften, 7 (Göttingen, 1966); Karl Otmar Freiherr von Aretin, *Heiliges Römisches Reich, 1776–1806: Reichsverfassung und Staatssouveränität*, vol. 1, Veröffentlichungen des Instituts für Europäische Geschichte Mainz, 38 (Wiesbaden, 1967), 51–68. Beside these important books, see in general Rudolf Vierhaus, *Staaten und Stände: Vom Westfälischen Frieden bis zum Hubertusburger Frieden, 1648 bis 1763*, Propyläen Geschichte Deutschlands, vol. 5 (Berlin, 1984); John G. Gagliardo, *Reich and Nation: The Holy Roman Empire as Idea and Reality, 1763–1806* (Bloomington, IN, 1980), 3–46; Hans Thieme, "Das Heilige Römische Reich und seine Glieder: Ein Beitrag zum Problem des Föderalismus," *Juristische Schulung* 21 (1981): 449–556; Gerhard Oestreich, "Verfassungsgeschichte vom Ende des Mittelalters bis zum Ende des alten Reiches," in Herbert Grundmann, ed., *Gebhardt: Handbuch der deutschen Geschichte*, vol. 2 (Stuttgart, 1970), 360–436; Hans Erich Feine, "Zur Verfassungsentwicklung des Heiligen Römischen Reiches seit dem Westfälischen Frieden," *Zeitschrift der Savigny-Stiftung für Rechtsgeschichte, Germanistische Abteilung* 52 (1932): 65–133; and a collection of essays by Karl Otmar Freiherr von Aretin, *Das Reich: Friedensgarantie und europäisches Gleichgewicht, 1648–1806* (Stuttgart, 1986).

34. Conrad, ed., *Recht und Verfassung des Reiches in der Zeit Maria Theresias* (see n. 26), 530–37.

Elector Karl Theodor of the Palatinate united his electorate with that of Bavaria, there were major changes only in the group of the imperial counts. The group increased to 99 members. In the year when the last emperor of the Holy Roman Empire, Francis II, was elected, there were 294 Imperial Estates.[35]

But the estates of the Holy Roman Empire were marked by a high degree of inequality. Each estate enjoyed a number of privileges, rights, and customs. These privileges, rights, and customs defined the position and status of each estate, thus separating it from the others. Politically this meant that only the electors who formed a council of their own (*Kurfürstenrat*) in the Imperial Diet and the ecclesiastical and secular imperial princes each had one vote (*Virilstimme*) in the council of electors or in the council of princes (*Reichsfürstenrat*). The imperial prelates (*Reichsprälaten*), who also belonged to the council of imperial princes, were divided into two benches defined by regional connection and had two curial votes (*Kuriatstimme*) at their disposal; by combining their territories, the even larger group of imperial counts had altogether four votes. Just as imperial prelates and counts had one vote (*Virilstimme*) each in their individual groups, this rule also applied to the imperial cities which, however, as the electors, formed their own council in the Imperial Diet. When obtaining the *votum decisivum* in the Peace of Westphalia in 1648,[36] they had, as council of imperial cities (*Reichsstädterat*), received full voting rights and were as such de jure on the same level as the councils of electors and imperial princes. However, as to their political importance in the procedure of consultations and resolutions, they still ranked behind the other Imperial Estates because, for each imperial decision, consent between the councils of electors and princes was absolutely necessary, and this could not be replaced by consent between one of these two councils and the imperial cities.[37]

35. See "Der deutsche Reichstag in seiner Zusammensetzung im Jahre 1792," in Karl Zeumer, ed., *Quellensammlung zur Geschichte der Deutschen Reichsverfassung in Mittelalter und Neuzeit* (Tübingen, ²1913), no. 220, 552–55.

36. "Instrumentum pacis Osnabrugense" (IPO) Art. VIII, §4, in Zeumer, ed., *Quellensammlung zur Geschichte der Deutschen Reichsverfassung in Mittelalter und Neuzeit* (see n. 35), no. 197, 416.

37. On the "Eternal Diet" in the eighteenth century, see Aretin, *Heiliges Römisches Reich, 1776–1806* (see n. 33), 51–68; Gagliardo, *Reich and Nation* (see n. 33), 21–26; for the history of the early modern Imperial Diet, see Schubert, *Die deutschen Reichstage in der Staatslehre der frühen Neuzeit* (see n. 33); Gerhard Oestreich,

This highly intricate picture of the estates of the Holy Roman Empire becomes even more complicated when one includes the groups subordinate only to the empire, which were not represented in the Imperial Diet. Apart from imperial villages (*Reichsdörfer*) – they are really negligible – of which there were still five by the end of the eighteenth century (Gochsheim, Sennfeld, Sulzbach, Soden, the free people of Leutkircher Heide), which were at times defined as small states (*kleine Staaten*),[38] the great number of imperial knights (*Reichsritter*) should above all be mentioned.[39] It is true that owing to a change in warfare at the end of the Middle Ages, they had lost both their military and political importance, but they were able to evade mediatization by the rising territorial states and, thanks to the emperor's strong support, to gain a quasi-territorial authority (*Landeshoheit*) which, in the Peace of Westphalia, was also sanctioned by imperial law.[40] Since the sixteenth century they had been organized in circles of imperial knights (*Ritterkreise*). And in

---

"Zur parlamentarischen Arbeitsweise der deutschen Reichstage unter Karl V. (1519–1556): Kuriensystem und Ausschußbildung," *Mitteilungen des Österreichischen Staatsarchivs* 25 (1972): 217–43; Helmut Neuhaus, *Reichstag und Supplikationsausschuß: Ein Beitrag zur Reichsverfassungsgeschichte der ersten Hälfte des 16. Jahrhunderts*, Schriften zur Verfassungsgeschichte, 24 (Berlin, 1977), 22–73; Rosemarie Aulinger, *Das Bild des Reichstages im 16. Jahrhundert: Beiträge zu einer typologischen Analyse schriftlicher und bildlicher Quellen*, Schriftenreihe der Historischen Kommission bei der Bayerischen Akademie der Wissenschaften, 18 (Göttingen, 1980), 99–138, 167–262; Peter Moraw, "Versuche über die Entstehung des Reichstages," in Hermann Weber, ed., *Politische Ordnungen und soziale Kräfte in Alten Reich* (Wiesbaden, 1980), 1–36; Anton Schindling, "Der Westfälische Frieden und der Reichstag," in Hermann Weber, ed., *Politische Ordnungen und soziale Kräfte im Alten Reich* (Wiesbaden, 1980), 113–53; Anton Schindling, "Reichstag und europäischer Frieden: Leopold I., Ludwig XIV. und die Reichsverfassung nach dem Frieden von Nimwegen (1679)," *Zeitschrift für historische Forschung* 8 (1981): 159–77; Heinrich Lutz and Alfred Kohler, eds., *Aus der Arbeit an den Reichstagen unter Kaiser Karl V.: Sieben Beiträge zu Fragen der Forschung und Edition*, Schriftenreihe der Historischen Kommission bei der Bayerischen Akademie der Wissenschaften, 26 (Göttingen, 1986); Helmut Neuhaus, "Wandlungen der Reichstagsorganisation in der ersten Hälfte des 16. Jahrhunderts," in Johannes Kunisch, ed., *Neue Studien zur frühneuzeitlichen Reichsgeschichte* (Berlin, 1987), 113–40.

38. Ekkehard Kaufmann, "Reichsdörfer," in Adalbert Erler and Ekkehard Kaufmann, eds., *Handwörterbuch zur deutschen Rechtsgeschichte*, vol. 4 (Berlin, 1986), 561–64; Archivar Hugo, "Verzeichnis der freien Reichsdörfer in Deutschland," *Zeitschrift für Archivkunde, Diplomatik und Geschichte* 2 (1836): 446–76.

39. Volker Press, "Reichsritterschaft," in Erler and Kaufmann, eds., *Handwörterbuch zur deutschen Rechtsgeschichte* (see n. 38), 4: 743–48; idem, "Reichsritterschaften," in Kurt G.A. Jeserich, Hans Pohl, and Georg-Christoph von Unruh, eds., *Deutsche Verwaltungsgeschichte* (Stuttgart, 1983), 1: 679–89.

40. IPO Art. V, §28 (see n. 36), 408.

spite of strong attempts at annexation on the part of the imperial princes, the Suabian, Franconian, and Rhenish circles, subdivided into fourteen (five, six, and three) administrative districts called cantons (*Ritterkantone*), remained in existence until the end of the Old Empire (1806). Spanning the three circles of imperial knights, these cantons (for example, Odenwald, Neckar-Schwarzwald, Kraichgau, and Mittelrhein), as regional associations of individual members, entered into different negotiations directly with the emperor by diets and/or managing directories, made decisions on strictly voluntary financial offerings (*subsidia charitativa*) beyond the Imperial Diet, and looked after their special privileges and rights.

All these different estates of the Holy Roman Empire shaped, as well as were affected by, the changes wrought on the Old Empire. Two were of special importance: the transfer of rights (*regalia*), originally due only to the king/emperor, to estates and, second, the acquisition and maintenance of other rights and privileges by estates. However, this participation varied in manner and success. Whereas the imperial knights were barely in a position to maintain imperial immediacy (*Reichsunmittelbarkeit*),[41] the imperial princes, owners of extensive landed property, were able to enlarge their stock of regalia, rights, and privileges to whole territorial states. Although this development occurred at the cost of emperor and empire, there was no loss of imperial unity, with the emperor remaining the most important person within the orientation of every Imperial Estate and knight. Up to the time of the *Federalist Papers*, the empire's feudal and legal systems kept all diverging forces together – not uncontested, but ultimately successfully.

This was due to the fundamental law of 1648, the Peace of Westphalia.[42] On the one hand it endorsed the individual achievements of the estates of the Holy Roman Empire and confirmed their participation, at a level equal to that of the emperor, in all imperial decisions[43] – for example, decisions relating to war and

41. Cf. Gagliardo, *Reich and Nation* (see n. 33), 4–5.
42. IPO (n. 36), 395–434, and "Instrumentum pacis Monasteriense" (IPM), in Zeumer, ed., *Quellensammlung zur Geschichte der Deutschen Reichsverfassung in Mittelalter und Neuzeit* (see n. 35), no. 198, 434–43. Cf. Fritz Dickmann, *Der Westfälische Frieden* (Münster, ⁴1972); Fritz Dickmann, "Der Westfälische Friede und die Reichsverfassung," in *Forschungen und Studien zur Geschichte des Westfälischen Friedens: Vorträge bei dem Colloquium französischer und deutscher Historiker vom 28. April–30. April 1963 in Münster* (Münster, 1965), 5–32.
43. IPO Art VIII, §§1–2 (see n. 36), 416.

peace or levying of taxes – but on the other hand it did not express their full independence of the Holy Roman Empire or their complete sovereignty. In particular it was that paragraph of the Treaty of Münster and Osnabrück (1648) in which the individual Imperial Estates were granted the right to form alliances among themselves or with foreign countries for the sake of preservation and security where they were explicitly reminded of the oath binding them to emperor and empire. No alliance was to be directed against the emperor, the Holy Roman Empire, the general public peace, or the stipulations of the Peace of Westphalia.[44] Fritz Dickmann, one of the most knowledgeable experts on the Treaty of Münster and Osnabrück, gave the following definition: the members of the Holy Roman Empire were at least by law, but to a large extent also in practice, subject to a superior power, bound by law common to all, and obliged to a peaceful settlement of their issues.[45]

Just as the *Federalist Papers* misinterpreted the estates of the Holy Roman Empire as "representatives" and "sovereigns" and did not do justice to their extreme dissimilarities and varieties, they also underestimated the importance of the imperial circles (*Reichskreise*) for the Old Empire. Apart from the fact that the Holy Roman Empire was not divided into "nine or ten circles or districts," but that from 1512 to its end there were exactly ten circles in existence, one does not do justice to this firm constitutional institution by describing it as an "experiment."[46] The circles played a decisive part in keeping the Old Empire alive up to its end in 1806, although split up into so many territorial states and other districts of authority, because they provided a kind of intermediate-level organization that kept the Holy Roman Empire and its members together as a whole.

In the first instance the division of the Holy Roman Empire into

44. Ibid., §2, 416. Cf. Ernst-Wolfgang Böckenförde, "Der Westfälische Frieden und das Bündnisrecht der Reichsstände." *Der Staat* 8 (1969): 449–78.

45. Dickmann, "Der Westfälische Friede und die Reichsverfassung" (see n. 42), 32: "Er [der Westfälische Frieden] bewirkte die allmähliche Umwandlung des Reiches in einen Verband von Staaten, die ihre gegenseitigen Beziehungen weithin nach völkerrechtlichen Prinzipien und Regeln gestalteten, dabei aber immer noch mindestens rechtlich, aber in weitem Umfang auch faktisch einer übergeordneten Gewalt unterworfen, an eine gemeinsame Rechtsordnung gebunden und in ihren Streitfragen untereinander zu friedlichem Austrag verpflichtet blieben."

46. Cooke, ed., *Federalist* (see n. 1), no. 19, 121.

ten circles[47] had been made for regional considerations, as can be seen by their names: Franconian, Bavarian, Suabian, Upper Rhenish, Lower Rhenish-Westphalian, Lower Saxon Circles. These six old circles, formed during the process of the so-called reform of the empire (*Reichsreform*) at the end of the fifteenth and early sixteenth centuries, were joined by another four – this was decided upon at the Cologne Diet in 1512, where the Austrian and the Burgundian Circles were formed by the Habsburg hereditary countries and the Rhenish Electoral and the Upper Saxon Circles were created, above all, by the electors of Mayence, Cologne, Trier, and the Palatinate as well as by the electors of Saxonia and Brandenburg.[48] Apart from the kingdom and electorate of Bohemia and its side lines (Moravia, Lausitz, Silesia) and Italian imperial feuds, several small dominions, and the whole of the imperial knighthood (*Reichsritterschaft*), all members of the estates of the Holy Roman Empire belonged to a circle. As a result of the principles on which these divisions were made, a varying number of estates belonged to the individual circles: only a few belonged to the Austrian, Burgundian, or Rhenish Electoral Circles; however, a great number, for instance, took part in the Suabian and Franconian Circles, which included numerous imperial prelates, counts, and cities as members, apart from ecclesiastical and secular imperial princes.[49] Changes within the estates of the empire, for example, those due to a change of sovereign, could mean that one imperial prince might

47. See in general Heinz Mohnhaupt, "Die verfassungsrechtliche Einordnung der Reichskreise in die Reichsorganisation," in Karl Otmar Freiherr von Aretin, ed., *Der Kurfürst von Mainz und die Kreisassoziationen, 1648–1746: Zur verfassungsmäßigen Stellung der Reichskreise nach dem Westfälischen Frieden* (Wiesbaden, 1975), 1–29; Hanns Hubert Hofmann, "Reichsidee und Staatspolitik: Die Vorderen Reichskreise im 18. Jahrhundert," *Zeitschrift für bayerische Landesgeschichte* 33 (1970): 969–85; idem, "Heiliges Römisches Reich," *Der Staat* 9 (1970): 241–50; idem, "Reichskreis und Kreisassoziation: Prolegomena zu einer Geschichte des fränkischen Kreises, zugleich als Beitrag zur Phänomenologie des deutschen Föderalismus," *Zeitschrift für bayerische Landesgeschichte* 25 (1962): 377–413.
48. See *Neue und vollständigere sammlung, welche von den zeiten kaiser Konrads II. bis jetzo auf den Teutschen reichstägen abgefasst worden, samt den wichtigsten reichsschlüssen, so auf dem noch fürwährenden reichstage zur richtigkeit gekommen sind*, vol. 2 (Frankfurt/Main, 1747), 138, §§11, 12.
49. See, e.g., "Der kayserlichen Majestät und gemeiner Stände des Heil. Röm. Reichs Teutscher Nation, Ordnung der zehen Crayß, unter welchen Crayß ein jeder Stand gehöre, gemacht und aufgericht zu Wormbs 1521," in *Neue und vollständigere sammlung der reichsabschiede* (see n. 48), 211–16; or "Usual-Matrikel des Kammergerichts" (1745), in Zeumer, ed., *Quellensammlung zur Geschichte der Deutschen Reichsverfassung in Mittelalter und Neuzeit* (see n. 35), no. 209, 500–505.

belong to several circles at the same time. From the seventeenth century onward this applied, for instance, to the electors of Brandenburg, who were members not only of the Upper Saxon, but also of the Lower Rhenish-Westphalian and the Lower Saxon Circles.[50]

In each circle its members, who were appointed by imperial resolution, formed a Circle Diet (Kreistag) as a central committee for consultations and resolutions.[51] From the 1530s and 1540s

---

50. See, e.g., Volker Press, "Friedrich der Große als Reichspolitiker," in Heinz Duchhardt, ed., *Friedrich der Große, Franken und das Reich* (Cologne, 1986), 38.

51. For some Imperial Circles see Fritz Hartung, *Geschichte des Fränkischen Kreises: Darstellung und Akten*, vol. 1, Veröffentlichungen der Gesellschaft für Fränkische Geschichte, 2. Reihe, 1 (Leipzig, 1910); Bernhard Sicken, *Der Fränkische Reichskreis: Seine Ämter und Einrichtungen im 18. Jahrhundert*, Veröffentlichungen der Gesellschaft für Fränkische Geschichte, Fotodruckreihe, 1 (Würzburg, 1970); Rudolf Endres, "Der Fränkische Reichskreis," in Jeserich, Pohl, and von Unruh, eds., *Deutsche Verwaltungsgeschichte* (see n. 39), 599–615; Adolf Laufs, *Der Schwäbische Kreis: Studien über Einungswesen und Reichsverfassung im deutschen Südwesten zu Beginn der Neuzeit*, Untersuchungen zur deutschen Staats- und Rechtsgeschichte, Neue Folge, 16 (Aalen, 1971); James Allen Vann, *The Swabian Kreis: Institutional Growth in the Holy Roman Empire, 1648–1715*, Studies Presented to the International Commission for the History of Representative and Parliamentary Institutions, 53 (Brussels, 1975); Peter-Christoph Storm, *Der Schwäbische Kreis als Feldherr: Untersuchungen zur Wehrverfassung des Schwäbischen Reichskreises in der Zeit von 1648 bis 1732*, Schriften zur Verfassungsgeschichte, 21 (Berlin, 1974); Traugott Malzan, *Geschichte und Verfassung des oberrheinischen Kreises von den Anfängen bis zum Beginn des Dreißigjährigen Krieges*, Ph.D. thesis (Mainz, 1951); Gustav Adolf Süß, "Geschichte des oberrheinischen Kreises und der Kreisassoziationen in der Zeit des spanischen Erbfolgekrieges (1697–1714)," *Zeitschrift für die Geschichte des Oberrheins* 103 (1955): 317–425, 104 (1956): 145–224; Anton Karl Mally, *Der Österreichische Kreis in der Exekutionsordnung des Römisch-Deutschen Reiches*, Wiener Dissertationen aus dem Gebiete der Geschichte, 8 (Vienna, 1967); Günther Loch, *Der Kurrheinische Kreis von Ryswijk bis zum Frieden von Rastatt und Baden (1697–1714)*, Ph.D. thesis (Bonn, 1951); Helmut Neuhaus, "Die rheinischen Kurfürsten, der Kurrheinische Kreis und das Reich im 16. Jahrhundert," *Rheinische Vierteljahrsblätter* 48 (1984): 138–60; Winfried Dotzauer, "Der Kurrheinische Reichskreis in der Verfassung des Alten Reiches," *Nassauische Annalen* 98 (1987): 61–104; Albert Neukirch, *Der Niedersächsische Kreis und die Kreisverfassung bis 1542*, Quellen und Darstellungen aus der Geschichte des Reformationsjahrhunderts, 10 (Leipzig, 1909); Walther Schmidt, "Geschichte des Niedersächsischen Kreises vom Jahre 1673 bis zum Zusammenbruch der Kreisverfassung," *Niedersächsisches Jahrbuch für Landesgeschichte* 7 (1930): 1–134; Eustach Schwend, *Entwicklungsgeschichte der bayrischen Kreisverfassung von 1531 bis 1542*, Beilage zum Jahresbericht 1918/19 der Luitpold-Kreisoberrealschule München (Munich, 1919); Andreas Schneider, *Der Niederrheinisch-Westfälische Kreis im 16. Jahrhundert: Geschichte, Struktur und Funktion eines Verfassungsorgans des Alten Reiches*, Düsseldorfer Schriften zur Neueren Landesgeschichte und zur Geschichte Nordrhein-Westfalens, 16 (Düsseldorf, 1985); Winfried Dotzauer, *Die deutschen Reichskreise in der Verfassung des Alten Reiches und ihr Eigenleben (1500–1800)* (Darmstadt, 1989).

onwards these diets met more and more frequently on the invitation of the prince-conveners (*kreisausschreibende Fürsten*), who had been appointed by emperor and empire at a time when the Imperial Diets were transferring an increasing number of tasks to the Circle Diets and at the same time inducing them to organize themselves and to carry out directive and administrative functions.[52] In the Circle Diets the estates were divided – according to the strength of their group – into benches (*Bänke*) or curiae (*Kurien*). This meant, for instance, that owing to the numerous ecclesiastical and secular imperial princes, prelates, counts and cities, the Suabian Circle had five benches, whereas there were only two in a less differentiated circle like the Bavarian. In contrast to the Imperial Diet, each member of the Circle Diets had his own vote irrespective of rank, thereby creating a political revaluation of the small estates in the Holy Roman Empire. Since the emperor was not allowed to participate in the Circle Diets but was informed of them and had the opportunity to send envoys as observers, resolutions taken at such a diet were based exclusively on the members' consent.

The tasks of the circles, which were organizations consisting only of estates, resulted from the fact that there were only a few executive and administrative institutions at the Holy Roman Empire's disposal. Originally the circles had been created for the sole purpose of settling local or regional disturbances of public peace (*Landfriede*) in the vast empire in those instances where an individual imperial prince or several princes alone were not in a position to do so. Already in the Middle Ages a centrally directed protection of public peace had not been possible. With the establishment in 1495 of the imperial cameral court (*Reichskammergericht*), which remained in existence for more than three hundred years,[53] and the setting up of an imperial government (*Reichsregiment*) which met for two short periods only (1500–1502 and 1521–30),[54] the six senior circles were assigned the task of electing members for these central imperial institutions, whereas the four junior circles were

---

52. Cf. Helmut Neuhaus, *Reichsständische Repräsentationsformen im 16. Jahrhundert: Reichstag – Reichskreistag – Reichsdeputationstag*, Schriften zur Verfassungsgeschichte, 33 (Berlin, 1982); Helmut Neuhaus, "Der Augsburger Reichstag des Jahres 1530: Ein Forschungsbericht," *Zeitschrift für historische Forschung* 9 (1982): 167–211, 199–201.

53. Rudolf Smend, *Das Reichskammergericht: Geschichte und Verfassung* (Weimar, 1911).

54. Heinz Angermeier, "Die Reichsregimenter und ihre Staatsidee," *Historische Zeitschrift* 211 (1970): 265–315.

represented by the delegates of the emperor and the electors. In 1555 the ordinary imperial deputation (*ordentlicher Reichsdeputationstag*) was set up by the Augsburg Diet, and from 1570 onward provisions were made that at least one Imperial Estate from each of the ten circles was to be a member of this new institution.[55] Within the framework of the *Reichsexekutionsordnung* (September 25, 1555), which finally made the circles responsible for the maintenance and restoration of public peace in the Holy Roman Empire as well as for the execution of the sentences passed by the Imperial Cameral Court, the Ordinary Imperial Deputation's task was to carry out imperial resolutions more effectively.[56]

Further tasks the Holy Roman Empire bestowed on the circles as far back as the sixteenth century referred to taxation, coinage, and *policey*, but also to the public proclamation of imperial laws. The circles' role for the empire's defense against attacks from outside was of particular importance. In this capacity they were responsible for the integration of the Holy Roman Empire as well as for the maintenance of internal peace. They became a constitutional institution superior to the individual Imperial Estates.

It was after the first siege of Vienna by the Turks in 1529 that the Augsburg Diet one year later engaged the ten Imperial Circles, which up to then had hardly been in evidence, for the purpose of warding off the Muhammedans.[57] As there was no permanent army within the circles, the contingents of troops to be raised by the individual Imperial Estates according to the imperial tax base of 1521 (*Reichsmatrikel*) were to be gathered and placed under the command of a captain (*Kreishauptmann*) elected by the diets of the circles. The imperial army, thus composed according to circles, was to be led by an imperial commander in chief (*Reichshauptmann*) appointed by emperor and empire. Although at the beginning of the 1530s this procedure was carried out only in a rudimentary way, the Holy Roman Empire fell back on it a decade later after the

---

55. Neuhaus, *Reichsständische Repräsentationsformen im 16. Jahrhundert* (see n. 52), 423–92; Helmut Neuhaus, "Zwänge und Entwicklungsmöglichkeiten reichsständischer Beratungsformen in der zweiten Hälfte des 16. Jahrhunderts," *Zeitschrift für historische Forschung* 10 (1983): 279–98, 288–90, 297.

56. See *Neue und vollständigere sammlung der reichsabschiede* (see n. 48), 3: §§60–69, 26–28.

57. Mohnhaupt, "Die verfassungsrechtliche Einordnung der Reichskreise in die Reichsorganisation" (see n. 47), 8; Neuhaus, "Der Augsburger Reichstag des Jahres 1530" (see n. 52), 199–200.

conquest of Ofen by the Turks. This time each circle had to appoint war councils (*Kriegsräte*) as advisors to Elector Joachim II, who was commander in chief of the imperial troops. But it was not until 1681 that the circles received their imperial political function, again not accidentally in a foreign political crisis, when the empire was threatened in the southeast by the Turks (second siege of Vienna in 1683) and in the west by the French king Louis XIV's politics of reunion. According to the imperial defense order (*Reichsdefensional-ordnung*, consisting of six decisions of the Imperial Diet concerning matters of imperial war, ratified by Emperor Leopold I between May 1681 and April 1682),[58] each circle had to raise stipulated infantry and cavalry contingents of 40,000 men for the imperial army, and each was obliged to establish a fund for food, equipment, and pay for their soldiers. The Austrian Circle had to supply 20.07 percent of the imperial troops; the Burgundian, Upper Saxon, Suabian, Lower Rhenish-Westphalian, and Lower Saxon Circles 10.07 percent each; the Upper Rhenish Circle 8.36 percent; the Rhenish Electoral Circle 8.27 percent; 7.21 percent had to be supplied by the Franconian Circle; and 5.74 percent by the Bavarian Circle. These contingents were commanded by generals of their circles who were, in turn, subordinate to imperial generals appointed by emperor and empire.

After the Peace of Westphalia in 1648, there was much argument about the principles of an imperial defense order finally ratified in 1681.[59] In view of the empire's weakness, these arguments were marked in particular by the struggle for either a centralistic or federal formation of the Holy Roman Empire; this struggle between monarch and estates is characteristic of a large part of the early modern history of the Old Empire and had by no means been decided upon in 1648. In the opinion of Emperor Leopold I, an up-to-date reform of the *Reichsexekutionsordnung* would fulfill the

58. Helmut Neuhaus, "Das Problem der militärischen Exekutive in der Spätphase des Alten Reiches," in Johannes Kunisch, ed., *Staatsverfassung und Heeresverfassung in der europäischen Geschichte der frühen Neuzeit* (Berlin, 1986), 307–15.

59. Cf. Rudolf Vierhaus, "Land, Staat und Reich in der politischen Vorstellungswelt deutscher Landstände im 18. Jahrhundert," *Historische Zeitschrift* 223 (1976): 40–60, 47–48; Volker Press, "Landtage im Alten Reich und Deutschen Bund: Voraussetzungen ständischer und konstitutioneller Entwicklungen, 1750–1830," *Zeitschrift für württembergische Landesgeschichte* 39 (1980): 100–40; Karl Otmar von Aretin, "Das Reich in seiner letzten Phase, 1648–1806: Das Problem der Regierbarkeit im Heiligen Römischen Reich," in idem, *Das Reich* (see n. 33), 32–34.

empire's need for protection when applied in cases of foreign threats. Since this raised general opposition among the more powerful Imperial Estates, which were armed, the estates thought it necessary to be entrusted with the Holy Roman Empire's safety. Accordingly, they now asked that the decisions of the *Jüngste Reichsabschied* of 1654 be further extended. This *Jüngste Reichsabschied* had stipulated that the estates (*Landstände*) and their subjects were obliged by imperial decision to contribute from time to time to the financing of necessary territorial military installations and services.[60] The emperor vehemently opposed such demands and was able to protect the interests of the smaller Imperial Estates, the imperial cities, and the landed gentry,[61] which in the long run considerably strengthened his position in the Holy Roman Empire. A compromise indicative of the distribution of power within the empire solved the conflict: in 1681 emperor and imperial princes agreed that the circles were the most important level of the empire's military affairs. From then on, until the end of the Holy Roman Empire, its military was no longer at the emperor's free disposal or dependent on arbitrary actions on the part of the armed estates,[62] and the smaller Imperial Estates, via the circles, also had a part in the empire's defense against foreign aggressions.

The 1681 decision in one of the most important spheres of state organization meant, as Nikolaus Thaddäus Gönner (1764–1827) said, that the circles finally functioned at an intermediate level, thus linking the territorial lordship with the central government of the Holy Roman Empire.[63] It is, therefore, shortsighted to interpret the history of the Holy Roman Empire's last century according to

---

60. "Jüngster Reichsabschied," in *Neue und vollständigere sammlung der reichsabschiede* (see n. 48), 3: §180, 674.

61. See "Reichsgutachten" of October 29, 1670, and "Kaiserliches Kommissionsdekret" of February 13, 1671, in Johann Joseph Pachner von Eggenstorff, ed., *Vollständige Sammlung Aller Von Anfang des noch fürwährenden Teutschen Reichs-Tags de Anno 1663 biß anhero abgefaßten Reichs-Schlüsse*, vol. 1 (Regensburg, 1740), no. CCXCI, 494–97, no. CCCIII, 518–20, and "Kayserliche Resolution über die verlangte Extension des § [180] Und gleichwie vorigen Reichs-Abschieds de Anno 1654, die Collectation der Unterthanen betreffend, de Anno 1670," in Johann Jacob Schmauß, ed., *Corpus Juris Publici* (Leipzig, 1774), no. LXXII, 1077–79.

62. Fritz Hartung, *Deutsche Verfassungsgeschichte vom 15. Jahrhundert bis zur Gegenwart* (Stuttgart, [8]1964), 155.

63. Nikolaus Thaddäus Gönner, *Teutsches Staatsrecht* (Landshut, 1804), 310: "Zwischenrad, wodurch die Landeshoheit mit der Centralregierung des Reichs in Verbindung gesetzt wird."

the provisions of the Peace of Westphalia, which granted the Imperial Estates the limited right to form alliances. The Imperial Circles deserve more attention; they prevented the empire's dissolution in favor of the larger Imperial Estates. For the problems of the Old Empire could only be solved in the circles' limited area and with a more balanced equality of power – in a federal manner.[64]

The circles were able to do so because their new task prompted them to improve their internal development, which differed greatly owing to their heterogeneousness. Far-reaching developments took place in circles divided among many members, above all in the Suabian, Franconian, and Upper Rhenish Circles, which were thus in a position to improve their internal integration. In contrast to the Old Empire as a whole, the Suabian and Franconian Circles even managed to establish a standing army, granting them elements of modern statehood.[65] The individual circle could become a sovereign responsible to itself alone and an independent political factor,[66] as is shown by membership in foreign political alliances.[67] These circles' geopolitical situation can partially account for this development because they were exposed more than others to pressure from France. On the other hand, such developments did not take place in those circles composed not so much by many small estates, but by few powerful imperial princes, electors, or by the emperor's influence. The armed Imperial Estates, which belonged to several circles and often possessed their most important offices, were not prepared to let the contingent of each individual circle have its share of soldiers separately; on the contrary, they insisted on keeping their troops together.[68]

64. See Hofmann, "Reichskreis und Kreisassoziation" (see n. 47), 378: "Denn allein in ihrem begrenzten Raum und bei ihrem besser ausbalancierbaren Gleichgewicht der Kräfte war das überhaupt noch zu lösen – und zwar föderativ."

65. See Storm, *Der Schwäbische Kreis als Feldherr* (see n. 51), 94: "Das Stehende Heer, der miles perpetuus circuli, verlieh dem Kreis ein Stück Staatlichkeit."

66. Rudolf Endres, "Zur Geschichte des fränkischen Reichskreises," *Würzburger Diözesan-Geschichtsblätter* 29 (1967): 179, describes the circle as a "selbstverantwortlicher Hoheitsträger und selbständiger politischer Faktor."

67. See, for instance, Imperial Circles as members of the Alliance of the Hague (September 7, 1701): J. Du Mont, ed., *Corps universel diplomatique du droit des gens*, vol. 7/1 (Amsterdam, 1731), no. XIII, 89–92; Ludwig Bittner, ed., *Chronologisches Verzeichnis der Österreichischen Staatsverträge*, vol. 1, Veröffentlichungen der Kommission für Neuere Geschichte Österreichs (Vienna, 1903), nos. 626, 631, 633, 635, 636, 120–21.

68. See Elector Frederick William of Brandenburg's letter of January 15, 1681, to his envoy, Gottfried of Jena, at the Regensburg Imperial Diet, in Ferdinand Hirsch,

The strengthening of the circles in 1681 also revived federal thoughts regarding their cooperation on behalf of the Holy Roman Empire as a whole. A beginning in this direction had already been made in the sixteenth century, when diets of all circles (*Reichskreistage*) and other intercircular assemblies had been in consultation – parallel to or in place of Imperial Diets – on imperial matters relating to the completion of the *Exekutionsordnung*, the reform of the imperial tax base, imperial coinage, or public peace.[69] Deputies from the individual circles met in these diets and assemblies and carried out a mandate on behalf of their circles, not on behalf of individual Imperial Estates. However, this is the very reason why these diets of all circles and other intercircular assemblies were in the long run ineffective; their leveling of the differences between Imperial Estates was, in particular, not in the interest of the imperial princes.

Following the tradition of intercircular cooperation, the *Kreisassoziationen*[70] were, according to imperial law, an independent type of alliance. Their existence did not result from the right to form alliances granted to the Imperial Estates in 1648, but dated back to the unions of circles provided for in the 1555 *Reichsexekutionsordnung* for the restoration of public peace and put into effect sporadically. Like these, the circular associations of the second half

---

ed., *Urkunden und Actenstücke zur Geschichte des Kurfürsten Friedrich Wilhelm von Brandenburg, Politische Verhandlungen*, 12, Urkunden und Actenstücke zur Geschichte des Kurfürsten Friedrich Wilhelm von Brandenburg, 19 (Berlin, 1906), 730–31.

69. Neuhaus, *Reichsständische Repräsentationsformen im 16. Jahrhundert* (see n. 52), 36–442.

70. See, in general, Bernd Wunder, "Die Kreisassoziationen, 1672–1748," *Zeitschrift für die Geschichte des Oberrheins* 128 (1980): 167–266; Karl Otmar Freiherr von Aretin, "Die Kreisassoziationen in der Politik der Mainzer Kurfürsten Johann Philipp und Lothar Franz von Schönborn, 1648–1711," in Aretin, *Das Reich* (see n. 33), 167–208, first printed in Aretin, ed., *Der Kurfürst von Mainz und die Kreisassoziationen, 1648–1746* (see n. 47), 31–67; Alfred Schröcker, "Kurmainz und die Kreisassoziation zur Zeit des Kurfürsten Lothar Franz von Schönborn," in Aretin, ed., *Der Kurfürst von Mainz und die Kreisassoziationen, 1648–1746* (see n. 47), 69–77; Notker Hammerstein, "Zur Geschichte der Kreis-Assoziationen und der Assoziationsversuche zwischen 1714 und 1746," in Aretin, ed., *Der Kurfürst von Mainz und die Kreisassoziationen, 1648–1746* (see n. 47), 79–120; idem, "Johann Wilhelm Graf von Wurmbrand und die Association der vorderen Reichs-Kreise im Jahre 1727," *Zeitschrift für die Geschichte des Oberrheins* 119 (1971): 323–86; Hofmann, "Reichsidee und Staatspolitik" (see n. 47); Hofmann, "Reichskreis und Kreisassoziation" (see n. 47).

of the seventeenth and the eighteenth centuries had to maintain peace; they were primarily defensive alliances aimed not only at internal disturbances of the public peace, but also at external enemies. They replaced the Holy Roman Empire as a whole with their armed forces because, in spite of the 1681 resolutions, the empire was either not in a position to set up an imperial army, as in the Palatinate War of Succession (Pfälzischer Erbfolgekrieg) (1689–97), or required supplements for the totally inadequate imperial army, as in the Spanish War of Succession. After the Spanish War of Succession, the Frankfurt Association of June 20, 1714, consisting of the Rhenish Electoral, Austrian, Franconian, Suabian, and Upper Rhenish Circles, for a long time fulfilled the task of maintaining peace within the circles.[71] In contrast to some of its predecessors, it was clearly under Austrian domination, that is, under the influence of the emperor, which shows that his position had been strengthened again, particularly in the so-called *Vordere Reich*. The reason why the 1714 Frankfurt Association of Circles did not extend to all ten circles was that the more powerful armed Imperial Estates of the North did not require the circles. Furthermore, in the second half of the eighteenth century, the circles played a less important role in an era marked by the dualism between the Brandenburg elector and Prussian king Frederick II on the one hand and the Austrian archduchess, Hungarian, and Bohemian queen Maria Theresa and Emperor Joseph II on the other. Reflections like those of the Osnabrück official, historian, and publicist Justus Möser (1720–94) on strengthening the Imperial Circles' significance compared with the secular principalities[72] had no chance of being realized in view of the political state of affairs in the empire. Yet the German League of Princes of 1785 (Deutscher Fürstenbund),[73] which once again revived the idea of organizing

---

71. Johann Adam Kopp, ed., *Beylagen zur Gründlichen Abhandlung Von der Association Derer Vordern Reichs-Craysse* (Frankfurt/Main, 1739), no. XXXIII, 141–45; Hammerstein, "Zur Geschichte der Kreis-Assoziationen und der Assoziationsversuche zwischen 1714 und 1746" (see n. 70), 92–97; Wunder, "Die Kreisassoziationen, 1672–1748" (see n. 70), 250–52.

72. Ludwig Schirmeyer, ed., *Justus Mösers sämtliche Werke, Historisch-kritische Ausgabe in 14 Bänden*, vol. 4, *Patriotische Phantasien, I* (Oldenburg, 1943), 172–74; William F. Sheldon, *The Intellectual Development of Justus Möser: The Growth of a German Patriot*, Osnabrücker Geschichtsquellen und Forschungen, 15 (Osnabrück, 1970), 112, 114, 118.

73. Aretin, *Heiliges Römisches Reich, 1776–1806* (see n. 33), 162–240.

the Old Empire with the help of a union of Imperial Estates, was a failure too.

In summing up, I would like to point out that the Holy Roman Empire of the early modern period was a highly complex political structure. Since the formation of strong central power could not be achieved, the federal principle inherent in the feudal system developed although the Old Empire did not become a federation in the sense of a confederation (*Staatenbund*) or a federal state (*Bundesstaat*). This was opposed by the Imperial Estates, those very heterogeneous members of the empire characterized by a maximum of inequality and a lack of full sovereignty. It was the Holy Roman Empire's division into ten circles and the possibility of temporary alliances in associations that brought the federal principle to the fore. The Imperial Circles prevented, so to speak, a microfederal solution of the Holy Roman Empire's constitutional problems in accordance with the more powerful armed Imperial Estates and at the cost of the smaller unarmed estates. At the same time they made a "macrofederal" solution on the level above the Imperial Estates possible, while maintaining the whole Imperial Estate diversity, and became the actual pillars of the executive in the Holy Roman Empire.

This is just one of the answers to the question raised repeatedly in the second half of the eighteenth century, a question also raised by the authors of the *Federalist Papers* at the end of their selective remarks on the Holy Roman Empire as a negative example of state organization: "It may be asked, perhaps, what has so long kept this disjointed machine from falling entirely to pieces?"[74] The Old Empire was not so weak as to fall apart, is how one has to sum up part of the answer given in the *Federalist Papers*, and it was not only the emperor who held it together.[75] To a large extent it was the Imperial Circles which, on the additional level that they created, gathered divergent forces. Seen as alliances, they contributed to the concept of the Holy Roman Empire, as Montesquieu put it, as an eternal republic.[76] Altogether it was the basic federal structure of

---

74. Cooke, ed., *Federalist* (see n. 1), no. 19, 121.

75. See also Robert C. Binkley, "The Holy Roman Empire versus the United States: Patterns for Constitution Making in Central Europe," in Conyers Read and Richard B. Morris, eds., *The Constitution Reconsidered* (New York, 1968), 275.

76. Gressaye, ed., *Montesquieu, De l'esprit des loix* (see n. 29), IX, 1, 6: "république éternelle."

the imperial constitution which, up to the beginning of the nineteenth century, secured the empire's existence. In contrast to the
opinion of the *Federalist Papers*, it was this form which simultaneously guaranteed internal peace and external security to the
empire over a long period of time, in an eighteenth-century Europe
that was otherwise so belligerent. The Holy Roman Empire as "a
union without linkage, an association without concord, a community without common interests, and a society with members
pursuing their own benefits only"[77] – to this definition of the Old
Empire given by Johann August Reuß in 1799 we can no longer
agree.

---

77. *Johann August von Reuß, ed., Teutsche Staatskanzlei,* vol. 7 (Ulm, 1799), 5.

2
American Federalism and the Politics of Expansion

Peter S. Onuf

The great achievement of the American founders was to establish a federal union capable of expansion across the continent. On the eve of the Constitutional Convention it was by no means certain that the American union could be preserved, much less perfected.

The British Empire had been in practice, if not in theory, a federal polity, but the independent states could not simply reconstruct the familiar division of power. Americans rejected monarchical authority – the theoretical foundation of the old empire – and were reluctant to accord extensive powers to any central government, even one of their own creation. At the same time, the separate states were jealous of their autonomy. Article II of the Confederation (ratified in 1781) specified that "each State retains its sovereignty, freedom and independence, and every power, jurisdiction and right, which is not by this confederation expressly delegated to the United States in Congress assembled."[1]

The history of reformers' frustrated efforts to amend the Articles of Confederation and endow Congress with effective power is familiar. Attributing their failures to the excesses of "state sovereignty," many "nationalists" would have liked to jettison the states altogether. But Antifederalists warned against just such a "consolidation" of the states, and proponents of the new system – whatever their inclinations – had to convince wary voters they really were "Federalists." This was possible, I will show, because reformers had already begun to deal successfully with the practical problems of federalism. Resolution of territorial controversies and the Continental Congress's provision for the orderly expansion of

1. Andrew McLaughlin, "The Background of American Federalism," *American Political Science Review* 12 (1918): 215–40; Jack P. Greene, *Peripheries and Center: Constitutional Development in the Extended Polities of the British Empire and the United States, 1607–1788* (Athens, GA, 1986).

the union through the creation of new states pointed toward a new distribution of power. Western policymakers affirmed the crucial premise that republican government could be preserved in a polity of imperial dimensions. By reconciling the authority of the central government and the claims of new states, Congress showed that the interests of center and periphery could be effectively balanced without sacrificing republican liberty.

Federalism

Emphasis on Madison's tenth *Federalist* has led scholars to slight the role of states, old or new, in reconstructing the founders' solution to the problem of the nation's enormous size.[2] Madison, more or less influenced by Hume, effectively countered Montesquieu's dictum that republican government could only survive in small states by suggesting that republican excesses could be more easily contained in a large republic. But Madison was solving a problem of his own creation. Emphasizing the unitary, "consolidated" character of the new regime, nationalists invited their opponents to invoke Montesquieu's authority. It is doubtful whether the campaign for ratification was advanced by Madison's insistence that the United States was a single republic in which the separate state establishments seemed like so many selfish interest groups.

Madison's neglect of the states was redressed in subsequent numbers in the *Federalist* series.[3] Elsewhere, moderate Federalists like John Dickinson understood that the most effective way to

2. Douglass Adair, "'That Politics May Be Reduced to a Science': David Hume, James Madison, and the Tenth Federalist," in H. Trevor Colbourn, ed., *Fame and the Founding Fathers: Essays by Douglass Adair* (New York, 1974), 93–106; Robert J. Morgan, "Madison's Theory of Representation in the Tenth Federalist," *Journal of Politics* 37 (1974): 852–85; David F. Epstein, *The Political Theory of the Federalist* (Chicago, IL, 1984), 59–110. Jean Yarbrough focuses on no. 35 in discussing the importance of large electoral districts for the "refinement" of representation. (Jean Yarbrough, "Representation and Republicanism: Two Views," *Publius* 9 [1979]: 77–98, and "Thoughts on the *Federalist*'s View of Representation," *Polity* 12 [1979]: 65–82.) I have found Albert Furtwangler, *The Authority of Publius* (Ithaca, NY, 1984), esp. 112–45, particularly useful in distinguishing Madison from Publius and emphasizing the rhetorical exigencies under which the series was composed.

3. Notably nos. 14, 51, and 63, Jacob E. Cooke, ed., *The Federalist* (Middletown, CT, 1961). Furtwangler, *Authority of Publius* (see n. 2), 118–24, shows how Madison's extended sphere argument changed in successive formulations. Epstein concludes that "*The Federalist*'s . . . position is on the whole unsympathetic to the . . .

assuage Antifederalist anxiety was to insist on the agency of the states in the new federal order. Translating Madison's formula into federal terms, Dickinson wrote, "THE EXTENT of our territory, and the NUMBER of states within it, vastly increase the difficulty of any political disorder diffusing its contagion."[4] Madison's extended republic was not infinitely extensible; to establish the proper balance of representatives to represented, it could be neither too large nor too small. Thus, if Madison was right in postulating that the existing union was of optimal size, his logic worked against further expansion.[5] But Dickinson's conception of a federal republic avoided these problems: the addition of new states mitigated "political disorder." The "true size" of the union, Marylander Alexander Contee Hanson concluded, was not fixed: it "is neither greater nor less than that, which may comprehend all the states, which by their contiquity, may become enemies." Thus, it followed, a "true federal republic is always capable of accession by the peaceable and friendly admission of new single states."[6]

The argument for a federal republic may seem disingenuous, particularly when set forth by large-state nationalists like James Wilson. Its proponents would reduce the problem of continental union to one of collective security, ignoring the evident dangers of overextension; they would appropriate Montesquieu's and Vattel's endorsements of confederations for their "partly federal and partly national" regime. Nonetheless, they recognized that the true test of the new union was, in Wilson's words, its "expanding quality," its

---

states," in Epstein, *Political Theory of the Federalist* (see n. 2), 51–58, quotation at 54. See also Martin Diamond, "What the Framers Meant by Federalism," in Robert A. Goldwin, ed., *A Nation of States* (Chicago, IL, 1961), 24–41. For an interesting discussion of the framers' initial distrust of federalism and its implications for republicanism, see Jean Yarbrough, "Federalism in the Foundation and Preservation of the American Republic," *Publius* 6 (1976): 43–60.

4. John Dickinson, *The Letters of Fabius* (Wilmington, DE, 1797), 60.

5. Madison wrote: "In too small a sphere oppressive combinations may be too easily formed against the weaker party; so in too extensive a one, a defensive concert may be rendered too difficult against the oppression of those entrusted with the administration." Madison to Thomas Jefferson, October 24, 1787, cited and discussed in Morgan, "Madison's Theory of Representation" (see n. 2), 858. Morgan also notes Madison's concern with creating and preserving a "constitutional equilibrium between North and South," ibid., 864.

6. Aristides [Alexander Contee Hanson], *Remarks on the Proposed Plan* (Annapolis, MD, 1788), 33.

capacity for admitting new members.[7] By this standard the Confederation had been a failure. Madison might dwell – at his own
risk – on the failure of republican government in the states. But
moderate, mainstream Federalists instead emphasized the "imbecility" of a central government that could not secure the interests of
the old states nor provide for the creation of new ones. Under the
Articles the union was incapable of further extension; if anything, it
appeared more likely to contract, by fracturing into separate regional confederations.[8]

Madison's approach to the problem of the extended republic was
anomalous, attesting to his extensive reading and theoretical bent –
and to his lingering attachment to the idea of a true national
government. The problem of size was hardly a new one to policymakers (including Madison), who had long sought to maintain the
extended union. Their most immediate and pressing concern was
admitting new states and preserving their connection with the old.
Here was a compelling rationale for a stronger national government: the survival of the states as well as the union depended on the
character of the federal government, both on its "energy" and on
its constitutional responsibility.

This paper offers a brief analysis of the problem of new state
formation in the early republic.[9] Americans experimented with
two distinct general solutions to the problem of expansion prior to
the jurisdictional settlement embodied in the Northwest Ordinance
and federal Constitution. I will discuss the failure of the union to
accommodate expansion, either by admitting new states under the
provisions of the Articles of Confederation or by permitting the
division of existing states. In 1785–87 Congress finally fashioned a
western policy that apparently protected the old states, secured
national property interests, and at least prospectively recognized

7. "The Substance of a Speech Delivered by James Wilson" (Philadelphia, PA,
1787), in Merrill Jensen et al., eds., *The Documentary History of the Ratification of the
Constitution*, 7 vols. to date (Madison, WI, 1976–), 2: 340–50, quotation at 342.

8. See the informative discussion in Jensen et al., eds., *Documentary History* (see n.
7), 3: 54–57.

9. For more extended discussion see Peter S. Onuf, *The Origins of the Federal
Republic: Jurisdictional Controversies in the United States, 1775–1787* (Philadelphia, PA,
1983); Cathy Matson and Peter S. Onuf, "Toward a Republican Empire: Interest
and Ideology in Revolutionary America," *American Quarterly* 37 (1985): 496–531;
Peter S. Onuf, "Liberty, Development, and Union: Visions of the West in the
1780s," *William and Mary Quarterly*, 3d ser. 43 (1986): 179–213; and Peter S. Onuf,
Statehood and Union: A History of the Northwest Ordinance (Bloomington, IN, 1987).

westerners' political aspirations. But these provisions for extending the republic and the hopes for a harmonious and prospering union on which they were premised depended, in turn, on a revitalized central government. The discrepancy between prospects for expansion and the ominous portents of contraction and disintegration in the existing union reflected the ambivalence of many Americans in the "critical" period.

The Articles of Confederation

Because a true confederation preserves the sovereignty of member states, there are no obvious obstacles to its expansion: a new member gains security without sacrificing its integrity. These were the advantages, cited by "peace planners" and other proponents of federalism, that Americans hoped to enjoy under the Articles of Confederation.[10] The adjudication of *Connecticut v. Pennsylvania* (1782), "a peaceable and conclusive settlement of a dispute between . . . powerful sovereign States," epitomized the happy prospects of the new system.[11] And just as the Articles enabled the existing states to keep the peace with each other, they also provided for the admission of new states. Americans enthusiastically predicted that their system would rapidly spread across the continent, ultimately inspiring the oppressed peoples of Europe to follow their lead.

Yet many Americans soon lost confidence in the Confederation, notwithstanding its notable success in containing interstate conflict.

10. On the peace-plan tradition see F.H. Hinsley, *Power and the Pursuit of Peace* (Cambridge, 1961). For American attitudes toward world politics see Gerald Stourzh, *Benjamin Franklin and American Foreign Policy* (Chicago, IL, 1969); Felix Gilbert, *To the Farewell Address: Ideas of Early American Foreign Policy* (Princeton, NJ, 1961); James H. Hutson, *John Adams and the Diplomacy of the American Revolution* (Lexington, KY, 1980); Daniel George Lang, *Foreign Policy in the Early Republic: The Law of Nations and the Balance of Power* (Baton Rouge, LA, 1985); and Peter S. Onuf and Nicholas G. Onuf, "American Constitutionalism and the Emergence of a Liberal World Order," paper delivered at the Organization of American Historians, Minneapolis, 1985.

11. Pennsylvania Council minutes, January 24, 1783, in Julian P. Boyd and Robert J. Taylor, eds., *The Susquehannah Company Papers*, 11 vols. (Wilkes-Barre, PA, and Ithaca, NY, 1930–71), 7: 257–58. A special court set up under Article IX upheld Pennsylvania's jurisdiction over the Wyoming Valley, rejecting Connecticut's charter claims to the same area. See Robert J. Taylor, "Trial at Trenton," *William and Mary Quarterly*, 3d Ser. 26 (1969): 521–547.

The failure to add new states helps to illuminate this malaise. According to Article XI, "Canada acceding to this confederation, and joining in the measures of the United States, shall be admitted into, and entitled to all the advantages of this Union: but no other colony shall be admitted into the same, unless such admission be agreed to by nine States." When the Articles were drafted, the liberation of Canada tested the appeal of republicanism and the flexibility of the union as well as constituting a key strategic objective in the war effort.[12] Prudence dictated a more circumspect posture toward other "colonies," whose addition might overextend American resources or offend the new nation's European allies. Because Canada or any "other colony" was by definition *outside* the area presently claimed by the thirteen states, Article XI took on the character of a belligerent manifesto: American expansion was defined in relation to the claims of imperial powers, particularly Britain. Given the Americans' lack of success on the battlefield, it is not surprising that this article remained inoperative.

If the promise of expansion under Article XI depended on conquest – French Canadians showed little interest in their own liberation – the formation of new states within the vast domain claimed by the United States faced insuperable constitutional obstacles. As Congress repeatedly declared, the American union was premised on the territorial monopoly of its original members: "No State shall be deprived of territory for the benefit of the United States" (Article IX).[13] The admission of any new state (as opposed to foreign colony) would be an amendment to the Articles that would have to be "confirmed by the Legislatures of every State" – including the state out of which it was formed.

No elaborate explanation for the illusory character of constitutionally sanctioned expansion under the Articles is required.

12. For an excellent brief discussion of the importance of Canada see Charles Royster, *A Revolutionary People at War: The Continental Army and American Character, 1775–1783* (Chapel Hill, NC, 1979), 98–102.

13. For Congress's determination to uphold the territorial monopoly of the original states see resolutions of June 30, 1777, and May 23, 1780, in Worthington C. Ford, ed., *Journals of the Continental Congress*, 34 vols. (Washington, DC, 1904–37), 8: 508–13, 17: 452. On constitutional obstacles to admitting new states see Madison to Edmund Pendleton. January 22, 1782, in Robert A. Rutland et al., eds., *The Papers of James Madison*, 15 vols. to date (Chicago, IL, 1962–), 4: 38–39, and Ezra L'Hommedieu to Gov. George Clinton, September 8, 1781, in Edmund Cody Burnett, ed., *Letters of the Members of the Continental Congress*, 8 vols. (Washington, DC, 1921–26), 6: 212.

Congressmen tried to avoid divisive controversies among the states that would entail a challenge to existing boundaries, and their provisions for expansion were naturally shaped by the exigencies of war. But there were conceptual as well as prudential obstacles to expansion under the Articles. Having only recently and reluctantly broken from the empire, Americans continued to look at their world from a colonial perspective. Resistance leaders had sought to preserve colonial rights by reforming the imperial constitution. Although the need for foreign assistance, particularly from the French, pushed Americans toward declaring their independence and formalizing their union under the Articles, the goals of resistance remained unchanged. With its elaborate guarantees of states' rights and its provisions for adding Canada and other "colonies" to the union, the Confederation contemplated an idealized, reformed British Empire in America.[14]

Crucial to the idea of expansion implicit in the Articles was the assumption that any new state would already be a colony, like the thirteen colonies that had made themselves states. States succeeded – and thus were defined by – their colonial antecedents; the union was grounded on their equal status as mature, semiautonomous polities.[15] Paradoxically, however, this new-state equality principle constituted an impediment to the expansion of the union: no existing colony presented itself for admission and no provision could be made for bringing entirely new states into existence without risking jurisdictional chaos. Detached from the implicit imperial framework of revolutionary war – in which the "liberation" of British colonies obviously would weaken the enemy and strengthen the patriot cause – the addition of new, equal states simply promised to complicate and immobilize continental government. Even if new states could have been created without subverting old-state claims – an impossibility before the western land

14. On the American understanding of "empire" see Richard Koebner, *Empire* (Cambridge, 1961), chap. 4; and Norbert Kilian, "New Wines in Old Skins? American Definitions of Empire and the Emergence of a New Concept," in Erich Angermann, Marie-Luise Frings, and Hermann Wellenreuther, eds., *New Wines in Old Skins: A Comparative View of Socio-Political Structures and Values Affecting the American Revolution* (Stuttgart, 1976), 135–52. The "neocolonial" mentality of the founding generation is discussed in Robert H. Wiebe, *The Opening of American Society* (New York, 1984), 7–125.

15. For the "statehood" of the colonies and development of "state succession" doctrine see Onuf, *Origins of the Federal Republic* (see n. 9), 24–29.

cessions of the 1780s – their addition offered few advantages to the old states to offset their proportionally diminished power in Congress. For the American union to expand, it would have to become something more complicated than a simple confederation of equal states: in crucial respects, namely in jurisdiction over the public lands, new states would have to be less than equal.

The failure to add new states under Article XI, combined with the success of American negotiators at the Paris Peace Treaty Conference in securing the new nation's title to the western lands, led to a reconception of the problem of expansion.[16] As Americans looked west they began to think in new ways about the character of new states and their relation to the union. As they did so, however, the immanent contradictions of the union created by the Articles became manifest.

State Division

Given the failure of existing colonies to join the union, the only possibility for adding new states was through the division of the old states. Proposals for state division came from the two sources. First, from 1776 on, the generally small, "landless" states (New Hampshire, Rhode Island, New Jersey, Delaware, Pennsylvania, and Maryland) sought to circumscribe their large "landed" neighbors (Massachusetts, Connecticut, New York, Virginia, North Carolina, South Carolina, and Georgia). Meanwhile, frontier separatists agitated for the division of the large states in order to create their own new states: the western "sons of freedom yet value their privileges too high" to long submit to the "invidious policy" of the old states.[17]

As long as the landed states refused to relinquish their claims, the goals of the small old states and would-be new states converged. But landless-state support for separatism disappeared when the

16. The territorial provisions, including recognition of American jurisdiction to the Mississippi, are in Article II of the Treaty of Paris (September 3, 1783), in Fred L. Israel, ed., *Major Peace Treaties of Modern History, 1648–1967, with an Introductory Essay by Arnold Toynbee*, 4 vols. (New York, 1967), 1: 346–47.

17. On the Western-lands controversy see Thomas Perkins Abernethy, *Western Lands and the American Revolution* (New York, 1937); Merrill Jensen, "The Cession of the Old Northwest," *Mississippi Valley Historical Review* 23 (1936): 27–48; Merrill Jensen, "The Creation of the National Domain, 1781–1784," *Mississippi Valley*

landed states (particularly Virginia in 1784) ceded their western lands to Congress. The landless states then agreed to recognize large-state claims over existing frontier settlements in exchange for a share in the future development of the unsettled region further to the north and west. State division was thus dissociated from any immediate prospect of new-state creation.

Proposals for expansion of the union through state division were both inspired and defeated by the unequal size of the old states. As settlement spread into frontier areas of the large states, the "unwieldiness of our present governments in extent of territory" became increasingly apparent; therefore separations "must sooner or later take place."[18] But inequality in state size meant that different states stood to gain or lose unequally in any renegotiation of boundaries. And the Articles of Confederation tended to institutionalize the jurisdictional status quo by enabling small groups of states or even individual states to check hostile policy initiatives and thus preserve their relative advantage.[19] Proponents of state division therefore were driven to challenge the basic organization of the union. Fearing that ratification would freeze existing inequalities and hoping to force large-state concessions, landless Maryland refused to assent to the Articles until 1781. The large states would not capitulate to this pressure. Virginia, the most important landed state and Maryland's chief antagonist, was prepared to give up a portion of its western claims, but only under stringent conditions that secured state interests, pledged Congress to form new states,

Historical Review 26 (1939): 323–42; and Onuf, *Origins of the Federal Republic* (see n. 9), 75–102 and passim. For a good recent survey of separatist activity emphasizing the persistence of intersectional conflict well beyond this period, see Thomas P. Slaughter, *The Whiskey Rebellion: Frontier Epilogue to the American Revolution* (New York, 1986), 28–60. See also Onuf, *Origins of the Federal Republic* (see n. 9), 33–41, 127–45 (on Vermont), and 155–58; and Frederick Jackson Turner, "Western State-Making in the Revolutionary Era," *American Historical Review* 1 (1895/96), 70–87, 251–69.

18. *Freeman's Journal* (Philadelphia, PA), June 15, 1785; Onuf, *Origins of the Federal Republic* (see n. 9), 34–36.

19. Jack N. Rakove, "The Articles of Confederation," in Jack P. Greene, ed., *The Encyclopedia of American Political History*, 3 vols. (New York, 1984), 1: 83–91, and Peter S. Onuf, "The Articles of Confederation," in Leonard Levy and Dennis Mahoney, eds., *The Constitution: A History of Its Framing and Ratification* (New York, 1987). The best general account of Confederation politics is Jack N. Rakove, *The Beginnings of National Politics: An Interpretive History of the Continental Congress* (New York, 1979).

and invalidated private speculations in Indian lands. Dominated by small-state delegations with shares in these speculative ventures, Congress insisted on more extensive, unconditional offers. The resulting stalemate lasted until 1784.

The western-lands controversy centered primarily on adjusting the territorial claims of the old states and only incidentally on the formation of new states. Nationalization of the frontier promised the small states equal access to the western lands while redressing imbalances in state size. But when these goals were finally achieved with cessions by New York (1782), Virginia (1784), Massachusetts (1785), and Connecticut (1786), the addition of any new state was effectively postponed. Henceforth large and small states would have a common interest in upholding a jurisdictional settlement that secured old-state claims over existing western settlements and preempted separatism. Statehood for the largely ungranted and unsettled national domain was only a distant prospect.

Resolution of the claims controversy did not lead to the sudden expansion of the union, even though Congress announced its intention to admit new states in the territorial government ordinance of April 23, 1784. Because the ordinance described boundaries for new states throughout the West, including territory not yet ceded to Congress, separatists in every part of the country were led to believe that Congress was now ready to welcome new members. "The Continental Congress, by their resolves, invite us" to separate from North Carolina, leaders of the new state of Franklin proclaimed.[20] But the cessions left existing frontier settlements, the most eligible candidates for statehood, under old-state control. In subsequent years, Congressmen retreated from the grand design of 1784, devoting their efforts to planning for new "states" in the unsettled Northwest.

Western policymakers rejected separatist pleas for further state divisions. Separatism, that "epidemic . . . Spirit of making new States," was tantamount to disunion and therefore the most

---

20. Committee report of second Franklin convention, Jonesborough, December 14, 1784, reprinted in Samuel Cole Williams, *History of the Lost State of Franklin* (New York, 1933), 40. See also "Address to the Western Inhabitants," enclosed in Charles Cummings to the Pres. of Congress, April 7, 1785, in *Papers of the Continental Congress* (National Archives, Washington, DC), 48: 289, and "Impartialis Secundus," *Falmouth Gazette* (Portland, MA), July 9, 1785.

dangerous form of factionalism in an extended republic.[21] If Congress did not resolutely resist separatism, Thomas Jefferson warned, "our several states will crumble to atoms by the spirit of establishing every little canton into a separate state."[22] Of course, separatists denied they were factious, claiming instead that the oppressive rule of the old states distorted and deflected loyalties and interests naturally inclined toward the union: they were the true nationalists. Memorialists from western Virginia thus suggested that the multiplication (and division) of the states would strengthen the union: "An increase of states in the federal Union will conduce to the strength and dignity of that union, just as our increase of individual citizens will increase the strength and dignity of a state."[23] "Nature" (in the form of impassable mountains and great distances) decreed the division of the large states. A Franklinite concluded that "Nature" – not factiousness – "has separated us" from North Carolina.[24] When boundaries were adjusted accordingly, new-state proponents concluded, factional conflict would cease.

Separatist arguments inspired little enthusiasm among delegates dedicated to upholding old-state claims, particularly after the cessions compromise was in place. Moreover, by insisting on the inevitability of conflict between the old states and their frontier settlements, separatists inadvertently raised questions about the survival of the union. Would the union be more harmonious when these conflicting interests were represented in separate states capable of pursuing independent policies? Opponents of separatism did not think so. They charged that self-proclaimed new states would be founded in factionalism, beginning with internal divisions over the statehood question, and would spread factional discord throughout the union. Conflicts between old and new states – over boundaries and property rights – would simply widen the sphere of jurisdictional conflicts that already stretched the bands of union to the breaking point. If the frontier settlements were

21. Hugh Williamson to Gov. Alexander Martin, November 18, 1782, in Burnett, ed., *Letters of the Members* (see n. 13), 6: 545.
22. Jefferson to Richard Henry Lee, July 12, 1785, in Julian P. Boyd et al., eds., *The Papers of Thomas Jefferson*, 22 vols. (Princeton, NJ, 1950–86), 8: 287.
23. Memorial reprinted in *Freeman's Journal* (Philadelphia, PA), January 12, 1785.
24. Judge David Campbell to Gov. Richard Caswell, November 30, 1786, reprinted in Williams, *Lost State of Franklin* (see n. 20), 116. For the same argument see "Copy of a letter from a gentleman to his friend in the county of York," *Falmouth Gazette* (Portland, MA), February 2, 1786.

really so naturally distinct from the older settlements to the east, there was no hope for the union. Many contemporaries agreed with Rufus King that "no paper engagements" could preserve the connection between East and West.[25]

Separatists wanted to guarantee the privileges of local self-government to all parts of the union by multiplying the number of states. They saw expansion on a horizontal plane: the character of the union would remain unchanged as new political societies came into being in the frontier regions of the old. But the ultimate result of "multiplying the parts of the Machine," Madison wrote in 1784, would be to immobilize the central government.[26] Reflecting on the near impossibility of effective action in the existing union, a British writer wondered "what degree of unanimity may be expected among [an even larger] number of states."[27] These questions were directed more at the tottering American union than at expansion per se: the Articles of Confederation would have to be reformed simply to keep the existing union from flying apart.

Although separatists could appeal to basic republican values in promoting their claims to "independence," their agitation was increasingly identified with the centrifugal forces threatening the union. By pointing toward the progressive fragmentation and ultimate destruction of the original members of the union, separatists posed a serious challenge to the future of the extended republic. Yet if the separatist movements of the 1780s would be suppressed, their message could not be ignored. Clearly, the creation and admission of new states was essential for the extension of republican government across the continent. The challenge to policymakers was to provide for expansion without weakening the bonds of union or jeopardizing the rights and interests of the old states.

25. Rufus King to Elbridge Gerry, June 4, 1786, in Burnett, ed., *Letters of the Members* (see n. 13), 8: 380.

26. Madison to Jefferson, August 20, 1784, in Rutland et al., eds., *Papers of James Madison* (see n. 13), 8: 108; see also Madison to Marquis de Lafayette, March 20, 1785, in Rutland et al., eds., *Papers of James Madison* (see n. 13), 8: 252. For the corollary idea that the "extent of territory" was dangerous to the Union see Nestor [Benjamin Rush], "To the People of the United States," *Independent Gazetteer* (Philadelphia, PA), June 3, 1786. The idea that the United States was "already too large" was lampooned by Lycurgus, in *New Haven Gazette and Connecticut Magazine* (New Haven, CT), February 23, 1786.

27. "Extract of a letter from London," dated October 14, 1784, *New-York Gazetteer* (New York), January 11, 1785.

The Making of New States

How could the United States expand if other colonies could not be convinced or coerced into joining the union or if the old states successfully resisted division efforts? The answer was that Congress would *make* new states in the cessions region north of the Ohio River. From 1784 to 1787 policymakers perfected a new system for regulating settlement and preserving law and order on the frontier prior to the creation and admission of new states into the union. Congress's great innovation was to invent a new jurisdictional category, the "territory," that permitted the central government to exercise effective authority while settlements remained scattered and before strong bonds of common interest with the old states developed.[28]

For separatists, "statehood" agitation spontaneously expressed the naturally distinct (and implicitly hostile) interests of frontier settlers. New-state proponents assumed their political competence and fitness for membership in the union: it was incumbent on the old states to recognize their self-evidently valid claims. But the new idea of territory enabled policymakers to counter the separatists' assumption and thus to distinguish expansion from the simple addition of new states. In Congress's new western policy territories might become states, but statehood was not an a priori assumption. Therefore expansion did not necessarily imply the disintegration of the old states and the promiscuous proliferation of new ones. Meanwhile, because policymakers would play an active role in making, and not simply recognizing, new states, they could develop solutions to the problems of overextension. Statehood would be attained only *after* new settlements had been carefully prepared for the burdens of self-government and the obligations of the union.

In the immediate context of the "critical period," Congress's new territorial policy constituted a rejection of separatist pretensions and a determination to limit the number of new states and delay their admission. In the mid-1780s many observers anticipated

---

28. Onuf, *Statehood and Union* (see n. 9), chap. 3; Onuf, "Territories and Statehood," in Greene, ed., *Encyclopedia of American Political History* (see n. 19), 3: 1283–1304; Robert F. Berkhofer, Jr., "The Northwest Ordinance and the Principle of Territorial Evolution," in John Porter Bloom, ed., *The American Territorial System* (Athens, OH, 1973), 45–55.

that the union would soon double in size.[29] But between 1784 and 1787 Congress reduced the number of projected new states in the Northwest (from ten in the 1784 Ordinance to three to five in the Northwest Ordinance), while refusing to entertain new-state pleas from other parts of the country. Sectional polarization further dimmed prospects for expansion. In the wake of the furor over the closure of the Mississippi, the growing consciousness of distinctive sectional interests raised questions about the prospective alignments of new states.[30] In these circumstances, and given continuing constitutional obstacles to expansion, it is questionable whether any new state ever could have been admitted under the Confederation.[31]

Congress had to respond effectively to the practical and theoretical issues raised by antiseparatists and antiexpansionists before new states could be admitted to the union. But policymakers also realized that the West would be lost if they failed to provide for the temporary government and future statehood of the new western settlements. Thus, even before the debate over the new Constitution brought the issue of size to the fore, Congressmen had to fashion a workable solution to the problem of the extended republic. For them, the "crisis of the union" – its apparent tendency

29. Determined to protect its territories from American encroachments, Spain blocked the free navigation of the lower Mississippi in 1784. In August 1786, Congress, by a close sectional vote, authorized negotiator John Jay to forgo American claims to free use of the river in exchange for an advantageous commercial treaty with Spain that would have benefited northern traders. It is doubtful that such a treaty – had negotiations ever been completed – would have gained the necessary nine state votes for congressional ratification.

30. "A correspondent says . . . ," dated New York, *New-York Gazetteer* (New York), February 11, 1785; "Extract of a letter" (see n. 27).

31. For an excellent recent discussion of sectionalism see Drew R. McCoy, "James Madison and Visions of American Nationality in the Confederation Period: A Regional Perspective," in Richard Beeman et al., eds., *Beyond Confederation: Origins of the Constitution and American National Identity* (Chapel Hill, NC, 1987), 226–58. See also Staughton Lynd, "The Compromise of 1787," reprinted in *Class Conflict, Slavery, and the United States Constitution* (Indianapolis, IN, 1967), 185–213; H. James Henderson, "The Structure of Politics in the Continental Congress," in Stephen G. Kurtz and James H. Hutson, eds., *Essays on the American Revolution* (Chapel Hill, NC, 1974), 157–96, esp. 170–78; Joseph L. Davis, *Sectionalism in American Politics, 1774–1787* (Madison, WI, 1977); and Slaughter, *Whiskey Rebellion* (see n. 17). For contemporary discussion of the constitutional obstacles to expansion see Jefferson's Answers to Demeunier's First Queries, January 24, 1786, in Boyd et al., eds., *Papers of Thomas Jefferson* (see n. 22) 10: 14; Nathan Dane to Samuel Phillips, January 20, 1786, in Nathan Dane Miscellaneous Manuscripts (Library of Congress, Washington, DC), and Cooke, ed., *Federalist* (see n. 3), no. 38.

to collapse into "anarchy" – was more than overheated rhetoric. The failure of the existing union to accommodate expansion was increasingly conspicuous, however well the American experiment in republican government was succeeding in the states.

The chief concern of western policymakers was to preserve the "union" of East and West.[32] This was imperative for several, related reasons: first, Congress looked to the sale of its trans-Ohio lands for desperately needed revenue; second, proponents of regional and continental economic development saw the Ohio Valley as a valuable hinterland for coastal commercial and manufacturing centers; and finally, national security seemed to depend on preventing a vacuum of effective authority that might lead westerners to form alliances with the neighboring imperial powers, British and Spanish. While growing sectional mistrust led many Americans to question the value of union among the old states, few doubted the crucial importance of holding on to the western lands. But the common interest of easterners in exploiting and developing the West had to be balanced against demands by discontented westerners for political privileges and a place in the union.

Congress's proposed solution, set forth in the Land Ordinance of 1785 and Northwest Ordinance of 1787, was to provide a broad framework for western development which would lead toward statehood. Controlled expansion would guarantee the rapid settlement of the near frontier region, thus raising federal land values while promoting infrastructural development and commercial agriculture. These new communities would be much easier to govern – and much sooner eligible to govern themselves – than would more scattered settlements. Perhaps most important, common interests between commercial farmers in the West and their eastern trading partners would establish durable bonds of union. The political and commercial advantages of improving the navigation of the Potomac and linking East and West were thus inextricable: "It will be one of the grandest Chains for preserving the federal Union[;] the Western World will have free access to us, and we shall be one and the same People, whatever System of European Politics may be adopted."[33]

32. This theme is developed at length in Onuf, "Liberty, Development, and Union" (see n. 9).

33. Item dated Alexandria, November 15, 1784, *Virginia Journal* (Alexandria, VA), November 25, 1784. See also George Washington to Henry Knox, December

By focusing on the settlement process, policymakers transposed the problem of union from the realm of politics, where the addition of new states only promised progressive complications, to the realm of political economy. If the union did not depend for its very existence on concessions and compromises among independent sovereignties (whose political interests were always potentially hostile), but was instead grounded on common interests transcending state boundaries, anxieties about expansion could be allayed. It was easier to portray the national economy as dynamic and expansive than to make similar claims about the American union, defined in narrow political terms. Lycurgus, among many others, thus celebrated the "fertile and flourishing" American landscape, with its prospects "of wealth and commerce which future ages alone can realize."[34] The economists' "union" grew stronger as its scope was extended: expansion into fertile new lands meant growing wealth and population for the country as a whole. Once westerners understood their role in the continental economy they would be less inclined to seek advantage elsewhere; and, when they were at last admitted to the union, their fundamental (economic) interest in preserving the union would counteract the centrifugal tendencies of distinct state (political) interests.

This basic reconception of the future of the West depended on coordinating the political development of embryonic states, or territories, toward statehood simultaneously with their economic development. According to the Northwest Ordinance, in the earliest stage of settlement, direct congressional rule would impose conditions of law and order essential to productive private enterprise, simultaneously securing national property interests and upholding national sovereignty against European and native American enemies. But economic development, by substituting bonds of

---

5, 1784, in John C. Fitzpatrick, ed., *The Writings of George Washington*, 39 vols. (Washington, DC, 1931–44), 28: 3.

34. Lycurgus, "Observations on the Present Situation and Future Prospects of This and the United States," *New-Haven Gazette* (New Haven, CT), February 16, 1786. For the best introduction to early American political economic thought see Drew R. McCoy, *The Elusive Republic: Political Economy in Jeffersonian America* (Chapel Hill, NC, 1980). Michael Lienesch's "Development: The Economics of Expansion," a chapter in his *A New Order of the Ages: The American Constitution and the Making of Modern Republican Thought* (Princeton, NJ, 1989), alerted me to the importance of economic development in contemporary thought.

interest for this temporary "colonial" regime, would permit the progressive relaxation of federal authority and the extension of the privileges of self-government. The ultimate attainment of statehood would bring westerners into the union, in the culmination of a protracted, integrative process that grounded local liberty in national prosperity and strength.[35]

Congress's new system was designed to allay misgivings about the fragmentation of the states and weakening of the union that expansion traditionally inspired. In order to protect the old states from further jurisdictional challenges, Congress turned a deaf ear to separatists while asserting its exclusive control over the state-making process. Territorial officials would uphold national authority, carefully supervising the gradual steps toward statehood and self-government. The old states' interest in the future new states' public lands would be enforced by the territorial government until economic development created reciprocal interests in sustaining the union.

Congressional western policy promised expansion without its supposedly inevitable disintegrative concommitants. Instead, policy-makers laid the foundation for an expanding republican empire. As Dickinson suggested, the extending sphere would mitigate faction-alism by multiplying state interests. But it also promised to unlock the natural wealth of the continent and secure the new nation's prosperity and power.

The vision of a dynamic national economy tied to opening the West helped change perceptions about relations between old states as well as between old and new. Thus Marylanders and Virginians, old adversaries in the western-lands controversy, now combined forces to develop the Potomac route to the Ohio Valley and share in the anticipated benefits of the new western trade.[36] The same logic that posited a harmony of interest between East and West based on distinctive, though complementary, roles in the continental economy could help Americans reconceive relations in the existing union.

35. Arthur Bestor, "Constitutionalism and the Settlement of the West: The Attainment of Consensus, 1754–1784," in Bloom, ed, *Territorial System* (see n. 28), 13–44. On the development of American "colonial" policy see Jack Ericson Eblen, *The First and Second United States Empires: Governors and Territorial Government, 1784–1912* (Pittsburgh, PA, 1968).
36. Norman K. Risjord, *Chesapeake Politics, 1781–1800* (New York, 1978), 241–44; Matson and Onuf, "Toward a Republican Empire" (see n. 9).

The Extended Republic

During the Confederation era, the conflict of interests over the direction of national and state politics encouraged a static, even deflationary view of possible outcomes: every gain was someone else's loss. At the national level, the tendency of such conflicts was to immobilize Congress and "contract the sphere." For many increasingly pessimistic commentators, the only apparent hope for implementing policy and securing state interests was to promote "union" on a regional level. A widely circulated proposal therefore suggested that the New England states withdraw from the present union and institute "a new Congress, as the Representative of the nation of New-England, and leave the rest of the Continent to pursue their own imbecile and disjointed plans."[37] But the development of western policy constituted a striking exception to this tendency. Thus, even while the national government virtually ceased to function and disunion seemed ever more likely, the opening of the West raised new hopes for the expansion of the union and its growing prosperity and power.

Plans for western development clarified the common interest of the old states in preserving and extending the union at a time when a true national interest seemed elusive. So too, by affirming the possibility of mutually beneficial union between East and West, Congress offered a solution to the problem of the extended republic. Long before Antifederalists raised the cry of "consolidation," antiexpansionists invoked Montesquieu's logic, equating expansion with anarchy and predicting the inevitable despotic reaction – or at least alliance with a neighboring imperial power.[38] But the authors of congressional land and territorial government ordinances denied the necessity of this familiar sequence. Instead, they argued, anarchy would be the necessary consequence of *failing* to develop a coherent policy and permitting settlement to proceed willy-nilly.

Congressional western policy was premised on the distinction between unregulated and regulated expansion. Policymakers insisted

37. Letter in *Independent Chronicle* (Boston, MA), February 15, 1787, reprinted in Jensen et al., eds., *Documentary History* (see n. 7), 13: 57.
38. Onuf, *Origins of the Federal Republic* (see n. 9), 158–60. See also Samuel Williams, "On the Fallacy . . . that Civil Liberty can only exist in a Small territory," *Columbian Museum* 6 (March 1791): 144.

that disintegrative tendencies could be controlled if the process of settlement was coordinated with the extension of law and order, transportation, and market relations.[39] Regulation was compatible with liberty because it facilitated private enterprise and accumulation that would be impossible under unregulated, anarchic conditions. These private initiatives, moreover, would provide the "cement" of enduring union, enabling the temporary rule of federal officials to become progressively milder and less "despotic." The eventual attainment of statehood would eliminate the last vestiges of national authority. Thus, where antiexpansionists assumed that expansion meant anarchy leading inexorably toward despotism, western policymakers projected the gradual relaxation of Congress's "despotic" authority over the new settlements until they finally enjoyed the full extent of political liberty.

Just as western statehood was supposed to be compatible with a stronger union, Federalists would argue in the ratification campaign that the new Constitution would secure states' rights and interests while strengthening the national government. The argument in both instances was inflationary, premising outcomes that would benefit all parties. It was an argument that Madison, the reluctant federalist, was not yet prepared to make in *Federalist* no. 10. Only when he began to see the advantages of distinct state interests in preserving liberty did Madison embrace the extended *federal* republic with real enthusiasm. Then, in his essay on "Consolidation" in the *National Gazette* in 1791, Madison argued that the real, enduring basis of union was reciprocal interest. "If a consolidation of the States into one government be an event so justly to be avoided, it is not less to be desired . . . that a consolidation should prevail in their interests and affections".[40] If the states were now seen as bulwarks against incipient despotism, "complication" of the machinery of continental government and the multiplicity of potentially conflicting *political* interests seemed less threatening

39. Pelatiah Webster, "Essay on the Extent and Value of Our Western Unlocated Lands," dated Phila., April 25, 1782, reprinted in *Political Essays on the Nature and Operation of Money, Public Finances, and Other Subjects* (Philadelphia, PA, 1791), 485–500, 495; Washington to Jacob Read, November 3, 1784, and to William Grayson, March 15, 1787, in Fitzpatrick, ed., *Writings of Washington* (see n. 33), 27: 487.

40. [Madison], "Consolidation," dated December 3, 1791, *National Gazette* (Philadelphia, PA), December 5, 1791. On Madison's belated appreciation of the states' role see Yarbrough, "Federalism in the Foundation" (see n. 3), 50–53.

than it had in 1784 or 1787. As a result, the states – so conspicuously absent in *Federalist* no. 10 – now emerged as vitally important components in preserving the essential balance between power and liberty and national authority and local autonomy that alone could guarantee the survival and continuing expansion of the extended republic.

American federalism was based on the faith Madison expressed in an ultimate harmony of interests across the continent that permitted the division of political authority between state and federal governments. Assuming this harmony, it was possible for Americans to see the expansion of their union as a source of prosperity and power. As optimists looked westward, inflationary expectations supplanted the debilitating, deflationary suspicions that threatened to destroy the original union. Of course, the subsequent course of American history showed that neither intersectional conflict nor the threat presented by the states' claims to sovereignty could be so easily suppressed: the West soon emerged as a distinct section with its own interests and growing tensions between North and South eventually tore the union apart. Yet Americans were convinced they had solved the problem of the extended republic; their version of federalism – constantly evolving and never defined – ultimately proved compatible with continental expansion and world power.

3.1
The Confederations of the Netherlands and Switzerland and the American Constitution

Hans R. Guggisberg

Let me begin by acknowledging that I have learned many things from the two preceding papers. The main insight I have gained from Dr. Neuhaus's presentation concerns the fact that a comparison between the American Confederation and the German Empire of the eighteenth century is practically impossible and that the founding fathers were quite aware of this. Both political entities were based upon the federal principle, it is true, but the empire was dominated by monarchical traditions while the new American nation was a republic of republics held together by the ideology of republicanism. This is perhaps more important than the equally well known fact that the imperial estates were of very unequal status within the empire while the American states were given equal status under the Articles of Confederation as well as under the federal Constitution. In addition to this, the American nation – Dr. Onuf's paper has shown this quite convincingly – was fundamentally expansionist on its own continent in a way that no European country could aspire to be.

All this does not mean, however, that it does not make sense to study the founding fathers' notions of European confederations of their time. I do not have the competence to discuss this topic in a systematic way. Neither do I have the competence to present a critical appraisal of the two preceding papers. Instead Professor Wellenreuther has asked me to do something different, and this I shall try to do. He has requested that I comment briefly on the two European confederations that may in some way be better suited for comparison with the American Confederation than is the German Empire, namely, the Netherlands and Switzerland.

My remarks may deviate somewhat from the general theme of this conference, but I shall indeed try to be as brief as possible. My discussion will consist of two parts: the first will be devoted to the two confederations and to what some founding fathers thought of them. My emphasis will be on the statements on Switzerland because they may be less well known than those on the Dutch republic. In the second part of my contribution I will comment on the influence of the U.S. federal Constitution on the Swiss federal Constitution of 1848.

Both the Dutch and Swiss Confederations were characterized by three distinctive features: they were confederations of republics; their central administrations, weak as they might be, were organized on the basis of the republican principle; and their full member states had equal status vis-à-vis the central authorities. For these reasons some of the founding fathers of the American nation showed a certain interest in the two small European countries and studied their histories and institutions. But they knew what we know: neither the Dutch nor the Swiss Confederation was based upon a republican tradition comparable to the one that had grown up and was to be maintained in America. Within the Dutch Confederation of the Seven Provinces an old dynastic tradition existed which had often been at odds with republican institutions. It was to remain strong enough to survive the revolutionary period and to assert itself as a unifying force when the monarchy was established in 1813. The Swiss cantons had no traditions of this sort, it is true, but in the late eighteenth century all of them were ruled by oligarchic elites. This applied also to the rural cantons, in spite of the fact that the famous citizens' meetings (*Landsgemeinden*) still existed in many of them.

The Dutch States General (Staten-Generaal) and the Swiss Diet (Tagsatzung) could indeed be compared with the Continental Congress. They were conferences of delegates in which each province or canton was equally represented. But both confederations also contained territorial units of lesser status. From 1648 the States General administered a number of frontier territories in the South, the so-called *Generaliteitslanden*. In addition to the thirteen full member cantons, the Swiss Confederation of the late eighteenth century also contained fourteen associate members (*zugewandte Orte*) of varying status and a number of jointly administered territories (*gemeine Herrschaften*). There was also a certain amount of inequality among the full member states of both confederations. The province of Holland always tended to dominate the other

Dutch provinces, and the same can be said of Berne and Zurich vis-à-vis the other cantons of the Swiss Confederation.

American observers were aware of these shortcomings and of many others as well. When studying their opinions on the two European confederations, it is worthwhile to recall some general reflections which Jan Willem Schulte Nordholt expressed on the opening pages of his recent article on "The Example of the Dutch Republic for American Federalism." The Dutch historian stated that when the founding fathers looked at European history and institutions they did it in a way characteristic of the Enlightenment. They did not try to understand the past for its own sake, but they chose between good and evil, between the customs which were suited and those which were unsuited to man's nature. They believed in history as a chain of events that linked the past to the present, but at the same time they tried to break that chain because they were convinced that in a new world a new beginning could really be made. James Madison, one of the foremost spokesmen also in respect to our topic, found all the institutions of the past exclusively bad and therefore unusable.[1]

It is, of course, quite impossible here to discuss all the statements concerning the Dutch and Swiss Confederations made in late eighteenth-century America. They vary from moderately enthusiastic praise to harsh criticism, the latter tendency distinctly predominating. Most of the relevant statements can be found in the "Records of the Federal Convention" of 1787, in the *Federalist Papers*, and in a number of political pamphlets. As far as the Netherlands is concerned, they have been convincingly analyzed by Schulte Nordholt, and there is no need to repeat his analysis here. The main conclusion is that for the Federalists the history of the Netherlands was an example of the tragic failure of a republic. What was wrong with the Dutch Confederation, as they saw it, was its eternal inner dissension, the extreme individualism of its inhabitants, the putting of local above national interest, and the usurpation of power by small oligarchies.[2]

---

1. Jan Willem Schulte Nordholt, "The Example of the Dutch Republic for American Federalism," in Johan Christiaan Boogman and G.N. van der Plaat, eds., *Federalism: History and Current Significance of a Form of Government* (The Hague, 1980), 65–77, esp. 66. Cf. also Jan Willem Schulte Nordholt, *The Dutch Republic and American Independence* (Chapel Hill, NC, 1982).
   2. Schulte Nordholt, "The Example of the Dutch Republic" (see n. 1), 74.

What Schulte Nordholt has said of the general tendency of the founding fathers' statements on the Netherlands also applies to their opinions concerning Switzerland. They knew Swiss history and institutions from articles in current encyclopedias and journals as well as from surveys published in French. None of the American authors who expressed their opinions on Switzerland, however, had actually been there.[3]

Very often the Dutch and Swiss Confederations were jointly referred to, but on the whole references to the Netherlands are considerably more numerous and also lengthier than those to Switzerland. This is easily explained by the fact that, as a colonial and maritime power, the Dutch republic was of much greater interest to most Americans than the confederation of the Swiss cantons.

In *Common Sense*, Thomas Paine had praised both the Netherlands and Switzerland as countries without wars, domestic and foreign. Rather naively, he had based this glaringly erroneous statement on the fact that both countries were republics. But he also saw the dangers of inner dissension, at least in the case of the Netherlands.[4] John Adams was well informed about Swiss history and institutions too, but he was mainly interested in the constitutional structures of the cantons. He thought that he had discovered in them the principle of separation of powers.[5]

Of the references to Switzerland in the *Records of the Federal Convention*, I can only mention the most important. On June 4, 1787, George Mason of Virginia made a speech in which he emphasized the necessity to create and strengthen a sense of patriotism in the new American nation, for only by that means would it be possible to defend the country effectively if it were attacked by foreign powers. Here he referred to Switzerland which, he said,

---

3. The most recent study of the influence of Switzerland on the American Constitution is by Paul Widmer, "Der Einfluß der Schweiz auf die amerikanische Verfassung von 1787," *Schweizerische Zeitschrift für Geschichte* 38 (1988): 359–89. I am grateful to Dr. Widmer (Embassy of Switzerland, Washington, DC) for having allowed me to read his manuscript before its publication.

4. Philip S. Foner, ed., *The Life and Major Writings of Thomas Paine* (Secaucus, NJ, 1974), 27.

5. John Adams, *A Defence of the Constitutions of Government of the United States of America against the Attack of M. Turgot*, 3 vols. (Philadelphia, PA, [3]1797), 1: 22ff. Cf. especially the remarks on the Canton of Zug, 1: 31f.

had only been able to maintain its independence because its inhabitants had always been ready to take the greatest sacrifices upon themselves in order to defend their homeland.[6] George Mason's somewhat idealized opinion was to be taken up and developed further by such Antifederalist politicians as Patrick Henry. Many of them praised the institutional pluralism of the Swiss Confederation. To Patrick Henry, the Swiss example proved that the American nation did not need a federal constitution.[7] Quite generally it can be observed that Antifederalist writers and orators tended to express more favorable opinions concerning the Swiss Confederation of the ancien régime than their Federalist opponents.[8] A much less positive verdict on Switzerland than that of George Mason was made by Alexander Hamilton in a long speech of June 18. The knowledgeable delegate from New York very vigorously urged the strengthening of the American union and declared with conviction that confederations with a weak central government were

6. Max Farrand, ed., *The Records of the Federal Convention of 1787*, 4 vols. (New Haven, CT, 1937, repr. 1966), 1: 112.

7. In the Virginia Convention debates of 1788 Patrick Henry said, "The history of Switzerland clearly proves that we might be in amicable alliance with those states [i.e., the other American states] without adopting this constitution." Cf. Cecelia M. Kenyon, ed., *The Antifederalists*, The American Heritage Series, 38 (Indianapolis, IN, 1966), 261.

8. Among many examples of this tendency in Antifederalist writings I would like to quote only one: an anonymous author who called himself "A Farmer" published an essay in the *Maryland Gazette and Baltimore Adviser* of March 7, 1788, in which he described the Swiss Confederation in most enthusiastic terms. He stated that "the honor of supporting the dignity of the human character, seems reserved to the hardy Helvetians alone," and then he added the following remark: "Whether national government will be productive of internal peace, is too uncertain to admit of decided opinion. I only hazard a conjecture when I say, that our state disputes, in a confederacy, would be disputes of levity and passion, which would subside before injury. The people being free, government having no right to them, but they to government, they would separate and divide as interest or inclination prompted – as they do at this day, and always have done, in Switzerland. In a national government, unless cautiously and fortunately administered, the disputes will be deep-rooted differences of interest, where part of the empire must be injured by the operation of general law; and then should the sword of government be once drawn (which Heaven avert) I fear it will not be sheathed, until we have waded through that series of desolation, which France, Spain, and the other great kingdoms of the world have suffered." Cf. Morton Borden, ed., *The Antifederalist Papers* (Ann Arbor, MI, 1965), 7; see also 46, 49f., 78. For other, lengthier and truly idealizing references to Switzerland in the same *Maryland Gazette* (March 25 and 28, 1788) see H.J. Storing, ed., *The Anti-Federalist* (Chicago, IL, 1985), 265–72. I am grateful to Prof. Ralph Ketcham for having drawn my attention to these texts which would indeed deserve further discussion.

bound to break down sooner or later. His principal examples were the German Empire and, first and foremost, the Swiss Confederation: in his opinion the Swiss no longer possessed a real union; the cantons were divided by questions of religion and politics; some were in mercenary league with France, others with the Netherlands; and there was not even a single and truly competent diet. The federation of the cantons had become completely "inefficient." Hamilton obviously thought that the Swiss Confederation would perish soon if it came under attack from another power. In this assumption he was not at all wrong.[9] James Madison made similar statements on June 19. He found that the confederation hardly deserved its name anymore: it was weak both inside and out; its existence was threatened by the Habsburgs and France; and it could not in any way be regarded as a model for America.[10] James Wilson of Pennsylvania was of the opinion that there were no historical models at all for the consolidated American union. Something new was being created in the New World, and the Old World was of no help there. Switzerland, he very correctly stated, was only held together as a nation by common dangers from the outside which threatened all of its parts equally (June 20).[11]

In the course of the lengthy debate on the relations between the individual member states and those between each of the states and the central government, Luther Martin of Maryland at least had something positive to say about Switzerland. He stressed the fact that the principle of equality had always been upheld among the full member cantons although Berne would have been quite capable of setting up and maintaining a permanent hegemony. On the whole, however, Martin too perceived more weaknesses than virtues in the Swiss Confederation (June 28).[12] Charles Pinckney of South Carolina also suggested that Switzerland might in the near future suffer a fate similar to that of the Greek republics at the time of the Macedonian invasion. He expressed this view in his widely circulated *Observations on the Plan of Government Submitted to the Federal Convention on the 28th of May 1787.*[13]

9. Farrand, ed., *Records of the Federal Convention* (see n. 6), 1: 285f., 296.
10. Ibid., 1: 317f.
11. Ibid., 1: 343. For Antifederalist reactions to Wilson's critical view of Switzerland cf. Borden, ed., *The Antifederalist Papers* (see n. 8), 50, 78.
12. Farrand, ed., *Records of the Federal Convention* (see n. 6), 1: 454.
13. Ibid., 3: 115.

The *Federalist Papers* do not divulge a basically different tendency in their assessment. The most interesting reference to Switzerland is in no. 19. Here Madison not only reveals an astonishing familiarity with the institutional structures and problems of the Swiss Confederation, but also – like Hamilton – a very clear perception of the dangers which threatened it in the late eighteenth century. Switzerland was full of inner conflicts. Among these the religious discord was particularly fatal because it paralyzed the functioning of the central government:

> The controversies on the subject of religion, which in three instances have kindled violent and bloody contests, may be said, in fact, to have severed the league. The Protestant and Catholic cantons have since had their separate diets, where all the most important concerns are adjusted, and which have left the general diet little other business than to take care of the common bailages.

The religious conflict had frozen the political and social life of the whole confederation. Worse than that, it had produced opposing alliances with foreign powers: Protestant Berne was tied to the Netherlands, Catholic Lucerne to France. If the confederation had not fallen apart a long time ago, it was for a number of very commonplace reasons: "They [the Swiss] are kept together by the peculiarity of their topographical position; by their individual weakness and insignificancy; by the fear of powerful neighbors . . . ; by their joint interest in their dependent possessions." In Madison's opinion, Switzerland very clearly could not serve as an example to the American nation. The only thing Americans could derive from it was the absolute necessity to establish a strong central government.[14] To prove this necessity was, as everyone knows, the main point of the *Federalist Papers*.

Summing up, we may say that the founding fathers generally did not think very highly of the Swiss Confederation. They considered it a republic in decline (like the Dutch Confederation) whose existence was jeopardized by the fact that it lacked a strong central government. They did not glance back at its early history, and there is no trace in their writings of an idealized conception of its origins. The myth of William Tell spread in the United States only

---

14. Clinton Rossiter, ed., *The Federalist Papers* (New York, 1961), 133f.

at the very end of the eighteenth and during the early decades of the nineteenth century.[15]

Every Swiss schoolchild knows that the U.S. Constitution of 1787 exerted an influence of fundamental importance upon the Swiss federal Constitution of 1848. This is mentioned in every textbook, but very often the reader is left in doubt about the essence of this American influence and about the way it manifested itself in Switzerland. The facts are very simple: what the creators of the Swiss Constitution of 1848 took over from the American Constitution was essentially the bicameral system. The federal legislature was divided up into the Council of States (Ständerat) and the National Council (Nationalrat). The first body corresponded to the Senate, the second to the House of Representatives. This structure was left untouched by the constitutional revision of 1874, and it has remained unchanged up to the present day.

Behind the institutional imitation of 1848 lay a historical experience that the Swiss nation shared with the American nation, namely, the transition from confederation (*Staatenbund*) to federal union (*Bundesstaat*). In the United States this transition had taken ten years (1777–87), in Switzerland it took thirty-three years (1815–48).

After the downfall of the Napoleonic hegemony, Switzerland reconstituted itself as a confederation of twenty-two equal and sovereign cantons. The diet was restored in its old weakness. Its only real authority lay in the organization of national defense and in decisions about war and peace. Everything else was left to the cantons, including the right to enter into mercenary treaties with foreign powers or into special alliances among themselves. The new constitutional arrangement was based upon the treaty of confederation (*Bundesvertrag*) of 1815, a document in many ways comparable to the Articles of Confederation.

After 1830 a movement toward establishing a federal union emerged. It was supported by the industrial interests in the economically more advanced cantons whose governments wanted to put down the obstacles to free commercial exchange within the confederation. The establishment of a strong federal government

---

15. Leo Schelbert, "Der Wilhelm-Tell-Mythos in der Tradition der Vereinigten Staaten von Nordamerika," in Lilly Stunzi, ed., *Tell: Werden und Wandern eines Mythos* (Berne, 1973), 313–30.

was vehemently opposed, however, by the still predominantly agricultural (and Roman Catholic) cantons of central Switzerland who concluded a special defensive alliance (*Sonderbund*) among themselves in 1845. Two years later civil war broke out. After the defeat of the *Sonderbund*, the way was clear for the federal union.

The diet appointed a committee of delegates from the cantons to act as a constitutional convention of sorts.[16] It sat from February through June 1848, that is, during five months when Europe was shaken by revolutions. Although it was a much less dignified gathering than the Philadelphia Convention of 1787, the constitutional committee very soon found itself confronted with the same problems. The most difficult issue was the question of how the cantons should be represented in the federal legislature. As in Philadelphia sixty years before, several proposals were submitted. They ranged from virtual restoration of the 1815 confederation to the establishment of a centralized republic. After several weeks of debating, a stalemate was reached. At this critical moment some delegates decided to seek outside advice. They addressed themselves to Ignaz Paul Vital Troxler, a well-known liberal politician from Lucerne who had played a very prominent part in the constitutional debates of the 1830s and was now teaching philosophy at the University of Berne. Troxler was able to come up with substantial advice. He presented the committee with a pamphlet he had just written and published on his own initiative (January 1848). Its title was *Die Verfassung der Vereinigten Staaten von Amerika als Musterbild der schweizerischen Bundesreform* (The Constitution of the United States . . . as a model for the constitutional reform of Switzerland).[17]

In this pamphlet Troxler recommended the adoption of the bicameral system according to the example of the American Constitution for the new federal Constitution of Switzerland. The constitutional committee very quickly accepted Troxler's advice on March 22, 1848. One of the committee members, Joseph Munzin-

---

16. William E. Rappard, *Die Bundesverfassung der Schweizerischen Eidgenossenschaft, 1848–1948* (Zurich, 1948), 121f. Cf. Myron L. Tripp, *Der schweizerische und der amerikanische Bundesstaat* (Zurich, 1942); Leonhard Haas, "Die Schweiz und die Vereinigten Staaten von Nordamerika," *Zeitschrift für schweizerische Geschichte* 20 (1940): 228–63; Johann Jakob Rüttimann, *Das nordamerikanische Bundesstaatsrecht, verglichen mit den politischen Einrichtungen der Schweiz*, 2 vols. (Zurich, 1867–76).

17. The tract had been printed in Schaffhausen and had appeared in early January 1848 ("Zum Neujahr 1848").

ger of Solothurn, who had been an ardent supporter of Troxler's idea right from the beginning, made an interesting statement on the following day. He said, "Surely the decision has fallen from heaven, because it was the birthday of Nicholas von Flüe."[18] Nicholas von Flüe, canonized in 1947, was the famous hermit who had given advice and established peace among the dissenting Swiss in 1481, at the time of another and by no means less dangerous crisis in the confederation.

This is the reason why, when reflecting upon the influence of the American upon the Swiss federal Constitution, Swiss historians must and Swiss schoolchildren ought to remember Ignaz P.V. Troxler and – even if very briefly – Saint Nicholas von Flüe. For an international conference like ours, however, these historical connections certainly cannot claim general relevance.

---

18. Hans Haefliger, *Bundesrat Josef Munzinger* (Solothurn, 1953), 249; Emil Spiess, *Ignaz Paul Vital Troxler* (Berne, 1967), 894ff. Nicholas von Flüe had allegedly been born on March 21 (not on March 22), 1417.

3.2
Another Look at Federalism in the Holy Roman Empire

Hartmut Lehmann

There is a long history of writing the history, of evaluating the merits and shortcomings, of the Holy Roman Empire. Furthermore, this particular part of historiography is characterized by remarkable fluctuations in judgment. In the early nineteenth century, for example, shortly after the dissolution of the Old Empire in 1806, there was little understanding of the problems of the era just expired. Criticism of the Holy Roman Empire climaxed after the unification of Germany in 1871. Seen from the perspective of a strong and unified Germany led by Prussia, the Old Empire appeared weak because it was divided into what were called egoistic, particularistic entities. This led to trenchant criticism both of the constitutional framework and of the political achievements of the empire. German history before 1806 appeared to teach the lesson that political strength was based on military power, political unity, and economic progress.

Since 1945 this view has been significantly reevaluated. After the devastating experiences with power politics in the First and Second World Wars, which in both cases led to nothing but defeat, the premises on which the criticism of the Old Empire had been founded were themselves criticized. Many German historians now argued that a special value was attached to the decentralized constitutional, political, and cultural order of the Holy Roman Empire. They now discovered the meaning of the rule of law in the Old Empire and praised its peacekeeping function in central Europe.

In the past twenty years this kind of revisionism has, perhaps, been carried too far. Helmut Neuhaus, for example, explains in his paper the peculiar legal order of the Holy Roman Empire at great length, while ignoring the social tensions that existed and neglecting the obvious political problems. In my view, in the eighteenth century the weakness of the Holy Roman Empire was never demonstrated as clearly as in 1740 when Frederick II conquered Silesia. By attacking Maria Theresa's realm, the ambitious Prussian king did not attack her in her capacity as archduchess of Austria or as queen of Bohemia, but as the daughter of the emperor who was considered by many contemporaries to represent the empire, although she did not officially hold the imperial crown.

As this episode shows, we should distinguish very clearly between legal tradition and political reality in the Holy Roman Empire. Certainly it is important to outline the constitutional provisions, as laid down by the Diet of Worms in 1495, the Capitulation of Election in 1519, and other laws and privileges, and as elaborately explained by Samuel Pufendorf, Johann Jacob Moser, and other seventeenth- and eighteenth-century imperial law experts. At the same time we should, however, keep in mind that the influence of the Holy Roman emperor was due less to the legal provisions defining his position than to the possessions he owned as head of the House of Habsburg, the income he derived from his vast lands, his role as the undisputed leader of the Catholic dynasties and territories of the empire, and his international connections, both through the members of his house who ruled in parts of Italy and Spain as well as through cordial relations with other ruling dynasties in other European countries.

Consequently, we should try to determine the kind of federalism that existed in the eighteenth-century empire not only from legal factors but also from an analysis of the political reality of the empire in the epoch after the Peace of Westphalia. In my view, we are still in need of a terminology appropriate for characterizing this political reality of the Holy Roman Empire in the era of the ancien régime. Obviously, legal terms as derived from an analysis of the constitutional framework are unsatisfactory. Neither the laws of the states, or territories, nor an interpretation of the Holy Roman Empire in terms of international law can help us in this respect, not to speak of the often-found, yet anachronistic manner of describing conditions in the Old Empire with legal terms taken from the Bismarckian Empire of 1871. In my view, Pufendorf's formula that the Holy Roman Empire resembled *irregulare aliquod corpus* and was *monstro simile* also evades the real issue, as this much-quoted orderly formula forbids a comparison of the conditions in the empire with other examples and therefore renders any kind of historical judgment practically impossible. As far as the search for appropriate, distinctive terms helpful in characterizing the political reality of the Holy Roman Empire is concerned, we are, or at least we should be as I see it, at the beginning and not, as Neuhaus's paper would have us believe, at the end of a meaningful discussion.

Within the political reality of the empire as I see it, distinct spheres or regions of predominant influence of certain powers or dynasties existed. In my view, it is not so important to know the exact number of ecclesiastical princes in the empire or the number of imperial prelates, counts, or others. What we should attempt to discover and what we should consider in our historical analysis are, however, the specific spheres or regions of predominant influence of certain powers, or dynasties, to which these smaller entities belonged. What we must focus on is, therefore, the question of the primary political loyalty, the obedience paid and rewarded, the protection given and accepted, of these smaller and weaker entities in relation to the larger and stronger entities within the political framework of the empire. In this perspective, we should proceed beyond an admiration of the liberty of princes as the root of federalism. We should instead try to detect the open and hidden means of building empires within the empire: such as having junior members of certain ruling dynasties elected in ecclesiastical territories; placing younger members of certain houses as sovereign rulers in other secular territories; winning and retaining the allegiance of free imperial cities; and then, the most frequently attempted but not always successful tactic, the linking of interests and territories by marriage.

Coming back to terminology, I should like to add that it is not easy to find categories well suited to depict such a system of family connections, of patronage, of fear and trust, of blackmailing and dependence. The players in this game were only equals in theory, not in practice (even if they all enjoyed the liberty of princes). They were all subordinates of the emperor, yet they were involved in political dealings in which the emperor himself was an active (although not always decisive or successful) partner. Only in one decade, in the 1630s, did the sense of a common destiny among all princes of the empire lead a majority to nourish a feeling of *Reichspatriotismus*, a kind of loyalty to the common order, which should not be confused with the later category, or notion, of nationalism.

The differences between this system and the Bismarckian empire are striking. The sovereignty of the emperor in foreign affairs and military matters, together with their financing, were the minimal requirements of imperial power in the Bismarckian era. Moreover, this system was dominated by the king of Prussia, who ruled over about two-thirds of the empire. In contrast, in his realm the emperor of the Holy Roman Empire neither had a hegemonial position comparable to that of the Prussian king after 1871 nor a command over substantial financial means to conduct foreign affairs or maintain an imperial army. In contrast to the Hohenzollern after 1871, the Habsburgs before 1806 had to rely, in matters of power politics, on the resources of their own house.

It should also be stressed that the spheres, or regions, of predominant influence of certain powers, or dynasties, were not identical with the imperial circles (*Reichskreise*). Some of the imperial circles functioned well, for example, the Suabian Circle; some did not function well at all, for example, the Lower Rhenish Circle; some had been perverted into provinces ruled by one power only, as was the case for the Austrian and Bavarian Circles after 1620; and some, such as the Burgundian Circle, should be called fictitious, because they did not contribute to the defense of any part of the empire and existed only on paper. The sphere of predominant influence I mentioned should rather be seen as the domain of certain leading dynasties such as the Habsburgs and Hohenzollern, the Wittelsbacher and Wettiner, and the Houses of Hanover and Württemberg.

These domains were extended beyond the actual possessions of their princes and consisted of areas of direct and indirect influence. We should also stress that, in the eighteenth century, the leading dynasties of the empire no longer corresponded with the group of electors around the emperor. The electors were, to be sure, the leading dynasties of the mid-fourteenth century. In the eighteenth century, by contrast, the influence of the archbishops of Mayence, Trier, and Cologne had declined; their sees were occupied, moreover, by members of the leading dynasties. The Palatinate had not fully recovered from the severe setbacks suffered in the course of the seventeenth century. On the other hand, the elector of Saxony had risen to become king of Poland; the elector of Brandenburg had proclaimed himself king in Prussia in 1701 and had become the hegemonial power in northern Germany. During the Thirty Years' War, Bavaria had been added to the list of electors and half a century later, Hanover. But while Bavaria remained strong within the empire, the dynasty of Hanover soon moved to Great Britain, and Hanover proper became a somewhat neglected part of the British Empire.

As these examples indicate, the group of leading dynasties, and the spheres of influence they had, was unstable. From the late sixteenth to the late eighteenth century, for example, the see of the archbishop of Cologne was occupied by a member of the House of Wittelsbach. It was a major change of the political balance in the lower Rhine region when Maria Theresa managed to have one of her sons, Max Franz, a younger brother of Joseph II, elected archbishop of Cologne. Through this move she incorporated the region around the cities of Cologne and Bonn into the Habsburg sphere of influence.

What we should consider in the context of our discussion is the fact that the federal principle within the Holy Roman Empire was based on the coexistence, as well as the cooperation, of not more than half a dozen, at the most a dozen, dynasties that shared power within the empire. No doubt the domains of these dynasties had a long-lasting effect on the course of German history. Thus the territories ruled directly and indirectly by them can be seen as forming the basis for eighteenth-century federalism in Germany. These same territories can be found when one analyzes the political structure of the *Deutsche Bund* in nineteenth-century Germany and they reappear, though in a somewhat modified combination, in the states of the Federal Republic of Germany after 1949. In his paper Helmut Neuhaus has stressed that the imperial circles should be seen as the core of the federal principle in the eighteenth-century Holy Roman Empire. In my view, his analysis can be sustained only in so far as some of the leading dynasties mentioned above were at the same time the leading powers within certain imperial circles.

Neuhaus took as a point of departure the description of the Holy Roman Empire that can be found in the *Federalist Papers*.[1] In my view, the section he quotes should not be criticized so sharply because it contains much truth. To follow up on some of the remarks we find there:

---

1. Helmut Neuhaus, "The Federal Principle and the Holy Roman Empire," above, 28–29.

– "Licentiousness of the strong." When commenting on this judgment we should remember that the empire failed to recover Silesia after the Prussian attack in 1740, although some of its members did make an effort to do so.
– "Oppression of the weak." Leaving aside a consideration of the weak in social terms, in the political field the small and weak territories of the empire could only defend themselves as long as they were protected by one of the leading and powerful dynasties.
– "Foreign intrusions." We do not take a nationally biased view when we remember that after 1648 many principalities in the west and southwest of the empire looked for and did in fact receive protection from France, while some in the north were protected by Denmark or Sweden.
– "General imbecility, confusion and misery." In evaluating these strong words of criticism we should keep in mind that the institutions of the empire were, for example, incapable of providing even that relief which was possible during the major crisis caused by the famine in 1771 and 1772, which lasted into 1773. Perhaps it was this event that James Madison, the author of the passage on the empire in the *Federalist Papers*, had in mind when he spoke of "general imbecility, confusion and misery" and not the seemingly well balanced cosmos of legal provisions and privileges that Helmut Neuhaus has described so well.

3.3
The Concept of Federalism and Its Consequences

Hermann Wellenreuther

To Noah Webster's *Compendious Dictionary of the English Language* of 1806 the words "federalism" as well as "federation" are unknown. Only the adjective "federal" is defined as "of or relating to a league or compact."[1] This definition is rather close to that of the Göttingen scholar Johann Stephan Pütter, whose definition of the Holy Roman Empire as "an Empire, which is divided into separate states, which are, however, all united under a joint supreme authority in the form of a composite state,"[2] also associates the word "federal" with a formal structural relationship. Without enlarging at present on both definitions, I think one can say that there was a transatlantic agreement at the end of the eighteenth century that "federation" meant a consociation of states, in which each partner retained his distinctive *Staatlichkeit* while submitting to a jointly constituted sovereignty above it – ideas probably indebted to Althusius's theory of organic federations.[3]

Yet does this, too, mean that the principles embodied in the American Constitution did not transcend those floating about in contemporary Old Europe? In turning to the writings of the founding fathers, both Federalist and Antifederalist, it immediately becomes apparent that there is another aspect to the American idea of federalism which in those days was very much in the minds of American politicians. European thinkers of the eighteenth century seem to have been unconcerned with this particular aspect, although it, too, had clearly been part of the seventeenth-century

---

1. Noah Webster, *A Compendius Dictionary of the English Language: A Facsimile of the First (1806) Edition* (New York, 1970), 61, 115.
2. Johann Stephan Pütter, *Beyträge zum Teutschen Staats- und Fürstenrechte*, 2 vols. (Göttingen, 1777–79), 1: 86.
3. Michael Dreyer, *Föderalismus als ordnungspolitisches und normative Prinzip: Das föderative Denken der Deutschen im 19. Jahrhundert* (Frankfurt/Main, 1987), 32–36.

German notion of federalism. Samuel Pufendorf, for one, considered it as one of the main tasks of a federation of individual states "to maintain and establish inner unity. The most necessary task therefore is, to guarantee each members' rights and privileges and to make sure that no one be allowed to suppress the weaker. Thus to ensure that despite apparent unequality in power equality in the sphere of rights, liberty and security be maintained."[4] Similarly we read in James Madison's *Federalist* essay, no. 51, that in the "federal system of America" or in "the compound republic . . . power surrendered by the people, is first divided between two distinct governments, and then the portion allotted to each, subdivided among distinct and separate departments. The different governments," he concludes, "will control each other." He further believed that the "federal republic of the United States," because of her federal character, would provide better safeguards for the rights of minorities than ordinary republics, where the "majority be united by a common interest" and therefore "the rights of the minority will be insecure."[5] Clearly, this is not the same as what Pufendorf had said but both share the idea that the principle of federalism refers not only to the structural relationship *between* sovereign states, but to the dynamics of power relations between smaller and larger states supposedly on equal footings with each other in general and to the problem of safeguarding rights of weaker states in particular.

These general remarks suggest that both papers, fine and delicate discussions of difficult problems indeed, probably put too much emphasis on the formal legal structural aspects of federalism and ignore too much the internal consequences stemming from the concept of federalism. I think that Dr. Neuhaus has put us all in his debt for his clear and concise description of the federal structure of the Holy Roman Empire. Yet I wonder whether he would not like to push his analysis a bit further into the inner workings of, as well as the relationship between, federated powers. Did the *Reichskammergericht* and then the emperor indeed not fulfill functions similar to those described by Madison as qualities of federalism and thus

---

4. Samuel Pufendorf, *Severinus de Mozambano* (1667); my translation is based on Ellinor von Puttkamer, ed., *Föderative Elemente im deutschen Staatsrecht seit 1648*, Quellensammlung zur Kulturgeschichte, 7 (Göttingen, 1955), 41.
5. Jacob E. Cooke, ed., *The Federalist* (Middletown, CT, 1961), 350–51. Cf. David F. Epstein, *The Political Theory of the Federalist* (Chicago, IL, 1984), 54.

provide a shield – for example, in the case of the Württemberg estates against their duke or in that of numerous cities, Dortmund, for example, comes to mind, against their *Landesherren* – and can it therefore not be said that the federal structure of the Holy Roman Empire provided safeguards for minorities similar to those that Madison mentioned for America?

Dr. Onuf's fine paper raises similar issues when stating that "in crucial respects, namely, in jurisdiction over the public lands, new states would have to be less than equal."[6] Yet this was of course the position at the beginning of the 1780s and prevailed only so long as the discussion between landless old states, "western 'sons of freedom,'"[7] and defenders of land-rich states like Virginia continued. After these states had ceded their western lands to the Confederation, the "western 'sons of freedom'" lost support. For "nationalization of the frontier promised the small states equal access to the western lands while redressing imbalances in state size,"[8] thus uniting small and large states against separatist sentiments advocating local self-government on the frontier. This was now considered a threat to the "survival of the union."[9] Caught between these two irreconcilable positions, Congress in 1784 developed "a new jurisdictional category, the 'territory,'"[10] which guaranteed control over western lands and secured these against western separatist tendencies and inferences of foreign powers,[11] culminating in the "broad framework of western development" embodied in the Land Ordinance of 1785 and the Northwest Ordinance of 1787.[12] Dr. Onuf interprets this solution as the result of a transfer of this thorny problem from the "realm of politics . . . to the realm of political economy."[13] The plan was simple: initially western settlement would be under "direct congressional rule" designed to "impose conditions of law and order essential to productive private enterprise,"[14] which would be gradually eased

---

6. Peter S. Onuf, "American Federalism and the Politics of Expansion," above, 57.

7. Ibid., 57.
8. Ibid., 59.
9. Ibid., 60.
10. Ibid., 62.
11. Ibid., 63.
12. Ibid., 64.
13. Ibid., 65.
14. Ibid.

by increasing "privileges of self-government" to the new settlements[15] that would ultimately lead to statehood and membership within the union. According to Dr. Onuf this congressional "regulation was compatible with liberty because it facilitated private enterprise and accumulation that would be impossible under unregulated, anarchic conditions." Viewing "private enterprise as providing 'cement' of enduring union," Dr. Onuf assigns to it the function of a laxative for congressional control.[16]

This argument raises some fundamental issues which I think need further exploration: clearly congressional western policy was based not so much on the idea of safeguarding the rights of individuals and nascent communities in the western regions by granting them local self-government at the earliest possible moment, as the concept of federalism suggested, but on a conjunction of, to recall Madison's words in *Federalist* no. 51, "a common interest" of the old states and the "rights of the minority"[17] in the western regions, with the latter clearly losing to the former. The least one must say is that one of the most important features of federalism, protection of the right of the minority, was, as far as the concept of western expansion is concerned, suspended. And that was no mean act for a young republic basing her origins on revolutionary principles.

That indeed was the decisive difference between European and American federalist notions: safeguarding rights in Europe meant those of sovereigns, of estates, and of corporations, but of course by and large not those of individual citizens. In North America, on the other hand, safeguarding the rights of states was a most important feature of federalism – but that of safeguarding the rights of individual citizens was the other important aspect of American federalism. Indeed, I am pretty sure that at least for the founding generation one cannot divest the discussion of federalism from that of republican ideology and thinking. Dr. Onuf is naturally well aware of this, and by pointing to contemporary descriptions of territorial government as "despotic" or "colonial,"[18] I suppose he intended to remind us of this context.

Yet my feeling is that here he does not quite do justice to the

15. Ibid., 66.
16. Ibid., 68.
17. Cooke, ed., *Federalist* (see n. 5), 351.
18. Onuf, "American Federalism" (see n. 6), 66, 68.

complexity of the relationship between these two concepts. While I agree with him that the problem of western lands after 1785 was discussed relatively more often in terms of political economy, those questions belonging to the "realm of politics" remained very much in the picture. The Reverend Manasseh Cutler, no mean authority indeed, certainly viewed the issues in a broader context. Writing to Winthrop Sargent on October 6, 1786, he confessed that in his mind

> it seems to be more problematical than ever whether mankind are in a state for enjoying all ye natural rights of humanity, and are possessed of virtue sufficient for ye support of a purely republican Government. Equal liberty in civil Community appears finely on paper, but ye question is, can it be realized? America is the first Nation on earth, who have had an opportunity for making a fair experiment, and will ere long decide one of ye most important questions in ye philosophical world. You will perhaps begin to think me a tory. I wish for liberty – but not at ye expence of Government.

And with an eye on the future government in the Ohio region for which Cutler was at this time negotiating in Washington, he continued: "The new States I hope, when they come to form Constitutions, will guard against ye evils in ye Old and realize that coercive Government is as necessary for ye existence of civil Society, as ye soul for ye existence of ye body."[19]

Even if we must allow Shays's Rebellion a large share in prompting such sentiments, it is evident that in the minds of contemporary old-state proponents of western states probably more was at stake than just the orderly process of western expansion. Cutler, and his feelings were shared by others as well, clearly felt that the nature of republican government needed rethinking not because of the chaos George Washington, John Jay, and others saw reigning in the West, but because it seemed to bring down political

19. The letter is in Frederick S. Alis, Jr., and Roy Bartolomei, eds., *The Winthrop Sargent Papers*, Massachusetts Historical Society, Microfilm Publication No. 1, 7 reels (Boston, MA, 1965), reel 2, exposures 647–48, cited in Hermann Wellenreuther, "'First Principles of Freedom' und die Vereinigten Staaten als Kolonialmacht, 1787–1803: Die Northwest Ordinance von 1787 und ihre Verwirklichung im Northwest Territory," in Erich Angermann, ed., "Revolution und Bewahrung: Untersuchungen zum Spannungsgefüge von revolutionärem Selbstverständnis und politischer Praxis in den Vereinigten Staaten von Amerika," *Historische Zeitschrift*, Beiheft 5 (1979): 131.

order in the East. While John Jay was haunted by the vision of the western regions being filled "with white savages,"[20] the future secretary of the Northwest Territory and thereafter governor of the Mississippi Territory, Winthrop Sargent, sitting in his tent near Pittsburgh, scribbled in his diary under July 19, 1786: "We talked over and anticipated a future Establishment in this country, where the veteran soldier and honest Man should find a Retreat from Ingratitude – never more to visit the Atlantic States but in their Children and like Goths and Vandals, to deluge a People more vicious and villianeous [*sic*] than ever the Pretorian Bands of ancient Rome."[21] True republican virtues – which of course meant different things to different people – traveled West and to that a lot of settlers in the Northwest Territory soon agreed. Indeed the lively debates in the territory between 1788 and the ratification of the Ohio Constitution in 1802 used revolutionary experience and thinking to an astonishing extent. One example must suffice: when in 1793 five judges of the peace returned their appointments as judges "during pleasure," they used "the Language of 1774, 75 of Liberty Privilege &ca, &ca, &ca," wrote Winthrop Sargent to Governor St. Clair.[22]

Put differently, what made politicians in the East proud, made those citizens who had settled in the West and who under the Northwest Ordinance, at least until the attainment of statehood, were denied the sweet taste of citizenship angry, bitter, and resentful. To those living in the Northwest Territory between 1788 and 1802, the mere notion of having become "white savages" and thus unworthy to partake in a civilized and republican government smacked of despotism indeed, of living under a "true transcript of our old English Colonial Governments," as Justice of the Peace William Goforth wrote President Thomas Jefferson in 1802.[23]

Dr. Onuf is probably right in insisting that, from a bird's-eye view in the Washington sky, regulated expansion as embodied in the Northwest Ordinance was a feasible and sensible solution to a

20. Henry P. Johnston, ed., *The Correspondence and Public Papers of John Jay*, 4 vols. (New York, 1890–93), 3: 222–24.

21. "Winthrop Sargent Diary," 18 June–26 October, 1786, in Alis, Jr., and Bartolomei, eds., *The Winthrop Sargent Papers* (see n. 19), reel 1, exposure 125.

22. Winthrop Sargent to Governor St. Clair, February 7, 1793, in Clarence Edwin Carter and John Porter Blooms, eds., *The Territorial Papers of the United States*, 29 vols. to date (Washington, DC 1934–[1979]), 2: 432.

23. Carter and Blooms, eds., *Territorial Papers* (see n. 22), 3: 198.

number of pressing and confusing problems; but I am not yet convinced that this "regulation was compatible with liberty because it facilitated private enterprise and accumulation that would be impossible under unregulated, anarchic conditions."[24] In the Northwest Territory this regulation certainly was viewed as a flagrant retraction of republican principles and a substitution of British colonial rule for celebrated Revolution principles. Western settlers were bitter, even if only temporarily, about being denied the fruits of their labors during the Revolution. To them, at least, the supposed advantages of federalism were nonexistent.

24. Onuf, "American Federalism" (see n. 6), 68.

3.4
Discussion

HERMANN WELLENREUTHER: Mr. Guggisberg and Mr. Neuhaus have argued conclusively that neither the Holy Roman Empire nor the Swiss or Dutch examples were sources for American federalist concepts. I would like to ask Mr. Stourzh about traits in English legal thought in the eighteenth century to which American concepts of federalism could be traced.

GERALD STOURZH: Probably there are none. Great Britain was of course an empire that consisted of various composite units; moreover, as a state England was not so unified as we sometimes tend to think. Thus the very growth of assorted subordinate entities endowed with various degrees of autonomy certainly had, I think, particularly in North America as well as elsewhere, encouraged the idea of a political entity consisting not only of political subjects subject to *the* sovereign individually but also of a larger political entity composed of a number of subentities. To that extent I think – but that has of course been said before – that the United States did grow out of the experience shaped by the past; it was not wholly new.

Overall, however, I continue to be more impressed with the newness of the thoughts of men like Jefferson and Madison. But this raises the interesting problem of rhetorical strategies, especially those of persuasion and dissimulation. On the one hand, the founding fathers were, as Madison has said, trying to create a new kind of government because there were two levels – the state and federal levels – that affected individuals very much. On the other hand, the authors of the *Federalist* de-emphasized the newness of the design by conscientiously employing a language more traditional than the concept of government they were trying to push through warranted. This strategy should make us weary of taking the comments of The *Federalist* too literally.

ERICH ANGERMANN: Don't we have to be aware that the term "federalism" underwent a very severe change of meaning at the time of the Constitution so that the founding fathers in fact never thought of patterning their concept after anything European? One simply had to be aware of the old concepts of "confederation" and then start out with the intention of doing something entirely new, namely, creating a strong national government. The founders chose to call it a federal government because that was a much more apt designation at the time than the terms "national" or "consolidated government" would have been.

GERALD STOURZH: I agree with Mr. Angermann that the American founders and Madison and Hamilton in particular used old language for a new thing. The old language was not a clear-cut one because in Montesquieu you do get the word *confédération* but you also get the expression that states will get together to form a "federal constitution"; the very expression *constitution fédéral*, not *fédérative*, occurs in Montesquieu's *Esprit des lois*. This idea of federal constitution was taken up by the Americans who indeed, as we all know, did look very closely at Montesquieu's work, which for them was a kind of textbook.

GRETE KLINGENSTEIN: It seems to me that the American concept of federalism was already based on a very new, and let us call it modern, idea of statecraft. Very recently I read the works of two Cologne scholars, Barbara Stollberg-Rilinger,[1] who wrote on the idea of state and the state as a machine, and Harm Klueting,[2] on the new concept of power in foreign relations as it evolved in both Prussia and Austria. It occurred to me in reading these books that the idea of the Holy Roman Empire as a federal state was a very old medieval idea and could no longer be adopted to the new mechanistic systematic thinking proposed by men such as Montesquieu. It seems to me that the idea of empire contained, and here I may draw your attention to Marsilius of Padua, an assortment or variety of politics including cities, villages, small and large territories, and ecclesiastic as well as secular areas whereas, if I am correct in this comparison, the new idea of American federalism was a mechan-

1. Barbara Stollberg-Rilinger, *Der Staat als Maschine: Zur politischen Metaphorik des absoluten Fürstenstaats*, Historische Forschungen, 30 (Berlin, 1986).
2. Harm Klueting, *Die Lehre von der Macht der Staaten: Das außenpolitische Machtproblem in der "politischen Wissenschaft" und in der praktischen Politik im 18. Jahrhundert*, Historische Forschungen, 29 (Berlin, 1986).

istic one based principally on the idea of equality.

In this context, minorities have a very different position in the Holy Roman Empire than they do in the United States. There is, to put it very briefly, a concept of quantities in the United States that is opposed to the concept of qualities in the Holy Roman Empire.

KNUD KRAKAU: In reading these papers I was struck by the idea that no one directly addressed the question whether federalism was really compatible with the notion of monarchy, or to turn the question upside down, whether republicanism was a precondition for a functioning federalism. Put that way I doubt it very much, but the problem is that the basic monarchical principle of *iure divino* is intrinsically incompatible with any kind of federation in the modern sense of the term. Such organizations may join together in all kinds of leagues, confederations, or *Staatenbünde*, but I do not think they could be constitutionally integrated into the complicated mechanism of a federal system that simultaneously transposed the composite parts of the league to the higher entity, as the modern notion suggests.

PETER S. ONUF: On the question of whether monarchies fit into a federal union, I think the answer is clearly "no" and the whole thrust of the American system is toward an equalization of states. It is certainly true that the definition of equality is problematic in terms of territory, population, power – in that sense it certainly was a product of power politics, as Gerald Stourzh has already said. There was some considerable discussion in the 1780s over what form a federal government should take and the kind of constitution you would have to have for all the states collectively. Because the Confederate Congress was such an inadequate model the idea was bandied about that perhaps only a government that could exercise powers usually associated with a monarchy could work on the level of the entire continent. Indeed, in many ways Congress itself had assumed some of the powers of the British monarch. Yet I think that your [that is, Knud Krakau's] point about their absolute incompatibility is completely correct – but contemporaries were not aware of that. There was still a free play of thinking about this.

ROBERT C. POST: The central question posed by this session is whether there are any analytic categories that would enable us to compare the American Constitution with the Holy Roman Empire. One approach would be to focus on the antecedent social realities that enabled nation builders to create one kind of political system rather than another. In that light, let me propose the sociological category of nationalism. To me, one of the most interesting points of Peter Onuf's paper is its conjunction of federalism with nationalism. Contemporary Americans normally think of federalism and nationalism as pointing in opposite directions. We associate nationalism with centralization and view it as a centripetal force. We think of federalism, on the other hand, as local and centrifugal. This same tension was in the minds of the framers. Yet Peter Onuf proposes the fascinating hypothesis that federalism was in the early American Republic harnessed to nationalism and to the concept of a centralized government. This was possible because of the antecedent political identity of those Americans who went out to the West. How does this compare to the European context? Was there a sense of nationalism in Germany, in the Netherlands, or in the Swiss cantons, which would have created the possibility of a similar blending of nationalism and federalism? Are we dealing with situations that are sociologically similar or not?

HARTMUT LEHMANN: "Nationalism" should be translated into German as *Reichspatriotismus*. The last period in which we speak of *Reichspatriotismus* is that of the 1630s, where something like patriotism for the empire as such existed, but not in the 1740s, or the 1770s, or in the stages of agony in the 1790s and so on.

TIMOTHY H. BREEN: Over the last twenty years social historians in the United States have raised some important questions about community development and structure. These issues have in turn evolved new problems, however, and that is the pointillism of social history; we lack a sense of coherence. It strikes me that meetings like this have the potential to reintroduce process into community development in the sense of something happening to them all.

The process we are talking about in this session is "federalism," "federalization," "consociation." In both papers there are suggestions about people to whom federalism "happens" – peasants in Germany who fight wars, till lands, or pay taxes – this thing "federalism" visits them one day, and there are these westerners (in North America) who are either barbarians or model citizens, depending on which way you are looking: but still, federalism comes to them.

Historians ought to develop some more sophisticated models that would escape what I would call the "legal-political-intellectual approach," which is the dominant discourse here. Instead they should think of how to tie in the local histories, including demographics and local cultural studies, with these larger processes and how to in some way link both. At the very least, this model I have in mind would be a dialectical one that would include some kind of reciprocal relationship between the frontiers in North America, the peasants in Germany – because they are not passive victims of federalization, they have a say in their lives, but not so much of a say that they can say we do not want federalism. And then, if you push this just one more stage, you would discover that the West is just as diverse as the East; the Kentucky frontier bears almost no relationship to the Ohio frontier. There is no West, and I think you would quickly discover, too, that there is no federalism in this time but a chorus of possible voices and concepts.

FRED L. MORRISON: I may be the only dissenter here on monarchy and federalism. Once you start talking about a monarchy whose authority is somewhat circumscribed by a constitution, then you are talking about the possibility that the monarch is only one of a series of actors in a process; and then, I believe, a federal system becomes possible.

GERHARD A. RITTER: I would like to add that another aspect of federalism comes up in the nineteenth century, the concept of hegemonial federalism, that is, a federation in which one of the members is a hegemonial power, like Prussia in Bismarck's empire, or earlier, the province of Holland in the Netherlands.

Second, I would like to point out that in 1867 or 1871, during the debates on the constitutions, Bismarck was very much aware of what was just said. I mean that he conscientiously constructed the *Bundesrat* in a way that opposed parliamentarism and furthered democratization because he rightly thought that the monarchs of the individual member states especially would oppose this development in the interest of their own states and that the parliaments in the individual states, too, would help in this. Federalism in Bismarck's construction was meant as a barrier against certain developments of democratization and parliamentarization. Thus clearly, in the case of Germany, a limited monarchy did allow federalism.

PAUL FINKELMAN: We are now talking about federalism in the way it was done in Philadelphia in 1787 and not in the context of federalism and expansion. It strikes me that the really big difference is that in Europe a federal state cannot conceive of expansion without contemplating conquering someone else, whereas the Americans were struggling with what they wanted to do with vacant land. That of course again raises the whole issue of what kind of liberty you give them. I just wonder whether there is a theoretical and historical difference between thinking about federalism in North America in terms of deciding what kind of federation they want and thinking about federalism vis-à-vis territories which you then later incorporate into the state.

GERALD STOURZH: In Europe we do have expansion without conquest. The Austrian historian Otto Brunner suggested the well-known formula, a monarchical union of corporate states or estate-oriented states. In early modern history this is one very important model of state formation and above all of the formation of larger entities. I do think that the idea of a monarchical union of states, that retained to some extent their own autonomous institutions and local institutions, the *Ständestaaten*, could serve as a European equivalent for the American idea of conquest and expansion.

HAROLD MELVIN HYMAN: Could you try to translate the term *Ständestaat* for us?

GERALD STOURZH: Well, *Ständestaat* is a state with estates, for instance, England with the House of Lords and the House of Commons or Scotland for that matter. The idea is that there has been an expansion by one monarch or dynasty that obtained control of a country with autonomous estates and these estates were actually retained although they got a different ruler. One classical case is the continuance of the estates of Hungary within the Habsburg Empire.

Part 2
The Idea of the Ruler
in the Eighteenth Century

4
Concepts of Presidential Leadership, Citizenship, and Good Government in the United States during the Founding Era

Ralph Ketcham

Two sets of writings, the Politics of Aristotle (ca. 350 B.C.) and certain sections from the classics traditionally attributed to Confucius, the *Analects*, the *Great Learning*, and the *Spring and Autumn Annals* (ca. 500 B.C.), quite likely rank as the most influential works on public philosophy in all of recorded human history. Some other works, such as parts of the Koran, Locke's *Second Treatise on Government*, and Lenin's *State and Society*, have had extraordinary significance in many places and for long periods of time, but for illuminating the nature of the political in human life and for outlining the place, purpose, and design of government in society, the Greek philosopher and the Chinese sage alone surely hold the first rank. The richness of their concern for the *social* nature of the human species and for the vast potential of the state in nourishing "not life only, but the good life," make them the world's preeminent *political* (or social) philosophers.

The measure of their achievement is not that either offered a particularly profound ideology envisioning some substantial, theoretical future for society – as, for example, Plato, or Marx, or Rousseau, or Mao Zedong can be said to have done – but rather that each affords deep insight into the very nature of the political itself. One finds in the writings of each, that is, an indelible sense of human life in relationship rather than in isolation, of the vast increment derivable from public accord and from shared effort and purposes, and of the critically important, uniquely beneficial contribution a well-ordered, properly empowered, and public-spirited government can make. To see the point, one need only observe that Aristotle and Confucius were poignantly aware that attention or failure to govern well produces the catastrophes of chaos, civil strife, tyranny, and war. The Greek and Chinese histories known to Aristotle and Confucius provided abundant evidence of that equation. Each not only explained theoretically the usefulness of good government, but also described the means to achieve it. Their teachings, then, seek not so much to provide blueprints or dogma or system (though, especially in Confucius's case, followers have sought to impose such) as to furnish a point of view toward government and rules of thumb, frameworks of political analysis, and widely applicable guidelines for good government. One learns from each the inevitability of the social, the potential for the political, and the standards needed to judge the quality of government. Though Confucius and his followers paid particular attention to the education of the officials who would advise the emperor and administer the vast, centralized empire (Confucian thought contains no idea of the people taking part in government), and Aristotle wrote about the enlightenment of all citizens who would participate in government (still in Athenian Greece a small portion of the population), in effect they were both concerned about the wisdom and competence of those who would guide the polity's public life.

Something of their significance can be seen in the limitations of other notable and in some ways brilliant thinkers. Consider, for example, Saint Augustine, John Locke, and Henry David Thoreau. Each offers profound insight into the nature of the human mind and spirit (or soul) that have inspired and transformed countless people. Yet each is deeply flawed as a *political* thinker partly because, in attending so incisively to the individual, he has only a subordinated, even superficial concern for relations among human beings and for social context. No one probes the recesses of the soul or the bond between God and man more compellingly than Augustine – but is his view of the earthly city and its government cognizant of anything like the scope and potential inherent in the Greek idea of polis? Locke offers profound and liberating analysis of the human mind and of the implications for freedom and government by consent – but do the Lockean concepts of social *contract* and government for the *convenience* of individuals begin to grasp the complexities and opportunities of human society or of the uses of good government? Thoreau brilliantly challenges the imagination of unfettered individuals – but isn't his sense of society ("any man more right than his neighbors constitutes a majority of one already")[1] so uncomprehending of political obligation and human accord as to be, finally, "irretrievably absurd"? Any reading of Confucius or of Aristotle's *Politics* in the presence of such political superficiality evokes a sense of rediscovering a substantial and indispensable realm of human experience. Thoreau's world, or Augustine's, or Locke's seems narrow and unfulfilled, almost perversely antisocial compared, for example, to the *public* virtues and *civic* achievements of Pericles' Athens or the early years of the Sung dynasty in China, the politics of which have perhaps best embodied the Greek and Chinese ideals.

Lest this seem unfair to the three "individualists" (and many others with similar orientation and genius), we must add quickly that there is no intention to disparage them – as far as they go. Human history and human life have been immeasurably enriched by their thought and writings. But it is also true that without more profound and substantial *political* ideas than any of them articulate, human society would not only be stunted generally but would even be unlikely to provide the ordered, receptive context needed to allow individual genius to survive and flourish. One need only recall the sufferings of the people of Argentina or Poland or Iran or China or Germany during much of the twentieth century (to choose among many available examples) to see the appalling liabilities of poor government. The substantial and educing foundation required, then, is not hostile or contradictory to the contributions of artistic or religious creativity. But a fuller, more intricate, more enlarging sense of human society and a deliberate attention to the positive contributions good government can make to human life are also essentials. In Aristotle's own words, "He who by nature and not by mere accident is without a state, is either above humanity or below it."[2]

When Aristotle wrote that "man is a political animal," he meant that part of human nature, an essential, ennobling part, was to have a concern for the public good, to have an opportunity to discuss and help resolve public matters, and to have pride in the quality of the shared life of the community – that is, to be a *citizen* of the polis.

1. Henry David Thoreau, *Essay on Civil Disobedience* (1848).
2. *Aristotle's Politics*, trans. Benjamin Jowett, introd. Max Lerner (New York, 1943), bk. I, chap. 2.

Without such participation, such fulfillment of that part of our nature which welcomes and enjoys effective public life, we simply undervalue and undernourish some of our humanness. "It is the nature of human beings living in society," as Max Lerner notes, "that they must work toward goals which have value" – and the state is the essential means of this axiom.[3] Just as Augustine, Locke, Adam Smith, Thoreau, and D.H. Lawrence evoke and challenge profoundly important aspects of our human nature, so too do Aristotle, Confucius, and other great *public* philosophers.

It is precisely this deep sense of publicness, exemplified in the approaches of Aristotle and Confucius, that is an often underemphasized part of the outlook of the founders of the American republic. Though they knew little or nothing of the Chinese sage, they were deeply influenced by the thought and culture of Greece and Rome. As they learned Latin and Greek, they absorbed the rich ideals of leadership and public life implicit in the writings of Homer, Cicero, Virgil, Livy, Plutarch, and others. Then, their first systematic study of politics was very likely cast in the conventional, Aristotelian framework: governments were by one, the few, or the many, and in each category there were good and bad forms. Kings could be tyrants or, in the eighteenth-century designation, "benevolent despots," the few could be oligarchs or aristocrats, while rule by the many could be turbulent and corrupt mob rule (what Aristotle termed *demo-cracy*) or good government under a constitutional polity. The key in any case was not the number who ruled, but the quality of government that resulted; whether, in Aristotle's terms, governments are good, ruling "with a view to the common interest," or "perversions," ruling "with a view to the private interest."[4]

The American founders, of course, were also well aware of more modern currents of political and social thought learned from Francis Bacon, Hobbes, Locke, "the English Cato," Bolingbroke,

3. Ibid., 21.
4. Ibid., bk. III, chap. 7. Meyer Reingold, *Classica Americana: The Greek and Roman Heritage in the United States* (Detroit, MI, 1984), explains more fully the influence in eighteenth century America of Aristotle and other classical thinkers. It is unlikely that the American founders had any knowledge of Confucius's thought – at least he is unmentioned in their extant writings, as far as I know (they were probably only aware that such a philosopher had existed in ancient China). Thus, reference to Confucius in this paper is only to enlarge understanding of the general approach to government of the American founders – an approach in some ways similar to that of Confucius, but of course not derived directly from his writings.

Adam Smith, Montesquieu, Hume, and others, but two factors controlled or even subordinated the impact of "modernity" on the founders. First, the "moderns" themselves, though preoccupied with new learning, were nonetheless Enlightenment figures stimulated by the revival of classical ideas. Thus, even the forward-looking thinkers so impressive to Americans – Jefferson's "trinity of immortals," Bacon, Newton, and Locke, for example – were learned classicists living within a worldview deeply responsive to the wisdom of Greece and Rome. David Hume, increasingly recognized as a major influence on Madison and other American founders, wrote that "a man, who is only susceptible of friendship, without public spirit or a regard to the community, is deficient in the most material part of virtue."[5] This publicly cognizant understanding of virtue, plus the implication of human "deficiency" if "public spirit" is missing, reveals the loud echoes of antiquity in the neoclassical world of the eighteenth century. Like Aristotle and Cicero, it was simply impossible for a Jefferson or a Hamilton to depreciate the political, to devalue the uses of good government, as a Thoreau, or a William Graham Sumner, or a Ronald Reagan would do in later centuries.

Second, the classical outlook was "second nature" to educated people of the eighteenth century because it was learned first, since pupils usually studied Latin and Greek before they had extensive contact with important modern writers. As students learned to read Cicero's eloquent Latin they also learned of the dangers posed by military control of politics, and as they read Livy's idealized history of the Roman republic they absorbed lessons in leadership and in the requirements of responsible citizenship. The wisdom of Greece and Rome, experienced as schoolboys, furnished, so to speak, the folklore, the "morality plays," and the basic concepts of human nature and society for the founding generation. Though they would later, for example, respond to Locke's insistence on the natural right of self-government or to the English Cato's stirring defense of free speech, these concepts were an overlay only on their already deeply ingrained, classical understanding of the political and its importance in human affairs.

This understanding of the political had an important and often

---

5. David Hume, "That Politics May Be Reduced to a Science" (1741), in Charles William Hendel, ed., *Political Essays* (Indianapolis, IN, 1953), 20.

overlooked or misconstrued influence on the ideas of leadership –
and citizenship – of those who drafted, supported, and opposed the
Constitution of 1787 in the United States. The debates both during
and after the Constitutional Convention reveal the essentially
qualitative emphasis of all concerned. That is, those drafting the
Constitution expected their work to be judged according to the
quality of government it would provide: would it "establish Justice,
insure domestic Tranquility, provide for the common defence,
promote the general Welfare, . . . secure the Blessings of Liberty"
and altogether "form a more perfect Union"? Note the capitalized
nouns emphasizing the essentials: Justice, Tranquility, Welfare,
Blessings of Liberty, Union – all qualities of the society vital to the
people and to be sustained by government – as Aristotle had
taught. With these agreed-upon goals, or "goods," the problem
then becomes one of framing a government – processes, institutions, and so on – that will be effectual to those ends.

As the debates of 1787–88 indicate clearly, all were aware that
government by one or the few *might*, theoretically, best sustain the
goals sought. Thus Hamilton countenanced an executive in office
for life, and John Adams upheld the uses of a candidly aristocratic
senate. In opposition, some Antifederalists supposed a division of
the union or a much-heightened emphasis on local, town-
meeting-type government would be best. These ideas, though, fell
outside the also-agreed-upon "American genius" for a republican
union, that is, a government deriving all its power, finally, from
the people (the majority principle); some form of representation
rather than "pure" democracy; and a federation that would retain
the states as important parts of the system. These were the procedural or institutional "givens" in 1787–88, but they were accepted
only because the revolutionary ideology and experience had validated them as peculiarly suited to the achievement of justice,
tranquility, welfare, and liberty – or, conversely, had invalidated
government by one or the few as peculiarly hostile to that achievement. Thus, what Americans were agreed on in 1787–88 was *both*
the Aristotelian emphasis that government should be an active
agent for pursuit of the public good (justice, etc.) *and* the Lockean
emphasis that government should derive from the consent of the
governed. But is was just as much agreed that to retain its validity,
the *procedure* of majority rule would have to be so organized as to
retain the *substantial* goal of nourishing the public good. Put

oppositely, the democratic process would deserve repudiation if it proved hostile to that good. The constant awareness by the revolutionary generation of their responsibility in "trying" government by consent, whether they would enhance or diminish its standing in the world, meant that they would have to "make it work," cause it to result in "the good life," reflect what Hume called "public spirit." Otherwise it would not merit praise or even survival.

Although the Constitutional Convention has been interpreted in many ways – as a "reform caucus," as a counterrevolutionary plot, as an assembly of demigods, and so on – it was most fundamentally an effort to restructure the confederation to make it both *good* government and *self*-government. The chorus of complaint and foreboding in the 1780s arose not so much from economic distress as from the widespread apprehension that governments were not working well. "The critical period" was quite real not as a description of depression or material deprivation but rather as a characterization of difficulties arising from the serious (and largely unexpected) "vices of the political system of the United States," as Madison put it.[6] In Washington's words, during the troubled winter of 1786–87, "No morning ever dawned more favorably than ours did; and no day was ever more clouded than the present. Wisdom and good examples are necessary at this time to rescue the *political* machine from the impending storm."[7]

By 1787, the revolutionary generation was much more aware than it had been in 1776 of the complexities of good self-government – of the difficulty of being *wise democrats*. Then, as during the long dispute with Britain leading up to independence, attention focused on the legislature. Drawing on the ancient English practice of restricting the people's voice in government to one branch of the legislature (the House of Commons) and on the colonial experience of the lower house as the place of effective assertion of local interests against imperial power, Americans in 1776 tended to think government by consent consisted largely of a fully empowered, responsive legislature. Somehow the "superior" and "inferior" offices – the executives who administer the law and the citizens who elect the legislators – were less attended to.

6. Robert A. Rutland et al., eds., *The Papers of James Madison*, 15 vols. to date (Chicago, IL, 1962–), 9: 345–58.
7. Washington to Madison, November 5, 1786, in ibid., 9: 161.

Thoughtful people realized, of course, that the character and qualifications of the electors were of ultimate importance. It was also clear that freedom and well-being in society depended critically on good or bad execution of the laws – Pope's oft-quoted couplet was

> For forms of government let fools contest –
> That which is best administered is best.[8]

But, initially at least, there was confidence in the capacity of the legislature to embody the public good.

Soon, though, difficulties appeared on all sides. Efforts by the Continental Congress to draft Articles of Confederation stalled first in Congress, then in the state legislatures, and resulted (after five years of bickering) in a document widely regarded as inferior to the ad hoc procedures it replaced. Among its obvious deficiencies were the lack of provision for executive power and a marked distancing of its officers from "the people." The states debated, drafted, and redrafted constitutions that increasingly reflected disenchantment with the assumption of legislative supremacy. Governors proved impotent to cope with problems of either war or peace, and whatever the voter qualifications or frequency of elections, the performances of the state legislatures were widely disapproved. The acts of the Maryland legislature "uniformly tended to disgust its citizens" (1784), North Carolina laws were "the vilest collection of trash" (1780), and the New York legislature "daily committed the most flagrant acts of injustice" (1787), according to not necessarily unbiased observers.[9] As disillusionment with legislative performance heightened, attention naturally shifted to executive power as a check or stimulant and to the *quality* (qualifications) of those who chose the legislators. That is, what were the uses of leadership and of citizenship in a self-governing polity? Might each need to be improved or exalted in order to contend with the palpable deficiencies of, as Madison put it in *Federalist* no. 48, "the legislative department . . . drawing all power into its impetuous vortex?"

Though these concerns, even fears, drove some critics back

8. Alexander Pope, "Essay on Man," in John Butt, ed., *Alexander Pope: The Poems*, 11 vols. (London, 1950–69), 3: 303–4.
9. All quoted from Gordon S. Wood, *Creation of the American Republic, 1776–1787* (Chapel Hill, NC, 1969), 406.

toward such antidemocratic devices as hereditary officeholding and more stringent limitations on suffrage, a much more creative and in the end more influential reaction turned to "republican solutions": how could executive energy be both derived from the people and enlisted on behalf of good (as opposed to tyrannical) government, and how could the "discretion of the people" be improved so they would choose better (more able, wiser) officials? The two directions were linked, moreover, because in order for the executive power to be both a substantial check on and a qualitative supplement to the flawed legislature and still remain within the republican principle, it too would require derivation from and dependence on a *qualified* electorate.

Debate in the Constitutional Convention revealed the close connection between the construction of the executive power and assumptions about the capacity of the people for self-government. The convention began with its members puzzled and uncertain about both problems. Madison had confessed to Washington a month before it opened that while he was convinced there must be a national executive, he had "scarcely ventured as yet to form [his] own opinion" about its selection or powers.[10] When the convention first considered executive power, Madison recorded for the only time that "a considerable pause ensued" – the members had no urgent or decided opinions on the subject. However, James Wilson, who had the clearest ideas about executive power and eventually had the greatest influence on its construction, early asserted two vital propositions: that "the executive consist of a single person" and that he be elected by the people. To Wilson the executive could be as thoroughly republican an officer as a legislator. "Prejudices against the Executive," he told the Constitutional Convention, "resulted from a misapplication of the adage that the parliament was the palladium of liberty." That may have been true "where the Executive was really formidable" and was independent of the people as in Great Britain, Wilson explained, but in a republic where the executive power was both limited and derived from the people, the situation was entirely different.[11]

Other members, though, revealed in the same debate that anti-

10. Madison to Washington, April 16, 1787, in Rutland et al., eds., *Papers of James Madison* (see n. 6), 9: 385.
11. Max Farrand, ed., *The Records of the Federal Convention of 1787*, 4 vols. (New Haven, CT, 1937, repr. 1966), 2: 301 (August 15, 1787).

executive prejudices remained strong. Bad experiences under George III and his colonial governors, wide reading in radical Whig tracts hostile to royal prerogative, and famous episodes in classical history of monarchs trampling republican liberties left many Americans convinced that executive power was inherently tyrannical. Roger Sherman of Connecticut (where for one hundred fifty years the colonial legislature had been the core of a widely admired government) voiced the basic reservation: "The Executive Magistracy is nothing more than an institution for carrying the will of the Legislature into effect, . . . and ought to be appointed by and accountable to the Legislature only, which was the depository of the supreme will of the Society." In this view, confirmed in many colonies when the legislatures struggled for power with royally appointed governors, the authentic voice of the people was found in their elected representatives in the legislature. Any other seat of power or even substantial check on it was thought to violate the very idea of self-government. Other reservations emphasized the danger inherent in a unitary executive. Edmund Randolph regarded that as "the fetus of monarchy."[12] Thus, between radical Whig prejudice in favor of legislatures and suspicions of any concentrations of power, the convention heard urgent arguments for a weak executive.

Yet sentiment during the 1780s had moved steadily to support a stronger executive. Madison argued that when legislative power (however democratically elected) was unchecked it was likely to threaten liberty because "wherever the real power in a Government lies, there is the danger of oppression." In the United States, where "the real power lies in the majority of the Community," oppression (laws neglectful "both of public Good and private rights") would most likely come "from acts in which the Government is the mere instrument of the major number of the constituents." This negative tendency, so apparent, Madison (and many other Federalists) thought, in the performances of state legislatures during the 1780s, was deeply troubling because it called "into question the fundamental principle of republican Government . . . according [to which] Right and power being both invested in the majority, are held to be synonymous."[13] This, of course, laid bare the root,

---

12. Debate of June 1, 1787, in ibid., 1: 65–66.
13. Madison, "Vices of the Political System," April 1787, and Madison to

nagging difficulty taken most seriously by theorists of self-government in the founding era: "If majorities are often wrong, on what grounds, or with the aid of what devices, can it be proper for them to rule?"

Madison's famous "Republican remedy for [the] disease[s] most incident to Republican government" in *Federalist* no. 10, to so "extend the sphere" of government that a factious majority would not be likely to form or coalesce, was a critically important tactical insight, but it was largely preventative. It suggested little about how "public Good and private rights" could receive positive support and enhancement. In addressing the problem Madison, Wilson, and other Federalists had, at least for the time being amid the 1780s "vices of the political system," little inclination to find "virtue" in legislative bodies. Instead they increasingly turned to the traditional source of "public Good," the executive authority, explained most eloquently for the revolutionary generation in Bolingbroke's *Idea of a Patriot King* (1749). The anti-executive bias of the American Revolution, general Whig distrust of any focus of power, and republican predilections to see deliberative assemblies as fountains of public virtue were serious obstacles to such a turn, but alternatives were getting hard to come by. How could the United States, its institutions of government unsettled yet widely regarded as having embarked on a critical testing of human capacity for self-rule, provide *good* government for its people?

Gouverneur Morris helped the convention of 1787 move away from legislative preoccupations by pointing out that since "the Legislature will continually seek to aggrandize and perpetuate themselves, . . . one great object of the Executive is to control the Legislature." Harking back to Roman and Tudor examples, Morris pointed out that "the Executive Magistrate should be the guardian of the people, even of the lower classes, against Legislative tyranny, against the Great and the wealthy who in the course of things will necessarily compose the legislative body." Proceeding to the question before the convention, of how to properly construct the executive department, Morris asserted that it "ought to be so constituted as to be the great protector of the Mass of the people." After rehearsing the arguments many delegates had made about the

---

Jefferson, October 17, 1788, in Rutland et al., eds., *Papers of James Madison* (see n. 6), 9: 354, 11: 298.

vices attendant on legislative election of the executive, Morris explained what he thought was the obvious answer to the troublesome problem of selection: "If [the executive] is to be the Guardian of the people let him be appointed by the people." They would, moreover, be the "best Judges" of the quality of the judicial appointments and the military duties of the president. Since the people would "feel the effects" of these important exercises of power, it was fitting that they have the authority to retain or remove those responsible for them. Morris thus favored a broadly empowered executive elected by the people and eligible for reelection to make him sensible while in office of the need to administer the laws in the public interest.[14]

James Wilson tied Morris's argument more closely to the republican character of the new constitution. He often insisted that the stability and justice of republican government required that it rest, like a pyramid, on the broad base of the people themselves. At the Pennsylvania State Constitutional Convention of 1790 he observed that good government had to be both "efficient and free. . . . But . . . to render government efficient, power must be given liberally; to render it free as well as efficient, those powers must be drawn from the people, as directly and as immediately as possible." This proposition was a commonplace among American Whigs of the revolutionary era in discussing *legislative* power, but Wilson moved boldly to apply it as well to the executive: "He who is to execute the laws will be as much the choice, as much the servant and, therefore, as much the friend of the people as he who makes them." In fact, Wilson found the granting of power to the executive necessary for "efficient" government safe and justifiable *only* if the executive was held directly responsible to the people. This "chain of connection," as he put it, would keep the executive attuned to "the interests of the whole," and generally less susceptible to the blandishments of special interests than the notoriously faction-ridden legislatures.[15]

In Wilson's argument the ancient idea, accepted by Morris, of the executive (monarch) as the protector and friend of the people received its legitimate foundation: far more than a hereditary,

14. Farrand, ed., *Records of the Federal Convention* (see n. 11), 2: 52–54 (July 19, 1787).

15. Speeches of January 1790; quoted in Geoffrey Seed, *James Wilson* (Millwood, NY, 1978), 134–37.

absolute monarch who might in some mystical way be sensitive to the rights and needs of "his people," a popularly selected executive would have immediate, practical attentiveness to those rights and needs. At least as much as the legislature, an elected executive would conform to the republican ideal of a responsible, public (-spirited) official acting in the interest of the community as a whole. American theories of a powerful "president of all the people" and the practices of such a presidency under Jackson, the two Roosevelts, and Lyndon Johnson have all simply worked out the implications of Wilson's argument. Thus, though the scope and structure of the contemporary presidency could not have been envisioned by the founders, led especially by Wilson, they fashioned an office consistent in spirit with its development in the hands of its most notable twentieth-century incumbents.

Even the device of the electoral college, so quickly rendered superfluous and now so irrelevant to the modes of modern presidential elections, was viewed by Wilson and others as an acceptable, relatively minor departure from the idea of executive dependence on the people. The bugaboo of corrupt, intriguing legislative election, which was nonetheless advocated by many delegates and even implanted in the first draft constitution of August 6, 1787, had been avoided. Wilson supposed that the presidential electors would be in substantial accord with the will of the people. The president, then, would indeed be their "friend" and advocate, giving voice and effect to the public will in a way that would not only prevent invasion of private rights but also allow and encourage the pursuit of programs for the good of the nation as a whole – precisely the guiding idea of republican government – and of traditional conceptions of patriot leadership.

The opposition to popular election of the president revealed how the question of executive leadership was tied to that of the competence of the electorate. In opposing direct election, George Mason "conceived it would be as unnatural to refer the choice of a proper character for Chief Magistrate to the people, as it would to refer a trial of colours to a blind man." The size of the country, he thought, would make it impossible for the people to properly "judge of the respective pretensions of the Candidates." Charles Pinckney feared that in popular elections the people would be misled by "a few active and designing men," while Elbridge Gerry thought such a mode of election "would certainly be the worst of all" because the people were "uninformed" and gullible. He believed, for example, that good governors of Massachusetts and New Hampshire, who had done their "duty" by insisting on necessary but unpopular fiscal restraints, had been "turned out for it" by the people in direct elections.[16] In fact, though a few delegates at the convention argued that direct election was theoretically attractive, most believed that in practice the incapacities of the voters would result in the choice of unqualified leaders. Thus the convention again faced the basic question of the ability of the people to fulfill *their office* as self-governing citizens wisely.

Members of the Constitutional Convention generally accepted the idea that citizenship, active participation in a self-governing society, required *qualification*, that is, some grounds for supposing that the voting (and, even more, officeholding) would be exercised with responsibility to the public good and with reason and a sense of justice. To some members this meant a version of the restriction, familiar in ancient Greece, modern Britain, and some of the new states, of suffrage to freeholders on the hallowed principle that those with "a stake in society," those who owned part of it (land), could be expected to vote responsibly and fairly. On the other hand, those without such a stake would be indifferent to the public good and unjust to those with property. John Dickinson stated the traditional argument that freeholders were "the best guardians of liberty. . . . The restriction of the right [to vote] to them [was] a necessary defence against the dangerous influence of those multitudes without property and without principle, with which our Country, like all others, will in time abound." Gouverneur Morris added: "Give the votes to people who have no property, and they will sell them to the rich who will be able to buy them." Furthermore, the growing class of "mechanics and manufacturers" who "receive their bread from their employers" would be dependent on them and thus not be able to "vote freely." Such a person, Morris argued, was not really participating, but rather was "represented" by "the man who dictates the vote." Charles Pinckney rehearsed these arguments in urging substantial property qualifications for the president, for federal judges, and for members of Congress. Only "possession of competent property," he insisted, would

16. Farrand, ed., *Records of the Federal Convention* (see n. 11), 2: 30–31, 56 (July 17 and 19, 1787).

"make them independent and respectable." To assure proper exercise of the great powers the proposed constitution conferred on all three departments, it was necessary "to connect the tie of property with that of reputation in securing a faithful administration."[17]

Other reservations about categories of people unfit to exercise the responsibilities of citizenship arose following Gouverneur Morris's motion to require "fourteen years instead of four years citizenship as a qualification for Senators." It was dangerous, he said, "to admit strangers into our public Councils." Charles Pinckney thought that those with "foreign attachments" would pose a "peculiar danger and impropriety" in a body dealing with foreign affairs. Pierce Butler, a native of Ireland, acknowledged that "his foreign habits, opinions, and attachments would have rendered him an improper agent in public affairs" during his first years in America. Morris further noted that all societies, from nations down to clubs, regulated admission of new members, so immigrants could not feel ill-treated at the proposed restriction, especially when "the privileges allowed to foreigners" in the United States exceeded those permitted in any other part of the world. He asserted further that he did not trust "those philosophical gentlemen, those Citizens of the World, as they call themselves," as prospective members of "our public Councils." He feared that "men who can shake off their attachments to their own Country can never love another." "Wholesome prejudices," Morris thought, normally give people a preference for their native land, so it would be incautious to bring such potentially traitorous biases into American government. Furthermore, Morris did not trust state legislatures to screen out "improper foreigners" in their choice of U.S. senators.[18]

Though the convention rejected all explicit property qualifications for either voting or officeholding and all severe restrictions on officeholding for nonnative citizens, the more liberal arguments objected not to the *idea* of voter qualification, but to the foolishness or injustice of the restrictions proposed. As was often the case during the convention, George Mason stated the republican ideal most forthrightly: "The true idea . . . was that every man having evidence of attachment to and permanent common interest with

17. Ibid., 2: 202–3, 248 (August 7 and 10, 1787).
18. Ibid., 2: 235–8 (August 9, 1787).

the Society ought to share in all its rights and privileges." This qualification, he thought, was not restricted to freeholders. Merchants, artisans, and financiers who owned no land and parents of children destined to live in the country might also feel the requisite "permanent attachment." Madison added that "the right of suffrage is certainly one of the fundamental articles of republican Government." Though he agreed with Dickinson that "the freeholders of the Country would be the safest repositories of Republican liberty," Madison was, like Mason, moving toward a broadened understanding of freehold suffrage: possession of land was surely not the only circumstance or quality that would make a person a responsible citizen. In fact, as some members pointed out, several states already permitted taxpayers, merchants, heads of families, and adult sons of "substantial farmers" as well as landowners to vote in some elections. Other members asked whether service in the armed forces during the Revolution was not sufficient evidence of attachment to the country. The difficulty of setting a uniform restriction for all the states and the awkwardness of having a federal restraint tighter than those for some state elections were mentioned as further practical considerations. Looking ahead to the need for the people to ratify the Constitution, John Rutledge thought the freehold restriction "a very unadvised one. It would create division among the people and make enemies of all those who should be excluded."[19] Clearly, members of the convention did not regard the traditional freehold restriction as entirely consistent with the emerging republican ideology of the new nation – but how could *responsible*, rather than selfish, manipulated, mindless, or factional participation be accentuated? Members were equally united in taking that question seriously.

In three short speeches, Benjamin Franklin discerned most profoundly the issues underlying the debate on suffrage and citizenship. He rejected outright the supposed connection between wealth (possession of property, landed or otherwise) and public virtue: "Some of the greatest rogues he was ever acquainted with, were the richest rogues." Though the poor were perhaps tempted to dishonesty to overcome poverty, Franklin thought the rich at least as much tempted because "the possession of property increased the desire of more property." Franklin noted that the Scripture required

19. Ibid., 2: 203–5 (August 7, 1787).

116

that "rulers . . . should be men hating covetousness." The author of *Poor Richard's Almanac* was well aware that the industrious tradesman and the yeoman farmer were at least as likely to develop in their occupations the essential moral qualities of citizenship as was the rich merchant or larger landholder – to say nothing of the slaveowner. If this were so, on what just grounds could suffrage and officeholding be conferred on some and denied to others?

Franklin then alluded to the high reputation American governments had in Europe and the value of this in attracting ambitious and talented immigrants. Should the Constitution "betray a great partiality to the rich," he observed, it would hurt the United States in "the esteem of the most liberal and enlightened men, . . . [and] discourage the common people from removing to this country." In urging quick qualification of new citizens for officeholding, Franklin thought their preference for the United States, evidenced by their choice and by their exertion in crossing the Atlantic, "is a proof of attachment [to America] which ought to excite our confidence and affection."[20] It was not wealth, then, that was the essential mark of the good American citizen, but rather attachment to the nation because of its freedom and justice and opportunity. Franklin had enlarged on the same point five years earlier in his advice on who should emigrate to the United States. A "mere Man of Quality," one without talent or virtue who merely prided himself on pedigree, wealth, or courtly sophistication, Franklin said, would be "despised and disregarded," while the farmer and artisan were "in honor [in America] because their employments are useful." The only encouragements offered to immigrants were "what are derived from good Laws and liberty." With such "advantages" poor but hardworking persons could soon own farms or "establish themselves in Business, marry, raise families" and, speaking of Pennsylvania, after "one or two years' residence [be given] all the Rights of a Citizen."[21] To Franklin, the qualifications for citizenship were clearly moral ones.

He even pointed out a critical linkage between granting rights of participation and encouraging the proper exercise of them. Great attention, he said, should be paid to "the virtue and public spirit of

20. Ibid., 2: 249, 236–37 (August 9 and 10, 1787).
21. "Information to Those Who Would Remove to America" (1782) in Ralph Ketcham, ed., *The Political Thought of Benjamin Franklin* (Indianapolis, IN, 1965), 336–46.

our common people." Those qualities were evident, he thought, among American seamen captured by the British during the Revolution who refused to purchase release from prison by "entering on board the Ships of the Enemies to their country." British prisoners, on the other hand, readily enlisted on board American ships. This "contrasting . . . patriotism," Franklin believed, "proceeded . . . from the different manner in which the common people were treated in America and Great Britain." To deny people the rights of citizenship, the right to vote and participate in government, would "depress" and "debase" their patriotism and sense of public responsibility. Thus, the extension of suffrage to the people (which in any case, under republican ideals, those already in office had no right to limit) would be a positive encouragement to their proper exercise of that right.[22] Franklin was formulating and urging implantation in the new constitution of a theory of citizenship linked to good leadership and good government: if ambitious, industrious people, grateful for the freedom and opportunity afforded by good laws and encouraged in virtue by the nature of their occupations, were given the rights of citizenship, the very exercise of those rights would help insure that the people would be able to choose good leaders. Franklin, that is, made the critical "wager" required at some stage in every effort to join self-government and good government – that the people were capable of attaining the skill and judgment needed to make wise and public-spirited choices. As Franklin put it, much, perhaps everything, depended on "the virtue and public spirit" of the people.

Where, then, were members of the convention headed in considering suffrage, the right to hold office, and the need for good leadership in a republic? At the urging of Franklin, Mason, Wilson, and others and with at least the hesitant support of all but a few delegates, the convention refused to tie the new government to schemes of land or wealth-restricted suffrage or officeholding. It did this in part for reasons of practical disagreements among the delegates, but more fundamentally because the old rationale for property-based, stake-in-society suffrage was revealed as deeply flawed. At the same time, the members were equally unwilling to assert on the face of it that everyone (even all white, adult males) in

22. Farrand, ed., *Records of the Federal Convention* (see n. 11), 2: 204–5, 249 (August 7 and 10, 1787).

a republic had a right to vote. They continued to accept the ancient equation between good government (results, not process) and properly qualified exercisers of power – as Confucius and Aristotle had taught. This meant, as Jefferson's thought and career would attest most profoundly, that the achievement of *good self-government* was complex and problematic, yet not impossible in a democratic society. Part of the hesitancy on the part of the convention arose, moreover, from its realization that the new United States was perhaps the first nation to address the question of good government in its new form: could the people, ultimately all of them in the internal logic of human equality, be so nurtured and organized politically that their self-rule might aspire to long-recognized standards of good government for a good society – for example, "establish Justice, insure domestic Tranquility, provide for the common defence, promote the general Welfare, and secure the Blessings of Liberty?"[23]

Three partially understood, perhaps problematic, yet portentous ideas, then, lurked in the "considerable pause" that ensued when the Constitutional Convention first took up the design of the executive department. First was the time-honored conviction that a purposeful government led by a powerful, active executive might be, as it always had been, the essential means to a beckoning national prosperity, freedom, and greatness. Second was the dawning awareness that this sort of executive might, in a republic, not be a threat to liberty and the public good but instead be the very instrument of that liberty and good. The principle of government empowered by consent, that is, could transform the often tyrannical executive into, in Wilson's words, "the servant and friend of the people." Finally, the members of the convention saw that the exciting prospects for such benign and constructive executive power depended, like so much else, on the existence among the people of, in Franklin's words, "virtue and public spirit."

The linkage of the ideas apparent to and accepted by all members of the convention (though some doubted or denied the premises of one or more of the three propositions), moreover, was both simple and crucial: only a properly qualified citizenry would be likely to elect a properly qualified executive fit to exercise the broad powers of leadership that good government itself required. Though many

---

23. Preamble of the U.S. Constitution.

other forces helped shape the office of the president, it is also clear that the provisions for the executive in the Constitution emerged in part from this linkage of ideas. In devising the Constitution, the framers *did* have in mind positive, Aristotelian ideas of active government, as well as ideas of consent (Locke, for example), separation of powers (Montesquieu, for example), refinement of representation (Hume, for example), and distrust of power (English Whigs, for example). The president *was* vested with "the executive Power" in its full eighteenth-century connotations, and his wide range of specific powers was such that they became a major target of opponents of the Constitution – but the authority had been conferred, was ratified, and remained in the document for presidents to use – as many have, I would argue legitimately and in the spirit of the framers, for two hundred years. And the president *was* to be elected, indirectly but unconditionally, by the people. The electoral college idea, as the convention debates clearly show, rested not on hostility to government by consent but on the earnest intention to protect that principle from two corruptions equally damaging to good government: mindless, demogogic, circuslike campaigns among the people at large and cabalistic, faction-ridden executive elections in Congress or in state legislatures. The convention *did* accept the essence of Morris's and Wilson's argument that the president could be depended upon to be the vigorous friend of the people if they were given the power to choose him. Finally, in refusing to limit suffrage in the Constitution itself and in allowing liberal provision for immigrants to become citizens, the convention attested at least a guarded confidence in the idea that the people – common people, from anywhere in the world – might possess or come to possess the "virtue and public spirit" to elect similarly qualified officials, especially in the amply empowered presidency.

In some ways the presidency of George Washington seemed to make the developing ideology of virtuous citizenship, vigorous leadership, and good government too easy. His unique standing in the country made boisterous electoral appeals to the people unnecessary, his known capacity for effective leadership precluded serious doubt on that score, and his acknowledged patriotism assured at least that his intentions would be on behalf of good government for the common welfare. Thus, though his presidency afforded little practice in the mechanisms of democracy and even left the qualifications of the people for responsible participation largely untested (though they *had* elected Washington), it did sustain the moral foundations of good government insisted upon by Confucius, Aristotle, and others. American government under him retained the emphasis on effective leadership in the public interest implanted in both the classical paradigm and in the Renaissance civic republican tradition derived from it. Washington was also entirely faithful to the ideas of ruling with the consent of the people and of nourishing, as much as possible within the limits of federal power, their well qualified participation in government. While maintaining what he regarded as a necessary dignity and formality in office, Washington always explicitly deferred to the people as well – any hint that he was not their clear, nonpartisan "choice" as president, for example, troubled him deeply and was taken as grounds for retirement to private life. He even considered public opinion, supportive of "consistent and wholesome plans, digested by common counsels and modified by mutual interests," as an essential guard against "the baneful effects of the spirit of party" which, left unchecked, would "perpetrate the most horrid enormities [and] . . . a frightful despotism."[24]

In order to encourage this constructive public opinion, Washington believed that Congress should use its "best endeavors to promote the education and manners of a people." He called specifically for a national university where "a portion of our youth from every quarter" of the nation could learn the common "principle, opinions, and manners" of a republican polity and receive instruction "in the science of government." Thus he accepted and promoted as best he could the assumptions undergirding discussion of his office at the Constitutional Convention; good government depended on effective, public-spirited leadership that rested on (and derived from) the active support of an enlightened citizenry.[25]

Though Washington's administration was often entangled in factional quarrels, and toward its end he himself became increasingly partisan, he viewed these developments with sadness and remorse. When confronted with what he regarded as "deliberate acts of . . . determined party" by members of his cabinet (Hamil-

---

24. "Farewell Address," September 17, 1796, in John Clement Fitzpatrick, ed., *George Washington: The Writings from the Original Manuscript Sources, 1745–1799*, 39 vols. (Washington, DC, 1931–43), 35: 226–28.
25. "Discarded Address," April 1789, in ibid., 30: 306–7.

ton and Jefferson), he begged them to subordinate their differences to the public good. Without that, he entoned, "everything must rub; the Wheels of Government will clog; our enemies will triumph. . . . Melancholy thought!"[26] Factional strife and party dispute, far from being signs of healthy differences of opinion or manifestations of diversity, were to Washington harmful to every one of the undergirding precepts: partisanship encouraged rancor and self-centeredness ("confusion and serious mischief," in Washington's words), it prevented the president from leading effectively in the public interest, and it poisoned the political harmony and elevated view vital to good government. Citizenship, leadership, and good government all suffered, that is, from the incessant party disputes and sharpening of conflict that the conventional wisdom of a later age would declare to be essential to the good health of democratic politics. The Constitution and the ideas of executive power that informed it, however, were generally the products of an earlier age. Washington, in the spirit of Aristotle and Confucius and in keeping with the intent of the convention of 1787 over which he had presided, thought of wisdom, active leadership, and concern for the common good, not party conflict, democratic process, and elite privilege, as essential to an admirable polity.

Thomas Jefferson's conception of leadership in a republic and his own remarkable presidency under the Constitution, though, furnish the keenest insight into the founders' understanding of that office. His experience as governor of Virginia convinced him (as it did Madison) of the need for a stronger executive power, more independent of the legislature. He approved of the much-strengthened executive department in the federal Constitution of 1787, but he urged, in order to make the president less subject to partisan politics, that he be elected for a single, perhaps longer term and that he be ineligible for reelection. Even though Jefferson came to be deeply troubled by Hamilton's manipulation of executive power during Washington's presidency and has often been pictured as a foe of such power, Hamilton himself testified that while they "were in the administration together, [Jefferson] was generally for a large construction of the Executive authority."[27] Then, in his own adminis-

---

26. Washington to Hamilton, August 26, 1792, and to Jefferson, August 23, 1792, in ibid., 32: 130–34.

27. Hamilton to James A. Bayard, January 16, 1801, in Harold C. Syrett et al., eds., *The Papers of Alexander Hamilton*, 27 vols. (New York, 1962–87), 25: 319–24.

trations, despite lingering Whig biases for legislative supremacy, executive limitation, and "mild" government, all heightened by a decade of opposition to Federalists in power, Jefferson provided vigorous leadership that has earned him a place on everyone's list of the half-dozen most able American presidents. He understood, advocated, and practiced the art of active leadership.

The basis for this executive vigor was Jefferson's own acceptance of an Aristotelian sense of both the uses of good government and the possibility of conducting it according to an objective idea of the public good. (His aphorism that that government is best which governs least applied especially to the federal government and to the excesses in it engineered during twelve years of Federalist rule.) He had left Congress after the Declaration of Independence, he later wrote, to return to Virginia, there to take part in removing the "vicious points" of "regal government" and instead to draft and enact laws "for a government truly republican." His efforts there on behalf of new laws for inheritance of lands, religious liberty, public education, administration of justice, and the gradual abolition of slavery amounted to active government of the most comprehensive sort. Jefferson believed that regimes could ruin or uplift a state or a nation. When his granddaughter wrote glowingly of the prosperity, beauty, and happiness of western Massachusetts in 1825, he replied, remembering his own earlier journey (1791) through what "was then mostly desert, . . . [that] it was now what thirty-four years of free and good government have made it." It simply would not have occurred to Jefferson to suppose that government was relatively unimportant in human affairs or that it was a largely negative agency best subordinated to economic or other private interests or energies. And far from being weak, Jefferson thought free and republican government, willingly supported by those consenting to it, would be "on the contrary, the strongest government on earth."[28] Though he believed earnestly in the beneficent potential of free individuals, he did not see this as in any way diminishing the need for pursuit of the public good through acts of government.

This general faith in the need for and the value of publicly

28. To Ellen Coolidge, August 27, 1825, and First Inaugural Address, March 4, 1801, in Adrienne Koch and William Peden, eds., *Thomas Jefferson: The Life and Selected Writings* (New York, 1944), 721, 323.

exercised power was also a key part of his concept of citizenship. A rather casual, largely defensive citizenship, tuned to the protection of individual rights and interests and vigilant against malfeasance in office, now often seen as the essence of public participation, had little appeal to Jefferson. To him it would have been grossly inadequate and a betrayal of the rich, positive connotations of an Aristotelian citizenship. In fact, like Aristotle, Jefferson believed an indispensable dimension of freedom was public liberty, the responsible participation in the affairs of the polity. His constant attention to the *quality* of citizenship – grounded in possession of land, education for all, and participation in local government – rested squarely on the need for the people to possess knowledge and virtue if they were to govern well. Even his conduct as president, sometimes regarded as retaining the age-old aristocratic bias, had vital overtones of educating and setting a moral tone for citizens as well as officeholders. Thus he introduced informality and pell-mell into presidential etiquette and social life; he worked with, even as he led, the people's representatives in Congress; and through letters and addresses he conducted a continuous campaign of public education.

Jefferson summarized his views in letters written at the beginning and at the end of his presidency. He would seek, he wrote in 1801, as the foundation of his administration, to move the "whole people, . . . the great machine of society," toward notions of "ideal right." Then, a year after leaving office, he wrote of the obligation of the president to "unite in himself the confidence of the whole people," thus to mobilize "the energy of the nation" in pursuit of the common good. These letters reveal often-misunderstood aspects of Jefferson's thought that led John Randolph of Roanoke, Henry Adams, and a whole school of modern historians to regard Jefferson as contradictory and even hypocritical. These letters, that is, seem not to conform evenly to his assertion before the election of 1801 that he was "for a government rigorously frugal and simple" that did not aggrandize either federal power over the states or executive power over legislative.[29] In office, in

29. Jefferson to Walter Jones, March 31, 1801, and to Garland Jefferson, January 25, 1810, in Paul L. Ford, ed., *The Writings of Thomas Jefferson* (New York, 1892–99), 8: 29, 9: 210; Jefferson to Elbridge Gerry, January 26, 1799, in Koch and Peden, eds., *Life and Selected Writings of Jefferson* (see n. 28), 545.

conformity to what Randolph and others thought were Jefferson's republican principles, he reduced the federal judiciary, the armed forces, the national debt, the bureaucracy, and taxes. But he also established the military academy, called for a national university and a national road, purchased Louisiana, dispatched the Lewis and Clark expedition, and secured passage of the embargo, all measures of active leadership, national purpose, and enlargement of government. His call for a constitutional amendment to authorize these "great objects of public education, roads, rivers, canals, and such other objects of public improvement as may be thought proper," because he believed powers to do these things "are not among those enumerated in the Constitution," reveals *both* his fidelity to constitutional government *and* his virtually unlimited willingness to use government, when appropriate, for public purposes. He meant to govern responsibly under a constitution ratified by the people, but he sought also to use the active agency of government and his leadership of it in the public interest. He intended, he said in the midst of delicate negotiations with Congress in 1806, to preside over a government of "design," not of "chance."[30]

The most creative, even radical aspect of Jefferson's thought, though, resting on his rather traditional (Aristotelian) ideas of the uses of government and of leadership in the public interest, was his determination to at the same time maintain the "inviolable republican principle" – government according to the consent of the governed registered through representative processes. He saw more clearly than the other founders the need for and worked more persistently to achieve improvement in the quality of citizenship essential to good, democratic government. Jefferson's equivocation on freedom of the press reveals his twin concerns. While president he complained bitterly of lying, slanderous newspapers as "polluted vehicles" that made a farce of reasoned public debate. He even approved "selected prosecution" of violently partisan newspapers, all part of his concern to improve and guide the people's understanding. But he also often expressed faith that the people could withstand "abuses of the press" and ultimately "discern between

---

30. "Sixth Annual Message," December 2, 1806, in Merrill Peterson, ed., *The Portable Thomas Jefferson* (New York, 1975), 326; Jefferson to Barnabas Bidwell, July 5, 1806, quoted in Noble Cunningham, *The Process of Government under Jefferson* (Princeton, NJ, 1978), 189.

truth and falsehood."[31] As a leader, he had a responsibility, that is, to attend to the *quality* of public debate in order to help create the informed citizenry essential to good government in a republic – a citizenry that, to complete the circle, would then be likely to elect wise and able leaders. By thus uniting in his own outlook and practice incessant attention both to providing active, purposeful leadership and to the development of an informed, public-spirited citizenry, he sought to combat charges that democracy would lack effective leadership and that it would be ruined by the ignorance and selfishness of the people. He knew that the solution of both problems was necessary – and the genius of his thought and of his presidency was to see that the two problems had to be solved *together* if they were to be solved at all. Even more than Washington, Jefferson sought to shape a presidential office empowered to lead actively on behalf of good government and devoted to the improvement of and respect for the voice of the people. In this way, he accepted the ancient wisdom of Aristotle and Confucius on the nature and benefits of good government, but added to it the dawning idealism of the Enlightenment that the people themselves (ultimately *all* the people), properly improved in their discretion, as Jefferson put it, could provide wisely for the conduct of their common concerns.

The American presidency, then, had its origin in a climate of political thought still steeped in the classical, civic republican convictions that a good society required good government, that good government required active leadership, and that active leaders required the support of public-spirited citizens. Though emphasis in characterizing the American constitution and American government under it has often been on "checks and balances" and on the Bill of Rights, all designed to restrain government and protect individual rights (fair enough up to a point), an additional emphasis on the uses of active government is also imbedded in the Constitution. In fact, its very ambiguity can be seen more properly as a creative opportunity than as a flaw or limitation. It arose because American government was founded in the flux that existed as the Western world moved into the modern age. Ideas of free trade, capitalist enterprise, industrial revolution, diversifying interests,

---

31. Jefferson to John Tyler, June 28, 1804, and to John Norvell, June 11, 1807, in Koch and Peden, eds., *Life and Selected Writings of Jefferson* (see n. 28), 576, 581–82.

individualism, and democratic politics burgeoned all around the Atlantic world of the founders. Yet more traditional ideas of community, moral purpose, political obligation, and patriot leadership remained strong. The founders were thus well aware not only of the debate over the moral dangers of commerce and self-seeking warned against by philosophers at least since Confucius, but also of their probably demeaning effect on the public virtue essential to social accord in a richly textured human community. The notion of citizenship they accepted, then, was *both* "modern" in its insistence on individual and increasingly universal participation and "classical" in its concern for political obligation and public virtue. And their conception of leadership, resting on the consent of the people but also positioned for active pursuit of "ideal right," was consistent with and dependent on such citizenship. The leader would, on the model of the duke of Chou, Nehemiah, Pericles, and other fabled leaders, have to rule actively, wisely, and selflessly for the public good, but in a new requirement, would also have to be chosen by the people and thus be responsible to them. These conceptions were evident in the debates of the convention of 1787 and also characterized the early presidencies, especially those of Washington and Jefferson.

5

A Republican Perception of German Rulers in the Late Eighteenth Century

Grete Klingenstein

In 1785, two years after winning their independence, Americans had not yet set their minds on traveling into central Europe. Yet Colonel William Stephens Smith was one who did. He had arrived in London in May to serve as secretary to John Adams, the first minister to the court of Saint James (1785–88).[1] In August, he left England and traveled into the Holy Roman Empire. But he was not to go on an official mission. Rather it was the fame of Frederick the Great which lured the former aide-de-camp to Marquis de Lafayette and George Washington away from London.

In fact, it is doubtful whether the colonel would have ventured into Germany if it had not been for his friend Francisco de Miranda, another veteran of the American war and five years his senior. The Venezuelan invited Smith to accompany him on his travels, at least as far as Berlin, from where he himself was to continue further south and east into Italy, Turkey, and Russia. Once in Berlin, Smith changed his mind, and before returning to London via Paris, made a detour to the Vienna of Joseph II.[2]

On August 10, the two gentlemen left Harwich, England, and disembarked the next day in Hellevoetsluis, Holland. It took them five days to see what grand-tour travelers considered remarkable in Rotterdam, Delft, The Hague, Leyden, Haarlem, and Amsterdam. On August 17, they crossed the border into the Prussian garrison town of Wesel on the Rhine. On their way to Hanover they

---

1. *Who Was Who in America: Historical Volume, 1607–1867* (Chicago, IL, rev. ed., 1976), 566. Dumas Malone, ed., *Dictionary of American Biography* (New York, 1964), 9: 368–69. Page Smith, *John Adams* (Garden City, NY, 1962), 2: 620–21, 647–48.
2. *Archivo del General Miranda: Viajes, Diarios, 1750–1785*, vol. 1 (Caracas, 1929), 352–435. The diary from London to Vienna was kept by Smith in English.

witnessed the territorial divisions and denominational differences ruling the western part of the Holy Roman Empire. Their next stop was Brunswick, the capital of a proper duchy, whose rulers, through family relations and military service, were intimately connected to the Prussian king. The heartland of Frederick II they entered on August 26. The town of Magdeburg drew their particular attention since it was the strongest fortress in the realm, with a huge arsenal and a formidable prison. Here, on August 28, they paid a first visit to Prince Ferdinand of Brunswick (1721–92), the famous victor of the battle of Minden (August 1, 1759), the site of which Smith and Miranda had already inspected. On August 28, they arrived in Potsdam via the town of Brandenburg and stayed for two days of sightseeing before continuing on to Berlin.

As traveling gentlemen, they were recommended by friends from town to town. Thus Miranda's connection to Bernardo del Campo, the Spanish envoy in London, which was apparently fortified by a Masonic network, opened the doors to the diplomatic corps in Berlin, as later was the case in Dresden.[3] Apparently it was in this society that Smith made contacts with a group of men whom he calls the literati. No names are mentioned.[4] Probably they were members of the so-called Montagsclub, an institution typical of enlightened sociability which had existed since 1749 and welcomed foreign visitors to its meetings. This was not the only occasion on which they had a glimpse of the Berlin enlightenment. It was an Austrian abbé, Johann Leonhard Gruber, who for four days acted as their guide through Berlin and introduced them to famous men of letters and the arts. He took the Americans first to Anton Friedrich Büsching (1724–93). The conversation was held in the geographer's garden, and Smith was favorably impressed with the open, liberal mind: "There is an independence in his manner and sentiments which is seldom met with in this country, and he professed himself a friend to liberty."[5] The next day, the abbé took them to Moses Mendelssohn (1729–86), the successful entrepreneur, philosopher, and advocate of Jewish emancipation. Smith

---

3. Ibid., 352, 404, 411.
4. Ibid., 381, 394.
5. Ibid., 381. Büsching was director of a grammar school and served as a member on the board of the *Oberkonsistorium*, which dealt with church matters and education.

described him as an "old antediluvian figure, very deformed," and not at all inclined to agree with Miranda's enthusiastic plea for "liberty and independence."[6]

On September 5, they saw the maneuvers outside Berlin for the first time; they were to attend these every morning from September 7 to 10 and again on the 16th. There they saw the king and his generals and met the international corps of military observers.[7] In one of the sham battles, fifteen thousand soldiers were involved. We need not interest ourselves here in the meticulous description of maneuvers and reviews, but must observe that the colonel had apparently never before seen such masses move in single lines.

They returned to Potsdam with the military society on September 19. This was also the day of two most important and interesting conversations. First, for two hours the two Americans again had the honor of a conversation with Prince Ferdinand of Brunswick. Then Marie Joseph de Lafayette, the celebrated French general and participant in the American War of Independence, entered the scene. Immediately upon his arrival in Potsdam from Vienna, he called on Smith and talked to him alone for three hours. In his company were General Duportail and Colonel Jean-Baptiste Gouvion, both veterans from America and as much imbued with American ideas as was Lafayette.[8] From the Prussian maneuvers in Silesia, he had made a detour to Vienna. What Lafayette had heard in his conversations with Joseph II, with the state chancellor Wenzel Anton von Kaunitz, and with ministers such as Count Karl Friedrich von Hatzfeld and Count Karl von Zinzendorf, former governor of Trieste and now president of the aulic chamber of accounting (*Hofrechenkammer*) and what he had seen in the Bohemian headquarters of Brandeis on the Elbe (Brandÿs), he appar-

6. Ibid., 384.

7. Reinhold Koser, *Friedrich der Große*, vol. 2 (Stuttgart, ³1905), 631. See also the famous painting by E.F. Cunningham, *The Return of Frederick II from Maneuvers, 1785; Diarios* (see n. 2), 378–93.

8. *Diarios* (see n. 2), 396–97. The entry concerning the conversation is brief, but its main lines can be reconstructed by means of Lafayette's letters to Washington, of February 2, 1786, and to John Jay, also from Paris, of February 11, 1786, in *Mémoires: Correspondance et manuscrits du général Lafayette* (Paris, 1837), 2: 130–47. See also Louis Gottschalk, *Lafayette between the American and the French Revolution* (Chicago, IL, 1950), 188–94. Notes on Lafayette's visit to Vienna in Wiener Diarium, September 7, 1785, and in the Diary of Karl von Zinzendorf, September 3, 4, and 7, in Haus-, Hof-, und Staatsarchiv, Vienna.

ently reported immediately to John Adams's secretary. For one of the main topics of conversation in Vienna was America and in particular commerce with America. With Lafayette's account of Vienna and probably with Gruber's suggestions, Smith's appetite was now sufficiently whetted. He decided to continue to Vienna in the company of Miranda. Lafayette's presence in Potsdam seems to have opened the doors of the dining hall of Sans Souci for the Americans on September 20. The old king, however, did not appear, having been struck by a severe fit of gout. It must also have been the marquis who presented the Americans to the king's more liberal-minded brother, Prince Henry.[9]

Finally, on September 24, Smith and Miranda left Potsdam for Leipzig, Meissen, and Dresden.[10] After a most agreeable sojourn in Saxony, they crossed the border into the Kingdom of Bohemia, where Prague had fine sights to offer.[11] They entered Vienna, the largest town of central Europe, inhabited by more than two hundred thousand people, on October 14 and stayed there for twelve days.[12]

On the first day, they strolled through the alleys of the Augarten, a former imperial park that Joseph had opened to the public. Then they visited the imperial library, "the most superb of any we have seen."[13] On Sunday, their program included the churches of Saint Stephen and the Augustinians, and in the afternoon they followed a crowd to a favorite pastime, the *Hetze*. In the evening they gazed in amazement at the Viennese dancing. Prince Eugene's Belvedere delighted them on Monday, and before watching navigation on the Danube, they visited the imperial arsenal. As on the evening of their arrival, on Monday they attended the theater, where the Emperor and his brother Maximilian, the elector archbishop of Cologne, were present. On Tuesday, as was customary with the aristocracy after theater, they joined a party of court ladies and gentlemen assembled at the French ambassador's. "Some handsome," he notes, "all brilliant to excess,"[14] because his guidebook[15]

9. *Diarios* (see n. 2), 398.
10. Ibid., 400–414.
11. Ibid., 415–19.
12. Ibid., 422–34.
13. Ibid., 423.
14. Ibid., 426.
15. William Guthrie, *A New Geographical, Historical, and Commercial Grammar and Present State of the Several Kingdoms of the World* (London, 1777 and 1782). According

had already drawn his attention to the rich jewelry worn by the aristocracy in Vienna. Smith did not mix with the card-crazy party.

On Wednesday, they visited the Hofburg, the imperial palace, and the university. On Thursday, rain forced them to stay in their lodgings at the hotel called Beuf Blanc, where they received visits "by several."[16] Whoever those were, the main topic of conversation was the person of the emperor and the conditions of trade and commerce. On Friday, they admired the elegance and simplicity of Schönbrunn, and in the evening attended the theater. Somebody must have encouraged them to attend a public examination at the school for the deaf and the dumb on Saturday before they proceeded to the customhouse and the warehouse for foreign merchandise, which had been the subject of dismal conversation two days before. On October 26, they left Vienna, which they considered "the best built town in this continent."[17]

Apparently, Miranda had been charmed by some Hungarian acquaintances and headed toward the Esterhazy estate in nearby Hungary. There he met the prince's musician, Joseph Haydn, and then proceeded to Pressburg (Bratislava), which was renowned since 1741 as the site of Maria Theresa's spectacular coronation as queen of Hungary. Trieste was his next destination. Smith in turn took the road to Jefferson in Paris, and from there he returned to London to assume his diplomatic duties. On June 11, 1786, the secretary married Adams's daughter.[18]

Smith was a man with firm judgments about politics and society both in America and in Europe.[19] They were rooted in his own and in his generation's republican convictions and revolutionary experience. In his diary, therefore, we find the patterns of the accomplished American Revolution and the apprehensions and expectancies of the Confederation applied to individuals, society, and politics in

---

to *Nouvelle biographie générale*, vol. 22 (Paris, 1888), the author is not William Guthrie. The name of the popular Scottish historian and geographer is supposed to have been used for sales' purposes by the publisher, John Knox.

16. *Diarios* (see n. 2), 427.

17. Ibid., 433.

18. Smith, *Adams* (see n. 1), 2: 675–76. Cf. Lester J. Cappon, ed., *The Adams-Jefferson Letters: The Complete Correspondence between Thomas Jefferson and Abigail and John Adams*, vol. 1 (New York, 1951).

19. The diary reveals a man of more intellectual capacities and a wider range of interests than Smith, *Adams* (see n. 1), 2: 675–76, admits.

monarchical Germany. His sympathy for the peasants and his denunciation of oppression by landlord and Catholic church can be classified as physiocratic. His views on trade, commerce, and manufacturing clearly bear the stamp of Adam Smith's *Wealth of Nations* (1776). As to Catholicism, he is a typical representative of enlightened Protestantism who welcomes the signs of a reasonable, simple, and tolerant church. His favorable opinion of Emperor Joseph II is due mainly to this ruler's church decrees. Looming large over all Germany are the figures of the two monarchs, Frederick II and Joseph II, competing with each other in the military, economic, and political areas, with each claiming philosophy as his adviser. But did the rulers leave room for their subjects' freedom? Like the Physiocrats, Smith would accept a monarchy where "wisdom and virtue centered in the prince."[20] Did he really encounter such a ruler? To the reader of Montesquieu, the Netherlands of 1785 held out warnings against the decline of republican liberties through partisan strife and renunciation of virtue, with its impending loss of independence to the neighboring powers of Austria and Prussia. Monarchical Germany, in turn, taught him "lessons for Republicans"[21] about the effects of liberty and oppression and demonstrated the transition of rulers from monarchs into tyrants. In Prussia he observed how encompassing a system despotism could be. The mild Austrian absolutism appeared far less offensive, though puzzling, while Saxony, lying peacefully between the heavily armed giants, seemed exempt from the ills of despotism.

The first signs of Prussian despotism were glimpsed by the travelers from the windows of their coach. They had left intensively cultivated England and passed through the prosperous Netherlands. In contrast to these countries, which were undergoing an agricultural revolution, large stretches of land in the western provinces of Prussia lay uncultivated, and the villagers lived in abject misery.[22] "[A]griculture lessens[!]" Smith comments, "and

---

20. *Diarios* (see n. 2), 364. On the problem of enlightened absolutism see Karl Otmar Freiherr von Aretin, ed., *Der aufgeklärte Absolutismus* (Cologne, 1974).
21. *Diarios* (see n. 2), 372.
22. Ibid., 362–363. On the state of agriculture and of the peasants see Gustavo Corni, "Das Agrarwesen," 319–23, and Clemens Zimmermann, "Die Bauern," 547–55, both in Jürgen Ziechmann, ed., *Panorama der friderizianischen Zeit* (Bremen, 1985).

the effects of despotism and sanguinary laws shew themselves."[23] Commenting on the discrepancy between the good soil and the poverty of the people, he states "There are but two degrees, the noble and the peasant, the master and the slave."[24] The companions of rural poverty were ignorance and blind submission, as demonstrated by a shepherd on a road. He knelt down as the coach of Smith and Miranda passed by, for he imagined it to contain persons of high station and dignity.

Signs of poverty also hovered about the Prussian towns and, when combined with military attributes, made a lasting impression on the American. "The soldiers," the colonel notes in Hamm, a town in the county of Mark, "out of their parade dress appear dirty and distressed, their pay is not sufficient to support them without hard labour, and they are not permitted to walk in any other street than where their quarters are."[25] These were the visible social and economic effects of the Prussian recruiting system. In the fortress of Magdeburg and even in the gardens of Sans Souci, the sentinels "with a hungry countenance"[26] would beg from the visitors. Even worse was the sight of prisoners in Magdeburg, who returned from hard labor to their dungeons in rags, "all chained and rattling thro the streets."[27] The citadel, he was told, held 260 prisoners of state, all victims, he was convinced, of arbitrary decisions taken by the king himself "in a capricious moment."[28] The prison of Spandau, which Smith saw weeks later, was a no more edifying sight. When he learned about the great number of deserters, he observed that the severity of discipline and the paltry allowance had undermined the morale of the troops. The king, concluded Washington's former

23. *Diarios* (see n. 2), 362.
24. Ibid., 365.
25. Ibid., 363. See Franz Mehring, "Friedrichs aufgeklärter Despotismus," in Otto Büsch and Wolfgang Neugebauer, eds., *Moderne preußische Geschichte, 1648–1947: Eine Anthologie*, Veröffentlichungen der Historischen Kommission zu Berlin, 52, 3 vols. (Berlin, 1981), 1: 152–53. Henri Brunschwig, *Gesellschaft und Romantik in Preußen im 18. Jahrhundert: Die Krise des preußischen Staates am Ende des 18. Jahrhunderts und die Entstehung der romantischen Mentalität* (Frankfurt/Main, 1975), 109–13 (orig. pub. in French as *La crise de l'état prussien à la fin du XVIIIe siècle et la genèse de la mentalité romantique* (Paris, 1947)); Otto Büsch, *Militärsystem und Sozialleben im alten Preußen, 1713–1807: Die Anfänge der sozialen Militarisierung der preußisch-deutschen Gesellschaft*, Veröffentlichungen der Berliner Historischen Kommission, vol. 7 (Berlin, 1962).
26. *Diarios* (see n. 2), 373.
27. Ibid., 372.
28. Ibid., 371.

aide, had failed to kindle the sentiments of affection and solidarity among his soldiers. Outside Prussia, some military leaders already valued these qualities as stronger stimuli for fighting than fear and discipline alone. In Smith's eyes, the Prussian soldiers were but "myrmidons with all the gaiety and splendour of dress," and from Austrian soil he calls them "slaves of power cloathed in military uniforms."[29] Thus the parades and maneuvers deceived the eye and concealed the true state of the Prussian army in decline. "The situation of his army as to discipline, and the skill of his officers cannot be exceeded but now they are at their zenith, Frederick is gliding rapidly down the current of time, and according to the course of nature, cannot float much longer on the surface."[30]

In the grip of despotism, the prospects for manufacture, the trades, and commerce were similarly bleak. Prohibition of imports, royal interference, the widespread use of monopolies, and even royal management were the rule. The king not only acted as the "grand merchant,"[31] but even disposed of private property, as in the case of tobacco grown by peasants. Such mercantilist practices, Smith observed, were another cause for rural poverty. Smith, whose economic thinking was based on a laissez-faire individualism, could not see any other cause but the king's tyrannical will behind the state's control, as was the case also for large-scale housing construction. He comments on the social and political effects of Frederick's stale mercantilism as follows: "The king possessing almost all the wealth of the country, keeps his subjects almost totally dependent on himself for a subsistence – he is constantly building new houses and superficially improving his capital and country villa and other palaces, he thus keeps his subjects constantly employed at a very cheap rate."[32] As a merchant, in negotiations the king was an unreliable partner. He had his reputation damaged by the depreciation of currency during the Seven Years' War.

With the king himself controlling the economy, it was no wonder

29. Ibid., 385, 419.
30. Ibid., 395. Cf. the critical assessment by Bernhard R. Kroener, "Armee, Krieg und Gesellschaft im friderizianischen Preußen," in Karl Otmar Freiherr von Aretin, ed., *Friedrich der Große* (Gütersloh, 1985), 104; idem, "Armee und Staat," 393–404, and Ulrich Marwitz, "Das innere Gefüge der Armee," 404–17, both in Ziechmann, ed., *Panorama* (see n. 22).
31. *Diarios* (see n. 2), 384.
32. Ibid., 384.

that the merchant society of Berlin displayed neither comfortable wealth nor the social attitudes accompanying the blessings of prosperity. Smith found the riches in town confined to Jews and to a few families "who made their fortunes by the Seven Years War, and the monopolizers."[33] He experienced a shocking lack of social refinement at a dinner in the house of David Splitgerber, the banker and entrepreneur, who had supplied arms and ammunition to the Americans during the war.[34] Smith and Miranda left immediately after dinner, "with no favourable idea of the politeness and civility of the Prussian mercantile character."[35] These were no good portents for commercial relations between America and Prussia. By comparison, the military comes off much better, for here "great gentility prevails."[36]

And finally the center of despotism, the king himself. He was an old man of seventy-three whom Smith saw on horseback reviewing and commanding the troops during maneuvers. It was the military role and posture which had carried the king's fame through all of Europe and across the sea. But now the sham attack by the Prussian cavalry drew sharp criticism from Washington's former aide-de-camp. Furthermore, what the American had heard about the king's morality and habits did not please him either. Admitted to Sans Souci for sightseeing, as had become customary for visitors of rank in royal and aristocratic palaces, Smith could see with his own eyes how the king lived. The scenery offended his Puritan sense of cleanliness:

> Library and lodging chambers finished with the greatest elegance and taste – furniture the most magnificent – in the midst of this grandeur, a pile of wood is in his dining room and his bed set off in a corner by a screen, appear too filthy for a monk – it is a common Dutch bunk – the curtains and furniture are rich, but being used in the absence of a pocket handkerchief, appear very disgusting.[37]

---

33. Ibid., 388. On the role of the Jews in Prussia see Heinz Duchhardt, "Die Juden," in Ziechmann, ed., *Panorama* (see n. 22), 565–70; and Achim von Borries, "Die Rolle der Juden und ihre Existenzbedingungen unter Friedrich II." in Aretin, ed., *Friedrich der Große* (see n. 30), 163–68.

34. *Diarios* (see n. 2), 379f. Cf. Wilhelm Treue, "David Splitgerber, 1683–1764: Ein Unternehmer im preußischen Merkantilismus," *Vierteljahrshefte für Sozial- und Wirtschaftsgeschichte* 41 (1954): 253–67.

35. Ibid., 380.

36. Ibid., 380.

37. Ibid., 375. On the aging king see Karl Otmar Freiherr von Aretin, *Friedrich*

What conclusion could Smith then draw, when the king himself gave such an example of slovenliness and when he traveled without retinue and lived without queen and court? All the splendors of Sans Souci could serve but one purpose – sheer conspicuousness of power. It appeared to Smith as another cause of public poverty. A couple of days later, Smith assured himself of the vile and false character of the king: "He tarnishes actions which can proceed only from an elevated soul, with the most contemptible meanness and avarice – he covers filth and poverty with sperficial [*sic*] grandeur and elegance.[38] More than, a month later, in Emperor Joseph's Vienna, Smith drew the following conclusion: "In a tyrannical government, as Prussia, Le Roi is their terrestrial good, and his subjects will freely sacrafice [*sic*] their lives to his caprice and humour, they gaze at him with reverence, view him as a mighty stranger, and in dread retire."[39] Fear, the reader of Montesquieu knew, was the principle of despotic governments.

With the ruler, the whole system of government was rotten at the core, and there was no remedy. The king did not even speak to his crown prince, who in turn "seems void both of dignity and ability, and only promises to give a loose to vice and dissipation."[40] Thus the evils of despotism lay in the will and passion of the holders of unlimited power, who were living in self-imposed isolation, and succeeded each other by sheer coincidence of consanguinity, not by deliberation or consent of the people. But was it not also the people who submitted themselves by their own free will to tyranny and payed their respects?

How different then was Saxony. The country, again seen from the coach, presented "a most pleasing scene, the hills well cultivated and settled,"[41] and neither in the villages nor in the towns did hordes of beggars give offense to the eye. The fortress of Königstein differed remarkably from Spandau and Magdeburg. Overlooking a "most rural romantic and luxuriant scene," with the Elbe meandering through the mountains, it appeared "pleasant and

---

der Große: Größe und Grenzen des Preußenkönigs, Bilder und Gegenbilder (Freiburg, 1985), 120–48.
38. *Diarios* (see n. 2), 385.
39. Ibid., 429.
40. Ibid., 395.
41. Ibid., 404.

healthy,"[42] holding only three prisoners. Leipzig was all to the taste of the New York merchant's son. It was a town of trade, commerce, and learning. Smith arrived there when it was shedding its fortified character, as did many towns then, and trees were being planted on the ramparts for the amenity of its inhabitants. The houses and gardens of the merchants rivaled royal palaces in elegance and wealth. He took this mercantile prosperity as a plain proof of his own conviction that "this can spring from no other source than the liberty they enjoy superior to their neighbours."[43] It was thus liberty of trade and commerce that procured for the Saxons the means to improve their lives and obtain happiness. In Prussia, by contrast, all wealth, according to Smith, passed through the hands of the despot to fill his treasury, while his subjects were kept poor and miserable.

In the shade of liberty, the arts and sciences also flourished in Saxony, to "contradict the assertion that commerce is unfriendly to the science."[44] The graduate of Princeton (1774) stood in awe at the University of Leipzig, where he found a library "similar to that of Cambridge in Boston" and "very industrious" students.[45] He visited a private collection of pictures, owned by a merchant. The wholesome effects of liberty reached even further, for "the very face of nature declares it."[46] Did not the Prussian experience show how tyranny misshaped the landscape and the villages? Even the outward appearance of the Saxons and their behavior bore the stamp of liberty. "The people in general here are handsomer, better made and more polished in their manners than any we have met with on the continent."[47] Montesquieu had propounded the theory of nature's influence on the spirit of laws and on the forms of government. Now Smith sought traces of the spirit upon the faces and bodies of men and in their surroundings. Apparently he was familiar with Aristotle, who ascribed different physical shapes to free man and slave.[48]

42. Ibid., 410.
43. Ibid., 403.
44. ibid., 402.
45. Ibid., 401.
46. Ibid., 402.
47. Ibid., 404–5.
48. It is unlikely that Smith knew Johann Kaspar Lavater's *Physiognomische Fragmente zur Beförderung der Menschenkenntnis und Menschenliebe* (Leipzig, 1775–78). That the soul gave shape to the body, as Georg Christoph Lichtenberg would also

Thus Saxony boasted all the blessings of liberty hailed in contemporary economic and political tracts, for which Smith himself
had fought. There was only one flaw, namely, Elector Frederick
August III's passion for palaces, gardens, and art galleries. Not that
Smith himself did not cherish the arts and entertainment as embel-
lishments of life and sources of sociability. It was the origin and use
of wealth that his utilitarian and philanthropic mind called into
question. On the whole, however, Smith found that "the appearance of his subjects and country do him honour."[49] Let us now
leave the happy and prosperous Saxony and enter the domain of
Emperor Joseph II.

With the American travelers the forty-four-year-old Habsburg
enjoyed a far more favorable reputation than the old Prussian king.
While Frederick "tramples on the rights of society and conquers
only to enslave,"[50] the Austrian ruler was credited with genuine
"philanthropy and wisdom."[51] He seemed "generally disposed to
serve his people by his arrangements"[52] and had accomplished
more in his as yet brief reign than his mother had done in forty
years. Similarly, Jefferson in Paris hailed Joseph's "internal regulation," although in European affairs he distrusted the emperor's
"eccentric character."[53] Even in the face of Joseph's project to
exchange the distant Austrian Netherlands for the adjacent Electorate of Bavaria and of Frederick's countermove in the League of
Princes, Smith persisted in ascribing "philosophy" to Joseph's
mind and expected him to preserve peace in Germany.[54] Philosophy and wisdom's only enemy was Joseph's ambition. But, then,
would this dangerous passion in the end not be controlled by reason?

---

maintain, seems to have become a common conviction by the 1780s, cf. Georg
Christoph Lichtenberg, "Über Physiognomik," in Peter Platt, ed., *Georg Christoph
Lichtenberg: Werke in einem Band* (Hamburg, 1967), 371–407.

49. *Diarios* (see n. 2), 407.

50. Ibid., 421.

51. Ibid., 395.

52. Ibid., 427f.

53. Rudolf Friebel, "Österreich und die Vereinigten Staaten von Amerika bis
zum Gesandtenaustausch im Jahre 1838," 3 pts., unpublished Ph.D. thesis, Innsbruck, 1955, pt. 1: 69.

54. *Diarios* (see n. 2), 395. Cf. Karl Otmar Freiherr von Aretin, *Heiliges Römisches
Reich, 1776–1806: Reichsverfassung und Staatssouveränität*, 2 vols., vol. 1, *Darstellung*,
Veröffentlichungen des Instituts für Europäische Geschichte Mainz, vol. 38 (Wies-
baden, 1967), chap. 3; Paul P. Bernard, *Joseph II and Bavaria: Two Eighteenth Century
Attempts at German Unification* (The Hague, 1965).

It is likely that one of the main sources for Smith's friendly predisposition toward Joseph was Benjamin Franklin, although not in a direct way. For among American diplomats it was Franklin who obtained firsthand information from Vienna, where his friend, the scientist Jan Ingen-Housz, had already served as an intermediary to transmit messages from Franklin to Maria Theresa and from Kaunitz to Franklin in Paris. Frequently, the inquisitive emperor visited the chemical laboratory to observe Ingen-Housz's experiments.[55] In addition, the English physician Dr. John Moore spread the most favorable opinion about the emperor in his travel guide.[56] Would these impressions, gained by reading and hearsay, hold up against the realities?

First there was Bohemia. The soil was fertile and the country well cultivated. But the villages were poor, the peasants downtrodden and worn out. In the outskirts of the villages noble mansions demonstrated for whom the peasants labored. Apparently the emperor's reforms to relieve the situation of the peasants were not a matter of conversation in Prague or Vienna and therefore escaped Smith's attention. However, Joseph's church reforms did not. Like all Protestants, Smith was convinced that in Catholic countries such as the kingdom of Bohemia the church oppressed the people: "[T]he villages are poor and the inhabitants as wretched as priestcraft can make them."[57] In Bohemia, he saw town and country filled with "the engines of popery and blind superstition." The huge building of Strahov monastery, magnificently situated on a hill above Prague, confirmed his enlightened opinion that the clergy exploited the people. For "here they live on the fat of the land and all ranks treat them with respect." However, the members of the Premonstrate order did not quite fit the Protestant's preju-

55. Julius Wiesner, *Jan Ingen-Housz: Sein Leben und sein Wirken als Naturforscher und Arzt* (Vienna, 1905), 43. Hanns Schlitter, *Die Beziehungen Österreichs zu den Vereinigten Staaten von Amerika, 1778–1787* (Innsbruck, 1885), 66, mentions a visit by Franklin to Vienna scheduled in 1783 which, however, was not realized.

56. John Moore, *A View of Society and Manners in France, Switzerland, and Germany, with Anecdotes Relating to Some Eminent Characters*, vol. 2 (London, 1777), 333–34; cf. Michel Sutschek, *Die Darstellung der europäischen Nationen im Werk von Dr. John Moore, 1729–1802: Ein Beitrag zum Problem des Ausländertypos in Reisebericht und Roman*, Ph.D. thesis (Graz, 1973).

57. *Diarios* (see n. 2), 421. On agrarian conditions see Joseph Koci, "Die Reformen der Untertänigkeitsverhältnisse in den böhmischen Ländern unter Maria Theresia und Joseph II," in Richard Plaschka and Grete Klingenstein, eds., *Österreich im Europa der Aufklärung*, vol. 1 (Vienna, 1985), 121–38.

dice against the regular clergy. For the monks were neither filthy nor ignorant, but presented themselves as "the civilest people we meet with," not to speak of their librarian Bartholotti, who was a friend of the American Revolution.[58]

Smith's optimism rose higher when he happened to watch Jews in one of the Prague churches sort out ecclesiastic gold and silver, which Joseph had decreed to be sold at public auction, and when he heard of monasteries being closed. "These circumstances," his prophesy ran, "must in a very few years produce a very material alteration in this country, and is a proof of the decline even here of the superstition of the popish establishment."[59] That the incoming money was destined for the support of parish priests and for poor relief was of great satisfaction to him. But it seemed strange to the American that the emperor himself, that is, the state, should make all the necessary arrangements. "He becomes a banker,"[60] he concluded curtly in Prague, just as in Berlin Frederick had acted as "merchant." Later, in Vienna, voices of discontent would explain to him that Joseph's apparent philanthropy rested solely upon "mercenary principles" and "irreverence and heresy."[61]

Thus it was in Prague that the American witnessed Joseph's brand of enlightened Catholicism in action. Similarly, it was Prague that offered the sight of an army that was not only well exercised, but also very well kept. Besides Dr. Moore, it must have been Lafayette who, earlier in Potsdam, had drawn Smith's attention to the far superior Austrian military organization. Smith himself observed after a visit to the barracks that the "soldiers [were] well cloathed . . . well lodged two in a bed and allowed two grotien per day – they are healthy smart men and in general young."[62] Prague, the largest garrison in the monarchy, thus confirmed Smith's opinion of the emperor's military strength. But let us now head toward Vienna, which had quite different sights and insights to offer.

---

58. *Diarios* (see n. 2), 418.
59. Ibid., 417. Cf. Elisabeth Kovács, ed., *Katholische Aufklärung und Josephinismus* (Vienna, 1979).
60. *Diarios* (see n. 2), 417.
61. Ibid., 429.
62. Ibid., 416–17. Cf. Lafayette, *Mémoires* (see n. 8), 2: 134; Moore, *View* (see n. 56), 2: 305. On the state of the army see Edith Kotasek, *Feldmarschall Franz Moritz Graf von Lacy, 1725–1801: Ein Leben für Österreichs Heer*, Ph.D. thesis (Horn, 1956), 169–84.

Since roads in the travel- and commerce-minded eighteenth century were becoming indicators of a government's accomplishments, Smith was most impressed with the good condition of the road between Prague and Vienna, which was "thronged with lodded waggons passing to and from this capital to the manufacturing towns, Prague, etc."; safety seemed assured, for in Lower Austria he observed vaults of wine dug into the hills outside the villages: "A proof," he notes, "of the good police of this country, through the whole of which I have not even heard of robbery or insult."[63] "Equal to the English"[64] was the highest praise for a road on the Continent. The villages and towns in Moravia and Lower Austria were "neat and well arranged" and offered surprising sights of prosperity, as did the countryside full of vineyards.

The excellence of the roads thus promised to encourage commerce and therefore to pave the way for "a very great alteration in this country." Vienna's social institutions gave evidence of Joseph's best humanitarian intentions, and the institutions for the promotion of the arts and the sciences deserved the highest praise. It was of great satisfaction to the republican that the aristocracy employed their wealth in amassing art collections and in cultivating good taste and that none of the imperial palaces displayed superfluous splendor.

Taking sociability and entertainment as another indicator of good government, Smith had much to praise in Joseph's capital. In Vienna, the theater was open every night. Founded in 1776 by Joseph to become the national stage of the Holy Roman Empire, it was "large and elegant, and presents a company unmixed and superior in appearance to the opera of the Hay Market."[65] Besides these public entertainments, the Viennese privately engaged in the exchange of dinner invitations and conversations that was highly pleasing because women also participated. Vienna was indeed a town unsurpassed by any in Germany. Viennese society was most enticing, and the emperor himself appeared to be the most philanthropic of all the rulers, "superior," as Smith found, "to all the crowned heads of Europe." From the gentlemen-in-waiting at the Hofburg, the foreign visitors readily received information that the

63. *Diarios* (see n. 2), 422.
64. Ibid., 421.
65. Ibid., 433. Cf. Heinz Kindermann, *Theatergeschichte Europas*, vol. 5 (Salzburg, 1962), chaps. 6b and 9b.

emperor was "a very temperate man"[66] who pursued duties and leisure with daily regularity. But, then, these favorable opinions and impressions were strangely marred, plunging Smith into astonishment and confusion. First, he observed that , as regards the particular kind of entertainment and sociability that he considered public, the Viennese contented themselves with theater only. Coming from London, he had apparently expected such places of public entertainment as Vauxhall, where people of all stations could meet and mix, have drinks, dinners and discussions, and watch performances of all sorts. Instead, the Viennese enjoyed entertainments that filled the American with horror and contempt. One of the entertainments was *Hetze*, where in an amphitheater he found a polite circle entertaining themselves by watching animals fight and kill each other. Smith and Miranda witnessed another entertainment, seemingly less brutal, but similarly absurd, on a Sunday evening in three different assemblies in town. It was dancing, which was apparently so different from what he had seen in Berlin and knew from England and America that he gave a detailed description of what today is considered the evolution of the waltz. "The dance consists of minuets of six or eight couples – at a time and when the music chooses they change and the pairs, clasped in each other's arms, keep a constant twirling around the room, the spectators being in the centre and at small sideboards, with cold suppers – this is a giddy movement and devoid of grace, but is the only dance they have ."[67] On Monday, then, the diary carries the entry on the incomprehensible character of the Viennese, who on Sunday mornings went to church, then in the afternoon enjoyed themselves seeing the blood of animals being spilled, and finally in the evenings indulged in riotous dancing. "Oh man," the puzzled American concludes, "of what inconsistent particles art thou formed, running headlong into extremes."[68]

If, in Vienna, his enlightened faith in the people became uncertain and ambiguous, it became all the more so when he heard them talk about the emperor and watched them behave in his very presence. Smith agreed wholeheartedly with the discontented merchants that all laws prohibiting imports were detrimental for as he was told, the country "has neither materials nor capital to establish

---

66. *Diarios* (see n. 2), 427.
67. Ibid., 424.
68. Ibid., 425.

such manufactures as can supply the wants of the people."[69] A visit
to the customhouse, to the repository of foreign merchandise
withheld from circulation, and to the banks confirmed the merchants' talk. "The banks," he observed himself, "do not be much
troubled . . . they did not appear to be over-stocked with business
– in the national one," as he apparently called the Wiener Stadt-
Banco, "there were no applicants." Thus he concluded that Joseph
"undoubtedly is in an error."[70] But again, errors could be mended
if reason prevailed.

It was in mercantile circles that he heard the gossip about the
emperor, who "uses women of the town when he chooses to send
for them and condemns others to public punishment who are guilty
of it."[71] So Joseph the philosopher could act arbitrarily and exempt
his own person from the law of the land, which he himself made.
But against that Smith mentions a criminal case in which Joseph,
according to the American, meted out justice against the privileged
in an exemplary way.[72] Wagging tongues in the same circles also
spread the opinion that Joseph was "a prince of no great education,
who seldom takes a book in his hand."[73]

Apparently, they themselves were readers of the latest economic
tracts and of other literature. Smith readily believed these tales
about Joseph's education and about the absence of extraordinary
talents. Yet he persisted in calling him a "a prince of great pen-
etration, of a philosophical turn of mind."[74] He based this opinion
on the practical experience that Joseph had gained by "travel and an
early acquaintance with different nations" and by his own effort to
study the wants of the people. Thus, the grumblings against Joseph

69. Ibid., 428. Cf. Helen P. Liebel-Weckowicz, "Count Karl von Zinzendorf and
the Liberal Revolt against Joseph II's Economic Reforms, 1783–1790," in Hans
Ulrich Wehler, ed., *Sozialgeschichte Heute: Festschrift für Hans Rosenberg zum 70.
Geburtstag*, Kritische Studien zur Geschichtswissenschaft, 11 (Göttingen, 1974),
69–85.

70. *Diarios* (see n. 2), 428.

71. Ibid., 428.

72. Ibid., 425. A pamphlet about the punishment of Ladislaus Freiherr von
Székely was published in 1786, cf. Leslie Bodi, *Tauwetter in Wien: Zur Prosa der
österreichischen Aufklärung* (Frankfurt/Main, 1977), 283–88.

73. *Diarios* (see n. 2), 427. On Joseph's thorough education see Derek Beales,
"Writing a Life of Joseph II: The Problem of His Education," *Wiener Beiträge zur
Geschichte der Neuzeit* 6 (1979): 183–207, and Anna Benna, "Jugend und Erziehung
Josephs II," in *Österreich zur Zeit Josephs II: Katalog der Ausstellung* (Vienna, 1980),
31–34.

74. *Diarios* (see n. 2), 429.

could not deter Smith from his unlimited trust in the ruler's good intentions. As to internal reforms, Joseph's image remained untainted.

And yet, Smith was alarmed by the large amount of voluble discontent with Joseph's rule. If it was only soldiers hankering after the florins that Maria Theresa had tossed them for a drink, Smith could have attributed it to the shallow minds of the lower classes, who were not capable of grasping Joseph's grandiose schemes. But the way in which not only the merchants, but also the educated audience at the national theater, behaved toward the emperor baffled the American.

Twice he saw the emperor attend the theater in the company of his brother Maximilian, the elector and archbishop of Cologne. The Emperor's dress and behavior were all up to Smith's expectancies. He wore the plain uniform of his regiment. With ease, familiarity, and affability, Joseph mixed with the audience, applauded the actors and actresses, and joined in the encore. But nobody in the audience, not even the military, paid attention to the monarch. No gesture of respect, of reverence and obeisance; nothing but utter indifference surrounded the ruler. Dr. John Moore had supplied his readers with the account of a similar reception of Joseph in an aristocratic salon and had applauded the emperor's modesty and the lack of subservience on the part of the aristocracy.[75] What disturbed the American was apparently the transfer of these very attitudes from the private circle of the court aristocracy to the public sphere of the national theater. This was an entirely new feature in Smith's grammar of government and in the scale of political behavior familiar to him. It ranged from the natural reverence and admiration that republicans in America showed George Washington to the total submission and trembling fear in tyrannical Prussia. In Vienna, however, authority was neither openly admired and loved, nor openly hated and feared. The ruler was the object of gossip and of tales, brewed of ridicule and contempt, of derogatory and vile opinions, and of simple disregard. Therefore Joseph's government, though absolute, could never be judged tyrannical to the degree that the Prussian one was, but appeared instead as a "mild administration."[76]

75. Moore, *View* (see n. 56), 2: 333–34.
76. *Diarios* (see n. 2), 429; Bodi, *Tauwetter* (see n. 72), 153–66; and the full length critique of Joseph by his brother Leopold in Adam Wandruszka, *Leopold II:*

Listening to the Viennese, Smith began to shudder at the thought that it was the ruled themselves who would not tolerate a monarch who descended from his throne, and that this was the main reason why Joseph was not respected: "The free intercourse with his subjects and ease of his deportment, they attribute to a trifling mind incapable of amusing itself in that dignified line which would be more becoming his station."[77] The emperor did not meet the expectations of his people, who wanted "to respect and reverence what is out of their reach and view."[78] By lowering himself, the emperor invited the people to detect in his comportment deficiencies and errors, which they now could attribute to avarice, self-conceit, obstinacy, and other vices common among ordinary men.

What lesson then could be drawn from such a ruler and such a people? "My pen revolts at the idea of considering mankind in themselves, as favouring tyrannical establishments, but in every other situation we find them turbulent and uneasy, always pressing to a change until they get so overcome by the pressure of the yoke that they find no redress but to grin and bear it."[79] Expecting the clear-cut lines of liberty and oppression, of revolt and submission familiar to him through his own revolutionary experience, the American surrendered to the perplexing inconsistencies and contradictions of government in Vienna.

The trip to the German courts was probably only a fleeting episode in Smith's rather sedate career as a member of the U.S. establishment and in the more rugged life of the Venezuelan. After brief diplomatic missions to Paris and Portugal in 1787, Smith returned to America to assume the post of surveyor of the port of New York. Miranda, all the more inflamed in 1789 for liberty, entered the French revolutionary army.[80] In 1806 he led a private military expedition to Caracas, which failed. His friend Smith had

---

Erzherzog von Österreich, Großherzog von Toskana, König von Ungarn und Böhmen, Römischer Kaiser, vol. 1, 1747–1780, 356–57, vol. 2, 1780–1792, 92–100 (Vienna, 1963 and 1965).

77. *Diarios* (see n. 2), 430.

78. Ibid., 428.

79. Ibid., 430.

80. Cf. Victor Andres Belaunde, *Bolivar and the Political Thought of the Spanish American Revolution* (New York, [2]1967), chap. 5. Alfonso Rumazo Gonzales, *Miranda protolider de la independencia americana* (Caracas, 1985), and W.E. Robertson, *The Life of Miranda*, 2 vols. (1929) were not available.

been his foremost financier in the United States, and as a consequence, having broken neutrality, Smith was discredited and lost his position. In 1813, however, he was elected to Congress, where he served for the Federalist party until 1815. He died on June 10, 1816.

Meanwhile, Miranda had continued on the path of revolution. With Simon Bolivar he fought for the independence of Venezuela in 1810–11. Discord among the two heroes and the Spanish reconquest in 1812 then delivered the aging Miranda into the hands of the Spanish. A prisoner in Cadiz, Spain, he died on July 14, 1816.[81]

81. A different version of this article, under the title "Lessons for Republicans: An American Critique of Enlightened Absolutism in Central Europe," appeared in *The Mirror of History: Essays in Honor of Fritz Fellner*, ed. Solomon Wank et al. (Santa Barbara, 1988), 181–212.

6.1
Ideology and Experience in Eighteenth-Century American Political Culture and the Concept of the "Good Ruler"

Timothy H. Breen

Colonial American historians are rarely called upon to discuss the drafting of the Constitution or even the creation of a new nation state. These events are usually seen as the beginning of a long political and constitutional development which, for better or worse, has made the U.S. government what it is today. It is not surprising, therefore, that in this bicentennial year we hear a good deal about a "living document," an enduring political framework in which the American people have struggled to define adequately civil rights, executive power, and due process.

Though this view of the Constitution is perfectly agreeable, there is obviously another perspective, one that perceives the document not as a starting point, but rather as a culmination, a moment when various strands of experience and ideology, some of them quite old, were powerfully woven together in a document that has acquired mythic status. The two papers presented at this session have in a constructive sense provoked these reflections, and my comments today are intended less as a critique of the work of Professors Ketcham and Klingenstein than as a preliminary sketch of how we might think about the Constitution within a genuinely eighteenth-century context.

For some time, intellectual historians have shaped our basic understanding of the politics of this period. This is the idealist position associated with scholars such as Bernard Bailyn, Gordon S. Wood, Morton White, and J.G.A. Pocock. They view the Constitution as a peculiarly eighteenth-century expression of an ideological discourse, a crystallization of abstract thought. These writers disagree, of course, about the precise character of this bundle of ideas. For our purposes, however, it does not much matter whether the chief component of this ideology was civic humanism, Scottish realism, or Lockean liberalism. The challenge of historiography has been to trace the genealogy of these various ideas or clusters of ideas, suggesting in the process how members of a colonial elite – the delegates to the Constitutional Convention, for example – might have acquired these views, an approach that has transformed much of the scholarship of this period into a kind of sociology of knowledge for the American gentry.

Though this intellectual history is often brilliantly conceived, I must confess that I have never found it altogether persuasive. Something seems to be missing; the explanative puzzle remains incomplete. The causal arrows always appear to be pointing from ideology to event, and though the American people surely acted on principle – ideas *did* matter – they also lived, and thought, and wrote constitutions within social contexts that gave special meaning to the very language in which they expressed political ideas. I object, in other words, to the radical divorce of ideology and experience, a demurral that seems additionally justified by the fact that these historians usually concentrate their attention on the ideas of a small group of gentry leaders.

Progressive or, more recently, neo-progressive historians have flipped the problem on its head, insisting that late eighteenth-century Americans viewed the Constitution through the lens of special material interests. These people, we learn, subscribed to ideas that the modern scholar decides must have been especially appropriate to artisans, or yeomen, or precapitalists, or slave-holders, or whatever vocational identity allowed them to survive. There is no reason here to review this literature. Although much of it is quite stimulating, it suffers from an interpretive circularity that makes causality largely a function of material condition.

I suspect that historians of the Constitution should take a longer and broader perspective, analyzing the political experiences of ordinary men and women as they developed over the course of the eighteenth century and interpreting them as a kind of evolving, collective memory, where a shared sense of how things ought to be done responded to a fluid social environment. What I have in mind is not the study of past politics – institutional structures and electoral returns – nor even an investigation of ideas about politics – an analysis of election sermons and pamphlets, for example. Rather

149

I am advocating something looser, the exploration of an eighteenth-century American political culture that was itself a product of ideas, attitudes, and assumptions, on the one hand, and material conditions, on the other.

Let us start where many scholars have begun, with the political philosophy of John Locke. In his famous controversy with Filmer, Locke divorced government from society. This was a radical move. Suddenly the entire structure of traditional, organic society appeared unnatural, arbitrary, and illegitimate. He destroyed the argument for absolutism, and as he did so, he opened up the possibility of a new, liberal society, a natural order composed of reasoning individuals.

All this is familiar material. What Anglo-American historians of the eighteenth century have tended to overlook, however, is that this was also the period during which a centralizing British state was rapidly transforming itself into the most powerful economic and political force in the world. As historian Joanna Innes recently observed, "In the English case . . . the same decades which saw the country firmly constituting itself as a limited monarchy, with a 'mixed' government constrained by 'checks and balances,' also saw the nation's 'rise to power' – a development only a government exceptionally well placed to mobilize and deploy domestic resources could possibly have brought about." We find ourselves confronted with what appears an insolvable conundrum. How can we square Locke's liberal individual with a strong state apparatus? According to students of British society like Innes and Linda Colley, the answer is that within the political context of the eighteenth century this was a nonproblem. A liberal vision of society coexisted quite successfully with centralized authority.

This was also the world of the colonial Americans. Though many of them owned their own land and grew their own food, they were not the self-sufficient yeomen of Jeffersonian mythology. Nor is it analytically very helpful to think of these people as premodern, or preindustrial, or "pre" anything else. By the second quarter of the eighteenth century, they had been fully integrated into a complex world market. As Russell Menard and John McCusker have demonstrated so persuasively, these "independent" American yeomen produced all sorts of staples that coursed through the British economy, with southern rice, tobacco, and indigo carried directly to the mother country and timber, fish, and foodstuffs from the Middle Atlantic and New England colonies transported to the Caribbean, where slaves manufactured sugar.[1] Historians know a good deal about this flow of New World exports. Only recently have they begun to pay adequate attention to the flood of British consumer goods – what Samuel Adams called the "baubles of Britain" – that helped transform the character of colonial society during the eighteenth century. The point is that by the 1740s these Americans were undeniably part of a sophisticated capitalist system, one that linked even the most humble frontier farmers to distant British manufacturers.

Let me expand on this set of relationships. Some social historians working in this period have stressed the capacity of individual Americans or groups of Americans to shape their own lives. We are told that these men and women decided whether to enter the capitalist economy and on what terms. They could – in so much as they willed to do so – preserve their own independence. But a moment's reflection reveals the problems with this position. As Carole Shammas and others have discovered, the yeomen of the northern colonies were both creditors and debtors, dependent and independent, people whose social position was defined within a chain of relationships. And James Oakes, among others, has shown that even the great slaveholders of the South, men who presumably possessed absolute power over their slaves and who bragged to each other that their plantations were little "rocks of independency" were, in fact, beholden to distant suppliers; and however much these gentlemen claimed to be paternalists who looked after the welfare of their blacks, they frequently had to sell their dependents because they too were dependent on the merchants of London or Glasgow.

I am not suggesting that there was anything darkly conspiratorial about the spread of eighteenth-century capitalism. Most whites in the colonies eagerly embraced the consumer economy, purchasing goods that presumably made their lives warmer, healthier, more beautiful, that brought them – especially the women – a measure of leisure. And given a chance, they produced surpluses to pay for these items, more tobacco, more rice, more wheat, fueling a commercial system in which almost everyone by midcentury was

---

1. John J. McCusker and Russell R. Menard, *The Economy of British America, 1607–1789* (Chapel Hill, NC, 1985), passim.

both a giver and receiver of credit. This *was* a liberal society – at least for whites – exactly what Locke had envisioned. And the key element within this commercial empire was property, access to it, security in possessing it, distribution of it. The opportunity to acquire land drew thousands of Germans, Scotch-Irish, and Irish to America during this period. They were in search of the prosperity that had eluded them in the Old World. The shock of William Smith – the curious American traveler whom Professor Klingenstein described – at the inequities of Prussian society was not a measure of his republicanism. Rather he judged this regime through liberal eyes; it insulted his economic sense of fair play.

How then does all this relate to notions about the "good ruler" of the eighteenth century, much less to the writing of the U.S. Constitution? The answer is that colonial Americans had experience with two quite different types of rulers. Many of the colonies were governed, at least nominally, by an appointed royal governor. These individuals tended to be second-rate placemen, persons who owed their position to favor rather than to talent. In the normal course of events, how the royal governors behaved in office did not matter much to the great mass of ordinary Americans.

But this was not true of the legislators elected to the various colonial assemblies. In the eyes of the colonists, the lower houses were the heart of the political system. This is why Professor Ketcham can state – quite correctly in my estimation – "Drawing on the ancient English practice of restricting the people's voice in government to one branch of the legislature (the House of Commons) and on the colonial experience of the lower house as the place of effective assertion of local interests against imperial power, Americans in 1776 tended to think government by consent consisted largely of a fully empowered, responsive legislature."[2] We know that the franchise requirements of the eighteenth century were not very restrictive. The fact that the "independent" voters of colonial America usually selected members of the gentry to sit in these assemblies should not be interpreted to mean that ordinary folk did not possess strong ideas about who could best represent their interest in the legislatures. They did. It was not unusual for colonial voters to drop a representative. In Massachusetts the

2. Ralph Ketcham, "Concepts of Presidential Leadership, Citizenship, and Good Government in the United States during the Founding Era," above, 107.

freeholders often provided instructions for delegates to the lower house.

Most eighteenth-century Americans expected the "good ruler" – which in this context meant the good legislator – to do as little as possible. Or, to state the proposition somewhat differently, the colonial assemblymen were urged to nourish the expansion of a liberal society, and in practical terms that involved keeping down taxation, doing their best to stimulate trade with Native Americans, keeping officious British bureaucrats off the backs of local merchants, opening up new western lands, and protecting the rights of property which, among other things, involved the strict enforcement of the slave codes.

For the most part the burden of colonial government was not very great. To be sure, the expense of waging war against the French could upset this set of expectations. But even in the great contest for empire what was at stake was land, the dreams of parents in densely populated eastern farm villages and worn-out tidewater communities to locate their children or their children's children on the rich soil of the Ohio Valley. Western expansion was, in fact, a liberal dream, one well worth the sacrifice of men and money. "Salutary neglect" – at all levels of eighteenth-century Anglo-American government – was a policy that allowed individuals to acquire property freely, to produce and consume to the fullest of their abilities within an expanding capitalist economy. This arrangement was the driving engine behind the prosperity of the British Empire. Strong nations were built upon liberal societies. Adam Smith was not the only one who appreciated the logic of this formulation.

This is the rough outline of a late eighteenth-century political culture, a bundle of assumptions rooted in a century of experience that was shared by the founding fathers as well as the mass of less-renowned Americans. It powerfully influenced decisions made in Philadelphia in the summer of 1787. By the time that these men convened, there was no question about the centrality of elected rulers in the new system of government, and though a few delegates may have entertained aristocratic or monarchical fantasies, they knew full well that the American people would never accept such political innovation.

And whatever else contemporaries said about the "good" constitutional ruler, it was clear that they expected him to preserve property, the foundation of a liberal society. As Benjamin Franklin reminded his colleagues at the convention, European immigrants to this country were drawn by "good Laws and liberty." With diligence, Franklin declared, such persons could expect to "establish themselves in Business, marry, raise families . . . [and after] one or two years' residence [acquire] all the Rights of a Citizen." Here we again encounter the formula for effective government in a liberal society – free individuals busily developing economic opportunities under what Professor Ketcham calls "active leadership." Jefferson as well as Hamilton understood these relations, and as Joyce Appleby among others has reminded us, even the most apparently doctrinaire republicans actually welcomed commerce.

The question before the founding generation was not whether they would accept participation in a capitalist economy, but rather on what terms they would do so. That is what Ketcham seems to be suggesting when he notes the ambiguity of the Constitution: it protected individual rights as well as promoted "active government." This apparent tension within the system, he concludes, "arose because American government was founded in the flux that existed as the Western World moved into the modern age."[3] Ideas of free trade, capitalist enterprise, industrial revolution, diversifying interests, individuals, and democratic politics burgeoned all around the Atlantic world of the founders. But, as I have tried to argue here, the ambiguity is actually an illusion. Individual rights and "active" government went hand in hand in the eighteenth century. And it was because of the centrality of property in this framework that the delegates to the Constitutional Convention refused to deal with human bondage. The crucial props that sustained the liberal state – the sanctity of property and individual rights – also maintained the institution of slavery.

The burden of these reflections on the Constitution is not that we should reject intellectual history or conclude that the teachings of the classical republicans, the Scottish common-sense realists, the Enlightenment philosophers, and all the rest did not matter. To the gentry leaders of this period, they obviously mattered very much. But however these various ideas may have shaped political discourse, they did not *cause* the Constitution. Nor, by the same token, am I dismissing the study of particular economic and social

3. Ibid., 126.

strains during the 1780s. Such tensions unquestionably heightened anxieties – especially among the old colonial elites – and served as catalysts for the creation of a new system of government. My point is simply that these short-term dislocations and the shrill republican ideas about power, virtue, and corruption took on meaning within the context of a liberal political culture that was already a century old when the delegates to the Constitutional Convention gathered at Philadelphia.

6.2
The "Act of Governing" and the American Constitution

James H. Hutson

Professor Ketcham's paper is a subtle rebuke to the Reagan administration, which apparently scorns activist government as unjustified by American history. Ketcham argues that it was the original intention of the framers of the Constitution to establish a vigorous, energetic executive. Edward S. Corwin made this point in a celebrated article in the *American Historical Review* decades ago,[1] where he argued that the impetus for an energetic executive was the framers' revulsion at the excesses of the unbridled state legislatures in the 1780s. While not contesting Corwin, Professor Ketcham locates the impulse for a strong executive in the classical political philosophy with which the framers were familiar, thus adding an intellectual dimension to Corwin's thesis.

Missing from Professor Ketcham's paper is an exploration of what he called the act of governing, for it appears to me that the framers of the Constitution, while in the abstract favoring an energetic executive, did not supply their executive with the means to govern energetically.

The means of governing – what Professor Ketcham called the act of governing – were discussed sparingly in the convention. Aside from George Mason and Edmund Randolph, who were keen on establishing a statutory council to assist the executive in discharging his duties, only Alexander Hamilton and John Frances Mercer appear to have thought about the mechanics of governing. Both men observed that the executive could operate by force or influence. Since force was precluded in a free republic, both favored investing the executive with influence, which Hamilton on June 18

---

1. Edward S. Corwin, "The Progress of Constitutional Theory between the Declaration of Independence and the Philadelphia Convention," *American Historical Review* 30 (1925): 511–36.

described as "a dispensation of those regular honors and emoluments which produce an attachment to the Government."[2] The art of governing Hamilton was proposing was made famous or – depending on one's views – infamous by Sir Robert Walpole earlier in the century – the disposition of patronage – "places and pensions" in the jargon of the time – to build a party through which an executive could implement a program. Walpole's enemies denounced government by patronage as corruption and Hamilton was obliged to preface his proposal of June 18 with a disclaimer that "he did not mean corruption."[3] Nevertheless he was advocating – and every delegate knew he was advocating – Walpole's art of governing, the techniques of Sir Robert's Court Party. Hamilton appeared to have reasoned that if the convention wanted a strong executive, which the Court party in England favored, it would have to provide the Court's tools, influence, to obtain its objectives.

The proposal to arm the executive with influence was crushed in the convention. The Constitution, Article I, section 6, proscribed placeholding and other forms of influence by forbidding members of Congress to accept executive branch offices. Occasional suggestions on the floor of the convention to legitimize influence by deleting this provision were rebuffed by delegates like Edmund Randolph who asserted on August 14 that he "should continue uniformly opposed to striking out the clause as opening a door for influence and corruption."[4] Closing the door against influence and corruption was the crusade of the Country party in England and in following its example by denying the executive access to influence the convention acted in vintage Country fashion. And in this connection I think we should applaud Professor Ketcham's insight that the framers took Bolingbroke's *Idea of a Patriot King*, one of the holy writs of the Country party, for their model in structuring the executive. *The Idea of a Patriot King*, written as a polemic against Walpole in 1738, was a philippic against corruption and influence and against the governing by party which the Court party permitted. "Governing by party," wrote Bolingbroke, "must always end

2. Hamilton, speech of June 18, 1787, in Max Farrand, ed., *The Records of the Federal Convention of 1787*, 4 vols. (New Haven, CT, 1937 repr. 1966), 1: 285.
3. Hamilton in ibid.
4. Randolph in ibid., 2: 290.

in the government of a faction" and "as party is a political evil, faction is the worst of all parties."[5]

With this condemnation of party to which the framers subscribed ringing in our ears, I would put the following question to Professor Ketcham. Was there not a contradiction in the way the framers conceived the executive? Did they not establish what John Adams in another connection called a solecism in politics – an executive half Court and half Country, an executive theoretically energetic but actually weak because it was bereft of the tools needed to govern? Washington, it is true, governed like the "patriot king," establishing his policies by the sober charisma Bolingbroke prescribed for his ruler. But many of Washington's successors, lacking his unique endowments, have not been able to govern well.

I think it is significant that at present, a group in the United States led by Lloyd Cutler and Douglas Dillon is proposing, as the best way to celebrate the bicentennial of the Constitution, a revision in the structure of government that is distinctly Walpolian – a strengthening of parties by allowing them to dispense more patronage, with a simultaneous movement toward parliamentary government by allowing members of the executive branch to serve in the legislature. The justification for these proposed changes is that in our system the executive does not have sufficient power consistently to pass a program in the legislative branch. To Professor Ketcham I would, in closing, put this quesion: if this analysis is true, were the seeds not planted in a defective structuring of the executive in 1787, where that officer was deprived of the means to employ the art of governing through patronage and party and should this subject, on which he has written elsewhere, not have been included in his paper?

Professor Klingenstein describes the travels of William Smith and Francisco de Miranda in Prussia, Saxony, and Austria during 1785 and records their impressions of the government and economy in those countries. Since she is describing the reaction of the travelers to the sights they see and the people they meet, she might better have called her paper "American Impressions of German Rulers in the Eighteenth Century." Professor Klingenstein shows with an understated irony that Smith and Miranda were prisoners of their own preconceptions in assessing German governments,

---

5. David Mallet, ed., *Viscount Bolingbroke, Works* (Hildesheim, 1968), 3: 83.

that they were prepared to give Joseph II the benefit of every doubt because Benjamin Franklin had given them a favorable account of him and that they were prepared to dismiss Frederick as a tyrant because he was so regarded by the American habitués of the salons of Paris. The appearances which Smith and Miranda recorded were, Professor Klingenstein suggests, far from the realities of the situation. What is missing in her paper is a description of those realities. What were the Prussian and Austrian conceptions of a ruler? Did they differ, and if so, how? Was government in Prussia the "benevolent despotism" described in my high school textbooks or was it the relentless tyranny Smith and Miranda thought they observed? Professor Klingenstein knows the answers to these questions and may have assumed that her audience does as well. But I confess my own superficial grasp of them and wished she had enlightened us about them.

6.3
The Positions of Rulers in Eighteenth-Century Germany and America

Hartmut Lehmann

Let me start with some remarks by Franz von Zeiller, a law expert in Vienna and tutor of the law of states to the Habsburg princes. In this capacity, in the mid-1790s Zeiller explained the position of the emperor to Archduke Anton Victor as follows: "Whoever wants to be elected emperor has to be a just, benevolent, and useful man of proper descent, that is, of high nobility, a count or a duke. As he will have no income to speak of as emperor, he should have command over considerable means of his own." According to Zeiller it was "a mattter of controversy whether he had to be a German and a Catholic, nor was it clear," as Zeiller continued, "whether the candidate had to be of age."[1]

If we compare Zeiller's definition with the observations made by Colonel Smith and repeated to us by Grete Klingenstein, two matters appear worth mentioning: first, that Smith's views were derived from political rumors rather than from formal or legal definitions of the position and image of an ideal ruler and were therefore more a matter of arbitrary judgment than of notions comparable to the kind of prerequisites Zeiller endeavored to define; and second, that Smith's own bias with regard to matters of religion would appear to have colored his views more than any information he may have gathered during his trip.

If we compare Zeiller's definition with Ralph Ketcham's most interesting remarks on the American views of leadership and good government in the late 1780s, two matters also appear worth mentioning: first, that the attributes of an emperor as defined by

---

1. Wolfgang Wagner, ed., *Das Staatsrecht des Heiligen Römischen Reiches Deutscher Nation: Eine Darstellung der Reichsverfassung gegen Ende des 18. Jahrhunderts nach einer Handschrift der Wiener Nationalbibliothek* (Karlsruhe, 1968), 44.

Zeiller – that an emperor should be a just, benevolent, and useful man – could easily be found and applied with regard to the position of the American president; second, while Zeiller insisted that a candidate for the position of emperor should have considerable means of his own, he did not nor did he need to, given the legal situation, mention public support as a prerequisite. In contrast, American leaders, while also requiring certain private means, did in fact need and believed themselves to need the consent of approval of a majority of the people.

Of course, Zeiller's definition is very brief and should not be pressed too much. In order to compare the position of a ruler in late eighteenth-century Germany and America, let me now introduce additional source material. Early in 1765, for example, when Archduke Leopold, Joseph's younger brother, was being prepared for his new task as duke of Tuscany, a position he was to assume in the course of that year, his father, Emperor Francis, wrote instructions in which he tried to explain to Leopold the duties of a ruler.[2] Leopold was to read these instructions four times a year, Emperor Francis remarked, and then decide whether his advice, which he described as nothing but a testimony of fatherly love and concern, was in any way helpful to him.

Leopold should examine his conscience daily, Francis wrote, and go to communion often, for only in so doing would he lose the fear of sudden death (which in fact did occur both to Francis and Leopold). Leopold should mistrust his own desires and prejudices, the father continued, echoing Fénelon's *Les aventures de Télémaque*, just as he should always mistrust flatterers. He should always keep in mind that he bears responsibility for all the people of his country; he should be aware that his example influences the behavior of his subjects; his family should therefore excel in unity and virtue, just as he should always remain loyal to the dynasty to which he belonged.

Furthermore, Leopold should strive to attain an attitude of *douceur*, of mildness and considerateness. This would help him win the love of those he governed. *Douceur* should be complimented by *politesse*, a friendliness and politeness to people of all social ranks, high as well as low. In financial matters he should neither spend too

2. Adam Wandruszka, *Leopold II: Erzherzog von Österreich, Großherzog von Toskana, König von Ungarn und Böhmen, Römischer Kaiser*, 2 vols. (Vienna, 1963), 1: 82–86.

much nor too little, and in Francis's view a small and financially healthy court, as he put it, was more desirable than a large and splendid court with many debts.

In keeping with the philosophy of enlightenment, but also in the tradition of classical philosophy and Christian morals, Francis reminded Leopold that he should always attempt to fulfill his duties as a ruler and that he should never postpone any official tasks, such as administering justice, due to private pleasures. In short, Leopold should follow the principle that he who tries to make others happy is happiest himself.

In August 1765, only a few days after Francis's sudden death and shortly before Leopold left for Tuscany, his mother, Maria Theresa, sat down to write instructions of her own in which she modified some of the remarks her husband had made.[3] For example, in Maria Theresa's view, Leopold should not be too friendly with people of low origin, he should be prepared to accept good advice from experienced councillors, he should publicly profess to the Catholic religion, he should attend church services regularly, and he should suppress books undermining religion. He should honor the pope, Maria Theresa continued, yet never let the pope interfere in his political affairs. At court he should not tolerate scandals and should insist on modest dress, decent behavior, and conversations without slander. Never should he engage in intrigues, nor censure his ministers in the presence of their subordinates. He should try to promote the practical arts, but should eliminate from his palace pictures that depicted nudes and should discourage those who painted such pictures. In conclusion, Maria Theresa stressed that Leopold should always observe the law, inform himself before making any decisions, and be aware of people's needs: "As sovereign, as father of your peoples, try to fulfill your duties. Do always look after their welfare, try to help, to give support and courage."[4]

This is not the place to discuss in detail the differences between the instructions given by Emperor Francis and those given by Maria Theresa. Nor do I have the time to supplement these documents with more eighteenth-century material from other dynasties, such as the Hohenzollern. Instead, I will attempt to compare the instructions by Leopold's parents with the conclusion of Pro-

3. Ibid., 1: 110–19.
4. Ibid.

fessor Ketcham's paper. Leaving aside minor aspects, three major points should be made:

1. While the American founding fathers were deeply influenced by the thought and culture of Greece and Rome, late eighteenth-century German rulers were much less exposed to classical ideas of leadership. In Germany the revival of classical learning would appear to have been more a matter involving the educated and enlightened middle class, which was occasionally close to those in power but was in fact powerless aside from its role in the world of letters. Of course, enlightened rulers in German territories had been taught a certain amount of classical learning as part of a general enlightened worldview and education. When it came to questions of power or rather the sharing of power, however, they put aside all theories concerning intermediate powers or constitutional responsibility and relied on the traditional monarchical principle, modified perhaps by the position granted to trusted councillors.

2. While the American founding fathers were intimately acquainted with modern political thinkers such as Hobbes and Montesquieu, German rulers were far less schooled in political theory. They were instead expected to observe the tradition of their respective dynasties. Sometimes they were also told by their advisers to follow the example of some outstanding member of another dynasty or to imitate the example of another court. It should be added that within specific dynasties the appreciation of certain examples underwent considerable change from generation to generation. The Prussian King Frederick William I, for example, did not choose his father, King Frederick I, as the ruler whose policies he wished to follow, but rather his grandfather, Duke Elector Frederick William; the son of Frederick William I, Frederick the Great, in turn, broke with much that his father had cherished and returned to some of the policies of his grandfather, Frederick I.

3. Both German rulers and the American founding fathers were convinced that their governing should serve the public good. In the case of the founding fathers the idea of good government was closely linked to the principle of self-government; in the case of the Habsburg dynasty, on the other hand, the power and tradition of the monarchy, and not the power and the interests

of the people over whom they ruled, formed the basis of their obligation to a policy of good government.

We should therefore not be blinded by certain similarities we may find in late eighteenth-century statements about good rulers in America and Germany. Serving the public good and depending on public trust gave strength to the presidency in America. In German principalities and kingdoms, on the other hand, enlightened reform and the despotism of princes could not be merged into a coherent and successful policy in foreign and domestic affairs, in economics and finance, in justice and education. This was as true for the Prussia of Frederick the Great as for the Austria of Joseph II. In this matter, I think, Grete Klingenstein's chief witness, Colonel Smith, who praised Joseph II as a ruler while sharply criticizing Frederick the Great, would appear to have been mistaken.

6.4
The Social Context of the Idea of the Ruler in Eighteenth-Century Germany

Diethelm Klippel

The idea of a ruler in the eighteenth century is strictly speaking ambiguous: it can refer to theory or practice, to the viewpoints of different groups of people or to different stages in time. When the idea of a ruler refers to German political theory in the eighteenth century, a survey of the various schools of thought may indicate what ideas we can expect about the sovereign and his position. Applying this method, it should become clear that although the authors of the period of enlightened absolutism, in particular, were very concerned about the theoretical and practical aspects of the education of their future rulers – in our discussion we mentioned Christian August Beck and Josef von Sonnenfels as examples – they represented one aspect, albeit important, of German political theory of the time. The whole range of German political theory also shows that at the end of the eighteenth century the differences between the German and the North American political cultures are less distinct than usually expected.[1]

It is true that in the eighteenth century the political schools of thought can mainly be divided into two parts: they either represent enlightened absolutism or the interests of the estates against the aspirations of absolute rulers. Especially over the last twenty years, research has shown, however, that at the end of the eighteenth century liberal and democratic theories were formed in Germany too, and they were directed against enlightened absolutism and the

1. I am grateful to S. McCaskill for this translation. Leonard Krieger, for example, perceives a specifically German idea of freedom in contrast to "the individual secular liberty familiar to the western political tradition," in Leonard Krieger, *The German Idea of Freedom: History of a Political Tradition* (repr. Chicago, IL and London, 1972), ix. This concept is ultimately based on the idea of a German *Sonderweg* in history.

Ständestaat (a system in which the different estates are represented in a Diet) of the ancien régime.[2] Therefore, it is obvious that the concepts about the sovereign and his responsibilities change as well. A few examples, mainly taken from the literature of natural-rights philosophy, may serve to illustrate this point.

Absolutism conceives of the ruler as a *legibus solutus*: "The laws of a state are binding for the subjects but not for the sovereign in relation to his subjects."[3] However, Adam Friedrich Glafey adds, "unless decreed otherwise by a fundamental law, constitution of an empire or state"; this statement points to the concept of *leges fundamentales* and uses the terminology of the natural-rights doctrine, *limites pactitii*, which describes how the rights and privileges of the estates curtail the power of a ruler. Neither in theory nor in practice, however, is this taken as seriously binding.[4]

Johann Jacob Moser, a confirmed defender of the interests of the estates in the eighteenth century, therefore speaks with some justification of legal "Masters of the guild of sovereignty makers" and criticizes the desire for absolutism of numerous German princes who are "increasingly beginning to exert their power in a sovereign or despotic fashion and who want to hear less and less about worthy members of the Diet, about wider consultation with others, and about allowing them to participate in any decisions."[5]

The rights of the subjects or the duties of the ruler, as they are

---

2. See, for instance, Zwi Batscha, *Studien zur politischen Theorie des deutschen Frühliberalismus* (Frankfurt/Main, 1981); Otto Büsch and Walter Grab, eds., *Die demokratische Bewegung in Mitteleuropa im ausgehenden 18. und frühen 19. Jahrhundert* (Berlin, 1980); Walter Grab, *Ein Volk muß seine Freiheit selbst erobern: Zur Geschichte der deutschen Jakobiner* (Frankfurt/Main, 1984); Diethelm Klippel, *Politische Freiheit und Freiheitsrechte im deutschen Naturrecht des 18. Jahrhunderts* (Paderborn, 1976); Helmut Reinalter, *Der Jakobinismus in Mitteleuropa: Eine Einführung* (Stuttgart, 1981); Inge Stephan, *Literarischer Jakobinismus in Deutschland, 1789–1806* (Stuttgart, 1976). See also the editions by Jörn Garber, ed., *Revolutionäre Vernunft: Texte zur jakobinischen und liberalen Revolutionsrezeption in Deutschland, 1789–1810* (Kronberg/Ts., 1974); Zwi Batscha and Jörn Garber, eds., *Von der ständischen zur bürgerlichen Gesellschaft: Politisch-soziale Theorien im Deutschland der zweiten Hälfte des 18. Jahrhunderts* (Frankfurt/Main, 1981).

3. Adam Friedrich Glafey, *Recht der Vernunfft* (Franfurt/Main, [2]1732), 831.

4. Part of the natural rights doctrine relieves the ruler from paying attention to such limitations, see for example Justus Henning Boehmer, *Introductio in ius publicum universale* (Halle, [2]1726), 300, 598f.

5. Johann Jacob Moser, "Von der Landeshoheit derer Teutschen Reichsstände überhaupt," in Johann Jacob Moser, *Neues Teutsches Staatsrecht* (Frankfurt/Main, 1773), 14: 256, 252f.

formulated in the doctrine of natural rights (*limites naturales*), can be considered as a further constraint on the power of a ruler. Right up to the last decades of the eighteenth century the authors of the doctrine of natural rights still do not see these limitations as legally binding for the ruler: in terms of natural rights he only has "imperfect," that is, moral responsibilities: "imperans parentibus ex iure naturae imperfecte . . . obligatus est; obligatio imperantis ad leges iuris publici universalis est imperfecta."[6] At best, this allows for an appeal to the ruler to limit his own power for the sake of the freedom of his subjects: "The legal freedom in a state requires . . . that the prince himself . . . has to set limits to his orders and decisions."[7]

In the two last decades of the eighteenth century, all this changes fundamentally with the German doctrine of natural rights. According to Leopold Friedrich Fredersdorff, the sovereign is obliged "to follow the laws which he has given to his people. It is an act of servile flattery to try to make the prince believe that he is above the law."[8] It is accepted practice at this stage for the authors to begin to formulate fundamental concepts of natural rights which are characteristic of liberal political thinking and which, at the same time, are considered as legally binding for all states and rulers.[9] There are, for instance, human-rights catalogs (especially freedom of the press, freedom of trade and industry) designed to protect the individual and society from the state; furthermore, the liberal concept of property, the denial of the rights of the estates, the theory of the separation of powers, and the demand for written constitutions in our modern sense are all advocated. Thus, the theoretical foundations for the constitutionalism of the nineteenth century were now established in Germany as well.

In addition, Rousseau's doctrine of the sovereignty of the people is occasionally applied and even a monarch who is bound by a constitution is disposable for the sake of the republic, but this is

6. Gottfried Ernst Fritsch, *Ius publicum universale et pragmaticum* (Jena, 1734), 54, 61; see Christian Wolff, *Grundsätze des Natur- und Völckerrechts* (Halle, 1754, repr. 1980), §1085.

7. Heinrich Gottfried Scheidemantel, *Das Staatsrecht nach der Vernunft und den Sitten der vornehmsten Völker betrachtet*, vol. 3 (Jena, 1773), 203.

8. Leopold Friedrich Fredersdorff, *System des Rechts der Natur, auf bürgerliche Gesellschaften: Gesetzgebung und das Völkerrecht angewandt* (Braunschweig, 1790), 521.

9. For this and the following see Klippel, *Politische Freiheit und Freiheitsrechte* (see n. 2), 113ff.

done in favor of a different concept of ruling and of the people who exert power. Johann Adam Bergk, for example, views the "democratic republic" as "the only legal form" of a state. In his opinion, even "the North American free states . . . cannot be seen as perfect democracies because those people who own property or money have been granted privileges."[10]

10. Johann Adam Bergk, *Untersuchungen aus dem Natur-, Staats- und Völkerrechte* (Leipzig, 1796), 94, 100.

6.5
Discussion

GRETE KLINGENSTEIN: Let me concentrate on the idea of the ruler as it was formulated and transported by political and legal theory both of German and foreign, that is to say French, origin. There are four common denominators as far as rulers are concerned. The first and most important is that the rulers, if we read the papers of Frederick II, Maria Theresa, and Joseph II, should rule themselves. This was considered progress in comparison with the earlier rulers of absolutism.

Second, there is a heightened sense of responsibility for the material and spiritual welfare of the people, their security, and of course for foreign policy and defense as well. In this context the phrase "servant of the state" first proclaimed by Frederick II and then imitated by many of the German rulers acquired its meaning. From this heightened sense of responsibility the ruler became an *active* ruler. This ruler was restless, was supposed to be constantly travelling, had to view and inspect the country. Economic conditions, social conditions, church conditions, and last but not least, the military situation had to be inspected by the ruler himself. This activism is especially pronounced in the image of the ruler as a creative legislator and as a supreme commander.

Third, as part of this image the idea looms large that the ruler should rule according to preordained fundamental laws – of course there is a good portion of Montesquieu in this area. The main object is to bind the successor, whose character and actions could not be foreseen, to the wholesome laws that the enlightened ruler would pass. There is one example of a ruler, namely Leopold, Pietro Leopoldo of Toscany, the brother of Joseph II, who from 1779 to 1782 himself proposed a constitution for the Grand Duchy of Toscany.

In conclusion let me suggest the hypothesis that in the later part of the eighteenth century the government of rulers in Germany was future-oriented, whereas in the first half of the eighteenth century traditional rulers were geared to deal with ad hoc situations. Yet the later concept had its peculiar dilemma: most laws instituting or initiating reforms in enlightened Germany were based on well deliberated plans of bureaucrats and counselors whose importance must be stressed here. However, at least in Austria most laws were ad hoc decisions of the ruler himself. This dilemma between the image of the rulers and the reality of rule could not be solved before 1789.

HERMANN WELLENREUTHER: I would like to shift the emphasis by asking how rule was experienced by people on both sides of the Atlantic. Timothy Breen has already raised that question. I think he is right that rule was experienced in North America in the doings of the justices of the peace. The county courts were extremely import-ant in the southern as well as in the middle colonies. One measure by which to determine how important these institutions were is to ask where people thought things were decided. This can be dis-covered by tracing the flow of petitions. In the northern colonies petitions would flow by the hundreds per year to the houses of representatives, while in the middle colonies they were sent to the county courts and only seldom to the houses of representatives. In Virginia it was the county court and the vestries on one side and the House of Burgesses on the other. As one moves further south the vestry eventually becomes the central institution where you experi-ence local rule – that at least is true for South Carolina, where the courts in Charleston were too far away for most people. Rule in North America was thus experienced in very different ways. The institutions that meted out justice and were competent to make decisions changed from colony to colony. I think that Timothy Breen is very right that the least important person in this game was the governor of the colony.

I think there are similarities in Europe which can be pointed out. How was rule experienced by people in Lower Saxony and es-pecially in Göttingen? In Göttingen in the beginning of the eight-eenth century no one got the idea to look to Hanover, to the *Geheime Rat*, or to the king, who after 1714 was far away in London. Those considered rulers were the magistrates of the town. The charter of the city asked the citizens to pay absolute obedience to the magistracy. That is true for all the charters I have seen. There are only a few exceptions in Prussia. For the citizen, authority, rulers, and rule converged in the institution called *Stadtmagistrat*. What *they* did represented the reality of rule.

170

The magistracy was responsible for the preservation of order. Now there are instructions, there are lists of what a *Magistrat* was supposed to do – some of these are indeed very elaborate. What is your duty as a ruler in a town? He is obliged to further the public good – at least in Prussia this had some concrete meaning. Often, however, it is difficult to distinguish rhetoric from concrete meaning. Certainly a couple of things that the magistracy considered important linked that office to some extent to the functions cherished by elected representatives in North America. To keep taxes low was very important, and to further the local economy was another important self-imposed task, although by the middle of the eighteenth century the latter was increasingly and sometimes not really voluntarily ceded to the sovereign, the king, or the duke.

There are, at least in the German towns I have looked at, two conflicting tendencies: while magistracy on the local level tried to produce as little governmental action as possible the tendency on the part of the ruler was to do exactly the opposite. The speed and flow of ordinances and orders from Hanover to Göttingen increased between the 1690s and the 1780s. In ever greater detail every aspect of town life became subject to the sovereign's rules. And that likewise meant that the independence of the local town magistracy gradually withered. By the end of the eighteenth century the role of the town magistracy in a lot of German towns had changed dramatically: rule was now experienced in a different way, and with that the notion of rule as experienced by the citizens changed too. For now the local magistracy had degenerated into being nothing but a dependent organ of the central government; in a parallel development, citizens now also turned increasingly to the central government if need be and expected relief from the center, where before they had walked up to the town hall as their focus of power and rule.

Thus in the first half of the eighteenth century rule was experienced in Göttingen and in Philadelphia or South Carolina in similar ways – but not in New England! Yet while participatory elements on the local, regional, and national levels increased in North America as the century progressed they decreased in Germany, especially in German towns, until the middle of the nineteenth century. While rule in Germany became something distant, anonymous, it became much more of a personal concern in North America.

FRED L. MORRISON: In Germany there existed quite clearly the notion that the government has the duty to govern. In the United States that notion simply does not exist. The president has "to faithfully execute the laws." And that is something quite different. It is something which says there may be a stalemate – I think it was an intentional stalemate. I would draw a distinction between the current parliamentary systems: in the *Grundgesetz* there is a provision for a *Notstandsgesetzgebung* (emergency legislation) in case of a stalemate between the executive and the legislature which would provide for the issuance of new laws in order to ensure that the government was in a position to govern. In contrast, in the United States in the case of a budget deficit, as well as in any number of other cases, we find a stalemate quite acceptable.

RALPH KETCHAM: You seem to suggest that the founding fathers intended a kind of paralysis, a stalemate. I cannot imagine that this was so. It seems to me that there was a liberal concern for checking and balancing power. I think you can read this in *Federalist* no. 10, where the intention was not that the checks and balances would lead to a stalemate as much as it was that they would neutralize factional forces in a polity.

GERALD STOURZH: I would like to turn to a problem which lends itself to comparative analysis and that is the question of the ruler and the law. The problem is that American leaders sometimes thought that they should conscientiously break the law in order to observe some higher law, the *salus publica*. In Mr. Ketcham's paper the Louisiana Purchase is mentioned. Jefferson certainly thought that he was breaking the Constitution when he purchased Louisiana. And afterward he appealed to the conscience of his countrymen, pleading with them that they should understand that he really did it for the best of the country, which he certainly did. When Abraham Lincoln suspended habeas corpus at the beginning of the Civil War that was a similar problem.

There is one issue hidden here: at the time of the Constitutional Convention what happened to the prerogative of England? Prerogative disappears and executive power emerges. Although the Americans were very much aware of the existence of prerogative, they never mentioned it. They spoke about executive power – I agree with Mr. Morrison that executive power means, literally speaking, "to execute the laws." I really do think that there is a tension and an unsolved dilemma in the relationship of the ruler to the laws and various levels of laws.

GRETE KLINGENSTEIN: I would like to take up the discussion of the task of the ruler begun by Mr. Morrison. In central Europe we have two models of rulers, an old model and a new one. The old model, and Montesquieu pointed to this in his travel diary, was a ruler who not so much obeyed the law or rather the laws of the land, but instead kept the existing laws; rule in this respect meant rather to retain the status quo – a status quo which, and I am now turning to the local conditions, I think, in central Europe was divided among various local governments that had guaranteed rights and liberties. Now in this respect foreign politics have to be taken into account. The new concept of a ruler was formulated under the impact of power contests, especially those in central Europe.

At the heart of this new concept of the ruler is not so much the notion of keeping the law, but first of all, of compiling existing laws. Just a small detail to illustrate the problems associated with rule in central Europe: in 1759, for the first time in Austria, the government asked several administrators in the provinces to make a survey of the constitutions of the various realms and provinces for the purposes of the princes' education. As a reason for this request Maria Theresa herself recorded that "my father did not know the constitutions of his realms"; this is very interesting because he had left the government of the various provinces, she concludes, to the estates and their representatives.

Let me sketch this new model of a ruler: his first duty would be to compile various laws, which meant keeping the rights and liberties of the people, their autonomies; his second would be to improve these existing laws, a very important task indeed; and the third then – and this of course is an idealistic step – was to create a new law. Due to this succession of legislative tasks the ruler and his counselors became creators of new law.

RALPH KETCHAM: I take it then that the second model you speak of is in accord with the notion of the enlightened and benevolent despot?

GRETE KLINGENSTEIN: Yes. May I just add that in the new

model the idea of equality of rights and liberties became very strong. The main object was to create equal laws for all parts of society and for all diverse territories of the realm. Thus the notion of one law for the entire realm originated. In this respect I would also like to propose the hypothesis that in central Europe there was a shift from personal loyalty on the local level, on the town level, to abstract loyalty on the national level. In these shifts I think the dilemma and the tensions that arose and the criticism that was directed against enlightened monarchs were due to the fact that traditional rights and liberties – the plural form of the law – were violated.

RALPH KETCHAM: This again suggests to me that the Americans were quite willing to admire and see as good government the governments of these enlightened despots even apart from any democratic forms – that is really what William Smith was looking for.

ERICH ANGERMANN: I just keep wondering why no one thus far has referred to the Declaration of Independence. After all, the picture of George III is the perfect picture of a good ruler turned into the negative. You can find almost all the elements of a good ruler turned upside down: he has to take care of the public good – he did not. What is the public good? Peace, justice, and prosperity. All these are points brought against George III. So I think that the foil of this negative picture is what we always have to keep in mind when looking at the leadership of the executive in the Constitution of 1787. As a modern man, one always tends to forget that these people really wanted only as little government as necessary.

WILLIAM M. WIECEK: In the period of German political thought and practice that we are discussing was there anything comparable to the concept of the rule of law? It struck me specifically, when Mr. Morrison earlier quoted the sentence "Regierungen haben die Aufgabe zu regieren" ["Governments have the duty to govern"], that the English language does not have an equivalent to the noun *Regierung* except in the phrase "rule of law."

GRETE KLINGENSTEIN: Yes, there was a growing discussion about the rule of law. *Regierung* is probably "administration"; I think in German one would have to introduce the word *Verwaltung*, which probably has greater importance than *Regierung*. *Verwaltung* emanating from a central government can also felt on a local level, while the rule of law as such usually cannot. For central Europe I would not conceive of local rule coming from a national ruler, but there are local individual rulers – that is, town magistrates – administering laws coming from a national ruler. In the latter part of the century, however, there was wide agreement that all these various functionaries of administration should be bound by one and the same law.

WILLIAM M. WIECEK: Is the prince bound by the law?

GRETE KLINGENSTEIN: Yes, also the prince.

HARTMUT LEHMANN: There are more problems with translating things here; just to throw light on some of them let me again quote Maria Theresa's instructions to Leopold, that he should always observe the "law." Now what does this mean, *das Recht*? What is *das Recht*, is it "constitution," or is it "justice," *Recht* as *Gesetz*, *Gerechtigkeit*, *Gesetz* in the sense of *Verfassung*, or *Gerechtigkeit* in the sense of "inner conscience"? What is meant obviously lies somewhere between all these terms – thus, it too is wide open to many interpretations. Leopold himself, incidentally, interpreted the term at one stage of his life as meaning "constitution," but later he went back to the much more traditional interpretation of "customary laws and habits."

There is another point I would like to make concerning Ms. Klingenstein's new model for rulers. There are some frictions one should see. How was it brought to the attention of those who ruled how rule was experienced? In central Europe there was no effective way of doing that, for there was no body of local representatives meeting regularly, writing up their grievances, and bringing them to the attention of the ruler, only reports by local officials like the *Gerichtsschulze*. Very often what it comes down to then is the advice given to rulers to be distrustful of flatterers.

The other limitation which I see hindering the new model from becoming very effective is the education of the princes. Now in the sixteenth century we have a lot of literature about how to educate a prince, and in the seventeenth century much is also written about educating those who educate the princes, but in the eighteenth century in the new model it is the educated prince himself, the enlightened despot, who instructs and supervises the education of his successors. In my mind there is a shrinking of horizons with regard to all kinds of things. This then is a much more vulnerable model than those of the sixteenth and seventeenth centuries.

GRETE KLINGENSTEIN: As far as the new model is concerned I am sceptical about it. I proposed the new model more or less as a Weberian *Idealtyp*, knowing very well that political reality was very different indeed. Since the topic was "The Idea of a Ruler," I tried to present some kind of an "ideal."

With regard to the education of the princes, I was struck myself by the very large literature on educating princes existing in the eighteenth century in Germany, France, England, and Italy. I believe scholarship has concentrated on the sixteenth and seventeenth centuries and has too often neglected the eighteenth century.

GERHARD A. RITTER: At the very end of the eighteenth century the training of civil servants changes from the *Kameralistik* mode of education to legal training. This of course should be seen in connection with the duty of the civil servant: he was to apply the law, therefore he was supposed to study the law first. Instituting this change was not successful everywhere; there are other traditions, particularly in Southwest Germany, where a civil servant should be trained in many practical affairs considered to be at least as important as being trained in the law.

Behind these differences, to some degree, are different notions of how much good government should intervene in people's affairs. I was struck by the judgment of William Smith: he did not call it "despotic," etc., but he judged what he saw by the effects; people were not "prosperous," they were "poor" and therefore conditions were bad. Toward the end of the eighteenth century, in North America as well as in Germany, the concept of the "pursuit of happiness," of *Glückseligkeit*, became current; both terms have the same meaning, but they differ in the way how to reach that goal. The *Kameralistik* mode of reaching *Glückseligkeit* was through as much intervention as possible in people's lives and affairs: this was at the center of the idea of the good ruler.

In America of course the "pursuit of happiness" is reached by not intervening too much in people's lives and affairs. Adam Smith has been very differently received on both sides of the Atlantic. In Germany in the very beginning people pointed out that perhaps Smith was right and we should turn away from the old *Wohlfahrtsstaat* (welfare state created by constant intervention), but so these continued, we cannot adopt the English concept for the smaller states. They insisted that it simply would not work and an active intervening government was still needed; the concept of good government is certainly *gute Verwaltung* (effective administration), as Freiherr von Stein among others insisted. It is of course not by chance that people in Prussia or Bavaria continued to talk about "enlightened bureaucracy," "farsighted bureaucracy"; there was reform from above by civil servants brought up on these ideas. Typically, in the legislatures later more than half of the members were sometimes civil servants of this type; in contrast to England, it was the parliamentarians themselves who insisted that civil servants should be members of parliament. There was a long debate with Bismarck about whether civil servants should be in the Reichstag and Bismarck finally agreed to it because he thought that it would not be possible to run a good government and control it if those who are the government did not participate in the Reichstag.

Part 3
Civil Rights and
National Unity

7
The Fourteenth Amendment and Civil Rights after 1866

Harold Melvin Hyman

"Haiti is sick because it has eaten too many constitutions," insisted a sloganeer in that harassed island-nation's 1986 constitutional referendum. Although popular excitements from the ousting of "Baby Doc" Duvalier linger in Haiti, a *New York Times* report later that year from Port-au-Prince noted that "over the years there has been a sort of devaluation of constitutions in Haiti. There have been 22 since the country gained independence from France in 1804. Basically they have all been pretty good documents. The problem has been that they were never respected."[1] America's sharply differing history is characterized in part by a strikingly consistent and largely respectful view of its now two-centuries-old Constitution. Despite this nation's vicissitudes, especially during the Civil War and Reconstruction, the Depression, and Vietnam, as a society Americans retain the habit of looking on the 1787 Constitution as "a machine that would go of itself."[2]

Yet we know also that at times, and sometimes for long periods of time, the Constitution has not been self-starting and that for extended decades locally or regionally disfavored minorities have not enjoyed realistic protections for the exercise of either their civil rights or liberties merely because national and state constitutions existed. Sporadically in our history demands have arisen, through politics or litigations or both, for the nation to intervene on behalf of individuals and/or groups who claimed to suffer by reason of community or state injustices that in some instances state constitutions and laws forbade. On many of these occasions opponents to federal interventions have insisted that only the formal texts of the 1787 Constitution and its implementing statutes be considered in determining if a debated federal action was constitutional or even

1. *New York Times* (October 13, 1986), Y9.
2. Michael G. Kammen, *A Machine That Would Go of Itself* (New York, 1986).

politic. In overbrief terms, this recurring argument is that if a proposed federal policy could not be squared with the formal texts of constitution and statutes, it was inadmissible and undesirable. This attitude has often been expressed in constitutional argumentations as "strict constructionism" and, in doctrines of law, as "legal positivism."

Further definition follows shortly. Before it does, the scheme of this paper warrants mention. An emphasis of recent historical scholarship, to which this paper will later turn, affirms that no Berlin Wall separates legal doctrines from constitutional decisions or either or both from their historical contexts. Instead they all mix to configure controversial public policies and are shaped by these policies.

Thus, for an ordinary legal or civil (that is, a property) right a losing claimant in a lower court may elect to pay his attorney to argue in an appeal court that the controverted claim had constitutional supports, either as an inadmissible constraint by the relevant government (First or Fourteenth Amendment right, as in speech, assembly, petition, etc.) or as a duty that the relevant government failed to perform (Fifth or Fourteenth Amendment's due process arguments). Such reciprocations have been particularly significant and numerous since the Civil War and Reconstruction. The Thirteenth and Fourteenth Amendments to the Constitution and their implementing legislation, especially the 1866 Civil Rights Act, created potentially vastly wide legal bridges across the federal system. However tragically deferred, these bridges from the 1860s provided transit for the 1954 *Brown v. Board* decision.

Like other Americans, law academics and practitioners take all sides in the ongoing debate about the wisdom and rectitude of *Brown*. Their passions were evident in the Senate's recent hearings on the nominations of Chief Justice William Rehnquist, Justices Antonin Scalia and Sandra O'Connor, and Judge Clarence Manion. Along with hundreds of other recent Reagan appointees to lower federal courts, these appointees are now settling into their tenured lifetime work. High on the agendas of the federal courts in this constitutional bicentennial period are litigations involving the validity of the so-called New Deal–Square Deal–Warren Court "rev-

3. See Attorney General Edwin Meese III on *Cooper v. Aaron*, in *New York Times* (October 23, 1986), 1; "High Court to Rule on . . . 1866 Civil-Rights Law . . . ," *Chronicle of Higher Education* (October 15, 1986), 24–25.

olutions."[3] These litigations will predictably test whether the 1787 Constitution can or should continue to evolve in a manner receptive to social change and the raised aspirations of long-disfavored racial, ethnic, religious, and gender groups. The prohibitions and duties the federal Bill of Rights imposes on the national government in areas of civil liberties and, as "incorporated" into the Fourteenth Amendment, on states and local communities as well,[4] are, many fear and others hope, up for grabs.

Now extreme legal positivists want to reverse changes in the relationships both of the races and of the nation and states that were triggered or accelerated by *Brown* and its progeny. This paper will suggest from a new body of constitutional-legal history scholarship that this reversal is inappropriate.

To definitions. Strict constructionism in constitutional discourse and legal positivism in legal culture share elements with the creationist versus evolutionist schism in pedagogy. The strict construction argument may be considered self-defining for this audience. But "legal positivism" is less well known. It has been clutched closely to the bosoms of the legal profession, obscured by the jargon of both technical law experts and legal philosophers and left largely unexplored by nonlawyer historians and allied researchers.

Translated from lawyerese into plainer English, legal positivism is definable as a means of identifying what legitimate law is. A recent law encyclopedia suggests that major architects of positivism, including John Austin and Hans Kelsen, "sought to identify law by total separation from [ethics and] moral justice." They and their disciples, taking cues from Jeremy Bentham, insist that law has "objective meaning drawn from the provisions themselves." Therefore positivists "concentrated on the formal analysis of the terms and concepts of the law in force." In their approach to law as the obligations of a society, positivists "seek to be entirely formal, and free from all taint of history, ethics, politics, sociology, idealism, and other external influences." In sum, to positivists laws and constitutions are "a hierarchy of normative relations."[5]

This air of austere amoralism and priestly oracularity attends much legal positivistic discourse. Persons of this mind, including

---

4. See Arthur Selwyn Miller, *Social Change and Fundamental Law: America's Evolving Constitution*, Contributions in American Studies, 41 (Westport, CT, 1979).
5. David M. Walker, ed., *The Oxford Companion to Law* (Oxford, 1980), 970.

some present Supreme Court justices, insist, in creationist terms, that only the formal texts of the 1787 Constitution and derivative statutes legitimately define public policies and private rights. They at least imply that they themselves, and perhaps only they, understand those texts, that the texts are unambiguous especially to judges and lawyers, and that no mere history-based arguments should intrude. Yet, paradoxically, by positivistic definitions history is perceived as a "blinding light" mirroring also from such external canonized sources as the *Federalist Papers* and Madison's *Notes*, but from little else. Only this thin list of sources is properly usable for policy purposes by legislators, jurists, and lawyers.

These users and abusers of history rarely, if ever, allow nonlawyers reciprocal competence in their trade. All of which so irked normally mild-mannered Princeton legal historian Stanley Katz as to provoke his recent comment to a journalist: "Lawyers are arrogant, and think they can do anything including write history. Well, they can't."[6]

For their parts, critics of positivistic positions have insisted that, as in *Brown*, the law must serve as a democratically responsive social force more than as a repository of negative technical legal doctrines. Failure to rank justice at the apex of concerns in a legal system erodes the quality of political democracy and federalism, these critics have argued. The Constitution has simply not been a fully revealed oracle, a phonograph, or a jukebox playing predictable tunes as requested by its high priests and sole legitimate interpreters, the lawyers.

Historians know that from John Marshall's time to our own, high judges and other law officers possessed of goal-oriented purposes defined and redefined the Constitution by arguments concerning the framers' intentions. As an example, Roger Taney found proof from the framers for his *Dred Scott* and *Merryman* excesses. In those opinions Taney invented histories about, respectively, blacks and habeas corpus. One of our greatest constitutionalists, Abraham Lincoln, during the Civil War's gloomiest period for the Union, advised his countrymen that positivist ideas doomed the nation. He

6. Stanley Katz in *New York Times* (May 3, 1986); and Paul Gerwitz in *New York Times* (July 8, 1986). See also John G. Wofford, "The Blinding Light: The Uses of History in Constitutional Interpretation," *University of Chicago Law Review* 31 (1964): 502–33. Wilcomb E. Washburn, "The Supreme Court's Use and Abuse of History," *Organization of American Historians Newsletter* (August 1983).

said that "the dogmas of the quiet past are inadequate to the stormy present." A year later, the Union's military fortunes having greatly improved and his decisions favoring the military emancipation of slaves as a war aim and the arming of black bluecoats made, Lincoln told the nation that it "must not lose sight of the fact that the war power [of the Constitution] is our main reliance."[7] That is, the evolved, dynamic, non–positivistically interpreted Constitution could cope with change, a position that Appomattox, the Thirteenth Amendment, the 1866 civil rights law, and the Fourteenth Amendment affirmed.

Fifty years after Appomattox, a loose coterie of then-youngish law practitioners and academics had become increasingly itchy about the formalistic positivism that had come to dominate the profession since the early 1870s in the wake of Christopher Columbus Langdell's paper-chasing case method at Harvard Law School and the Supreme Court's *Slaughterhouse* decision. Calling themselves "legal realists," these dissidents in the law echoed the substance of Lincoln's evolutionary, adapting, adequacy constitutionalism. In the words of one legal realist, positivism was "transcendental nonsense." All law was politics, realists asserted. Law must allow for human idiosyncracies, recognize the reality of racial, ethnic, religious, and gender prejudices, and reflect the fallibility even of legislators, lawyers, and judges.

Clemson University historian John Johnson concluded that John Marshall and Joseph Story in the nation's early decades and Oliver Wendell Holmes, Louis Brandeis, Karl Llewellyn, James Frank, and William Douglas in the late nineteenth and twentieth centuries "were instrumental in prompting American legal culture to accommodate itself to externalities – to interest groups, to legal reformers, to the insights provided by extra-legal disciplines: in short, to what Holmes once called the 'felt necessities of the time.'"[8]

But the realist surge peaked and, as noted, renascent legal positivists in the highest echelons of the Reagan administration,

---

7. James Daniel Richardson, ed., *A Compilation of the Messages and Papers of the Presidents, 1789–1897*, 10 vols. (Washington, DC, 1896–99), 6: 142, 191.

8. John Johnson, "Creativity and Adaptation: A Reassessment of American Jurisprudence, 1801–1857 and 1908–1940," *Rutgers-Camden Law Journal* 7 (1976): 647. See also Laura Kalman, *Legal Realism at Yale, 1927–1960* (Chapel Hill, NC, 1986), passim.

including the Supreme Court and major funding agencies, have grown large in number, loud in voice, and influential in policy decisions. Perhaps it was the tone of this revival as well as its immediate and potential retrograde effects that provoked Justice William Brennan, Jr.'s spectacular outburst of 1985, in which he criticized positivist views as "little more than arrogance cloaked as humility."[9]

Strong language from a sitting justice. It evoked counterblasts from Brennan's probable primary target, U.S. Attorney General Edwin Meese III. The latter had publicly and repetitively extolled the need to restrict public policies and constitutional interpretations to the specific intentions of the Constitution's framers, as "the only reliable guide" for interpretation.

Former justice Arthur Goldberg, taking sides with Brennan, noted that the real roots of discord were less in 1787 than in 1868, in that now eight-decades-old question of whether the Fourteenth Amendment to the U.S. Constitution properly incorporated the Bill of Rights against the states.[10] Scholars are sharply adversary about incorporation. Little wonder. Now, as in 1868 when state voters ratified the Fourteenth Amendment, incorporation touches America's most vital, urgent, and tender relationships and policies, including racial equality, nation-state federalism, and an uncertain galaxy of individual civil rights and liberties. Every undergraduate constitutional history textbook and freshman constitutional law casebook surveys that declension of U.S. Supreme Court decisions on the Fourteenth Amendment, from *Slaughterhouse* in 1873 to the 1883 civil rights cases and *Plessy v. Ferguson* (1896). These and other decisions set parameters for the amendment which, by the 1930s, had made it almost irrelevant as a libertarian protection.

Then in his 1937 *Palko v. Connecticut* opinion, Justice Cardozo, though rejecting counsel's argument that the Fourteenth Amendment incorporated all of the Bill of Rights, held that the most fundamental federal rights did apply against the states by a "process of absorption." Eleven years later Justice Black, after reviewing the history of the Fourteenth Amendment's framing and ratification, read into *Adamson v. California* (1948) his conviction that total

9. William Brennan, Jr., in *New York Times* (October 13, 1985).
10. Goldberg in *Houston Post* (Feb. 21, 1986); and see Meese in *New York Times* (see n. 3), 1. In *New York Times* (April 16, 1986), Y18, Brennan insisted that he had not been responding to Meese specifically.

incorporation of the first eight amendments of the Bill of Rights was intended in 1866–68. Going further, Justices Douglas, Murphy, and Rutledge extended due process limitations to any fundamental right, whether or not it was included in the Bill of Rights.

These extended views triggered great debates among legal writers and practitioners, academic constitutionalists, and elective politicos. The debates reached new heights with the 1954 school desegregation decision, *Brown v. Board of Education*, and its progeny.

Both pro-incorporation and anti-incorporation have a rich literature to employ.[11] Where does this large and, fearfully, still enlarging incorporation literature leave us? Without much comfort, if we look back only a few years to Vietnam, or yesterday to Lebanon, or today in Nicaragua and "Irangate," and ask: what are the Constitution's precise limits on the president's martial powers in undeclared wars? Few respondents concerning Vietnam, for example, failed confidently to evoke the framers' intentions, though often to support opposing conclusions. I know no one among the prides of

11. Horace Edgar Flack's *The Adoption of the Fourteenth Amendment*, John Hopkins University Studies in Historical and Political Science, 26 (Baltimore, MD, 1908, repr. Gloucester, MA, 1965); Jacobus ten Broek's *The Antislavery Sources of Antislavery Constitutionalism in America* (Berkeley, CA, 1951); Howard Jay Graham's *Everyman's Constitution: Historical Essays on the Fourteenth Amendment, the "Conspiracy Theory," and American Constitutionalism* (Madison, WI, 1968); Harold Melvin Hyman and William Michael Wiecek's *Equal Justice under Law: Constitutional Development, 1835–75* (New York, 1982); Judith A. Baer's *Equality under the Constitution: Reclaiming the Fourteenth Amendment* (Ithaca, NY, 1983); Robert Kaczorowski's *The Politics of Judicial Interpretation: The Federal Courts, Department of Justice, and Civil Rights, 1866–76* (New York, 1985); and the New York University School of Law series in Legal History offer pro-incorporation analyses. Anti-incorporation supporters use powerful and durable articles by, respectively, Alexander M. Bickel, "The Original Understanding and the Segregation Decision," *Harvard Law Review* 69 (1955): 1–65; and Charles Fairman, "Does the Fourteenth Amendment Incorporate the Bill of Rights? Original Understanding," *Stanford Law Review* 2 (1949): 5–139 (included, with much else, in Charles Fairman and Stanley Morrison, *The Fourteenth Amendment and the Bill of Rights: The Incorporation Theory*, Intr. by Leonard William Levy [New York, 1970]). They concluded that the amendment's creators and ratifiers did not intend to apply the Bill of Rights to the states or to desegregate schools. This narrow interpretation received impressive emphasis in Raoul Berger's *Government by Judiciary: The Transformation of the Fourteenth Amendment* (Cambridge, MA, 1977); and in Bernard Siegan's *The Supreme Court's Constitution* (New Brunswick, NJ, 1987). Not yet in print at this writing, two large-scale reevaluations of the incorporation question by Earl Maltz (tentatively entitled *The Politics of Section One of the Fourteenth Amendment*) and William Nelson (tentatively entitled *The Adoption and Early Interpretation of the Fourteenth Amendment*), while searching out moderate supportable positions and responding to the imperatives of the new legal history, lean toward the relatively narrow interpretive positions.

scholars who testified to Congress or wrote on the war powers who exceeded Henry Monaghan's wisdom: "We do not know and can not know, what, specifically, . . . [the framers] would have thought about a world so different from their own. . . . The central fact is that the framers left us a structure of government sufficiently fluid to accommodate a good deal of shifting between the Congress and the President."[12]

Do useful middle grounds exist between polar views, however footnoted? Praising the 1787 framers as practical politicians rather than "ideologues, theoreticians, [or] theologians," Paul Bator noted recently that "Time and time again in the history of our Constitution we have developed needs that seem to have been unperceived or only dimly perceived by the Framers; yet we have succeeded, in an improvisational and somewhat untidy way, to adapt their document to these needs, while at the same time adapting our own expediences to their fundamental ideas and aspirations."[13] Referring now to the Brennan-Meese exchange, Bator's fellow University of Chicago Law School colleague Philip B. Kurland asserted similarly that neither the justice nor the attorney general knew a formula "for resolving the ambiguities inherent in the cases that are to be governed by the periphery of the Constitution. . . . Certainly the answers are not to be found in any formula, such as [Franklin] Roosevelt's 'back to the Constitution' or Nixon's 'strict construction,' or Meese's 'original intent,' or Brennan's 'will of the people.'" Continuing, Kurland advised judges among his audiences that if they "are to be true to the spirit of 1787, they will recognize that ideally judicial controversies ought to be resolved by articulatable reasons, of which history may be one."[14]

"Of which history may be one." Splendid! But then the question arises, what history? The vast interpretive literature on the inten-

---

12. Henry P. Monaghan, "Presidential War-Making," *Boston University Law Review* 50 (1970): passim; Harold Melvin Hyman, *Quiet Past and Stormy Present? War Powers in American History: Bicentennial Essays on the Constitution* (Washington, DC, 1986), passim.

13. This "saving sense of the practical" gave Bator hope that "as a society, . . . we do not swallow wholehog the love affair the professors are having with theory and methodology. The American style of common sense has been a saving solvent of our constitutional development. I hope we do not abandon it." Paul Bator, "The Constitution and the Art of Practical Government," *University of Chicago Law School Record* 32 (1986): 8–12, passim.

14. Philip B. Kurland in *University of Chicago Law School Record* 32 (1986): 3–5.

tions of the framers of both 1787 and 1866, and on the incorporation of the Bill of Rights as duties and restraints on the states through the Fourteenth Amendment, has brought us to the present condition of the positivists' excessive definiteness as opposed to those who insist on its boundless elasticity. A relatively new kid on history's block, one known as constitutional-legal history or, in shorthand, as legal history, may help us better to recognize ourselves. The conceptual coupling of legal and constitutional historians has generated an impressive outpouring of books, articles, and papers. It is an energetic newcomer, having already inspired the creation of two specialist associations and a like number of periodicals and justified the publication in 1985 of a major analytical book that surveys this burgeoning, eclectic field. Both coauthors of this survey are historian-lawyers. They concluded that "today it would be presumptuous to attempt to define the boundaries of the discipline of legal history or to specify the sorts of scholarship upon which practitioners in the field should work."[15]

In markedly interdisciplinary manner, legal history traverses eclectic orbits and exploits the accumulated scholarship of diverse law and nonlaw areas. The latter includes history and law, plus anthropology, economics, linguistics, philosophy, and political science. Further to illustrate the new legal history's eclecticism, as recently as the early 1970s many "straight" constitutional historians still concentrated on textual analyses and high judges' glosses of government's fundamental charters. Therefore in 1975 a compiler of a conceptually traditional bibliography of the specialization required only 100 smallish pages to list approximately 1,000 titles. But in 1984 a bibliography of the new constitutional-legal history required not one thin volume but five fat ones, totalling 3,400 pages and listing 68,000 titles.[16]

In sum, as a teaching field in non–law schools as well as in law schools and as a markedly diverse and eclectic research area, American legal history "is booming," to quote Stanford Law's Lawrence Friedman. Many of the best law schools now offer legal history

15. William Edward Nelson and John Phillip Reid, *The Literature of American Legal History*, New York University School of Law Series in Legal History, 1 (New York, 1985).

16. Cf. Stephen M. Millett, *A Selected Bibliography of American Constitutional History* (Santa Barbara, CA, 1975); Kermit L. Hall, *A Comprehensive Bibliography of American Constitutional and Legal History, 1869–1979* (Millword, NY, 1984).

courses, and in several instances nonlawyer historians teach them.[17] Legal history flourishes in part because traditional legal education, research, and practice had become a "flawed system," in the opinion of Harvard's sitting president and former law dean, Derek Bok.[18]

But legal history's very eclecticism concerning allowable sources displeases many law-focused professionals, including positivists of course. The latter, it will be recalled, suggest that useful research can derive only from the formal texts of constitutions and laws, from the official records of the legislative process, from high court case decisional law, and from rare and canonized extra-official commentaries such as the *Federalist Papers*. "There is absolutely no point in setting up a separate category of legal writing (or . . . teaching) to be known as 'legal history,'" groused the late, eminent Yale law academic, Grant Gilmore. Yet, though Gilmore acknowledged that a "fascinating story" exists in "the development of our legal institutions," he insisted nevertheless that this subject was "irrelevant to our discussion."[19]

To many legal historians this seemingly homely, workaday topic, the history of legal institutions, is of central importance. As examples, legal historians are now inquiring into the history of the standards of solo and corporate law practice, the "inside" stories of nineteenth-century law schools and bar associations, the changing views of writers of early law casebooks and textbooks and of law publishers, and the purposes of fee-paying litigants in courts of first resort as well as in highest appeal tribunals. Legal biography is enjoying a renascence. It offers intimate insights into the lives of real people in actual circumstances far removed from that famous 1787 Philadelphia meeting hall or the Supreme Court's rococo chambers. Much of this context-respecting new research helps to illuminate the intentions of the framers and ratifiers of the Fourteenth Amendment concerning many centrally important matters, especially that of incorporation of the Bill of Rights against the states.

17. Lawrence M. Friedman, "American Legal History: Past and Present," *Journal of Legal Education* 34 (1984): 563–76; Paul Finkelman, "Exploring Southern Legal History," *North Carolina Law Review* 64 (1985): 77–116.

18. Derek C. Bok, "A Flawed System of Law Practice and Training," *Journal of Legal Education* 33 (1983): 570–85.

19. Grant Gilmore, *The Ages of American Law*, Yale Law School, Storrs Lectures on Jurisprudence 1974 (New Haven, CT, 1977), 8, 146, and see 102–4.

I have argued elsewhere[20] that the recurring, passionate focus on the Fourteenth Amendment's incorporation of the Bill of Rights against the states has ignored a vital dimension, that of the Thirteenth Amendment, whose brief, unambiguous terms embrace nation, states, territories, and private persons. It is a universal prohibition against both formal slavery and all its "persisting incidents" or equivalents of "involuntary servitude." In the views of many central actors of 1865 involved in creating the Thirteenth Amendment, *it* incorporated the Bill of Rights, not only against the nation-states as entities but also against or for all individuals as well. The Thirteenth imposes duties to equal justice as well as a denial of a property right to own humans. The men who wrote and ratified the Thirteenth Amendment did not know that a Fourteenth was to come. The Fourteenth did not repeal the Thirteenth. In short, the Thirteenth deserves reevaluation on its own terms not, as in the 1873 *Slaughterhouse* decision in the Supreme Court, as a mixed pair created virtually simultaneously with the Fourteenth, but rather as one of a pair in which the Thirteenth was a finished job. The Thirteenth was not of lesser importance than the Fourteenth because its initial mighty purpose, the delegalization of state-defined property rights in people, was achieved and confirmed in 1865 at Appomattox.

This perception developed in part from ongoing research into the lives of three strikingly different "yuppie" lawyers who were to make the Thirteenth Amendment possible and were among its most important early implementers as well as architects. The three were two Ohioans, Salmon Portland Chase and Edwin McMasters Stanton (who moved to Pennsylvania), and the Illinoisan Abraham Lincoln.

All were born between 1808 and 1814. The trio shared upbringings in intensely racist Ohio River Valley states embraced by the antislavery provisions of the Northwest Ordinance. Concerning social origins, initial class expectations, and legal training, the three midwesterners differed from one another as sharply as white Jacksonian America allowed. Chase's genealogy, Dartmouth education, and formal law preparation gave him elite status. Stanton attended Kenyon College but did not graduate, and his professional training was less lofty and systematic than Chase's, placing him in

20. Hyman and Wiecek, *Equal Justice under Law* (see n. 11), chap. 11.

some middling rank. And Lincoln's mudsill origins and haphazard education started him on lowly rungs. But all became consummately successful law practitioners who welcomed all manner of civil and criminal cases and other commonplace legal business.

Of the three, Chase alone was a pioneer antislavery activist, a hazardous role for an aspiring jack-of-all-cases novice lawyer in southward-looking Cincinnati. Until secession and Civil War, Stanton kept his feelings on these tender matters largely to himself. Lincoln, as Republican presidential candidate in 1860, accommodated the party's plank that, despite *Dred Scott*, stipulated against the further extension of slavery in the federal territories, those states in the process of becoming.

No pushover for anyone, a demythicized Lincoln was a very tough lawyer and politician. He brought both Chase and Stanton into the two most vital wartime cabinet offices, Chase as secretary of the treasury and Stanton as secretary of war, and in 1864 named Chase to succeed the tardily defunct Roger Taney as chief justice. Grant was to name Stanton to the Supreme Court in 1869, but the latter died before taking his seat. *Slaughterhouse* might have had a differing outcome had Stanton lived to join in Chase's minority arguments. For by 1862–63 both secretaries and their president were becoming committed to prewar evolutionary, antipositivist "freedom national" ideas of the most advanced abolitionists. The three men – Lincoln, Chase, and Stanton – educated each other, in short.

If variously expressed, freedom national ideas, especially as Chase developed them, centered on redefining the nation's and the states' duty to all individual Americans. No centralizers, the espousers of freedom national ideas stressed the familiar Madisonian theme of dual citizenship, but in an evolved form. As citizens of both nation and state of residence in this federal system, Americans should, at a minimum, enjoy federal definition of bedrock protections, equality before their state's civil and criminal laws. Abolitionist lawyers argued that this concept pervaded the Declaration of Independence, the Bill of Rights, and the Northwest Ordinance and allowed emancipation *and* equality. Intrastate equality would alter treasured federalism as little as possible, while improving political democracy and stabilizing economic capitalism.[21]

21. Louis Gerteis's *Morality and Utility in American Antislavery Reform* (Chapel

Similar perceptions and conclusions became multiplied among a majority of Congressmen and voters including, through 1865, masses of voters in uniform. The latter included black bluecoats. By 1865, when the Thirteenth Amendment was created, Lincoln and much of white America had evidenced spectacular educability about race and constitutionalism during the war years. He had dared, first, military emancipation of disloyalists' slaves by commander-in-chief war power orders, then the recruitment of negroes into Union Army ranks, and finally, the political reconstructions of whole crumpling Confederate states as slaveless states in the reunifying union.

The Thirteenth Amendment aimed to insure that freedom was indeed national in the union, not only in 1865 but thereafter. The Thirteenth equalized all Americans' access to land, public education, and legal remedies by placing them on the same legal footing with respect to the benefits of the wartime Morrill, homestead, and habeas corpus-jurisdiction laws. That amendment embraced not only the South and border states, but also the unseceded, racist "black code" Northwest Ordinance states like Illinois and Ohio, the homes of Lincoln, Chase, and Stanton. Federal law had always forbidden slavery there. Now federal supreme law would also strike at inequality, there and nationwide. Precisely because the Thirteenth Amendment so clearly was a commitment to color-blind equality within all states, thus creating what John Wilkes Booth called "nigger citizenship," he decided to kill Lincoln and other high officials.[22]

As we know, Andrew Johnson reversed the unfamiliar, complex, fragile equalitarian tide, placing Booth and Johnson, respectively, among the ranks of history's most successful assassins and racially reactionary heads of state. Post-Appomattox Reconstruction became an account of white America's declining concerns about race equality, an equality that Republicans had hoped to plant

Hill, NC, 1987) explores these matters. See also Robert D. Sawrey, "Ohioans and the Fourteenth Amendment: Initial Perceptions and Expectations," *The Old Northwest* 10 (1984/85): 389–407.

22. William Hanchett, *The Lincoln Murder Conspiracies: Being an Account of the Hatred Felt by Many Americans for President Abraham Lincoln during the Civil War* (Urbana, IL, 1983): Harold Melvin Hyman, *American Singularity: The 1787 Northwest Ordinance, the 1862 Homestead-Morrill Acts, and the 1944 GI Bill*, The Richard B. Russel Lecturers, 5 (Athens, GA, 1986).

permanently in public policy in a second Lincoln term that was supposed to last until March 4, 1869, not Good Friday, 1865. Chase, now an aging chief justice, feared correctly that though brave "freedom national" goals had ennobled the Civil War effort, they were less able to shape the peace. For by 1873, as in *Slaughterhouse*, Chase found himself one of a minority of justices as the Court majority enshrined into constitutional law an ominously narrowing sense of the outreach of both the Thirteenth and Fourteenth Amendments. Chase died later that year, sadly aware that basic changes adverse to his "freedom national" vision were occurring in American society and law.

The changes were gradual. In the late 1860s and through the early 1880s questions kept arising about persisting "involuntary servitudes." No neat catalog had been thought necessary in 1865, precisely because the Thirteenth Amendment accommodated interstate diversity in laws and customs while encouraging intrastate equality. Then, in 1883, almost three decades after the "year of jubilee," the Supreme Court decided the Civil Rights Cases. They began in lawsuits initiated by activist northern blacks to gain equal access to public facilities including licensed entertainments. But the Court insisted tragically and, I believe incorrectly, that the amendment's postemancipation task was finished, that if remnant "badges of slavery," including racial discriminations in workplaces and leisure facilities, still infested America, these private bigotries were not after all comprehended by the framers of the postwar amendments.

In a biting dissent, Justice John Marshall Harlan noted that race segregation relegated blacks to inferior public conveniences, education, jobs, housing, credit, and aspirations and that private discriminations could not exist without the states' participation. The discriminations included federal and state laws and myriads of community customs that made skin pigment a visible proof of inferiority and a justification for lesser access to local equality in both marketplace and justice terms. In contrast to his robed brethren, Harlan proved to be a far more realistic reporter and prophet of a Supreme Court that was already well on the road to *Plessy*.

In part these changes both shaped and were configured by developments in legal education and practice from 1870 to 1900. Recall that Chase, Lincoln, and Stanton were either self-taught or products of mixed collegiate-apprenticeship preparations. For decades prominent lawyers and jurists had criticized such uncoordinated and variable kinds of legal educations. With some justice they argued that in order to improve the profession the education and admission requirements for practice had to be both standardized and raised. Some self-styled law reformers also unjustifiably insisted that "undesirables," by which they meant Catholics, Jews, blacks, and women, must be kept excluded from practice and, if possible, from legal education. Some law spokesmen feared the democratizing effects of the Jackson-Lincoln decades. They were anxious to limit the tendencies of state legislators to interfere in marketplace transactions, including the regulation of lawyers by licensing.

Such elements had already mixed together in the Supreme Court's 1867 *Test Oath* and 1873 *Slaughterhouse* decisions. The latter's origins are in rights that very inventive lawyers claimed under both the Thirteenth and Fourteenth Amendments not for black clients, but for white butchers of New Orleans who had missed out on a lucrative licensed monopoly created in a state law aimed at safeguarding public health.[23] Chase had feared correctly that the majestic universals of the Thirteenth Amendment would become trivialized by the Fourteenth Amendment's state-action focus on such questions as the limits of federal authority to determine access to state-licensed butchering. His fears became despair when the *Slaughterhouse* majority of justices limited defendable federal rights to such irrelevancies to the interests of the great majority of Americans, especially blacks, as travel abroad and fishing in interstate waters.

Trivialized and made inconsistent as well. In the 1870s and 1880s the Court found it inoffensive when states, despite both amendments, denied highly qualified white women access to jury duty and to legal and medical practices and barred black men and women from access to state ballots, to fair criminal trials, to equal protection against murderers and lynchers and other supposedly available shields of state laws and due processes.

Behind *Slaughterhouse* and its fateful offspring, deep currents of change in legal practice and training were swirling. When Chase died in 1873 a new tribe of law academics and practitioners was

---

23. Harold Melvin Hyman, *A More Perfect Union: The Impact of the Civil War and Reconstruction on the Constitution* (New York, 1973), chaps. 18–28.

already growing in influence and in succeeding decades would swell in number. This new breed viewed individuals' rights and remedies differently from his, Lincoln's, and Stanton's perspectives.

The shift in perspectives is visible in the novel kinds of law schools that, beginning in the early 1870s, were coming into existence and incorporated into their curricula not freedom national ideas but those from *Slaughterhouse* and the Civil Rights decisions. These law schools, having increasingly modeled themselves on the "socially scientific" lines that Christopher Columbus Langdell initiated at Harvard, affiliated with universities. Gradually they raised admission requirements from possession of a high school diploma to possession of a college degree. Over decades the new law schools developed their own full-time faculties, libraries with peculiar finding aids, specially trained librarians, casebooks supplied by specialized publishers, and budgets that in practice often were independent of other budgets on a campus. In these new law schools, students no longer apprenticed haphazardly to practitioners and no longer dealt with real people in life situations. Instead paper-chasing law students searched for controlling legal doctrines and constitutional principles in high court cases including *Slaughterhouse*. That case overwhelmingly headed the tables of contents of widely used standardized textbooks and textbooklike commentaries such as Thomas McIntyre Cooley's *A Treatise on the Constitutional Limitations Which Rest upon the Legislative Power of the States of the American Union*. Published first in 1868 and destined after dozens of revised editions to serve as a law school textbook well into the 1930s, Cooley praised the *Slaughterhouse* decision.[24]

In high court jurists such tendencies generated certain common and commonly inflexible reactions to popular aspirations for reform through government action and to individuals' petitions for justice defined as equality. These hardened reactions exhibited themselves repetitively in the 1895–1937 decades in highly formalistic and often positivistic decisions of imprudent jurisprudents, ranging from *Plessy* (separate-but-allegedly-equal Jim Crow public transportation facilities) to famous litigations of the Progressive and New Deal periods that invalidated major reform efforts.

Yet, despite the long triumph of negativistic interpretations of

24. Robert Stevens, *The Law Schools* (Chapel Hill, NC, 1985), passim.

the Fourteenth Amendment, combined with almost total disregard of the Thirteenth Amendment, more generous reform interpretations did not die with Lincoln, Stanton, and Chase. Instead, the once-sharp focus of antislavery Civil War reformers diffused into many concerns, almost all of which were insensitive to racial equality. These included abused animals and children, polygamy, corporations, and votes for women. In politics the Grangers of the 1870s, the Alliance and Populist associators of the 1880s–1890s, and the Progressive and New Deal activists of the 1900s–1930s perpetuated aspects of the Lincoln-Chase-Stanton emphases and hopes of the 1860s.

Paralleling these political movements were the currents in the American legal universe noted earlier. Under such labels as "legal realism" or under no labels, these currents were carried from the Reconstruction years to our time by those who sympathized with the morally sensitive, evolutionary imperatives for law and constitutionalism of the sorts that Lincoln, Chase, and Stanton had espoused earlier. In 1954 these joined in the Supreme Court's unanimous *Brown v. Board of Education* decision. It rejected race segregation in education because segregation made impossible equality in the quality of learning. Despite the ongoing efforts of misreaders of American history to reverse the *Brown* current, it continues, at least to the present, to answer a question posed by the beat poet Jack Kerouac: "Whither goes thou America, in thy shiny new car?"

Perhaps present critics of *Brown* should review the contributions of the two Ohio lawyers, Chase and Stanton, and the Illinois lawyer, Lincoln, to basic elements of the Thirteenth as well as the Fourteenth Amendments. Such a review justifies *Brown* as sound constitutional doctrine because in 1954 it built better on history than had a century of historical constitutional law concerning the 1876 *Slaughterhouse* decision. On this point, the careful, history-sensitive 1984 estimate of Robert Palmer deserves attention:

> Legal analysis grafts new conclusions onto existing lines of construction, often inappropriately. . . . [T]he crucial question for practicing lawyers was not what *Slaughter-House* actually said but which construction *Slaughter-House* was actually following. That pragmatic feature of legal analysis leads away from constitutional meaning. Court-established tests assume a decided superiority to constitutional language. . . . *Slaughter-*

House had done that. The . . . case, misunderstood and unexamined, shielded subsequent cases from the force of the fourteenth amendment's language. . . . Of course, incorporation of the enumerated rights via the privileges or immunities clause was not the historical original intent. The historical intent encompassed numerous different understandings. However, the appropriate point is that incorporating enumerated rights through the privileges or immunities clause is the only construction that responds both to the varied motivations behind the amendment and to the constitutional language. . . . Whatever approach the [present Supreme] Court takes, however, the Court cannot use *Slaughter-House* to justify the nullification of the privileges or immunities clause [of the 14th Amendment).[25]

In 1971, Charles Fairman's useful massive survey of Reconstruction constitutionalism surveyed the "perplexing and touchy" problems the national government faced in the 1860s to secure the rights of free Americans "in the face of hostile forces entrenched behind local law and custom." "What Congress did [in the 1860s] in the prosecution of its efforts to restore the Union on the basis of the Fourteenth Amendment is entitled to a far more discriminating consideration than it has generally received."[26]

Agreed. The new legal history is reviewing these matters and reestimating what the Lincoln, Chase, and Stanton generation among antislavery lawyers intended and did in shaping and implementing the Reconstruction amendments. The evidence suggests that they wished to shape and direct it further, toward greater liberty and equality as measured by racial equality and enlarged access to land, education, and justice. These were the widest-known avenues to a more perfect union. In our time these avenues helped to lead to *Brown*. Will they, in our Constitution's bicentennial season, take us beyond *Brown*, to shores still only dimly seen, to new frontiers of more truly equal racial and gender justice and of liberty in law? Or will renascent positivism reverse the fragile drift?

---

25. Robert Palmer, "The Parameters of Constitutional Reconstruction: Slaughter-House (*Slaughter-House* Cases, 83 U.S. 36), Cruikshank (United States v. Cruikshank, 92 U.S. 542), and the Fourteenth Amendment," *University of Illinois Law Review* (1984): 739, 769–70.

26. Charles Fairman, *Reconstruction and Reunion, 1864–88*, History of the Supreme Court of the United States, 6 (New York, 1971), 342–43; Harold Melvin Hyman, *Lincoln's Reconstruction: Neither Failure of Vision nor Vision of Failure* (Fort Wayne, IN, 1980), 25 and passim.

8
Civil Rights and German Constitutional Thought, 1848–1871

Jörg-Detlef Kühne

Principles

1848: A Turning Point

Because of the many ways in which civil rights issues arose in the period of this report, they can only be treated briefly.[1] "Civil rights" includes the rights of the individual and also those of associations and groups. In order for these rights to become part of the constitutional system they must first be given an explicit legal definition and their durability must be insured by constitutional amendment procedures which make them difficult to change. Starting from this basic definition of civil rights, two points can initially be made:

1. During the period covered by this report, civil rights were much discussed at the level of the German nation, within the German *Bund*, and also at the level of the individual German states and principalities.
2. There were resulting conflicts between the protection of civil rights and the structural parts of the Constitutions, since each of these was dependent on the other.

1. I am very grateful to Professor Fred L. Morrison, University of Minnesota, for his congenial translation. For the general history of the period see Thomas Nipperdey, *Deutsche Geschichte, 1800–1866* (Munich, 1983), 595ff., with more detailed literature cited on 807ff., and Theodore S. Hamerow, *Restauration, Revolution, Reaction: Economics and Politics in Germany, 1815–1871* (Princeton, NJ, 1958); for constitutional history, Ernst Rudolf Huber, *Deutsche Verfassungsgeschichte seit 1789*, 3 vols. (Stuttgart, ²1975–78), and John A. Hawgood, *Modern Constitutions since 1787* (London, 1939). Texts of the Constitutions, if not otherwise noted, are from Ernst Rudolf Huber, ed., *Dokumente zur deutschen Verfassungsgeschichte*, 2 vols. (Stuttgart, ³1978–86); and for Austria, Heinz Fischer and Gerhard Silvestri, eds., *Texte zur österreichischen Verfassungsgeschichte* (Vienna, 1970).

At the time of this report, the notion of "constitutionalism," as it is now understood, was not fully accepted in Germany. That notion, long accepted in the United States, is perhaps best defined as follows: two fundamental ideas are commonly implied in the term constitution – one refers to the regulation of the form of government, and the other to the securing of the liberties of the people.[2]

The Constitutions of the German *Bund*[3] and of the German Empire contained no more than rudimentary lists of civil rights. One must remember, however, that between 1850 and 1866 the Constitution of the German *Bund* was much like the organic instrument of an international organization. Such organizations, even today, do not normally have bills of rights. Rather, that Constitution contained a list of rules for relationships between relatively independent states.

The year 1848 is significant because it presented Germany with the opportunity to move to a constitutional understanding much more like what prevails today. It was a year of revolution in Germany. The Frankfurt Assembly was established and began work on its proposed Constitution in the Paulskirche. The civil rights concepts in that Constitution were so carefully elaborated that they continued to have significant effect long after the Revolution had failed and the Constitution itself had no hope of enactment.[4] The liberal and democratic movements which prepared that document established a standard that provided a basis for later German constitutional history. It was a standard which, even in comparison with other Western constitutions, served as a distinctive step forward for the German liberal tradition.

---

2. Henry C. Black, *Handbook of American Constitutional Law* (St. Paul, MN, [4]1927), 2.

3. For the German Confederation see Huber, *Deutsche Verfassungsgeschichte* (see n. 1), 1: 475ff.; Hawgood, *Modern Constitutions* (see n. 1), 111ff.; Enno E. Kraehe, *History of the German Confederation, 1850–1866* (Minneapolis, MN, 1948).

4. For the Paulskirche Assembly cf. Veit Valentin, *Geschichte der deutschen Revolution von 1848/49*, 2 vols. (1930/31, repr. Cologne, 1970) or a condensed English translation, *1848: Chapters of German History* (London, 1940); Günter Wollstein, *Deutsche Geschichte 1848/49* (Stuttgart, 1986); Frank Eyck, *Deutschlands große Hoffnung: Die Frankfurter Nationalversammlung, 1848–49* (Munich, 1973), first published in English as *The Frankfurt Parliament, 1848–1849* (London, 1968); for the Frankfurt Constitution, Manfred Botzenhart, *Deutscher Parlamentarismus, 1848–1850* (Düsseldorf, 1977), 651ff.; Jörg-Detlef Kühne, *Die Reichsverfassung der Paulskirche* (Frankfurt/Main, 1985); the best English equivalent is Hawgood, *Modern Constitu-*

The standard established at Frankfurt can be used to measure the degree of freedom protected by other German constitutional systems, both before and after it. Since a complete list of the civil rights provided by Frankfurt has not been published in English, an official translation of the so-called Plan of the Committee of Seventeen[5] will be outlined here. It was a plan prepared by a committee some weeks before the Frankfurt Assembly. It became the model for the work of the assembly, although the final Constitution[6] was much more detailed in its elaboration of individual rights. The Plan of the Committee of Seventeen was as follows:

Article 4
Fundamental Rights of the German People
§25: The empire guarantees to the German people the following fundamental laws, which are also to serve as the basis of the constitution of each German state.

a. A popular representative body with a deliberative voice for legislation and imposts and with responsibility of ministers to the representatives of the people.

b. Publicity of sessions of the Diets.

c. A free municipal constitutional government based upon an indepen-

---

tions (see n. 1), 197ff.; summarizing Eyck, *Deutschlands große Hoffnung: Die Frankfurter Nationalversammlung, 1848–49* (see n. 4), 206ff., 377ff.; James J. Sheehan, *German Liberalism in the Nineteenth Century* (Chicago, IL, 1978), 65ff.

5. English text in "Project of the Fundamental Law of the Empire of Germany" (from April 26, 1848), National Archives, Washington, DC: Diplomatic dispatch no. 80 from U.S. minister A.J. Donelson to the secretary of state, May 5, 1848. On the Seventeen's Committee and its preparing role between the pre-Parliament and the Frankfurt Parliament cf. Rudolf Hübner, "Der Verfassungsentwurf der 17 Vertrauensmänner: Ein Beitrag zur Vorgeschichte des Frankfurter Verfassungswerkes," in *Festschrift Eduard Rosenthal* (Jena, 1923), 109–68; Paul Vinogradoff, ed., *Essays in Legal History* (Oxford, 1913), 384–96; and Hawgood, *Modern Constitutions* (see n. 1), 206ff.

6. A complete English translation of the Frankfurt Constitution from March 28, 1848, is unavailable up to the present time. Investigations in archives and libraries in Washington and London have so far had no results. The English minister in Frankfurt, Lord Cowley, sent his government a partial French translation of the *Grundrechte* (cf. Lord Cowley's despatch no. 9 of 13. January 1859–FO 30/122, P.R.O., London), which later was published in Georg Friedrich Martens, *Nouveau recueil géneral des traités*, 2d series, 35 vols. (Göttingen, 1876–1910), 13: 348–54. For a partial English translation, especially of the *Grundrechte*, cf. Louis L. Snyder, ed., *Documents of German History* (repr. Westport, CT, 1976), 180ff.; and Frank Eyck, *The Revolutions of 1848–49* (Edinburgh, 1972), 149–56. A partial English translation of the Constitution for an edition of historical constitutions is being prepared by Albert P. Blaustein.

dent administration in communal affairs.

d. Independence of tribunals, the *inamovibilité* of the judges unless in virtue of a sentence, orality and publicity of debates in judicial matters with a jury for criminal causes and for all political misdemeanors, the execution throughout the whole German Empire of sentences rendered by German tribunals.

e. Equality of all classes in matters concerning offices of state, of the communes, and capacity to fill the functions.

f. Establishment of a national guard.

g. The right to hold meetings, under reserve of a law against abuses.

h. Unlimited right of petition for private individuals, as well as for corporations.

i. Right of accusation against any functionary before the Diet of the country, after having in vain addressed the established authorities, and before one of the two chambers of the Diet in case of violation of the laws of the empire, with demand for their intervention for the redress of wrongs [j. is missing in the original].

k. Liberty of the press, freedom from all censorship, privileges and guarantees; misdemeanors of the press to be decided only by juries.

l. Inviolability of letters and the fixing by law of the necesssary restrictions in criminal cases and in case of war.

m. Security of the person against arbitrary arrest and search of private houses by an act of habeas corpus.

n. The right of every citizen of the empire of Germany to fix his own domicile in any state and in each place, to acquire real estate, and to exercise his profession under the same conditions as the natives of the country.

o. Right of emigration.

p. Right to choose a profession and to study in German as well as in foreign countries.

q. The establishment of academic freedom.

r. Religious liberty and that of public and private worship; equality of all confessions in civil and political rights.

s. Liberty to advance the development of the people as well as that of the races non-Germanic, granting to their languages the same rights in matters concerning educational and interior administration.

Western commentators[7] later recognized that Germany would have succeeded in becoming one of the most advanced states in

7. The Swiss scholar Hans Fehr, *Deutsche Rechtsgeschichte* (Berlin, [6]1962), 287; also Hawgood, *Modern Constitutions* (see n. 1), 198, remarked that it "had advantages both over the American constitution of 1787 and the Swiss of 1848 . . ."; more general, Robert G. Neumann, *European and Comparative Government* (New York,

Europe in the field of protection of human rights. This observation was not an exaggeration. On the other hand, these rights were never in effect for any long period. Thus they did not serve, either in Germany or abroad, to establish an operative liberal tradition. Despite its brief legal validity, the promulgation of the Frankfurt Constitution had substantial effects both inside and outside of Germany. That Constitution serves as an indicator of the liberality of later constitutional concepts within Germany.

The Contemporary Western View of German Constitutional Conditions

When one seeks to examine the contemporary reaction of other Western observers, especially that of Anglo-American observers, it immediately becomes apparent that contemporary Western scholarship did not regard constitutional developments in Germany as important. Except for a few unpublished notes by diplomatic specialists[8] little was written in English. Indeed, texts of the German Constitutions of this time and of proposed drafts for them were not available in English until 1918. To some extent, they are still inaccessible in foreign languages.[9] Even if one considers the failure of German information policies abroad, there was apparently little interest in the United States in translating the pertinent sections. If one seeks to trace the reasons for this remarkable disinterest, some basic prejudices of the time should be noted. The nineteenth-century French scholar Esmain, for example, disregarded

---

1951), 309: "an excellent instrument"; Snyder, ed., *Documents of German History* (see n. 6), 179: "an extraordinarily fine achievement."

8. Cf. Günter Moltmann, *Atlantische Blockpolitik im 19. Jahrhundert* (Düsseldorf, 1973), 88ff., 208ff.

9. Cf. nn. 5 and 6; Constitution of the North German Federation from April 16, 1867, in *British and Foreign State Papers*, Foreign Office Publications (London, 1871), 57: 296ff.; more often the Constitution of the German Empire from April 16, 1871, in *British and Foreign State Papers*, Foreign Office Publications (London, 1877), 63: 58ff.; other sources are listed in Hawgood, *Modern Constitutions* (see n. 1), 500ff.; Edwin Hermann Zeydel, ed., *Constitutions of the German Empire and German States* (Washington, DC, 1919, repr. Wilmington, DE, 1974), 8ff.; Otis H. Fisk, *Germany's Constitutions of 1871 and 1919: Texts* (Cincinnati, OH, 1924); Snyder, ed., *Documents of German History* (see n. 6), 188ff.; Robert I. Vexler, *Germany: A Chronology and Fact Book* (Dobbs Ferry, NY, 1973), 108ff.; cf. nn. 26, 27, and 37 for English translations of German state constitutions.

the German Constitution in his work on comparative constitutional law. He did so because he only took into account "liberal constitutions . . . which have public liberty for their direct purpose."[10]

Even if one dismisses this kind of negative commentary as merely chauvinistic, a view which is perhaps confirmed by Esmain's method of analysis, his evaluation is not atypical for Western scholars. For many, Germany was the westernmost Eastern country. For example, there is an English quotation that "the Prussians are like the Russians." In the Dutch language, the nickname for Germans is *Moffen*, which means something like "out of date, musty, or disused." Compared to the New World of America, the Old World of Germany seemed especially out of date, musty, and disused. Its division into territorial principalities contrasted with the relatively nationalistic and centralized states elsewhere in Western Europe. Thus there was a particular indistinctness and subjection to local custom in German constitutional law and constitutional thought. In contrast, various regional groups and countries such as Great Britain had developed a uniformity of language and law. Germany, in comparison, constituted an especially sharp contrast to the New World, particularly because of its multiplicity of states.

This is reinforced by a notion of a European "cultural slope" from West to East, which was especially prevalent during the last century. Its Western high point was found in the impulses toward liberty and legal modernization initiated by the French Revolution and in the experiences of openness and flexibility in the unwritten constitution of England. Its Eastern low point might be found in the czarism of Russia.

In contrast, the German classic and romantic poets and composers had been positively received by Western countries throughout the nineteenth century.[11] Their cultural influence was, however, unable to change the constitutional and political remoteness of Germany. The same was true for the later admiration and imitation of the German universities' academic freedom. At the end of the last

10. Adhémar Esmain, *Eléments de Droit Constitutionel français et comparé* (Paris, [2]1898), x; similar to James T. Shotwell, *The Dong Way to Freedom* (Indianapolis, IN, 1960), 382ff.

11. Eudo D. Mason, *Deutsche und englische Romantik* (Göttingen, [2]1966); Anthony Thorlby, *The Romantic Movement* (London, 1927).

century, the preeminence of those universities was epitomized by the expression "every scholar in the world has two native countries: his own and Germany."[12] The scholars, however, preferred the intellectual life of the German university and the political life of their home country.

Finally, one might have supposed that the massive German emigration of the 1800s would have lessened the remoteness of Germany in this respect. About 2.5 million persons had emigrated by 1871; 90 percent of them had gone to the United States. Theoretically, this stream of people could have stimulated an interest in German constitutional and legal rights. This does not, however, appear to have happened. Since the emigrants came mostly from the lower social classes they were less interested in their own past and more interested in the future of their new country. This holds true especially for those who emigrated after the Revolutions of 1830 and 1848. In a sense they may be considered emigrants "from the constitution," indeed, some of those who emigrated in 1848 were virtual refugees.[13] The period after the failure of the 1848 Revolution, which is commonly known as the reactionary or neo-absolutist period, was perceived as so oppressive that some German states, including Württemberg, Baden, and the two Mecklenburgs, lost an eighth of their population within four years. Such emigrants simply wanted to have nothing to do with constitutional developments in Germany which for them had failed. A few exceptions, such as the "forty-eighters" Hans Kudlich and Carl Schurz, will be discussed later. As far as can be determined there was no careful constitutional analysis of German developments in any other country during this period.

In contrast, within Germany the situation was totally different. Many German studies were directed to the examination of constitutional institutions in England and in the United States.[14] This

12. Cf. Peter Wapnewski, *Von Forschung und Lehre und der Problematik des Elitebegriffs* (Münster, 1982), 11.
13. Carl Wittke, *Refugees of the Revolution* (Philadelphia, PA, 1952); Adolf E. Zucker, ed., *The Fourty-Eighters* (New York, 1950).
14. Charles E. McClelland, *The German Historians and England* (Cambridge, 1971); Moltmann, *Atlantische Blockpolitik im 19. Jahrhundert* (see n. 8); John A. Hawgood, *Political and Economic Relations between the United States of America and the German Provisional Central Government in Frankfurt am Main in 1848–49* (Heidelberg, 1928); Sigmund Skard, *American Studies in Europe*, 2 vols. (Philadelphia, PA, 1958), 1: 209–357, 229f.; and especially the legal scholars Albert Hänel, *Die Unionsverfassung:*

trend was established by the Frenchman de Tocqueville[15] in 1835 and had become part of the general intellectual life of this country. Indeed, it contributed to the increasing inclination to emigrate. In only two instances, in 1848 and 1871, was there a reciprocal under-standing or discussion of German constitutional developments.

In 1848–49 there was an attempted "revolution from below" in which a liberal federal constitution was proposed for the German nation. This was the first time that such a constitution had been put forward in modern German history. That was a basic decision followed in later German constitutions. In 1867–71 there was, under Bismarck, a "revolution from above," which finally accomplished federal unification. While that Constitution provided federal unification, it did not provide for individual rights. Provisions for the protection of human rights were viewed as a task for later constitutional development,[16] just as the Bill of Rights followed the adoption of the Constitution in the United States. In both periods, the parallels between constitutional developments in the United States and Germany cannot be ignored, and indeed, they were noted in official messages from the presidents of the United States.

In 1848–49 President Polk was the only foreign head of state who directed greetings to the Frankfurt Assembly. After receiving the credentials of the diplomatic minister sent to Washington in June 1848 by the provisional central authority, President Polk answered:

> The government and people of the United States have taken a deep and lively interest in the great events which have transpired in Germany

---

Annalen des Deutschen Reichs (Leipzig, 1878), 796–806; Max von Seydel, "Verfassung und Verfassungsgeschichte der Vereinigten Staaten von Amerika" (1891), in idem, *Staatsrechtliche und politische Abhandlungen: Neue Folge* (Tübingen, 1902), 33–58; and Otto von Gierke, "German Constitutional Law in Its Relation to the American Constitution," *Harvard Law Review* 23 (1909/10): 273–90.

15. His work, *De la démocratie en Amérique* (1835/40) had already been translated into German one year after its original publication, cf. Eckart G. Franz, *Das Amerikabild der deutschen Revolution von 1848/49* (Heidelberg, 1958), 15ff.

16. Kühne, *Reichsverfassung der Paulskirche* (see n. 4), 118, 126; also Heinrich von Sybel, "Das neue Deutsche Reich" (first in *English Fortnightly Review*, January 1, 1871), in *Vorträge und Aufsätze* (Berlin, 1874), 324f.; similar to Carl Schurz in an unpublished letter, cf. Hans L. Trefousse, "The German-American Immigrants and the Newly Founded *Reich*," in Frank Trommler and Joseph McVeigh, eds., *America and the Germans*, 2 vols. (Philadelphia, PA, 1985), 1: 160–75; for Hans Kudlich cf. Friedrich Prinz, "Hans Kudlich," in *Hans Kudlich und die Bauernbefreiung in Niederösterreich: Katalog des Niederösterreichischen Landesmuseums* (Vienna, 1983), 55.

during the past year . . . all our sympathies have been enlisted for the success of the efforts of Germany to establish legal liberty and unity in the government of confederated states. This feeling of sympathy was natural to a people, themselves enjoying the fullest liberty under a confederation of sovereign states, such as your countrymen seek to establish.[17]

Similarly in 1871, a message from the president of the United States extended a friendly welcome to the new German union and emphasized parallels with the American Constitution. In this instance, however, the expectations of liberal freedom were articulated more as hopes than as accomplished results:

The union of the states of Germany into a form of government similar in many respects to that of the American union is an event that cannot fail to touch deeply the sympathies of the American people to the United States. . . . In it the American people see an attempt to reproduce in Europe some of the best features of our own Constitution. . . . The cherished aspiration of national unity which for ages has inspired the many intentions of people speaking the same language, inhabiting a contiguous and compact territory, but unnaturally separated and divided by dynastic jealousies . . . has been attained. . . . The bringing of great masses of thoughtful and free people under a single government must tend to make governments what alone they should be – the representatives of the will and the organization of the power of the people.

The adoption in Europe of the American system of union under the control and direction of a free people, educated to self-restraint, cannot fail to extend popular institutions and to enlarge peaceful influence of American ideas.[18]

At the very least, these two passages clarify one dimension of our discussion. They point beyond the nucleus of traditional civil rights to political rights. The former are comparable to the French Declaration of the Rights of Man, but the rights cited in items a–f above

17. Cf. Valentin, *Geschichte der Deutschen Revolution* (see n. 4), 119. Complete text in the *Daily Union*, Washington, DC, January 31, 1849 (Bundesarchiv, Außenstelle Frankfurt/Main – DB 60–VIII/1); about the German minister in Washington, Friedrich von Roenne, see John A. Hawgood, "Friedrich von Roenne, A German Tocqueville," *University of Birmingham Historical Journal* 3 (1951): 81–94.

18. Special message to Congress, February 7, 1871, in Janette Keim, *Forty Years of German-American Political Relations* (Philadelphia, PA, 1919), 32; Bruno Siemers, "Die Vereinigten Staaten und die deutsche Einigung," in *Geschichtliche Kräfte und Entscheidungen: Festschrift Otto Becker* (Wiesbaden, 1954), 200ff.

(in the list of the Plan of the Committee of Seventeen) show emphatically the close relationship of those fundamental rights to political rights. Their separation would be both arbitrary and impossible.

Both presidential statements should certainly be seen as high points in German-American relations in the last century. This was, however, only an occasional and sporadic friendship. After the failure of the Revolution of 1848–49, the initially harmonious relationship cooled due to a distancing of the United States from the situation in the German *Bund*, which the American minister to Prussia, A.J. Donelson, correctly characterized as follows:

> In the existing German Confederation the decrees of the Diet were enforced to the mediation and instrumentality of the states, but its diction was so limited and its influence so feeble that it has lost almost the name of a government. It served rather as a bond by which the abuses of monarchy escaped responsibility than as a means of security to the states which comprised it. It created no navy, encouraged no commerce, projected no international improvements, and if it could have executed no laws lessening the hereditary privileges in the unreasonable priority possessed by the princes and nobility in the public service and legislation.[19]

This description of the status quo was again true after 1850. In any case, Donelson points out the disparity that existed up to 1867 between the internal conditions in Germany and the United States. That disparity can be summarized as follows:

Germany	United States
a loose quasi-international law, the product of the *Bund*	a federal state that experienced its crisis and test in the Civil War
monarchies, the rights of	a republic

19. Cited in Günter Moltmann, "Zwei amerikanische Beiträge zur deutschen Verfassungsdiskussion, 1848," *Jahrbuch für Amerikastudien* 12 (1967): 264; cf. too his positive interpretation of the new Constitution: "By the constitution now proposed these features of weakness are all changed. Universal suffrage opens the door of public honor to the humblest citizen. The government is subjected to the scrutiny of the people, who are guaranteed the freedom of debate, the liberty of the press, the *Habeas Corpus* and the trial by Jury . . . an immense stride from absolutism to a democratic system . . . . it will perhaps come nearer to our system than will the new republic of France."

which went far beyond the
powers of the British crown

feudal-like estates with clear feudal public and private privileges	at least for the white population, economic and political equality
dominating conservative powers with only a small place for moderate liberals	the dominance of democratic liberalism

German Civil Rights Issues – Between Freedom and Unity

The Amount of Freedom

Like the fundamental rights included in the Paulskirche Constitution, the fundamental rights proposed by the Committee of
Seventeen included individual rights (items e and h–r), institutional
rights for associations (item g), the special protection of associ-
ational rights (items c and s), as well as organic provisions for the
organization of government (items a, b, d, and f). These concepts
of fundamental rights, which appeared in German constitutional
law for the first time, were derived from the debates of the
pre-Parliament, the body which called the Frankfurt National
Assembly into session. These concepts established the minimum
standards of "German popular freedom."[20] Because of the wide
variety of rights included, the concept of fundamental rights was
thought to be comprehensive. It was not restricted to individual
rights but even included rights which the French Declaration had
omitted (see items c–g, o–q, and s). It also went further than the
American Bill of Rights (see items a–c, n–q, and s).

The breadth of human rights protected had two consequences:

1. The inseparability of civil rights and political freedom was
   unmistakably recognized. This connection was already well

---

20. Cf. the debates of the Preliminary Parliament, *Verhandlungen des Deutschen
Parlaments: Officielle Ausgabe*, 1. Lieferung (Frankfurt/Main 1848), 174; and the
takeover of the Seventeen's committee by Ludwig Uhland in Rudolf Hübner, ed.,
*Aktenstücke und Aufzeichnungen zur Geschichte der Frankfurter Nationalversammlung aus
dem Nachlaß von Johann Gustav Droysen* (1924, repr. Osnabrück, 1973), 73.

established in Western European and American thought.
2. There was an unmistakably strong restriction on the state, which found its expression in the regulations for a vertical separation of powers (items a–c). In this respect the German concept of freedom was contrary to the then-existing civil rights catalogs that implicitly rested on a dualism of state and society. The strong individualistic character of most of the other human rights' catalogs was thus avoided. In its place a catalog of basic rights was positively established which went beyond the rights of the individuals and dealt with state-related and social rights.[21] One reason for this was that the state which was to secure these freedoms had itself yet to be established. The tradition of the Old German Empire, the Holy Roman Empire, which had granted special privileges to certain groups within the states, also had a strong influence in this direction.[22]

The meshing of the constitutional catalog of rights with the organizational parts of the Constitution was intentional. In 1848 it was especially important: basic rights had to be an integral part of the Constitution. As colorfully stated, these rights should form the foundation upon which the building of the state would then be erected. Even more concretely, one of the goals of 1848 was the creation of an unified Germany with a rule of law and the abolition of repression and feudal privileges in the society.[23]

The interrelationship of the fundamental rights section and the organizational section of the Constitution did not survive the failure of the Revolution. The political power of the monarchical elements in the reestablished states of the German *Bund* restricted the content of individual rights and their authority.

The constitutional basis of the German *Bund* was the *Bundesakte*,[24] which once again came into effect after the failure of the Revolution. The *Bundesakte* contained only the most rudimen-

21. Kühne, *Reichsverfassung der Paulskirche* (see n. 4), 171ff.

22. See Leonard Krieger, *The German Idea of Freedom* (Boston, MA, 1957).

23. Cf. Georg Beseler for the Constitutional Committee of the Frankfurt Parliament in Franz Wigard, ed., *Stenographischer Bericht über die Verhandlungen der Deutschen Konstituirenden Nationalversammlung zu Frankfurt a.M.* (Frankfurt/Main, 1848), 1: 700f.; Kühne, *Reichsverfassung der Paulskirche* (see n. 4), 180.

24. English translation in *The Annual Register, 1815* (London, 1816), 309ff.; also in Robert I. Vexler, *Austria: A Chronology and Fact Book* (Dobbs Ferry, NY, 1975), 65ff.

tary provisions with regard to fundamental rights and the constitutional law of the several states. Its Article 16 required religious equality for the three recognized Christian confessions (Lutheran, Calvinist, and Roman Catholic); Article 18 regulated the right to travel within German territory, as well as the right to own property and the military service obligation of citizens. It also promised to regulate press freedom. These provisions might have been used, both before and after 1848, and expanded in order to protect fundamental rights; however, the opposite was the case. The freedom-of-press provision was transformed into an obligation to censor and supervise the press, the consequences of which led to many difficulties.[25] These negative developments on the confederated level could have been cut short if the constitutions of the several principalities had provided for human rights. This was, however, only partially the case. Article 13 of the *Bundesakte* required each state to adopt a constitution. This was accomplished in each of the individual states. By 1848 each had a kind of civil rights' catalog which dealt with the legal status of public officials, the church, the nobility, the military and national guard units, municipalities, and educational institutions.[26] Such state constitutions, with their civil rights provisions, were formally quite similar to the American concept of constitutionalism. They provided for an equal "regulation of the form of government and the securing of the liberties of the people." But in spite of their literal similarity, closer inspection revealed significant differences both in their content and in the applicability of their constitutional provisions.

The protections that would have been provided by these constitutional provisions were not fully available in the member states of

25. Cf. Wolfgang Häusler, "Vom Standrecht zum Rechtsstaat: Politik und Justiz in Österreich (1848-1867)," in Erika Weinzierl and Karl R. Stadler, eds., *Justiz und Zeitgeschichte* (Vienna, 1977), 16ff.; Wolfram Siemann, ed., *Der Polizeiverein deutscher Staaten: Eine Dokumentation zur Überwachung der Öffentlichkeit nach der Revolution von 1848/49* (Tübingen, 1983), 157f.; inhibition from May 22, 1858 onward of American newspapers in the German language.

26. Cf. for example the Constitutions of Baden 1818, §§7ff. in *British and Foreign State Papers* (see n. 9) (London, 1837), 5: 161ff.; of Bavaria 1818, Title IV §1ff. in ibid., 1055ff.; of Hanover 1840, §§27ff. in *British and Foreign State Papers* (see n. 9) (London, 1857), 29: 1244ff.; of the Electorate of Hesse 1831, §§19ff., 132ff. in *British and Foreign State Papers* (see n. 9) (London, 1834), 19: 599ff.; of Saxony 1831, §§24ff. in *British and Foreign State Papers* (see n. 9) (London, 1836), 20: 47ff.; the Constitutions of Bavaria, Baden, and Saxony are printed also in Zeydel, ed., *Constitutions of the German Empire and German States* (see n. 9), 35ff., 51ff., 272ff.

the German *Bund*. The two great powers of the *Bund*, Prussia and Austria, exercised enough influence to effect a suspension of laws implementing these freedoms as well as a rejection of proposals for new laws. The *Bund* became a reactionary force against the liberal constitutional movement. Examples can be seen in the destruction of the so-called March accomplishments by the formal repeal of the basic rights of Frankfurt in 1851 and in the very restrictive federal press and federal association laws enacted in 1854. Neither Prussia nor Austria had done their duty and had established state constitutions until 1848, and indeed, Austria did not take this obligation seriously until 1860.[27]

Repression from above, both before and after the Revolution, was the reason that some liberals were prepared to separate the goals of unity and freedom. They had thought that, in the process of transformation of the German *Bund* into a truly federal state, individual freedom could have been established in the national Constitution. Some, however, held the opposite view that individual liberty should be established in the separate states first and then adopted at the federal level. Pursuing both goals, which the 1848 Revolution tried to do, was later regarded as a tactical mistake.[28] Bismarck subsequently decided this question in favor of the priority of national unity.

There was a further weakening of liberties in the division of civil and political rights, a division which is even less understandable for Americans. Article 16 of the *Bundesakte* had already established this division. Item r of the "Fundamental Rights of the German People"

---

27. Revised Constitution of Prussia 1850, in *British and Foreign State Papers* (see n. 9) (London, 1863), 39: 1025ff.; also in Zeydel, ed., *Constitutions of the German Empire and German States* (see n. 9), 225ff.; Constitution of Austria 1861, in *British and Foreign State Papers* (see n. 9) (London, 1863), 43: 1216ff.; also Vexler, *Austria* (see n. 24), 76ff.

28. Cf. Ludwig August von Rochau, *Grundsätze der Realpolitik*, 2 vols. (1853/69), new ed. by Hans-Ulrich Wehler (Frankfurt/Main, 1972), 242: "wäre . . . nur die Einheit ohne die Freiheit, oder die Freiheit ohne die Einheit für uns erreichbar, so müßten wir . . . nach der Einheit . . . greifen. Mit ihr wäre wenigstens die deutsche Zukunft gerettet; ohne dieselbe hingegen . . . ein polnisches Schicksal . . . gewiß." Similarly the former minister of the Frankfurt Parliament, the Austrian Liberal, and Minister Schmerling thought (in Huber, *Deutsche Verfassungsgeschichte*, (see n. 1), 3: 382, n. 32): "alle Verfassungsfragen sind Fragen der Macht . . . Ich selbst habe immer für verfassungsmäßige Zustände gedacht, gesorgt und gehandelt; ich war kein Absolutist, aber . . . ein Gegner derjenigen Bestimmungen, die rein theoretischer Natur sind, nie zur faktischen Anwendung kommen und nur gegeben sind, um gewissen Postulaten des Rechtsbewußtseins und der Freiheit zu entsprechen."

had attempted to counteract this.

Judicial decisions also weakened the applicability of individual rights in Germany. In the United States, Chief Justice Marshall had set the tone for judicial protection of individual rights in his famous decision, *Marbury v. Madison*:

> The Constitution is either a superior paramount law unchangeable by ordinary means or it is on a level with ordinary legislative acts, like other acts and is alterable when the legislature is pleased to alter it. If the former part of the alternative be true, then a legislative act contrary to the Constitution is not law: if the latter part be true then written constitutions are absurd attempts, on the part of the people, to limit the power in its own nature illimitable.[29]

Such direct application of constitutional norms was planned in 1848–49, and the proposed *Reichsgericht* was to have that kind of jurisdiction. Subsequently, however, the attitude toward direct application of the Constitution was much more restricted. Contemporaries consciously stressed the difference between the German and American systems.[30] The German system could be described as one in which the substantive agreement of a statute with a constitutional mandate was not required; it could be applied without such an inquiry.

The German form of constitutionalism not only adopted the two simple alternatives of Chief Justice Marshall but added a third. This was a dubious accomplishment with somewhat absurd implications. The constitutional provisions for civil rights were seen as goals for achieving rather than for establishing norms and were perceived as goals for the adoption of ordinary legislation by the state legislatures without any time limitation or judicial supervision. Constitutional rights were thus only partially and slowly realized. In part this was so because the composition of state legislatures was influenced by massive manipulation of the electoral laws for the benefit of conservative parties.[31] Nevertheless, the tradition of this so-called program theory of the constitution, that

29. 1 Cranch 137; cf. Klaus Stern, *Das Staatsrecht der Bundesrepublik Deutschland*, vol. 1 (Munich, [2]1984), 81ff.
30. Cf. §126 of the Frankfurt Constitution; Kühne, *Reichsverfassung der Paulskirche* (see n. 4), 185ff.
31. For a good summary cf. Dolf Sternberger and Bernhard Vogel, eds., *Die Wahl der Parlamente und anderer Staatsorgane*, 2 vols. (Berlin, 1969–78), 1: 201f., 207f.

is, the necessity for legislative reenactment of constitutional provisions if they were to be directly applicable, was so strong that there were no directly enforceable rights in the constitutions of the North German *Bund* of 1867 or in the German Empire of 1871. Constitutional rights were, as it was then thought, not directly applicable; ordinary legislation was always necessary for their implementation.[32] Thus the Constitution of 1871 gave the central government legislative power to enact certain basic rights for the people. But the actual enactment of such laws nevertheless occurred only slowly. In contrast, Austria, which had been expelled from the German *Bund* in 1866, had already established a remarkable codification of individual rights with constitutional judicial protection between 1862 and 1867. That codification continues to exist even today.[33]

In addition to looking at the purely hortatory provisions on human rights in the 1850 Constitution of the German *Bund*, one should also examine its organizational structure. The failure to create a constitutional court, which the 1848 Constitution would have established, is also of significance. The view was expressed that Germany's acceptance of the American system of direct constitutional application would be "historically impossible" because of the dualistic order of the state in constitutional life.[34] I mention this because in 1848–49 the issue of constitutionalism under the slogan "popular freedom in the individual state" became part of planned human rights (item a). This aspiration had also played a key role in the establishment of other basic rights.

Freedom in Constitutionalism

To Americans it must sound tautological that since the early nineteenth century Germans have spoken of a "constitutional constitution." This repetitiveness had, however, a meaning. In contrast to North America, Germany had enjoyed a constitution much

---

32. Kühne, *Reichsverfassung der Paulskirche* (see n. 4), 114.

33. For the German Empire cf. Ernst Rudolf Huber, "Grundrechte im Bismarckschen Reichssystem," in *Festschrift Ulrich Scheuner* (Berlin, 1973), 161–81; for Austria cf. Felix Ermacora, *Handbuch der Grundfreiheiten und der Menschenrechte* (Vienna, 1963).

34. Rainer Wahl, "Der Vorrang der Verfassung," *Der Staat* 20 (1981): 495.

earlier – the institutional constitution of the Holy Roman Empire. The term "constitutional constitution," in contrast, expressed the influence of Western models and especially that of the United States. The constitutional constitution made the individual rather than groups or classes (*Stände*) the centerpiece of the state.[35] The government was to be the concern of all citizens. How this was to be accomplished remained controversial throughout the nineteenth century.

Article 13 of the *Bundesakte* of 1815 provided for institutional constitutions in each of the German states. This article was again in force after 1850 and was a key concept of German constitutionalism. Originally established as a bulwark against the extension of power by the monarchs of the individual states, it represented a compromise between the democratic principle, representation of the individual, and the monarchical principle, dominance of a monarch in a state. Article 57 of the Vienna Act of 1820 had placed the predominant weight on the latter principle: "Since the German *Bund*, with the exception of the free cities, consists of sovereign princes, the basic concepts given herein with regard to the authority of the state must remain unified in the head of the state, and the sovereign can be bound to obtain the cooperation of the estates by the state constitution only in the exercise of certain powers."

This norm meant two things for the German notion of constitutionalism.[36] First of all, it can be understood as a rejection of the principle of separation of powers. After 1848 this understanding was in practice set aside. The liberal democratic demand for a rule of law with the goal of institutional and personal separation of legislative, executive, and judicial power was a powerful counterforce, as was the distinction between formal and real holders of power. This interpretation increasingly limited the monarch to functioning as a symbol of state unity. The situation is, however, quite different when one reflects that Article 57 of the Vienna Act was also a counterweight to the democratic principle. This was achieved in three ways:

1. It meant that there could be no purely democratic constitutions. The effort of Paulskirche failed in 1849 when faced with armed

---

35. Cf. Reinhart Koselleck, *Preußen zwischen Reform und Revolution* (Stuttgart, ³1981), 164; McClelland, *The German Historians and England* (see n. 14), 69ff., 268ff.
36. Huber, *Deutsche Verfassungsgeschichte* (see n. 1), 1: 640ff.

resistance by the monarchs. At best the Constitution was a compromise between the people and the monarchs. In other cases differences of opinion between the prince and the people either led to indefinite delay in adoption of a constitution or to the unilateral proclamation of a constitution by the monarch himself. The latter occurred in Prussia and Austria at the end of 1848 and the beginning of 1849.[37]

2. Article 57 of the Vienna Act also served as a counterweight to further expansion of the concept of the state constitution. With its decided emphasis on the monarchical principle, it was, however, possible to take into consideration the "new estates," property owners, independent professionals, and merchants' communities as well as the old estates of nobility and clergy. The realistic consequence of this broadening of representation was that in the individual German state legislatures elements from a broad range of views were represented. A certain tendency toward a representative system was unmistakable after 1848 but it was nevertheless limited by the continuing influence of the old estates. That influence was to have been abolished by the concept of the equality of citizens in the 1848–49 Constitution (item e),[38] but after the failure of the Revolution the old estates continued to exert considerable influence especially in the upper houses of the normally bicameral legislatures. It is difficult to underestimate the potential of these bodies to block constitutional modernization in Germany. The type of nobility represented in the upper houses was perhaps illustrated by the Prussian Junker, but it was present in other states too. All the upper chambers played significant roles as vetoing bodies.

At the national level the Constitution of 1848–49 had provided for an upper chamber (*Staatenhaus*) representative of the estates and for a lower chamber (*Volkshaus*) representative of the people. This arrangement would partially live on in the *Bundesrat* and in the Reichstag after 1867.[39] In both cases this was a

---

37. Prussia, Constitution from Dec. 5, 1848, in *British and Foreign State Papers* (see n. 9), (London, 1862), 37: 1378ff.; Austria, Proclamation of Political Rights, from March 4, 1849, in Ibid.

38. Kühne, *Reichsverfassung der Paulskirche* (see n. 4), 221ff., 457ff.

39. James Harvey Robinson, *The German Bundesrath* (Philadelphia, PA, 1891); Stephen King-Hall and Richard K. Ullmann, *German Parliaments: A Study of the Development of Representative Institutions in Germany* (New York, 1954).

progressive development because of the direct and general right of men to vote for members of the lower chamber.

3. The third point was at the core of German constitutionalism – the influence (or lack thereof) of state parliaments on the formation of state governments. For the early democratic writer Georg Büchner,[40] state parliaments were no more than "slow blockades, which one could now and then shove in the path of the greed of princes and their ministers, but on which one could not build a secure fortress for German freedom." That view was widely applicable. It was based on the fact that the composition of governments was, with the exception of the brief period of the Revolution, understood to be a prerogative of the monarch, which could be exercised without any review by the legislative bodies.

This arrangement was only superficially similar to the English constitutional model. Its godfather was more likely the reactionary model of the French Charter of 1814. In France, however, the Revolution of 1830 had already transformed that provision into a general predominance of Parliament similar to that in England. In the individual German constitutions, the right of parliaments to impeach ministers for crimes against the Constitution was supposed to be the counterweight to the dominance of the monarch in the executive. But in 1862 that model had permitted, for example, the naming of Bismarck as the Prussian premier against a massive majority of liberals in the lower house. Nevertheless such impeachments were largely a matter of theory.[41] The veto of the upper chamber usually made it impossible for a resolution of impeachment to be passed by both houses. In addition the state courts necessary for trial of impeachments were frequently not established, so trials could not be held. Despite many attempts to create such tribunals, such laws were passed neither in Prussia after 1849 nor in the national Constitution after 1867. Laws regulating the right to impeach ministers which were put forward in the legislative bodies seven

40. Georg Büchner, "Der hessische Landbote" (1835), in *Gesammelte Werke* (Munich, 1961), 177.

41. Kühne, *Reichsverfassung der Paulskirche* (see n. 4), 463ff.; Rudolf Hoke, "Verfassungsgerichtsbarkeit in deutschen Ländern in der Tradition der deutschen Staatsgerichtsbarkeit," in Klaus Stern and Christian Starck, eds., *Landesverfassungsgerichtsbarkeit*, vol. 1 (Baden-Baden, 1983), 61ff.

times during this period were never enacted; the right to impeach thus remained an empty promise.[42]

All attempts to establish a popular monarchy which would be legally based on an interrelationship of monarchical and democratic principles in the Constitution failed in Germany. Such attempts only led to de facto temporary cooperation between both groups, as in Baden in the second half of the nineteenth century and in the Reichstag in the period from 1867 to 1879.[43] The Revolution of 1848–49 had produced, in contrast, a remarkable proposal for a compromise between monarchical and parliamentary government, which can be designated as the high point of German constitutionalism. In the naming of the government, the proposal had sought to establish an exact parity between the prince and the people; both parties would have been forced to compromise. This would have been insured by a series of balanced legal instruments: to the Crown belonged the formal power to name ministers and the right to dissolve the Parliament; to the Parliament pertained the right of each chamber to bring accusations against ministers as well as the power to reject laws and budgets.[44] Yet this model was not realized in the period under discussion. Not only did the impediments to the impeachment of ministers work to the disadvantage of the legislative bodies but, even more so, the manipulation of the electoral law for both chambers had the same effect. These manipulations were frequently put into effect by way of unilateral monarchical edict. In contrast to the prevailing conservative view,[45] defeated supporters of liberal democratic constitutions bitterly denounced this as "false constitutionalism."[46] In part, these political forces turned to the municipal level where so-called mu-

---

42. Erich Hahn, "Ministerial Responsibility and Impeachment in Prussia, 1848–63," *Central European History* 10 (1977): 3–28; and the essays of Manfred Botzenhart, Günter Grünthal, and Klaus Erich Pollmann in Gerhard A. Ritter, ed., *Regierung, Bürokratie und Parlament in Preußen und Deutschland von 1848 bis zur Gegenwart* (Düsseldorf, 1983).

43. Lother Gall, *Der Liberalismus als regierende Partei* (Wiesbaden, 1968).

44. Kühne, *Reichsverfassung der Paulskirche* (see n. 4), 467ff.; for a more statistical approach cf. Donald I. Mattheisen, "Liberal Constitutionalism in the Frankfurt Parliament of 1848," *Central European History* 12 (1979): 124–42.

45. Cf. especially Franzjörg Baumgart, *Die verdrängte Revolution* (Düsseldorf, 1976); Theodore S. Hamerow, "History and the German Revolution of 1848," *American Historical Review* 60 (1954): 28.

46. Cf. Rochau, *Grundsätze der Realpolitik* (see n. 28), 127, 233; Kühne, *Reichsver-*

nicipal constitutionalism (item c) provided opportunities. Yet even there, they were confronted with a legally unregulated monarchical authority appointing or confirming incumbents to the highest municipal offices.

After 1850 there was no longer a real general protection of popular freedom in the German Constitution. Unity between prince and people was replaced by a dualism between prince and people. The liberal jurist Robert von Mohl, minister of justice,[47] identified this trend and compared it with developments in other Western countries. Positive participation of the legislatures in the formation of governments was never a possibility. In contrast to England, the ministers did not bring together the will of the chief of state and the views of the popular assembly. In contrast to France after 1830, ministerial positions did not go to the leaders of the parties represented in the state parliament. This accounts for the nature of state governments in Germany, which always sought their protection in the monarch and thereby themselves became a party in all controversies. This unhappy dualism led to a steady criticism of state administrations by the legislative chambers, which, in turn, prompted efforts by the governments to influence the composition of the chambers. The consequence was not only a dualism between the state and society, but also a lack of interest in the political system on behalf of the public who believed it to be beyond their influence. This in turn impeded the creation of a responsible and recognizable popular will.

The result was obvious – the conscious hindering of the constitutionally mandated equality of authority of prince and people resulted in a dualism of state and society. The French aphorism, "The king reigns, but he does not govern," did not apply in Germany; judicial enforcement of the Constitution could possibly have impaired monarchical priorities. The real cause for the failure of constitutionalism, however, was not dualism but rather the

---

fassung der Paulskirche (see n. 4), 473 with note 303; in a conservative sense today, Ernst Nolte, "Deutscher Scheinkonstitutionalismus?" *Historische Zeitschrift* 228 (1979): 533ff.

47. Robert von Mohl, "Über die verschiedenen Auffassungen des repräsentativen Systems in England, Frankreich und Deutschland," in Robert von Mohl, ed., *Staatsrecht, Völkerrecht und Politik*, vol. 1 (Tübingen, 1860, repr. Graz, 1962), 49ff.; about Mohl see Erich Angermann, *Robert von Mohl, 1799–1875: Leben und Werk eines altliberalen Staatsgelehrten*, Politica, 8 (Neuwied, 1962).

monarchical principle that was enforced without consideration of the popular will.

Further Aspects

Theoretical Bases

An explanation of the tensions in German constitutional thought would be superficial, if it did not mention the theoretical constitutional structure that contributed to them. Germany lacked the simple formula on which American constitutional thought was based for the benefit of the individual, that is, Jefferson's natural law, "pursuit of happiness." In its place, one finds the so-called "philosophical public law," which provided for a multitude of different theories on the true legitimacy of the state and of the Constitution. These mirror not only the strength and conviction of the rival views of state order, but also reflect doubts about the legitimacy of monarchically created constitutions.[48]

The notion of pursuit of individual happiness[49] was rejected as a basis for the Constitution because it was contrary to the notion of the state. Not only conservatives, but other groups too opposed this notion. The state had a being and existence separate and apart from the good of the individual citizen. Since its inception this theory implied the rawest and most forceful materialism; it thus tended to negate the moral notion of the state. A theory of morality, which was erected as a barrier to libertarianism, went beyond that to a recognition of the individual commands of morality. It was, however, doubted that the law could regulate all aspects of conduct.

A few examples will serve to show that German constitutional thought included superindividual and community protections in contrast to an individualistic understanding of constitutionally protected civil liberties. Historicism is to account for this as much as the romantic-religious ideas of the state as an organism.[50] In

48. Klaus Hespe, *Die Entwicklung der Staatszwecklehre in der deutschen Staatsrechtswissenschaft des 19. Jahrhunderts* (Cologne, 1964), 74; Georg Jellinek, *Allgemeine Staatslehre* (Berlin, ³1922), 239ff.

49. Cf. Joseph Held, *System des Verfassungsrechts der monarchischen Staaten Deutschlands*, vol. 1 (Würzburg, 1856), 279ff.

50. Karl-Georg Faber, "Ausprägungen des Historismus," *Historische Zeitschrift*

contrast to American constitutional thought, natural law ideas were less apparent. Rather, there is an orientation toward the concept of a state as an entity or a conscious consideration of the limits of civil liberties that goes beyond pure individualism. This peculiarity can best be understood as a result of persistent German efforts to seek both freedom and unity. In contrast to the France of 1789, German efforts at creating a constitution were not only a matter of making an existing state more free. Rather, a state had to be formed in the process of creating that freedom.

The liberal concept of constitutionalism sought to establish a state with popular freedom. The theoretical background of this unrealized conception was a view of the state that was based on democratic–natural law ideas of social contract and conservative–romantic theories based on the idea of the community as an organism.[51] It perceived the prince and the people as a unity by seeking to pull together the monarchical and democratic principles.

Finally, another theoretical development occurring after the failure of the Revolution of 1848–49 deserves mention because it also discouraged the development of progressive constitutional thought – the introduction of doctrines of positivism into juristic thought.[52] Positivism sought to link constitutional norms inseparably to their political-historical background, to what is called "frozen history." Ideally, in the realm of realpolitik this enabled the liberals of that day to compromise with their conservative opponents on issues of basic rights, thus preparing the ground for the compromise between liberal constitutional demands and conservative constitutional ideas in the German Constitutions of 1867–71. The failure to include a list of fundamental rights in those Constitutions was not unintentional. Yet Germans continued to hope and trust, with the American president, that this Constitution would progress toward a recognition of basic rights.[53] In part, however, the Con-

---

228 (1979): 5ff.; Georg G. Iggers, *The German Conception of History* (Middletown, CT, 1968); Francis W. Coker, *Organismic Theories of the State* (New York, 1910).

51. Jörg-Detlef Kühne, "Die Bedeutung der Genossenschaftslehre für die moderne Verfassung," *Zeitschrift für Parlamentsfragen* 15 (1984): 559ff.; John D. Lewis, *The Genossenschafts-Theory of Otto von Gierke: A Study in Political Thought* (Madison, WI, 1935).

52. Cf. Michael Stolleis, "Verwaltungslehre und Verwaltungswissenschaft, 1803–1866," in Kurt G.A. Jeserich et al., eds., *Deutsche Verwaltungsgeschichte*, vol. 2 (Stuttgart, 1983), 78ff.

53. See Rochau, *Grundsätze der Realpolitik* (see n. 28), n. 16.

stitution sought to offer a new alternative to the extreme of Western ideas of individual freedom on the one hand and czarism on the other.[54]

Political Forces in the Community

Our discussion of the contemporary development of constitutional rights would be incomplete without a brief look at the political forces shaping the formation of constitutional ideas. For my purpose it may be sufficient to recall the German five-party system[55] which offered opponents of the Constitution the option of using the tactic of "divide and rule." Yet in 1848–49, of the five principal political groups or forces – Liberal, Democratic, Conservative, Catholic, and Socialist – only the first three played any meaningful role. Moreover, with the exception of the Conservatives, all groups were in favor of fundamental rights. The strongest proponents of civil liberties, as well as of constitutionalism, were the Liberals, with a share of about 45 percent of the constitutional coalition in the National Assembly. The Liberals were, however, split into several groups. The principal Liberal groups consisted of delegates from southwestern Germany, who placed a stronger emphasis on individual liberties, and of delegates from northern Germany, who adhered to a more state-oriented organizational liberalism. For historical reasons, both subgroups supported constitutional monarchy and were repelled by the terror of the French Revolution. Their notions of fundamental rights were primarily derived from middle-class values; and it was to the middle class that they were prepared to give overwhelming influence in the state

---

54. The slogans used to distance it from Western constitutions were Ireland, Indians, slavery, and corrupt parties in parliament. Cf. Rochau, *Grundsätze der Realpolitik* (see n. 28), 212 (Indians); on L. Bucher, see McClelland, *The German Historians and England* (see n. 14), 116f. (party corruption in England); Hänel, *Die Unionsverfassung* (see n. 14), 796 (party corruption in the United States), 801 (limitations of civil rights); Seydel, "Verfassung und Verfassungsgeschichte" (see n. 14), 54 (*Dred Scott* case and no-coercion doctrine). For a favorable view in the sense of a positive German compensatory replacement for further guarantees of freedom in France and England through strong decentralization by richly outlined bodies of self-government, Fritz Fleiner, "Beamtenstaat und Volksstaat (1916)," in Fanny Fleiner, ed., *Ausgewählte Reden und Schriften* (Zurich, 1941), 143; Otto von Gierke, *Der germanische Staatsgedanke* (Berlin, 1919), 24; in general, Bernd Faulenbach, *Ideologie des deutschen Weges* (Munich, 1980), 5ff., 214ff.

55. Huber, *Deutsche Verfassungsgeschichte* (see n. 1), 2: 324ff.

through the electoral system.[56] This most competent and creative coalition for constitutional development, as an organizational unity, did not survive the failure of the Revolution because the reaction restricted its scope through massive limitations on the freedom of association (cf. item g). After 1850, political associations were only permitted during an election and only for the purpose of nominating candidates. Except for that limited period standing party organizations were strictly prohibited; this limitation was only allowed to lapse at the end of the nineteenth century.[57] This prevented the creation of a strong Liberal party organization as well as the emergence of any distinct Liberal leadership.

The Democrats, who represented about 25 percent of the delegates in the National Assembly, had their roots in the middle class. They were republican egalitarians and thus stood for unlimited electoral rights, even of the lower classes. Interestingly enough, this group did not experience any growth despite the failure of the Revolution; the Liberals did not adopt their views. The famous case of G.G. Gervinus was an exception; yet even he was more moderate. He had "full sympathy"[58] for all efforts on behalf of the masses, but in comparison with the American democracy he preferred the English monarchy. The Democratic movement left the political arena after 1850 by exile and emigration of its leaders, by electoral boycott as a protest against the reaction, and because of police repression, which sought to block its coalition with labor movements. Until the middle of the 1860s, Democrats were predominately found in the left segments of the Liberal groupings, while a smaller portion of them joined the growing Socialist party.[59]

The Socialist and Catholic parties were the only ones based on a

56. Cf. Botzenhart, *Deutscher Parlamentarismus* (see n. 4), 132ff., 663ff.; Rose Carol, "The Issue of Parliamentary Suffrage at the Frankfurt National Assembly," *Central European History* 5 (1972): 139ff.

57. Kühne, *Reichsverfassung der Paulskirche* (see n. 4), 409ff.

58. Cf. Jonathan F. Wagner, "Georg Gottfried Gervinus nach der Revolution," in Christian Probst, ed., *Darstellungen und Quellen zur Geschichte der deutschen Einheitsbewegung im 19. und 20. Jahrhundert* (Heidelberg, 1978), 177, letter to Baron von Rutenberg dated May 6, 1851.

59. For the forty-eighters cf. J. Fröbel, who became liberal: Rainer Koch, *Demokratie und Staat bei Julius Fröbel, 1805–1893* (Wiesbaden, 1978); and J. Jacoby, who became socialist: Edmund Silberner, *Johann Jacoby* (Bonn, 1976).

distinct weltanschauung. The Socialists stood for the battle of workers against industrial and other poverty and favored fundamental rights. The Catholics had their own concerns, including the effort to have Austria incorporated in the German nation in order to maintain the numerical parity of religions.[60]

Finally there were the Conservatives, whose motto, "authority instead of majority," revealed them as the only party opposed to all changes. Their conservatism was thoroughly monarchical and thus had no parallel in the United States.[61] Conservative constitutional notions were based upon the idea of restricting the predominance of the monarchy as little as possible. Basically, the Conservatives envisioned an administrative rather than a constitutional state. Carl Schurz put it well in a conversation with Bismarck, when he stated that in a monarchy individual things are handled very well, but the greater issues can go very badly.[62] In view of the minimal support which they had from the public, with only about 12 percent of the seats in the National Assembly, the Conservatives owed their political successes to support from the monarchs. This included the state governments, the upper chambers, the professional civil service, and not the least, the military.[63] It also included the advantageous electoral edicts, which added to their numbers.

Despite this opposition to the popular will, both in Austria and in Prussia, after the mid-1860s the Conservatives began to cooperate with the Liberals, producing successes in the field of fundamental rights through ordinary legislation. The famous Berlin law professor and social theorist Otto Gierke,[64] in commenting on an aphorism of Lincoln, put his finger on the central difference be-

---

60. On socialism and pauperism cf. Karl Jantke and Dietrich Hilger, *Die Eigentumslosen* (Freiburg and Munich, 1965); Paul H. Noyes, *Organization and Revolution: Working-Class Associations in the German Revolution of 1848/49* (Princeton, NJ, 1966); on Catholicism cf. Georg G. Windell, *The Catholics and German Unity, 1866–71* (Minneapolis, MN, 1954), 5ff.

61. On American conservatism cf. Günter Doeker, "Konservativismus in den Vereinigten Staaten," *Der Staat* 12 (1973): 369f.

62. Cf. *Otto von Bismarck: Die gesammelten Werke*, vol. 7 (Berlin, ²1924), 238f., conversation with Carl Schurz on January 28/29, 1868.

63. Cf. the pertinent good observations in Gierke, "German Constitutional Law in Its Relation to the American Constitution" (see n. 14), 289; Kühne, *Reichsverfassung der Paulskirche* (see n. 4), 297ff.

64. Gierke, *Der germanische Staatsgedanke* (see n. 54), 19; in his Gettysburg address on November 19, 1863: Lincoln had said, "the government of the people, by the people, and for the people."

tween the Prussian monarchical and the American republican systems: the former, although consisting of most able experts, could only be a government for the people and not a government of and by the people.

Other Aspects of Achieving Freedom

Constitutional Structure

The Rule of Law

Not only was constitutionalism not achieved after 1848–49, but other basic rights were also not fully realized. A joke common in Berlin had it that the only lasting success of the constitutional reforms was the right to smoke in public.[65] Nevertheless, the demands for basic individual rights continued to be an important goal. Through their discussion in the Frankfurt Parliament and their elaboration in the Paulskirche Constitution as well as in the constituent assemblies of the German states, they became a major element in the political demands of the people. They influenced the political consciousness so strongly that even the reaction to the Revolution did not seek to overturn them completely. That was particularly true of those rights (item d) that sought to establish the rule of law in place of administrative or police arbitrariness.

The demand for rule of law is a specific German form of the modern desire for freedom. Functionally, the demand for rule of law was designed to bypass the Conservatives' blockade of state legislatures by assigning to the third branch of government, the judiciary, a new and crucial role. The special meaning and importance of the German concept *Rechtsstaat* stems from the fact that, in contrast to most Western European states, legal modernization took place through the judiciary and not through the legislative branch.

The demand for a *Rechtsstaat*[66] called for the institutional separation of executive and judicial branches. This aspiration was largely accomplished in the period covered by this report; but it was

65. Rudolf Stadelmann, *Soziale und politische Geschichte der Revolution von 1848* (Darmstadt, ²1962), 195.
66. Kühne, *Reichsverfassung der Paulskirche* (see n. 4), 334ff.

accomplished at the expense of the administrative unity that had been established to overcome the privileges of the feudal courts. For similar reasons the personal independence of judges was also realized at the same time. The Conservative forces were limited to efforts to influence the organization of the courts and the division of their jurisdiction.

After the lawlessness of the police state during the reaction of the 1850s, the *Rechtsstaat* began to gain ground in the course of the 1860s, slowly binding the state administration to statutes and laws. The Paulskirche Constitution would have accomplished this same goal through the formula of equality before the law.

Establishment of the principle of rule of law was particularly helped by the introduction of trial by jury established in 1848–49 (items d, k). Because of their liberal Democratic roots, juries opposed reactionary legal demands by producing acquittal rates as high as 70 to 80 percent in trials involving political offenses; no wonder that in the 1850s Conservatives succeeded in sharply curtailing jury activity in this field. Here, as in the case of other basic rights, regional differences appeared. The two states that showed the greatest resistance to these March proposals for juries were those which, through their intransigence, had caused the failure of the Paulskirche Constitution, Prussia and Austria. Other states either accommodated themselves or like Bavaria and Württemberg sought to camouflage the results. After 1850 they no longer published the acquittal rates for jury trials.[67]

Limitation of the use of the jury, however, stood in contrast to the creation of another special jurisdiction in the 1860s, which even today has no full counterpart in the Anglo-Saxon world – the administrative law courts, which included lay members. Here citizens could seek justice against administrative decisions which affected them. The actions of the police in particular were subject to this jurisdiction.[68]

On the other hand, constitutional adjudication was more limited. It was generally made available in Austria after 1867. The form of constitutional jurisdiction there may have alleviated monarchical concerns because the court had no authority to set aside adminis-

67. Ibid., 404; for Bavaria, Information of the Hauptstaatsarchiv München.
68. Walter Jellinek, *Verwaltungsrecht* (Berlin, ³1931), 92ff.; for the Swiss, Fritz Fleiner, "Deutschlands Verfassungswandlungen (1919)," in Fleiner, ed., *Ausgewählte Schriften und Reden* (see n. 54), 401.

trative decisions but only the jurisdiction to state the proper rule of law.[69] At the same time, however, the constituent Reichstag of the North German Confederation declined to include a constitutional court in its Constitution. It is interesting to note that this was done on the basis of the experience of the American Civil War: opponents noted that constitutional adjudication had not been able to prevent that war.[70]

The material elements of rule of law should also be discussed. These are the concepts of justice included in all of the fundamental rights, particularly personal and economic freedom, freedom of movement, equality, freedom of the press, freedom of religion, academic freedom, and freedom of assembly. These rights were realized only very slowly. The most progressive example and much copied model was the Judiciary Act of Hanover which provided for the right to habeas corpus.[71]

The provision for the protection of ethnic minorities (item s), which was influenced by the Austrian experience, is worth a special note. This provision for dealing with the very serious problem of equal treatment of ethnic minorities in central Europe reflected a kind of supranational patriotism shaped in large part by the transnational consciousness of the Old Empire of 1806, which differed substantially from later European nationalism.[72] In 1867 Austria developed norms for minority rights that are still in many instances unsurpassed. They represent the most significant contribution of that country to the development of modern human rights.[73]

Up to 1867 other basic rights, especially those which depended upon German unity, such as freedom of movement (item n), were

69. Cf. Ermacora, *Handbuch der Grundfreiheiten und der Menschenrechte* (see n. 33), 1, n. 2; Robert Walter, "Die Organisation des Verfassungsgerichtshofs in historischer Sicht," in *Festschrift Karl Hellbling* (Salzburg, 1971), 731–81. On the jurisdiction of the Austrian *Reichsgericht* and ethnic rights cf. Gerald Stourzh, *Die Gleichberechtigung der Nationalstaaten in der Verfassung und Verwaltung Österreichs, 1848–1918* (Vienna, 1985).

70. Kühne, *Reichsverfassung der Paulskirche* (see n. 4), 115f.

71. Huber, *Deutsche Verfassungsgeschichte* (see n. 1), 3: 209; Thomas Klein, "Königreich Hannover," in Kurt G.A. Jeserich et al., eds., *Deutsche Verwaltungsgeschichte* (see n. 52), 2: 708ff.

72. Valentin, *Geschichte der Deutschen Revolution* (see n. 4), 2: 583ff.; Hans Rothfels, "1848–1948 – One Hundred Years After," *Journal of Modern History* 20 (1948): 296.

73. Karl Gottfried Hugelmann, ed., *Das Nationalitätenrecht im alten Österreich* (Vienna, 1934); Stourzh, *Die Gleichberechtigung der Nationalstaaten* (see n. 69).

particularly restricted. Until 1866, within the German *Bund* this right was limited to freedom of movement within the territory of one's own principality. Movement between German states was burdened by charges for new residents, by massive property requirements for entry, and by the authority of police to deport unwanted citizens of other principalities. After 1867, restrictions were swept away in the several states by unified parallel legislation.[74]

It is worth noting that Conservative resistance to basic rights was reduced when it became obvious that those rights led to increased antipathy between groups in society. By doing so, they reduced resistance to monarchical groups. Such was the case with geographical mobility, which in 1848–49 had been intentionally provided for self-employed persons as well as for workers. One-sided restriction of the right for workers only served after 1850 to increase conflicts between capitalists and workers.[75]

Provisions for the Social State

From a modern perspective it is surprising that the basic rights listed above did not contain a guarantee for private property. Guarantee of private property against the state was not a significant issue in that period. The real problem was, as the Paulskirche Constitution made clear, one of freeing property from feudal limitations. The American observer must find it rather strange that as late as the middle of the last century substantial elements of medieval duties (taxes, feudal dues, personal service, etc.) were still being exacted in rural areas. The freeing of peasants from such obligations, accomplished in France by the Revolution, first started in Germany at the beginning of the nineteenth century but, despite substantial progress, had not yet been completed. The Revolution of 1848 gave the last push toward defeudalization and immediate allotment of land. The governments accomplished this by providing partial reimbursement to feudal lords through special agencies. Thus freed from feudal dues, property owners not only won

---

74. Mack Walker, *German Hometowns* (Ithaca, NY, 1971); Kühne, *Reichsverfassung der Paulskirche* (see n. 4), 208ff.

75. Dieter Langewiesche, *Liberalismus und Demokratie in Württemberg zwischen Revolution und Reichsgründung* (Düsseldorf, 1974), 223; Kühne, *Reichsverfassung der Paulskirche* (see n. 4), 238ff.

immediate freehold rights but were in return required to remit payments to the same agencies over a long period of time. This rural transition led to sweeping changes in Austria, in Württemberg, and, with respect to hunting rights, in Prussia. It ensured that, even during 1848–49, the peasants remained satisfied with their situation and refrained from supporting the Revolution.[76]

The social state provisions of 1848–49 were not intended to be limited to the rural world. For artisans and craftsmen, the inclusion of geographical mobility (item n) was intended to restore the favorable aspects of the former guilds. Here the Paulskirche Constitution provided not only for sickness, accident, and old-age insurance for workers in industry but also for workers' participation in the management of factories, an extraordinary provision at that time. Both solutions were not fully realized in the period of this report; but they demonstrate the extraordinarily far-reaching views of the drafters of the Constitution.[77] They provided the fundamental basis both for Bismarck's social legislation and for the later creation of the social state in Germany, the latter viewed as the most important contribution of Germany to modern constitutional thought.

Other social state measures, which were partially successful, are:[78]

- The elimination of financial burdens on printers (item k) in order to make newspapers less expensive and further the political education of the masses
- In education (item p), support of teachers' salaries through the state and elimination of tuition for primary schools and for those unable to pay even for secondary schools
- In the area of freedom of emigration (item o), the state's concern for human dignity in ocean transportation, protection against financial swindles, and information about desirable areas for settlement

76. Christof Dipper, *Die Bauernbefreiung in Deutschland* (Stuttgart, 1980); for Austria cf. Ernst Bruckmüller, "Die Grundherren, die Bauern, und die Revolution," in *Hans Kudlich und die Bauernbefreiung in Niederösterreich* (see n. 16), 57–76.

77. Hans-Jürgen Teuteberg, *Geschichte der industriellen Mitbestimmung* (Tübingen, 1961), 59ff.; Donald G. Rohr, *The Origins of Social Liberalism in Germany* (Chicago, IL and London, 1963), 158ff.

78. Cf. Kühne, *Reichsverfassung der Paulskirche* (see n. 4), 224ff., 395f., 507ff.

Individual Examples

Freedom of Assembly and Freedom of the Press

As already indicated, these two basic rights (items g and k) were not fully realized before 1871. Since they were based upon a division between private and political use of basic rights, however, they were partially accepted. This led to the following rule – as claims of basic rights were increasingly considered private, that is, of an unpolitical nature, they had to cope with increasingly less obstacle, and vice versa.

In concrete terms this meant that literature, societies, and associations experienced extraordinary growth as long as they were apolitical, for example, scholarly. Political organizations, however, were faced with the major restrictions of freedom of assembly and press; previously mentioned prohibitions on the creation of political parties, as well as prohibitions of coalitions of workers, remained in force. The latter were repealed for business and industrial workers in the middle of the 1860s, but were maintained for agricultural workers through 1918.[79] Even freedom of religious association (item r) was limited to the three great churches. A strong movement toward sects that would have led to a multiplication of churches and provided cultural support for democratic ideals was thus restricted.[80]

In the political area press freedom was more severely restricted. The press was influenced by the state through a mixture of financial support for newspapers and police repression of opposition journals. As a consequence in Prussia within a period of only six months in 1850 the number of opposition newspapers was limited, while progovernment or politically neutral papers declined by only 10 percent; in Bavaria opposition papers fell from about 30 to 16 percent by 1853. On average no more than a quarter of the newspapers could be classified as critical of state governments. In addition, seizure of press runs and trials of editors remained threats

79. Cf. Kühne, *Reichsverfassung der Paulskirche* (see n. 4), 244f., 405ff.
80. Ferdinand Kampe, *Geschichte der religiösen Bewegung der neueren Zeit*, vol. 4: *Geschichte des Deutschkatholicismus und freien Protestantismus in Deutschland und Nordamerika von 1848–1858* (Leipzig, 1860), 209ff.; Kühne, *Reichsverfassung der Paulskirche* (see n. 4), 304ff., 487f.

against the press especially after – contrary to the right expressed in item k – the right to jury trial had been withdrawn in the first half of the 1850s. As late as the 1870s the acquittal rate in press trials without juries was about 50 percent lower than in southern Germany, where the jury trial for press freedom cases had been retained.[81] It requires no further elaboration to say that these inhibitions also reduced the freedom of voters to elect members of the legislatures. After 1867 hopes for improved civil liberty provisions in the Constitution focused principally on these rights. Yet liberals such as H. Kudlich and C. Schurz,[82] who had emigrated to America, as well as those in Germany were again disappointed.

Substitutes for the Right of Resistance

While there was no normative formulation of a right of resistance in 1848–49, the Paulskirche Constitution contained certain substitutes: the creation of a militia (item f), the right of petition (item h), the right to emigrate (item o), and freedom of belief (item r).

These were realized in different ways. After 1848 the right to petition was widely accepted. In the 1850s the courts even admitted within limits a direct application of the Constitution as law in order to mitigate widespread fears of a second revolution. This led to the use of the right of petition as a way of ventilating complaints without making commitments to change anything. In a similar way, there were also concessions in the field of freedom of belief. Despite close connections between church and state, after 1848 people were not only allowed to move from one denomination to another but even to leave churches altogether and to adopt atheism as their creed. Here too the courts accepted the direct application of individual rights, at least to some extent. Freedom of emigration was seen as a useful tool against pauperism and as a means to ease social and political pressures. Certain state limitations nevertheless remained, such as the duty to serve in the military. But after 1871 all financial charges for emigration were eliminated.[83]

The creation of an armed militia – the Paulskirche Constitution

81. Kühne, *Reichsverfassung der Paulskirche* (see n. 4), 403ff.
82. Ref. to Kudlich, cf. Wittke, *Refugees of the Revolution* (see n. 13), 364; ref. to Carl Schurz, cf. Trefousse, "The German-American Immigrants and the Newly Founded *Reich*" (see n. 16), 164ff.
83. Kühne, *Reichsverfassung der Paulskirche* (see n. 4), 219ff., 422ff., 479ff.

had originally conceived the militia in terms of the right of the people to arm themselves – was dropped in view of the opposition of the Prussian monarch, with whom the liberal constitutional movement wished to ally itself. In 1848–49 militias were formed in many areas, but after 1850 they were sharply reduced, even where they had existed before 1848. In 1860, Prussia eliminated the militia that it had created during the Napoleonic wars. Württemberg formally adopted this constitutional idea once again in 1868, only to have it repealed after the unification of 1871 for the sake of conformity with the common military laws of the New Empire.[84]

The systematic restrictions of these rights revealed once more the naked face of monarchical power, which in this period not only opposed revolutionary, but also evolutionary introduction of basic political rights. Yet this statement must be qualified, for at this time basic freedoms, in the narrowest sense, were available to individuals. But as soon as their exercise became closely associated with political action or with the forming of political associations, they encountered more opposition. This prevented any decisive influence of the people on the government of the states.

These restraints had direct results on the people's perception of the foreign policy of the German *Bund*. For its ingeniously regulated concept of a balance between German expansion and foreign invasion was not only poorly understood but increasingly rejected. The results for Europe are well known. The alternative of greater freedom within the German *Bund* unfortunately remained untried.[85] Without speculating too much, it appears that greater freedoms could have not only limited emigration but provided opportunities for the repeatedly proposed inner colonization of the eastern areas of Austria and Prussia. Thus German lack of greater political freedom became advantageous to the United States.

---

84. Manfred Messerschmidt, "Die politische Geschichte der preußisch-deutschen Armee," in Militärgeschichtliches Forschungsamt, ed., *Handbuch der deutschen Militärgeschichte*, vol. 2 (Munich, 1972), 79ff.; Paul Sauer, *Das württembergische Heer in der Zeit des Deutschen und Norddeutschen Bundes* (Stuttgart, 1958).

85. Cf. Theodor Schieder, "Vom Deutschen Bund zum Deutschen Reich," in Bruno Gebhardt, ed., *Handbuch der deutschen Geschichte*, 4 vols. (Stuttgart, ⁹1970), 3: 105f.; typical of the refusals is Rochau, *Grundzüge der Realpolitik* (see n. 28), 246ff.. For the corresponding foreign contentment with the German federation and foreign discontent with German unification see Otto Pflanze, ed., *The Unification of Germany, 1848–1871* (New York, 1968); Werner E. Mosse, *The European Powers and the German Question, 1848–1871* (New York, 1969).

9.1
The Evolution of Civil Rights Legislation into Practice

Fred L. Morrison

These comments are divided into three parts. Two of the parts are directed to the two papers individually. The third states some general propositions, providing parallels between the two papers and setting forth some hypotheses for further discussion.

Comments on Professor Hyman's Paper

Professor Hyman's paper presents an interesting critique of the interpretation of the Fourteenth Amendment (and of the broader implications of the Thirteenth Amendment) in the period from roughly 1880 through 1954. The basic theme of the paper is one well recognized in legal and historical scholarship in the United States. Some of the commentary, however, seems to me to be unsupportable.

It is clear that the "original intent" of the post–Civil War amendments, the Thirteenth, Fourteenth, and Fifteenth, was to protect slaves or former slaves. That original understanding was first implemented in legislation and in litigation that protected the rights of blacks in the United States. The protection was even extended, in the *Slaughterhouse* cases, to other groups in the United States. Within two decades, however, that purpose was subverted, and the protections of the Civil War amendments were turned to quite different purposes. It was only in the current generation that these protections were again truly extended to black Americans, in *Brown v. Board of Education* and subsequent cases. I will comment further about the underlying causes of this diversion in a subsequent part of this presentation.

Professor Hyman suggests that an emergence of legal positivism is responsible for this development. I would argue that quite the

233

opposite is true. A "positivist" interpretation of these amendments would have led to the opposite result. Indeed, the dissent of the elder justice Harlan in *Plessy v. Ferguson* is the epitome of a positivist argument; it focuses on the text and on the purpose of constitutional legislator at the time of the adoption and ratification of the Fourteenth Amendment. The majority in *Plessy*, like the majority in *Lochner v. New York*, is *not* overtly positivistic; rather it is teleological in its orientation, attempting to use the Constitution to achieve a certain result. After all, in his famous statement about Herbert Spencer's *Social Statics* in *Lochner*, Justice Holmes did not complain of an overly narrow and technical legal interpretation of the due process clause, but rather of the importation of extraneous social and historical concepts. The positivists of this time were the dissenters Harlan and Holmes, respectively, not the majority of the Court.

Likewise, I would be critical of the suggestion that there was a gap in the use of the Fourteenth Amendment from roughly the 1870s to 1937. There were a number of instances in which the amendment was effectively applied against state governments. It was used to impose "substantive" due process limitations on their legislation and was the apparent theoretical basis for the assertion of constitutional free speech and religious liberty claims in cases like *Near* and *Society of Sisters*. The Fourteenth Amendment did not die or go into hibernation from 1870 to 1937; rather it was diverted to other uses.

The reasons for the changes in constitutional interpretation in the latter part of the nineteenth century are complex. They range from intentional misrepresentation of the legislative history of the amendments by advocates for certain positions to waning political enthusiasm for Reconstruction. Positivism was, in itself, hardly a factor.

Finally, I would come to the defense of my former teacher, the late Grant Gilmore. I do not think he was "grousing" about legal history in the comment quoted. Anyone who has read his work would know that he was instead asserting that legal scholarship cannot be properly done without adequate consideration of the historical perspective. Far from repudiating historians, he was saying that we should all be historians.

Comments on Professor Kühne's Paper

My comments on Professor Kühne's paper must be more limited. The evaluation of German legal history must come from the German historians and lawyers present here today.

Professor Kühne's discussion is unfortunately too limited to the legal aspects of constitutional rights and does not place them clearly into the context of the political, social, and economic history of the time. Perhaps, as a foreigner, I require more explicit background than do my German colleagues. I suggest that German constitutional thought of the time was attempting to limit governmental power, to "build down" from a tradition that had included near-absolute monarchical power. In contrast, American constitutional thought was "building up" by granting powers to government, albeit subject to a bill of rights, from a basic proposition under which Englishmen had certain rights according to common law, even without constitutional protection. This has a great impact on constitutional interpretation. Comparisons must bear that difference in mind.

I would also give emphasis to the legal context of the time. Professor Kühne's paper is restricted primarily to the constitutional limitations on great acts of state: limits on statutes, ordinances, and other sovereign acts. There is another aspect of constitutional law that is also important – its use to limit the administration of government. In the United States, the vast bulk of constitutional law practice is directed to preventing administrators from violating constitutional rights rather than testing the validity of statutes. By definition, in Germany that falls outside the sphere of constitutional law, in the fields of administrative or public law, as they are more broadly defined. Yet in these areas, individual rights were receiving substantial protection from the petty abuses of petty (and not-so-petty) bureaucrats through the administrative law reforms introduced by Stein and others. In this respect German law during this period was introducing principles of constitutionalism, but was calling them something else. Professor Kühne mentions this in passing, but it is really a significant development.

General Propositions

Finally, I would like to propose two general propositions about the rights discussed in these two papers.

Proposition A

In the presentations in these two papers, we see two noble mid-nineteenth-century experiments to protect individual rights. Both were eclipsed. The Constitution of the Frankfurt Paulskirche was eclipsed by the forces of monarchy and nationalism and never came into being; the Prussian king and Bismarck prevailed in the short run. The Civil War amendments came into force, but were rapidly diverted to purposes other than those intended by their framers; they protected railroads and economic investors, rather than individuals, for most of the period 1880–1950.

In both cases, the full original purpose was eventually realized. The catalog of rights of Frankfurt of 1849 was largely incorporated into the Weimar Constitution of 1919, and has more recently been taken up in the *Grundgesetz*. The protections of the Fourteeth Amendment of 1868 were eventually more fully realized in *Brown* in 1954. In each case roughly seventy to eighty years intervened between the first articulation of these rights and their real legal efficacy. Such a time lapse may have been necessary in order to digest them and their implications into the functioning legal system.

My hypothesis is that, in both systems, the emergence of a greater national economic uniformity was a necessary precondition to the establishment of national civil and political rights. So long as individuals thought of themselves as Pennsylvanians or as Bavarians, they would have little concern about the political or civil rights of those in other states. Only when they thought of themselves, in first instances, as Americans or Germans, would their reaction change from "they can't do that *there*" to "they can't do that *here*." That change is essential to human-rights thinking.

I would suggest that in our time two great evolutions have contributed to this change. The first was an economic revolution that centered around improved transportation. The emergence of the railroad made interstate commerce much more competitive with local industries. In Germany this led to the elimination of customs barriers and demands for the unification of civil and commercial law, originally through parallel legislation and ultimately through the adoption of the Civil Code. In the United States it led to demands by interstate railroads and other businesses for protection of their property and of other economic interests against local discriminatory legislation. (This accounts for much of the deviation from the original purpose of the Fourteenth Amendment discussed above.) Economic interests of out-of-state traders and investors did not immediately lead to a parallel interest in political and civil rights throughout the nation.

The second was a revolution of communications and of personal mobility. The economic changes introduced by free trade certainly contributed to it, for investors and businessmen moved more easily from state to state. Technological improvements in communications were also a great force. The end of legally sanctioned racial discrimination in the United States coincided with the emergence of nationally broadcast television news. Events on the streets of the South suddenly became "our problem" rather than "their problem," and the political will to deal with them suddenly increased. Economic unification may have been a necessary precondition to this sense of political unity which is, in turn, necessary to a *Grundnorm* establishing a constitutional system.

Proposition B

My second hypothesis is principally directed to the paper by Professor Hyman. It is simple. The genius of American constitutional interpretation is neither its faithfulness to constitutional text, nor its regard for history, but rather its adjustment to current, but long-term, political understandings. After the abolition of the legal institution of slavery, the popular interest in human equality waned; the most visible excess of discrimination had been eliminated. The political imagination turned toward the opening of the West and the development of American economic institutions. The Supreme Court followed that change in the intellectual current of the United States and applied the Fourteenth Amendment for the protection of the interests of business. Only when the conscience of America was awakened to the plight of minorities, in part through

237

the Second World War, did constitutional interpretation return to the original intent of the Fourteenth Amendment.

I might add that the single major counterexample to this proposition is to be found in *Dred Scott*. The Supreme Court may have decided that case in conformity to the text of the Constitution, but contrary to a rapidly expanding social conscience against slavery. The result was civil war.

In this context, I would contrast the extremely detailed provisions of most of the German constitutional instruments with the broad general principles of the American document. The broad provisions of the latter text and the traditions of common law have given the U.S. Supreme Court more of an opportunity for flexibility of interpretation than has been present in Germany. That flexibility may be a factor in the durability of the U.S. Constitution and may have made it possible for us to celebrate a two-hundredth birthday this year.

9.2
The Theoretical Precociousness of German Civil Rights

Diethelm Klippel

There are two objections to the general validity of a German *Sonderweg* in history, which supposedly lasted for a number of centuries.[1] On the one hand, this concept does not reflect its theoretical preconditions, which require at least a comparative approach and rule out recourse to a very general contrast within the Western tradition. However, I do not intend to comment on this point at present. On the other hand, influenced by such a concept, early modern historiography has neglected historical material that would modify the idea of a German *Sonderweg* in certain periods of history, refute that notion, or apply reductio ad absurdum to it. This is the topic of my comment today.

The latter argument relates to the history of the German concept of freedom, which cannot be regarded as having been either "unpolitical" or "authoritarian"[2] over the past centuries, as Leonard Krieger has suggested.[3] Furthermore, it is not true that the history of the basic freedoms in Germany has not evolved in the context of a theory of the separation of state and society and therefore did not take the individual into account.[4] Both aspects have been evident since the end of the eighteenth century, when liberal and occasionally democratic political ideas emerged.

Liberal and democratic rights that correspond to those of the

---

1. I am grateful to S. McCaskill for this translation. See David Blackbourn and Geoff Eley, *The Peculiarities of German History: Bourgeois Society and Politics in 19th-Century Germany* (Oxford, 1984); *Deutscher Sonderweg – Mythos oder Realität?* Kolloquien des Instituts für Zeitgeschichte (Munich, 1982).

2. Cf. only the article "Freiheit" in Otto Brunner, Werner Conze, and Reinhart Koselleck, eds., *Geschichtliche Grundbegriffe historisches Lexikon zur politisch-sozialen Sprache in Deutschland*, 6 vols. to date (Stuttgart, 1972–), 2: 425–542.

3. *The German Idea of Freedom: History of a Political Tradition* (1957, repr. Chicago, IL and London, 1972).

4. For a different view cf. Jörg-Detlef Kühne, "Civil Rights and German Constitutional Thought, 1848–1871," above, 199–232.

American Bill of Rights and the French Declaration of the Rights of Man can be found in Germany as early as the last quarter of the eighteenth century.[5] Contemporary writing, especially that focusing on natural-rights philosophy, developed whole catalogs of human rights that are referred to as inalienable, absolute, unchangeable, and holy. They include, among other rights, the human right to one's personality, profession, trade, property, expression, press and religion, and in part, equality. No doubt all these rights were deduced from the nature of man and, in particular, his personality. The formulation of these rights is directed against the state and is resistant to it: "Those with whom the highest power resides have to accept as their first and foremost law the respect for the rights of mankind."[6]

The process of the conceptual division of state and society also originated in the eighteenth century; since that time the basic freedoms cannot be understood solely as a claim of the individual but of the civic society as a whole. Since about 1780, the concepts of "civic society" (*societas civilis*) and "state" (*civitas, res publica*) have gradually ceased to be used as synonyms in Germany.[7] As early as 1782, in the works of Samuel Simon Witte, we find a surprisingly farsighted theory of the separation of state and society as well as the notion of the state's obligation to respect the autonomous aims of the civic society, regarded essentially as a freely trading competing society consisting of proprietors and tradesmen. The "alliance, which can be referred to as an alliance of power, a political or state alliance," has to be clearly distinguished from the "civic society," the "society of property," the "alliance which aims at the mutual satisfaction of needs by means of a mutual free turnover of products, of abilities or of properties and goods";[8] Witte eventually states the "principle that the state alliance has to be subordinated to the civic alliance because the former is merely an instrument to further the purpose of the latter."[9]

5. For this and the following see Diethelm Klippel, *Politische Freiheit und Freiheitsrechte im deutschen Naturrecht des 18. Jahrhunderts* (Paderborn, 1976), 113ff.

6. Leopold Friedrich Fredersdorff, *System des Rechts der Natur* (Braunschweig, 1790), 421.

7. See Manfred Riedel, "Gesellschaft, bürgerliche," in Brunner, Conze, and Koselleck, eds., *Geschichtliche Grundbegriffe* (see n. 2), 2: 753.

8. Samuel Simon Witte, *Ueber die Schicklichkeit der Aufwandsgesetze* (Leipzig, 1782), 62.

9. Ibid., 64.

The fact that the concepts illustrated above – that is, those relating the rights of freedom to the individual as well as to the theoretical separation of state and society – were an ongoing concern in the political theory of the nineteenth century is of major importance. This has often been demonstrated for the separation of state and society;[10] it is, for the nineteenth as well as for the twentieth century, a basic proposition accepted not only in liberal political and economic teachings. It is also true for the deduction of the basic freedoms of the individual; for many nineteenth-century authors, arguments involving the nature of the human personality form the basis for the deduction of fundamental and human rights, even if the theory of birthrights is losing ground with the waning influence of liberal natural-rights philosophy.[11]

10. See Riedel, "Gesellschaft, bürgerliche," in Brunner, Conze, and Koselleck, eds., *Geschichtliche Grundbegriffe* (see n. 2), 2: 753; and for example, Werner Conze, "Das Spannungsfeld von Staat und Gesellschaft im Vormärz," in Werner Conze, ed., *Staat und Gesellschaft im deutschen Vormärz, 1815–1848* (Stuttgart, 1962), 207–69; Ernst-Wolfgang Böckenförde, *Die verfassungstheoretische Unterscheidung von Staat und Gesellschaft als Bedingung der individuellen Freiheit* (Opladen, 1973).
11. See Wolfgang von Rimscha, *Die Grundrechte im süddeutschen Konstitutionalismus* (Cologne, 1973); Diethelm Klippel, "Persönlichkeit und Freiheit: Das 'Recht der Persönlichkeit' in der Entwicklung der Freiheitsrechte im 18. und 19. Jahrhundert," in Günter Birtsch, ed., *Grund- und Freiheitsrechte von der ständischen zur spätbürgerlichen Gesellschaft* (Göttingen, 1987), 269–90.

9.3
Jurisdictional Unity, Cultural Hegemony, and the Impetus for Human Rights

Robert C. Post

The subject of this session is "Civil Rights and National Unity." At first blush the conjunction seems to be an odd one, for what exactly is the relationship between civil rights and national unity? The question is sharply posed by the 1848 list of *Grundrechte* provided by Professor Kühne. The list embraces an astonishingly broad array of civil and political rights, and yet these rights were designed to apply to a diverse group of German states with different and distinct political, civil, and economic cultures. What is the possible connection between these rights and the notion of national unity?

In one sense, of course, the answer to the question is obvious. The uniform enforcement of civil and political rights under the aegis of a national government implies the existence of an unitary national jurisdiction, and this jurisdiction is itself a form of national unity. But the meaning of this unity, as Professor Hyman's discussion of the Thirteenth and Fourteenth Amendments to the U.S. Constitution should remind us, is far from clear. In the United States the Civil War was necessary in order to clarify the issue of national jurisdiction. When the North won, its physical domination of the South was assured, and on the basis of this domination it immediately imposed upon the South a series of civil rights derived from the civil and political culture of the North, rights that were based upon notions of free labor and "freedom national" ideas. The underlying concept was to use federal courts as administrative agencies to transform the culture and customs of the South.

Although after 1865 there was never any real challenge to the concept of national unity based upon the physical supremacy of the North and its ability to assert jurisdiction in the South, the fate of the civil rights created during Reconstruction illustrates the limited nature of this national unity. For when the North lost interest in creating a truly national culture, these rights were largely drained of meaning. As Hyman notes, they received restrictive interpretations and were largely unenforced. Their promise of imposing northern cultural values upon the South went unfulfilled. They abolished slavery, but left in its place a caste system based upon race. In effect they lay fallow until the nation decided after the Second World War to seriously attempt to create a national culture. And for the forty years after the Second World War, Reconstruction constitutional amendments and statutory rights, with some modern additions, were used as the basis of a renewed and determined effort to destroy local southern mores and the caste system they created. Although these rights had remained on the books unchanged for well over seventy years, they were now reinterpreted, revitalized, and renewed.

The lesson, I take it, is that civil and political rights can have a rather complicated relationship to national unity. Such rights can merely be evidence of a national monopoly of force and of a national unity of jurisdiction. Like the sword of Damocles, they can hang in the statute books, letting all know where ultimate power resides. Or, more actively, they can also be the instruments of an aggressive attempt to impose upon local customs the hegemony of a particular political culture. In this context a large and diverse nation can use legal rights as a means of determining which of its many local cultures will survive and dominate and which will be stigmatized as deviant. In this sense, civil rights can imply a national unity not only of power and jurisdiction, but also of ideology as well.

The distinction has interesting implications for the concept of a constitution, which we are all here this week to explore. To examine a relatively simple example, take item g listed by Professor Kühne: "The right of holding meetings under the reserve of a law against abuses." It does not take much thought to see that the issue of when a meeting becomes abusive and thus can be regulated by the law is an intricate and somewhat delicate question. The mere statement of the right does not answer this question. It does not tell us whether meetings are abusive if they are used to advocate illegal acts or if (and only if) they present a clear and present danger of the performance of such acts; it does not clarify if meetings are abusive if they are held on public property without permission or if they disturb the neighbors with amplified sound. The bare statement of the right does not tell us if those wanting to hold a meeting can be required to obtain a permit, and if so, on what terms, or if they can be required to pay a fee or obtain insurance, or if meetings can be subject to time, place, and manner regulations, or if meetings can be regulated if they have cultural rather than explicitly political objectives, and so forth. The shape and nature of the right in Professor Kühne's list thus lies in its actual implementation, which is to say that it depends upon the answers to questions like those that I have raised. No codification of a right, however detailed, can avoid being substantially shaped in response to the infinite number of such unanticipated questions. And the point is that these questions cannot coherently be answered in the absence of a political culture whose assumptions and ideas will permit the generation of coherent principles of analysis. To put the point in the somewhat inflammatory terms of Hans-Georg Gadamer, the interpretation of any right will depend upon existing cultural "prejudices."

Gadamer's point is illustrated by the fact that the line between abusive and nonabusive meetings will depend primarily upon why one wants to protect meetings in the first place, and the answer to that question will in turn presuppose some kind of relationship between, for example, the holding of political meetings and the conduct of government. In the United States it is thought that political sovereignty rests with the people, and so the right to hold meetings is conceived as the right of the sovereign people to decide their own minds so as to instruct their servants, who are government officials, as to how the government is to be conducted. This is a very culturally specific way of interpreting the right.

In the context of the Germany of 1848 in which the *Grundrechte* listed by Professor Kühne were proposed, however, there were numerous diverse states with radically different political cultures ranging from free states to conservative monarchies. In such a context I would argue that item g listed by Professor Kühne could not possibly have been given coherent national application, *unless* one political culture were to dominate all the others. Without such hegemony the right, even if embodied in a national constitution, could remain little more than an abstract symbol of a national unity of jurisdiction.

I elaborate this example to stress the point that constitutions can reflect various kinds and degrees of national unity. This implies that the relationship between constitutional civil rights and principles of federalism is of especial importance. In a federal system it is always necessary to inquire into the nature of national unity, for in varying historical circumstances that unity could reflect fundamentally different social situations. For instance, it could be a unity comprised merely of national jurisdiction, or it could reflect a preexisting political and cultural homogeneity, or it could be founded upon the hegemony of one of a number of competing cultures. In the United States, for example, we have in the past fifty years developed a fascinating situation in which national civil rights regarding freedom of expression rest on cultural concepts of individual autonomy that differ in significant ways from virtually all local or regional American cultures.[1] We have, in other words, seen the rise of civil rights derived from a distinctively national political outlook. The situation should be contrasted with that which obtained during the 1950s and 1960s in the area of racial discrimination, where national civil rights reflected the domination of southern customs by the regional culture of the West and North.

Historical questions regarding the cultural origins and social foundations of national civil rights are thus deeply important, and yet these questions would not even be visible unless civil rights were understood as a form of cultural expression. This point is not, after Durkheim, theoretically controversial. It is now clear that law is itself a cultural artifact. But the historical implications of this insight have yet to be fully exploited. One of the fundamental achievements of the great American historian Perry Miller was to examine the theological writings of the New England Puritans and to demonstrate the cultural meanings that underlay them. Miller, so to speak, appropriated theological doctrine away from the theologians. American legal history still needs its Perry Miller: it is waiting for the historian to take legal doctrine, in all its formidable complexity, away from the lawyers and to illuminate the cultural dynamics that lie beneath it.

The task is so very difficult because in interpreting law we are torn between three conflicting tendencies. The first is to view law as a purely abstract and formal system of rules that create rights, duties, obligations, remedies, and so forth. When, congratulating ourselves on our realism and realpolitik, we reject this view, we often fall into the opposite perspective of seeing law as merely

---

1. Robert C. Post, "The Social Foundations of Defamation Law: Reputation and the Constitution," *California Law Review* 74 (1986): 691–742.

expressive of underlying conditions of economic structure and power. And when we recoil from the cynicism of this Marxist outlook, we fall into yet a third perspective that views law normatively as the aspiration toward universal values of justice. Of course in some sense law is all of these things. But it is also, and here we have found difficulty capturing the right voice – perhaps because law is so much our own contemporary theology – a system of cultural expression like any other.

The task of interpreting law in this way is of particular importance for the study of federal societies, like those in Germany and the United States. This is because federal systems must ultimately be understood as societies in which political power is in some significant ways distributed according to regional cultural distinctions. If society is culturally uniform, I would predict that even the decentralization of national power would not be understood as a form of federalism, but would instead be conceptualized as a question of administration, as an issue in the proper application of instrumental reason.

In the United States, for example, where cultural homogenization is well underway, political scientists have already begun to transform questions of federalism into questions of what they call Intergovernmental Relations, or IGR.[2] The change in vocabulary is important because the ultimate issue for IGR is how to administer large territories efficiently, whereas the question for federalism is always at root one of political, not technocratic, ordering.

If this analysis is accurate, then precisely because of the clash of cultural diversity, national unity will always be problematic in federal states. This is certainly true in the United States, where the meaning of "Americanism" has long been the subject of profound and anguished debate. If I am correct that law can be "read" as a cultural text and if civil rights are for this reason the most systematic and authoritative cultural expression of the values associated with public obligations and the duties and rights of citizenship, then the study of civil rights should prove of central importance in understanding the problematics of national unity in federal societies. Certainly the value of that study is aptly illustrated in the excellent papers by Professors Kühne and Hyman.

2. Harry N. Scheiber, "Federalism and Legal Process: Historical and Contemporary Analysis of the American System," *Law and Society Review* 14 (1980): 663–722.

9.4
Discussion

GERALD STOURZH: I would like to draw your attention to an Austrian development diverging from the German experience. The liberal heritage of the 1848 constitutional achievements – which in Germany took seventy years to realize fully in the Weimar Constitution – only nineteen years later scored a great victory in Austria. For various reasons the compromise of Hungary and the Crown granted great concessions of a liberal constitutional nature, a Bill of Rights in 1867, which is still in force today, and a constitutional court under the name of imperial court (*Reichsgericht*), which started operating in 1869. Thus Austria did become the first country where adjudication of constitutionally guaranteed rights began in the 1870s, continued to 1918, and then were completed and refined under the influence of Hans Kelsen after the First World War, in the Austrian Constitutional Court.

Among the articles of the Austrian Bill of Rights was – and this is interesting in view of the recent Supreme Court decision on ethnic groups – a right guaranteeing to the ethnic groups of Austria equality of language rights in offices, schools, and common life, and from it there developed a judicature of about 150 cases which are of extreme interest.

In Austria, next to the Constitutional Court a high administrative court was set up in 1875 which again, within its competence, has played a very great role in guaranteeing the rights of citizens and individuals against violations of the law by agencies of the state.

JÖRG-DETLEF KÜHNE: There are parallels between Mr. Stourzh's and Mr. Hyman's remarks: The imperial court of Austria has interpreted the *Staatsgrundgesetz* in a very restricted way; today the Constitutional Court is allowed to nullify an administrative act or a statute; the imperial court in Austria, however, had only the right to say that something was against the Constitution and nothing more. Indeed people hoped at the time that the imperial court's declaring something unconstitutional would be accepted by the

247

administration. One has to realize, of course, that such a Constitutional Court was a rather strange animal in a monarchy because the monarchical idea after all presupposed only one seat of final legal competence, that is, the monarch.

GERALD STOURZH: The deficiency Mr. Kühne has mentioned was remedied in 1919 due to the insistence of Hans Kelsen. However, I have examined those cases in which the court ruled something unconstitutional and have found that, in the vast majority, the administration indeed accepted the sentence of the court.

ERICH ANGERMANN: I would like to raise another point. Our national anthem contains one line of text that I believe to be important in the context of our discussion, that is, "Einigkeit und Recht und Freiheit." What this line meant, at least in the mind of the author, Hoffman von Fallersleben, is that the movement for national unity behind all this promised more freedom, more *Grundrechte*, more civil rights. It was the small states of Germany, at least some of them, which restricted that freedom. On the surface there is some similarity to the American situation. I think that, in order to achieve freedom for blacks in the South, it was absolutely necessary to unify the country in terms of its legal structure.

HARTMUT LEHMANN: In the course of the discussion it was suggested that it was perhaps the lack of a unified political culture as a precondition for the effective implementation of civil rights which was missing at that time; Erich Angermann's remark points in the same direction. Now my impression is that in this context we have to treat nationalism very carefully. For nationalism seems to me to be an ambivalent force; on the one hand it certainly serves to unify and create the kind of preconditions mentioned, while on the other hand national unity expressing itself as nationalism might also have generated a kind of nationalism associated with a white Anglo-Saxon Protestant or Prussian Protestant mode of thought. This may have been another reason why civil rights were not given the top priority which they would have otherwise deserved.

JÖRG-DETLEF KÜHNE: "Einigkeit und Recht und Freiheit" are vey important topics in the nineteenth century. Mr. Angermann has advanced the thesis that Germans wanted to achieve "freedom by unification." Yet the other formula, "unification by freedom," was likewise current at the time. To achieve both was the goal of the Paulskirche.

ERICH ANGERMANN: But they did not succeed!

JÖRG-DETLEF KÜHNE: You are correct of course. But this certainly resulted in the *Realpolitiker* losing the connection between freedom and unification; thereafter they wanted unification first and freedom second. My feeling is that in the 1860s the idea of unification joined hands with nationalism while the idea of freedom gradually faded into the background, thus starting the dangerous combination mentioned by Mr. Lehmann.

ERICH ANGERMANN: I must disagree. For I think that even in the 1860s the thrust behind the movement was for freedom. People hoped to achieve it even if they did not succeed to the extent they wanted. Yet it still holds true for the movement as such, despite the failure.

HAROLD MELVIN HYMAN: Professor Morrison illustrated brilliantly why Harvard president and former law dean Derek C. Bok called the teaching and practice of law a flawed system because the kind of professional fossa he employed in his excellent commentary suggests why lawyers and judges desperately need legal history to assist them in their governing task. To illustrate very briefly: he talked about *Yick Wo.* and *Near*, decisions very famous and important but in a sense almost irrelevant to the major thrust of American race relations, federal-state relations involving civil liberties, etc. *Yick Wo.* and *Near* might well be compared to the great efficiency of the federal governmet and state governments involved during the same decades, for example, in collecting federal revenue for whiskey. Federal government could not enforce civil rights or liberties but could collect taxes in remote Kentucky hamlets. What is the great difference? Government likes to collect money – government does not like to enforce civil liberties? I think that is too simple. According to the reports, federal tax commissioners in large part did not provoke a Whiskey Rebellion all through those decades; instead the federal government was able to get plenty of local people to inform on their neighbors and did not encounter obstacles in the form of local peace officers who cooperated with lawbreakers, as was true with respect to the violation of civil liberties. The practical local level of the law plus federal policy had a great deal to do with it.

In 1873, the year of *Slaughterhouse* and two years after reforms began at Harvard Law School, the statutes of the United States were revised, not quite codified but put into a more coherent form. For some unknown reason the Civil Rights Act of 1866 lost its caption and its paragraphs and clauses were divided haphazardly among all the statutes of the United States. Imagine yourself a solo lawyer with a private practice in the years until the 1911 restatements – a whole generation – to whom a client without much money comes asking for help in a civil rights matter; you go to the available books in the local law library to try to find a law – and cannot find it. I wonder if the realities of that aspect of our constitutional history that did not happen in a sense deserve exploration on this humble level of legal-practice history.

What is the life of law in terms of civil rights and civil liberties in ordinary workaday situations? *Yick Wo.* and *Near* are important illustrations of what could happen under certain circumstances. *Slaughterhouse* is what did happen under rather peculiar circumstances. But in 1873 also *West Publishing* began to feed the legal pedagogues as the legal pedagogues began to feed *West Publishing* and other legal publishers. I do not know what that conjunction of events in 1873 means yet but I am trying to find out.

PAUL FINKELMAN: There is a difference between collecting taxes on whiskey and the enforcement of civil rights. Once you have a license to produce whiskey or once the moonshiner is reported, the revenue agent goes in, but this is not the same as the necessity of day-to-day enforcement of civil rights. There are similar situations to which we can point: the white primary is struck down by court decision but later we discover that the white primary is still in effect after it had been struck down. This is true too for other discriminatory acts in the South which are struck down by court decisions and then are reinstated after a way around the court decision is found. It is not simply a willingness to enforce but the necessity to constantly enforce that is at issue here.

JÖRG-DETLEF KÜHNE: There is a possible similarity between

German and American constitutional law: I found our *Grundrechte* in the period of the restoration, that is in the 1850s, were not self-executing – they were, in other words, in the Constitution but they were worthless in real life. In the United States the Fourteenth Amendment was self-executing but the interpretation of the amendment was so restricted that in the end it likewise became worthless in real life.

HAROLD MELVIN HYMAN: There is certainly a set of parallels. The question of implementation for self-executing laws, however, deserves further exploration. The Thirteenth, Fourteenth, and Fifteenth Amendments are the first to contain precise authorities to the Congress to enforce them. Congress included those phrases to avoid any discussion as to whether there was such national congressional authority. And so, in a sense, the commitment then is that they are not self-executing but that implementation would be needed. But I do think that in more fundamental terms you are correct. I get the impression from plowing through the mountains of papers on the subject that a great many people assumed that defeated southern whites would obey the verdict of defeat, would obey the changed law. And so in a sense the advantage lay with those who would disobey because one had to react and, as in guerrilla warfare, each time the disobedience repeated itself a positive implementation had to occur. American government, both state and national, had very little experience with systematic implementation of almost anything up to that time, and so this wholly new area of civil rights' implementation proved to be beyond actual possibilities. Thus southern whites had time on this.

HERMANN WELLENREUTHER: I want to draw your attention to two very simple and not very learned points. First, from the eighteenth to the nineteenth century there is a change in scale as far as constitutional developments and people affected are concerned. In the eighteenth century very few people enjoyed the same rights. Citizens living in a chartered town enjoyed the same rights and privileges, citizens living in privileged villages enjoyed the same rights, citizens living in one colony might enjoy the same rights. After the Declaration of Independence and the Constitution these individual groups suddenly found themselves enjoying exactly the same rights and privileges as did their fellow citizens in Maryland.

What had been one, two, or three thousands before in one particular political entity now became a matter of hundreds of thousands. And that is even more true as we turn to constitutional developments in central Europe, something that was preceded by dismantling chartered towns and substituting the idea of the *Bürger* as a person enjoying the special privileges of one walled region with the concept of the *Untertan* in the second half of the eighteenth century. Now that must have had fantastic consequences for any government trying to implement laws. In the eighteenth century a law would be directed toward a municipality, toward a small region. But a law, for example a *Recess* of the Imperial Diet, was worthless unless it was specially proclaimed and implemented on the local level by a particular ordinance sent down from the particular sovereign. In the nineteenth century, of course, all this changes. A law touched large numbers of people who now had similar or the same rights; to implement a law required dramatically different types of measures and means. I think that parallel to this the methods of resisting state regulations change from the eighteenth to the nineteenth century. In the eighteenth century the typical method of resistance was the "riot." In Germany, in England, in France we have tax riots, smuggling riots, bread riots, rent riots, etc. These were typical old forms of resistance. In the nineteenth century, my feeling is that as we move on riots go out of favor and are being replaced by a more important form of resistance, the habit of ignoring something and behaving as if the law did not exist. And that is why the question of scale becomes so important. When we talk about enforcing or implementing something we have to envision this administrative task in dramatically changed contexts. In the eighteenth century it was reasonably easy to enforce something because the corporate entity in which the measure had to be enforced was much smaller. In the nineteenth century, before adequate bureaucratic systems had been developed, it was next to impossible to achieve the same. Mr. Hyman has made the same point. Both suggest that we focus our attention on the development of administrative apparatus in Germany as well as in the United States.

WILLIAM M. WIECEK: Thus far we have said very little about the meaning of the term "equality." For the period of Reconstruction it is conventional to divide the Congress into radicals and moderates.

I never thought that this distinction was very helpful until it occurred to me that what truly distinguishes the Republican factions is their sense of what equality means. The very small number of radicals in the Reconstruction Congresses believed that equality meant "literal equality of all people before the law," particularly with respect to equality of opportunities available to them. The moderate faction of Republicans in Congress believed in an older, northern conception of equality before the law, which was something different and simply meant that law would treat all people equally and not deferentially on the basis of irrational factors such as race.

I would be interested to hear from our German colleagues what equality meant in German thought in the same period.

GERTRUDE LÜBBE-WOLFF: I think in the nineteenth century we had not even gotten as far as equality before the law, at least not in the sense that one could bring it before the courts. The difference between formal equality before the law and factual equality is something we discussed in the 1970s but not in the nineteenth century.

STANLEY N. KATZ: Two points: one is that there was a good deal of civil rights litigation in the second part of the nineteenth century but it was in the state courts rather than in the federal Supreme Court. Historians have not looked at these trials much until recently; we are now discovering how much litigation there was. Some individuals were indeed finding protection in the state courts; this should not be ignored. The second is to note what was happening with relation to the development of black codes in the South: a new and powerful customary law was allowed to develop in the southern states. In *Plessy v. Ferguson* the federal Supreme Court was really saying that this new customary law was not inconsistent with the prescripts of the Fourteenth Amendment. That was a really powerful statement. Whats was so dramatically important about *Brown v. Board of Education* is its declaration that local common law on these matters could not be superior to constitutional law. If you look at the situation that way it becomes more consistent with the discussion of European law we have had; for then *Brown* really does say something about the interaction between the nation and the localities.

RALPH KETCHAM: I meant to raise a somewhat broader question by way of amplification of two sentences in Mr. Kühne's paper. The first sentence reads like this: "The German concept of freedom was contrary to the then-existing civil rights catalogs that implicitly rested on a dualism of state and society. The strong individualistic character of most of the other human rights' catalogs was thus avoided."[1] The second reads as follows: "Germany lacked the simple formula on which American constitutional thought was based for the benefit of the individual, that is, Jefferson's natural law, 'pursuit of happiness.'"[2] Both of these sentences deny the existence in German tradition of an individualist tradition. And what I am really interested in is the effect of this, its place in German political culture, and the liabilities of that lack of individualistic tradition.

DIETHELM KLIPPEL: I do not agree with Mr. Kühne's just-cited statements. From the end of the eighteenth century in Germany there were books on natural law that strongly advocated the liberty of the individual and in fact established something like the division between society and state (*Staat und Gesellschaft*). I suppose that this natural law was alive in the nineteenth century as well; I am sure about the first part of the century at least, but am unsure about the later decades.

KNUD KRAKAU: With regard to the notion of individualistic rights, my German history colleagues may not agree with me but I would like to take a middle view between the two of you (Kühne and Klippel), agreeing with Mr. Kühne about politics but disagreeing with him on their function in bourgeois culture. As a reaction in this country to the challenge of enlightenment, which did not lead to anything comparable to the restructuring of society on either the French or American model but created expectations and hopes for such a restructuring in our society, did not succeed, I think that these activities were diverted to the bourgeois cultural sphere where individualism developed to the extreme in philosophy and in cultural productions. But the necessary complemen-

---

1. Jörg-Detlef Kühne, "Civil Rights and German Constitutional Thought, 1848–1871," above, 210.
2. Ibid., 220.

tary attitude on the political side was abstention from political activities; in this context I agree with Mr. Kühne that there was no individualistic approach to the concepts of constitution building or nation building. This led to a peculiar cultural consciousness in this country, characterized by a disdain for political activity and for rational attempts to recreate society and emphasizing, on the other hand, the romantic insistence on the historical role of community forms and institutions – an attitude that could be distinguished as a means of escape for the intellectual elite until very recent times.

GERHARD A. RITTER: I would like to add to what Mr. Krakau said and change the emphasis a bit. I do think that in the 1849 Constitution and in the *Grundrecht* you do have individualistic human rights seen as individual rights. But you also have, as you yourself pointed out, rights related to communities (*Gemeinden*), to churches, and to schools, in short, positive rights as they would be called; this whole tradition had its roots in the 1848 debate. To give some examples: free education is a positive right that the state should provide you with – the Weimar Constitution is of course full of these social rights. The state is not just there to guarantee you your liberty to do what you want as an individual person but should also guarantee your social rights, the right to live, not to be poor, the right to be ensured. There is a whole concept in the *Sozialstaatsklausel* and that I hold to be a very specific tradition; it is probably one of the reasons why Bismarck and not an American president invented social insurance!

ERICH ANGERMANN: I disagree with these statements that there was no tradition of individual liberty. You just have to read the protocols of the Württemberg, Baden, and Hesse diets and you will find that they were continually talking about the liberty of the press, individual liberty from imprisonment, the individual right to own property, in short, all the aspects you find in the French and American debates. The same holds true for the constitutional charters. There is no part of Germany which did not work toward individual liberty in the Western sense.

KNUD KRAKAU: Of course you are right. But one might add that after all it failed and thus the failure determined the broad picture of political reality.

Part 4
Federalism in the Nineteenth Century

10
Federalism as an Issue in the German Constitutions of 1849 and 1871

Hans Boldt

Generally speaking, political development in Germany between 1848 and 1871 was a process of nation building: the German people became united into the so-called small-German national state (that is, Germany without Austria), epitomized in the *Reichsverfassungen* (Constitutions of the German Empire) of 1849 and 1871.[1] In both cases, one of the core problems was to build a federation, a so-called *Bundesstaat*, and construct a strong federal government while preserving the then-existing states, which continued to have a say in national matters. The Constitutions of 1848–49 (the so-called *Paulskirchenverfassung* in Frankfurt), of 1867 (the foundation of the *Norddeutsche Bund*, the North German Confederation), and of 1871 (the *Bismarcksche Reichsverfassung*) were variations on the same – federal – theme.

Surprisingly enough, even in 1848, when the political situation was much more in flux than in 1867–71, hardly anyone opposed the federal idea. Only the radical left demanded the abolition of German monarchies and establishment of a unitary national state.[2] Yet these centralist movements were without good prospects when one takes into account that monarchy was firmly rooted in the minds of the German people and that there was a particularistic tradition of local government in Germany stretching back to the Middle Ages.

The odds were against the confederative principle too. It had been discredited by the *Deutsche Bund*, which since its inception in 1815, was renowned for its suppression of civic liberties and for

---

1. I am grateful to Werner Reh for translating the text into English.
2. For the different political affiliations in the National Assembly and their programs cf. Gottfried Eisenmann, *Die Parteyen der teutschen Reichsversammlung* (Erlangen, 1848); and Manfred Botzenhart, *Deutscher Parlamentarismus, 1848–1850* (Düsseldorf, 1977), 315ff.

acting as an obstacle to economic and political development. The *Bundesstaat* promised a stronger economy, more freedom, legal and national unity, and the power Germany needed to lay claim to its fair share among nations. These domestic and international aims went beyond confederative organization and called for a "federation"; in Germany they required a "national" union, that is, the combination of "national" and "federal elements" that had already been regarded as distinctive features of the *Bundesstaat* in the *Federalist Papers*.

At the time of the 1848 Revolution, the concept of a *Bundesstaat* was well known in Germany.[3] Even before the Revolution, Deputy Friedrich Daniel Bassermann, in his famous motion in the second chamber in Baden on February 12, 1848, demanded "political federation." Bassermann pleaded for the establishment of a national representation of the people on the federal level. He quickly found many followers. They all wanted a central government and a national representation additional to that of the states, in short, a *Bundesstaat*. Later, in the Constitution ratified on March 28, 1849, the nostalgic expression *Reich* (empire) was used. But nevertheless this term stood for *Bundesstaat*,[4] as was the case in the German "Empire" in 1871.

In 1849 the effort at German nation building via federalism failed, as is known. But a temporary compromise was found in 1867 and the issue was finally settled in 1871. The solution of 1867–71 was rather different from that envisioned 1848–49. Yet there is more continuity than one might perceive at first glance. We will treat both solutions successively and emphasize the parallels between them.

The Constitution of 1849

In the German Revolution at the end of February 1848,[5] which led to the Constitution of March 23, 1849, different positions clashed:

3. Cf. Ernst Deuerlein, *Föderalismus* (Munich, 1972), 79ff.
4. Cf. §1 of the draft of the Constitution by the Committee of Seventeen of the German *Bundestag* (cf. n. 16).
5. Cf. Veit Valentin, *Geschichte der deutschen Revolution von 1848–49*, 2 vols. (Berlin, 1930/31); and Wolfram Siemann, *Die deutsche Revolution von 1848/49* (Frankfurt/Main, 1985).

claims of civic liberties, intellectual and economic freedom, but also social demands by peasants and the underprivileged classes were simultaneously placed on the political agenda. Certainly of equal importance were the issues of national identity and of legal and economic unity – but without destroying the states. Germany was in search of a free and federative nation-state.

In that formative process the ideal of the United States of America played a part that cannot be overrated. Sixty years earlier the United States had presented the first example of individual states forming a firm union without abolishing the autonomy and independence of the member states; the solution proposed succeeded in simultaneously combining civic liberties, the flourishing of member states, and a powerful central government. It is small wonder that this nonmonarchical but republican, nonunitary but federative union roused the interest of many Europeans, especially the Germans. The United States was talked of as the "marvel of the time."[6]

There had been attempts to formulate German federalist theories since the "Holy Roman Empire" had decayed into a loose association of many territories, yet the American example was undoubtedly the main source of inspiration for the *Bundesstaat* in the nineteenth century. Even though this observation remained true after 1871, one then took pride in stressing one's own federalist tradition.[7] The American model was discussed intensely. As early as 1824 the well-known liberal deputy and professor of law Robert von Mohl published a book on the federal Constitution of the United States (*Bundes-Staatsrecht der Vereinigten Staaten von Amerika*). Georg Waitz, the leading German theorist of federalism of the time up to 1871, fully accepted the Tocqueville-American

6. Cf. Robert von Mohl, *Das Bundes-Staatsrecht der Vereinigten Staaten von Nord-Amerika* (Stuttgart, 1824), VII. For the impact of the American model cf. Eckhart G. Franz, *Das Amerikabild der deutschen Revolution, 1848/49* (Heidelberg, 1958); Erich Angermann, "Der deutsche Frühkonstitutionalismus und das amerikanische Vorbild," *Historische Zeitschrift* 219 (1974): 1–32; Anton Scholl, *Einfluß der nordamerikanischen Verfassung auf die Verfassung des Deutschen Reiches vom 28. März 1849* (Borna and Leipzig, 1913); Thomas Ellwein, *Der Einfluß des nordamerikanischen Bundesverfassungsrechts auf die Verhandlungen der Frankfurter Nationalversammlung im Jahre 1848/49* (Erlanger juristische Dissertation, 1950).

7. Cf. Siegfried Brie, *Der Bundesstaat, I: Geschichte der Lehre vom Bundesstaate* (Leipzig, 1874); cf. also Michael Dreyer, *Föderalismus als ordnungspolitisches und normatives Prinzip: Das föderative Denken der Deutschen im 19. Jahrhundert* (Frankfurt/Main, 1987).

federalist doctrine, yet only, it is true, after the German Revolution had definitely failed.[8] Nevertheless, in the years before 1848 American federalism had been godfather to the efforts to distinguish between the (desired) "federation" and the (undesired) "confederation."[9]

In the Revolution of 1848 everybody spoke of the American example. Already in his motion of February 12th mentioned above, Deputy Bassermann had drawn attention to the example of the United States. In those days pamphlets that dealt with constitutional problems were also full of allusions to the United States. Perhaps even more important, the first draft of the Constitution, conceived by the Committee of Seventeen of the *Bundestag*, the federal organ of the old confederation, sticks very close to the American model.[10] The radical left, too, demanded a "federal Constitution modelled after the constitution of the North American Free States [i.e. United States of America]."[11] And when in October 1848 Professor Carl Josef Anton Mittermaier, the referee of the Constitutional Committee (the *Verfassungsausschuß*) in the National Assembly, remarked in his report on the organizational part of the Constitution that America had resolved the problem of the "true federal state" by "harmonizing a powerful central government with the fullest possibility of a prospering development of the member states," he too opted for the American ideal.[12]

The borrowings from the American experience in the *Reichsverfassung* of 1849 are numerous. One finds not only word-for-word translations, for example, regarding the responsibilities of central government, but also some basic rights.[13] Regulations concerning

8. Georg Waitz, "Das Wesen des Bundesstaats," *Allgemeine Monatsschrift für Wissenschaft und Literatur* 3 (1853): 494ff.

9. Cf. the representative article by Carl Theodor Welcker, "Bund," in Carl von Rotteck and Carl Theodor Welcker, eds., *Staats-Lexikon oder Enzyklopädie der Staatswissenschaften*, 15 vols. (Altona, 1834–43), 3: 76–116.

10. See the reprint in Ernst Rudolf Huber, ed., *Dokumente zur deutschen Verfassungsgeschichte*, 2 vols. (Stuttgart, 1961), 1: no. 91; cf. Christian Carl Josias Bunsen, *Die deutsche Bundesverfassung und ihr eigentümliches Verhältnis zu den Verfassungen Englands und der Vereinigten Staaten* (Frankfurt/Main, 1848).

11. Cf. the demands of the German radical Peter Struwe documented in Huber, ed., *Dokumente zur deutschen Verfassungsgeschichte* (see n. 10), 1: no. 77.

12. For Mittermaier's report see Franz Wigard, ed., *Stenographischer Bericht über die Verhandlungen der Deutschen Konstituirenden Nationalversammlung zu Frankfurt a.M.*, 9 vols. (Frankfurt/Main, 1848–49), 4: 2722ff., 2724.

13. Cf. the compilation of Scholl, *Einfluß der nordamerikanischen Verfassung* (see n. 6).

the representation of the states on the federal level, the relationships of state and church or the position of the military power, and many more points were debated and resolved with the American model in mind. Some deputies even demanded a special federal district around the city of Erfurt in Thuringia. Not only the liberals and the radical republican left felt at ease in citing the American example. Occasionally even the conservatives joined in, though mainly in order to puzzle their opponents. Once a member of Parliament ironically began his speech with the words, "This time I have news from America, too."[14]

Yet the deputies did not cling slavishly to the American example. For even its admirers knew that German traditions could not be ignored and that one had to find specific solutions to German problems. In some respects the German situation was rather different from that of America in the eighteenth century. In the first place Germany had a complex state or "territorial" development over centuries. In 1848 thirty-nine German states still remained to be unified. Among them were ministates of a few thousand but also states with millions of inhabitants; very ancient monarchies as well as city-states; unimportant *Duodez-Fürstentümer* and great European powers like Austria and Prussia. Contrary to the United States of America, the German states could not draw on a unitary legal system based on common law, and despite the Prussian-dominated *Zollverein* of 1833, economic unity was rather deficient. Furthermore, in opposition to the liberal tradition in the United States, the German states had an authoritarian, feudal-absolutistic tradition.

Second, the German lack of economic prosperity, so different from the American example, was often mentioned; it accelerated the revolutionary tendencies in the years of crisis between 1845 and 1847. At the same time poverty had created a proletariat. From the analysis of social conditions, different conclusions have been drawn: on the one hand, demands for social policies were raised, while on the other hand, the exclusion from the right to vote was debated.

A third point of interest is the long tradition of restorative tendencies in the *Deutsche Bund*, which had been hostile to freedom and progress. Furthermore, Germany, like the United States, had

14. Cf. Franz, *Das Amerikabild der deutschen Revolution, 1848/49* (see n. 6), 116, n. 107.

no political center, but in a deviation from the American model, instead had two powers competing for hegemony, namely, Austria and Prussia.

In short, in the Germany of 1848 the question of nation building was posited in a very different manner. In America it was all about the separation from a political center, from London, and about the gradual formation of a nation. In Germany the aim was to unite different sovereign states with rather distinctive peculiarities and to create a powerful central government in opposition to internal particularistic forces but also in opposition to the great powers in Europe, which were not interested in the formation of a new powerful state.

These different issues prompted the deputies in the *Nationalversammlung* to stress, respectively, popular sovereignty or the sovereignty of the national Parliament, as well as basic rights, as an expression of the new legal system and of freedom from the old, particularistic forces on the one hand, while paying regard to the rights of the states on the other. It is characteristic for the Germany of 1848 that the dividing line of political movements was not between supporters of a confederation and of the *Bundesstaat*, but between moderate liberals (*Konstitutionelle*) and republican-minded, radical *Demokraten*. Both wanted to go beyond the confederative solution to a federation; the former more by agreement with the old powers and by guaranteeing the classical individual liberties, the latter by breaking with the tradition and founding a republic based on popular sovereignty according to the example of the United States, but with the addition of welfare-state demands. However, those on the left were not simply more centralistic than the moderates. Among the latter were many who favored a strong government, while on the left many argued for states' rights because they were concerned about the new central government's lack of progressiveness.[15]

For these reasons the new Constitution of the empire became somewhat more centralistic than the model Constitution of the United States. On the one hand, it was indeed necessary to bring about a more unitary system. On the other hand, there were also stronger particularistic trends for conceding to the states a more powerful position. A special problem was the resolution of the

15. Cf. Franz, *Das Amerikabild der deutschen Revolution, 1848/49* (see n. 6), 127.

dualism between Austria and Prussia in the federation envisioned. After all, this was the reason why the federative effort would be doomed to failure in 1848–49. But before we come to this point let us first look at the Constitution which was passed in March 1849 after somewhat longish deliberations.[16]

The Constitution of 1871

The Constitution of the empire is divided into 7 chapters and 197 paragraphs. It begins with a short chapter about "das Reich" (§§1–5). The National Assembly had decided very late to put this in front of the following articles. These first paragraphs deal with the problem of founding a national federation in Germany. Resistance to this part of the document led to the failure of the constitutional venture altogether. We shall come back to this.

The first chapter is followed by a second about the "Reichsgewalt" (§§6–67) containing the catalog of federal areas of competence. After that the organization of federal power is described in chapter three, "das Reichsoberhaupt" (§§68–84); in chapter four, "der Reichstag" (§§85–124), which includes important regulations on the "Staatenhaus" (§§86–92); and in chapter five on the "Reichsgericht," the federal supreme court (§§125–29). Chapter six contains basic rights (§§130–89) and the last chapter, "die Gewähr der Verfassung," the regulations safeguarding the Constitution (§§190–97).

The construction of the *Reichsverfassung* stresses federative thought, whereas in the Constitution of the United States the

16. For the *Reichsverfassung* of 1849 and its formation cf. Ernst Rudolf Huber, *Deutsche Verfassungsgeschichte seit 1789*, 3 vols. (Stuttgart, 1960–63), 2: 502ff. For the plenary discussions of the National Assembly cf. Wigard, ed., *Stenographischer Bericht über die Verhandlungen der Deutschen Konstituirenden Nationalversammlung* (see n. 12), 4: 2722ff. For the Verfassungsausschuß cf. Johann Gustav Droysen, *Die Verhandlungen des Verfassungs-Ausschusses der deutschen Nationalversammlung*, vol. 1 (Leipzig, 1849, repr. Vaduz, 1985); and Rudolf Hübner, ed., *Aktenstücke und Aufzeichnungen zur Geschichte der Frankfurter Nationalversammlung aus dem Nachlaß von Johann Gustav Droysen* (1924, repr. Osnabrück, 1973). For several important documents cf. Paul Roth–Heinrich Merck, ed., *Quellensammlung zum deutschen öffentlichen Recht seit 1848*, 2 vols. (Erlangen, 1850/52). See also the synopsis of the Constitution of 1849 and its drafts in Ludwig Bergsträsser, *Die Verfassung des Deutschen Reiches vom Jahre 1849* (Bonn, 1913). For its impact cf. Jörg-Detlef Kühne, *Die Reichsverfassung der Paulskirche: Vorbild und Verwirklichung im späteren Rechtsleben* (Frankfurt/Main, 1985).

concept of checks and balances between the Congress, president, and Supreme Court dominates. Thus the German constitutional draft of 1849 proceeds from the allocation of competences between the federal government and the states, the central problem of every federative organization (cf. §5). This is followed by a discussion of the powers of the federal organs. Here the position of the national chief executive is assigned particular privileges vis-à-vis the national parliament.

The federative (*bundesstaatliche*) character of the Constitution is very clear. In an organization quite different from a confederation, the empire first has a territory of its own, namely, the whole of the territories of the individual states (§1). Second, the citizens of the states are at the same time citizens of the empire and are immediately affected by the actions of the national government (§132). Questions of citizenship and immigration are regulated by the central power (§57). Third, the empire possesses an independent *Reichsgewalt* with numerous organs and competences. Let us begin with an examination of these competences and their division between the federal government and the states, since this is, as we said before, one of the most important problems of federalism.

Areas of Responsibility

In its hierarchy of competences, the Frankfurt *Paulskirchenverfassung* takes over the principle of allocation from the American Constitution: the responsibilities of the national government are enumerated, whereas the states fulfill all other tasks. Explicitly §5 states: "The individual German states retain that part of their independence which is not affected and restricted by the Constitution of the empire; they enjoy all these sovereign rights and privileges which are not expressly by this Constitution transferred to the empire." This is equivalent to the Tenth Amendment of the U.S. Constitution and is similar to Article II of the Act of Confederation of 1777.

The fourteen articles in the second chapter of the Constitution enumerate, among others, the following responsibilities of the federal government: foreign relations; decisions on war and peace; guarantees of internal law and order; federal income policy; regulations concerning tax and trade, currency, measures and weights, copyright and patents, immigration and citizenship, post and telegraphy, railways, navigation, achievement of unitary law in all important legal and economic domains, and finally, the establishment of guidelines for the preservation of health. This catalog far exceeds the powers of the *Deutsche Bund* which, as a confederation, was essentially restricted to the external and internal security of the member states. Now a number of competences in the spheres of economy and traffic are added that underline the importance of achieving unitary economic conditions. In this respect too, the German Constitution follows the American example. This holds true even for §62, which stipulates that the national government has, whenever it seems necessary for the execution of the enumerated competences, the right to legislate in all cases unspecified by the Constitution. Here the deputies evoked a doctrine of "implied powers" drawn from the "necessary and proper clause" of the American Constitution.[17]

In several respects they went beyond the American model. They not only provided the opportunity to make comprehensive decisions on economic questions at the national level[18] and assigned the responsibilities for railways and telegraphy – recent inventions – to the empire, but they also empowered the national government to accomplish the unity of law in Germany in a very general sense, which even included measures of health care (cf. §§61 and 64). Finally, the unitary trend is strongly epitomized in the so-called competence-competence which gives the national government the right to change the rights of the states by altering the imperial federal Constitution (cf. §63).

These tendencies of German federalism, more centralist in comparison to the United States, are already apparent in the first drafts of the Constitution of 1848. The inventory of national competences is already visible in the draft of the above-mentioned Committee of Seventeen of April 1848. This document is marked by the obvious intention to assign the national government all responsibilities pertaining to the national interest. Compared to these strong centralist notions, which were shared by the Verfassungsausschuß of

17. Cf. The Constitution of the United States of America, I, 8, 18.
18. For this function in the United States the interstate commerce clause is used; see I, 8, 3 in the Constitution. For the debate in the National Assembly cf. Franz, *Das Amerikabild der deutschen Revolution 1848/49* (see n. 6), 128ff.; and Ellwein, *Der Einfluß des nordamerikanischen Bundesverfassungsrechts auf die Verhandlungen der Frankfurter Nationalversammlung* (see n. 6), 292ff.

the National Assembly, the final solution signifies a certain weakening of the centralist drive. Many of the legislative competences were assigned to the national government, no longer in an obligatory, but in a facultative manner. Only foreign relations and the decisions about war and peace remained the exclusive domain of the national government (cf. §§6 and 10). These regulations, however, nullified sovereign rights especially important to the great powers of Austria and Prussia. For, according to the "mitigated" version of the Frankfurt Constitution, only the right to make contracts with non-German neighbor states (§8) remained with the states.

With regard to military affairs, however, things looked rather different. Here only the navy was earmarked exclusively as the national domain (§19), while only general organizational principles were stated with regard to the army. The armed forces, built up by contingents, remained under the sovereignty of the states. It did not seem possible to take this paramount instrument of power and control, especially the selection of leaders and officers, away from the monarchs of the states. Only in times of war was the authority of command to be transferred to the national level (§§11 seq.).

In many other cases the competences of the empire are only facultative. The empire may act but does not have to. Sometimes its activity is tied to the "Interest of general communication" (see, for example, §§28–32). But if the central government passes a regulation, its laws are superior to state regulations (§66).

These provisions must be seen as the attempt to prepare the way for the establishment of a national unitary law and policy while paying due regard to the rights of the states. The German construction of the *Bundesstaat* is characterized by a specific unitarian-particularistic ambivalence. This ambivalence is particularly evident in a regulation that was first introduced into the Constitution of 1849 and has become typical for German federalism up to now: we are talking of the vertical division of power apart from the horizontal one. This feature has no parallel in the American model, where the spheres of competence are clearly assigned to either the national or the state level. Once a task has been transferred to the central government, that government assumes complete responsibility. It passes the laws and has them executed by federal agencies. Quite the contrary is true for Germany: here the national assembly thought that the execution of federal laws had to be left to the member states, since the monarchical character of the states was not to be destroyed.[19] For the same reasons, in the military as well as in the civil sectors the executive apparatus remained in the hands of the state governments because the monarchs were not to be deprived of the bureaucracies as the traditional bases of their powers.

The *Zollverein* had proved that such an arrangement was able to function; in that confederacy the states had been responsible for raising and administrating the revenues according to general regulations. This regulation was now incorporated into the new Constitution. In general the national government was only assigned the right to pass laws and the right to exercise supervision (*Oberaufsicht*) over the state in order to ensure and enforce the execution of federal laws. As in the case of certain marine and coastal establishments, the national government was merely given an *Oberaufsichtsrecht* (cf. §21); in other instances it was only accorded the right to legislate (cf. §§59 and 64). Only in a very few cases did the Constitution establish a separate national administration; this was the case with respect to the construction of national fortresses (§18) and the navy (§19). In the case of the mail, however, the national government got only the competence for general regulation and supervision (cf. §41). It may well be asked, however, whether such a division of tasks does not represent an even stronger encroachment on states' rights than a strict separation after the North American model. For it clearly implied the danger that states would become mere executive organs of the central power subject to central control and regulation. This problem epitomizes the ambivalence of the unitarian-particularistic German approach very clearly.

Conflict Resolution

Of course, such a regulation was bound to generate many conflicts between the central government and the states. This had been taken into account through the establishment of a national supreme court, the *Reichsgericht*. Its necessity was never questioned. On the contrary it was thought to be the appropriate "Cornerstone of the Constitution," and once more, one referred to the American

19. Cf. Wigard, ed., *Stenographischer Bericht über die Verhandlungen der Deutschen Konstituirenden Nationalversammlung* (see n. 12), 4: 3157 passim, 8: 5444ff.

example. It is true that the left feared that, as a result of suits against federal laws, the German supreme court could jeopardize the sovereignty of the national Parliament. But the opinion prevailed that a court could only render decisions in certain concrete cases and, therefore, was unable to assume the function of the legislator or perform acts of sovereignty.

Furthermore, it was argued that political issues should not be brought before the courts. Yet the belief was widely shared that in a modern state only courts could make decisions about conflicts when those conclusions had to be deduced from laws. This conviction was not only derived from the American experience but was deeply rooted in German traditions. Although the *Deutsche Bund* had only institutionalized a facultative arbitration – the so-called *Austrägalverfahren* – rather than an obligatory judicial ruling, the Old Empire had had central courts (*Reichsgerichte*) for the settlement of various issues. These traditions and precedents explain the rather comprehensive catalog of competences of the new national court.

In this paper we can only name a few instances of judicial review (cf. §126a–n). They included conflicts between the central government and states (§126a) and conflicts between states (§126c), but also conflicts between the Parliament and the executive of member states about the interpretation of their Constitution (§126e) – all cases with which the *Reichsgerichte* of the Holy Roman Empire had already had to deal. Others, like the right to impeach ministers of the central and state governments (§126i, k), were based on a constitutional tradition. Conflicts between the two houses on the federal level and between one of these and the federal government (§126b) seem to be more modern, however. The same applies to the right of citizens to sue when their rights, as guaranteed by the *Reichsverfassung* (§126g), were violated. These rights have been revived by the constitutional court in the Federal Republic of Germany (the so-called *Organstreitigkeiten* and *Verfassungsbeschwerden*).

The Frankfurt Constitution of 1849 says nothing about the organization of the federal court. According to then-existing plans, one-third of its members were to be chosen from the federal executive and one-third from the *Staatenhaus* and the national Parliament, respectively. But the final decision was left to a special law (§128). This law was also to regulate the enforcement of sentences. Irrespective of that, the Constitution provided the central power with the right for direct intervention

- If one state endangered the peace of another member state
- If peace was broken in a member state and the state government either explicitly required help from the national government or was incapable of restoring peace, or if the peace of the empire as such was endangered
- If the constitution of a member state was destroyed or changed either by force or unilaterally (§54)

These regulations aimed at dangers to inter- and intrastate peace. Under these circumstances the central government might seize power in a state by means of decrees, by appointing commissionaries, or by using the armed forces (§55); in case of insurgency human rights might be suspended too (§197). These kinds of federal intervention also corresponded to German traditions. We find similar provisions in the Constitutions of the *Deutsche Bund* and in the later federal Constitution. But in contrast to all later Constitutions, the Frankfurt Constitution did not authorize immediate intervention in case of an insubordination of a member state against orders "from above." It was believed to be sufficient that the national government could go to court against disobedient states (cf. §126a).

Organization of the Federal Power

In the Paulskirche Constitution the responsibilities of the federal powers are divided between different organs. At first glance their relationship resembles that of the United States. We see a head of state (*Reichsoberhaupt*); a Parliament (Reichstag) consisting of two houses, the "representatives' house" (*Volkshaus*) and the "states' house" (*Staatenhaus*); and the already-mentioned federal court. But the Frankfurt Constitution does not contain the strict division of powers of the American Constitution. It has often been suggested that the British system served as a model. It seems, however, more convincing to argue that this Constitution followed the German tradition which had been established from the beginning of the nineteenth century.

The head of the empire in the Frankfurt Constitution is not, like the president of the United States, an elected chief executive, but a monarch commanding departments responsible to parliament. Yet it is not clear what kind of responsibility is meant or which possibilities for control the Reichstag had since the Constitution refrains from being more specific (cf. §§68–73). In any case the monarchical head of state (according to the German tradition, the Kaiser) and his government are not strictly separated from Parliament. On the contrary, the Kaiser as head of state convokes Parliament, terminates its sessions, and may even dissolve the *Volkshaus* (§79). He also has the right to initiate legislation. According to §80 he shares the legislative power with the Reichstag ("in Gemeinschaft mit dem Reichstage"). Obviously, in 1848 Germany was on its way to a parliamentary government. A strict separation of powers was not intended. And if the federal government had a suspensive veto against decisions of the Reichstag, this derived from the example of Norway rather than from that of the United States. For, as in Norway, parliamentary decisions became law if, after a veto, they were confirmed by parliament in three consecutive sessions (§101); in the United States, on the other hand, a presidential veto can only be overruled by a two-thirds majority of both houses of Congress.

In the American Constitution, as well as in the German Constitution of 1849, the members of the house of representatives are to be elected in general elections according to the principle of "one man, one vote." Detailed regulations were laid down in a special law, the *Reichswahlgesetz* of April 24, 1849. Yet from our federative point of view, the second chamber of the Reichstag, the *Staatenhaus*, is more interesting. In the Germany of 1848 it was widely held that, apart from the national representative body, a federation must also have an organ representing the states. The radical left's demand for one chamber only was never shared by a majority. Yet, due to German peculiarities, the difficulties involved in construction of the second chamber did not allow for copying the American Senate.

In the first place the question of whether all small and large states, some of which owed their territorial shape to dynastic casualties, were to survive had to be answered. The left wanted to dissolve all states and in their stead create ten *Reichskreise* of nearly equal shape. After intensive discussion in the Constitutional Committee of the National Assembly a plan was developed for either joining together the smallest states or incorporating them into larger ones (the so-called *Mediatisierungsplan*), which would have left seventeen states and four free cities. But this plan turned out to be so delicate that it was soon dropped in the plenary session. Although the Constitution did not guarantee the existence and the territories of the states, both were implicitly recognized by their admission as members of the second chamber (cf. §§86f. and 90).

The agreement about the territorial issue opened the way for a settlement of the question of how the states were to be represented in the federative organ. Contrary to the U.S. model, the smallest states in Germany had only a few thousand inhabitants, yet the largest ones had several million. This prompted the suggestion that the old German tradition of giving the small states together only one vote (the so-called *Kurialstimmen*) be revived. The great powers especially insisted on distinguishing between large and small states: "Liechtenstein may not have the same weight as Prussia." Accordingly, the Constitution distributed the 192 members of the federal chamber on the basis of the size of the states: Prussia was to have 40, Austria 38, Bavaria 18 and so forth, but every state was to enjoy at least one vote (§87).

As in the United States, members had to be thirty years of age and citizens of the states they represented. Half were to be appointed by the state parliaments (as was the case in the United States at that time), the other half by the state governments. Their period of office was fixed at six years; every third year half of the members were to be reelected (§88 seq.). The Constitution did not stipulate – as in the United States – that the states must be republics. The states were obliged to respect human rights (§130), to pass no law violating the *Reichsverfassung* (§194), and to adopt a constitution with a representative organ of the people to which the government was responsible. The rights of the state parliaments were enumerated in §187. Changing the constitution of a member state required the approval of the federal government (§195).

With the exception of the budgetary right, the Frankfurt Constitution granted both chambers equal powers (§103, nos. 5 and 6), but the states were not satisfied with this solution, especially since the members of the *Staatenhaus*, like American senators, were given a free mandate and not bound to instructions (§96). They therefore demanded another second chamber apart from the *Staatenhaus*, to be called the *Reichsrat* and used to counsel the federal government on legislative matters. It should consist of members of the state governments and be instructed by them, thus establishing a direct link between the state and federal governments (the *Reichsrat* as the "Organ der Versöhnung"). Yet in the constitutional assembly this resumption of a feature from the old German confederation was fiercely opposed by the leftists and they succeeded in undermining the project. Later German constitutions, however, again revived the tradition of sending representatives instructed by state governments into the second chamber.

The Failure of the Constitution of 1849

The solution found in 1849 for the vertical distribution of competences, for conflict resolution, and for the organization of the federal powers underlines the anxious need to mediate between the unitary requirements of a truly national government and the particularistic interests of the traditional states. Yet in 1848–49, the question of centralism and particularism was not the main problem of German constitution making. Equally difficult problems were posed by the issues of nationhood and the dualism between Prussia and Austria. Both questions further complicated the selection of the head of the central government.

The question of establishing a central government above the numerous sovereign monarchies existing in 1848 had already occupied the national convent when in June it had to decide about a provisional central government; the issue was again debated in autumn, when the organizational part of the Constitution was discussed. In June the democrats were for putting the government into the hands of a committee chosen from the assembly, which was only to execute the assembly's decisions. Thus they were frank supporters of the principle of "convent government." Apart from that they tried to strengthen the republican idea at the federal level by pleading for an elected president as head of state. The moderates considered such a solution not viable because of the monarchical character of the German states. They also did not wish to snub the monarchs because they needed their backing against the radicals. Therefore, they pleaded for a monarchical head of state, a kaiser, who was to be above the German monarchs. This, however, raised further problems: should the kaiser be an elected or a hereditary emperor? And if elected, should he be elected by Parliament or by the people? Unfortunately, two pretenders were available, the Austrian and Prussian monarchs. Who should be preferred? Faced with these problems, a third solution was advanced – a directory consisting of three or more princes. The proposal was an attempt to overcome the insoluble Austrian-Prussian antagonism and at the same time to integrate the smaller and medium-sized states into the national government. In such a directory the chairmanship could alternate between Austria and Prussia, and the everyday work was to be done by a ministry subject to the directorate and controlled by Parliament. But neither of these proposals gained a majority either in the Constitutional Committee or in the plenary sessions. It is significant that during the first reading of the Constitution this problem could not be settled. It touched upon the most delicate problem for the foundation of the empire in 1848, the integration of Austria into a national and federative German state. For an explanation we have to go further back.

As mentioned above, the aim of the Revolution and of the in Frankfurt 1848–49 assembly was the formation of a nation-state. But that was easier said than done. The National Assembly proceeded from the territorial status quo, that is, the *Deutsche Bund* (cf. §1). Strictly speaking, this implied that the territory of the Holy Roman Empire should be the same as that of the new empire. The trouble, however, was that the former did not include all regions occupied by Germans. There were areas with German inhabitants, such as East Prussia, which did not belong to the *Deutsche Bund*. In 1848 these were immediately incorporated into the new federation. On the other hand, there were areas with non-German inhabitants, for example, North Schleswig, Italian-speaking Tyrol, or parts of Posen with traditionally close connections to the German states, which the national convent did not want to renounce. In some areas drawing a borderline was difficult because Germans and non-Germans were mingled, as in Bohemia or in Posen, where a division was tried. Finally, some areas that belonged to the *Deutsche Bund* – such as Limburg, Luxembourg, and Holstein or regions populated by Germans, such as Schleswig – were ruled by foreign monarchs, namely, the kings of the Netherlands and Denmark, respectively. And conversely, it was also possible for a German monarch to rule German and foreign lands, as was the case with the

Habsburg monarchy. For all of these individual situations, a national solution had to be found.

In the latter cases the Frankfurt Constitution had provided for a division of the monarchies (§§2–4). As members of the German federation, the areas belonging to the *Deutsche Bund* were to obtain separate constitutions, governments, and administrations. In other words, the connection with the non-German parts could only persist in the form of a personal union with its ruler. But this proposal was not acceptable for Austria because it implied the breaking up of the Habsburg monarchy, as the Austrian government emphasized in November 1848 after this issue had been decided in the assembly. The provisional government under Heinrich von Gagern therefore took refuge in the old Prussian scheme of a "smaller" and a "larger" federation (the so-called *Doppelbund*). This plan envisioned a Germany united in an "engeren Bund" without Austria, which was again to be loosely confederated with the Habsburg monarchy. It divided the assembly into the *Kleindeutschen* or *Erbkaiserlichen*, who opted for the Prussian dynasty as future German emperors, and the so-called *Großdeutschen*, an antiborussic front of conservatives and radical democrats who continued to fight for the integration of Austria and for a directorial government. But this group had no answer to the question of how to include the non-German parts of the Habsburg monarchy in the new empire. Since the Austrian government emphatically rejected any suggestion for the separation of its territories, only the small-German option remained (with the possibility that Austria join the empire with only those parts formerly belonging to the *Deutsche Bund*, cf. §87). In March 1849 the *Erbkaiserlichen* were able to assert themselves at the end of the second reading of the Constitution. But the costs were high: as a tribute to the democrats, the so-called Simon-Gagern agreement provided that the future government should only have a suspensive veto against the decisions of Parliament, and that the national Parliament was to be elected according to universal, democratic suffrage. In addition, the idea of a *Reichsrat* was dropped.

On the basis of this compromise, on March 28, 1849 the Constitution was ratified. Almost immediately, however, the Prussian king, Friedrich Wilhelm IV, rejected the emperor's crown. He wished to receive the crown not from deputies of the people, but from representatives of his own rank. He was also offended by the way the Constitution was drafted. According to him, it should have been negotiated between the people represented by the national convent and those member states that wanted to join. Now it proved to be a fault that from the very beginning the national convent had regarded itself alone entitled to make the Constitution as the sole representative of the people in contact with the states, but not subject to their explicit approval. Only after the first reading in January 1849 did the convent establish some kind of relationship to the states. Certainly it would have been better to open permanent negotiations with a delegation of the states; yet in 1848 everyone had been glad to be rid of former institutions like the *Bundestag*.

Yet this problem could be resolved. On April 14, 1849, twenty-eight out of thirty-nine state governments recognized the *Reichsverfassung* without conditions. Even Prussia was not disinclined to lead a smaller federation provided that some conditions were met and the other member states' consent given. Accordingly, in May 1849 the *Reichsverfassung* was modified along the lines suggested by a Prussian draft; this revised constitution not only met with the fundamental approval of most states but also with that of the Reichstag that was convened in Erfurt the following year. First, this *Erfurter Reichsverfassung* contained a *Fürstenkollegium* that was to participate in legislation beside the *Reichstag*; second, it replaced the suspensive veto with an absolute veto and universal suffrage with a censuslike franchise of three classes. The *Kompetenzkompetenz* of §63 was canceled. Some other regulations were altered too.[20]

This Constitution could have been accepted even though the democrats boycotted the Reichstag in Erfurt, for both conservatives as well as democrats were quite willing to compromise on key issues. The real problem was Austria's opposition. Austria rejected closer union under the hegemony of Prussia, to be supplemented by an alliance with Austria, and instead proposed to include the whole of Austria in a federation. According to this plan, the new union would have comprised seventy million inhabitants with Austria alone representing thirty-eight million in the house of states. But this scheme too had no chance for approval. At any rate, Austrian opposition also encouraged Bavaria and Württemberg to

---

20. Cf. Karl Binding, "Der deutsche Bundesstaat auf dem Erfurter Parlament von 1850," in idem, *Zum Werden und Leben der Staaten* (Munich, 1920), 55ff.

reject the Prussian plan. As a result neither the Austrian idea of a union of seventy million people nor the Prussian plan for a small German federation could be realized. The efforts of 1848–49 to build a federative German nation had a strange result: the *Deutsche Bund*, an instrument of oppression, was restored in May 1851.

This attempt to found a German federation did not fail because of the antagonism between *Konstitutionellen* (moderates) and *Demokraten* (radicals), as has often been maintained. Both had demonstrated their ability to compromise. Nor did it fail because of the antagonism between popular sovereignty and the monarchical principle; for the coexistence of the national Parliament and monarchical governments was a practical as well as an acceptable possibility. Nor did it fail because king Friedrich Wilhelm IV had rejected acceptance of the imperial crown, since this monarch continued to favor a federative solution and Prussian leadership. The effort failed because Prussia and Austria could not bury their old rivalry. In 1849 the making of a German union foundered on the "Zerstückelung Österreichs" (*großdeutsche* solution) or the "Zerstückelung Deutschlands" (*kleindeutsche* solution). Austria rejected both proposals. Only after Prussia had beaten Austria into accepting the Prussian plan through military means did the door once again open for the formation of a German federation.

The Foundation of the Federative Nation-State, 1849–1871

The failure to build a federative nation-state in 1848 did not mean that these endeavors were abandoned. On the contrary, after only ten years they were again in full swing. The chief contributory factors responsible for this development were the outbreak of the Industrial Revolution, the weakening of Austria in the war against Italy, and the dawning of the "new era" in Prussia. In 1859 this new national thrust was symbolized by the foundation of the *Deutsche Nationalverein* as well as other associations and by the suggestion for a *Bundesreform*.[21]

Austria's reform proposals as well as those of the German middle

---

21. For a discussion of federalism at that time cf. Rudolf Ullner, *Die Idee des Föderalismus im Jahrzehnt der deutschen Einigungskriege* (Lübeck and Hamburg, 1965).

states aimed at the organization of a tripartite federation (the so-called trias plans) with but a weak, directorial central power, no genuine popular representation, and no provision for the establishment of real economic and legal unity. The difficulties in uniting Germany and Austria became obvious in the failure to integrate the weak Austrian economy, which needed protection, into the German *Zollverein* dedicated to free trade. For Prussia, on the other hand, the *Zollverein* was a functioning and promising trading union. Therefore Prussia was at ease in calling for further development toward more economic and political unity as well as for a democratically elected national Parliament. The German national movement thus allied itself to Prussia, which was determined to establish its hegemony even though the southern German states at first seemed reluctant to submit to Prussian domination. But Austria was not in a position to offer an attractive alternative to the Germans. The resulting deadlock persisted until it was resolved on the battlefield in 1866.

The questions often raised in German historiography are whether other options, for example, a *großdeutsche* solution, would have been viable, and whether a solution could have been achieved peacefully. But a *großdeutsche Lösung*, even if we see it nowadays with more sympathy, was at that time out of reach. It is difficult to see how the necessary economic, legal, and political unity could have been brought about, and how the rivalry between Austria and Prussia could have been settled without a war. Certainly Bismarck's way of describing the problems is less than satisfactory. His dictum, "Nicht durch Reden und Majoritätsbeschlüsse werden die großen Fragen der Zeit entschieden – das ist der große Fehler von 1848 und 1849 gewesen – sondern durch Eisen und Blut," is, in a general sense, not true.[22] Yet the situation of 1848 and 1866 is well characterized in his saying. There seem to be deadlocks in the development of federations where civil war becomes inevitable – a lesson taught by the American Civil War and the *Sonderbundskrieg* in Switzerland 1847.

Be that as it may, the war of 1866 changed the constellation for the establishment of the German nation-state completely. Now

---

22. Cf. Bismarck's speech in the budgetary committee of the Prussian house of representatives on September 30, 1862, in Huber, ed., *Dokumente zur deutschen Verfassungsgeschichte* (see n. 10), 2: no. 46.

foundation became possible. By forced separation from Austria, the inhibitive influence of the Austrian-Prussian dualism was removed. First, Prussia became the recognized hegemonial power in Germany. Second, the initiative for the new Constitution came from the state governments. The Constitution of the *Norddeutsche Bund* of 1867 was mainly worked out by the Prussian government according to Bismarck's directives and not by a national convention.[23] Third, the draft of the Constitution was not only harmonized with the allied governments, but debated by and passed in agreement with the people's representatives assembled in the first Reichstag of the *Norddeutsche Bund*. Thus the demand for the participation of the people in the constitutional process was also fulfilled because the Reichstag had been elected according to the election law of April 24, 1849, which had introduced universal and direct suffrage. However, under the pressure of the governments the Reichstag could only deliberate in plenary sessions and for a rather short period of time. The Constitution was not only accepted by the federal Parliament but by the parliaments of the states too.

To summarize, abolition of Austrian-Prussian dualism, Prussia's resolute lead in the national movement and in drafting the Constitution, and last but not least, the arrangement between the state governments and the national popular representatives are the most important elements of the changed historical context that characterized and made possible the new constitutional process of 1867. The joining of the southern German states in 1870 did not fundamentally alter this situation. It merely caused nominal changes: the *Norddeutsche Bund* changed into the German Reich and the Prussian king became the German kaiser.

Comparison of the Constitutions of 1849 and 1871

The *Reichsverfassung* of April 16, 1871, is divided into fourteen chapters containing seventy-eight articles altogether.[24] It is signifi-

---

23. For the making of the Constitution cf. Otto Becker, *Bismarcks Ringen um Deutschlands Gestaltung* (Heidelberg, 1958).

24. Cf. Huber, *Deutsche Verfassungsgeschichte seit 1789* (see n. 16), 3: 641ff.; Hans Boldt, "Deutscher Konstitutionalismus und Bismarckreich," in Michael Stürmer, ed., *Das kaiserliche Deutschland* (Düsseldorf, 1970), 119ff.; Wolfgang Mommsen,

cantly shorter than the Constitution of 1849. The chapter on basic laws is missing. The passage about the "Bundesgebiet" (Article 1) is followed by those concerning national legislation (*Reichsgesetzgebung*, Articles 2–5), comprising the significant competences of the Reichstag and the central government. Chapters on the organization of federal institutions follow: III, *Bundesrat* (Articles 6–10); IV, *Präsidium* (Articles 11–19); and V, Reichstag (Articles 20–32). The following passages elaborate on the federative legislative responsibilities: VI, *Zoll- und Handelswesen* (Articles 33–40); VII, *Eisenbahnwesen* (Articles 41–47); VIII, *Post- und Telegraphenwesen* (Articles 48–52); IX, *Marine und Schiffahrt* (Articles 53–55); X, *Konsulatswesen* (Article 56); XI, *Reichskriegswesen* (Articles 57–68); XII, *Reichsfinanzen* (Articles 69–73). The Constitution ends with chapters XIII, *Schlichtungen von Streitigkeiten und Strafbestimmungen* (Articles 74–77) and XIV, *Allgemeine Bestimmungen* (Article 78), regulating the procedure for changing and amending the Constitution.

That the preamble of the *Reichsverfassung* of 1871 mentions only that the monarchs of the member states have joined in an everlasting union (in opposition to the Constitution of 1849 but similar to the confederative act of the *Deutsche Bund*, 1815), as well as that the federal representation of the state governments, the *Bundesrat*, plays a major part, has induced some scholars to say that in reality the German Empire of 1871 was a mere confederation of sovereign monarchs (a *Fürstenbund*) rather than a federation.[25] Nevertheless, a different conclusion is inevitable if one considers that the new federative power had a territory of its own (Article 1) with its own national citizenship (Article 2), that the federal government as such was set up with strong and independent powers (Article 6 seq.), and that, finally, there existed a clear division of competences between federation and states – for these are features of a *Bundesstaat*. In the Constitution of 1871 this conclusion is supported by

---

"Die Verfassung des Deutschen Reichs von 1871 als dilatorischer Herrschaftskompromiß," in Otto Pflanze, ed., *Innenpolitische Probleme des Bismarck-Reiches* (Munich, 1983), 195ff. The drafts and a synopsis of the Constitution of the *Norddeutsche Bund* and of the *Deutsche Reich* are printed in Karl Binding, ed., *Deutsche Staatsgrundgesetze*, vol. 1 (Leipzig, 1904). For the discussions in the Reichstag cf. Ernst Bezold, ed., *Materialien zur deutschen Reichsverfassung*, 3 vols. (Berlin, 1872–73).

25. Cf. Max von Seydel, "Der Bundesstaatsbegriff: Eine staatsrechtliche Untersuchung," *Zeitschrift für die gesamte Staatswissenschaft* 28 (1872): 185ff. Seydel refers to the doctrines of Calhoun in opposition to the absolutely dominant trend in the German *Staatsrechtslehre*.

the definition of the purpose of the state, which exists not only for the "security" but also for the "welfare" of its citizens. This definition was more comprehensive than it would have been had a mere confederation been intended.

Positions of the States

Contrary to the Constitution of 1849, the twenty-five states forming the German Empire are named in the first article, thus eliminating all uncertainties about the extent of the empire.[26] The question about the extent of nationality had been answered unequivocally in favor of the *kleindeutsche* solution. Since in 1871 new territorial arrangements had not been on the political agenda (apart from some annexations by Prussia in 1866), constitutional provisions safeguarding the existence or territorial status quo were unnecessary. The monarchies were considered as the natural preconditions of the New Empire; their status was confirmed by their participation in the *Bundesrat* (Article 6). A provision for territorial reorganization comparable to §90 of the Frankfurt Constitution seemed superfluous. Equally, there are no prescriptions pertaining to the inner structure of the member states. On the other hand, it was more than likely that the example of national representatives elected according to universal suffrage would sooner or later have some impact on the states; however, the specter of republicanism no longer haunted Germany; this was to remain the case until 1918.

Competences of the Federation

Following the example of its predecessor of 1849, the Constitution of 1871 enumerates the federal competences (cf. Article 4 and passim, for example, Article 11, foreign relations as well as decisions on war and peace). Indeed, the catalog of federal competences resembles that of 1849 very strongly. Due to the intervention of the North German Reichstag of 1867 that catalog

---

26. Austria, Liechtenstein, Luxembourg, and Limburg no longer belonged to the new federation. Schleswig and the so-called *Reichsland* Alsace-Lorraine were joined. Prussia, with all of its territories, was part of the empire.

became, however, even more voluminous. The competences are characterized, in particular, by the endeavor to establish more unity in economic and legal affairs and by the desire to facilitate communication through mail, telegraphy, railways, unitary coins, and banks. Germany is explicitly declared to be a unitary tariff and trade zone (Article 33): the *Deutsche Zollverein* is succeeded by the *Deutsche Reich*. The merchant marine is unified too (Article 54). Although basic rights are not enumerated, important sectors such as the press and associations enjoy comparable protection and are subject only to federal legislation (cf. Article 4, no. 16). Later laws breathed a liberal spirit and epitomized the unitary liberal thrust that fueled the process of nation building. The *Kompetenzkompetenz* too, contained a centralist-unifying tendency, that is, the possibility of altering the Constitution through the federal organs alone. Although neither the "implied powers" nor this competence was explicitly included in the Constitution of 1871, the scholarly community and practicing lawyers generally assumed their validity.

Some regulations of federal legislation (in chapters VI–XI) are very detailed; this can be traced back to the participation of certain Prussian ministries, like the Ministry of Trade, in the drafting of the Constitution. In other areas subjects for legislation themselves suggested modifications: as in 1849, in 1871 it was a delicate question as to how far uniformity in military affairs could be pushed in a monarchical federation. In opposition to the navy, which from the beginning of the negotiations was held to be a federal matter (cf. Article 53), the army consisted of various contingents that were brought together as a "einheitliches Heer" under the high command of the emperor (cf. Article 63 seq.). Organizational principles and supreme command became uniform. Yet the states, or rather their monarchs, still retained original rights in military matters. Hence there was no minister of war or secretary of state on the national level, but ministers in most, but not all, states. Among them, the Prussian minister of war was the most important. On the whole, this is a curiosity of a monarchical federation and that is why it deserves to be mentioned here.

The structure of federal finance is more important. With the extension of the federal areas of competence, the need for more revenue and higher spending increased. Important projects could only be financed by credit to a small degree, as the building of battleships at the beginning of this century proved. The main sources of revenue consisted of customs (Article 80) and excise taxes (*Verbrauchssteuern*, cf. Article 35) and of revenues produced by the mail and telegraph services (cf. Article 49). In addition, the states had to make contributions (the so-called *Matrikularbeiträge*) to cover federal deficits. Hence the empire was sometimes called the *Kostgänger* of the states. This regulation corresponded to that of the Constitution of 1849 (cf. §§49 and 50), which had been considerably improved by the *Norddeutsche Reichstag* in 1867: at the request of the federal government the Reichstag had accepted a provision which stated that federal legislation no longer be restricted to customs and indirect taxes but to embrace all "für die Zwecke des Reichs zu verwendenden Steuern" (Article 4, no. 2). Thus it became possible for the empire to levy direct taxes; however, that was not actually done before the beginning of the twentieth century.

Contrary to the United States, German federalism has never had concurrent tax legislation on the national and state levels. Although the empire's competences are not exclusive powers, it was recognized in theory and practice that certain matters could only be decided by the national government, for example, foreign relations or tariff legislation (cf. Article 35). Most competences were regarded as facultative or *konkurrierend*. But this does not imply that the states could pass laws on these matters freely. On the contrary, as in 1849, federal laws in these cases abrogated state laws (cf. Article 2, "Reichsgesetze gehen den Landesgesetzen vor"). That meant that laws passed on the national level replaced state laws and this also applies to finances.

No doubt these provisions favored the federal government, but its power was of course not unlimited. The Constitution of 1871 followed the pattern established in 1849 by distinguishing even more sharply between the competence of the federation as to legislation on the one hand and the execution of the laws on the other. According to Article 4, federal activities were explicitly restricted to legislation and supervision. The Constitution pointedly states that the empire only has the right to regulate certain spheres of life by laws and to supervise the execution of the laws in these spheres. But the states retain control over the administrative apparatus. This peculiarity of German federalism still exists today. Even the activity of collecting the customs of the empire remained – as it had been during the *Zollverein* – a state matter (cf. Article 36).

Only a few proper national bureaucracies were installed, for example, for the mail and for the navy (cf. 48 and 53). The particularistic tendencies fostered by this specific division are emphasized in the Constitution of 1871 by making the state governments participate in the legislation of the union via the *Bundesrat*. We shall come back to this.

Conflict Resolution

There are differences between the Constitutions of 1849 and 1871. And one of them is that the latter contains no provisions for the resolution of federal conflicts by a supreme court. Throughout the *Kaiserreich* a judicial review of "political" issues was rejected. Perhaps Bismarck's experience with an opposition that wanted to sue him for violation of the Constitution during the Prussian constitutional conflict may account for this omission. The Constitution of 1871 offers no possibilities for complaints and politico-judicial claims comparable to the detailed list in the Frankfurt Constitution. As a result, unlike American federalism German federalism developed a tradition of constitutional courts very late. In its stead, the *Bundesrat* was declared responsible for the resolution of "interstate" constitutional conflicts and even for "intrastate" problems (Article 76). Whenever the federal government discovered shortcomings in the administration of its laws (cf. Article 17), the *Bundesrat* was empowered to take the proper measures (Article 7, no. 3). Likewise, it was to decide on and order federal intervention (*Bundesexekution*) if a state violated its constitutional obligation (Article 19). In the case of riots in a member state or in the empire, however, the emperor was entitled to impose martial law (Article 68). The *Reichsgericht* was, however, entitled to subject state laws to judicial review and pass judgment on their conformity with the imperial Constitution. It also enjoyed final jurisdiction in civic and criminal matters.

Organization of the Federal Power: Emperor and Reichstag

Like the Frankfurt Constitution of 1849, the Constitution of 1871 provided for a monarchical head of state. But in 1871 this question, which had contributed to the failure of the former Constitution, was no longer an issue. It had been settled by Prussia's hegemony in Germany. In 1867 and in 1871 there was widespread agreement that there would be neither a republican head of state nor a directorial solution on the federal level and that the Prussian king would take over the *Präsidium des Bundes*, as it had been cautiously labeled in 1867. After the foundation of the German Empire, the king of Prussia was to bear the title *Deutscher Kaiser*. His competences resembled those of the *Kaiser der Deutschen* of 1849. Among other things, he was to represent the nation in matters of international law, decide about war and peace, exercise the supreme command over army and navy, and summon the national Parliament. He was vested with the supreme executive power of the empire. On the other hand he no longer had the right of codetermination in legislative matters, as had been common in monarchical traditions (cf. Articles 5 and 17), and he did not possess the right to initiate legislation. In practice this regulation could be circumvented, however, by resorting to the so-called *Präsidialvorlagen*. This institutional arrangement contained elements of the balance-of-power principle.

As parliamentary institutions, the Reichstag and *Bundesrat* confront the emperor. Yet the Reichstag of 1871 consists of only one chamber. It is the *Volkshaus* of 1849, the democratic-unitary element of the federal government in which the parties – generally organized on the national level – dominate. The important role of the Reichstag in the legislative process, especially in the budgetary decision, contributed much to the flourishing of political parties and to the development of a multiparty system on the national level. Within this system it proved difficult to find majorities. The importance of the national Parliament increased with the political development of the empire. For the originally federative construction of the Constitution, however, the *Bundesrat* is more important.

Organization of the Federal Power: Bundesrat *and* Chancellor

The Constitution of 1849 had established as a second chamber a *Staatenhaus* which had some features similar to those of the American Senate, like the representative character of the deputies and their election by parliaments of the states. Originally the intention too had been to found a *Reichsrat* as a federative organ of the state governments. For a proper understanding of the *Reichsverfassung* of 1871, it is eminently important to realize that it neither followed the example of the *Staatenhaus* of 1849 nor that of the American Senate, but returned to the concept of a *Bundesrat* as it has been embodied in the *Reichsratplan* of 1849. The authors of the new Constitution consciously went back to the *Bundesversammlung* of the *Deutsche Bund* of 1815 and continued the tradition of delegates on the federal level instructed by their governments, as it was known from the Reichstag of the Holy Roman Empire. In 1867 the *Demokraten* sharply criticized this return to a confederative element. Bismarck, who strongly supported this solution, wanted to facilitate the joining of the monarchs and governments of the states under Prussia's leadership; at the same he favored the *Bundesrat* as an effective counterbalance to the Reichstag.

Article 6 of the *Reichsverfassung* of 1871 stipulates that the *Bundesrat* is composed of the mandatories of the state governments, who are bound to instructions. As in the *Staatenhaus* of 1849, the number of deputies differs according to the size of the states. Since the mandatories do not deliberate and decide independently but instead hand in the vote of their government, split votes are not possible for a single state. Thus even one deputy alone may represent and vote for his state. What is important is the number of votes and not the number of delegates present. The distribution of votes was fixed after the gradation of 1815. In consideration of the territories annexed in 1866 Prussia received seventeen votes, Bavaria four, etc., but every state received at least one. Together these amounted to forty-three votes and, after the accession of the southern German states in 1871, to fifty-eight.

The *Bundesrat* (not the emperor!) and the Reichstag together constitute the legislative power (Article 5). But the *Bundesrat*'s competences reach far beyond that into the executive domain. Like the Reichstag, it not only participates in the ratification of international treaties, but also has to approve declarations of war (Article 11). It decides on administrative regulations (*Verwaltungsvorschriften*) necessary for the implementation of federal laws, examines grievances concerning the execution of laws, and orders federal intervention in disobedient member states (Articles 7 and 19). To a certain extent it replaces the federal ministry that is missing in the

Constitution of 1871. It may well be maintained that the core of the political system of the empire was a *Bundesrat* government.

In the Reichstag of the North German Confederation, the moderates criticized the lack of federal departments responsible to Parliament. Yet this was exactly what Bismarck wanted. In his famous Putbuser dictations he pleaded for the establishment of a confederative organ instead of a *Zentralbehörde*.[27] Its special committees (cf. Article 8 of the *Reichsverfassung*) were to prepare legislation. The members of the *Bundesrat* should form a "bench of forty-three ministers." Article 9 allows them to visit the sessions of the Reichstag and to speak there. According to Article 24, the *Bundesrat* (the approval of the emperor presupposed) may even exert the monarchical prerogative to dissolve the national Parliament. This demonstrates that the *Bundesrat* is not merely a "co-legislative" organ, but virtually is the government of the empire.

Yet the Constitution also created a *Reichskanzler* who was to preside at the *Bundesrat* and is nominated by the emperor (Article 15). The chancellor is obviously more than a mandatory of the emperor in the *Bundesrat*, for he has to accept responsibility for all the orders and decrees (*Anordnungen und Verfügungen*) of the emperor in the same sense that a constitutional minister takes responsibility (Article 17). Thus he may be seen as a representative of the central government, a one-man government, just as Bismarck – annoyed about the Prussian collegiate cabinet over which he had presided as a prime minister – wished it to be. As a matter of fact, such a chancellor government with subordinated secretaries of state as heads of departments had become a reality in the *Kaiserreich*. Probably from the very beginning Bismarck had been interested in taking over the role of the chief in such a government; how else could he govern the empire?[28] He had not been reluctant to accept the (political) responsibility the North German Reichstag had postulated for the chancellor. For such a regulation (as it was inserted in Article 17) could only strengthen his position vis-à-vis the emperor.

27. Cf. Gustav Adolf Rein and Wilhelm Schüßler, eds., *Otto von Bismarck: Jahrhundertausgabe zum 23. September 1862*, Ausgewählte Quellen zur deutschen Geschichte der Neuzeit, 3–10, 8 vols. (Darmstadt, 1962–83), 4: 7ff.

28. About the controversy concerning Bismarck's intentions and the so-called *lex Benningsen* cf. Becker, *Bismarcks Ringen um Deutschlands Gestaltung* (see n. 23), 242ff., 264ff., 388ff.

These provisions in the Constitution did not imply a transition to a parliamentary system of government. This was effectively prevented by the decision that not the chancellor, but the *Bundesrat* as the government, faced the Reichstag. The right of the chancellor to appear in Parliament resulted only from his membership in the *Bundesrat*. On the other hand, no member of the *Bundesrat* was obliged to present political declarations or justifications to the Reichstag or to answer its interpellations. On top of that, incompatibility of membership in *Bundesrat* and Reichstag (Article 9) further reduced the Reichstag's possibilities of control. Bismarck was fully aware of the antiparliamentary effects of this conception of federalism. Not surprisingly, from 1871 onward "federalism" and "parliamentary system" have been regarded as incompatible in Germany.[29]

It is rather difficult to grasp all the peculiarities of the *Reichsverfassung* of 1871. At first glance one recognizes similarities with the American constitutional system – a kind of presidential government with a chancellor and a strict separation of powers between him and the Reichstag. However, the monarchical aspect and the *Bundesrat* do not lend themselves to clear-cut classifications. Emperor and chancellor form something like a double-headed executive, *Bundesrat* and Reichstag face them as something like a legislature divided in two chambers. But since the *Bundesrat* also has executive powers and is – with the chancellor as its chairman – the governmental counterpart to the Reichstag, it is necessary to speak not only of an imperial chancellor government but also of a *Bundesratsregierung*, that is, of two executive parts linked by the person of the chancellor. Within this constellation, the chancellor represents the monocratic and anticollegiate, the emperor the Prussian-monarchical, and the *Bundesrat* the confederative-antiparliamentarian aspect of the political institutions of the empire.

Summary

1. The *Reichsverfassung* of 1871 contains, as the *Paulskirchenverfassung* did in 1849, a unitarian-particularistic ambivalence. A

29. Cf. for example Erich Kaufmann, *Bismarcks Erbe in der Reichsverfassung* (Berlin, 1917).

unitary centralistic tendency emanates from the allocation of competences and from the so-called *Kompetenzkompetenz* favoring the empire. The Reichstag and the institutions of the emperor and chancellor produce similar effects. Particularistic effects are the result of the reduction of the federal competence to legislation; the administrative apparatus remains in the hands of the states. Particularism is also embodied in the *Bundesrat*, which provides the state governments with important rights for determining national matters. The Constitution even grants special rights (*Reservatrechte*) to certain southern German states by renouncing federal competences, for example, in the sphere of mail policy and the army, in order to enable their joining the *Deutsche Bund* in 1870. After Article 78, a minority veto of fourteen votes in the *Bundesrat* sufficed to prevent constitutional changes.

2. While the *Reichsverfassung* of 1871 on the one hand shares the unitarian-particularistic ambivalence of the Frankfurt Constitution, on the other the Austrian-Prussian rivalry had been overcome and was replaced by Prussian domination. The *Deutsche Reich* of 1871 was a hegemonial federation. Prussia ruled two-thirds of the national territories and two-thirds of the inhabitants of the empire, which manifested itself in the number of Prussian members in the Reichstag. With the *Ruhrgebiet* and the industrial region in Upper Silesia, Prussia was also the most important economic power. Her capital was the capital of the empire, her king was the emperor of Germany. Her administrative apparatus was important not only in the drafting of the legislation of the empire, but in the execution of imperial policies as well. Regularly, there was a personal union between the office of Prussian prime minister and that of federal chancellor. The *Reichskanzler* was not only minister of external affairs but was also entitled to instruct the Prussian votes in the *Bundesrat*. The Prussian war minister in practice exercised the functions of the national war minister. For all that, it is less significant that Prussia commanded only seventeen votes in the *Bundesrat*. Since fourteen votes were enough to prevent alterations of the Constitution and since the emperor had a veto in military affairs and in matters of tariffs and taxation (cf. Article 5, nos. 35 and 37), Prussia's position was indeed strong, even without commanding a majority of votes. In the time after 1871 it was less often

the case that other states opposed Prussia than that the interests of Prussia and those of the empire came into conflict. Thus the federal chancellor and Prussian prime minister had to defend his policies twice, namely, before the national Parliament and before the Prussian house of representatives, which was called the *heimliche zweite Kammer*. But the dualism between the empire and Prussia became a conspicuous element in the Weimar Republic after the identity of personnel between the central and Prussian governments had ceased.

3. Through the *Reichsverfassung* of 1849 a federal tradition had been founded in Germany that influenced the Constitutions of 1867 and 1871. The tradition is that of a monarchical-democratic federation with the strong legislative powers of the empire that at the same time preserves the administrative responsibility of the states. In 1867–71 this system was modified to some extent. We find a monarchical-democratic federation again, but due to the replacement of the federal ministry conceived in 1849 with the chancellor government and the replacement of the house of states with the *Bundesrat*, it acquired particularistic-antiparliamentary and Prussian-hegemonial traits. But the development of German federalism did not end there. As Bismarck had already predicted in his Putbuser dictations, the importance of the emperor and federal government led by the chancellor increased in significance, while the *Bundesrat* lost in importance. The institution, which according to the Constitution possessed plenty of power, became a second chamber dominated by bureaucratic specialists of the member states. It could neither prevent the "parliamentarization" of the federal power nor the "republicanization" of the empire in 1918–19. The unitary trend, too, gained momentum in the Weimar Republic. It is true that in 1945 West Germany experienced a federalist revival while the hegemonial power of Prussia was destroyed, but this could not stop the development leading to what was called a "unitarische Bundesstaat."[30] The unitary trend persisted, while at the same time a feeling of belonging to the new states formed by the Allied powers after the war took root. The *Bundesrat* also persisted, as well as the separation of tasks between federal legislation on the one hand and state responsibility for the

30. Cf. Konrad Hesse, *Der unitarische Bundesstaat* (Karlsruhe, 1962).

administration of laws on the other. It was only in the 1960s that a new trend toward the so-called "cooperative federalism" appeared, which once again evokes a similarity to the United States of America.

11
States' Rights, Federalism, and Criminal Extradition in Antebellum America: The New York–Virginia Controversy, 1839–1846

Paul Finkelman

The political structure of the Constitution of 1787 created an inherent tension between the states and the national government. Where the rights of the states ended and the power of the national government began was uncertain. Before 1861 arguments about states' rights were usually raised when the national government pursued policies that specific states or regions disliked.

Most studies of states' rights focus on the conflicts between the states and the central government. Assertions of states' rights are usually viewed as those made by states in their struggle against the federal government. Between 1787 and 1861 the relationship between the national government and the states led to four levels of states' rights policies or arguments.

At its least controversial level, states' rights simply meant the right of states to pursue their own interests independently of or concurrently with the national government. The states claimed concurrent jurisdiction over taxation, navigation, economic regulation, and even some forms of interstate commerce. Such claims, which did not threaten the national government, were either tolerated or encouraged by various presidents, Congresses, and Supreme Court justices. Thus the high court found it was constitutionally permissible for states to prohibit the sale of certain goods, like lottery tickets, liquor, or slaves, even though such legislation affected interstate commerce.[1] Assertions of states' rights at

---

1. *Cohens v. Virginia*, 6 Wheat. 264 (1821) upheld a conviction for selling federally approved lottery tickets in violation of Virginia law; *Groves v. Slaughter*, 15 Peters 449 (1841) declared that a state, by appropriate legislation, could prohibit the importation of slaves as articles of commerce; *The License Cases*, 5 Howard 504

this level did not usually disrupt the federal system, not did it challenge the power of the national government.

More dangerous to the federal union were assertions by states that they did not have to help the national government enforce its laws and that, to a limited extent, they might obstruct such laws. The refusal of individual northern judges to aid in the surrender of fugitive slaves is a good example of this.[2] So too were the northern personal liberty laws that prohibited the use of state facilities in the return of fugitive slaves.[3] Such assertions of states' rights did not directly challenge the power of the national government, although they certainly reduced its ability to enforce the fugitive slave laws. While we generally think of states' rights as a southern phenomenon, northerners vigorously adopted this application of states' rights theory.

State interposition and/or nullification, the third level of states' rights argumentation, was a far greater threat to the federal government. Here the states claimed they had a right to actually prevent the enforcement of a federal law. Before 1820 claims for this power were made in the North and South. In 1788 Jeffersonians in Virginia opposed the enforcement of the Sedition Act by arguing that a state has a right and a duty "to interpose" to prevent federal authority from interfering with the "rights and liberties" of the people. A more extreme position was taken by Kentucky, which declared the Sedition Act "which does abridge the freedom of the press, is not law, but is altogether void and of no effect."[4] Similarly, during the War of 1812 representatives of the New England

---

(1847) upheld a state tax on liquor produced in other states on the ground that this was part of the state's inherent police power.

2. This is discussed in Paul Finkelman, *"Prigg v. Pennsylvania* and Northern State Courts: Antislavery Use of a Proslavery Decision," *Civil War History* 25 (1979): 5–35.

3. See generally Thomas D. Morris, *Free Men All: The Personal Liberty Laws of the North, 1780–1861* (Baltimore, MD, 1974).

4. "Resolution of the Commonwealth of Kentucky," November 16, 1798; "Resolution of the Commonwealth of Virginia," December 24, 1798. Both resolutions have been reprinted in numerous places, including Henry Steele Commager, ed., *Documents of American History* (New York, 1934), passim. "The Sedition Act, Act of July 14, 1798," *U.S. Statutes at Large*, 1: 596–97, allowed the prosecution of "any person [who] shall write, print, utter, or publish . . . any false scandalous and malicious writing or writings against the government of the United States, or either house of the Congress or the President of the United States, with intent to defame the said government, . . . the said Congress, or the said President, or to bring them, . . . into contempt or disrepute." The law was passed by the Federalist-

states, meeting in Hartford, Connecticut, urged their legislatures "to adopt all such measures as may be necessary effectually to protect the citizens of said states from the operations and effects of all acts which have been or may be passed by Congress . . . subjecting the militia or other citizens to forcible drafts, conscriptions, or impressments, not authorized by the constitution of the United States."[5]

After the War of 1812 nullification became primarily a southern doctrine. In ordering the abolitionist Sherman Booth's release from federal custody and in later ordering the arrest of the federal marshal, the Wisconsin Supreme Court came close to adopting interposition. However, Wisconsin acquiesced in the Supreme Court's decision ordering the rearrest of Booth.[6] In the South nullification was more common. In 1818 the state of Maryland tried to prevent the operation of the federally chartered Bank of the United States through the state's taxing powers. Chief Justice Marshall held unconstitutional this novel attempt of a state to effectively nullify a federal law.[7] The state of Georgia effectively annulled the Supreme Court decision in *Worcester v. Georgia* in 1832. South Carolina went so far as to formally adopt an ordinance nullifying the tariff of 1832.[8]

---

dominated Congress to help suppress the Jeffersonian Republicans in the upcoming presidential election. The political nature of the law was underscored by the fact that the law would be in force only until March 3, 1801 – the day before the president elected in 1800 would take office. Some twenty-five persons, mostly supporters of Jefferson, were prosecuted under the law. Ten, including Congressman Matthew Lyon of Vermont, were convicted and sentenced to jail. Although the act was probably unconstitutional, its validity was never determined by the U.S. Supreme Court. President Jefferson pardoned all persons convicted under the law and ultimately Congress remitted their fines. The Virginia resolution protesting this act was written by James Madison while the Kentucky resolution was secretly authored by Thomas Jefferson, who was then vice-president of the United States. Significantly, the act punished libels against the president and the Congress, but not against the vice-president. The best study of the act is James Morton Smith, *Freedom's Fetters: The Alien and Sedition Laws and American Civil Liberties* (Ithaca, NY, 1956).

5. "Report and Resolutions of the Hartford Convention," January 4, 1815 (Hartford, CT, 1815), reprinted in Commager, ed., *Documents of American History* (see n. 4), 209.

6. *In re Booth*, 3 Wis. 1 (1854); *Ex parte Booth*, 3 Wis. 145 (1854); *In re Booth and Rycraft*, 3 Wis. 157 (1854); *Ableman v. Booth*, 21 Howard (U.S.) 506 (1858).

7. *McCulloch v. Maryland*, 4 Wheat. (U.S.) 316 (1819) at 431.

8. *Worcester v. Georgia*, 6 Peters (U.S.) 515 (1832); "An Ordinance to Nullify certain acts of the Congress of the United States," resolution of November 2, 1832, *The Statutes at Large of South Carolina*, 1: 329.

The fourth, and most extreme, level of states' rights arguments asserted that states had a right to secede from the union. New England Federalists made this claim during the War of 1812. However, this position garnered little sympathy in that region and was abandoned with the end of the war. Secession was never again seriously advocated in the North. Although the Garrisonian abolitionists demanded "No Union With Slaveowners," they were a tiny minority, disdained in the North in part because of their anti-union slogan.[9]

For many southerners, on the other hand, the idea of secession – and ultimately the desire for it – was a powerful intellectual and political force. The concept of secession helps differentiate constitutional thought, development, and action in the South from that of the North. Arthur Bestor has cogently argued, "Secession was the *alternative* to, not the proposed *outcome* of, the constitutional program that proslavery forces advocated, in the name of state sovereignty, during the controversy over slavery in the territories."[10] Significantly, however, the South viewed secession as a viable – indeed an inevitable – alternative, while the North did not. From the very beginning of the nation, the South believed in a right to secede if the national government threatened slavery. The peculiar institution led the South to have a peculiar commitment to the union.

Even before the union was solidified, southerners suggested that they might secede. In the debates over the Articles of Confederation, South Carolina's Thomas Lynch declared that, "If it is debated, whether their slaves are their property, there is an end of the confederation."[11] Similar threats were made at the Philadelphia Convention. During the debate over representation North Carolina's William R. Davie told the delegates that his state would "never

9. Even the Garrisonians never argued in favor of disunion per se. Rather, they wanted an end to a union with slaveowners. They were perfectly content to remain within a union once slavery was abolished. The pro-union position of most Garrisonians after the beginning of the Civil War supports this analysis.

10. Arthur Bestor, "State Sovereignty and Slavery: A Reinterpretation of Proslavery Constitutional Doctrine, 1846–1860," *Journal of the Illinois State Historical Society* 54 (1961): 119.

11. Worthington C. Ford, ed., *Journals of the Continental Congress, 1777–1789*, 34 vols. (Washington, DC, 1904–37), 6: 1080, debate of July 30, 1776. As Bestor noted, the term "states' rights" did not appear in the American political vocabulary until 1798. Thus, the concept of secession may have preceded the articulation of the concept of states' rights. Bestor, "State Sovereignty and Slavery" (see n. 10), 145.

confederate" unless slaves were counted for representation. General Charles Cotesworth Pinckney warned that a prohibition of the African slave trade would be "an exclusion of South Carolina from the Union." Indeed throughout the Convention the southerners made it clear that if they did not get substantial protection for slavery they would not join the union.[12] Only southerners talked of leaving the convention or of not accepting the Constitution if they did not get their way.

The southern commitment to the union remained uncertain from 1787 until 1861. From the 1820s on "southerners repeatedly threatened to secede."[13] During the nullification crisis of 1832–33, South Carolina took the theory to the brink of reality. In 1850 southern leaders called disunion conventions, which were thwarted only by the compromise of 1850. After 1854 southerners warned that a Republican victory would lead to secession. In 1860–61 they acted on this threat. Northerners reacted to this turn of events with surprise because "the simple fact was that the disunion alarm had been sounded so often that only a few were willing to heed it any longer."[14]

The result of secession, as many had long predicted, was civil war. That is no doubt why most Americans – North and South – resisted carrying states' rights arguments to their ultimate conclusion.

States' Rights between the States

The tensions between the states and the national government were not, however, the only conflicts which led to the articulation of states' rights doctrine in the nineteenth century. Equally important, although far less studied, was the use of states' rights arguments in interstate disputes. Disputes between states on both sides of the

---

12. Max Farrand, ed., *The Records of the Federal Convention of 1787*, 4 vols. (New Haven, CT, 1937, repr. 1966), 1: 593. The problem of slavery at the convention is dealt with in Paul Finkelman, "Slavery and the Constitutional Convention: Making a Covenant with Death," in Richard Beeman et al., eds., *Beyond Confederation: Origins of the Constitution and American National Identity* (Chapel Hill, NC, 1987), 188–225.
13. Kenneth Stampp, *And the War Came: The North and the Secession Crisis, 1860–1861* (Baton Rouge, LA, 1950, repr. 1970), 5.
14. Ibid., 8.

Mason-Dixon line put great stress on the union. There were a number of areas of public policy in which states applied these theories. Many, perhaps most, were related to slavery.[15] A few of these, such as the problem of comity and the interstate transit of slaves, have been studied in great detail.[16] Other problems, such as the refusal of southern states to respect the rights of northern free black seamen, have only been briefly examined.[17] Virtually unstudied but equally important for an understanding of states' rights in this period are the responses of southern and northern governors to requests for extraditions of persons charged with slavery-related crimes.

Before 1861 most criminal extraditions were pro forma matters and only rarely caused controversy. The one exception to this rule concerned extraditions involving slavery and race. Southern

15. After 1820 there were two major antebellum examples of state resistance to federal law which were not immediately related to slavery. Georgia ignored the Supreme Court's ruling in *Worcester v. Georgia*, 6 Peters (U.S.) 515 (1832), but the state's governor pardoned the plaintiffs in the case, thus mooting its states' rights opposition to the decision. This compromise was tied to the response of Georgia officials and President Jackson to the nullification crisis in South Carolina. Alfred H. Kelly, Winfred A. Harbison, and Herman Belz, *The American Constitution* (New York, [4]1983), 212–13. More famous was South Carolina's nullification of a federal tariff in 1832. However, William W. Freehling in *Prelude to Civil War: The Nullification Controversy in South Carolina, 1816–1836* (New York, 1967), persuasively argues that the nullification controversy was directly tied to South Carolina's self-conscious development as a slave society. While slavery was not the immediate issue in the crisis, it was certainly the underlying cause of the crisis.

16. Paul Finkelman, *An Imperfect Union: Slavery, Federalism, and Comity* (Chapel Hill, NC, 1981).

17. This is explored in Paul Finkelman, "Antebellum States' Rights, North and South," in Kermit Hall and James Ely, eds., *An Uncertain Tradition: Constitutionalism and the History of the South* (Athens, GA, 1988). Earlier discussions of the issue are found in Philip M. Hamer, "Great Britain, the United States, and the Negro Seamen Acts, 1822–1848," and "British Consuls and the Negro Seamen Acts, 1850–1860," *Journal of Southern History* 1 (1935): 3–28, 138–68; Donald G. Morgan, *Justice William Johnson: The First Dissenter* (Columbia, SC, 1954), 184–206; William M. Wiecek, *The Sources of Antislavery Constitutionalism* (Ithaca, NY, 1978), 132–40; and Freehling, *Prelude to Civil War* (see n. 15), 113–15. A history of the Negro Seamen's Acts, which has never been written, would add much to our understanding of the development and implementation of southern constitutional theory. For primary-source material on this problem see *Elkison v. Deliesseline*, 8 F. Cas. 433 (1823); "The Argument of Benj. Faneuil Hunt, in the case of the arrest of the Person claiming to be a British Seaman . . . before the Hon. Judge Johnson, Circuit Judge of the United States, for 6th Circuit" (Charleston, SC, 1823), 12–14, reprinted in Paul Finkelman, ed., *Slavery, Race, and the American Legal System, 1700–1872* (New York, 1987).

governors often refused to extradite whites accused of kidnapping free blacks in the North. Similarly, some northern governors refused to cooperate in the extradition to the South of persons charged with slavery-related crimes. These controversies helped to gradually erode the bonds of union. Northern noncooperation with southern states may have led southerners to assume that the North was not committed to the union. This proved to be a tragic miscalculation.

Interstate Comity and the Rendition of Fugitives from Justice

Between 1787 and 1861 claims of states' rights, complicated by slavery and race, undermined the constitutional clause which required that governors allow the extradition of accused criminals. This clause, found in Article IV, declared: "A Person charged in any State with Treason, Felony, or other Crime, who shall flee from Justice, and be found in another State, shall on Demand of the executive Authority of the State from which he fled, be delivered up, to be removed to the State having Jurisdiction of the Crime."[18] Before 1861 controversies over criminal extradition, complicated by slavery and race, occurred between Pennsylvania and Virginia, Pennsylvania and Maryland, Missouri and Illinois, Maine and Georgia, New York and Virginia, New York and Georgia, Ohio and Virginia, and Ohio and Kentucky.[19] Although governors in both sections of the country justified their refusals to accede to

18. The Constitution of the United States of America, IV, 2, 2. This clause was almost identical to a similar clause in Article IV of the Articles of Confederation: "If any person guilty of, or charged with treason, felony, or other high misdemeanor in any State, shall flee from justice, and be found in any of the United States, he shall upon demand of the Governor or Executive power, of the State from which he fled, be delivered up and removed to the State having jurisdiction of his offence."

19. Some of these controversies are discussed in Finkelman, "Antebellum States' Rights" (see n. 17). For further information see Thomas Mifflin, governor of Pennsylvania, to President Washington, July 18, 1791, *American State Papers, Miscellaneous* 1: 38–43; Fred Somkin, "The Strange Career of Fugitivity in the History of Interstate Extradition," *Utah Law Review* 35 (1984): 511–31; and I.T. Hoague, "Extradition between States: Executive Discretion," *American Law Review* 13 (1879): 181–243. Austin King, governor of Missouri to Augustus French, governor of Illinois, June 30, 1849; French to King, July 20, 1849; King to French, July 27, 1849; French to King, August 28, 1849, all reprinted in Evarts B. Greene and Charles M. Thompson, eds., *Collections of the Illinois State Historical Society*, vol. 7;

extradition requisitions on states' rights grounds, there was nevertheless a striking difference in the way these arguments were used.

Northerners tended to use states' rights arguments where they were convenient, but without any real conviction. Thus, northern governors and legislatures were willing to turn to the president, the Congress, or the federal courts to vindicate their policies. With the exception of one case argued late in the antebellum period, southerners rarely turned to the national government to solve interstate disputes.[20] To have done so would have meant acknowledging the supremacy of the national government – something that ran counter to southern states' rights theory.

Southern states' rights responses differed from the northern arguments and positions in three other critical ways. First, southerners were willing to appeal to other states for support in their verbal battles with northern states. For example, during its lengthy dispute with New York, Virginia appealed to other slave states for support. Resolutions from South Carolina, Maryland, Kentucky, and elsewhere followed. Northern states never sought or presented such a "united front" on issues involving interstate conflicts.

Similarly, southerners were quick to threaten retaliation against the North for policies they did not like. The threats of Governor George Gilmer of Georgia during his dispute with Maine illustrate this. Gilmer demanded the extradition of two Maine sailors accused

---

Governors' Letter-Books, 1840–1853 (Springfield, IL, 1911), 207–9, 212–16. French to "The Governor of Missouri," February 17, 1852, in Greene and Thompson, eds., *Collections of the Illinois State Historical Society*, 7: 244–45. In 1851 the free black relatives of Peyton Polly were kidnapped in Ohio and taken to Kentucky. Some of the Polly family were sold there, and the rest were taken to Virginia. The Pollys in Kentucky were eventually recovered through the intervention of the Ohio government. After nearly ten years of negotiation and litigation, including a case taken to the Court of Appeals of Virginia, the Pollys in that state remained enslaved. There is no published history of this case. Records of it are found in the papers of Ohio governors in the Ohio Historical Society. See also *Journal of the Senate of Ohio* (1851): 530, 586, 825, 847; "Annual Message of the Governor of Ohio, January 5, 1852," *Executive Documents, Ohio, Fiftieth General Assembly*, vol. 16, pt. 1 (Columbus, OH, 1852), 19–20; *Ratcliff v. Polly & als.*, 12 Gratt (Va.) 528 (1855); "Joint Resolution relative to the Kidnapping of the Polly Family," resolution of March 10, 1860, *Ohio Laws 57* (1860), 149. There was also a small controversy between New York and Louisiana over a fugitive slave charged with theft in Louisiana. See extradition papers of April 13, 1839, from governor of Louisiana to governor of New York, *In re Stephen Johnson*; Seward to the secretary of state, n.d.; and Seward to the governor of Louisiana, July 29, 1839, draft of letter, Seward Papers, Extradition Files (Stephen Johnson), Univ. of Rochester.

20. *Kentucky v. Dennison*, 24 Howard (U.S.) 66 (1861).

of helping a slave escape from Georgia. Gilmer sought the sailors even though the escaped slave had been captured and returned to his master. The governor of Maine refused to comply with the requisition. Governor Gilmer responded that if Maine did not acquiesce to Georgia's demand, Georgia "must necessarily protect the rights of its citizens from the danger to which their slave property will be thus exposed from Mainers coming from Maine into her ports." Gilmer ominously concluded, "I shall not attempt to trace out the consequences to which such a state of things must lead."[21] Georgia declined to pass such legislation in 1839. However, in 1841, in response to a similar controversy with New York, Georgia adopted "An Act the better to secure and protect the citizens of Georgia in possession of their Slaves," which required northern shippers entering the state to post a bond guaranteeing that no slaves would leave the state on their ships.[22]

A final difference between southern and northern states' rights arguments concerned secession. During these controversies southern governors and legislatures repeatedly declared that the behavior of their northern counterparts would lead to a dissolution of the union. For example, during the Maine-Georgia controversy, the Georgia legislature declared that Maine's refusal to extradite the two sailors meant that Georgia was "no longer *bound by any obligations to the common compact*" and was free "to seek and provide protection for her *own people in her own way*." The legislature resolved that if Maine did not return the two indicted sailors, the governor should call a statewide convention "to take into consideration the state of the Commonwealth of Georgia, and to devise the course of her future policy, and provide all necessary safeguards for the protection of her people."[23] In other words, Georgia was willing to consider a dissolution of the union over the refusal of

21. Governor George Gilmer to Governor Edward Kent, August 23, 1838, printed in Governor of Maine [Edward Kent], *Message to the Senate and House of Representatives of Maine* (Augusta, 1839), 25. For the Maine-Georgia controversy see Finkelman, "Antebellum States' Rights, North and South" (see n. 17), 125–58.

22. "An Act to better secure and protect the citizens of Georgia in the possession of their slaves," act of December 11, 1841, *Georgia Laws* (1841), 125–28.

23. Georgia House of Representatives, "Report of the Joint Committee on the State of the Republic," printed in Governor of Maine [Edward Kent], *Message to the Senate and House of Representatives of Maine* (see n. 21), 32–33 [emphasis in the original].

Maine to extradite two sailors.

Between 1837 and 1845 Georgia, Louisiana, and Virginia attempted to extradite from Maine and New York free black sailors, fugitive slaves, and whites who were charged with crimes in the South. These attempts were frustrated by the governors of Maine and New York and led to controversies that reached national politics. The New York-Virginia controversy illustrates the utility and limitations of northern states' rights arguments. The New York-Virginia controversy also reveals the restricted options available for southern politicians disgruntled by northern applications of states' rights doctrines. In the late 1850s this problem reemerged in a dispute between Ohio and Kentucky that reached the Supreme Court.[24] In these controversies the North took a strong states' rights position, while the South, when not threatening retaliation or secession, cloaked itself in the rhetoric of nationalism. The ironies were not lost on the participants. As Governor William H. Seward of New York pointed out to his Virginia counterpart:

> I must be permitted to express, with all due deference, my belief that if this question had arisen in any case not supposed to involve a peculiar interest of Virginia, that state would have been very unwilling to maintain a construction of the Constitution, which, if it is not altogether misunderstood on my part, is incompatible with the true dignity and sovereignty of the states.[25]

The rest of this article examines in detail the extradition controversy between Virginia and New York over three black sailors accused of helping a slave escape from Virginia to New York. This examination reveals the manner in which states' rights arguments were used in the growing war of words between the states. This investigation also demonstrates that in the emerging sectional controversy states' rights were far more important to the South than the North.

---

24. *Kentucky v. Dennison*, 24 Howard (U.S.) 66 (1861).

25. Seward to Thomas W. Gilmer, governor of the state of Virginia, November 9, 1840, printed version in *Message of the Governor of Virginia, Communicating a Correspondence between the Governors of Virginia and New York in Relation to Certain Fugitives from Justice* (Richmond, VA, 1840), 36.

The New York–Virginia Controversy

In July 1839 three free black sailors, Peter Johnson, Edward Smith, and Isaac Gansey, helped a slave named Isaac escape from Norfolk, Virginia, on the *Robert Center*, a New York–based schooner. Isaac's absence was immediately noted, and agents for the state of Virginia went to New York City, where they were waiting when the *Robert Center* docked. Isaac was captured without incident while Johnson, Smith, and Gansey were arrested under a Virginia warrant. One of the Virginia agents, James Caphart, then went to Albany, where he presented to Governor William H. Seward an extradition requisition for the three sailors, signed by Henry L. Hopkins, Virginia's lieutenant governor. Seward informally declined to approve the extradition requisition, at least in part because it was not accompanied by a grand-jury indictment. Seward told Caphart that the three sailors should be given "an opportunity to be heard before deciding the question." Caphart returned to Virginia with the slave Isaac. Meanwhile, the three sailors obtained a writ of habeas corpus and were released from custody.[26]

Seward's refusal on technical grounds was a reasonable response to an extradition requisition. It neither raised states' rights questions nor implied that a sectional or political crisis would develop. Seward's response was within the accepted parameters of theories about the extradition clause; he did not refuse to extradite the three men but only postponed a decision because the form of the requisition was incomplete. Seward's refusal was procedural rather than substantive and on its face legitimate as long as procedural questions remained.[27]

In September Seward received a letter from Lieutenant Governor Hopkins, asking for a formal explanation of his failure to extradite the black sailors. This was the beginning of a voluminous three years' correspondence between Seward and five Virginia chief executives. The conflict led to special messages from governors in

---

26. Seward to Hopkins, September 16, 1839, and Samuel Blatchford to [James Caphart], July 30, 1839, both in *Message from the Governor*, "Correspondence between the Governor of New-York and the Executive of Virginia," New York State Senate, no. 1, January 5, 1841, 42–43 [hereafter cited as *Governors' Correspondence*]. See also Glyndon G. Van Deusen, *William Henry Seward* (New York, 1967), 65–66.

27. Seward to Hopkins, September 16, 1839, in *Governors' Correspondence* (see n. 26), 42.

both states. It became a subject for their annual messages. The legislatures of both states eventually passed resolutions on the controversy and enacted statutes because of it. A number of other states also became involved through legislation and resolutions. A satisfactory conclusion was never reached, and as a political issue it lingered until 1846.[28]

The New York–Virginia controversy involved the antislavery movement in New York and the developing proslavery ideology in Virginia. Seward's adamant defense of the rights of three black sailors also suggests the willingness of some northern politicians, as early as 1839, to fight for justice for free blacks. This suggests that the alleged racism of antebellum northerners may not have been as pervasive as many scholars believe.[29] The controversy also raised questions of states' rights and federalism central to the antebellum crisis. Finally, this controversy helped solidify the emerging concept of executive discretion in extradition cases. By the time the controversy was over, Seward had set an important precedent for governors' refusing to comply with extradition requisitions for reasons that went beyond questions of procedure.

In his response to Hopkins's September letter, Seward noted the many technical and procedural problems with the extradition requisition. But Seward did not rely on these insufficiencies or technicalities in denying Virginia's demand. Instead, Seward directly confronted the question of who should determine the validity of an extradition requisition. His conclusion was blunt: "Waiving all the defects in the affidavit, I cannot surrender the

28. Hopkins to Seward, August 30, 1839; Robert H. Morris, recorder of the City of New York to Seward, July, 1839; Seward to Hopkins, September 16, 1839, in Virginia House of Delegates, doc. no. 1, *Annual Message of the Governor of the Commonwealth and Accompanying Documents*, December 2, 1839, 31, 34–35, 35–38 [hereafter cited as *Virginia Annual Message, 1839*]. Frederick W. Seward, ed., *Autobiography of William H. Seward*, 3 vols. (New York, 1877), 1: 428–29, 439. There is no adequate history of these events. They are briefly discussed in Edward Everett Hale, Jr., *William H. Seward* (Philadelphia, PA, 1910), 158–64; Frederick Bancroft, *The Life of William H. Seward*, 2 vols. (New York, 1900), 101–7. Van Deusen, *William Henry Seward* (see n. 26) barely mentions the issue at 65–66. Although only briefly focusing on the issue, Jane H. Pease, "The Road to the Higher Law," *New York History* 40 (1959): 117, 121–23, is the best available analysis of the New York–Virginia controversy.

29. See, for example, Leon Litwack, *North of Slavery* (Chicago, IL, 1961). For an extended reevaluation of the thesis that the antebellum North was almost totally negrophobic, see Paul Finkelman, "Prelude to the Fourteenth Amendment: Black Legal Rights in the Antebellum North," *Rutgers Law Journal* 17 (1986): 415–82.

supposed fugitives to be carried to Virginia for trial under the statute of that State."[30] This conclusion was based on an analysis that applied both states' rights arguments and international law to American federalism.

Seward explained that as a state governor he had the authority and obligation to determine the validity of any extradition requisition he received. After "due consideration" he concluded that the Constitution's extradition clause "applies only to those acts which, if committed within the jurisdiction of the State in which the person accused is found, would be treasonable, felonious or criminal, by the laws of that State." This was a well recognized concept of international law, which to this day is valid.[31] Seward asserted that his refusal to extradite the blacks stemmed from his responsibility as a governor to protect the "civil liberty" of his citizens. He found that "there is no law of this State which recognizes slavery, no statute which admits that one man can be the property of another, or that one man can be stolen from another." Nor did the common law recognize slavery. Seward refused to extradite the three black sailors because he concluded that the offense of slave stealing was "not a felony nor a crime within the meaning of the Constitution."[32]

Seward then analyzed the issue within a framework of international law. He noted that "the right to demand and the reciprocal obligation to surrender fugitives from justice between sovereign and independent nations, as defined by the law of nations, include only those cases in which the acts constituting the offence charged are recognized as crimes by the universal laws of all civilized countries." Seward implied that the Constitution's extradition clause was similar to a treaty between sovereign nations. Seward asserted that the "well understood" purpose of the provision "was to recognize and establish this principle in the mutual relations of the States, as independent, equal and sovereign communities." Since these states "could form no treaties between themselves, it was necessarily engrafted in the Constitution." Because slavery

---

30. Hopkins to Seward, August 30, 1839; Seward to Hopkins, September 16, 1839. *Governors' Correspondence* (see n. 26), 41, 45, 46, 44. See also Seward, ed., *Autobiography of William H. Seward* (see n. 28), 437–38.

31. *Governors' Correspondence* (see n. 26), 44, 45; 31 *Am. Jur. 2d*, 962–65.

32. Seward to Hopkins, September 16, 1839. *Governors' Correspondence* (see n. 26), 45–46.

was not recognized by international law, Seward could not return the fugitives.[33]

Seward's analysis was a correct statement of international law. It dovetailed perfectly with his analysis that a state need only return a fugitive if that fugitive was charged with a crime recognized in the state where he was seeking asylum.[34] In doing so, Seward effectively equated New York and Virginia with independent nations. However, the limits of Seward's state-sovereignty arguments must be understood. Unlike the nullification position of South Carolina in the 1830s, Seward was not asserting his state's independence from national or federal authority. Rather, he was simply asserting New York's equality with Virginia.

Hopkins found Seward's answer to be "at war with the language and spirit of the federal constitution – inconsistent with the true relations, rights, and duties of the States, and calculated to disturb the general harmony of the country." The argument that slaves could not be stolen was unacceptable because Hopkins understood "*stealing* to be recognized as *crime* by all laws, human and divine." Hopkins asserted that as a "free, independent and sovereign state" Virginia had "an unquestionable right to devise its own system of jurisprudence" and New York had no right to question its laws. "Neither the government nor the citizens of any other country can rightfully interfere with its municipal regulations in any way." He warned Seward that on the subject of slavery "Virginia knows her rights and will at all times maintain them."[35] Thus, Hopkins confronted Seward's assertions of states' rights with those of his own. While basing some of his response on the U.S. Constitution, Hopkins seemed more comfortable in asserting a states' rights argument.

Seward answered Virginia's assertions of states' rights with assertions of his own. He did "not question the constitutional right of a state to make such a penal code as it shall deem necessary or expedient." Seward readily "admitted the sovereignty of the several states" as Hopkins had so "strenuously insist[ed]." Indeed, Seward declared that "no person can maintain more firmly than I do the principle that the states are sovereign and independent in

33. *Governors' Correspondence* (cf. n. 26), 44–45.
34. Ibid., 44–45; 31 *Am. Jur. 2d*, 962–65.
35. Hopkins to Seward, October 4, 1839, *Virginia Annual Message, 1839* (cf. n. 28), 31–34 [emphasis in the original].

regard to all matters except those . . . expressly . . . transferred to the federal government." With just a touch of irony, Seward pointed out to Hopkins that "I have at least believed that my non-compliance with the requisition made upon me in the present case would be regarded as maintaining the equal sovereignty and independence of this state, and by necessary consequence those of all other states." This fidelity to states' rights led Seward to reiterate his position that New York could not extradite men charged with stealing slaves because that crime was not recognized by New York.[36]

This civil war of words soon shifted to the annual messages of the governors. In December David Campbell, Virginia's new governor, told his legislature that because of the policies of New York and Maine, the latter of which was involved in a similar controversy with Goergia,[37] "It is impossible that the Union can continue long." He accused Seward of following "the fanatic doctrines" of the abolitionists, which "jeopardize the tranquility and hazard the dissolution of the Union."[38] This response reflected a major theme of southern states' rights argumentation – the willingness to threaten secession whenever confronted with northern politicians who would not accept their demands.

In January Seward expressed regret "that a construction of the constitution manifestly necessary to maintain the sovereignty of this State, and the personal rights of her citizens, should be regarded by the Executive of Virginia as justifying, in any contingency, a menace of secession for the Union."[39] Seward no doubt found it difficult to comprehend that Virginia would even threaten a dissolution of the union over something as minor as the extradition of three alleged thieves.

Seward's refusal to extradite the three fugitives, his reasons for not doing so, and Virginia's immediate response illustrate the

36. Seward to Hopkins, October 24, 1839, *Virginia Annual Message, 1839* (see n. 28), 38–43; Seward, ed., *Autobiography of William H. Seward* (see n. 28), 438.

37. See nn. 22–23 above. This controversy is also mentioned briefly in Ulrich B. Phillips, *Georgia and State Rights* (1902, repr. Yellow Spring, OH, 1968), 139–40.

38. "Message of Governor Campbell," *Virginia Annual Message, 1839,* (see n. 28), 1–7; "Annual Message to the Legislature, January 7, 1840," in Charles Z. Lincoln, ed., *Messages from the Governors of the State of New York,* 4 vols. (Albany, NY, 1909), 3: 778.

39. "Annual Message to the Legislature, January 7, 1840," in Lincoln, ed., *Messages from the Governors* (see n. 38), 3: 778.

nature of the states' rights debate at this point. As a state governor, Seward asserted his power to reject an extradition requisition that did not meet with New York's definition of a crime. He also asserted that as chief executive of the state he was empowered, indeed obligated, to protect his citizens from the improper demands of another state. This was what states' rights meant to Seward. For Virginia, on the other hand, states' rights meant getting its way with another state *or* threatening to leave the union. However, the secession threat was, at least in 1839, a hollow one. Thus Virginia considered its other options.

In March 1840 Virginia's legislature passed a fourteen-page preamble and a series of resolutions on the conflict. The preamble, presenting the history of the controversy, reminded New York that the Constitution was written "to form a more perfect union," that its provisions "are the supreme law of the land," and that the fugitives-from-justice clause secured "to one state the most unlimited right to demand" while "imposing upon another the most unqualified duty to surrender fugitives from justice."[40]

Not surprisingly, Virginia denied that its request went beyond the Constitution, asserting that this was a simple case of stealing. In a rather novel use of the secession threat, the legislature declared that "should any state . . . erect herself into a place of refuge for the thieves and robbers who might escape from the offended justice of any of her sister states" the union would be worthless and Virginia would "take proper measures to extricate herself from such an unholy alliance!"[41]

While Virginia found Seward's position dangerous and a threat to the union, the Old Dominion was less certain how to respond. The legislature ruled out a suit in the Supreme Court or a petition to Congress because either "would bring the authorities of the federal government and of the states in collision." In addition, an appeal to the Congress would give "the abolitionists the long wished for opportunity of denouncing" slavery "in the national legislature . . . and of franking their incendiary effusions to the

40. "Preamble and Resolutions Relative to the Demand by the Executive of Virginia upon the Executive of the State of New York, for the Surrender of Three Fugitives from Justice," resolution of March 17, 1840, *Acts of Virginia, 1840*, 155–68.

41. Ibid., 164. A similar argument was made by the Georgia legislature in a petition to Congress over Maine's refusal to extradite two white sailors accused of helping slaves escape from Maine. "Resolutions concerning the delivery of fugitives from Justice," December 24, 1839, *Georgia Acts, 1839*, 229–31.

four quarters of the Union."[42] Virginia's own commitment to states' rights and the need to protect slavery precluded an appeal to the national government.

The legislature thought that appointing inspectors for all ships entering Virginia would be a constitutionally permissible response "specific to the wrong." However, it would also be "harassing and vexatious," difficult to enforce, and "would operate equally upon those who had wronged us, and those who had not." It too was rejected.[43] Also rejected was a "requirement of security for good behavior from the citizens of New York." The legislature acknowledged that such a proposal would violate the Constitution. But this was not the reason for its rejection. Indeed, the legislature rationalized that New York had already "broken" the "compact between the states" and once "broken by one party, it ceases to be binding on the rest." Nevertheless, the legislature thought it best "not *now* to take this ground" in hopes that New York might abandon "her unconstitutional course."[44]

Having eliminated so many of its options, the legislature resolved to make "a solemn appeal" to the New York legislature and "await the action" of that body. However, the Virginians also asserted their willingness "to make common cause with Georgia" in its controversy with Maine. They argued that although the position of the governor of Maine was "much less exceptionable" than Seward's, both were "untenable" and had "too severely taxed" the "patience of the South."[45] Here the Virginians displayed an aspect of states' rights argumentation peculiar to the South. While New York viewed itself as involved in a controversy between two states, Virginia characterized the dispute in sectional terms. Even though Virginia had not had any dealings with Maine, Virginia was ready to condemn that state and offer solidarity with Georgia. In contrast, Seward and the New York legislature never mentioned the Maine-Georgia controversy, much less took a position on it.

Following this detailed preamble, the Virginia legislature passed resolutions calling on New York to change its position, condemning Seward's actions, and authorizing the governor of Virginia "to

42. *Acts of Virginia, 1840*, 165. At p. 166 the same point is reiterated.
43. Ibid., 166–67.
44. Ibid., 167.
45. Ibid., 167–69.

open a correspondence with the executive of each of the slaveholding states, requesting their co-operation in any necessary and
proper measures of redress which Virginia may be forced to
adopt."[46] Here again Virginia indicated that it viewed the conflict
as a sectional one and not as one between two states.

In April 1840 Virginia's new governor, Thomas Gilmer, sent the
legislature's resolutions to Seward. Gilmer told Seward that Virginia "cannot admit the right of *New York*, or any other state, to call
in question either the legality or policy of those domestic institutions" existing in the states at the time the Constitution was
adopted. Gilmer asserted Virginia's "perfect and exclusive right to
regulate her own domestic affairs in her own way." Gilmer could
not resist defending slavery with his version of the emerging
proslavery argument. Gilmer did not question New York's decision to end slavery, but asserted that New York's actions ending
slavery were limited by the Constitution's supremacy clause and
the fugitives-from-justice clause.[47] In essence, Gilmer argued that
New York's freedom to end slavery was restricted, but Virginia's
freedom to maintain slavery was constitutionally protected and
open-ended. In Gilmer's eyes Virginia's state rights were superior
to those of New York.

In April Seward forwarded Gilmer's message to the legislature.
Initially the legislature did not respond directly to the resolutions.
Instead, in a show of support for Seward, the legislature acted on
two pending personal-liberty laws. On May 6, the state adopted

46. Ibid., 168; *Message of the Governor of Virginia, Communicating a Correspondence between the Governors of Virginia and New York* (see n. 25), 18; Lincoln, ed., *Messages from the Governors*, 3: 852–53.

47. *Message of the Governor of Virginia, Communicating a Correspondence between the Governors of Virginia and New York* (see n. 25), 23, 25. Throughout this correspondence the legislature and governors of Virginia stressed the fact that slavery had existed in all but one state at the time the Constitution was adopted. The Virginians tied this fact to an "original intention of the framers" argument which asserted that, because slavery was found throughout the nation in 1787, the rights of slaveholders and the slave states were perpetually protected by the Constitution. While an "original intention" argument is now not confined to any one section of the country, it seems that type of argumentation may have been particularly southern before the Civil War. It was used by Chief Justice Taney in *Dred Scott v. Sandford* to argue that blacks could not be citizens of the nation. Similarly, it was used by the South after the Civil War to argue that the Fourteenth Amendment did not prohibit segregation. For more discussion on Taney's use of original intent, see Paul Finkelman, "The Constitution and the Intentions of the Framers: The Limits of Historical Analysis," *University of Pittsburgh Law Review* 50 (1989): 349–98.

"An act to extend the right of trial by jury." Eight days later the legislature authorized the governor to appoint agents to help rescue free blacks taken to the South as fugitive slaves.[48] Both acts exacerbated the growing conflict between the two states.

The jury-trial bill had been on the legislative agenda for more than a year. In 1839 a similar bill passed the Assembly and was reported out of the Senate Committee on the Judiciary. The legislature adjourned, however, before completing action on the bill. It was reintroduced in February 1840, but languished until April. This law guaranteed that persons seized as fugitive slaves could have their status determined by a jury. If the jury found against the claimant, the alleged fugitive would "be forthwith set at liberty, and shall never thereafter be molested upon the same claim." Anyone attempting to resurrect a claim or actually remove the person from the state would be guilty of kidnapping and subject to ten years in prison. The law also required county district attorneys to intervene on behalf of persons claimed as fugitive slaves. Finally, anyone seizing a fugitive in the state had to give bond "in the penal sum of one thousand dollars" to guarantee court costs if the person seized was not a runaway slave.[49] This law made it extremely difficult for slaveowners to legally remove fugitives from New York.

Unlike the jury-trial law, the law authorizing the appointment of agents to seek kidnapped New Yorkers did not directly affect slaveowners. However, it did affect the growing controversy between New York and Virginia. The act symbolized the legislature's support for Seward. It also indicated that New Yorkers believed kidnapping was a problem, which implied that New Yorkers believed southerners were kidnappers and manstealers. To a limited extent, the New York legislature had enacted into law the arguments and slogans of the antislavery movement.

Between June and November Governor Gilmer wrote five letters to Seward, asking for a response. While Seward acknowledged Gilmer's letters, he did not provide a full response until November, after the New York legislature had reviewed the matter and sustained

48. "An Act to extend the right of trial by Jury," act of May 6, 1840, *Laws of New York, 1840,* 174; "An Act more effectually to protect the free citizens of this state from being kidnapped or reduced to slavery," act of May 14, 1840, *Laws of New York, 1840,* 319.
49. "An Act to extend the right of trial by Jury," see n. 48.

Seward's position. Meanwhile, a private correspondent informed Seward that Gilmer honestly hoped to avoid a confrontation. Gilmer "had fondly flattered himself with the hope, that upon full and mature reflection" Seward would change his mind. Such a change would have relieved Gilmer "of the most alarming consequences to our happy confederacy" that the controversy would cause.[50] Once again a Virginian used an implied threat of disunion in an effort to change Seward's mind.

Seward's response of November 1840 was hardly what Gilmer had hoped for. Relying on a combination of constitutional law, international law, and states' rights theory Seward presented a thirty-three-page defense of his position. Presenting few new arguments, Seward gave numerous examples of cases unrelated to slavery in which extradition had been denied. Such denials were based "on the duty of a state government to its own citizens." He asserted that his decision was not based on any desire to interfere with "the domestic interests" of Virginia, but rather "for the protection of the domestic rights of the citizens" of New York, and did not derive from "a desire to invade or assail the institutions of other states." Finally, Seward suggested that, if Virginia was unhappy with this state of affairs, the "constitution provides a practicable mode of negotiations upon every question which can arise between the states, by contemplating amendments of the compact between them." He ended this battle of words by assuring Governor Gilmer that he would "very cheerfully abide such further examination of the principles I have adopted, as they may receive from the other states, whose attention is invoked by the state of *Virginia.*"[51]

Virginia had already invoked the attention of other states. In a long letter to "the governors of the slaveholding states," Virginia sought the cooperation of its southern neighbors because "common interests and common dangers require that there should be mutual confidence and concert between us." This letter urged support of the Constitution because "the incalculable benefits of the

50. Morris, *Free Men All* (see n. 3), 28–34. C.S. Morgan to Seward, Richmond, July 15, 1840, Seward Papers, Univ. of Rochester.
51. Seward to Gilmer, November 9, 1840, Seward Papers, Univ. of Rochester. This thirty-three-page letter is reprinted in *Message of the Governor of Virginia, Communicating a Correspondence between the Governors of Virginia and New York* (see n. 25), 34–49; quotations from the printed version at 42, 45–46, and 49.

union, are too dear to every Virginian to be abandoned, while there remains a hope of their preservation." However, if that hope faded, Virginia was prepared to call for retaliation against New York and any other state that followed Seward's lead.[52] This letter combined the three major tendencies of southern states' rights arguments: the conceptualization of interstate conflicts as sectional conflicts; a willingness to call for retaliation against the North; and a threat of secession. As always, these tendencies were prefaced by a self-proclaimed love of the union and the Constitution.

In March 1841, the New York-Virginia controversy entered a new phase when Seward received a resolution from Mississippi attacking New York's conduct in the affair. Resolutions from other southern states followed. Alabama declared its willingness to "sustain the State of Virginia in all needfull and proper measures to redress the wrongs complained of, and to prevent their recurrence." South Carolina went further by adopting legislation that discriminated against New York ships and shippers.[53]

These resolutions and laws revealed that other southern states accepted Virginia's concept of the conflict as a regional one. The slave states not only agreed on the sectional nature of the dispute, but also on the legitimacy of threats of retaliation (or actual retaliation) and of threats of secession. The other slave states agreed that

52. *Message of the Governor of Virginia, Communicating a Correspondence between the Governors of Virginia and New York* (see n. 25), 52–58, quotations at 56f. Virginia's letter was received with interest by most southern states. The Kentucky House of Representatives, for example, printed 150 copies of ther letter and accompanying documents "for the use of the members of the General Assembly." *Journal of the House of Representatives of Kentucky, 1840* (Frankfort, KY, 1840): 92.

53. Lincoln, ed., *Messages from the Governors* (see n. 38), 3: 810. "Resolutions in Relation to Fugitives from Justice," chap. 38, approved April 6, 1841, *Laws of Mississippi, 1841*, 155–56. See also, "Preamble and Joint Resolutions of the General Assembly of the State of Alabama," approved April 27, 1841, *Acts of Alabama, 1841*, 19; "Joint Resolution in Relation to a Controversy between the States of New York and Virginia," approved February 14, 1843, *Alabama Acts, 1842*, 225; "Report and Resolutions in Relation to the Constitutional Rights of Slaveholders," resolution no. 9, of April 6, 1841, *Maryland Laws, 1841*. Resolution of Missouri, approved February 16, 1841, *Missouri Laws, 1841*, 336–37. Resolution of Louisiana, no. 110, approved March 16, 1842, *Louisiana Laws, 1842*, 288–90. Both the Louisiana and Missouri resolutions attacked New York's jury-trial law as well as the Empire State's conduct toward Virginia. "An Act to prevent the citizens of New York from carrying slaves, or persons held to service out of this State," act of December 20, 1841, *South Carolina Laws, 1841*, 149–52. South Carolina ultimately sent a copy of this law to the Congress, and it is reprinted in *House of Representatives*, 27th Cong., 2d Sess., doc. no. 135, "South Carolina, Virginia, and New York Controversy," March 17, 1845.

New York's conduct was an assault on their domestic institutions and not just on Virginia's. Thus, Virginia sought and received the solidarity and aid of other states, and the controversy evolved from a dispute between two states to a dispute between one state and a group of states. New York, on the other hand, refused to approach the dispute as a sectional problem. From Seward's perspective it was a disagreement between two state governors and not the basis of schism within the union.

More serious was Virginia's retaliation for Seward's actions. In February 1841 Seward requested the extradition of Robert Curry, a forger who had fled to Virginia. Governor Gilmer did not deny the "regularity of the requisition." Nor was there anything controversial about Curry's crime. Nevertheless, Gilmer refused to extradite Curry until Seward agreed to extradite the three black sailors. At the same time, Virginia adopted legislation requiring inspections of all New York ships leaving Virginia and placing restrictions on other New Yorkers sailing to Virginia. This new legislation, passed in February 1841, would go into effect on May 1, 1842. Virginia's governor was empowered to suspend the law if New York turned over the three black sailors and also repealed its 1840 act guaranteeing a jury trial for alleged fugitive slaves.[54]

Virginia's law was extraordinary. It undermined states' rights and federalism by holding one state hostage through what Seward described as "onerous and offensive" laws. In March 1841 Seward responded. Taking the high road of federalism, he declared that New York would continue to honor constitutionally sound extradition requests from Virginia. But, he asserted "that measures of retaliation, injury and reprisal, are deemed equally unworthy the dignity of this State and inconsistent with its federal relations." Seward declared that the Constitution and laws of the United States provided "ample remedies for any injuries the citizens of this State may suffer from the unconstitutional proceedings on the part of Virginia."[55]

A week after the passage of its anti–New York law, the Virginia

54. "Message to the Senate, March 26, 1841," in Lincoln, ed., *Messages from the Governors* (see n. 38), 3: 910–13; "An Act to Prevent the Citizens of New York From Carrying Slaves Out of this Commonwealth." chap. 72, act of March 13, 1841, *Acts of Virginia, 1841*, 79–82. "An Act to Extend the Right of Trial by Jury," *New York Laws, 1840*, 174–77.

55. "Message to the Senate, March 26, 1841," in Lincoln, ed., *Messages from the Governors* (see n. 38), 3: 910–13.

legislature urged Virginia's governor to approve the extradition of Curry. The legislature realized that Virginia could not consistently demand the free blacks from New York and also reject Seward's requisition for Curry. The legislature declared that "the duty of the executive of each state to surrender fugitives legally charged with a crime . . . is one imperiously enjoyed by the constitution and laws." John M. Patton, who had recently replaced Gilmer as governor, immediately communicated this change of policy to Seward. In doing so he reminded Seward of the three fugitives Virginia sought. He accused New York of becoming "an asylum for felons and runaway slaves," but declared that although New York "refused to comply with the Constitution," his state would "scrupulously obey it." Patton proclaimed that Virginia was "ready to perform our duties, rather than quick to retaliate injuries" and he urged Seward to do the same. Patton warned that Virginia would "not submit to those aggressions of New York which have occasioned the existing controversy."[56] Obviously Governor Patton failed to see the irony of his claims of Virginia's fidelity to interstate harmony and the passage of its law retaliating against New York, adopted a week earlier.

Seward happily acknowledged Virginia's cooperation in arresting Curry, but he refused to equate the case with that of the black sailors. Instead, Seward responded with a detailed recapitulation of the controversy, placing the blame for its escalation on the authorities of Virginia. At the heart of Seward's politely firm letter, which ran to ten printed pages, was the assertion that Virginia sought to undermine the sovereignty of New York and the stability of the union over a minor dispute that Virginia had made into a national issue with potentially dangerous consequences.[57]

Seward pointed out that he had never questioned Virginia's right to maintain slavery. On the contrary, he had been "careful to avoid even any seeming interference with the institutions or municipal affairs of the other States" because he believed such a discussion "could not be agreeable to the people of Virginia." But, Seward

56. "Preamble and Resolution Relative to the Surrender of a Fugitive from Justice," adopted March 20, 1841, *Acts of Virginia, 1841,* 157. "Patton to Seward, March 22, 1841," in Lincoln, ed., *Messages from the Governors* (see n. 38), 3: 915–18.
57. "Seward to John H. Patton, Lieutenant and Acting Governor of Virginia, or His Successor in Office," April 6, 1841, in Lincoln, ed., *Messages from the Governors* (see n. 38), 3: 915–18.

noted, the governors of Virginia had "invited" such a discussion. Seward categorically denied that his refusal to extradite the three men was "designed as an aggression upon Virginia." He admitted that Virginia was "sovereign within her territory, in the enactment of her own laws," but denied that Virginia "could extend her legislative power" to dictate the actions of a governor of New York. Seward also noted that it was the authorities in Virginia who chose to call this controversy "a flagrant invasion of the rights of that Commonwealth" that would justify secession. Seward accused Virginia of violating New York's sovereignty by offering "large pecuniary rewards" to anyone who would "seize, within the jurisdiction of New York and in violation of its laws, and convey to Virginia" the three free blacks. Seward noted that his Virginia counterpart "addressed public circular letters to" the slave states "inviting them to make common cause against New York." In addition, the Virginia legislature passed "an act attempting to impose invidious restrictions and onerous impositions upon" New York citizens in order to compel the governor to change his mind and the legislature to repeal a statute. Seward concluded by asserting that "there is no good reason to believe that the interests of the citizens of this State are less carefully regarded by its Legislature, than the supposed interests of the citizens of Virginia are by the General Assembly of that Commonwealth."[58] This analysis and history of the affair blamed Virginia for violating New York's state rights.

Seward's defense of New York and his complaints against Virginia for interfering with New York's state rights did not end the controversy. It did, however, put Virginia's next governor, John B. Rutherford, on the defensive. Before responding to Seward, Rutherford sought the advice of one of the Virginia's leading legal theorists, Judge Henry St. George Tucker. Much as he disliked Seward's position, Tucker had grudging admiration for his style. He found Seward's last communication "courteous and eminently diplomatic" and so carefully phrased that it was "difficult to extract his distinct opinions or to determine the precise points on which he is working." Furthermore, by skillfully combining "the defect of the process" and "the retaliation of Virginia" with New York's loyalty to the Constitution, Tucker found that Seward was able to

58. Lincoln, ed., *Messages from the Governors* (see n. 38), 3: 922–25, 927.

avoid the "grave constitutional question which he was respectfully asked to reconsider." Tucker "severely" regretted the actions of the previous governor and the Virginia legislature, which "enabled" Seward "to divert the public indignation from himself by endeavouring to excite odium against us." These acts put Virginia at a "great disadvantage" and he warned Rutherford that "on the subject of the last measures of Virginia you cannot enter heartily upon all that has been *said* & done on our part." Yet, he commiserated with the governor, "on the other hand your position forbids you to disavow or abandon them." Given these constraints, Tucker advised Rutherford "to confine yourself to the expression of regret that the Executive of New York declares an unshaken adherence to a construction" of the Constitution "repugnant to its form & its spirit" and "subversive to the rights of the South."[59] Tucker thus spelled out the difficulty Virginia had placed itself in: by adopting an extreme states' rights policy, Virginia made Seward appear to be the offended party.

Rutherford's careful answer was remarkably conciliatory. It contained neither bombast nor threats of retaliation or secession. Rutherford clearly sought a reconciliation. He asserted that Virginia did not seek the three fugitives in a "vindictive spirit" and admitted that the state "might indeed be satisfied without their surrender, were it not for the principles avowed" by Seward. Rutherford praised New York's fidelity to the Constitution, while firmly objecting to Seward's behavior in this case and to the passage of the New York personal-liberty law of 1840. After giving his own version of the events of the past two years, Rutherford rejected Seward's contention that "it rests with Virginia to restore harmony" between the two states. He emphatically declared that Virginia "is the party aggrieved" and it was up to New York to restore "peace and harmony" between "the confederated States of our glorious and happy union." Meanwhile, he promised that Virginia would "continue to fulfill with good faith her constitutional duties."[60]

59. Henry St. George Tucker to John Rutherford, April 23, 1841, Rutherford Papers, Perkins Library, Duke Univ.

60. Rutherford to Seward, April 30, 1841 (first draft); May 3, 1841 (second draft), Rutherford Papers, Perkins Library, Duke Univ. Seward transmitted Rutherford's answer to the New York Senate on May 15, "Message to the Senate," in Lincoln, ed., *Messages from the Governors* (see n. 38), 3: 932.

However much Rutherford hoped for reconciliation, he doubted it would come about. Even before he finished this letter, Rutherford confided to his son that it was time to consider the matter "*as at rest*" because Seward would "do nothing to prevent the collision which must inevitably ensue between" the two states "unless the people" of New York changed their minds "or Congress shall do something to restore harmony."[61] In his private correspondence Rutherford revealed an expectation of doom – an end to the union or at least a "collision" between the largest state in each section over the extradition of three minor felons.

In October Rutherford reported that he had heard "nothing further from Gov. Seward." But in a few days he received Seward's answer to his letter of the previous May. In this letter Seward attacked the constitutionality of Virginia's inspection law, which would go into effect in 1842. He indignantly denounced the notion that Virginia thought it could dictate to New York what laws that state should pass and what actions its executive should take. He noted that if Virginia could "make discriminating regulations" of commerce that "New York and any other state may exercise like powers." This, Seward asserted, "would produce anarchy and end in dissolution" of the union. This was not a threat of secession, but an argument in favor of the unconstitutionality of the Virginia law. Seward concluded that "inasmuch as the parties are equals, if a reconciliation is to be accomplished, Virginia ought to make the first advance."[62]

In response Rutherford regretted that Seward's letter "affords no ground to believe that a longer continuance of our correspondence will tend to promote an adjustment of the differences which unhappily exist between our respective states." He adamantly refused to "make the first advance" toward a reconciliation, blaming New York for starting the controversy. This letter ended the official correspondence between the two states. Although unsuccessful, Rutherford was at least "gratified that Judge Tucker" approved his "communications with Gov. Seward."[63]

61. John Rutherford to John C. Rutherford, April 20, 1841, Rutherford Papers, Perkins Library, Duke Univ.

62. John Rutherford to John C. Rutherford, October 10, 1841, Rutherford Papers, Perkins Library, Duke Univ. Seward to Rutherford, October 8, 1841, Seward Papers, Univ. of Rochester.

63. Rutherford to Seward, October 28, 1841, and Rutherford to John C. Rutherford, January 28, 1842, Rutherford Papers, Perkins Library, Duke Univ.

The end of formal communications between the states did not end the controversy. In his 1842 annual message Seward suggested that the Virginia act regulating New York shipping should be challenged in the Supreme Court. He also noted that a similar controversy had arisen between New York and Georgia. In February, South Carolina notified New York that, in sympathy with Virginia, it had passed restrictive legislation directed at New York ships. In April, the recently elected Democratic majority in the New York state legislature passed a resolution opposing Seward's policy on the extradition of the black sailors. Seward refused to transmit this resolution to Virginia. In August, Seward requested authority from the legislature to test the Virginia law in federal court. At the end of the year Seward left office, with no resolution of the issues. The new Democratic governor repudiated most of Seward's positions, but did not take any steps to extradite the three sailors. Meanwhile, attempts to repeal the jury-trial law failed. Defenders of the existing statute argued that a repeal at this point would be a "humiliation" and a capitulation to Virginia, which had been "so unfriendly and menacing to New York." The Democrats ignored these arguments, and passed a repeal measure in the House in 1843. The legislature adjourned before the Democratic majority in the Senate could act.[64] There were no further attempts at repeal. From both states' rights and antislavery perspectives, New York's honor remained secure.

The New York–Georgia Controversy

In April 1841 New York became involved with Georgia in yet another extradition controversy. Here the states' rights arguments, especially those by Georgia governor Charles J. McDonald, were even more heated. Even New York's comptroller, John Collier, a conservative generally unsympathetic to Seward's antislavery policies, characterized McDonald's correspondence as "exceptionable,

---

64. "Governor's Annual Message, January 4, 1842," in Lincoln, ed., *Messages from the Governors* (see n. 38), 3: 934–37. "Message to the Legislature, February 11, 1842," 3: 980–83. "Message to the Legislature, April 12, 1842," 3: 1029–32. "Message to the Senate and Assembly, August 16, 1842," 3: 1033–37. *House of Representatives*, 27th Cong., 2d Sess., doc. no. 135, "South Carolina, Virginia, and New York Controversy," March 17, 1845.

undignified and . . . *provoking.*"[65]

The New York–Georgia controversy began when Seward refused to order the extradition of one John Greenman, a white charged with trying to help a slave escape from Georgia. Seward argued that the affidavits in Greenman's case were insufficient, but also declared that he would not extradite anyone on "the charge of stealing the slave," who "being of full age, left her home on her own free will."[66]

In his response to Seward's initial refusal to approve the extradition, McDonald declared, "I will remind your Excellency, that the crimes of which Greenman is charged, and in which the demand is made, are crimes against the laws of Georgia, as enacted by her Legislature, construed and enforced by her courts, and not offences against the laws of New-York." He berated Seward with a series of questions that indicated McDonald's irritation and anger with the New Yorker's position. The Georgian asked:

> Are the laws of other States establishing or recognizing the relation of master and slave, held in New-York to contravene any portion of the Constitution of the United States? If so, what provision? Is it held in New-York that the Constitution and laws of the United States passed in pursuance thereof, do not recognize in the States the existence of the relation of master and slave, and of property of the master in the slaves? Is it held in New-York, that in other States, the legislative authority has not the power to secure to the people the possession of their property to penal enactments? And if so, by what authority does she assume to say what shall be the policy of other States, and the rights of their people?

McDonald sarcastically concluded, "If I am informed upon these points, I shall be the better enabled to comprehend the doctrine which is held by New-York, and appreciate the reasoning of your Excellency."[67]

65. John A. Collier to [Seward], Friday morning, 8 October [1841], Seward Papers, Univ. of Rochester, commenting on McDonald to Seward, September 3, 1841, *New York State Assembly Document, No. 2, January 4, 1842: Documents Accompanying Governor's Message, Document B: Correspondence between the Governor of New York and the Governor of Georgia*, 58–59 [hereafter cited as *New York–Georgia Correspondence*].

66. *New York–Georgia Correspondence* (see n. 65), 58–59, and McDonald to Justice of the Peace Robert Raiford, July 19, 1841, copy in *Governors' Letterbooks*, 1841–43, Georgia Archives, 162–63.

67. McDonald to Seward, June 28, 1841, reprinted in *New York–Georgia Correspondence* (see n. 65), 58–59.

McDonald's letter indicated that he would not seek conciliation or negotiation. This response may have been a function of the ongoing controversy between Georgia and Maine. The frustrations and anger caused by that case may have spilled over into the New York extradition controversy. McDonald may have felt that he had no reason to try diplomacy with Seward because the New York–Virginia controversy had taught him that Seward was not likely to be forthcoming.[68]

Seward's answer was a model of careful, lawyerly analysis. He explained in great detail why the affidavits in support of the extradition were inadequate. Seward did not, however, indicate that he would comply with a properly framed requisition based on a grand-jury indictment. On the contrary, he specifically reserved "the question whether, if this case had been presented by indictment, it would not be within my power to inquire into the facts and circumstances" at issue. Similarly, Seward refused "to enter into a controversy concerning the powers vested in the executive authorities of the States in deciding upon requisitions for the surrender of fugitives." But Seward warned that, if forced to engage in such a discussion, he "might maintain that the Executive of a State can not be obliged by any law of Congress, to arrest a person and deliver him over to the authorities of another State." Seward based his refusal on the insufficiencies in the extradition requisition and diplomatically ignored the battery of questions McDonald had fired off in the previous letter. However, Seward ended his letter by declaring that if the time came to engage in a discussion of the Constitution, the right of a slave to walk away from her master, and the duty of a governor to extradite someone who helped that slave, Seward would "maintain the inalienable rights of man, the sovereignty of the States, and the integrity of the Federal Union."[69]

McDonald thought Seward's argument was "one that fanaticism itself will scarcely recognize as legitimate." McDonald expressed pleasure that Seward "sought to preserve the integrity of the Federal Union" but he argued that this could only be done if Seward complied with the extradition request. He urged Seward to

---

68. McDonald to Justice of the Peace Robert Raiford, July 19, 1841, copy in *Governors' Letterbooks, 1841–43* (see n. 66).

69. Seward to McDonald, July 14, 1841, reprinted in *New York–Georgia Correspondence* (see n. 65), 62–65.

"defend the honor of the people of New-York by not permitting that great State to become the sanctuary of thieves and robbers, who plunder the plantations of the people of her sister States." McDonald concluded that "no good can result from a further discussion of the difficulties presented" by Seward.[70]

Further correspondence bore out this conclusion.[71] After 1841 Georgia officials ceased communicating with Seward. In December of that year the governor signed into law "An Act the better to secure and protect the citizens of Georgia in possession of their Slaves." Unlike Virginia's legislation on this subject, the Georgia law was not directed solely at New York, and it did not require onerous inspections. Rather, the law required that all northern shippers post a bond to guarantee that they would not illegally remove slaves from the state.[72]

Interstate States' Rights and the Antebellum Crisis

The New York–Georgia controversy was tied to both the Maine-Georgia controversy and the New York–Virginia controversy. None of these interstate conflicts led to satisfactory solutions. Both

70. McDonald to Seward, September 3, 1841, reprinted in *New York–Georgia Correspondence* (see n. 65), 65–68.

71. In October McDonald sent Seward a copy of the indictment for one "Alanson" Greenman for attempting to steal a slave named Kezia, owned by Robert Flournoy. McDonald to Seward, October 8, 1841, and Indictments of Alanson Greenman, reprinted in *New York–Georgia Correspondence* (see n. 65), 74–75. McDonald was quite angry with Flournoy, the owner of the slave Kezia, for initially swearing out an affidavit against *John* Greenman. Throughout their correspondence Seward had stressed the insufficiency of an affidavit as the basis for an extradition requisition because of potential inaccuracies. McDonald argued that an affidavit was as good as an indictment. Thus McDonald's anger over the mistake in names is understandable. McDonald also feared this would "give rise to some difficulty in the future progress of the case." McDonald to Justice of the Peace Robert Raiford, July 19, 1841, copy in *Governors' Letterbooks, 1841–43* (see n. 66), 162–63. The date of this letter indicates that McDonald exacerbated these problems. He apparently knew of the name difference in July, but continued his correspondence with Seward until October, alleging throughout that the affidavits provided a basis for extraditing Greenman. *Alanson* Greenman was actually indicted on May 1, 1841. It is impossible to explain why McDonald waited until October to send Seward the indictment. Seward to McDonald, December 27, 1841, reprinted New York–Georgia Correspondence (see n. 65), 80–84.

72. "An Act to better secure and protect the citizens of Georgia in the possession of their slaves," act of December 11, 1841, *Georgia Laws, 1841*, 125–28.

New York and Maine, relying on states' rights, refused to extradite the alleged criminals to Virginia and Georgia. The two southern states had few viable options. Threats of an end to the union and resolutions from other slave states had no effect on Maine or New York. Both Virginia and Georgia (as well as South Carolina) passed restrictive legislation aimed at northern ships and crews. The North, as Seward had pointed out, was also capable of passing such legislation. However, the southern states were probably aware that retaliatory legislation would have been unlikely from such staunch nationists as Seward. But, even without northern retaliation, the disadvantages faced by Virginia and Georgia from a disruption of commerce were more numerous than any advantages they may have gained from preventing the escape of slaves. This was apparent to representatives from Savannah, Georgia, who opposed an 1839 bill aimed at Maine ships entering the state. Savannah was the place from which slaves were most likely to escape, but it was also the city most likely to suffer from a decline in interstate trade. The leaders of that city preferred to lose a few slaves than to lose their commerce.[73] Nor did such legislation always prevent escapes. George Latimer, after all, found it just as convenient to escape from Virginia on a Massachusetts ship as he would have on one from New York or Maine.[74]

By the mid-1840s Virginia and Georgia had abandoned their efforts at retaliation.[75] Neither Virginia nor Georgia wished to take the issues involved to the Supreme Court, because this would have violated their sense of state sovereignty and states' rights. At one point the Georgia legislature contemplated taking their controversy

73. *Journal of the Senate of the State of Georgia, 1839* (Milledgeville, GA, 1840): 53–53, 118–19, 258–59, 290–91, 306–7, 340–41, 346–47, 358–63.

74. William M. Wiecek, "Latimer, Lawyers, Abolitionists, and the Problem of Unjust Laws," in Lewis Perry and Michael Fellman, eds., *Antislavery Reconsidered: New Perspectives on the Abolitionists* (Baton Rouge, LA, 1979), 219–37.

75. The Virginia act was repealed by "An Act amending the act, entitled, 'an Act to prevent the citizens of New York from carrying slaves out of this commonwealth, and to prevent the escape of persons charged with commission of any offence,' passed March 13th, 1841, and all acts amendatory thereto," act of March 5, 1846, *Acts of Virginia, 1845–1846*, 67–68. A similar act passed by Georgia, "An Act the better to secure and protect the citizens of Georgia in the possession of their Slaves," act of December 11, 1841, *Acts of Georgia, 1841*, 125–28, was repealed "so far as relates to the Port of Savannah" a year later. "An Act to repeal an act the better to secure and protect the citizens of Georgia . . . ," act of December 27, 1842, *Acts of Georgia, 1842*, 166. Savannah was the only port where this law would have been important.

with Maine to Congress and asking for legislation allowing federal judges to enforce extradition requisitions. Georgia's congressional delegation successfully headed off this idea. The Georgia Congressmen argued that such a law would be unconstitutional because only governors had the power to extradite fugitives from justice. They also argued that such a law would place Georgia's "great sovereign and constitutional right . . . under the absolute control and decision" of a federal judge, and perhaps, a jury "whose judgment might, and probably would be swayed by his, or their, own prejudices." Such a law, the congressmen felt, would not "protect the sacred rights" of Georgia's "citizens in their slave property." The congressmen suggested that the refusal of a governor to extradite a fugitive criminal would be a "just cause of war," but they were unwilling to submit it to Congress.[76]

Seward, on the other hand, suggested congressional legislation or a constitutional amendment as alternatives when his southern correspondents threatened secession. More significantly, Seward was anxious to challenge Virginia's inspection of New York ships in the Supreme Court. Seward's willingness to litigate this issue suggests that his commitment to states' rights differed from that of his southern counterparts. States' rights was an argument to be used when helpful, not an ideology to be rigorously followed. Thus Seward was willing to abide by a Supreme Court decision. Seward probably expected the Court to deny the constitutionality of Virginia's inspection laws, which would have benefitted his state; any cost to states' rights theory would have been marginal to New York, since it was unlikely that New York would have attempted to restrict interstate commerce. On the other hand, if Virginia had taken New York to court and forced the extradition of the three black sailors, Virginia would have then been responsible for setting the precedent that the Supreme Court could order state governors to act. This was intolerable to states' rights proponents, at least in the 1840s.

In 1860 the staunchly states' rights governor of Kentucky did

76. "Resolutions of the General Assembly of Georgia," December 24, 1839, reprinted in Senate doc. no. 273, 26th Cong., 1st Sess., March 11, 1840. Congressmen Julius Alford, William C. Dawson, Richard W. Habersham, Thomas Butler King, Eugenius A. Nisbet, and Lott Warren to Governor Charles McDonald, March 16, 1840, McDonald Papers, Re: Requisitions Maine, Georgia Archives. See also Phillips, *Georgia and State Rights* (see n. 37), 139–40.

324

take such a case to the Supreme Court, in *Kentucky v. Dennison* (1861). In this case two successive governors of Ohio, Salmon P. Chase and William Dennison, refused to extradite a free black, Willis Lago, who was wanted for "stealing" a slave in Kentucky. The Ohio attorney general thought the indictment was faulty and would not be valid in Ohio "or wheresoever else the common law prevails." Equally important, what Lago did was not a crime in Ohio "or by the common law."[77]

Governor Beriah Magoffin of Kentucky found Dennison's positions unpersuasive. Magoffin noted that the Constitution "was the work of slaveholders" and that in 1787 "non-slaveholding states were then the *exception, not the rule.*" While not using the term directly, Magoffin argued that the original intent of the framers was to provide for extradition of people who helped slaves escape. Magoffin avoided any discussion of states' rights and state sovereignty. Instead, he accused Ohio of bad faith and of violating comity.[78] When Dennison refused to change his mind, Magoffin asked the Supreme Court for a writ of mandamus ordering Dennison to extradite Lago.

Kentucky v. Dennison presented a profound dilemma for the Taney court. In 1861 the court contained five southerners and two northern doughfaces. It was an overwhelmingly proslavery court, led by a chief justice who "had become privately a bitter sectionalist, seething with anger at 'Northern insult' and 'Northern aggression.'"[79] While sympathetic to Kentucky's position, Taney refused to issue the writ of mandamus. If he had done so, Taney would have set a precedent under which Congress or the Supreme Court had the power to order state executives to act. With a number of states having already seceded and others threatening to do so, Taney was unwilling to give the Lincoln administration a two-edged sword that could be turned against the South.

Thus a fanatically proslavery chief justice sustained the use of states' rights theory by antislavery governors in Maine, New York,

77. *Kentucky v. Dennison*, 24 Howard (65 U.S.) 66 (1861). Attorney General C.P. Wolcott to Governor William Dennison, April 14, 1860, Dennison Papers, Ohio Historical Society. This letter is reprinted in *Kentucky v. Dennison*, 24 Howard 66, at 67–70.

78. Governor Beriah Magoffin to Governor William Dennison, June 4, 1860, Dennison Papers, Ohio Historical Society.

79. Don E. Fehrenbacher, *The Dred Scott Case: Its Significance in American Law and Politics* (New York, 1978), 311.

and Ohio. Ironically, this occurred at the precise moment that antislavery politicians could abandon states' rights for an aggressive nationalism. The leaders of this new antislavery nationalism included Seward, the new secretary of state, and Chase, the new secretary of the treasury. These men had few regrets about abandoning their states' rights positions. They had been useful rhetorical tools, but they were easily jettisoned.

Executive Discretion and States' Rights

From 1783 until the 1830s interstate criminal extradition had raised few interstate problems. However, starting in the 1830s the theory of executive discretion arose, and governors sometimes refused to honor extradition requests from other states. Executive discretion developed because of extradition requisitions that were complicated by slavery and sectional tensions.[80] Once articulated, the theory was used in other cases.

The viability of executive discretion is possible because under a federal system all states are equal. Thus Virginia could not truly make any demands on New York, but could only request cooperation and hope for comity.[81] Even the national government lacked the power to force one state to act on the constitutionally protected claim of another state. In disputes between governors of two states, the Constitution seemed to make the federal government little more than a neutral observer. As Chief Justice Taney concluded in *Dennison,* "If the Governor of Ohio refuses to discharge this duty, there is no power delegated to the General Government, either

80. Hoague, "Extradition between States" (see n. 19), 239. This remained good law until 1987. *Drew v. Thaw,* 235 U.S. 432 (1914), at 439. 31 *Am. Jur.* 2d, 956, sec. 48. In 1950 Governor Williams of Michigan refused to approve the extradition of one of the Scottsboro Boys who had escaped from prison in Alabama. More recently, Governor Gerry Brown of California refused to extradite American Indian activist Russell Means to stand trial for crimes he allegedly committed in South Dakota. This precedent was overturned in *Puerto Rico v. Branstad,* 483 U.S. 219 (1987).

81. This concept was implied by Chief Justice Taney in *Strader v. Graham,* 10 Howard (U.S.) 82 (1850) at 93–94. In that case Taney asserted that "every state has an undoubted right to determine the *status,* or domestic and social condition, of the persons domiciled within its territory." Thus, Taney concluded that Kentucky did not have to accept the law of Ohio in determining the status of slaves who might be free in Ohio, but had returned to Kentucky. Ohio law, in other words, could have no force in Kentucky, except through comity.

through the Judicial Department or any other department, to use any coercive means to compel him."[82] For antebellum Americans, interstate disputes could only be arbitrated and negotiated; neither the national government nor a complaining state had the power to force another state to act.

The *Dennison* case revealed the underlying weakness of the states' rights arguments for the South. In *Dennison* Taney had to choose between protecting slavery and protecting states' rights. He chose to protect the latter, in hopes that this result would usually protect the former as well. But this solution did not really offer the South protection. Southern states' rights arguments stemmed from a fear that the national government would interfere with local institutions – the most important of which was slavery. Thus the South sought to preserve its states' rights against the national government.

The North, at least after 1820, never really feared the national government. Thus northerners were quite willing to challenge southern laws in federal court. The South, fearing the effects of a strong national government, almost always resisted an appeal to the federal courts. Ironically, in *Dennison*, the one time a southern state brought the states' rights issue to the Supreme Court, the South was in the uncomfortable position of arguing for national supremacy. Oddly enough, the case did not raise the kind of state-federal issues the South feared. Instead, it raised an issue of state equality. No matter how Taney decided it, the case was one that the South could not win. In protecting executive discretion, the Supreme Court supported one of the few aspects of states' rights arguments that the North had subscribed to and that the South found onerous. But, had Taney decided in favor of Kentucky, he would have given the national government power to invade the states. Either way, the South lost. In a time of great national crisis, states' rights proved a thin shield indeed for those who challenged the federal government to protect slavery.

82. *Kentucky v. Dennison*, 24 Howard (U.S.) 66 (1861), at 109–10.

12.1
American Federalism – Blueprint for Nineteen-Century Germany?

Michael Dreyer

In discussions of eighteenth-century federalism at the beginning of this conference and several times later on, we stressed the elements that distinguish the historico-political settings in Germany and in the United States from each other rather than concentrating on the similarities that do, beyond any doubt, exist. This will also be true for the discussion of nineteenth-century federalism.

The problems Professor Paul Finkelman's paper addresses were simply nonexistent in the German context. We never experienced a states' rights discussion worth mentioning. Only occasionally, for example, when in 1820 Wilhelm Joseph Behr defended the liberal Bavarian Constitution against the restorative policies of the *Bundestag*,[1] did German Liberals stress the *souveraineté* of the member states. However, this never led to anything like a consistent states' rights policy on the part of any of the state governments. Even in cases of severe conflict between one of the states and the *Deutsche Bund*, it was not the case that arguments were used that reflected the American example. Rather, the states tried to justify their position by referring to the constitutional law of the *Bund* or that of the states themselves.[2]

There are two reasons to explain this observation: on the one hand, in Germany there was no potential source of conflict comparable to slavery in the United States. The different legal situation of

---

1. Wilhelm Joseph Behr, *Von den rechtlichen Grenzen der Einwirkung des deutschen Bundes auf die Verfassung, Gesetzgebung und Rechtspflege seiner Glieder-Staaten* (Stuttgart, ²1820).
2. I looked at the *Braunschweiger Thronfolgestreit* (1827–30), the constitutional conflict in Hanover (1837), the *Bundesintervention* in Electoral Hesse and Holstein (1850), and the *Lippische Thronfolgestreit* of the 1890s.

Jews in the German states did not come close to a systemic conflict and therefore could not create similar problems; even more important, none of the state governments was ready to entangle itself in conflicts with the others over this problem. At least until the Revolution of 1848, the four republics as well as the thirty-four monarchies promoted state policies friendly to the *Bundestag* and united in suppression of liberalism. This situation changed – and here we approach the second reason – when the Prussian-Austrian differences could only be resolved temporarily at Olmütz. Conflict important enough to cause a meaningful states' rights debate could only arise between these two European powers, all other states being too insignificant. Great powers, however, usually resolve their conflicts neither by means of a states' rights debate nor by means of the *Austrägalverfahren* proposed by the *Bund*.

Prussian-Austrian dualism and, later on, Prussian hegemony made their mark on nineteenth-century federalism in Germany. The latter impressively shaped both constitutions, the one designed by the Paulskirchen assembly and the other written by Bismarck. Although – with only a few exceptions[3] – constitutional theorists of the empire denied the close relation of their document to that of 1848, Professor Boldt's paper conclusively shows the similarities between the two documents as exemplified by the distribution of competences, the organization of the Reichstag, and the electoral system. One should, however, be careful not to overrate these similarities: the enumerative principle can be found in almost all federal constitutions, as well as the principle of independence of the states in all matters not regulated by the federal government.[4] There are important distinctions too:

1. The legitimacy of the Constitution of 1849 was based on the Revolution and on the idea of the sovereignty of the people. On

3. The exception is Albert Hänel from Kiel.
4. For the enumerative principle cf., e.g., the German Constitutions of 1871 (Art. 4), 1919 (Art. 6 and 7), and 1949 (Art. 73 and 74), the Constitution of the GDR of 1949 (Art. 112), and even the Soviet Constitutions of 1936 (Art. 14) and 1977 (Art. 73). Independence or even sovereignty of the states is granted in §5 of the Paulskirche, in the Federal Republic (1949: Art. 30 and 70), in Switzerland (1874: Art. 3), in the GDR (1949: Art. 2), and again in both Soviet Constitutions (1936: Art. 76; 1977: Art. 15). The texts of the Soviet Constitutions even secured a right of secession (1936: Art. 72; 1977: Art. 17)!

the contrary, the Bismarck Constitution was enacted by the princes with the consent of the people assembled in the Reichstag.

2. Centerpieces were, respectively, the Reichstag in 1849 and the *Bundesrat* in 1867/71 – the latter, at least, according to the text and theory of the Constitution. In fact the emperor, the chancellor, and even the Reichstag soon circumscribed the role of the *Bundesrat* sharply – but this is another problem, irrelevant for us.

The *Bundesrat*, with its peculiar construction and its theoretically dominant role, posed no small problem for contemporary constitutional theorists. Despite its similarities to the old *Bundestag* and to the even older Reichstag of the Holy Roman Empire, the *Bundesrat* was a strange combination of elements of parliamentary, executive and judiciary bodies. Robert von Mohl's dictum, "proles sine matre creata,"[5] certainly demonstrated the helplessness of theorists more than it contributed to solving the problem. This also applies to Paul Laband's unsatisfactory construction that interpreted the *Bundesrat* as the collective head of state of a twenty-five-member republic! But all the same, this misleading interpretation gained decisive theoretical influence during the empire, mainly because of Laband's reputation as the foremost constitutional lawyer of his time. In fact, the *Bundesrat* came to be regarded as the essential element of federalism per se, against the lone voice of Hugo Preuß.[6]

Looking more closely at the political circumstances, however, one easily understands why it was impossible to conceive of another body. The princes had to be represented, German constitutional history suggested a *Bundesrat* solution, and – most important – after the *Verfassungskonflikt* Bismarck was certainly not willing to submit his regime to parliamentary control, which was the only alternative. The *Bundesrat* served him well as a means of

5. Robert von Mohl, *Das deutsche Reichsstaatsrecht: Rechtliche und politische Erörterungen* (Tübingen, 1873), 230.

6. Paul Laband's authoritative work was *Das Staatsrecht des Deutschen Reiches*, of which were published several editions between 1876 and 1911. For Hugo Preuß cf. several of his articles in his *Staat, Recht und Freiheit* (Tübingen, 1926). Cf. also Manfred Rauh, *Föderalismus und Parlamentarismus im Wilhelminischen Reich* (Düsseldorf, 1973); and Michael Dreyer, *Föderalismus als ordnungspolitisches und normatives Prinzip* (Frankfurt/Main, 1987), esp. chap. 5.

blocking the Reichstag. It was unable to take care of its positive duties, but it definitely was quite successful in pursuing these destructive functions.

But the living constitution is always more important than the written constitution; and the living constitution was shaped by Prussian hegemonial federalism, as Professor Boldt rightly shows.

Against a chorus of dissenting opinions, I completely agree with his statement that it was not the democratic parts of the Frankfurt Constitution that caused its downfall. It became unacceptable to Austria because of the ideas of *Personalunion* and of Heinrich von Gagern's *Doppelbund*. The same reasons were responsible for the failure of the *Erfurter Unionsplan*, which could definitely not be described as overdoing democracy.[7] And conversely, Schwarzenberg's idea of the *Siebzig-Millionen-Reich* was just as unacceptable to German national liberalism, to say nothing of Prussia, which would have been doomed to *seconda volta* for eternity.

The problems of 1849 can be summed up in three points:

1. Austria was not ready to leave Germany alone
2. Prussia was not able to force her to do so
3. Friedrich Wilhelm IV was not willing to accept the risk of war

All of these aspects can be regarded as combined in the term "Olmütz." In 1866, points 2 and 3, Prussia's objective and subjective inability to go to war, were reversed through Bismarck's energetic leadership, which in turn solved the problem of dualism in the well known, but perhaps inevitable war.

Following the elimination of obsolete dualism, however, a new but by no means minor structural problem emerged for the newly founded empire – Prussian hegemony. Is it really possible to build a federal state among equals, when one "partner" is so much larger then all of the others together? Moreover, is it possible to create a truly federal state that is at the same time a monarchical state composed of twenty-two other monarchies and three republics? And, considering these two basic structural problems of the empire, is it possible to seriously think of using the American example as the blueprint for Germany?

---

7. The *Doppelbund* was, in a manner of speaking, enacted later through Bismarck's foreign policy toward Austria.

These questions reflect the very core of my disagreement with Professor Boldt – and with most writers on nineteenth-century federalism.[8] Indeed, Professor Boldt does not overlook the important differences between Germany and the United States; moreover, he mentions them explicitly. But we have to examine critically two of his most important statements:

1. "In the Revolution of 1848 everybody spoke of the American example."
2. ". . . the American example was undoubtedly the main source of inspiration for the *Bundesstaat* in the nineteenth century."[9]

The former refers to the factual process of constructing the Constitution, the latter to the theory of the *Bundesstaat*.

One cannot deny – as Professor Boldt shows – that in 1849 numerous provisions were indeed modeled after the example of the United States. Even more, Professor Mittermaier, the spokesman for the liberal majority in the Constitutional Committee, praised the United States highly when he introduced the draft of the Constitution in the plenary meeting: "This country [the U.S.] has solved the problem of a central government with every opportunity for a most beneficial development of the member states. . . . No country can praise herself that her statesmen, equally great in theory and practice, have discussed the essence of a federal constitution as magnificently as men like Hamilton, Jefferson, Story, Kent, Rawle, Serjeant did."[10] And not only the liberal majority, but the democratic and conservative minorities in the Constitutional Committee and in the plenary meeting also quoted the American example to justify their completely divergent drafts![11]

This very fact, however, should make us think twice – it seems hardly permissible to speak of a serious reception when the liberal Mittermaier as well as the democrat Blum and the reactionary v. Lassaulx in unison quote the American model in their support. Their problem was that they just could not avoid doing so! The United States was a well-known *Bundesstaat*, and the *Bundesstaat*

---

8. Cf. Dreyer, *Föderalismus* (see n. 6).

9. Hans Boldt, "Federalism as an Issue in the German Constitutions of 1849 and 1871," above, 262 and 261.

10. In *Stenographische Berichte über die Verhandlungen der durch das allerhöchste Patent . . . einberufenen Kammern Session 1848/49*, 5 vols. (Berlin, 1849–), 4: 2724.

11. See Dreyer, *Föderalismus* (see n. 6), 552–53 and passim.

was the catchword for the German unitary movement, mainly on the liberal side. It seems readily understandable that the liberals exploited their "ideal" through somewhat skewed interpretations so that it could serve their needs, namely, to make in the legitimizing blueprint for the erection of a monarchical German *Bundesstaat* under entirely different conditions. Their opponents, on the other hand, could only hope to find an audience if they tied their criticism to a verbal reference to the American example.

It may be helpful to look, by way of comparison, at the situation in the first Reichstag of 1867, after the small German Empire had de facto been founded – and after the American example had been discredited during the long and bloody Civil War. Then no one spoke of the American example, especially not Miquel, the leader of the *Nationalliberale*:

> The draft, as it lies in front of us, reflects the political basis it developed from. It seems to be rough and unpolished at first glance; it does satisfy neither a political ideal, nor a theoretical ideal, nor a historical development; it cannot be compared either with the American federal Constitution or with the Swiss federal Constitution, nor can it be put in line with the Constitution of the Old Empire; it gives us neither a unitary state nor a federal state nor a confederation; it is completely original, just as the political situation is new and original, in the context of which it has to function. Great peoples don't copy, great peoples in great circumstances are always new.[12]

What we find here is the almost unqualified acceptance of the "model United States" in 1849 and its unqualified rejection in 1867 – and this for two constitutional drafts displaying many important similarities, as Professor Boldt himself has shown!

A similar observation can be made about the theoretical concept of the *Bundesstaat* but each political group in the *Paulskirchenversammlung* – as later in Erfurt – had their own divergent interpretations of the concept's meaning; the Paulskirche just did not follow a well-established theory. And they could not even do so, since there was no such theory. At best, Johann Ludwig Klüber's definition was generally accepted; according to it the *Bundesstaat* had two governments and followed constitutional law, whereas the

---

12. In *Stenographische Berichte über die Verhandlungen des Reichstages des norddeutschen Bundes im Jahre 1867* (Berlin, 1867), 1: 111–12.

Staatenbund followed international law.[13] This definition, however, was not very helpful for concrete political work. The extent to which the theory of the *Bundesstaat* was shaped by the political desires of the *Vormärz* is indicated by the widespread notion of a gradual transition from *Staatenbund* to *Bundesstaat* – a golden bridge, built by the Liberals for the *Deutsche Bund*, which, however, remained deaf to their desires.[14]

All this suggests that there was not much of a true reception of American concepts. To be sure, Mohl and Welcker, to mention only two theorists, certainly did derive some of their ideas on the construction of the *Bundesstaat* from the American model. But the former's work was forgotten almost instantly, whereas the latter's allegiance to a liberal monarchy did not allow him to understand fully the democratic federalism of the United States.[15] The most important witnesses for the "reception theory" are Georg Waitz and Max von Seydel, who allegedly did no more than copy Tocqueville and Calhoun, respectively.

Waitz's famous discourse on the *Bundesstaat* was published in a rather obscure place in 1853. It became well known only after it was republished in 1862 – and afterward it dominated the discussion for a decade.[16] To a large extent, Waitz refers to Tocqueville and through him to the United States – it can be left open whether the idealized picture the French nobleman gave of the United States, which was aimed at the corrupt morals back home, was as unrealistic as Montesquieu's deliberations on the English Constitution. To Waitz – referring to Tocqueville – the most important point is that in the *Bundesstaat* both the central government and the states are sovereign. Both enjoy their respective competences completely independent of the other.

One should not forget that Waitz first published this discourse as a book review on a work by Radowitz, who had already expressed

13. Johann Ludwig Klüber, *Oeffentliches Recht des Teutschen Bundes und der Bundesstaaten* (Frankfurt/Main, ³1831), 2, 109, and 137.

14. This is discussed in detail in Dreyer, *Föderalismus* (see n. 6), chap. 3.

15. Cf. Robert von Mohl, *Das Bundes-Staatsrecht der Vereinigten Staaten von Nord-Amerika* (Stuttgart, 1824); Carl Theodor Welcker, "Bund," in Carl von Rotteck and Carl Theodor Welcker, eds., *Staats-Lexikon oder Enzyklopädie der Staatswissenschaften*, 15 vols. (Altona, 1836), 3: 76–116.

16. Georg Waitz, "Das Wesen des Bundesstaates," *Kieler Monatsschrift* (1853): 494–530, and again in his *Grundzüge der Politik nebst einzelnen Ausführungen* (Kiel, 1862), 153–218.

these very thoughts – without referring to Tocqueville. Bluntschli and Dönniges (both well known to Waitz) had published similar ideas even earlier, and H.A. Zachariä developed the same theory in 1853 as well, once more without referring to either Waitz or Tocqueville.[17]

Obviously, the time was ripe for a theory of the *Bundesstaat* advocating the division of sovereignty – immediately after the failure of the unitary movement, which had been criticized by the states and mainly by Prussia for transferring the sovereign rights of the states to the central government. But there is even more to come: Waitz viewed an indirectly elected parliament as being feasible even for the *Staatenbund*. The member states of a *Bundesstaat* do not have to be of equal strength because they cannot be in each other's way at all due to their sovereignty. According to Waitz, unequal strength even poses a bigger problem for the *Staatenbund* than for the *Bundesstaat*. And in obvious contradiction to his own theory (and to America and Tocqueville), he wants to take German political realities into account by adding a *Reichsrat* or *Bundesrat* to the two houses of parliament to give the state governments direct influence in federal politics.[18]

Clearly, Waitz did not just copy Tocqueville. He wanted to suggest to the German princes and especially to Prussia that they were not going to lose their sovereignty in a *Bundesstaat*. These political implications helped to make his ideas the dominating theory for the last years of the *Deutsche Bund*, especially since he had successfully given extra legitimacy to his thoughts by excessively quoting a famous authority like Tocqueville.

These observations also help to understand that, after 1867–71, this theory was quickly dropped and completely forgotten once the long desired empire came into existence. That the theory was forgotten was due foremost to political changes and not so much to the fact that Seydel had shown the necessary unity of the concept of sovereignty in 1872.[19] Seydel's own construction of the empire as a *Staatenbund* was completely rejected by his German fellow theorists. After all, one had not fought for a *Bundesstaat* from the time of the

---

17. Johann Caspar Bluntschli, *Geschichte des schweizerischen Bundesrechtes von den ersten ewigen Bünden bis auf die Gegenwart*, vol. 1 (Zurich, 1849); Wilhelm Dönniges, *Die deutsche Verfassungsfrage und die deutschen Einzelstaaten*, 3 vols. (Munich, 1848); Heinrich Albert Zachariä, *Deutsches Staats- und Bundesrecht*, vol. 1 (Göttingen, [2]1853).
18. For a discussion of Waitz's theory see Dreyer, *Föderalismus* (see n. 6), 204–13.
19. Max von Seydel, "Der Bundesstaatsbegriff: Eine staatsrechtliche Untersuchung," *Zeitschrift für die gesammte Staatswissenschaft* 28 (1872): 185–256.

Vienna Congress just to acknowledge, at the very moment that your dreams were achieved, that there was no such thing as a *Bundesstaat*.

But Seydel, too, quotes Calhoun only in an illustrative, not constituent manner. This had to be so because their goals were too far apart: Calhoun wanted to prove that a citizen of South Carolina, as a citizen of this state and not as a citizen of the United States, was a part of "the sovereign." Seydel wanted to prove that the king of Bavaria was a sovereign head of state and not the hereditary chief of a provincial administration. The difference is too obvious to need further explanation.

As we have seen, in the nineteenth century the American example had no decisive influence on either the policies or the theory of federalism. That leaves us with a final question: was a serious reception of American ideas possible at all? To pose this question is to negate it; the structural problems of German federalism prevented such reception:

1. The existing monarchy was generally accepted by the German theory of state. German constitutional theorists, advocating the authoritarian monarchical Constitution, were unable to understand the American combination of federalism and democracy. They used the vocabulary but did not catch the spirit. The problem of sovereignty and of the nonsovereign state was not solved by a generation of German constitutional lawyers, and it was unsoluble indeed.[20]

2. Besides that, Prussian–Austrian dualism and later Prussian hegemony prevented a balanced federalism of the American type. A *Bundesstaat* that included two rival powers like Prussia and Austria is inconceivable. On the other hand, a federation between Prussia and Reuß-Schleiz-Lobenstein-Ebersdorf is just as impossible; the *Problem Preußen* permitted only a facade of federalism behind which the Iron Chancellor pursued his course, if necessary with an iron fist. This is aptly phrased in a statement of Constantin Frantz, the most important critic of Bismarck from the point of view of federalism: "The lion and the mouse cannot confederate."[21]

20. This was noticed only by Hugo Preuß, *Gemeinde, Staat, Reich als Gebietskörperschaften* (Berlin, 1889).

21. Constantin Frantz, *Der Föderalismus als das leitende Princip für die sociale, staatliche und internationale Organisation unter besonderer Bezugnahme auf Deutschland, kritisch nachgewiesen und constructiv dargestellt* (Mainz, 1879), 232.

12.2
States' Rights and Theories of the American Union

William M. Wiecek

Professor Paul Finkelman's perceptive study, which surveys the differing yet parallel uses made of states' rights arguments by northern and southern states before the Civil War, considers an old theme. To the limited extent that the phrase "states' rights" denotes a political theory (rather than merely being a slogan devoid of meaning), it implies a conception of federalism in the American political system that exalts the sovereign character and powers of the states vis-à-vis the national government.

Before the Civil War, the nature of the American union remained undefined. Competing theories of the union made widely divergent views of the states' power more plausible than they would be after 1865. These theories cluster around two poles. The first posits what has been termed the "compact theory" of the American union. In this view, the states, embodying the sovereign power of their people, preexisted the union and combined to form the national government under the Constitution of 1787. In doing so, they did not relinquish their sovereign authority. Rather, they delegated specified powers to the national government, chiefly in the areas of defense and foreign policy. But southern compact theorists like Roger B. Taney emphasized that none of these delegated federal powers could override the state's absolute and unqualified authority over their domestic institutions, including slavery. The states necessarily retained all power over persons and things within their jurisdictions. However, the compact theory provided no guidance as to how this power was to be reconciled with a like power retained by sister states when a state believed that its vital interests, like internal security, were threatened by the actions of persons outside its jurisdiction. The constitutional touchstone of compact theorists was the Tenth Amendment, which specified that "the powers not delegated to the United States by the

Constitution, nor prohibited by it to the States, are reserved to the States respectively, or to the people."

The antagonist theory rejected such compact reasoning and instead emphasized the primacy of the national government. It will be referred to here as the national-supremacy concept. As articulated first by Chief Justice John Marshall in *McCulloch v. Maryland* (1819) and then by Daniel Webster in his 1830 United States Senate debate with Robert Y. Hayne, the national-supremacy theory maintained that the union was formed by the aggregate of all the American people and that the Constitution was the expression of their collective national will. As such, it derived its authority directly from the whole American people; therefore that authority could not be resisted by any single state. As Marshall conceded in *McCulloch*, the powers of the national government might be limited, but within their sphere they were supreme. To Americans who thought like Marshall and Webster, the bases of the union were the supremacy clause of Article VI (specifying that "This Constitution, and the Laws of the United States which shall be made in pursuance thereof . . . shall be the supreme Law of the Land;") and the powers of the federal courts conferred by Article III.

In the antebellum era, these two general theories of the American union vied for acceptance, and they gave form to debates over the powers of the states. Those debates were vigorous and unresolved because the Constitution shed little light on the actual functioning of the union considered as a federation of states. In addition to the clauses referred to above, only Article IV provided guidance for the workings of federalism, and such directions as it gave were opaque because most of its provisions were couched in the passive voice (for example, "Full Faith and Credit shall be given . . .", which does not specify who must give that credit, how, or when). Perhaps the framers believed that the more powerful central authority that they created in 1787 would obviate the need for a more carefully detailed specification of the ways in which the states must interact with each other, but if they did, they did not foresee the strains on the union imposed by the nineteenth-century controversy over slavery.

Against this constitutional background, inconsistent theories and practices of states' rights flourished before the Civil War. We think of such theories as a shield held by the states against the intrusion of national authority, legitimating state, local, and regional resistance to federal authority. However, it was pointed out a generation ago that states' rights arguments served equally well as a sword of state aggression, a weapon by which the slaveholding states attempted to control the national government and use its power to force slavery into the territories and the free states.[1] And now Professor Finkelman has demonstrated the protean utility of states' rights theory as a device of interstate relations.

In the controversies reviewed by Professor Finkelman, the participants deployed states' rights arguments defensively. They opportunistically used such ideology to evade obligations that, others contended, were imposed on them by the national Constitution. States' rights theories are associated in the popular mind with southern constitutional positions, but that is due in large measure to the bastardized use of such arguments in modern times. Nevertheless there was an important strand of states' rights ideology that was developed by southern spokesmen in the antebellum period, and Professor Finkelman surveys one significant but neglected part of it. The story he tells here, of southern travail over the presence of black seamen in southern ports, was part of a larger ideological movement. The Negro Seamen's Acts controversy realigned the thinking of southern jurists, led by Chief Justice of the United States Roger B. Taney, in anti-nationalist directions, producing an unnatural hostility to the national treaty power and congressional authority over interstate commerce. This in turn developed concurrently with southern refinement of an anticonsolidationist ideology, originated not by John C. Calhoun, who was something of a Johnny-come-lately in this matter, but rather by John Taylor of Caroline, Thomas Cooper, and other, lesser-known Virginia and South Carolina ideologists. The product of these ideological innovations was a coherent and comprehensive southern worldview that was fully articulated by 1840 in time to rebut the constitutional offensive emanating from the northern states in the decade of the 1840s.

The other half of Professor Finkelman's story is less familiar. We do not usually associate state's rights constitutional argument with

---

1. Arthur Bestor, "State Sovereignty and Slavery – A Reinterpretation of Pro-slavery Constitutional Doctrine, 1846–1860," *Journal of the Illinois State Historical Society* 54 (1961): 117–80.

the free states of the North. That too is a result of northern victory in the Civil War and the consequent ratification of the nationalist theory of the union that became canonical for Republicans during the war. Yet states' rights flourished in the North for more than two generations before the war, beginning with Antifederalist resistance to ratification of the Constitution in 1788 and evolving through Wisconsin's defiance of national judicial authority in the case of *Ableman v. Booth* (1859). Northern determination to protect their free citizens from kidnapping and extradition formed an important part of this tradition, and Professor Finkelman has effectively traced out the contours of that ideological byway in early American constitutional development.

Professor Finkelman's novel exploration of antebellum incidents reminds us of the riches still to be found in areas thought to be overworked. We are enriched by the innovative uses he has made of sources hitherto known but overlooked.

12.3
Discussion

HANS R. GUGGISBERG: My first point is that the Swiss misread some of the important aspects of the American federal union just as the German liberals did. They were in general no better informed than the Germans and, if the Swiss experiment of 1848 did not fail, it was for reasons not relevant for our context. The fact as such should not be idealized.

My second point is that during the debates preceding the Civil War of autumn 1847 in Switzerland between the minority – consisting of agricultural, nonindustrial, and Roman Catholic cantons organized in the so-called *Sonderbund* to protect their own interests – and the other cantons – which were industrialized, more progressive in their political tendencies, and predominantly Protestant, a states' rights theory emerged which can in many ways be compared to the American states' rights theory, except of course for the arguments concerning slavery. Some of the arguments used by the Catholic cantons were quite comparable to American states' rights arguments. Another similarity is obvious – in Switzerland as in North America the civil wars were conflicts between agrarian and industrialized regions; in both cases the latter won.

My third point is that after Switzerland had become a union in 1849, it was the only republican federation in Europe, and of course American politicians and political writers of the nineteenth century knew and appreciated that fact. Many American political writings of the nineteenth century spoke of the uniqueness of the Swiss Alpine sister republic, and the similarity of national structure was strongly felt both in the United States and in Switzerland.

Let me just mention two facts to illustrate this: in 1863 after Lincoln's Emancipation Proclamation a very enthusiastic reaction in Switzerland resulted in the so-called address movement. This was a collection of hundreds of congratulatory letters to Lincoln and his government written by private persons but also by groups of people which was sent to the United States in an official memoir as an expression of enthusiastic support and also of the feeling that the Swiss Republic was in many ways very similar to the American Republic.

In 1894, to come to my second example, Emil Frey became president of the Swiss government. He had served in Lincoln's army during the Civil War and had also served as the first Swiss ambassador to the United States in the years 1882–88. So he was well known in America. And when he became president of the federal council (*Bundesrat*) many congratulatory letters and articles were published in American newspapers. Some of the American journalists who wrote about Frey in 1894 of course did not know that the Swiss presidency was something different from the American presidency but still they congratulated Frey. They noted that he was one of the most ideal people to be the head of the Alpine sister republic because, and I am now quoting from the *New York Times* of 1894, "he had been in the alpine democracy but then he had received his political education as a democratic politician in America."

STANLEY N. KATZ: In the United States today in the field of legal history the preference is to talk in behavioral and not in idealistic terms; constitutional history is still more formalistic and that has been a problem for those of us who are in both fields. Our problem lies in the combination of the assertion of realpolitik and the dominance of ideological considerations and the tension between the two. It is hard for me to believe that either aspect could provide an exclusive explanation. It does seem, however, that the resolution is in the collision of the two – realpolitik and ideological considerations – and indeed in all of Mr. Finkelman's examples both elements are present. Now I was wondering about the extent to which, in nineteenth-century Germany, there is a similar conflict between formalistic notions of constitutionalism (some obviously based on the American example) and the equally obvious pressure of individual interests and to what extent that conflict shaped or influenced German developments.

GERALD STOURZH: I would like to voice my skepticism about whether it is really correct to refer to a more formalistic approach as an idealistic one. Let me make two points: I have been impressed by a saying of Max Weber, "Form is the twin sister of liberty" ("Die Form ist die Zwillingsschwester der Freiheit"). I have always encountered difficulties in discussing with American colleagues what in German and also in French legal language is called *formeller Rechtsbegriff*; the dialogue becomes easier if one equates the German term *Form* with the English term "procedure." For then Max Weber's saying translates into "procedure is the twin sister of liberty," meaning that, according to Weber, procedure is a protection from arbitrariness and discretion.

This brings me to my second, again general, point. If we try to compare German and American experiences in federalism in the nineteenth century – an attempt obviously fraught with problems – I think one admittedly very general point made by Albert Dicey in the nineteenth century suggests possible comparisons. Comparing America not with Germany but with England, he wrote that "federalism really means legalism," suggesting that there is in every federal system a great need for the articulation of rules and of competences. Obviously this is a point similar to that suggested by Max Weber's term *Form*: the procedural aspect is of greater importance in a federal than in a unitary system. That is one explanation for the fact that I think proceduralism is a very important aspect in federal systems in spite what Mr. Katz has said about the formal side of legal history.

HANS BOLDT: I agree with you in both your arguments. *Form*, as Max Weber used the term, seems to me to mean in legal terms "law" and that is the *Gesetzesvorbehalt* we talked about yesterday. And "federalism" is to my mind a more legal system, for it needs more legal procedures than a unitary state does, for example, in deciding federal conflicts that lead to the establishment of a supreme court. This is the real cause for *Verfassungsgerichtsbarkeit*. This may have been so, too, with the Austrian case.

GERALD STOURZH: I am skeptical about the Austrian case. Here I am more of a Kelsian, believing that the more important source is the notion of the constitution as a paramount law, as I think was also so in America.

Let me address another point to Mr. Finkelman: I continue to reflect about one aspect of his paper, the connection of states' rights and sectional or regional problems. There is a difference between states' rights positions and states' rights arguments on the one hand and arguments and positions advanced and used in forming, on the other hand, a subentity between those states' rights and the national level. Apart from expressions of an awareness of the South as a cultural entity and of the slavery interest as a common bond, do you know of practical proposals for an institutional unification, a legal procedural unification of the southern States at an intermediary level between the states' rights and national levels prior to confederation?

PAUL FINKELMAN: Before the Civil War there is nothing like a southern caucus in Congress. Southern leaders, were they to be resurrected, would claim that they were acting as individual states; but since their interests were concurrent with those of other individual states, they simply wanted the aid of the other southern states to protect states' rights. Nevertheless, they were not yet prepared to come together and think of themselves as "the South" for political purposes. Yet we can see that this is obviously what they were really doing.

TIMOTHY H. BREEN: This is what happens when we use a too narrowly formalistic notion of politics. Of course there were southern regional institutions – they just were not political in a constitutional sense. The southern churches were one of these central-core binding powers within which powerful messages were exchanged. There certainly was a regional structure in the South outside of politics.

JÖRG-DETLEF KÜHNE: I would like to emphasize the specific importance of religion for the relationship between regions in Germany. Thus Catholic Austrians and Bavarians do not consort with the Protestants of lower Germany; in politics we had the Catholic party, the Deutsche Zentrumspartei, as an outgrowth of this religious regionalism.

HARTMUT LEHMANN: Let me add another observation. Looking at religious history in the second half of the nineteenth century, it seems to me that, from the point of view of the way Christianity in both societies has exerted an influence, that the spiritual basis for the system of federalism was corroded and corrupted. In building a Christian America, in building a Christian Germany, a larger unity was envisioned that applied and utilized the idea of a chosen nation and of chosen people evoked in the example of the people of Israel, who were collectively punished and collectively blessed. Note that it was not the single states that were blessed or punished but the idea of one nation under God, a unified Germany of 1871 under God, that was blessed. Being a *Württemberger*, or being a *Badener*, or being a *Hesse* was not so important anymore although the sovereigns of these states continued to rule until 1918. From this perspective not they but the Prussian king, who under God was the symbol and the exponent of *the* one German nation, was important. I believe that in that area too we can find quite a few similarities.

Another possible area of comparison is, and Hans Rudolf Guggisberg has also mentioned it, the notion of fundamental differences between North and South, of northern progressive industrialized cultures building the modern world and of southern backwardness and superstition. Looking through American schoolbooks of the 1880s and 1890s, I found that to their authors northern Germany seemed congenial not to the southern but to the northern American experience – Prussian history was interpreted in an extremely positive way while Austria disappeared from German history altogether, being superstitious and backward, etc. Contemporaries, it seems, were not as reluctant as we are to draw comparisons but were instead rather daring and straightforward in making very clear connections between the North and South in Germany and in the United States; Bismarck was to them the twin brother of Lincoln.

ROBERT C. POST: I have a question for our German colleagues. Mr. Finkelman's paper focuses not so much on federalism as a matter of vertical integration – on the relationship between the national government and states – as it does on the question of comity between states in a federal system. This question of comity goes very much to what it means to be a state, to the kinds of sovereignty that states retain or yield to sister states. Were these problems discussed in Germany? What was the situation in 1871 between the individual states in the Second German Empire?

FRED L. MORRISON: If you mean by "comity" the Full Faith and Credit Clause of the Constitution, then there is the provision in the German constitution that "Alle deutsche Urteile sind in ganz

Deutschland vollstreckbar" ["All German judgments are enforceable throughout Germany"].

ROBERT C. POST: To give an example, one state in the United States does not necessarily have to recognize another state's divorce.

HANS BOLDT: Well that is a problem of the *Rechtseinheit*. All the big German legal codifications derive from the time of the 1860s and the end of the nineteenth century.

PAUL FINKELMAN: Well, what happened to a citizen of one German state if he moved to another German state to take up permanent residence there or come as a visitor? Would he have all the privileges of citizenship, and are there German states that discriminate against certain classes of citizens and others that do not? I was told in a previous conversation, for example, that the emancipation of Jews took place in Prussia before it took place in the free city of Frankfurt. What happened then when a Jewish citizen of Prussia came to Frankfurt? Was he treated as a citizen of Prussia or was he treated as a Jew in Frankfurt would be treated?

HANS BOLDT: He retained the citizenship of Prussia. When a Prussian goes to Bavaria he still remains a Prussian. But he is an inhabitant (*Inländer*) too, meaning that he has all the rights of a citizen of Bavaria. Your example about the emancipation of the Jews really belongs to the period before the formation of the Second German Empire. Before 1871 there were indeed differences in citizenship status. After 1871 the legal situation with respect to citizenship was the same throughout the empire.

GERHARD A. RITTER: I would now like to draw your attention to those things which did not happen in Germany but happened in the United States. We assume that it is natural that there was no major debate on states' rights and no major conflict between states and the empire in Bismarck's Germany. Yet I think that this is by no means natural. If one compares the German situation with that of America one is struck by the differences between the two; yet there were strong similarities too, and strong sectional differences in Germany are one example which, astonishingly enough, however, did not lead to ruptures or major strains.

Let me take as an example tariff policy: there existed tremendous differences in economic interests between the different parts of Germany as far as protection was concerned. According to the influential liberal politician Rudolf von Bennigsen, the splitting of the National Liberal party, which was originally for German unity, by the tariff policy of 1880 endangered the existence of the German Empire. However, his fears did not become reality:

> We will see the formation of a new party which unlike the present National Liberal Party will not be a party for all of Germany and Prussia but a party originating in and being based on the special economic interests of individual regions . . . Once new political parties representing the interests of the East or the North against those of the South, the Middle or the West exist side by side with or even supplant the old political parties then we will witness a development which would sorely test any old unitary state but which the complicated structure of the German Empire never could sustain.[1]

Second, we have the *Kulturkampf,* a major policy against the Catholic church. There were in Germany predominantly Catholic states. How could it happen that in Bavaria, for instance, this *Kulturkampfgesetzgebung* was put into effect? Some explanation is offered by actual politics in this state: at that time Bavaria had a political setup where the liberals were very strong while the majority of the population was Catholic; by moderating the impact of the *Kulturkampfgesetze* the liberals were able to enforce them.

So clearly there were plenty of differences between the states – but why did these not develop into major fights over states' rights? I think the *Bundesrat* played a larger role than we normally think when focusing on actual politics, for all the major German states had their ambassadors accredited with the *Bundesrat,* and they negotiated before they met in the *Bundesrat,* which was very much a formal institution where major negotiations, especially those between Prussia and Bavaria, took place before formal meetings. In Bismarck's time we all know that he was very considerate with specific Bavarian wishes.

1. Bennigsen gave that speech in front of the convention of the National Liberal party in Hanover on September 19, 1880. Walther Schultze and Friedrich Thimme, eds., *Rudolf von Bennigsens Reden,* vol. 2, 1879–1901 (Halle/Saale, 1911), 85f.

Another factor preventing open ruptures may be found in the constitution itself; thus they did not dare to tax Bavarian beer for that was forbidden by the constitution and they did not take over the Bavarian railways and postal system – clearly there were arrangements that probably demanded some degree of moderation.

Another factor which might have prevented ruptures was the taxation system, which was very much geared to the individual states: And then of course, and this is a major difference between the Second German Empire and the United States, the administration of legislation was implemented by the state. Laws were put into effect by the state's administration and this meant that – and I have mentioned the Bavarian example – one could moderate to some degree the impact of particular laws while enforcing them.

DIETHELM KLIPPEL: Let me at least raise the question of whether economic factors influenced German federal thought and development, probably mediated through the codification of German law. A short description of this trend toward codification might throw some light on this problem.

After 1812 the Liberals in Germany wanted codes of law comparable to the French codes. They did not succeed. Instead the predominance of Roman law continued. In 1849 a code of commercial law was drafted but it remained a draft. Then in the 1850s the *Allgemeine Deutsche Wechselordnung*, a code regulating bills of exchange, was accepted by the *Deutsche Bund*, and in 1861 the *Allgemeine Deutsche Handelsgesetzbuch* (general code of commercial law) was accepted. Now, characteristic for these codes was that every state of the *Deutsche Bund* had to take it over as law. So it was not in force as a statute of the *Deutsche Bund*.

In the Second German Empire – I neglect its predecessor, the *Norddeutsche Bund* – several codes were enacted for the whole empire, starting in 1871 with the criminal code and the codes of criminal and civil procedures. As to private law, the Constitution of the empire had to be altered in order to vest the empire with the legislative competence to enact a code of private law. This resulted in the *Bürgerliche Gesetzbuch*, the BGB, put into force in January 1900.

This means that up to 1900, in the field of private law there was a sort of particularization in the German Empire. Roman law dominated; in some states left of the Rhine French law was in force; in most parts of Prussia the Prussian *Allgemeine Landrecht* was in force; and in Saxony from 1863 the Saxonian BGB was in force. Apart from the economic aspect of these developments, I suggest that this development can be viewed as a substitute for liberals who, in the first part of the nineteenth century, failed in their efforts to get a unified German state but who, in the second half of the century, at least got a *Reichsrechtseinheit* through codification and thus were able to establish a legal unity of the German states.

RALPH KETCHAM: What I would like to do so is to look at the problem of federalism in both countries over a span of time from 1848 to 1877. We could say that in some sense what happened in about 1850 in both countries was the same: the compromise of 1850 and the deliberations in the Paulskirche are in some way both failures. Federalism neither solves the basic problem of slavery in the United States, nor the opposition between Prussia and Austria in Germany. The result of the failure is that these problems are ultimately solved by blood and iron: there is a civil war in both countries in the 1860s. The war led to hegemony of sorts in both countries. In Germany it is quite clear that the Bismarckian Empire of 1871 is Prussian-dominated; in the United States I would like to suggest that the hegemony achieved by the North in the Civil War was briefly and ultimately unsuccessfully directed toward Reconstruction. But as many American historians have suggested what really happened was the settlement in 1877, which put an end to Reconstruction and left the hegemonic power in the hands of the Northern capitalists and developers of the economy; again we have the same thing happening in both countries. In the next generation or two the tremendous achievements in economic growth allowed Germany and America to dominate the world for parts of the twentieth century. This happened as a result of the hegemony achieved through those wars.

In some ways this reflection means shedding a tear for both countries for the demise of a political system that, until the two civil wars, had been resistant to the kinds of hegemonies that were achieved as a result of those wars. Without accepting the notion that federalism defended slavery, it still seems important to keep in mind that in another sense the demise of liberal federalism in both countries, where domination of the federation by a part of the federacy was resisted, may suggest some lessons.

MICHAEL DREYER: I would like to add to these remarks that federalism was also a failure as a theory because, for over one hundred years, German theorists were completely unable to advance a convincing theoretical solution to the federal problems of Germany. In sum, I believe that federalism really has been a great problem for nineteenth-century Germany.

Part 5
Safeguards of Civil and Constitutional Rights

13
Safeguards of Civil and Constitutional Rights – The Debate on the Role of the *Reichsgericht*

Gertrude Lübbe-Wolff

The German *Reichsgericht* was instituted in 1879, eight years after the foundation of the *Bismarck Reich*, as a federal court to top the most important – so-called ordinary – branch of the judiciary.[1] It was only under the Weimar Constitution, however, that the *Reichsgericht* began to play an important and much debated role in securing constitutionally guaranteed individual rights. Under that constitution, the *Reichsgericht* went into judicial review of federal statutes and thus assumed, for itself and for the courts in general, the role of safeguarding constitutional rights against intrusions by the federal legislature. To understand why this happened, why it happened more than a hundred years later than in the United States, and what it meant in the German context, we must take a short look back into the nineteenth century.

Nineteenth-Century Questions of Constitutional Rights and Judicial Review

In Germany, civil rights or *Grundrechte* first appeared in the modern state constitutions of the early nineteenth century.[2] These early nineteenth-century constitutions were at the same time the first to

---

1. On the foundation and history of the *Reichsgericht* see Arno Buschmann, "100 Jahre Gründungstag des Reichsgerichts," *Neue Juristische Wochenschrift* (1979): 1966–73; Walter Simons, "Das Reichsgericht," in Julius Magnus, ed., *Die höchsten Gerichte der Welt* (Leipzig, 1929), 1–28; Gerd Pfeiffer, "Das Reichsgericht und seine Rechtsprechung," *Deutsche Richterzeitung* (1979): 325–32; Elmar Wadle, "Das Reichsgericht im Widerschein denkwürdiger Tage," *Juristische Schulung* (1979): 841–47.

2. See, e.g., the famous Constitutions of Bavaria (1818), Baden (1818), and Württemberg (1819), reprinted in Ernst Rudolf Huber, ed., *Dokumente zur deutschen Verfassungsgeschichte*, 2 vols. (Stuttgart, 1961), 1: 141–200.

institute representative parliaments and give them a share in the exercise of legislative power. In that early constitutional framework, the idea of interpreting constitutionally guaranteed rights and liberties as potentially directed against the exercise of legislative power would not have made much sense, since the class primarily interested in them had just acquired an institutionally secured veto position in the legislative process itself. The thrust of civil liberties, then, was not antilegislative; it was, in the main, antifeudal in the sense of being directed against certain prominent traits of ancient society which, to a large extent, still existed in Germany at that time. Constitutionally guaranteed civil rights – freedom of the person, freedom of enterprise, civil equality, etc.[3] – *aimed at* a modern civil society but, like the famous French Declaration of the Rights of Man, could not by themselves put it into effect when in fact villeinage, guild monopolies, and privileges continued to exist. Intricate legislation was required to effect the real transition from feudal to modern society, and the function of civil liberties in that process was, for the most part, merely a programmatic one.[4] Legislative power, as the new constitutions had established it, was therefore seen not as a danger to civil rights but as the authority designed to really effect them.[5]

In the second half of the century, to the extent that constitutionally guaranteed civil rights had served their programmatic purpose, they came to be regarded as juridically superfluous declamations that might as well be renounced.[6] Consequently, the Reich's Con-

---

3. See, e.g., §§21, 24, 29, 31 of the Constitution of Württemberg in Huber, ed., *Dokumente zur deutschen Verfassungsgeschichte* (see n. 2), 1: 141–200.

4. Ulrich Scheuner, "Die rechtliche Tragweite der Grundrechte in der deutschen Verfassungsentwicklung," in *Festschrift für Ernst Rudolf Huber* (Göttingen, 1973), 139–65; Rainer Wahl, "Rechtliche Wirkungen und Funktionen der Grundrechte im deutschen Konstitutionalismus," *Der Staat* 18 (1979): 321–48; Gertrude Lübbe-Wolff, "Das wohlerworbene Recht als Grenze der Gesetzgebung im neunzehnten Jahrhundert," *Zeitschrift der Savigny-Stiftung für Rechtsgeschichte, Germanistische Abteilung*, 103 (1986): 104–39; idem, "Über das Fehlen von Grundrechten in Hegels Rechtsphilosophie," in Hans-Christian Lucas and Otto Pöggeler, eds., *Hegels Rechtsphilosophie im Zusammenhang der europäischen Verfassungsgeschichte* (Stuttgart, 1986), 421–46.

5. See Friedrich Giese, *Die Grundrechte* (Tübingen, 1905), 91. For further references see Lübbe-Wolff, "Das wohlerworbene Recht" (see n. 4), 105, n. 3.

6. See Georg Meyer, *Lehrbuch des deutschen Staatsrechtes* (Leipzig, 1878), 566–67. Conrad Bornhak, *Preußisches Staatsrecht*, vol. 1 (Breslau, [2]1911), 291–97. According to Georg Jellinek's classical analysis, constitutionally guaranteed civil rights were nothing more than special (and somewhat redundant) reformulations of the general

stitution of 1871 (like the French Constitution of 1875) did *not* contain any civil rights provisions.[7] However, constitutionally granted rights and liberties continued to exist on the level of state constitutions.

This very short and general outline should explain why in Germany, during the nineteenth century, judicial review was not an issue in connection with constitutionally guaranteed civil liberties. It was, however, discussed in connection with an older form of individual rights. It had been a principle of German law that vested rights (*wohlerworbene Rechte*) could not be taken or otherwise violated by the state except in cases of emergency and, in such cases, for due compensation. In the process of social and political reform undergone by the German territories in the first decades of the nineteenth century, the aggrieved parties never failed to invoke that ancient principle against the legislation depriving them of their former privileges.[8] For the courts, giving way to such claims would have meant giving the individual rights dating from the old order precedence over the civil rights proclamations of the new order that instigated the reform process. In fact, courts and jurisprudence, while maintaining that the principle of inviolability of vested rights continued to be valid, generally refused to admit judicial review of legislative acts for compatibility with that principle.[9] This doctrine, however, was never so firmly settled as to definitely discourage any attempts to get it reversed. The issue therefore remained relevant throughout the century. In 1883, the *Reichsgericht* dealt with it in a case concerning the transfer, by law, of certain rights to appropriate dike construction material. Confronted with the claim that the statute effecting that transfer was void because it violated vested rights, the *Reichsgericht* implicitly

---

principle, inherent in the rule of law, that the state may not *unlawfully* interfere with the liberty of its subjects, see Georg Jellinek, *System der subjektiven öffentlichen Rechte* (Tübingen, [2]1905), 103. For the history of the more rigorous principle that the state may interfere with liberty and property only on a statutory basis and for the interpretation of constitutionally granted liberties as expressions of that principle, see Ottmar Bühler, *Die subjektiven öffentlichen Rechte und ihr Schutz in der deutschen Verwaltungsrechtsprechung* (Berlin, 1914), 76–87.

7. On the relevant debates of the Reichstag see Giese, *Die Grundrechte* (see n. 5), 22.

8. See Lübbe-Wolff, "Das wohlerworbene Recht" (see n. 4), 113–28.

9. Ibid., 106–7 and passim.

treated the principle of inviolability of vested rights as a principle of constitutional rank, but decided that, although binding the legislator, it could not be enforced against him by the courts.[10] Later, in the Weimar discussion, this case was usually adduced as one of the main precedents against judicial review.[11]

So much for the issue of vested rights. Judicial review was, however, discussed in yet another context, namely, as a safeguard of the constitutional division of powers between parliament and the monarch or the executive. In that context, the central question, bound up with uncertainties concerning the scope of monarchic prerogative, was how to deal with norms promulgated by the monarch without the parliamentary consent required by the modern state constitutions.[12] During the first two-thirds of the nineteenth century, a great number of jurists advocated judicial review with respect to such cases.[13] Some, notably Robert von Mohl, even wrote in favor of judicial review quite generally, without limiting it to violations of the kind just mentioned. Mohl explicitly held that the courts were entitled to check not only the "formal constitutionality" of any legislative act, that is, its having been enacted in conformity with the lawmaking procedure prescribed by the constitution, but also its "substantive constitutionality," that is, the constitutionality of its content.[14] Mohl's position, however, did not become the dominant one. In the course of the last two decades of the century, along with the victory of legal positivism, the very restrictive doctrine advocated by Paul Laband came to prevail.

10. *Entscheidungen des Reichsgerichts in Zivilsachen* [hereafter RGZ], 9,232 (235).

11. For further *Reichsgericht* cases see n. 22–24 below.

12. See the report on the Third German Lawyers' Conference, held in 1862: *Verhandlungen des Dritten Deutschen Juristentages*, vol. 2 (Berlin, 1863), 20–61. For the period before 1848 see Ludwig Adamovich, *Die Prüfung der Gesetze und Verordnungen durch den österreichischen Verfassungsgerichtshof* (Leipzig, 1923), 8, with detailed references.

13. See the almost unanimous vote of the Third German Lawyers' Conference, *Verhandlungen des Dritten Deutschen Juristentages* (see n. 12), 61. Before 1848 opinions were more divided, see Adamovich, *Die Prüfung der Gesetze und Verordnungen* (see n. 12), 8. In a number of cases judicial review was in fact exercised by the courts: for an account of court practice see Christoph Gusy, *Richterliches Prüfungsrecht* (Berlin, 1985), 25–26.

14. Robert von Mohl, "Über die rechtliche Bedeutung verfassungswidriger Gesetze," in Robert von Mohl, *Staatsrecht, Völkerrecht, und Politik*, vol. 1 (Tübingen, 1860, repr. Graz, 1962), 66–95. On Mohl see Herbert Haller, *Die Prüfung von Gesetzen* (Vienna and New York, 1979), 8–14.

According to Laband, the constitutionality of a federal statute that had been engrossed and promulgated by the emperor in accordance with Article 17 of the Reich's Constitution was to be irrefutably presumed and therefore could not be questioned by the courts. Article 17, entrusting the emperor with the engrossment and promulgation of federal statutes, Laband argued, assigned to the emperor, and to him exclusively, the task of verifying that the constitutional lawmaking procedures had been correctly observed; proper promulgation (that is, publication) of a statute was therefore the only thing left to be verified by the courts.[15] At first sight this argument, if at all conclusive, seems to foreclose judicial review only with respect to most aspects of formal constitutionality, leaving to the courts the right to refuse the application of statutes found to be substantively unconstitutional. However, Laband's argument was in fact, more far-reaching. This was due to the doctrine of *Verfassungsdurchbrechung*. According to that fatal doctrine, which was later to cover the enabling law of 1933, any statute incompatible with the Constitution in its content was to be held valid if enacted in the form prescribed for changes of the Constitution (explicit change of the text of the Constitution not being among the formal requirements).[16] Under the doctrine of *Verfassungsdurchbrechung*, a statute found to be substantively incompatible with the Constitution could therefore be held unconstitutional only if it had *not* been enacted in accordance with these particular formal requirements, and a judicial statement to that effect was prohibited by Laband's presumption.[17]

Another line of argument running through the literature of the time starts out from a somewhat different point, denying that there was a difference in rank between "simple" statutes and provisions of the Constitution that would give the latter precedence over the former. According to that view, which can be found, for instance,

15. Paul Laband, *Das Staatsrecht des Deutschen Reiches*, vol. 2 (Tübingen, [5]1911, repr. Aalen, 1964), 44–52.

16. On the doctrine of *Verfassungsdurchbrechung* see Ernst Rudolf Huber, *Deutsche Verfassungsgeschichte seit 1789*, vol. 5 (Stuttgart, 1981), 421–27. For a critical approach to that doctrine in the Weimar period see Erwin Jacobi, "Reichsverfassungsänderung," in Otto Schreiber, ed., *Die Reichsgerichtspraxis im deutschen Rechtsleben*, vol. 1 (Berlin, 1929), 264–75.

17. For a similar observation see Hans Kelsen, "Wesen und Entwicklung der Staatsgerichtsbarkeit," in *Veröffentlichungen der Vereinigung der deutschen Staatsrechtslehrer*, vol. 5 (1928), 37.

in the renowned constitutional law compendium of Meyer and Anschütz,[18] conflicts between statutory provisions and provisions of the Constitution were to be resolved by the general principle that *lex posterior derogat legi priori*; the question of judicial review of the constitutionality of statutes, in that view, did not even have to be raised because constitutionality was not deemed prerequisite to the validity of a statute.

Note that both arguments just rendered, Laband's and Meyer-Anschütz's, were relevant only to judicial review of federal statutes. In fact, judicial review was unanimously accepted under the Constitution of 1871 with respect to ordinances and to state statutes. It was by then almost generally acknowledged that ordinances were admissible only on the basis and within the limits of statutory delegation; they could be reviewed for meeting these requirements.[19] As to state statutes, Article 2 of the Constitution was interpreted as clarifying that federal law had precedence over state law and thus allowed judicial review of state statutes.[20] This early and easy acceptance of judicial review may seem remarkable, particularly when compared with the development in the United States, where judicial review of state statutes was admitted later and with greater difficulties than judicial review of federal statutes.

The *Reichsgericht*, under the 1871 Constitution, can be said to have by and large followed and reinforced the prevailing doctrines just outlined, although not quite consistently in the matter of judicial review of federal statutes. Judicial review of ordinances and state legislation for compatibility with federal law, including the federal Constitution, was unambiguously admitted.[21] As to review of federal legislation, later advocates of judicial review could draw on an obiter dictum presenting the question as "controversial"[22] and on another obiter dictum which, in sweeping formulation, ascribed to the courts the competence to check the "validity" of

---

18. Georg Meyer and Gerhard Anschütz, *Lehrbuch des deutschen Staatsrechts*, vol. 3 (Munich and Leipzig, [7]1919), 743–44. The argument was taken up in a *Reichsgericht* decision refusing to go into judicial review of a federal statute; see RG, *Juristische Wochenschrift* (1916): 596–97.

19. See Mende, "Die Nachprüfung des Verordnungsrechts der 'Reichsregierung' durch die Gerichte," *Leipziger Zeitschrift für deutsches Recht* (1924): 705.

20. Meyer and Anschütz, *Lehrbuch des deutschen Staatsrechts* (see n. 18), 743, with further references.

21. RGZ 15, 27 (29); 24, 1 (3); 83, 54 (61); 93, 255 (260).

22. RGZ 24, 1 (3).

"norms."[23] In other, really pertinent cases, however, the *Reichsgericht* firmly refused to go into judicial review of federal statutes.[24]

Shifts of Doctrine under the Weimar Constitution

From a merely juridical point of view, the Reich's Constitution of 1919 would not have necessitated any change in the courts' and the legal sciences' previous attitude toward judicial review: the Weimar Constitution, like the Constitution of 1871, did not deal with the matter explicitly, and it was known that the Constitutional Committee of the National Assembly had, for its part, willingly decided to leave the question undecided.[25] The fact that the attitude toward judicial review nevertheless did change already indicates that points of view other than merely juridical were involved.

In 1921, in a case depending on the validity of a state ordinance regulating the housing market, the *Reichsgericht* boldly declared that it had always held the courts entitled to review all statutes and ordinances with respect to form and substance, unless a statute

23. RGZ 45, 267 (270); the case turned on a state police ordinance.
24. RGZ 48, 84 (88); 77, 229 (231); RG, *Juristische Wochenschrift* (1916): 596–97; RG, *Goldtammers Archiv* 55 (1908): 325–26; in RGZ 48, 88 and 77, 231, the court states that since the respective statutes in question had been decided upon by the *Bundesrat* and the Reichstag and were properly published, there was no reason to doubt that it had also been produced in accordance with Art. 78 of the Constitution (the article concerning the requirements for a change of the Constitution). Karl August Bettermann, "Reichsgericht und richterliches Prüfungsrecht," in *Festschrift für Johannes Broermann* (Berlin, 1982), 496–97, interprets these passages as showing that the court did assume judicial review in these cases. However, both cases clearly operate on the basis of Laband. In both cases the relevant statutes were substantively unconstitutional. If, nevertheless, the court treated them as valid under the doctrine of *Verfassungsdurchbrechung* (cf. text above with n. 16) *without* actually checking that the prerequisites stated in Art. 78 had been observed, it could do so only on the basis of Laband's doctrine that the monarchical engrossment of a statute (certified by the monarchical signature under the published text) irrefutably proved that the constitutional lawmaking procedure had, up to that point, been correctly observed. In fact, RGZ 77, 231 explicitly refers to a footnote in Laband's *Staatsrecht des Deutschen Reiches*; in that footnote, Laband, to buttress his doctrine of nonreview, hints at the disastrous consequences that the admission of judicial review would have. It would, says Laband, force the courts to find that in fact the *Reichsgericht* was an unconstitutional institution – and therefore to hold all its judgments null and void – since the federation had no constitutional power to establish a federal court. It is easy to imagine that this must have seemed a very convincing argument to the *Reichsgericht* judges.
25. See Gerhard Anschütz, *Die Verfassung des Deutschen Reichs* (Berlin, [12]1930), 223–24.

explicitly forbade them to do so.[26] The same phrase was repeated two and a half years later in a case concerning a federal ordinance.[27] Insofar as these dicta pretended that judicial review had been traditional in the *Reichsgericht*'s jurisprudence not only with respect to ordinances and state laws but also with respect to federal statutes, Walter Jellinek quite properly qualified them as "fairy tales."[28]

The *Reichsgericht*, however, unperturbed by such criticism and backed by a growing number of advocates of judicial review in the legal profession, continued to follow its new course. The famous or, depending on the spectator's predilection, infamous judgment of November 4, 1925 (RGZ 111, 320), made it clear beyond any doubt that the *Reichsgericht* now assumed the competence to review federal statutes. The statute at stake this time was the federal revalorization act of July 1925, a statute limiting the judicial revalorization of claims that had been devalued by inflation.[29] Considering the amount of paper and erudition spent on the subject for generations, the reasoning delivered by the *Reichsgericht* to justify its undertaking judicial review of that statute seemed remarkably short and unsophisticated:

The federal constitution has, in Article 102, taken up the principle, formulated before in §1 of the law instituting the ordinary courts (*Gerichtsverfassungsgesetz*), that the judges are independent and subject only to the law. This latter provision does not bar the judges from declaring a federal statute or particular provisions of such a statute void insofar as they are in conflict with other provisions of higher rank. Such is the case when a statute is at variance with a provision of the Constitution without having been enacted in accordance with the requirements for a change of the Constitution stated in Article 76 RV. For the provisions of the Constitution cannot be abrogated otherwise than by a properly enacted law having the force to change the Constitution. The provisions of the Constitution therefore remain binding for the judges also in the face of a divergent statute enacted later without observing the special requirements of Article 76 and force the judges to leave the contradicting provisions of the later statute unapplied. Since the federal constitution itself does not contain any provision withdrawing the

26. RGZ 102, 161 (164).
27. RGZ 107, 377 (379).
28. Walter Jellinek, "Das Märchen von der Überprüfung verfassungswidriger Gesetze durch das Reichsgericht," *Juristische Wochenschrift* (1925): 454–55.
29. Cf. below, text with nn. 32–36.

competence to decide on the constitutionality of federal statutes from the courts and transferring it to some other authority, the right and the duty of judges to review federal statutes must be acknowledged.[30]

Having stated this, the court turned to examine the statute in question and found it to be constitutional.

For the sake of completeness, it must be noted that before RGZ 111, 320, two other federal courts – the *Reichsfinanzhof* (federal tax court) and the *Reichsversorgungsgericht* (federal maintenance court) – had in fact undertaken judicial review of federal legislation, the latter even abating the statute reviewed.[31] Nevertheless, RGZ 111, 320 was and is generally regarded as the leading case in the matter of judicial review, whereas little attention was directed to the *Reichsversorgungsgericht* case. This was due not only to the fact that RGZ 111, 320 was more explicit and had bothered to give reasons for its undertaking, but mainly of course, to the greater importance of the *Reichsgericht* in terms of the range of its jurisdiction. Moreover, the matter of revalorization dealt with in RGZ 111, 320 was in itself of vital importance and had for years before constituted a battlefield on which the judiciary had tested the range of its power.

In 1923, at the peak of inflation, the *Reichsgericht* had decided that mortgage creditors did not have to accept payment at par in paper marks but could get their claims revalorized (by court decision) according to the circumstances of each case.[32] The court thus initiated a redistribution of inflationary profits and losses. Working on the assumption that the profits had until then mostly resided with big industry, while numberless middle-class creditors had been dispossessed of their fortunes,[33] the court's intervention might

---

30. RGZ 111, 320 (322–23).

31. *Reichsfinanzhof* E 5, 333; *Reichsversorgungsgericht* E 4, 168. *Reichsfinanzhof* E 7, 97, also often mentioned in this context, deals with a statute enacted before the Weimar Constitution came into effect; judicial review of such "preconstitutional" statutes was generally and unproblematically understood to be allowed by Art. 178, II of the Weimar Constitution (stating that a preconstitutional federal law remains in force unless incompatible with the Constitution), see Ernst von Hippel, "Das richterliche Prüfungsrecht," in Gerhard Anschütz and Richard Thoma, eds., *Handbuch des deutschen Staatsrechts*, vol. 2 (Tübingen, 1932), 552; Karl Heinrich Görres, "Besteht ein richterliches Prüfungsrecht gegenüber den Rechtsquellen nach der Reichs-Verfassung?" *Juristische Wochenschrift* (1924): 1565; Hartmut Maurer, "Das richterliche Prüfungsrecht zur Zeit der Weimarer Verfassung," *Die öffentliche Verwaltung* (1968): 684.

32. RGZ 107, 78.

33. James Goldschmidt, "Gesetzesdämmerung," *Juristische Wochenschrift* (1924):

be interpreted as an act of middle-class solidarity. At any rate the court had taken unusual methodological liberty in order to reach the desired result: it had set aside the statutory status of the paper mark as legal tender on the lofty ground that nominal payment of debts in paper marks would run contrary to the bona fides principle of §242 BGB.[34] To put it more bluntly, the court had turned §242 BGB from a principle demanding equitable behavior within the margins of statutory law into a principle apt to control and, if necessary, override statutory rules that offended the judges' sense of equity. Following that judgment, there were rumors in the newspapers that the government planned to stop judicial revalorization by a law explicitly prohibiting it. The association of *Reichsgericht* judges reacted to this with a declaration exhorting the government not to give way to "influences of a selfish kind" and announcing that the *Reichsgericht* might disobey such a law, finding it contrary to the supralegal principle of bona fides and to the constitutional guarantee of private property. The judges made it painstakingly clear that even a partial, limited statutory bar to judicial revalorization would cause the "serious danger" of such a finding.[35] In the sequel, however, the judges did not quite live up to these pronouncements. The third *Steuernotverordnung*, an emergency ordinance based on statutory delegation, which limited the revalorization of claims against private persons to 15 percent, was held to be valid in RGZ 107, 370, and the revalorization law replacing it in 1925 was examined and upheld in RGZ 111, 320. In the latter case the court prudently limited the inspection to questions of constitutionality, thus tacitly renouncing the pretension

---

246; Helmut Rittstieg, *Eigentum als Verfassungsproblem* (Darmstadt, 1975), 263, 265. See also the references in Norbert Hempel, *Richterleitbilder in der Weimarer Republik* (Frankfurt/Main, 1978), 49, n. 122. Hempel himself challenges the common assumption relying on critical remarks by Knut Borchardt, "Wachstum und Wechsellagen 1914–1970," in Hermann Aubin and Wolfgang Zorn, eds., *Handbuch der deutschen Wirtschafts- und Sozialgeschichte*, vol. 2 (Stuttgart, 1976), 701. Borchardt, however, at least partly agrees with that assumption when he supposes that inflation was to the advantage of entrepreneurial profits and to the disadvantage of (profits from) nonentrepreneurial property.

34. §242 *Bürgerliches Gesetzbuch* (Federal Civil Code): "Der Schuldner ist verpflichtet, die Leistung so zu bewirken, wie Treu und Glauben mit Rücksicht auf die Verkehrssitte es erfordern."

35. *Juristische Wochenschrift* (1924): 90. The declaration is reprinted in Ernst Rudolf Huber, ed., *Dokumente zur deutschen Verfassungsgeschichte*, vol. 3 (Stuttgart, 1966), 383–84.

that it could also review legislative acts for compatibility with bona fides or any other principles "of an allegedly supralegal nature."[36] The first case in which the court undertook to review a federal statute was thus presented as a case in which the virtue of judicial restraint had by no means been thrown overboard altogether.

The main constitutional issues dealt with in RGZ 111, 320 were the constitutional guarantees of private property (Article 153) and of equality before the law (Article 109). The doctrinal changes reflected here are of no less importance than the extension of judicial review to federal statutes. It is only in conjunction with a new understanding of the scope of constitutionally guaranteed civil rights that judicial review developed into an instrument of potentially comprehensive judicial control of the legislature, and it is only in conjunction with judicial review of legislative acts that the new understanding of constitutional rights could be made effective.

As was pointed out above, nineteenth-century legal theory in Germany did not see constitutional rights as directed against (and much less as juridically enforceable against) the exercise of constitutionally established legislative power. This attitude quickly changed under the democratic Weimar Constitution. Most civil rights were guaranteed by the Weimar Constitution – subject to statutory determination or restriction. Interpreters immediately set out, however, to restrict the admissibility of such restrictions. The most successful instrument for that purpose was the doctrine of "institutional guarantees," which stated that, where the constitution guaranteed legal institutions like private property or the right of inheritance in the form of a civil right,[37] the constitutionally recognized power of the legislature to regulate and restrict such rights did not imply the power to change the essence of the institution. Private property, in other words, was not to be turned

36. For an earlier refusal to review statutes and ordinances for equity and expedience see RGZ 60, 326 (329). Advocates of judicial review often made it clear that they did not mean to entrust the courts with some general equity control, see Kelsen, "Wesen und Entwicklung der Staatsgerichtsbarkeit" (see n. 17), 68–69; Carl Schmitt, "Das Reichsgericht als Hüter der Verfassung," in Otto Schreiber, ed., *Die Reichsgerichtspraxis im deutschen Rechtsleben*, vol. 1 (Berlin, 1929), 173. The delimitation between review for compatibility with the Constitution and review for compatibility with general principles of equity and justice became unclear where review for compatibility with the Constitution was held to include review for compatibility with the *general principles underlying the Constitution* (thus Hippel, "Das richterliche Prüfungsrecht" [see n. 31], 558).

37. Art. 153, 154 WRV.

into something that no longer deserved the name.[38] Similar doctrines were drawn up for civil rights in general.[39]

As to private property, legislative discretion was further restricted by a new extensive interpretation of the concepts of property and expropriation. The term "property" (*Eigentum*), which had formerly been used only with respect to corporeal objects, was now considered to cover all vested legal estates (*jedes vermögenswerte Recht*),[40] and the concept of "expropriation," formerly applied only to the transfer of property from one person to another by an administrative act, was extended to cover any significant abridgment of property rights, including statutory modifications of their content.[41] All kinds of statutory restrictions of legal rights, from billeting regulations to statutes limiting the judicial revalorization of creditors' claims, were thus brought into the scope of judicial review under the constitutional rule that expropriations are admissible only for due compensation provided for by statute (Article 153 WRV).[42] Since the Constitution itself allowed federal laws to make exceptions to that rule,[43] however, the new, extensive read-

38. Martin Wolff, "Reichsverfassung und Eigentum," in *Festschrift für Wilhelm Kahl* (Tübingen, 1923), 6 (separate numbering of pages for this article). More generally on institutional guarantees Carl Schmitt, "Freiheitsrechte und institutionelle Garantien der Reichsverfassung" (1931), in idem, *Verfassungsrechtliche Aufsätze* (Berlin, 1958), 140–73.

39. See, e.g., Carl Schmitt, "Grundrechte und Grundpflichten," in idem, *Verfassungsrechtliche Aufsätze* (see n. 38), 208–10. Albert Hensel, "Die Rangordnung der Rechtsquellen, insbesondere das Verhältnis von Reichs- und Landesgesetzgebung," in Anschütz and Thoma, eds., *Handbuch des deutschen Staatsrechts* (see n. 31), 2: 316, n. 2.

40. Wolff, "Reichsverfassung und Eigentum" (see n. 38), 3; RGZ 111, 320 (328). For a more comprehensive survey of the *Reichsgericht*'s property jurisdiction see Alexander von Brünneck, *Die Eigentumsgarantie des Grundgesetzes* (Baden-Baden, 1984), 29–38; Rittstieg, *Eigentum als Verfassungsproblem* (see n. 33), 252–69.

41. RGZ 116, 268 (272). See also Brünneck, *Die Eigentumsgarantie* (see n. 40), and Rittstieg, *Eigentum als Verfassungsproblem* (see n. 33), 252–69.

42. For the necessary distinction between expropriatory and nonexpropriatory restrictions of property rights, the *Reichsgericht*, in the sequel, adopted the doctrine of *Einzelakt* or *Sonderopfer*. According to that doctrine, restrictions of property rights are expropriatory when they are not perfectly general in character but, for the public good, charge particular individuals or groups with a special burden; see RGZ 128, 18 (29–30); 129, 146 (148–49); 132, 69 (73, 75); 137, 163 (170). In RGZ 116, 268 (271), that doctrine is not yet clearly developed or subscribed to.

43. Art. 153 II 1, 2: "Eine Enteignung kann nur zum Wohle der Allgemeinheit und auf gesetzlicher Grundlage vorgenommen werden. Sie erfolgt gegen angemessene Entschädigung, soweit nicht ein Reichsgesetz etwas anderes bestimmt." RGZ 107, 377 (382) generously allowed exceptions to be made tacitly, i.e., by simple failure to provide for compensation. Cf. on that point the obiter dictum in RGZ 102, 161 (166), which tends toward a more severe interpretation.

ing of the constitutional guarantee of private property was brought to bear mainly on state legislation. In fact, the only legislative acts which the *Reichsgericht* has held unconstitutional under Article 153 WRV were acts of state legislatures.[44]

A conspicuous antilegislative shift also took place in the interpretation of Article 109 I WRV, which states that all Germans "are equal before the law." Traditionally, constitutional provisions with the same wording had unanimously been taken to guarantee no more and no less than equal application of the law.[45] Under the Weimar Constitution, however, the idea quickly gained ground that Article 109, ruling out any arbitrary differentiation, was also binding on the legislature itself.[46] The *Reichsgericht*, while it had unambiguously adopted the extensive, antilegislative reading of Article 153, never clearly took sides in the controversy over Article 109. In a number of cases, the question of the scope of Article 109 was explicitly treated as one that could be left open, since the respective statutes under review could not be qualified as arbitrarily differentiating anyhow.[47]

Interpretations and Assessments

Looking at the doctrinal shifts described, one cannot fail to notice that they coincide with the shift of political and constitutional power that had occurred in the same period. Contemporary critics like Franz Neumann and Otto Kirchheimer were very clear on that point, qualifying judicial review and the extensive interpretation of constitutional rights as reactionary devices invented by the bourgeoisie to secure their interest against the exercise of a legislative power that could no longer be trusted since it had become

44. RGZ 103, 200; 109, 310; 111, 123; 112, 67; 128, 18; 132, 69.

45. See, e.g., Art. 4 of the Prussian Constitution of 1850.

46. The classical text is Heinrich Triepel, *Goldbilanzenverordnung und Vorzugsaktien* (Berlin and Leipzig, 1924), 26–32. Triepel extensively refers to the jurisdiction of the U.S. Supreme Court to buttress his view. For an account of the controversy over Art. 109 WRV see Anschütz, *Die Verfassung des Deutschen Reichs* (see n. 25), 459–67.

47. RGZ 111, 320 (329); 113, 6 (13); 125, 369 (372); 128, 165 (169); 136, 211 (221). An incidental remark in RGZ 126, 161 (163) comes closest to adopting the extensive interpretation; in RGZ 128, 165 (169), however, the question is again treated as undecided and open.

democratic.[48] Neumann, attacking one of the several (unsuccessful) law projects concerning judicial review initiated under the Weimar Republic,[49] adduced the defeat of American labor legislation by the Supreme Court as a warning example to buttress his view.[50] Gustav Radbruch also used the American example as an argument against judicial review and, in somewhat more measured words than Neumann and Kirchheimer, ascribed the advance of judicial review to the fact that quite a few citizens were apparently unwilling to give the new republican government as much credit as they had given to the former, monarchial one.[51] Hermann Heller described judicial review of legislative acts, along with the extensive interpretation of "equality before the law," as instruments created by the bourgeoisie to prevent the transformation of the liberal state into a social state of law.[52] In our time, Willibald Apelt, Helmut Rittstieg, and others have expressed similar views,[53] while on the other hand Karl August Bettermann, in a recent article has challenged the assumption on which these interpretations are based and has tried to show that the *Reichsgericht*'s doctrines on judicial review did not significantly change at all with the transition from the empire to the republic.[54] Bettermann is certainly right in drawing attention to the fact that with respect to certain kinds of norms – ordinances and state laws – judicial review was already clearly recognized by the *Reichsgericht* under the Constitution of 1871.[55]

---

48. Franz Neumann, "Gegen ein Gesetz über Nachprüfung der Verfassungsmäßigkeit von Reichsgesetzen," *Die Gesellschaft* (1929): 521–22; Franz Neumann, *Die Herrschaft des Gesetzes* (1936, repr. Frankfurt/Main, 1980), 327–28; Otto Kichheimer, *Die Grenzen der Enteignung* (Berlin, 1930), 34, 42–44. See also Ernst Fraenkel, "Die Krise des Rechtsstaats und die Justiz" (first published in 1931), in idem, *Zur Soziologie der Klassenjustiz und Aufsätze zur Verfassungskrise, 1931–1932* (Darmstadt, 1968), 43.

49. On these projects see Maurer, "Das richterliche Prüfungsrecht" (see n. 31), 686–87.

50. Neumann, "Gegen ein Gesetz über Nachprüfung der Verfassungsmäßigkeit von Reichsgesetzen" (see n. 48), 530–32.

51. Gustav Radbruch, "Richterliches Prüfungsrecht?" *Die Justiz* 1 (1925/26): 13–14.

52. Hermann Heller, "Rechtsstaat oder Diktatur," in *Gesammelte Schriften*, vol. 2 (Leiden, 1971), 450.

53. Willibald Apelt, *Geschichte der Weimarer Verfassung* (Munich, ²1964), 343–44; Rittstieg, *Eigentum als Verfassungsproblem* (see n. 33), 255, 269; Joachim Perels, *Kapitalismus und politische Demokratie: Privatrechtssystem und Gesellschaftsstruktur in der Weimarer Republik* (Frankfurt/Main, 1973), 39–45; Helmut D. Fangmann, *Justiz gegen Demokratie* (Frankfurt/Main and New York, 1979).

54. Bettermann, "Reichsgericht und richterliches Prüfungsrecht" (see n. 24).

His claim, however, that the same is true for judicial review of federal statutes is based on an erroneous reading of two relevant cases and on the failure to consider two other cases in which the court clearly refused to go into judicial review of federal statutes.[56]

The doctrinal shifts outlined above thus remain to be explained, and a closer look at the literature preceding and following the relevant *Reichsgericht* decisions uncontestably reveals that political discontent with the performance of the democratic legislature and, above all, fear of further and more far-reaching socialist developments were indeed driving motives in the process of doctrinal change. Heinrich Triepel, one of the leading scholars advocating judicial review, pointed out that what may be supportable under a constitutional monarchy may be insupportable under a parliamentary republic, and that in the latter state judicial review was indeed indispensable for the protection of liberty against the appetence of the legislature.[57] James Goldschmidt, having expressed his displeasure with the legislation for the protection of tenants and other interferences with private property and the free market, concluded that in the popular state (*Volksstaat*) judicial review was necessary to safeguard law and justice against the "absolutism of the majority."[58] Fritz Morstein-Marx bluntly stated that the question of judicial review was a question of trust rather than one of law and for his own part decided to trust the judges more than the legislature.[59] In Martin Wolff's classical article establishing the extensive, antilegislative interpretation of the constitutional

---

55. Inaccurate accounts are indeed quite common. It is often asserted without the necessary distinctions that judicial review of statutes has been assumed (only) under the Weimar Constitution: Rittstieg, *Eigentum als Verfassungsproblem* (see n. 33), 256; Brünneck, *Die Eigentumsgarantie des Grundgesetzes* (see n. 40), 29. Huber, *Deutsche Verfassungsgeschichte* (see n. 16), 561, maintains that before 1911 formal, but not substantive, review of statutes had been recognized.

56. Cf. n. 24. The cases not considered at all by Bettermann are RG, *Juristische Wochenschrift* (1916): 596, 597, and RG (St), *Goldtammers Archiv* 55 (1908): 352–53.

57. Heinrich Triepel, "Der Weg der Gesetzgebung nach der neuen Reichsverfassung," *Archiv für öffentliches Recht* 39 (1920): 537–38. See also Heinrich Triepel, "Streitigkeiten zwischen Reich und Ländern," in *Festschrift für Wilhelm Kahl* (Tübingen, 1923), 93, dealing with the question of judicial review of statutes by the *Staatsgerichtshof* in controversies between states and the empire (Art. 19 WRV).

58. James Goldschmidt, "Gesetzesdämmerung," *Juristische Wochenschrift* (1924): 248.

59. Fritz Morstein Marx, "Art. 13 Abs. 2 der Reichsverfassung und der Streit um die richterliche Prüfungszuständigkeit," *Archiv für öffentliches Recht*, n.s. 6 (1924): 223 and passim.

367

guarantee of private property, central doctrines were explicitly designed to counter "extreme leftist" ideas and plans.[60] Some other authors expressed their political preferences less frankly, but nevertheless distinctly enough. To Radbruch's warning, for instance, that judicial review would undermine the authority of the judiciary,[61] Ernst von Hippel coldly replied that, to say the least, the legislator's authority did not seem to be more firmly established than the authority of the judiciary,[62] and for precisely that reason, the exercise of the former needed to be controlled.

Where political points of view have to such an extent been made explicit in a juridical debate and where, in fact, the political relevance of juridical alternatives is as obvious as it was in the matter of judicial review and related interpretations of constitutional rights, it can be presumed that juridical sides are usually taken in conformity with political preferences even where such preferences do not appear on the face of the relevant juridical statements. It therefore also seems reasonable to suspect that when seemingly neutral arguments concerning tradition,[63] legal certainty,[64] the

60. Wolff, "Reichsverfassung und Eigentum" (see n. 38), 6, 18. For an analysis of political motives underlying the new interpretation of the constitutional guarantee of "equality before the law" see Max Rümelin, *Die Gleichheit vor dem Gesetz* (Tübingen, 1928), 19–20.

61. Radbruch, "Richterliches Prüfungsrecht?" (see n. 51), 15.

62. Hippel, "Das richterliche Prüfungsrecht" (see n. 31), 556. Hippel, by the way, found no deterrent in the way judicial review was exercised by the U.S. Supreme Court.

63. Richard Thoma, "Das richterliche Prüfungsrecht," *Archiv für öffentliches Recht* 43 (1922): 267–86, finding that the text of the Constitution offered no logically conclusive arguments for or against judicial review, argued that in the absence of cogent counterarguments, one had to stay with the relevant tradition. According to Thoma (274), *nonreview* was the German and even the European tradition. Views on what was the German tradition, however, strongly differed. Those opposing judicial review tended to find tradition supporting their view: Anschütz, *Die Verfassung des Deutschen Reichs* (see n. 25), 324; Neumann, "Gegen ein Gesetz über Nachprüfung der Verfassungsmäßigkeit von Reichsgesetzen" (see n. 48), 518; Radbruch, "Richterliches Prüfungsrecht?" (see n. 51), 13. Advocates of judicial review, when they went back to history, found doctrinal traditions to have at least varied over time: Wassertrüdinger, "Darf der Richter die Verfassungsmäßigkeit der Reichsgesetze nachprüfen?" *Juristische Wochenschrift* (1925): 44; Kleineberg, "Das richterliche Prüfungsrecht der Verfassungsmäßigkeit der Reichsgesetze," *Leipziger Zeitschrift* (1925): 630; Adamovich, *Die Prüfung der Gesetze und Verordnungen* (see n. 12), 1–13.

64. See, e.g., Anschütz, *Die Verfassung des Deutschen Reichs* (see n. 25), 326; Neumann, "Gegen ein Gesetz über Nachprüfung der Verfassungsmäßigkeit von Reichsgesetzen" (see n. 48), 521. Both see legal certainty endangered by judicial review. Cf. on the other side, Hippel, "Das richterliche Prüfungsrecht" (see n. 31), 556.

division of powers,[65] or the nature of the presidential promulgation of statutes[66] were adduced for or against judicial review, political motives had played a part in their choice and exposition. In fact, it has been observed that while, under the monarchy, judicial review was advocated by liberals and democrats, the Weimar adherents of judicial review are to be found on the conservative or reactionary side.[67] Generalizations of this kind are of course true only *cum grano salis*. Hans Kelsen, for instance, might be adduced as a counter-example.[68] It has also often been pointed out that in the Constitutional Committee of the National Assembly, attitudes toward judicial review had bridged party and coalition lines.[69]

To acknowledge the impact of political interests in the movement toward recognition of judicial review is not to say that judicial review was *usurped*[70] for the protection of such interests. Political motives were, of course, involved on both sides, and the juridical arguments in favor of judicial review were not all that bad. Weimar lawyers had to start out from the prerevolutionary doctrine that allowed judicial review with respect to ordinances and

65. For an account of the arguments used in this context see Maurer, "Das richterliche Prüfungsrecht" (see n. 31), 685.

66. For arguments fighting Laband's doctrine see Triepel, "Der Weg der Gesetzgebung" (see n. 57), 535–36; Hans Nawiasky, "Zur Frage des richterlichen Prüfungsrechts," *Deutsche Juristenzeitung* (1923): 40–41; Kleineberg, "Das richterliche Prüfungsrecht der Verfassungsmäßigkeit der Reichsgesetze" (see n. 63), 631–35; Wassertrüdinger, "Darf der Richter die Verfassungsmäßigkeit der Reichsgesetze nachprüfen?" (see n. 63), 45; Hermann Breiholdt, "Die Abstimmung im Reichstag," *Archiv für öffentliches Recht*, n.s. 10 (1926): 316f.

67. Karl Dietrich Bracher, *Die Auflösung der Weimarer Republik* (Düsseldorf, ⁵1984), 173. See also Neumann, "Gegen ein Gesetz über Nachprüfung der Verfassungsmäßigkeit von Reichsgesetzen" (see n. 48), 522. For a detailed and striking analysis considering party affiliations see Helge Wendenburg, *Die Debatte um die Verfassungsgerichtsbarkeit und der Methodenstreit der Staatsrechtslehre in der Weimarer Republik* (Göttingen, 1984), 226–31.

68. Kelsen, "Wesen und Entwicklung der Staatsgerichtsbarkeit" (see n. 17). Kelsen, of course, must be read against the particular Austrian background.

69. Anschütz, *Die Verfassung des Deutschen Reichs* (see n. 25), 323–24; Thoma, "Das richterliche Prüfungsrecht" (see n. 63), 268–69; Ludwig Bendix, "Recht und Pflicht des Richters zur Prüfung der materiellen Verfassungsmäßigkeit von Reichsgesetzen nach der Weimarer Verfassung," *Juristische Wochenschrift* (1924): 527. See, however, Wendenburg, *Die Debatte um die Verfassungsgerichtsbarkeit* (see n. 67), 226, explaining the seemingly irregular communist and radical socialist advocacy of judicial review of legislative acts in the Constitutional Committee as having been tied to the concept of an elective judiciary.

70. Fangmann, *Justiz gegen Demokratie* (see n. 53), 10. See also the formulation used by Fraenkel, "Die Krise des Rechtsstaats und die Justiz" (see n. 48), 43: "angemaßt."

state law, but foreclosed it with respect to federal statutes. From the empire to Weimar, the plausibility of the differences made here objectively diminished. Under the Constitution of 1871, review of state law had been uncontroversial on the basis of Article 2 I 1 RV, giving federal law precedence over state law. Under the Weimar Constitution, it was quite convincingly argued that if judicial review of state law follows from a rule giving federal law precedence over state law, judicial review of federal statutes must follow if it can be ascertained that the Constitution has precedence over "simple" statutory law. And the Weimar Constitution could indeed be seen as claiming that precedence more distinctly than the Constitution of 1871, since unlike its predecessor it demanded qualified majorities in both houses for its own change.[71]

The second distinction relevant under the older doctrine – the distinction between statutes and ordinances – was blurred by legislation itself. From 1914 to 1923, various enabling laws had delegated comprehensive legislative powers to the *Bundesrat* or, from 1919 on, to the government.[72] Since these delegations were practically unlimited,[73] it could well seem that they had not only endowed the government with sweeping power to make ordinances but that they had transformed the legislative process itself, conferring power to make statutes to the executive. Two of these enabling laws, enacted in 1919 and 1920, were indeed entitled "law on a simplified form of legislation for the purposes of the transitional economy."[74] This state of legal confusion concerning the proper delimitation of powers and concepts could not fail to have dis-

71. Eduard Bötticher, "Das Reichsgesetz vor dem Richterstuhl," *Leipziger Zeitschrift* (1925): 892–93; Wassertrüdinger, "Darf der Richter die Verfassungsmäßigkeit der Reichsgesetze nachprüfen?" (see n. 63), 44; Adamovich, *Die Prüfung der Gesetze und Verordnungen* (see n. 12), 17, 28–32. Adamovich gives a short account of the different views concerning the precedence of the Constitution over ordinary statutory law.

72. These enabling laws are reprinted in Huber, ed., *Dokumente zur deutschen Verfassungsgeschichte* (see n. 35), 185–88.

73. In spite of occasional criticism, German legal theory and practice (unlike the American) accepted sweeping delegations of this kind, and whatever might otherwise have given rise to certain doubts could always be justified under the doctrine of *Verfassungsdurchbrechung* (see text above with n. 16). For a comparative account see Carl Schmitt, "Vergleichender Überblick über die neueste Entwicklung des Problems der gesetzgeberischen Ermächtigungen," *Zeitschrift für ausländisches öffentliches Recht und Völkerrecht* 6 (1936): 252–68.

74. Gesetz über eine vereinfachte Form der Gesetzgebung für die Zwecke der Übergangswirtschaft vom 17. April 1919, RGBl. I, 394; Gesetz über die verein-

orienting effects also in the context of judicial review. It is probably not just by chance that the first case in which the *Reichsgericht* asserted that it had always considered the courts competent to review statutes and ordinances was a case concerning an ordinance issued under the 1919 "law on a simplified form of legislation."[75]

From the question of reasons and motives underlying the *Reichsgericht*'s exercise of judicial review, the question of its effects must be distinguished. The *Reichsgericht* may have assumed the right to review federal statutes in order to be able to set limits to socialist aspirations of the democratic legislature, but it cannot properly be said to have produced considerable *actual* effects of that sort. The Weimar Republic did not witness anything comparable to the defeat of New Deal legislation by the U.S. Supreme Court. As was already mentioned above, only state laws – two of them concerning property rights of the formerly ruling princes, two denying compensation for building restrictions, one cutting back coal rents, and another one granting a public right of preemption to be exercised also on the basis of void contracts – were declared unconstitutional by the *Reichsgericht* under Article 153 WRV.[76] Four more state laws were held to violate the vested rights of civil servants guaranteed by Article 129 WRV.[77] *Federal* laws were considered unconstitutional in two or three cases only, depending on whether you do or do not count one case in which the court, outside its regular competence, decided as a court of arbitration on the basis of a private agreement. Two of the federal law cases again turned on the constitutional guarantee of the vested rights of civil servants.[78] In the arbitration case a statutory suspension of certain judicial proceedings, as far as it applied to arbitration proceedings, was held to violate the consti-

---

fachte Form der Gesetzgebung für die Zwecke der Übergangswirtschaft vom 3. August 1920, RGB1. I, 1493. Cf. also Friedrich Klein, "Verordnungsermächtigungen nach deutschem Verfassungsrecht," in W.E. Genzer and W. Einbeck, eds., *Die Übertragung rechtsetzender Gewalt im Rechtsstaat* (Frankfurt/Main, 1952), 14–15.

75. RGZ 102, 161; cf. text above, with n. 26.

76. Cf. above, text with n. 43 and 44. In another case the court awarded compensation in the absence of any statutory provision either granting or denying it; RGZ 116, 268. On the impact of that decision see Brünneck, *Die Eigentumsgarantie des Grundgesetzes* (see n. 40), 38.

77. RGZ 107, 1; 120, 374; 124, 173; 134, 1.

78. RGZ 120, 324; 124, 173.

tutional guarantee of the "legal judge" (Article 105 WRV).[79] In many other cases, the *Reichsgericht* confirmed the validity of statutes and ordinances that had been challenged,[80] and retrospectively one may even wonder at the court's largesse, particularly in dealing with the practice of enabling laws.[81] In fact, the bulk of interventionist regulation subjected to judicial review fell into the category of crisis management, interfering with the market, but without hostility to the market system itself. If judicial review of legislative acts and an extensive interpretation of civil rights had been designed as medicaments against legislative anticapitalism, their use, under the Weimar Constitution, remained prophylactic[82] rather than curative, and this mainly because there was not much to be cured. The relevant *Reichsgericht* jurisdiction has probably deployed its greatest effects on an atmospherical level. Claiming judicial control of legislative acts, the highest court of the empire affiliated with those who viewed the parliamentary system with antipathy and distrust. The court may not have wanted to express anything like that, but such was the objective meaning of its jurisdiction under the given political circumstances and in the given context of discussion.

---

79. RGZ 126, 161. Maurer, "Das richterliche Prüfungsrecht" (see n. 31), 684, wrongly assumes that the decision of the *Reichsversorgungsgericht* E 4, 168 (quoted by Maurer after a report by Graßhoff) is the only case in which a federal statute was held unconstitutional and therefore inapplicable by a highest court. See also Gusy, *Richterliches Prüfungsrecht* (see n. 13), 84–85, naming only RGZ 124, 173 and RGZ 126, 161, and Wendenburg, *Die Debatte um die Verfassungsgerichtsbarkeit* (see n. 67), 55, naming only RGZ 124, 173. For highest court decisions declaring statutory provisions unconstitutional see also *Staatsgerichtshof*, in RGZ 122, Appendix, 17 (concerning a federal law) and *Staatsgerichtshof*, in RGZ 124, Appendix, 1 (concerning a state law); both these cases did not turn on civil rights.

80. See RGZ 107, 261; 107, 315; 107, 320; 107, 370; 107, 377; 109, 117; 111, 320; 112, 50; 113, 16; 114, 262; 128, 165; 129, 146 (this listing cannot claim to be complete, but should contain the most important cases).

81. Cf. n. 73; for a striking example see RGZ 103, 306.

82. Brünneck, *Die Eigentumsgarantie des Grundgesetzes* (see n. 40), 42.

14
The Liberal Critique of the U.S. Supreme Court

William M. Wiecek

Although the U.S. Supreme Court has been the object of controversy almost from the date of its founding,[1] for the first half of the twentieth century its foremost critics were political liberals. It is necessary at the outset to define that term of reference. For purposes of this paper, I adopt a crude, American, and common-sense definition of the adjective "liberal" as it might be applied to widely different persons, groups, and ideas over a century of rapid development. The term refers to persons who seek to create a society that is democratic and egalitarian; whose principal concern is for the interests of workers, minorities (racial, religious, ethnic), and organized labor; who hold expansive views of civil liberties issues, especially those involving the First Amendment or the rights of persons accused of crime; who support expanding levels of state-supported social welfare and who propose to finance such programs through a modest but progressive redistribution of wealth. Defined negatively, liberals oppose authoritarian, elitist, and hierarchical political and social ordering; they resist the influence of wealth and corporate power.

Since the Civil War, the period of liberal criticism of the U.S. Supreme Court encompassed the half century that began ca. 1890 and ended with the onset of the Second World War. Voices of liberal criticism were heard before this period and after; they remain vocal today. Nevertheless, the period of a distinctively liberal critique of judicial policy-making occurred contemporaneously with the Populist, Progressive, and New Deal eras. At

---

1. I have briefly surveyed criticism in the earlier period in William M. Wiecek, "The 'Imperial Judiciary' in Historical Perspective," *Yearbook of the Supreme Court Historical Society* (1984): 61–89, and am preparing a more detailed survey in "*Murdock v. Memphis* (1875): The Aborted Revolution in Federal Question Jurisdiction" (in progress).

other times, and particularly since the 1950s, the dominant voices of criticism have been conservative, challenging the Court because its decisions have unsettled extant, majoritarian social policies.

Criticism of the Supreme Court, of whatever ideological stripe, can only occur within some specific historical context; it is always aimed at particular decisions that have important political and social consequences. Thus before we can sensibly describe a body of critical thought, we must outline the matrix of decisions that provoked that criticism. The first outburst of modern criticism, that of the Populists and Progressives, reacted to a string of decisions in the 1890s that displayed undue solicitude for wealth and corporate power. The gist of this critique was that the Court protected the interests of a small and wealthy minority of society at the expense of the right of democratic majorities to govern. Though this theme of majoritarianism figured importantly in the liberal critique, it continues today as a major element of the conservative challenge.

The most prominent of the Court's wealth-protecting decisions handed down during the two decades of the Fuller court[2] were these:

1. *Chicago, Milwaukee, and St. Paul Railway Co. v. Minnesota* (1890)[3] and *Smyth v. Ames* (1898)[4] established the doctrine of substantive due process. Anticipated in the dissents of Justices Stephen J. Field and Joseph Bradley in the *Slaughterhouse* cases (1873)[5] and numerous state supreme court decisions of the 1880s,[6] this amorphous doctrine held that all individuals and corporations have substantive rights to liberty and property that state and federal legislatures may not infringe. This protean doctrine retained its vitality until 1937.

2. *Allgeyer v. Louisiana* (1897)[7] enunciated the major daughter doctrine of substantive due process, liberty of contract, which

2. Melville Weston Fuller, an Illinois Democrat of mediocre abilities, was chief justice of the United States from 1888 to his death in 1910.
   3. 134 U.S. 418 (1890).
   4. 169 U.S. 466 (1898).
   5. 16 Wall. (83 U.S.) 36 (1873).
   6. E.g., In re *Jacobs*, 98 N.Y. 98 (1885); *Godcharles v. Wigeman*, 113 Pa. 431 (1886); *People v. Budd*, 117 N.Y. 1 (1889) (Peckham, J. dissenting); *Commonwealth v. Perry*, 155 Mass. 117 (1891), to mention only the most prominent.
   7. 165 U.S. 578 (1897).

held that all persons have a constitutionally protected liberty interest in being able to make contracts freely, without state interference. This doctrine was most potent in the field of labor relations, where it was based on the formalist premise that both parties, employer and employee, stood on an equal bargaining footing.

3. *United States v. E.C. Knight Co.* (1895)[8] and *Adair v. United States* (1908)[9] struck at the federal police power, defined broadly as the power of the national government to regulate economic relationships in the interest of all the American people.

4. *Lochner v. New York* (1905)[10] was the major decision striking down an exercise of the states' police powers. Though in our times it has become a byword for bad adjudication, the decision exercised an incalculable influence, both affirmative and negative, in shaping the way Americans think about their Constitution and the role of the U.S. Supreme Court in interpreting it.

5. In *re Debs* (1895)[11] validated the labor injunction. This struck a blow at organized labor, gave conservative judges a powerful judicial weapon to be wielded in collusion with attorneys representing management, and grossly abused First Amendment liberties of speech, press, and assembly.

6. *Loewe v. Lawlor* (1908),[12] commonly known as the *Danbury Hatters* case, demonstrated the Court's antilabor bias at its most virulent. Reversing the premises of the *Knight* case, the Court held that the Sherman Anti-Trust Act could be used to protect the manufacturing activity struck by the *Danbury Hatters*, though in *Knight* it could not similarly reach the Sugar Trust, which engrossed far more of the national market than the Danbury hat manufacturers. It shared *Debs's* enthusiasm for using the federal police power for union-busting ends, though that power could not be used to protect the interests of workers.

7. The income tax cases (*Pollock v. Farmers Loan and Trust Co.*, 1895)[13] reveal the Court in its most febrile antisocialist mood. There it held the federal income tax unconstitutional despite two

8. 156 U.S. 1 (1895).
9. 208 U.S. 161 (1908).
10. 198 U.S. 45 (1905).
11. 158 U.S. 564 (1895).
12. 208 U.S. 274 (1908).
13. 157 U.S. 429 (1895); 158 U.S. 601 (1895).

contra precedents, goaded on by counsels' apocalyptic warnings of class warfare and expropriation of wealth.

8. The Court was at first hostile to the new federal regulatory commissions, as evidenced in *Cincinnati, New Orleans, and Texas Pacific Railway Co. v. Interstate Commerce Commission* (1896) and *Interstate Commerce Commission v. Alabama Midland Railway* (1897),[14] which respectively denied the Interstate Commerce Commission rate-setting powers and denied finality to the commission's fact-finding.

9. Finally, the Court legitimated racial segregation and black disfranchisement in *Plessy v. Ferguson* (1896), *Cumming v. Richmond County Board of Education* (1899), and *Williams v. Mississippi* (1898).[15] On this matter, however, few contemporaries condemned the Court's results or its reasoning; such criticism was deferred for half a century.

These decisions were "instances of a hidebound and retrograde conservatism on the part of courts in decisions which turn on the individual economic or sociological views of the judges," as the conservative president William Howard Taft put it,[16] and they called forth an outburst of liberal criticism. Such attacks on the Court took one of two avenues, political or scholarly. At first, after the shock of the 1895 decisions, critics limited themselves to calling on the judges to exercise self-restraint. *Lochner* persuaded many that such an approach was futile, and critics turned to a variety of radical measures that would defang the judges. In 1911, Oklahoma senator Robert Owen introduced a bill providing for recall of all federal judges and election of the lower federal court judges.[17] This measure was clearly unconstitutional, violating both the appointments clause of Article II and the good-behavior provision of Article III,[18] but it reflected the popularity of the recall in the western states as well as the triumph of the nineteenth-century movement for an elective bench. (Today every state provides for the election of some or all of its judges, though that election is often

14. 162 U.S. 184 (1896); 168 U.S. 144 (1897).
15. 163 U.S. 537 (1896); 175 U.S. 528 (1899); 170 U.S. 213 (1898).
16. Veto Message on the Arizona Enabling Bill, August 15, 1911, reprinted in *Congressional Record*, 62d Cong. 1st sess. 3964 (August 15, 1911) at 3966.
17. *Congressional Record* (see n. 16), 3359 (July 31, 1911).
18. U.S. Constitution, Art. II, 2, 2; Art. III, 1.

nominal or pro forma. Only the federal courts remain wholly appointive.) The Socialist party, considering itself a victim of the federal judiciary because of such things as the labor injunction, also called for election of federal judges and demanded the abolition of judicial review.[19] Some congressmen echoed this demand for the abolition of judicial review, proposing to enforce it by vacating the office of any federal judge who held a federal statute unconstitutional.[20] Such proposals were patently unconstitutional (unless achieved through amendment of the Constitution).

Some congressional critics of the Court recommended more modest measures. These included proposals for a legislative override of judicial "vetoes": that is, if the Court held a statute unconstitutional, Congress could reenact it by a two-thirds majority. Other measures would require a supermajority to hold either a federal or state statute unconstitutional – two-thirds of the justices or a unanimous bench.[21] Former president Theodore Roosevelt, who had become explicitly critical of the Court after his retirement from office, endorsed some of these measures in his Progressive party (Bull Moose) campaign for the presidency in 1912.[22] He actually went further than other Progressives in demanding recall of judicial decisions, a sort of popular veto of judicial "lawmaking." This controversial proposal divided even his followers in 1912.

These various proposals met with as little success as Roosevelt's bid for re-election. Congress in fact actually expanded the Supreme Court's appellate jurisdiction under the old section 25 of the 1789 Judiciary Act by permitting appeals to be taken where a state court decision was favorable to a right claimed under the federal Constitution, as well as where the result was adverse.[23] It later enhanced the power of the Supreme Court in the Judiciary Act of 1925 by abolishing appeal (a matter of right) in all constitutional issues,

19. 1908 Socialist party platform, reprinted in Kirk H. Porter and Donald B. Johnson, eds., *National Party Platforms, 1840–1964* (Urbana, IL, [3]1966), 166.
20. *Congressional Record*, 64th Cong. 2d sess. 1068 (January 9, 1917); *Congressional Record*, 65 Cong. 2d sess. 7433 (June 6, 1918).
21. *Congressional Record*, 54th Cong. 1st sess. 5441 (May 20, 1896); *Congressional Record*, 55 Cong. 2d sess. 430 (January 7, 1898).
22. Theodore Roosevelt, "Judges and Progress," *Outlook*, January 6, 1912, 40–48; "A Charter of Democracy," *Outlook*, February 24, 1912, 490–502; "The Right of the People to Rule," *Outlook*, March 23, 1912, 618–26.
23. Act of January 28, 1914, ch. 22, 38 Stat. 805.

substituting in its stead the discretionary writ of certiorari. At the same time, it freed the Court for consideration of the more significant constitutional cases coming before it by diverting much routine business of lesser importance to the circuit courts of appeals.[24] While neither of these measures was dramatic, they attested to the continuing confidence of a majority of Congress in the Court and demonstrated how little support could be mustered for stripping the Court of its jurisdiction because of unpopular decisions.

Several decisions of the Court were reversed by the political or amendment processes, though. In 1913, Congress and the states overturned the result of the income tax cases by adoption and ratification of the Sixteenth Amendment, giving Congress power to enact an income tax. (This was the third time a constitutional amendment had reversed a Court decision, the previous two being the Eleventh Amendment, reversing *Chisholm v. Georgia* [1793], and the Fourteenth Amendment, reversing the *Dred Scott* case [1857].) The Nineteenth Amendment, extending the vote to women, had the effect of nullifying the Court's decision in *Minor v. Happersett* (1875),[25] which had construed the equal protection clause of the Fourteenth Amendment not to require that the states permit women to vote.

In the Clayton Act of 1914, Congress attempted to abolish the labor injunction and to moderate the harsh anti-union impact of the *Danbury Hatters* case and similar decisions in the lower federal courts by providing that labor was "not a commodity or article of commerce."[26] Within a decade, Congress would discover that a conservative-minded Court could easily evade this indirect attempt to deflect regressive doctrine.

While the political critique of the Court produced mixed results, scholarly criticism had a substantial impact. At the most generalized philosophical level, Oliver Wendell Holmes and Roscoe Pound undercut the formalist bases of the Fuller court's more dubious decisions. Holmes' great aphorism, "The life of the law has not been logic: it has been experience,"[27] demolished the arid formalism of *Knight* and *Plessy*. In his *Lochner* dissent, Holmes insisted that "general propositions do not decide concrete cases.

24. Judiciary Act of 1925, ch. 229, 43 Stat. 936.
25. 21 Wall. (88 U.S.) 163 (1875).
26. Clayton Act of 1914, ch. 323, 38 Stat. 730.
27. Oliver Wendell Holmes, *The Common Law* (Boston, MA, 1881), 1.

The decision will depend on a judgment or intuition more subtle than any articulate major premise."[28] Pound, praising the Holmes *Lochner* dissent, called for the infusion of philosophical pragmatism into adjudication. Deriding what he called "mechanical jurisprudence," Pound instead outlined the bases of "sociological jurisprudence," an approach to judging that took into account competing social interests involved in the consequences of a decision and balancing them.[29] Taken together, these ideas laid the foundation for legal realism.

The Holmes-Pound criticisms were abstract and philosophical. Other legal scholars addressed themselves to more specific issues. Ernst Freund of the University of Chicago Law School, a giant almost forgotten today after he was banished to the fringes of legal education by the Langdellian case method of legal indoctrination exported by Harvard to Chicago, published a substantial treatise, *The Police Power, Public Policy, and Constitutional Rights*, in 1904.[30] Seeing the Court's substantive due process decisions as inimical to a broad conception of the police power as outlined in *Munn v. Illinois* (1877),[31] Freund attempted to present a comprehensive survey of police power doctrine that might shore up its foundation against the assaults of hostile judges like Fuller and Rufus Peckham, the author of the *Lochner* majority opinion. Others expressed skepticism about substantive due process and liberty of contract dogmas.[32]

Much of the abuse heaped on the Court after 1895 went beyond criticism of a particular bad decision to a condemnation of judicial review itself. Scholars turned their attention to the origins of this topic near the turn of the century and in the process produced a body of scholarly literature impressive in its range and depth. James Bradley Thayer of the Harvard Law School, in a landmark 1893 article that still repays reading nearly a century later, defended the institution of judicial review, which he termed "a great and stately

28. 198 U.S. at 76.

29. Roscoe Pound, "Mechanical Jurisprudence," *Columbia Law Review* 8 (1908): 605.

30. Ernst Freund, *The Police Power, Public Policy, and Constitutional Rights* (Chicago, IL, 1904).

31. 94 U.S. 113 (1877).

32. Roscoe Pound, "Liberty of Contract," *Yale Law Journal* 18 (1909): 454–87; Charles E. Shattuck, "The True Meaning of the Term 'Liberty' in Those Clauses in the Federal and State Constitutions Which Protect 'Life, Liberty, and Property,'" *Harvard Law Review* 4 (1891): 365–92.

jurisdiction," but he demanded that it be exercised with a much greater sensitivity to the need for judicial self-restraint than would be demonstrated in the ensuing years.[33] Other legal commentators filled law review pages with criticism of the Court couched in increasingly virulent terms, accusing the Court of being overtly politicized and subservient to an economic elite. These critics included state-court judges (albeit from the southern states, where an antebellum hostility to judicial nationalism lingered long enough to be transformed into a suspicion that the U.S. Supreme Court was abetting the economic subjugation and colonialization of the South) and an occasional law school professor or dean,[34] so they could not be written off as the ravings of a Populist lunatic fringe.

By the eve of World War I, from both scholarship and diatribe there emerged a more sophisticated understanding of the role that the Supreme Court occupies in American society and of its impact on policy-making, something the legal philosopher Morris Cohen termed "judicial legislation."[35] Though eminent scholars defended the Court, its legitimacy, and even the substance of its decisions,[36] it was obvious that the role of the Court in the new century would be far more contentious than it had been since the Civil War.

America's entry into the First World War diverted the nation's attention momentarily from the role of the Court, but a number of reactionary and unpopular decisions rendered by the White and Taft courts reawoke the sleeping dog of hostility to the Court by progressives.[37] These decisions again provided a matrix for criticism of the Court from the political left. They included:

33. James Bradley Thayer, "The Origin and Scope of the American Doctrine of Constitutional Law," *Harvard Law Review* 7 (1893): 129–56.

34. Walter D. Coles, "Politics and the Supreme Court of the United States," *American Law Review* 27 (1893): 182–208; John W. Akin, "Aggressions of the Federal Courts," *American Law Review* 32 (1898): 669–700; Robert G. Street, "The Irreconcilable Conflict," *American Law Review* 41 (1907): 685–95; William Trickett, "The Great Usurpation," *American Law Review* 40 (1906): 356–76; Walter Clark, "Is the Supreme Court Constitutional?" *The Independent* 63 (1907): 723–26; Walter Clark, "Back to the Constitution," *American Law Review* 50 (1916): 1–14.

35. Morris R. Cohen, "The Process of Judicial Legislation," *American Law Review* 48 (1914): 161–98.

36. E.g., Charles Warren, "The Progressiveness of the United States Supreme Court," *Columbia Law Review* 13 (1913): 290–313.

37. Edward Douglass White, a Confederate veteran and Louisiana Democrat given to impenetrable prose, succeeded Fuller as chief justice of the United States and sat from 1910 to 1921. He was succeeded by the Ohio Republican and former president, William Howard Taft, who was chief justice from 1921 to his death in 1930.

1. The problem of child labor: in *Hammer v. Dagenhart* (1918)[38] and *Bailey v. Drexel Furniture* (1922),[39] the Court negated federal efforts to eliminate child labor in mines and factories through exercise of its commerce-regulatory and taxing powers. So outraged was public reaction to these two decisions that Congress proposed, and the states nearly ratified, a constitutional amendment permitting Congress to regulate in this area.

2. The working conditions of women: in *Adkins v. Children's Hospital* (1923),[40] the Court resurrected *Lochner*, considered moribund by then, and extended it to void federal and state efforts to regulate the minimum wages of female employees.

3. Labor organization: in the Clayton Act of 1914, Congress had explicitly prohibited use of the labor injunction by federal courts. Nevertheless, in a series of decisions the Supreme Court revived use of the labor injunction to halt boycotts and picketing.[41] It held a state law prohibiting use of the labor injunction unconstitutional and voided state attempts to prohibit yellow-dog contracts.[42] The Court's reactionary mood was most evident in the cases involving labor and unions, to the point where these decisions were an embarrassment even to the Court's conservative supporters.

4. The powers of federal regulatory agencies: the Court repeated its original hostility to fact-finding and regulatory authority of federal agencies, this time the Federal Trade Commission.[43]

5. State police powers: in *Wolff Packing Co. v. Court of Industrial Relations* (1923),[44] the Court sharply narrowed the *Munn* category of "business affected with a public interest" that the state was permitted to regulate. And in a series of less widely noted decisions, the Court invalidated a variety of state police-power regulations involving such diverse topics as coal mining, baking, employment agencies, and commercial sales of ice.[45]

---

38. 247 U.S. 251 (1918).
39. 259 U.S. 20 (1922).
40. 261 U.S. 525 (1923).
41. *Duplex Printing Press Co. v. Deering*, 254 U.S. 433 (1921); *American Steel Foundries v. Tri-City Trades Council*, 257 U.S. 184 (1921); *Bedford Cut Stone Co. v. Journeymen Stone Cutters Assn.*, 274 U.S. 37 (1927).
42. *Truax v. Corrigan*, 257 U.S. 312 (1921); *Coppage v. Kansas*, 236 U.S. 1 (1915).
43. *FTC v. Gratz*, 253 U.S. 421 (1920); *FTC v. Curtis Publishing Co.*, 260 U.S. 568 (1923).
44. 262 U.S. 522 (1923).
45. *Pennsylvania Coal Co. v. Mahon*, 260 U.S. 393 (1922); *Jay Burns Baking Co. v.*

6. First Amendment: though these decisions were offensive only to persons sensitized to civil liberties concerns, the Court's first exploration of First Amendment freedom-of-speech cases in wartime and in the war's aftermath upheld convictions for expression of political opinion and evolved increasingly anti-libertarian criteria for the permissible federal and state regulation of speech.[46]

Once again, resistance to these backward-looking decisions took both political and scholarly forms. Political opposition was much more muted in the era of normalcy than it had been in the robust Populist years. Insurgent congressmen dusted off old proposals, including permitting Congress to override judicial decisions, if necessary by a supermajority; allowing recall of judges; or abolishing judicial review entirely.[47] The principal vehicle of Court criticism was the Progressive party during Robert La Follette's 1924 presidential campaign. The Progressives demanded popular election of judges, a ten-year judicial tenure, and a constitutional amendment permitting Congress to override a "judicial veto." The 1924 platform explained at length the basis for these proposals:

> The usurpation in recent years by the federal courts of the power to nullify laws duly enacted by the legislative branch of the government is a plain violation of the Constitution. . . . The federal courts are given no authority under the Constitution to veto acts of Congress. Since the federal courts have assumed to exercise such veto power, it is essential that the Constitution shall give the Congress the right to override such judicial veto, otherwise the Court will make itself master over the other coordinate branches of the government.[48]

But political criticism made no more headway than La Follette's unsuccessful campaign. More than a decade would go by before the

---

Burns, 264 U.S. 504 (1924); *Weaver v. Palmer Bros. Co.*, 270 U.S. 402 (1926); *Tyson v. Banton*, 273 U.S. 418 (1927); *Ribnik v. McBride*, 277 U.S. 350 (1928); *New State Ice Co. v. Liebmann*, 285 U.S. 262 (1932).

46. *Schenck v. United States*, 249 U.S. 47 (1919); *Abrams v. United States*, 250 U.S. 616 (1919); *Frohwerk v. United States*, 249 U.S. 204 (1919); *Debs v. United States*, 249 U.S. 211 (1919); *Pierce v. United States*, 252 U.S. 239 (1920).

47. *Congressional Record*, 66th Cong. 2d sess. 4567 (March 19, 1920); "Shall We Curb the Supreme Court?" *Forum* 71 (1924): 842–45.

48. Porter and Johnson, eds., *National Party Platforms* (see n. 19), 256.

American people and their political representatives would resist judicial usurpation again.

It was otherwise in academic circles. The jurisprudential assault on formalist postulates of judging triumphed in the legal realist movement of the 1920s.[49] The realists challenged what has since come to be called the "declaratory theory of law" – the idea that the law consisted of immutable, fundamental principles. In this view the U.S. Constitution, which was declarative of these principles, was absolute and fixed. Its meaning was unalterable except by formal amendment. The role of judges and courts was merely to "find" or "discover" the law and then to declare the results of their findings. In the declaratory view, constitutional adjudication transcends politics, which is its prime virtue.

Courts did not "make" law, much less make policy or political decisions. As nineteenth-century jurists expressed the idea, the job of the judge is *ius dicere non ius dare*. To perform this function, they relied exclusively on reason. Their path was laid out as scientifically as the investigations of a geometer. Neither personal bias nor individual views of policy were relevant, and in the older view, they seldom actually did contaminate the judicial process. As President Taft expressed it in his statement quoted earlier: "Individual instances of a hidebound and retrograde conservatism on the part of courts which turn on the individual economic or sociological views of the judges . . . are not many, and they do not call for radical action."[50] Thus judges are nearly infallible oracles; in fact, a variant name for this attitude is the "oracular theory of jurisprudence."

Formalism was an essential element of this judicial outlook. Judges had to abstract out of a specific case before them all the particular and specific human components of the situation that might bias judgment. Real human beings were reduced to A and B, appellant and respondent. Only in this way would judges be

49. To cite only two of the loci classici of "legal realism": Karl Llewellyn, "A Realistic Jurisprudence – The Next Step," *Columbia Law Review* 30 (1930): 431–65; Jerome Frank, *Law and the Modern Mind* (New York, 1930). Secondary literature on the realist movement has proliferated so much that exhaustive citation is impossible. Though selective citation is invidious, two book-length studies stand out: Edward A. Purcell, Jr., *The Crisis of Democratic Theory: Scientific Naturalism and the Problem of Values* (New York, 1973); and William Twining, *Karl Llewellyn and the Realist Movement* (London, 1973).

50. *Congressional Record* (see n. 16), 3966 (August 15, 1911).

able to discover the pure and abstract principles that alone should guide judgment, unpolluted by party, religious, ethnic, or class prejudices. Obviously, emotion had no place in the jural process, but neither did an abstract sense of justice. Justice would be achieved only by the unbiased discovery of governing principles and their unblinking application, not by a judge cutting the suit of reasoning to fit the cloth of an instinctive sense of right and wrong.

Such an outlook passed away half a century ago, and it is difficult for the modern mind to recapture its mood and assumptions. All modern legal thinkers, including conservatives, are the intellectual children of the realists who repudiated the postulates of the declaratory theory of law. Realism, its philosophical grandparent, pragmatism, and its academic parent, sociological jurisprudence, have taught us that law is an artifact, not the "brooding omnipresence in the sky" that was the object of Justice Holmes's sneering skepticism.[51] Law reflects and embodies social policies; indeed, it has no meaning except as an embodiment of policy. Hence judges in the creative aspects of their work do not simply find or deduce law: they make policy. In doing so, because they are humans and not angels, they are unavoidably influenced by their individual biases and preconceptions about desirable social goals.

Since judges do this, they may as well be forced to achieve social justice in their lawmaking function. At the least, the opposite tendency, by which judges like Fuller and Peckham protected the interests of economic and corporate elites at the expense of working people and insulated economic decision makers from the influence of democratic politics, had to be exposed as the class oppression that it was. This led judicial liberals in one of two directions, the one personified by Justice Holmes and the other by Justice Louis D. Brandeis.

The Holmes view maintained that legislative majorities should have their way; judges ought not to obstruct the policies made by legislatures unless "a rational and fair man necessarily would admit that the statute proposed would infringe fundamental principles as they have been understood by the traditions of our people and our law," as he put it in the *Lochner* dissent.[52] The other tradition was exemplified in the "Brandeis brief," composed by Brandeis and

51. *Southern Pacific Co. v. Jensen*, 244 U.S. 205 (1917), Holmes, J. dissenting at 222.
52. 198 U.S. at 76.

384

Josephine Goldmark for arguments in *Muller v. Oregon* (1908).[53] In Brandeis's view, since a judge's political and economic predispositions will unavoidably determine the result of his judging, a judicial opinion may as well be informed by sound, informed, and progressive views and by as much social-scientific data as possible.

By 1935, legal realism had triumphed in the academy, but it remained an alien, indeed dangerous, legal outlook to a majority of justices on the Supreme Court, despite the presence there of Brandeis, Benjamin N. Cardozo, and Harlan Fiske Stone. In that year, a tenuous but consistent majority of five or six justices coalesced in unalterable opposition not only to the New Deal but seemingly to all efforts by the federal government and the states to cope with the economic crisis of the Depression. This judicial posture again provided a matrix of decisions that called forth a liberal denunciation of the Court.

Because these decisions came down in a brief period of two years, they may be summarized quickly. What is significant for us is not so much their content as their direction. After two decisions in 1934 supporting state efforts to cope with worsened economic conditions[54] and two other decisions supporting important federal innovations,[55] the bloc of justices known as the Four Horsemen (Willis Van Devanter, James C. McReynolds, Pierce Butler, and George Sutherland) were joined by the erratic Owen J. Roberts and occasionally by Chief Justice Charles Evans Hughes in an ever-widening attack on governmental power.

Beginning with the reasonable and unanimous decision in *Schechter v. United States* (1935),[56] which struck down the code commissions established under the National Industrial Recovery Act, and with the six-to-three decision in *United States v. Butler* (1936),[57] voiding major provisions of the Agricultural Adjustment Act, the Court became obdurate in its resistance to all forms of economic regulation. In *Carter v. Carter Coal Co.* (1936),[58] the Court alarmed advocates of effective government by voiding an

53. 208 U.S. 412 (1908).

54. *Home Building and Loan Assn. v. Blaisdell*, 290 U.S. 398 (1934); *Nebbia v. New York*, 291 U.S. 502 (1934).

55. The *Gold Clause* cases, 294 U.S. 240 (1935), and 294 U.S. 317 (1935); *Ashwander v. Tennessee Valley Authority*, 297 U.S. 288 (1936).

56. 295 U.S. 495 (1935).

57. *United States v. Butler*, 297 U.S. 1 (1936).

58. 298 U.S. 238 (1936).

attempt to salvage something of the National Recovery Administration (NRA) codes for the soft coal industry. Its action was
particularly troubling because, in the name of states' rights, it
struck down a statute that all the coal-producing states, appearing
as *amici*, had urged it to uphold. What was worse, by disregarding
Congress's explicit statement of intent concerning the severability
of the act's provisions,[59] the Court seemed to be telling Congress
that the judges would ignore any statement of Congress's intent in
favor of some hypothetical intent fabricated by the judges, no
matter how much that pseudointent flew in the face of reality.

Then in *Morehead v. Tipaldo* (1936),[60] the Court appalled moderate observers by resurrecting *Adkins v. Childrens Hospital* and
with it, implicitly, the discredited *Lochner* line of precedents, to
strike down state efforts to provide a minimum wage for women.
It thereby imposed on the nation a judge-created condition of stasis
and impotence in the face of economic distress. President Roosevelt
summed up the result by stating that the judges had created a
no-man's-land where neither state nor nation could attempt to
ameliorate the Depression.[61] A discouraged Justice Stone privately
expressed his view that the October 1935 term was "in many ways
one of the most disastrous in [the Court's] history."[62]

The response was explosive, but this time it was wholly political.
There was neither time nor need for the more slowly paced evolution of a liberal scholarly critique of any broad scope. (There is
one exception to this generalization, the eminent Princeton political
scientist Edward S. Corwin, who was a host unto himself as a critic
of the Court.[63]) The reaction was led by the man most frustrated by
judicial obstruction, the president. Roosevelt at one time or another

59. Severability relates to a provision in the statute stating that should one section
or title be found unconstitutional, the remainder is to be judged on its merits rather
than being held unconstitutional simply because the other section had fallen. The
Court held that despite explicit language to this effect, Congress did not mean what
it said.

60. 298 U.S. 587 (1936).

61. Samuel I. Rosenman, ed., *The Public Papers and Addresses of Franklin D.
Roosevelt*, 13 vols. (New York, 1938–50), 5: 200.

62. Quoted in Alpheus T. Mason, *Harlan Fiske Stone: Pillar of the Law* (New
York, 1956), 425.

63. See the following book-length works by Edward S. Corwin, *The Twilight of
the Supreme Court* (New Haven, CT, 1934); *The Commerce Power versus States Rights*
(Princeton, NJ, 1936); *Court over Constitution* (Princeton, NJ, 1938). See also his
reprise in *Constitutional Revolution, Ltd.* (Claremont, CA, 1941).

considered one of four political responses.

The first was a constitutional amendment reversing a particular decision, particularly one granting Congress broader commerce-regulatory powers than the Court was willing to permit. The second comprised various techniques of restricting or reversing the appellate review powers of the Court, for example, by a constitutional amendment that would permit Congress to reenact legislation after it had been invalidated by the Court. The third was to "pack" the federal judiciary with new judges, as various British prime ministers had threatened to do to get around obstruction by the House of Lords through creation of numerous new life peers. The fourth and most radical was the vague idea that Roosevelt toyed with from time to time of simply ignoring the Court. As is well known, Roosevelt settled on the Court-packing plan and thereby lost a political battle but won the war of constitutional principle.

The details of the Court-packing fight, contemporary journalistic denunciation of the Four Horsemen and the "Nine Old Men," the "switch in time," the constitutional crisis of 1937, and the Court's dismantling of all its obstructive precedent noted in this paper constitute a well-known story and need not detain us here. Though defeated in the Senate, Roosevelt had the satisfaction of seeing his criteria for judicial statesmanship win acceptance on the Court. These were: judicial respect for the democratic process and majoritarian government as expressed in the electoral process, a proper respect for the role of Congress in the scheme of separation of powers, a commitment to what Roosevelt called "social justice," and an acceptance of the need for effective governmental power, federal and state, to deal with national emergencies.[64] The triumph of liberal views began in 1937, as the Court systematically undertook to reverse all its obstructive precedents. Its new orientation toward the future was announced in the celebrated *Carolene Products* footnote (1938),[65] where Justice Stone proclaimed a new liberal jurisprudence that was to dominate the work of the Court for the next half-century. It consisted of a three-part program:

1. the double standard or two-tier approach to economic and civil liberties, whereby the Court squinted at "legislation [that]

---

64. Rosenman, ed., *Public Papers of Roosevelt* (see n. 61), 5: 639; 6: 2.
65. *United States v. Carolene Products Co.*, 304 U.S. 144 (1938).

appears on its face to be within a specific prohibition of the Constitution, such as those of the first ten amendments," while according deference to economic-regulatory statutes;

2. a suspect status for laws restricting "those political processes which can ordinarily be expected to bring about repeal of undesirable legislation"; and

3. an even more suspect status for "statutes directed at particular religious . . . or national . . . or racial minorities." With that, the modern era of liberal constitutionalism had begun.

Liberal criticism of the U.S. Supreme Court has resurfaced intermittently since the constitutional revolution of 1937, but like the earlier critiques, it has been predictable. Particularly since the Burger court refused to continue on the trajectory established during the decade of Warren court liberal activism, 1963–73,[66] voices on the liberal end of the truncated American political spectrum have challenged the Court's comparative indifference to the causes of racial minorities, criminal defendants, and other objects of liberal solicitude or regretted that it terminated the Warren court's preoccupation with attaining justice.[67] This is not surprising, but it is not very interesting either. What lends the modern liberal view of the Court fresh interest is the curious ideological exchange that has taken place between progressives and their conservative opponents. Abraham Lincoln once related a story about two drunks engaged in a barroom brawl who, in the process of wrestling, exchanged coats. Something of that sort has occurred in recent times, as liberals find themselves in the unaccustomed posture of having reservations about the processes of majoritarian democracy and upholding judicial review, while conservatives now appear as the apostles of majoritarianism and denounce judicial interference with legislative policy decisions. To be more specific, Chief Justice

66. These terminal dates were chosen somewhat arbitrarily: the first marks the retirement of Justice Felix Frankfurter and his replacement by the much more activist Arthur Goldberg; the latter marks the accession of Justice William H. Rehnquist. Though arbitrary, the dates do encompass most of the decisions characterizing the activist years of the Warren Court.

67. See, e.g., Leonard W. Levy, *Against the Law: The Nixon Court and Criminal Justice* (New York, 1974); William F. Swindler, "The Court, the Constitution, and Chief Justice Burger," *Vanderbilt Law Review* 27 (1974): 443–74; Alpheus T. Mason, "The Burger Court in Historical Perspective," *Political Science Quarterly* 89 (1974): 27–45.

William H. Rehnquist has frequently stolen liberal thunder by castigating the Court for Lochnerizing, imposing the values of nonelected judges for those of the people's democratically chosen representatives, while liberals defending the results of Warren court activism have emphasized the need for judges to supervise and correct the policy decisions of legislatures.

To comprehend this liberal turnabout, it is necessary to understand something of the modern conservative attack on judicial activism, as exemplified by Chief Justice Rehnquist. Following an era of extraordinary judicial innovation in such areas as racial integration, busing, prayer in the schools, legislative reapportionment, freedom of speech, religious establishment and free exercise, and the rights of persons accused of crime, modern conservatives, unlike their ideological ancestors, put their faith in legislative majorities. Espousing a position close to pure ethical relativism, Rehnquist has contended that there is no objective criterion that enables us to identify constitutional values in a way that will command universal agreement.[68] Therefore, he insists, the only legitimate way to identify values to be applied in constitutional adjudication is through the political will of electoral majorities. The vice of bad judging is that the judges substitute their own conceptions of the good society for the values articulated through majoritarian democratic processes.

Herein lies a remarkable distinction between modern conservatives and their ideological ancestors. Peckham, Brewer, Fuller, and others of the turn-of-the-century generation of jurists feared democracy and majority rule, seeing judicial review as a means of thwarting the will of legislative majorities. Rehnquist today extols majority rule and is suspicious of precisely the institution – judicial review – that earlier jurists saw as the republic's salvation. Perhaps this contrast should not be carried too far, and perhaps the similarities outweigh differences. Both groups consider the meaning of the words of the Constitution to be fixed, certain, unchanging, and discoverable.

The extremist implications and conservative agenda of modern conservatives alarm liberals today. They have adopted ideas now seemingly discarded by the conservatives. Liberals continued to

---

68. William H. Rehnquist, "The Notion of a Living Constitution," *Texas Law Review* 54 (1976): 693–706.

address the two principal challenges identified in the *Lochner* era and after the Second World War: the legitimacy of judicial review and the possibility of its objectivity. Their principal concern is the tendency of democratic majorities to suppress the rights of minorities, but now majorities and minorities are no longer defined in economic terms; rather, minorities are seen as racial, religious, socioeconomic, and even affectational. This directed liberal attention to the problem of rights, a view expressed most vigorously by Laurence Tribe of the Harvard Law School: "We are talking, necessarily, about rights of individuals or groups against the larger community, and against the majority – even an overwhelming majority – of the society as a whole. Subject to all of the perils of antimajoritarian judgment, courts . . . must ultimately define and defend rights against government in terms independent of consensus or majority will."[69]

Liberal critics of constitutional fundamentalism adhere to varying versions of a doctrine Paul Brest has labeled "fundamental rights."[70] They reject Rehnquist's ethical relativism, insisting instead that there are fundamental values that can be objectively identified. In this approach, modern liberal critics harked back to a tradition of Supreme Court adjudication backed by the authority of Justices Holmes and Cardozo. In his *Lochner* dissent, Holmes had assumed the existence of "fundamental principles as they have been understood by the traditions of our people and our law."[71] Cardozo explicitly carried on this tradition in *Palko v. Connecticut* (1937),[72] incorporating comparable formulations into his opinion: "[a] principle of justice so rooted in the traditions and conscience of our people as to be ranked as fundamental," and "fundamental principles of liberty and justice which lie at the base of all our civil and political institutions."[73]

It was this tradition that modern liberals recurred to, changing only the emphasis from principles to rights. The liberal fundamental rights interpretation of the early 1970s contended that the

69. Laurence H. Tribe, *American Constitutional Law* (Mineola, NY, 1988), 1311.

70. Paul Brest, "The Fundamental Rights Controversy: The Essential Contradictions of Normative Constitutional Scholarship," *Yale Law Journal* 90 (1981): 1063–1109.

71. 198 U.S. at 76.

72. 302 U.S. 319 (1937).

73. From, respectively, *Snyder v. Massachusetts*, 291 U.S. 97 (1934) at 105, and *Hebert v. Louisiana*, 272 U.S. 312 (1926) at 316.

consensual values of the American people could be discovered through judicial inquiry and that these values, if correctly identified, would provide the requisite objectivity to judicial review. But unfortunately any liberal consensus on a fundamental values approach broke down almost immediately in the aftermath of the abortion decision, *Roe v. Wade* (1973).[74] Both the scope of judicial policy-making in the decision and its lack of precedential basis troubled many commentators who had hitherto supported the activist innovations of the Warren and Burger Courts, forcing them to rethink the whole problem of judicial review. John Hart Ely, an early critic of *Roe*,[75] provided an influential alternative to the fundamental values commitment in his 1980 essay, *Democracy and Distrust*.[76] He abandoned the effort to define substantive values, writing off the fundamental values enterprise as unpersuasive. In its place, he offered a process-oriented interpretation, what he termed a "representation-reinforcing" approach. Substantive values he left to the democratic marketplace, restricting judges to the limited task of policing that marketplace to assure its legitimate functioning. Judges had two tasks: they had to remove artificial barriers impeding access to that political marketplace (hence the soundness of the reapportionment decisions and First Amendment political-speech cases), and they had to assure the fair representation of minorities in political debates. This approach was persuasive to many: it seemed to get judges out of the sticky business of defining the substantive content of values at a time when such judicial efforts were proving controversial and unpopular, as in the abortion and death penalty cases.

After Ely's restatement of the problem in process terms, the whole enterprise of constitutional theory seemed to disintegrate. Liberals in particular lost all semblance of unity. Two preeminent scholarly commentators among them, Lawrence H. Tribe and Paul Brest, recommended that we abandon the whole enterprise because the century-old ideals of legitimacy and objectivity are unattainable. Brest adopted the axioms and program of critical legal studies, calling for a transformation of American society in the direction of

74. 410 U.S. 113 (1973).

75. John Hart Ely, "The Wages of Crying Wolf: A Comment on Roe v. Wade," *Yale Law Journal* 82 (1973): 920–49.

76. John Hart Ely, *Democracy and Distrust: A Theory of Judicial Review* (Cambridge, MA, 1980).

participatory democracy.[77] Tribe, weary and impatient of the whole controversy, dismissed the preceding century of debate as futile. Instead, he counseled, let us identify our value axioms and then get on with debate and judging.[78] Owen Fiss in turn desperately condemned values skepticism as a modern "nihilism," urging in its place a return to the belief that the Constitution embodies a public morality that judges can at least identify.[79]

And there, for the moment, the liberal critique rests. Skeptical of programmatic approaches, liberals seem to have little critical to say about the Supreme Court, perhaps for the good reason that the Burger court gave them little to arouse fundamental or embittered condemnation. Whether the Rehnquist court can or will change that remains to be seen; its first two years, on the whole, suggest that it will not. In any event, the future course of liberal criticism of the Supreme Court is utterly problematical today.

77. Brest, "The Fundamental Rights Controversy" (see n. 70).
78. Laurence H. Tribe, *Constitutional Choices* (Cambridge, MA, 1985), 3–8.
79. Owen M. Fiss, "Objectivity and Interpretation," *Stanford Law Review* 34 (1982): 739–63.

15.1
Liberal and Conservative Criticism of Judicial Review in the United States and Germany

Knud Krakau

It is worth noting that Professor Wiecek can take judicial review for granted: in the American context the Supreme Court *is* the chief and final guarantor of civil and constitutional rights, and judicial review is its major instrument. The paper's focus is on political and theoretical issues that arise when liberal and conservative forces use that instrument for the promotion of their competing concepts of such rights. By contrast, the German paper must concentrate on the process by which the *Reichsgericht*, late in German constitutional history and even then only gradually and with modest results, came to assume an at least somewhat similar role under the first national German democratic-republican (hence comparable) Constitution.

Here I shall make some brief comments on:

1. The interplay of liberal and conservative criticism of the Supreme Court
2. The meaning of that debate from the perspective of changing value orientations in American society
3. Some comparative remarks on the American and German cases

1. The present state of judicial review in the two countries is the result of different developments, different histories, to be sure. Whereas German debate on these issues often seems characterized by a certain naiveté and lack of historical depth, the American side may be suffering from the effects of the opposite experience: two hundred years of constitutional continuity appear to set limits upon the inventiveness of the human mind. This remark is prompted by two observations: first, looking at judicial decision making related to the U.S. Constitution and at the public debate it generates – political as well as scholarly – between liberal and conservative

forces, one often has the distinct sensation of déjà vu. Important issues were anticipated by eighteenth-century constitutional debate,[1] forgotten, and then recurrently pushed to the foreground again as the political-constitutional "mood" of the country shifted, very broadly speaking, from liberal (progressive) criticism of a conservative Supreme Court (1890s to the 1930s), with its emphasis on property rights, to conservative criticism of a liberal Supreme Court (beginning in the 1950s) whose attention was focused on individual civil and political rights. My second point, and one that is of course related to the previous observation, is that many of the arguments tend to recur on *both* sides of the liberal-conservative fence depending on context – the configuration of political and social forces, the particular value concepts involved, etc. In other words, structurally similar or identical arguments may be used by liberal *or* conservative critics of the Court, as time and context may demand.

It is easy to see why this should be so on the level and regarding the form of political responses to Supreme Court decisions – be they directed against New Deal measures or school-prayer provisions: political responses may consist of attempts to discipline the judges individually and call for their impeachment, recall, election instead of appointment, limitation of tenure, etc., or they may endeavor to curb judicial review powers of the Court by amending the judiciary acts or the Constitution.[2] These responses are legitimate – though hardly ever effective – instruments provided by the American political and constitutional system. They may be used equally for liberal and conservative political or ideological objectives.

Obviously, responses are more complex on the level of constitutional theory. Pragmatism, sociological jurisprudence, and legal realism probably have destroyed, even in the eyes of modern conservatives, the legitimacy of the *crude* identification of their value preferences with an allegedly scientific and value-free constitutional interpretation as it used to be practiced in the substantive

1. A careful rereading, e.g., of Hamilton's *Federalist*, no. 78, I think will illustrate my point.
2. See, e.g. *Supreme Court: Congressional Quarterly, Guide to Current American Government* (Washington, DC, 1987), 62–64; Daniel Patrick Moynihan, "What Do You Do When the Supreme Court Is Wrong?" *The Public Interest* 57 (1979): 3–24, esp. 6, 19–24.

due process era. But even if a milder version of that identification still persists, it is to be noted with irony that their liberal critics – the legal realists being only their extreme exponents – have proceeded along similar lines, if only more openly and for values they claim were better suited to modern American society, that is, individual liberties and civil rights, as opposed to the conservatives' emphasis on property and "right of contract" in the earlier phase. Nevertheless, today everyone seems to agree in theory that constitutional adjudication generally *is* judicial policy-making, *is* choice among or allocation of competing constitutionally recognized values; hence the need to justify and legitimize their nature and rank.[3]

In modified form, however, the claim to "science" as camouflage for subjectivism still lingers on – now draped up as historical-scholarly search for "original intent." Mr. Edwin Meese's position[4] and the debate he provoked among highly regarded judges and historical and legal scholars[5] hardly allow us (as Professor Wiecek does) to dismiss Meese's extremist textualist parody as the "laughing stock of American legal education." Though intellectually not

---

3. See, e.g., Robert A. Dahl, "Decision-Making in a Democracy: The Supreme Court as a National Policy-Maker," *Journal of Public Law* 6 (1957): 280–81.

4. Attorney General Edwin Meese, addresses to the American Bar Association, July 9 and 17, 1985, in Washington, DC and London, reprinted in Elder Witt, *A Different Justice: Reagan and the Supreme Court* (Washington, DC, 1986), 171–83.

5. In support of Meese's position see federal appeals court judge, then Supreme Court justice nominee Robert H. Bork, "What the Founders Intended," *Dialogue* 1 (1987): 29–32. His major opponent in the public discourse is Supreme Court judge William J. Brennan, address, October 12, 1985, at Georgetown Univ., reprinted in Witt, *A Different Justice* (see n. 4), 183–91; and his 1986 Harvard Univ. Oliver Wendell Holmes, Jr., lecture, "Constitutional Adjudication and the Death Penalty: A View from the Court," *Harvard Law Review* 100 (1986/87): 313–31. For balanced criticism see federal appeals court judge Irving R. Kaufman, "What Did the Founding Fathers Intend?" *New York Times Magazine* (February 23, 1986), 42–69. On the side of scholars: a) historians, see James H. Hutson's critical discussion of the state of the sources as critique of the original-intent argument, "The Creation of the Constitution: The Integrity of the Documentary Record," *Texas Law Review* 65 (1986/87): 1–39; already earlier John G. Wofford, "The Blinding Light: The Uses of History in Constitutional Interpretation," *Univ. Chicago Law Review* 31 (1963/64): 502–33; Wilcomb E. Washburn, "Justice Brennan's Challenge to Historians," *American Historical Association Perspectives* (December 1986): 19–20; John Anthony Scott, "A Response," and Joyce Appleby, ". . . And Another Response," *American Historical Association Perspectives* (February 1987): 14–15; b) constitutional lawyers, see (pro-Meese) Lino A. Graglia, "How the Constitution Disappeared," *Commentary* (February 1986): 19–27; (critically) Laurence H. Tribe, "The Limits of Original Intent," *Dialogue* 1 (1987): 29–32.

convincing, it is nevertheless politically powerful because it is obviously based on and expressive of a broad ground swell of conservative thinking and feeling in regard to these constitutional issues. And perhaps, when the respected scholar Raoul Berger bases his more serious conservative critique of the "government by judiciary" on the same kind of textualist and fundamentalist approach, the difference is only a matter of degree.[6] Even more disturbing in this respect is the influence of Myres S. McDougal and his "Yale school" in their widely argued, explicitly "policy-oriented" attempts at generating values from "scientifically [i.e., sociologically] observable facts."[7] On the other hand, Hugo L. Black or Alexander Meiklejohn, not exactly archconservatives, ground their First Amendment radicalism on a comparable fundamentalist-textualist-literalist reading of the Constitution.[8]

The fact that arguments tend to travel in pairs of claim and counterclaim makes it attractive to use them interchangeably for seemingly contradictory (liberal-conservative) objectives. One of the classical and probably best-known pairs – going back to the founders – is (a) the democratic-majoritarian argument against the nonelected, hence nonlegitimate judicial branch imposing its values on "the people" or their "democratically chosen representatives." But then we have as a corrective counterclaim (b) the defense of specific constitutionally recognized substantive values against the tyranny of a "factious (however democractic) majority" (Madison). It is not at all surprising that conservatives and liberals alike

6. Raoul Berger, *Government by Judiciary: The Transformation of the Fourteenth Amendment* (Cambridge, MA, 1977).

7. McDougal developed his explicitly policy [i.e., value]-oriented approach first in the context of international law (what he and his many associates called an "international law of human dignity") and then applied it also to constitutional law, see for a general critical discussion with many references Knud Krakau, *Missionsbewußtsein und Völkerrechtsdoktrin in den Vereinigten Staaten von Amerika* (Frankfurt/Main, 1967), chap. 15.

8. For Black see his dissent in *Dennis v. United States*, 341 U.S. 494 (1951); or Hugo L. Black, *A Constitutional Faith* (New York, 1968), chap. 3, "The First Amendment"; Everette E. Dennis, Donald Gillmor, and David L. Grey, eds., *Justice Hugo Black and the First Amendment* (Ames, IA, 1978); James J. Magee, *Mr. Justice Black: Absolutist on the Court* (Charlottesville, VA, 1980), passim. Alexander Meiklejohn, "Free Speech and Its Relation to Self-Government," in Alexander Meiklejohn, *Political Freedom: The Constitutional Powers of the People* (New York, 1948/1965), p. 1; Alexander Meiklejohn, "The First Amendment Is an Absolute," in Philip B. Kurland, ed., *Free Speech and Association: The Supreme Court and the First Amendment* (Chicago, IL, 1975), 1–22.

have used these arguments interchangeably, depending upon whether their value position has majoritarian backing or not. Populists and Progressives, New Dealers and other liberals stood for claim (a), but so do the conservatives of the 1970s and 1980s.[9] Economic conservatives of an earlier period ("substantive due process") held view (b), just as the liberal protagonists of "preferred freedoms" or of rights considered so basic that they are thought to be "implicit in the concept of ordered liberty" do in the later period, on and outside the Supreme Court.[10]

William Wiecek's paper eloquently describes the liberals' fear of democratic-majoritarian suppression of certain fundamental values "objectively identified" (another topos borrowed from the Supreme Court of the early 1900s) and defined as "rights." Both ideological or political camps have used both sets of claims. Which of them will be advanced depends to a large extent on whose views dominate the Supreme Court and/or have majority backing in American society.

The "and/or" should be noted because the crucial variable is not always and only the (liberal or conservative) dominance of the Supreme Court. The democratic-majoritarian claim being more "easily" argued in a democratic society, groups will be tempted to advance that claim whenever they sense a majoritarian trend in society and can identify with it, in society at large or in the Supreme Court. The following matrix summarizes the pattern of available argumentative choices with regard to one value issue. From a majority or minority position in society or the Supreme Court, the Court majority, or its dissenting minority, or its critics have these claims available along the lines described above under (a) democratic-majoritarian and (b) substantive-value descriptors:

---

9. See these perhaps representative examples from an extensive debate often bordering on the polemic, Nathan Glazer, "Towards an Imperial Judiciary?" *The Public Interest* 41 (1975): 104–23; William H. Rehnquist (then associate, now chief justice of the U.S. Supreme Court), "The Notion of a Living Constitution," *Texas Law Review* 54 (1975/76): 693–706; Daniel Patrick Moynihan, "What Do You Do When the Supreme Court Is Wrong?" (see n. 2); Dinesh D'Souza, "The New Liberal Censorship: The Ideological Assault on the Constitution, the Bible, and the Great Works of Western Thought," *Policy Review* 38 (1986): 8–15.

10. J. Benjamin Cardozo's felicitous phrase in *Palko v. Connecticut*, 302 U.S. 319 (1937). The basis of the preferred-freedom doctrine of cause is J.H. Stone's famous "footnote four" in *United States v. Carolene Products Co.*, 304 U.S. 144, at 152–53 (1938).

Supreme Court

		Minority	Majority
Society	Minority	(1) Substantive-value	(2) Substantive-value
	Majority	(3) Majortarian-democratic and substantive-value	(4) Majortarian-democratic and substantive-value★

★ *Probably restraint, emphasis on majoritarian-democratic trend*

Supreme Court policies and criticism of those policies since the 1890s can be broadly described and analyzed along these lines. It should be noted that in phases of broad agreement between the Court and societal values and majorities (4), for example, when Judge Bork might have joined the Court and a conservative ground swell in American society still persists, there may be more emphasis again on judicial restraint, deference to the political process, etc., though the value argument remains available. Similar issues arose in Germany in the Weimar Republic, though less in regard to the practice of judicial review than in regard to its introduction into the constitutional system.[11]

Another, if related, pair of arguments refers to the dichotomy of procedure/process versus substance/content. Again this is a recurrent phenomenon – on *both* sides of the dividing line. I refer back to claim (b) above: the substantive content of specific values was the concern of the *Lochner* Supreme Court as much as it was that of Raoul Berger and his liberal critics. On the other hand the "reasoned elaboration" approach, though mildly conservative, has attracted many liberals because of its emphasis on pubic discourse, on legitimization through reasoned justification instead of judicial fiat.[12] John Hart Ely is the outstanding example for process orientation on the liberal side (reacting to an overdose of substantive value orientation) – the judge as umpire watching over access to

11. See Gertrude Lübbe-Wolff, "Safeguards of Civil and Constitutional Rights – The Debate on the Role of the *Reichsgericht*," above; also Georg Christoph von Unruh, "Nordamerikanische Einflüsse auf die deutsche Verfassungsentwicklung," *Deutsches Verwaltungsblatt* (1976): 460–61.

12. See William Wiecek, "The Liberal Critique of the U.S. Supreme Court," above; and G. Edward White, "The Evolution of Reasoned Elaboration: Jurisprudential Criticism and Social Change," *Virginia Law Review* 59 (1973): 279–302.

and fair representation in the democratic marketplace of public political debate. Finally, Justice Rehnquist then assumes the role of the judicial value skeptic and argues for the electoral *political* process to decide the value issues[13] – a conservative cynic feeling comfortably sure of being on the side of a reigning (conservative) majority or the quintessential constitutional proceduralist?

It is important to note that this kind of proceduralism relates very specifically to what many analysts see as one of the major characteristics and strengths of the American Constitution – its primarily procedural nature which, to a large degree, leaves substantive value issues open to later determination by the political process regulated by these very procedural rules. Max Weber has argued that "form is the twin sister of freedom."[14] This relates to the Federalist argument against any Bill of Rights: because the whole body of the Constitution per se, with its elaborate balances of forces and procedural rules and safeguards establishing a limited government, was the best conceivable protection against possible encroachments upon individual rights and freedoms.[15] And the eventual Bill of Rights follows a similar philosophy through its negative command structure (which does not attempt to define the substance of protected rights) and its emphasis on "due process."

The other arguments discussed in this section are similarly related to fundamental tenets of American constitutionalism and hence partake of the legitimizing aura of the Constitution. That makes them readily available time and again to liberals and conservatives alike.

2. Whatever the details of the liberal-conservative debate, when viewed from the perspective of changing value paradigms in American society over time, the interplay of conservative-liberal positions serves a larger purpose. The preoccupations of the Supreme Court in the early 1900s – anarchy, violence, class warfare – are now forgotten issues. America's transition from industrial to

13. John Hart Ely, *Democracy and Distrust: A Theory of Judicial Review* (Cambridge, MA, 1980), passim, e.g., 101–5; Rehnquist, "The Notion of a Living Constitution" (see n. 9), 699, 704–6.

14. Gerald Stourzh gave this quotation from Weber during the discussion period. I could not locate it.

15. See Walter Berns, "The Constitution as Bill of Rights," in Robert A. Goldwin and William A. Schambra, eds., *How Does the Constitution Secure Rights?* (Washington, DC, 1985), 50–73; also Herbert J. Storing, "The Constitution and the Bill of Rights", in ibid., 27.

postindustrial society has produced different concerns. They relate to moral and social values that Michael Kammen has summarized under the paired headings "liberty and justice" or "liberty and equality."[16] The contest between liberals and conservatives is part of the process in which these new value orientations are unfolding. Whatever the relative merits of the individual liberal or conservative positions, the debate between the Supreme Court and its conservative-liberal critics helps clarify and define in toto the new paradigm.

3. In both countries judicial review (for the periods considered) was the product of judicial innovation and judicial opinions that justified it cursorily and apodictically rather than theoretically and systematically. Here similarity ends. In Germany civil liberties were generally still regarded as granted by – not preexisting – the Constitution. Germany never, not even in the Weimar Republic, developed the concept of "higher/fundamental/paramount law" so basic to American constitutionalism;[17] hence the halting development and weak state of judicial review; hence also the power of the Reichstag to dispose of the Constitution by accidental majorities.[18]

What is fascinating, however, is the way liberals and conservatives in Germany use the constitutional argument as an instrument for their political objectives, just as they do in the United States. Radical democrats invoke the majoritarian principle against its "restrictions" through the *Reichsgericht*; conservatives seek consolation in judicial review, substituting it for the monarch as guarantor of liberal rights (mostly meaning property, so-called vested rights, specifically *Beamtenrechte*) against the "tyranny of legislative majorities" (socialists, communists, and all the rest) and definitely trusting the justices more than the legislature.[19]

16. Michael Kammen, *Spheres of Liberty: Changing Perceptions of Liberty in American Culture* (Madison, WI, 1986), introd. 5, and pt. 3.
17. Edward S. Corwin, *The "Higher Law" Background of American Constitutional Law* (Ithaca, NY, 1963), repr. of the 1928 *Harvard Law Review* articles; Stanley N. Katz, "The American Constitution: A Revolutionary Interpretation," in Richard Beeman, Stephen Botein, and Edward C. Carter II, eds., *Beyond Confederation: Origins of the Constitution and American National Identity* (Chapel Hill, NC, 1987), 23–37.
18. Art. 76, Weimar Constitution, see Gerhard Anschütz, *Die Verfassung des Deutschen Reichs vom 11. August 1919: Ein Kommentar für Wissenschaft und Praxis* (Berlin, [14]1933, repr. Darmstadt, 1965), 401–3.
19. See Unruh, "Nordamerikanische Einflüsse" (see n. 11), 460–61.

In the German case the issue was the creation and viability of the institution of judicial review as guarantor of civil and constitutional rights; on the American side it was the fight about shifting emphases within a broadly accepted functioning framework of constitutionalized "higher law" and of judicial review as the instrument enforcing that law. Liberal or conservative criticism is an attempt to influence it. That criticism may reflect cynical opportunism and use of the constitutional argument for parochial ("factious") purposes; or it may be used for the highest idealistic objectives. Both these approaches are legitimate components of the American constitutional framework.

15.2
Discussion

JÖRG-DETLEF KÜHNE: I would like to turn your attention to civil rights. Under the Weimar Constitution civil rights judged by the *Reichsgericht* were only self-executing in the field of classical rights – which means those listed in the First Amendment of the American Constitution. The very important social rights were declared by the conservative *Reichsgericht* not to be self-executing – which means that they were to all intents and purposes voided.

My second point concerns the emergency clause in the Weimar Constitution. Article 48 of that constitution contained a special emergency clause. In 1919 that clause was directed against riots and public disturbances. As a police clause it was never intended to regulate civil emergencies. Yet soon its meaning was extended.

In Ms. Lübbe-Wolff's paper the emergency clause is referred to as "that fatal doctrine which was later to cover the enabling law of 1933."[1] I agree with this. But we have to keep in mind that initially Article 48 embodied a liberal doctrine dating back to the Second German Empire, and this liberal doctrine was to provide, except in the case of Article 48, for civil emergencies. The rationale behind it was that since the Reichstag had behaved so reasonably, as indeed was the case in the time before the First World War, it would, if necessary, pass enabling laws only for short periods of time and it would always be kept under control. In 1919 no one dreamt that this doctrine could be misused in later years and especially in 1933.

MICHAEL DREYER: After 1919 there was a debate on this theme in Germany. Carl Schmitt held that there were several components in the Weimar Constitution not open to change according to Article 76, and foremost among these was Article 76 itself. From this it followed that this school of thought held the enabling law of 1933 unconstitutional because it changed Article 76.

---

1. Gertrude Lübbe-Wolff, "Safeguards of Civil and Constitutional Rights – The Debate on the Role of the Reichsgericht," above, 357.

STANLEY N. KATZ: I do not understand the precise relationship between the legislature and the constitution, in particular the methods for changing the constitution. By American standards there would be an incompatibility between the legislature and the concept of constitutional change because the legislature itself could not change the constitution. If under the Weimar Constitution there had been a very expansive interpretation of Articles 1 or 9 by the *Reichsgericht*, could the legislature have done something on its own initiative to break it?

GERTRUDE LÜBBE-WOLFF: It certainly could. Under the doctrine of *Verfassungsdurchbrechung*, there was a provision in the Weimar Constitution saying that changes in the Constitution could be made in the normal course of legislation, except that special majorities were required. Under the Constitution of 1871 that was even easier, for there a qualified majority was required for the *Bundesrat*. A change of the Constitution was impossible if more than fourteen votes (and Prussia alone had seventeen votes in the *Bundesrat*!) were opposed to change. The point about the *Verfassungsdurchbrechung* was that you did not have to change the text of the Constitution itself but could just enact laws contrary to the Constitution as individual exceptions to it provided that it was done with the majorities required – that was a very weak protection for the Constitution.

STANLEY N. KATZ: That was what I thought. To American ears Max Weber's statement therefore sounds totally incomprehensible because "form" would seem to be "liberty's" enemy in a system like that.

HERMANN WELLENREUTHER: If it is true that it was much easier to change the German than the American Constitution, then this of course radically alters the position of the Constitution within German public life. Why do you think it was so easy to change the German Constitution?

GERHARD A. RITTER: This is the consequence of German legal thinking in the nineteenth century, which did not possess a clear understanding of what we now call *Vorrang der Verfassung*, an understanding that developed only under the Weimar Constitution.

KNUD KRAKAU: America did develop the concept of fundamental law fairly early. John Marshall uses these terms in his opinion in *Marbury v. Madison*. In terms of historical development this can be traced back to old colonial charter provisions, to the right of disallowance for the king, to the fundamentalist perceptions of the Bible, and to certain precedents in British constitutional and public law. All these combined to create this concept of higher law as a last resort which was incorporated into the Constitution itself. Thus the written Constitution partook of all these earlier notions of higher law, which could be referred to as a critical check on the validity of some given law by the positive lawmaker. These concepts were the basis for the development of judicial review and of the idea of a hierarchy of norms.

A very long development determined American political and constitutional thinking. The *pouvoir constituant* is not identical with, but only represented by, the ordinary legislature. This concept did not develop in the German context because of the historical monarchical tradition and the creation of the Constitution by compact between the several states. To a very large extent the Constitution of 1871 and, to a limited degree, even the Weimar Constitution are not an emanation of "we the people." The fundamental legitimacy of the Constitution according to the republican principle "we the people" had been tried in 1848 but had failed and did not really come up again until the Bonn *Grundgesetz*.

GERHARD A. RITTER: The Constitution of 1871 was understood by many people as a treaty between princes or the senates of Hamburg, Bremen, and Lübeck, and of course you cannot take away something given by a treaty. This had important implications. In the 1880s and again in 1890, during the crisis just before he was forced out, Bismarck argued that you could change the Constitution from above by dissolving the empire. The new Constitution, again a compact between princes and senates, could then contain different articles, in particular a new election law. Bismarck did not succeed but he always pressed his interpretation.

His interpretation was very one-sided because, apart from his view that the Constitution was a compact between princes and senates, it also had to be affirmed by the parliaments of the individual states, indicating that there was another element that he had overlooked. But this compact is emphasized and therefore these fourteen votes Ms. Lübbe-Wolff quoted are significant. It was difficult to change the 1871 Constitution when the seventeen Prussian votes or the fourteen votes of the bigger states like Bavaria, Württemberg, and Saxony were cast together in opposition to a proposal, but as far as the Reichstag was concerned, a simple majority would have been enough.

We always compare the Weimar Constitution to the American Constitution and say how easily it could be changed. But the point of course is that the Weimar Constitution looked to England, where there was a parliamentary government. Before 1918 everyone was looking to England, and in England of course a straightforward act of Parliament can change everything by a simple majority, even the Bill of Rights.

ERNST BENDA: Let me go back to the question raised by Mr. Wellenreuther which created this debate. I agree with Mr. Ritter that Mr. Krakau overlooked the importance of the nineteenth-century state constitutions and the long, and at least in the southern part of Germany, quite effective and fruitful fight for constitutions. I would contend that Germans who fought for constitutions from the beginning of the nineteenth century knew about the importance of a constitution.

If, as I assume, people knew about the importance of a constitution, then they must have felt that immanent conflict between the principle of democracy and a constitution. For if you have a constitution as a legal instrument it has to be adjudicated by a judge. Yet, whether you have the principle of judicial review or not, every judge will sooner or later encounter a case in which he feels that if he decides according to the law then he will violate his fundamental sense of fairness.

I recall meeting the president of the Norwegian Supreme Court. I asked my Norwegian colleague what he would do in a case where he had to apply the law and he felt that the law was unconstitutional because it infringed upon fundamental rights also contained, of course, in the Norwegian Constitution. He answered that in such a case he certainly would not apply the law. I asked him to cite an example. After a while he described a case of about thirty years ago which concerned property rights. His predecessor, he thought, declared this law unconstitutional . All I could do was to congratulate him for his good Parliament, which passed only constitutional laws. For that was at the time when the federal Constitutional Court, after having existed for only twenty-five years, had declared its three hundred fiftieth law unconstitutional.

Now to my real point: I would say that whether the criticism of the court is voiced by liberals or conservatives depends on the government in power, on the political complexion of the majority in Parliament, and in more general terms, on the spirit of the times.

I hope it is permitted even in a meeting of historians to lead up a bit to the present time. In our country we have a court that, being only thirty-six years old now, is young compared to the U.S. Supreme Court. Comparing the two is most interesting. Your Constitution, of course, does not state the principle of judicial review. It was only established in the decision *Marbury v. Madison*, which in the 1920s was certainly known to everyone, including the members of the *Reichsgericht*. On the occasion of the federal Constitutional Court's celebration of its twenty-fifth anniversary in 1977, Theodor Schieder very learnedly traced the principle of judicial review right back to the *Reichskammergericht* of 1495. Thus judicial review is not a completely new idea to our country.

If you were faced with the question of whether or not to write a judicial review clause into the Constitution, as the framers of the *Grundgesetz* were, you would necessarily encounter a conflict with a fundamental principle of democracy. Let me explain what I mean: even during the short time that we had judicial review in our country all the criticisms Mr. Wiecek described in his paper were voiced in Germany too. In the time after 1969 a more progressive, social democratic, liberal, reform-minded spirit prevailed. During this time – and I was chief justice of this court between 1971 and 1983 and thus know what I am talking about – the court did not intentionally decide to stop all these foolish reforms, although some members of the bench considered them acceptable while others did not think too highly of them. Of course every judge had his own personal, political, religious, and other convictions. Still I say it is natural that the court accepts the times. And this is the central issue: you could illustrate this beautifully from the long history of the U.S. Supreme Court. For a constitutional court like this I would contend that it is vital to accept Mr. Justice Harlan's dictum of 1916 that "a constitution is a living organism." The Constitution changes as the times change, which in itself is one justification for having an instrument like judicial review to allow it to adapt to change. A court like ours might not be the best instrument but nor is it the worst.

I tend to believe that a court like the federal Constitutional Court, which has tremendous powers and uses them, can in the long run not work against the spirit of the time. I am not talking about whether the court should. I am not trying to find out what a court of this character and status can achieve but what the court *can do* and this is enough for me. For it is not a small task to tell the rapidly changing opinion makers and the people who are in the field of politics: consider what you do, think twice and do think, do not just make laws but reconsider and try to find out whether they are good ideas.

Every major decision excites the people and the public. This is not amazing. In 1983, for example, we stopped the census – which was my last major decision. This law was passed by unanimous vote in Parliament and the state chamber (*Bundesrat*). Thus not even the opposition went to court and still the court declared it unconstitutional – no wonder everyone got excited. Of course there were immediately plans for packing the court or forcing the court to declare a law unconstitutional only if the judges were unanimous or voted in a very highly qualified majority – all déjà vu. But the fundamental problem nevertheless remains and will stay with us.

RALPH KETCHAM: I would like to raise a general question. It arises from the Netherlands' Constitution, which does not provide for judicial review. In comparing theirs with the American Constitution Dutch students asked, is judicial review an admissable and helpful concept in a democratic society? On the whole they defend their constitutional provision by saying that the idea of a court overseeing the acts of a democratically elected legislature is somehow a violation of the democratic principle.

ERNST BENDA: I do not quite agree with the fairly widely held theory of the difference between politics and law. What is the law? The law is the result of the political process, which means that you freeze a certain situation after a debate in the democratic process; then you may change a law and start again. The Constitution had as its main intention to make certain major decisions to save time and energy on questions agreed on in principle. If you look at the question raised by Mr. Ketcham from this point of view, you need some sort of instrument to see whether the democratic will of the fathers of the Constitution is in agreement and conformity with what the lawmakers do.

GERTRUDE LÜBBE-WOLFF: The answer to your question, Mr. Ketcham, really depends on whether you take it to be antidemocratic to want certain limits imposed on democracy. I think a constitution imposes certain limits on a democracy. The problem then is, how to get judges to speak out only within these limits and not reach out beyond them. That of course raises the problem of defining a line of demarcation.

The judiciary and the legislature have different functions. The judges differ from the legislature in that they have no initiative for policy-making, and are restricted to reviewing individual cases that are brought before them. Taking into consideration the fact that they have no executive power at their disposal but are dependent on the goodwill of the other powers, it becomes reasonable to suppose that these factors will work to keep the judiciary within certain limits.

ERNST BENDA: I do not know whether the argument that the court can only decide when called upon, which is true of course, carries far. If you get many cases you can do a lot. My second point is an addition to my former remarks: in the field of fundamental rights democracy has no role to play. If I have a fundamental right it is my own individual right and no one is going to vote on it whether I exercise the right or not – this has nothing to do with democracy but has to do with my individual rights.

ROBERT C. POST: One way of approaching Mr. Ketcham's question is to ask why we want democracy in the first place. Is it because we have a substantive notion of political happiness and because we believe that democracy is the best means of facilitating that kind of happiness? Or is it because we believe that anything that a majority may want is by definition conducive to political happiness? That question is obviously parallel to the current debate in philosophy between utilitarianism and human rights' theory.

KNUD KRAKAU: The first answer to this old question was of course given by Alexander Hamilton in the *Federalist*, no. 78, where he combines his theory of delegation with Montesquieu's saying that the exercise of judicial review by the court is not above the legislature but the Constitution is above both. So this solves the problem. A more pragmatic answer has been given by A. Cox in his Chichele Lectures at All Souls College, Oxford. There are, he says, so many antagonisms built into the system that it just cannot work without an umpire who just has to have the power to decide things in situations where a decision is usually needed.

RALPH KETCHAM: I believe that the judicial review function often goes beyond umpiring to the substance of a law. I think Mr. Post's comment is really to the point, that is, if you take judicial review beyond a certain point in declaring these principles, then you are engaging some form of natural-rights thinking.

CLYDE W. SUMMERS: It seems to me self-evident that the problem of judicial review entails the question of to what extent you allow decisions to be made through a majoritarian process and to what extent you create an agency that will say majoritarian, political decisions are not final decisions. And that seems to me to be the fundamental issue. Now in comparative terms there is a significant difference between systems, depending on the ease of amending their constitutions. If a constitution is relatively easy to amend then the judicial review process may, in a sense, be nothing more than a delaying action. And the judges may be quite prepared to apply constitutional limitations relatively freely knowing that they can be overruled without too much difficulty through the political processes.

But when you have a constitution such as ours, which is very difficult to amend, the judge's problem and the problem of judicial review become much more severe, much more difficult because the review process is likely to be the final word since the political processes simply cannot overturn the judge's sentence. In that circumstance judges have to think much more seriously about whether they will intervene and declare laws unconstitutional. From that standpoint the American system is constantly being confronted with the question of whether majority rule can overrule fundamental rights, but then comes the question of what the court shall treat as fundamental rights. And of course that issue is involved when we approach the outer fringes of freedom of speech, of press and religion, and the right of privacy, the combination of which leads us to the very difficult question of abortion. Is this a fundamental right or is it not a fundamental right? And basically the question is whether the courts should declare that majoritarian rule or the political process do not control this issue. Now once you focus on that then you are confronted with the question of designing some kind of general principles guide to determine what the court's limits are. It seems to me that we must ask the question in practical terms and in the context of one's own political system. One of the devices that we have arrived at in judicial review is what one might call "pseudo judicial review," where the court says that it will not pass on the constitutionality of a statute but will interpret the statute so as to avoid the constitutional questions. Having done that, the court leaves the legislative process free to rethink the process. That is really a kind of temporary veto. It seems to me that to compare the German and American systems one must approach the problem in terms of what the function of judicial review is within each political system.

ROBERT C. POST: For me these two excellent papers raise the question of the extent to which both lawyers and historians can view law as independent of the everyday practice of politics. I want to approach this question by asking whether we can evaluate the institution of judicial review independent of liberalism and conservatism, both conceived as political programs.

The first point that comes out of Mr. Wiecek's paper is that there is no necessary or intrinsic relationship between a liberal or conservative political program and one's attitude toward judicial review. Conservative jurists in the United States today, for example, are divided roughly into two camps. The first we might call "Frankfurtarian" conservatives. They would include figures like Chief Justice Rehnquist and Justice Scalia. These justices stress issues of judicial restraint and noninvolvement in the political process. The other camp, which we might call the "activist" conservatives, are associated with jurists like Richard Posner and Alexander Kozinski. They are committed to judicial activism in defense of property rights in a manner reminiscent of the Supreme Court during the 1920s. Thus within the same conservative political program we can find two very different attitudes toward the institution of judicial review.

This suggests that from the point of view of particular political programs, the institution of judicial review has no autonomous status. To evaluate the institution, therefore, we must adopt a standpoint that is independent of those particular political programs. This seems to imply that Mr. Wiecek's use of terms like "liberal" and "conservative" to evaluate the institution of judicial review are probably red herrings.

The association of the concept of "original intent" with a particular political program also seems to me to be a red herring. To give one example used by Paul Freund: the Constitution gives to Congress the power to make rules for the government and regulation of the land and naval forces. It does not mention the power to make rules for the government of the "air" forces, and it is clear that the framers in 1787 did not have the "intent" of giving Congress any such power. Yet no one would now conclude from this that Congress does not have this power. That is because we naturally and properly "interpret" the intent of the framers to be that Congress has the power to govern the nations's "military" forces.

This demonstrates that "original intent" can always be understood at different levels of generality or abstraction and thus that "original intent" is not a fact, but an interpretation. And this means that "original intent" cannot be used as a means of radically circumscribing the discretion of judges, as is sometimes now done in contemporary conservative politics.

PAUL FINKELMAN: First I want to ask whether "original intent" means anything to Germans? With relation to original intent in America, I think that people would argue that "original intent" is at issue whenever a court determines what a statute or a clause in the Constitution is; then they must at least take some account of what it was that this statute or clause is supposed to have accomplished.

There is something to be said for looking at a constitution if one decides on fundamental rights; then you must at least have some idea of what the framers meant by those fundamental rights, what those fundamental rights were. Now, perhaps we want to say that fundamental rights change with time. But there comes a time when you ask yourself what the words of the statute of the clause of the Constitution mean and part of that interpretation involves deciding whether six months means "lunar" or "calendar" months.

411

To illustrate this problem with another hot topic in America: as much as I abhor capital punishment, I find it strains the historical imagination to argue that the clause against cruel and unusual punishment means that we should abolish capital punishment. For it is clear that the intentions of the people who wrote that clause were not to abolish capital punishment, and if we want to do it then we should pass a constitutional amendment to that effect.

INGWER EBSEN: Before the First World War the German scholar Philip Heck discussed original intent. He distinguished between the concept of the legislature and the purpose for which it was intended. Now Heck held it necessary to be oriented to original intent because to him that was the same as obeying the law. But that obedience had to be a "thinking obedience" as he called it. Of course everyone knows that with this relativization all sorts of problems occur but there is still a great difference between whether a judge takes the position of "thinking obedience" or the position of making legislation himself.

WILLIAM WIECEK: This morning I argued against comparisons, I argued that things are so specific due to the social circumstances that they are ultimately incommensurable. Yet on reading Ms. Lübbe-Wolff's paper I was struck by how similar the German experience is to the American and I wonder if in any democratic society the institution of judicial review will not produce more or less the same arguments over time, perhaps in cycles as Mr. Krakau has suggested. Perhaps it is a case of *plus ça change plus c'est la même chose*.

Part 6
Constitutions and Change in Industrial Societies

16
The Supreme Court and Industrial Democracy

Clyde W. Summers

The role of the U.S. Supreme Court in protecting or promoting industrial democracy is inevitably a secondary and limited one. This is so for two reasons. First, federal courts protect the constitutional guarantee of individual rights and democratic process only from governmental action, not private action. The conduct of private employers and the rights of their employees are not governed by the Constitution. They are governed only by statute or common law, and the federal courts have no constitutional power to make common law. Second, the constitutional guarantees of freedom of speech and freedom of assembly protect the right to form and join unions, but they have never been extended to include the right of unions to engage in collective bargaining or economic action. Public employees may be denied the right to engage in collective bargaining and may be prohibited from striking or using other methods of collective economic pressure.

The Supreme Court's role is secondary to that of Congress and is limited to interpreting legislation passed by Congress. The function of interpreting, though bounded, is potentially broad because the relevant legislation is phrased in general and flexible terms. Both the National Labor Relations Act[1] (NLRA) and the Labor Management Reporting and Disclosure Act[2] (LMRDA) contain basic provisions of near-constitutional quality in which Congress has proclaimed principles more than prescribed rules. Wide latitude was left for administration and enforcement, with the last word in the Supreme Court. The Supreme Court, however, does not always fully exercise its interpreting function, but defers to the interpretation of the administrative agency. The Court has

1. 28 U.S.C. §§151 et seq.
2. 29 U.S.C. §§401 et seq.

repeatedly declared that "the construction of a statute by those charged with its execution should be followed unless there are compelling indications that it is wrong,"[3] and has at times upheld an interpretation by the National Labor Relations Board which, "though not required by the Act, is at least permissible under it."[4] But it remains for the Court to determine whether an interpretation is "permissible" or whether there are "compelling indications to the contrary," and these elastic terms impose little restraint on the Court.

Industrial democracy in the United States depends entirely on collective bargaining. The only voice of the employees is the union that represents them, and it speaks for them through the negotiation of collective agreements and the administration of them. There are no statutory works councils or enterprise committees; indeed, any representation of employees apart from the union is generally prohibited. The statutes relevant to industrial democracy, therefore, are the National Labor Relations Act, which has as its stated purpose "encouraging the practice and procedure of collective bargaining," and the Labor Management Reporting and Disclosure Act, which has as its purpose guaranteeing union members democratic rights and procedures in determining the policies and officers of their union. The Supreme Court's role in industrial democracy is to interpret these two statutes. The intention of this paper is to determine how the Court's decisions in interpreting these statutes have promoted or discouraged industrial democracy.

Historical Roots of Collective Bargaining

The theme that our system of political democracy should be matched by a system of industrial democracy has been a recurrent one in the United States. During the nineteenth century, efforts to achieve industrial democracy took varied forms, including utopian communities, worker ownership of factories, cooperatives, and public ownership. The path ultimately chosen was marked out by the American Federation of Labor. Workers were to achieve a voice by forming trade unions that, through collective bargaining, would

---

3. *NLRB v. Hendricks County Rural Electric Corp.*, 454 U.S. 170, 176 (1981).
4. *NLRB v. J. Weingarten, Inc.*, 420 U.S. 251, 266 (1975).

determine the terms and conditions of employment and the rules governing the workplace. This view was forcefully expressed in the final report of the Industrial Commission of 1902:

> By the organization of labor, and by no other means, it is possible to introduce an element of democracy into the government of industry. By this means only, the workers can effectively take part in determining the condition under which they work. This becomes true in the fullest and best sense only when employers frankly meet the representatives of the workmen, and deal with them as parties equally interested in the conduct of affairs. . . . To the mind of a union man . . . the union brings him a sense of greater liberty. . . . The union is a democratic government in which he had an equal voice with every other member. By its collective strength he is able to exert some direct influence upon the conditions of employment. As a part of it, the individual workman feels that he has a voice in fixing the terms on which he works.[5]

This theme was restated and amplified in 1916 by the Commission of Industrial Relations which called for "the rapid extension of the principles of democracy to industry."[6] The commission pointed out with great force and logic that "the struggle of labor for organization is not merely an attempt to secure an increased measure of the material comforts of life, but is a part of the age long struggle for liberty . . . even if men were well-fed they would still struggle to be free." The commission declared that "every means should be used to extend and strengthen organizations throughout the entire industrial field." It then recommended legislation protecting the right of individuals to form unions, prohibiting the discharge of workers because of union membership, investigating unfair treatment of labor, and prohibiting refusal to meet and confer with representatives of employees. This proposal, which sought to achieve industrial democracy through collective bargaining, was a precursor of the National Labor Relations Act enacted some twenty years later.

In 1935, when the National Labor Relations Act was adopted, collective bargaining was conceived as serving three basic functions. First, it would provide a better balance of bargaining power,

5. XIX final report of the Industrial Commission, H.R. doc. no. 380, 57th Cong., 1st sess. (1902), 805–7.
6. Final report of the U.S. Commission on Industrial Relations, sec. doc. no. 415, 64th Cong., 1st sess. (1916), 62–63.

enabling workers to obtain a larger share in production. Second, because workers would have sufficient bargaining power to protect their own interests, the need for protective legislation would be reduced, with reliance on the free collective labor market rather than government controls. The third and most fundamental function was to provide a measure of industrial democracy by giving workers an effective voice in determining the terms and conditions of their employment.

Senator Wagner, author of the act, explained its philosophy in these terms:

> The principles of my proposal were surprisingly simple. They were founded upon the accepted facts that we must have democracy in industry as well as government; that democracy in industry means fair participation by those who work, in the decisions vitally affecting their lives and livelihood; and that the workers in our great mass production industries can enjoy this participation only if allowed to organize and bargain collectively through representatives of their own choosing.[7]

The purpose and expectation of the statute were to establish a system of collective bargaining as the accepted form of industrial relations. Through collective bargaining employees would have an effective voice; unilateral dictation by the employer would be replaced by mutually accepted rules, and the divine right of employers would give way to democratic industrial government.

This brief tracing of the origins and the purposes of the National Labor Relations Act is necessary, for it is this statute that the Supreme Court interprets. The Supreme Court's role in protecting or promoting industrial democracy must be measured against the purposes of the statute and the function of collective bargaining. We now turn to particular decisions which, directly or indirectly, have had a significant impact on industrial democracy.

Court Decisions affecting Industrial Democracy

None of the Supreme Court decisions deals directly with industrial democracy. They deal with the process of unionization and the

7. M. Derber, *The American Idea of Industrial Democracy, 1865–1965* (1970), 6 citing *New York Times*, April 13, 1937, 20, col. 1.

establishment of collective bargaining and with the economic action used by unions and employers to reach agreement. However, these are the components of industrial democracy in the United States because collective bargaining is the instrument and process of industrial democracy.

Protection and Promotion of Unionization

The essential precondition for collective bargaining is the organization of unions. Because American employers historically opposed unionization, not only through their control of the workplace and employment but also through the use of spies, agents provocateurs, and physical threats and violence, the central focus and immediate goal of the Wagner Act of 1935 was to protect union members and the process of unionization from employer unfair labor practices. Section 7, the fundamental provision of the statute, declared: "Employees shall have the right to self-organization, to form, join or assist labor organizations, to bargain collectively through representatives of their own choosing, and to engage in other concerted activities for the purposes of collective bargaining or other mutual aid and protection." Section 8 then stated, "It shall be an unfair labor practice for an employer – (1) To interfere with, restrain, or coerce employees in the exercise of the rights guaranteed in Section 7." Subsection (3), elaborating subsection (1), added "by discrimination in regard to hire or tenure of employment, or any term or condition of employment to encourage or discourage membership in any labor organization."

In examining the Supreme Court's role in interpreting these broadly worded provisions, two crucial facts must be kept in mind. First, passage of the statute did not end employer anti-union practices, for most employers have never willingly accepted collective bargaining. They have continued to mount massive campaigns to prevent unionization, commonly going beyond the limits of the law and engaging in a nearly unlimited range of unfair labor practices. Second, the union's statutory right to represent employees for collective bargaining depends on its obtaining majority support of the employees in a bargaining unit. Majority support is normally determined by a representation election conducted by the National Labor Relations Board (NLRB). This means that, in the period before an election, there is often a bitter contest between the union and employer, each attempting to influence the vote. Two telling indications of the character of the contest are that although unions do not request an election until they have strong support and believe thay can win, they lose more than half of the elections; and that for every seven votes cast for the union, one union member is illegally discharged for union activity.

The Supreme Court, in interpreting the broad provisions of sections 7 and 8, has given a wavering and incomplete protection to the union efforts to organize. In *Republic Aviation Corp. v. NLRB*[8] three employees were discharged for wearing union steward buttons at work during an organizing drive, and another was discharged for soliciting union membership in the plant during his lunch period. The Supreme Court upheld a National Labor Relations Board decision that these discharges violated the statute. The Court approved the board's reasoning that the employer's right of control over the employees did not extend to curtailing the wearing of union steward buttons, "a reasonable and legitimate form of union activity"; and that the "employer's right to control his property" did not entitle him to enforce a rule prohibiting union solicitation by an employee outside of working hours. "Inconvenience, or even some dislocation of property rights may be necessary to safeguard the right to collective bargaining." The employer could enforce "reasonable rules" of conduct and require employees to work during working time, but "prohibiting union solicitation by an employee outside working hours although on company property" – before or after work, during lunch or rest periods – "is presumed to be an unreasonable impediment to self-organization." The employees' right to organize for collective bargaining outweighed the employer's right to control its property.

The Court, however, tipped the balance the opposite way in *NLRB v. Babcock & Wilcox Co.*[9] The employer refused to allow union organizers who were not its employees to come into the company-owned parking lot to distribute union literature. The NLRB ruled that this unreasonably interfered with the employees' right to self-organization because the place of work was the effective and appropriate place for communication of this information.

8. 324 U.S. 793 (1945).
9. 351 U.S. 105 (1956).

The Court rejected the board's reasoning because it did not give adequate weight to the employer's property right to exclude those who were not its employees. The employer could bar all access to its property by union organizers, said the Court, unless the location of the plant and the homes of the employees were beyond the reach of other methods of communications. The union was thus deprived of the most effective, and often only practicable, method of making initial contact with employees, although distribution in the parking lot would place no substantial burden on the employer. The employer's bare property right outweighed the right to organize for collective bargaining. The ability of the employer to use his control of property to prevent unionization was extended in *Central Hardware Co. v. NLRB*,[10] where the Court held that a retail store could bar union organizers from contacting employees in the customers' parking lot, which was generally open to all who had business with the store.

Three comments are necessary to make clear the negative character of the Court's decision in *Babcock & Wilcox* as contrasted with *Republic Aviation*. First, in *Babcock & Wilcox* the Court overruled the decision of the board. Although the Court verbally recognized the board's "responsibility of applying the Act's general prohibitory language" and declared itself "slow to overturn an administrative decision," it declared that the board's conclusions "rest on an erroneous foundation." Second, the line drawn by the Court between "employees" and "non-employees" has no basis in the act. On the contrary, the statutory definition of "employee" explicitly states that it "shall not be limited to the employees of a particular employer." Under the statute, the union organizers were clearly "employees" entitled to full protection of their rights under section 7 to "form, join or assist labor organizations." Third, the Court's decisions have seriously hampered unions in organizing because contacts cannot be made within the plant without employees becoming identified as union activists and risking reprisals by employers.

The Court has given similarly limited and ambivalent protection against employer activities designed to persuade or deter employees from joining the union. In *NLRB v. Virginia Electric & Power Co.*,[11]

10. 407 U.S. 539 (1972).
11. 314 U.S. 469 (1941).

the Court upheld the employer's right to distribute literature and to compel employees to listen to a "captive audience" speech on the plant premises urging employees not to join the union, under the condition that the literature and speeches with their surrounding circumstances were not coercive. This decision opened the door to employers engaging in massive propaganda campaigns to discredit unions as communist, corrupt, interested only in collecting dues, unable to gain benefits for the workers, and causing loss of jobs. The speeches avoid making overt threats that the employer will take economic reprisal, but "predict" that the union will bring economic disaster with strikes and loss of jobs. Such "predictions" are intended to, and do, discourage employees from unionizing. More than twenty-five years later the Court marginally curbed some of these excesses by holding that such "predictions" of economic consequences must be based on objective facts and be beyond the employer's control.

The Court stated, in *NLRB v. United Steelworkers of America*,[12] that the "opportunities for effectively reaching the employees with a pro-union message" should be "at least as great as the employer's ability to promote the legally authorized expression of his anti-union views." This declared even-handedness is empty of meaning. The Court has held that the employer can use its control over the employees and the plant premises to distribute anti-union literature and make "captive audience" speeches, while denying unions equal rights in distributing literature and making "captive audience" speeches.

The most coercive measure to discourage unionization is discrimination in employment because of union membership or activity. This is expressly prohibited by section 8(a)(3). The Supreme Court, in *Phelps Dodge Corp. v. NLRB*,[13] gave the broadest protection against such discrimination. Refusal to hire union activists was as much a violation as dismissing them, and the board could order the employer to hire, or "instate," such employees with back pay, just as it could order dismissed employees reinstated with back pay by the employer. Further, the board could order instatement or reinstatement of workers who had obtained substantially equivalent employment elsewhere. The Court, in arriving at these con-

12. 357 U.S. 357 (1958).
13. 313 U.S. 177 (1941).

clusions, read potentially limiting statutory words "as a means for accomplishment of the main object of the legislation" and "translating into concreteness the purpose of safeguarding and encouraging the right of self-organization."

This broad protection proved incomplete, however, in *Textile Workers Union v. Darlington Manufacturing Co.*[14] During a union organizing drive the employer threatened to close the plant if the employees voted for a union. When the union won a representation election, the employer made good its threat. The plant was closed and all the employees were dismissed. Although the employer's action fell squarely within the words of the statute – the employees were discriminated against because of union membership – the Court declared that "it is not the type of discrimination which is prohibited by the Act," although it recognized that its decision "may result in some deterrent effect on organizational activities." The Court treated the employer's right to go out of business as an absolute management prerogative not touched by the statute, even if the closing was a vindictive one intended to punish employees for joining the union.

One sharp symbolic blow was struck on behalf of establishing collective bargaining where the employer has engaged in unfair labor practice to prevent unionization. In *NLRB v. Gissel Packing Company*,[15] the Court held that an employer could be required to recognize and bargain with a union even though it failed to obtain a majority in a representation election, when the union had originally obtained the authorizing signatures of a majority but that majority had been undermined by the employer's unfair labor practices. The NLRB had discretion to order the employer to recognize the union and establish a collective bargaining relationship. This decision has had more symbolic than practical value, for the federal courts of appeal frequently overrule the NLRB when it exercises its discretion or orders bargaining, and the board has now indicated a reluctance to issue such orders. Instead, it will order a new election and the employer can repeat its anti-union practices.

The role of the Supreme Court in protecting unionization, the essential precondition of collective bargaining, cannot be easily summarized. However, the Court has clearly failed to give consistent

14. 380 U.S. 263 (1965).
15. 395 U.S. 575 (1969).

protection "to the right of employees to self-organization, to form, join or assist labor organizations." The right of unions to use the working place as a forum for persuading employees to form and join unions, recognized in *Republic Aviation*, was deprived of its major practical value in *Babcock & Wilcox*, and the employer was given free use of the working place as its forum for persuading employees not to form unions, even to the extent of compelling employees to listen to anti-union tirades. In their literature and captive audience speeches, employers can make predictions of economic consequences to discourage unionizations and can threaten and carry out the threat to close the plant rather than to bargain collectively. These restrictive results were not required by either the words or purposes of the statute. Indeed, in all of the restrictive cases, the Court overruled the interpretation of the NLRB. Because of these decisions, the court bears at least some of the responsibility for the fact that industrial democracy has a semblance of reality for only one-fifth of workers in the private sector.

The Establishment of Collective Bargaining

Certification of a union as statutory representative of the employees does not establish collective bargaining. In more than half of the cases in which the union is newly certified the union does not obtain a collective agreement. Employer opposition continues in the form of legally challenging the union's status through appeals that may take two to eight years, long enough for the employees to despair of obtaining benefits through collective bargaining. The employer may engage in "surface bargaining," taking positions which will guarantee not reaching agreement, or may drive the union to strike and then hire replacements to break the strike and destroy the union's majority.

The Supreme Court has been less than helpful in establishing the collective bargaining relationship when the employer resists. For example, two years after a union had been certified as the employees' representative, the NLRB found that the employer, by its conduct at the bargaining table, "was demanding in effect that the Union relinquish the basic rights conferred by the Act or it would not receive a contract." The board's order for the employer to bargain in good faith was upheld by the Court of Appeals. After another year of bargaining the board again found the employer guilty of bargaining in bad faith by refusing to agree to a "check-off," or deduction of union dues from employees' wages, not because of any inconvenience but to frustrate the making of an agreement, with the explanation that it was "not going to give aid and comfort to the union." The Court of Appeals again upheld the board, and when the employer continued to refuse to agree on this, the only unsettled issue, the employer was ordered to grant the union a contract clause for checkoff of union dues.

The Supreme Court, in *H.K. Porter Co., Inc. v. NLRB*,[16] rejected this remedy prescribed by the board and the Court of Appeals. The Court acknowledged that the employer had repeatedly refused to bargain in good faith in spite of board and Court of Appeals orders, that a literal interpretation of the statute would allow this remedy, and that the board and Court of Appeals relied on the "important policy of the Act that workers' rights to collective bargaining be secured." All of these, however, were secondary to what the Court declared was a "fundamental" policy of the act, "freedom of contract." The Court gave no suggestion as to what remedy could be used when an employer adamantly refused to agree to a particular provision for the sole purpose of frustrating the making of an agreement.

The Supreme Court has not always insisted so single-mindedly on freedom of contract. In *H.J. Heinz v. NLRB*,[17] it earlier upheld a board order that the employer, who had reached agreement with the union, sign a written contract embodying those terms. The refusal to sign an agreement "discredits the union, impairs the bargaining process, and tends to frustrate the aim of the statute to secure industrial peace through collective bargaining."

The Court's unhelpfulness in establishing a collective agreement is more than matched by its unhelpfulness in preserving the collective bargaining relation when established. In a pair of cases,[18] the Court held that when a going business was transferred to a new employer, the new employer was not bound by the collective

16. 397 U.S. 99 (1970).
17. 311 U.S. 514 (1941).
18. *NLRB v. Burns International Security Services, Inc.*, 406 U.S. 272 (1972); *Howard Johnson Co., Inc. v. Detroit Local Joint Board Hotel & Restaurant Employees*, 417, U.S. 249 (1974).

agreement. Moreover, the new employer was not bound to recognize and bargain with the union unless a majority of the employees of the old employer were hired by the new employer, and the new employer was not obligated to hire any of the old employees. In short, the new employer could discard the old employees and hire a new work force, even though the collective agreement with the old employer had a seniority provision and a prohibition of dismissal without just cause. The new employer would be free of the union and the collective agreement, and the collective bargaining relationship would be totally destroyed. These decisions were not required by any statutory language or general legal principles other than invocation of *H.K. Porter* and freedom of contract. Indeed, the Court had earlier held that a successor employer was bound by the arbitration clause in the collective agreement of the old employer, suggesting that the collective bargaining relationship and collective agreement survived the transfer of a business.[19] The Court seemingly lost its willingness to protect established bargaining relationships and made them totally vulnerable to business transfers.

Exclusion of Employees from Collective Bargaining

The Supreme Court has circumscribed industrial democracy by denying significant categories of employees protection under the statute and effectively excluding them from collective bargaining. The National Labor Relations Act, as enacted in 1935, was applicable to all employees in the private sector except agricultural laborers and domestic servants. When first-line foremen of an automobile manufacturer organized in a foremen's association totally separate from the production workers, the NLRB certified the association as their statutory representative and ordered the employer to bargain collectively. The employer refused, asserting that they were not entitled to the advantages of the act. In *Packard Motor Car Co. v. NLRB*,[20] the majority of the Court agreed with the board and held that foremen come within the statutory definition of employee. In response to the argument that those with supervis-

19. *John Wiley & Sons, Inc. v. Livingston*, 376 U.S. 543 (1964).
20. 330 U.S. 485 (1947).

ory authority "owed the employer faithful performance in his interests," the majority pointed out that all employees owed this duty and added: "Even those who act for the employer in some matters, including the service of standing between management and manual labor, still have interests of their own as employees. . . . He does not lose his right to serve himself in these respects because he serves his master in others."

The crucial opinion, however, was the dissent by four of the justices, for it articulated not only what ultimately became law but also the underlying reasoning crucial in later developments. The dissent acknowledged that, historically, one of the purposes of employee representation was "the need for narrowing the gap between management and labor, for allowing labor greater participation in policy decisions, for developing an industrial system in which cooperation rather than coercion was the dominant characteristic." The dissent further acknowledged that the Court's decision was a step in that direction because it tended to soften the line between labor and management. This, however, declared the dissent, could not have been what Congress had in mind. Management and labor were hostile forces, and "foremen were the arms and legs of management in executing labor policies." If foremen bargained collectively they would be both management and labor, with conflicting loyalties.

The dissent never explored the possibility that collective bargaining by first-line foremen and lower-level supervisors might be appropriate, particularly if represented by a separate union, but emphasized the potential problems if all employees from the president to the janitor bargained together in the same union. It ignored the fact that in some industries foremen did bargain collectively, and historically some unions had included foremen without creating debilitating conflicts of loyalty.

The dissenting opinion ultimately prevailed. When the statute was amended the following year, Congress embraced the dissent's perspective and excluded supervisory employees from protection of the act. The term "supervisor" was defined as one who had authority over employees to direct them responsibly, adjust their grievances, or effectively recommend such action.

The assumptions underlying the dissent were extended by the Court beyond "supervisors" to exclude employees who had no role in making or executing labor policies. In *NLRB v. Bell Aerospace*

Co.,[21] the NLRB certified a bargaining unit of buyers in the purchasing department. The Court held that these were "managerial employees" who "formulate and effectuate management policies by expressing and making operative the decisions of their employer." Although they were not susceptible to conflicts of interest in labor relations, they were "allied with management" and collective bargaining was not appropriate. This would work a "fundamental change in industrial philosophy" because "it would eviscerate the traditional distinction between labor and management. If Congress had intended a result so drastic it is not unreasonable to expect that it would have said so." There was no discussion of how collective bargaining by these buyers would interfere with their "managerial" functions.

The Court did not exclude "managerial" employees from collective representation on the basis that they had no need for collective participation in decision making in the enterprise. The Court never mentioned the interest in or value of participation, and for good reason these "managerial" employees had no voice in the enterprise beyond their narrow jobs. The logic was simple: they were members of the managerial class, the same as the top executives, and collective bargaining was therefore inappropriate.

The most significant decision, the full implications of which will be discussed later, is *NLRB v. Yeshiva University,*[22] in which the Court held that college professors were excluded from the act as "managerial" employees. Yeshiva University, like many American universities, had a system of committees in which faculty members participated in making decisions concerning curriculum, grading, admission standards, academic calendars, and class schedules. The faculty at each school or department made recommendations as to hiring, tenure, promotions, terminations, and sabbatical leaves. In some departments the faculty decided admission, expulsion and graduation of individual students, teaching load and enrollment level. The faculty had no substantial voice in making the budget or in setting salary scales, pensions, leave policies, or tenure standards.

The faculty members organized and the NLRB certified the union as majority representative, but the university refused to bargain, asserting that the faculty were managerial employees. The

21. 416 U.S. 267 (1974).
22. 440 U.S. 672 (1980).

Court reversed the NLRB, holding that the faculty were managerial and not entitled to collective representation under the act. Said the Court:

> In fact, the faculty's professional interests – as applied to governance at a university like Yeshiva can not be separated from those of the institutions. . . . Faculty members enhance their own standing and fulfill their professional mission by ensuring that the university's objectives are met. . . . The university requires faculty participation in governance because professional expertise is indispensable to the formulation and implementation of policy. . . . It is clear that Yeshiva and like universities must rely on their faculties to participate in the making and implementation of their policies.

The faculty's decisions were managerial and the board must "ensure that employees who exercise discretionary authority on behalf of the employer will not divide their loyalties between the employer and the union." The Court never discussed how the faculty, in bargaining concerning terms and conditions of employment, would make decisions any differently than they did in the existing committees or system of faculty governance or why there would be any difference in conflict of interest and loyalty. Nor did the Court see the irony in holding that the university was all managers, with no employees except clerical and maintenance workers.

The significance of these cases does not lie in the number of employees excluded from the system of their potential importance as key groups, but rather in the underlying assumptions and preconceptions of collective bargaining on which these decisions rest. This will be more fully explored at a later point.

Decision for Collective Bargaining

The substance of industrial democracy depends on the range of decisions of the enterprise in which the employees have a voice. In the American system these decisions are described in terms of subjects of collective bargaining. The Supreme Court has developed a dichotomy between mandatory subjects of bargaining and permissive subjects of bargaining.[23] If a subject such as wages is

---

23. *NLRB v. Wooster Division of Borg-Warner*, 356 U.S. 342 (1958).

mandatory, there are three consequences. First, the employer is required, on the union's request, to meet and bargain in good faith to impasse concerning the subject. Second, the employer cannot make any change in existing terms without first notifying the union and bargaining to impasse. Third, the union can strike or use other legal forms of economic pressure to enforce its demands. If a subject is permissive, the employer can act unilaterally and need not discuss the subject with the union, and the union is prohibited from using economic force to achieve its demands.

Obviously, the right to participate collectively in decisions is limited to mandatory subjects of bargaining. The employer may permit participation on other subjects but cannot, by law or economic pressure, be required to do so. Congress, in 1947, amended the act to define the duty to bargain, but it refused to specify the mandatory subjects of bargaining. Instead, it used the broad terms "wages, hours and other terms and conditions of employment."[24]

The Supreme Court has held that these words reach incidental matters, such as the quality and price of food in the company cafeteria,[25] but has been grudging in extending it to more significant matters such as the contracting out of work and plant closures. In *Fibreboard Paper Products Corp. v. NLRB*,[26] the employer decided, without informing the union, to contract out all plant maintenance work, resulting in dismissal of three hundred employees. The Court upheld the board's decision that contracting out was a mandatory subject of bargaining. It was a "problem of vital concern to labor and management," and subcontracting clauses in many agreements showed that it was amenable to collective bargaining. A concurring opinion endorsed by three justices restricted the impact and ultimately undermined the decision. The concurring opinion agreed that where contracting out simply substituted another group of workers doing the same work in the same place, there was a duty to bargain. The statutory words, however, were not to be read broadly to reach all decisions that directly affected job security. There was no duty to bargain "regarding such managerial decisions which lie at the core of entrepreneurial control," for example, "decisions concerning the commitment of investment capital and the basic scope of the enterprise . . . those

24. Section 8(d).
25. *Ford Motor Co. v. NLRB*, 441 U.S. 488 (1979).
26. 379 U.S. 203 (1964).

management decisions which are fundamental to the basic direction of the enterprise."

The concurring opinion was followed and elaborated in *First National Maintenance Corp. v. NLRB.*[27] The company, which was engaged in providing cleaning and maintenance service for various commercial customers, terminated its services at a nursing home because the operation was not sufficiently profitable. As a result, thirty-five employees of the company working at the nursing home were dismissed. The NLRB held that making the decision to close the operation without notifying or bargaining with the union violated the statutory duty to bargain. The Supreme Court reversed the board, stating that although the decision had a direct impact on employment, it "had as its focus only the economic profitability of the contract." The Court emphasized that it was "particularly important to consider whether bargaining over this decision will advance the neutral purposes of the Act," but reasoned:

> Congress had no expectation that the elected union representative would become an equal partner in the running of the business enterprise in which the union's members are employed. . . . Management must be free from the constraints of the bargaining process [possible use of strike power] to the extent necessary for the running of a profitable business. . . . In view of the employer's need for unencumbered decision making, bargaining over management decisions that have a substantial impact on the continued availability of employment should be required only if the benefits for labor management relations and the collective bargaining process, outweigh the burden placed on the conduct of business.

The Court could find no substantial benefit to labor management relations or collective bargaining in requiring the employer to notify and bargain with the employees' representative concerning the decision and found great dangers to necessary speed, flexibility, and secrecy in decision making, with consequent risks of loss and economic efficiency. The union was entitled to bargain concerning the effects of the decision–severance pay, right of transfer, etc. – but this is often of little practical value because economic pressure may be ineffective once the operation is closed.

27. 452 U.S. 666 (1981).

The impact of *First National Maintenance* is to deprive employees of any effective voice in decisions to close, relocate, or sell part or all of a plant or operation, even if that decision has the most devastating effect on their job security and future livelihood. They have no right to notice, no right to be heard, no right to negotiate, and no right to strike or use other economic action in protest. The employer is shielded by law to assert prerogatives unreachable by any employee participation. The Supreme Court has not only circumscribed the area of worker participation and prohibited the union from using its economic strength to enlarge the area of participation, but has authorized the employer's use of its economic strength to shrink the area of participation. In *NLRB v. American National Insurance Co.*,[28] the employer insisted on including in the collective agreement a "management prerogatives" clause that, during the contract period, would give the employer unilateral control over hiring, promotion, discharge, demotion, and scheduling of work to establish and change as it chose. The company refused to agree to a contract that did not contain this management prerogatives clause. The NLRB held that insistence on retaining unilateral control over these mandatory subjects was in derogation of the employees' statutory rights to bargain collectively. The Court, however, held that the employer fulfilled his duty when he bargained over whether he should have unilateral control over these decisions during the contract term. The employer could, by use of its economic strength, compel employees to surrender their voice in these decisions.

If we cast these decisions in terms of industrial democracy, employees have the right to a voice in a restricted range of decisions that affect their wages, hours, and working conditions, but they have no right to a voice in many decisions of the enterprise, although those decisions directly affect their work or even destroy their jobs. The employer retains its authoritarian control over "managerial" decisions and may use its economic strength to enlarge its prerogatives. These restrictions on industrial democracy and preservation of employer authoritarianism were not required either by the words of the statute or its policies. They were the creation of the Supreme Court, overruling decisions by the NLRB, the expert agency to which the Court gives lip-service deference.

---

28. 343 U.S. 395 (1952).

Access to Information

The ability of employees to participate and the union to bargain requires access to relevant information. The NLRB has ruled that the employer is required to provide the union with all information potentially relevant and reasonably necessary to mandatory subjects of bargaining. This includes job rates and classifications, incentive earnings of individual employees, and costs of group insurance, pensions, and other fringe benefits. However, the employer is not required to give financial information concerning the enterprise or its profitability. This limiting rule was inferentially approved by the Supreme Court in *NLRB v. Truiit Manufacturing Co.*,[29] where the Court upheld an exception when the employer pleaded inability to pay in bargaining over wages. In that case, the employer could be compelled to allow the union to examine the financial record to determine whether the claim of inability to pay was justified. The Court assumed that the profitability of an enterprise was normally of no concern to the union in determining its bargaining policy, even though the survival of the enterprise might be at stake.

This decision does more than deny the union access to information. It builds on the assumption that the profitability of the enterprise is of no concern to the union or the employees it represents. It denies the common interest that is the premise and essential ingredient of industrial democracy.

Protection of Economic Action

Regardless of the employees covered or the subjects of collective bargaining, the reality of employee participation ultimately depends on whether the employer listens to the employee's collective voice. In some countries, employers willingly hear that voice or even seek out the views of the workers' representatives. In the United States most employers actively resist collective representation, and the strength of the workers' voice ultimately depends on the union's economic strength. The law, to the extent that it protects or prohibits certain forms of economic actions, affects the

29. 351 U.S. 149 (1956).

realization of industrial democracy.

It would be burdensome to canvas here all of the Supreme Court's decisions concerning various forms of economic action by unions and employers, but four examples will provide a sense of direction. Section 7 of the National Labor Relations Act guarantees employees "the right to engage in concerted activities for material aid and protection," and section 8 prohibits employers from discriminating in employment against employees who engage in activities guaranteed by section 7. The Court, however, in *NLRB v. Mackay Radio and Telegraph Co.*,[30] refused to give these words their plain meaning. It held that although an employer could not discharge strikers, it could hire permanent replacements and at the end of the strike refuse to take back the strikers whose places had been filled by replacements. This plainly discriminates against strikers in derogation of section 7 rights, but the Court found, out of the air, a superior right in the employer "to protect and continue his business by supplying places left vacant by strikers" and to give assurances to those employed during the strike that their jobs would be permanent. This can be a powerful weapon for the employer and has been used regularly by employers to break strikes and sometimes to destroy the union by causing it to lose its majority status. The availability of this employer weapon seriously weakens the union's voice at the bargaining table.

In two other cases, the Supreme Court refused to protect "concerted activities for mutual aid and protection" by holding that the union's calling of union meetings at irregular times during working hours[31] or having employees refuse to work overtime,[32] as methods of bringing economic pressure on the employer, were not protected by section 7, and that employees who engage in such concerted activities could be discharged. The union was thus deprived of these potentially powerful economic weapons.

On the other hand, the Supreme Court upheld the right of an employer to lock out its employees as a method of bringing economic pressure on the union to accept its proposals[33] and,

30. 304 U.S. 333 (1938).
31. *United Automobile Workers v. Wisconsin Employment Relations Board*, 336 U.S. 245 (1949).
32. Lodge 76, *International Association of Machinists v. Wisconsin Employment Relations Board*, 427 U.S. 132 (1976).
33. *American Shipbuilding Co. v. NLRB*, 380 U.S. 300 (1965).

where the union struck one employer of an employer's association, to extend that lockout so that all of the other employers could also lock out their employees.[34] In other cases, the Court first strengthened the hand of the union by holding that it could fine union members who worked during a strike and sue in court to enforce the fines.[35] But the Court broke this union spear by holding that the union could not fine members who resigned from the union before returning to work[36] and could not limit their right to resign before or during a strike.[37] The union's weapon was thus made practically useless.

The Supreme Court has thus placed powerful and sometimes devastating economic weapons in the hands of the employer, but has denied or weakened weapons in the hands of the union. The vitality of industrial democracy is thereby significantly weakened.

The Sources of Denial of Industrial Democracy

The pattern of Supreme Court decisions is plain. At every point it has failed to promote or strengthen industrial democracy. On the contrary, it has failed to protect the process of unionization essential for establishing industrial democracy and has permitted employers deliberately to defeat and destroy unionization. To the extent that unions are able to organize and establish collective bargaining, the Court has allowed employers to frustrate bargaining and destroy the bargaining relationship. The Court has restricted those who have right to be represented and limited the subjects to be governed by the democratic process of collective bargaining. And even within this restricted area of employee participation the Court has weakened the effective voice of the union as the employee's representative.

This confronts us with the question: how could the Court, in interpreting a statute which has as one of its principal purposes the establishment of a system of industrial democracy, have so utterly

34. *NLRB v. Brown*, 380 U.S. 278 (1965).
35. *NLRB v. Alli-Chalmers Manufacturing Co.*, 388 U.S. 175 (1967).
36. *NLRB v. Granite State Board, Textile Workers Local* 1029, 409 U.S. 213 (1972).
37. Booster Lodge No. 405, International Association of Machinists, 412 U.S. 84 (1973); *Pattern Maker's League of North America v. NLRB*, 473 U.S. 95, 105 S.Ct. 3064 (1985).

failed to fulfill that purpose? The answer is not clear, but it was in part because the Court built on premises antithetical to some of the original purposes of the statute, of which it had lost sight. The responsibility does not rest entirely with the Court, for in some measure it reflected, as well as helped shape, the policies and assumptions of the larger society. The Court went astray at three crucial points.

Neutrality toward Collective Bargaining

The National Labor Relations Act in 1935 declared as national policy "protection by law of the right of employees to organize and bargain collectively" to the end of "encouraging the practice and procedures of collective bargaining."[38] This policy of establishing a system of collective bargaining, the instrument of industrial democracy, helped inform many of the earlier decisions of the Supreme Court, such as *Phelps Dodge* in 1941, giving broad protection against discrimination; *Republic Aviation* in 1946, giving employees the right to solicit for the union at the work place; and *Packard Motors* in 1948, giving foremen the right to bargain collectively. The support, however, was not consistent, as indicated in *Mackay Radio*, giving employers the right to replace strikers, and in the dissent in *Packard Motors*.

Later cases shifted the policy from one of protecting unionization and encouraging collective bargaining toward that of neutrality in the contest of the union to organize and the employer to defeat unionization. The Court viewed the statute as largely indifferent to whether employees organized and bargained collectively; the NLRB and the courts were only to referee the contest between the union and the employer.

Viewing the statute as neutral, however, reinstated common law concepts antithetical to encouraging unionization and establishing collective bargaining. In *Babcock & Wilcox* the right to engage in organizational activity at the workplace was truncated by allowing the employer to invoke common law property concepts to exclude union organizers from entering the employer's property. The employer's right of free speech, recognized in *Virginia Electric*

38. Section 1.

Power, was extended to allow the employer to use its control over its property and employees to compel those employees to attend the employer's anti-union speeches. The *Steelworkers* opinion purported to require equal access, but denied the union equal time and equal access to address the employees. In practice, neutrality returned to the employer many of the advantages enjoyed under common law.

Common law concepts overrode statutory rights in other decisions that frustrated or limited collective bargaining. The right of an employer to go out of business, carrying with it the right to threaten to go out of business as protected in *Darlington*, elevated the employer's property rights over the employee's statutory rights. The unwillingness of the Court to order H.K. Porter Co. to accept a checkoff provision made a fetish of freedom of contract. And management's prerogative of "unencumbered decision making" and its right to "be free from the constraints of the bargaining process to the extent necessary for running a business," shielded in *First National Maintenance*, protected common law property interests over the statutory purpose of industrial democracy.

Responsibility for this shift toward neutrality concerning unionization and collective bargaining does not rest solely on the Court. Congress, in amending the statute in 1947, betrayed an ambivalence toward its purpose. The statutory statement of policy in section 1 and the employer unfair labor practices in section 8 remained unchanged, except to prohibit closed and union shop agreements. However, to the words of section 7 guaranteeing employees the right to form and join unions, to bargain collectively, and to engage in concerted activities were added the words "and shall also have the right to refrain from any or all such activities." Also, union unfair labor practices were added, prohibiting unions from restraining or coercing employees in the exercise of those rights. None of the changes, on their face, gave employers greater freedom to oppose unionization or weakened the commitment to collective bargaining. The changes were aimed at protecting employees from coercion by unions. The legislative debates, however, carried strong overtones of hostility to unions and collective bargaining, often with an implication that employers were the protectors of employees' rights to refrain from joining unions and engage in collective bargaining.

Congressional ambivalence reflected a public attitude of ambivalence, which fostered development of a widespread conception that the decision about whether there was to be collective bargaining should be made in a contest between the union and the employer for the loyalty of the employees. The public had no interest in the outcome, and the law should be neutral. The Court decisions both reflected and fed these political and social attitudes.

Adversarial Collective Bargaining

The National Labor Relations Act carries mixed messages as to whether collective bargaining, when established, was envisioned as an adversarial or collaborative process. Section 1 states that: "Experience has proved that protection by law of the right of employees to organize and bargain collectively . . . [removes] certain recognized sources of industrial strife and unrest, by encouraging practices fundamental to the friendly adjustment of industrial disputes."

At the same time, in section 13, it guaranteed an undiminished right to strike. Also, section 8(2)I declared it to be an unfair labor practice for an employer "to dominate or interfere with the formation or administration of any labor organization or contribute financial or other support to it." Legislative reports declared that collective bargaining is "a sham when the employer sits on both sides of the table by supporting a particular organization with which he deals."[39]

Congress apparently envisioned collective bargaining with the parties sitting on opposite sides of the table, and the process was in this respect adversarial; but it also envisioned "practices fundamental to the friendly adjustment of industrial disputes." There was no inherent contradiction between management and union being independent parties seeking their own interests and collaborating for the good of the enterprise. Differences about shares of the return could coexist with a common interest in increasing those returns.

The Supreme Court has not recognized this common interest and the potential for collective bargaining serving it, but has viewed the union as an outside force representing a hostile interest.

39. House report no. 1147, 74th Cong., 1st sess. (1935), 3.

Bell Aerospace, echoing the dissent in *Packard Motors*, emphasized that management and labor were basic opposing forces, with employees allied with one or the other. For those allied with management, collective bargaining was not appropriate and would work a "fundamental change in industrial philosophy" because "it would eviscerate the traditional distinction between labor and management."

The Court was more explicit in *Yeshiva*. The exclusion of supervisory and managerial employees, said the Court, "grow[s] out of the same concern; that an employer is entitled to the undivided loyalty of its representatives." Collective bargaining, in the Court's view, was inconsistent with loyalty to the institution. "Faculty members enhance their own standing and fulfill their professional mission by ensuring that the university's objectives are met," said the Court. The faculty and the university share a common goal, "the quest for academic excellence and institutional distinction." It is because "the faculty's professional interests – as applied to governance at a university like Yeshiva – can not be separated from those of the institution" that collective bargaining by the faculty was contrary to the purposes of the statute. In short, collective bargaining requires adverse interests and divided loyalty; common interests and loyalty to the goals of the institution make collective bargaining inappropriate.

This conception of collective bargaining as an entirely adversary relationship which is inappropriate when employees and management have common interests in the enterprise leaves little room for industrial democracy as a function of collective bargaining. Shared decision making presupposes some unifying loyalty and common goals. The Court has, without discussion or understanding, acted on an unnecessary and unfortunate conception that forecloses any consideration of industrial democracy as one of the purposes of the statute.

Again, sole responsibility cannot be placed on the Court. Congress has given no clear direction. More important, employers' bitter resistance to unionization and the unions' response in organizing campaigns create a climate of hostility and distrust that carries over to the bargaining relationship. This is sharpened by the political battles between union and management over labor legislation. Collective bargaining in the United States is, in practice, predominantly adversarial, and the Court's decisions largely reflect existing realities. The Court's failure is to see what collective bargaining should be, and sometimes is, to achieve the purposes of the statute. The Court has led the evolution of collective bargaining toward conflict of interest, indeed insisted on it, rather than toward shared decision making and industrial democracy.

The Forgotten Purpose of Industrial Democracy

The Supreme Court has failed to promote or strengthen industrial democracy largely because it has forgotten this purpose of the statute. It is a telling fact that in the fifty years since the passage of the National Labor Relations Act the Supreme Court has only twice made passing reference to "industrial democracy."[40] In contrast, the Court has relied repeatedly upon the statutory purpose of promoting industrial peace, a purpose which is often but a foil to justify its decision.

The Court has not merely forgotten, but deliberately disowned, the goal of industrial democracy. In *First National Maintenance* the Court declared, "Congress had no expectation that the elected union representation would become an equal partner in the running of the business enterprise in which the union's members are employed." After genuflecting to the "fundamental aim" of the act as "the establishment of and maintenance of industrial peace," it cast the equation of weighing "the employer's need for unencumbered decision-making" for "the running of a profitable business" against "the benefit for labor-management relations and the collective bargaining process." No mention was made of the right of employees to have a voice in the decision to close an operation on which their lives depended, nor of the statutory purpose of industrial democracy. Those values had no weight; management prerogatives and profitability prevailed.

In *Yeshiva*, the denial of industrial democracy was less explicit but more profound. The union involved had as its declared policy that where it acted as collective bargaining representative it would, in addition to seeking better salaries and economic benefits, seek to establish a system of faculty governance for the institution, much as

---

40. *AFL v. American Sash & Door Co.*, 335 U.S. 538 at 548 (1949) and *Bay Ridge Operating Co., Inc. v. Aaron*, 334 U.S. 446 at 494 (1948).

Yeshiva University and many other universities had. That policy was based explicitly on the union's long-standing goal of creating democratic structures within institutions of higher learning – the college professor's version of industrial democracy. The Court's decision turned the statutory purpose on its head. Where there was industrial democracy, collective bargaining was not appropriate. If collective bargaining succeeded in establishing a measure of industrial democracy, the employees became managers and were no longer entitled to bargain collectively. Indeed, in another university exactly this happened. When the union was organized the school had no meaningful system of faculty governance and one of the arguments used to persuade faculty members to join the union was to establish such a system. When the union won bargaining rights and was certified, it negotiated a faculty governance provision in the collective agreement and implemented that provision with faculty committees similar to Yeshiva. The NLRB, following the 'eshiva decision, ruled that the faculty had now become managers and were no longer entitled to collective representation. The fulfillment of one of the purposes of collective bargaining required its destruction.

This harsh criticism of the Court should be tempered with acknowledgment that the Court is not alone in forgetting this original purpose of the statute. When the statute was amended in 1947, there was no discussion of this purpose, and there has been little academic writing and no public discussion of industrial democracy in the United States. Not even the unions have promoted the idea nor urged legislation in its name. The prevailing interest in industrial democracy in Europe has not been imported or become common in the American marketplace of ideas. It is the forgotten premise of American labor law.

Democracy in the Employee Representation

Industrial democracy requires democratic unions. An employee can have no voice in the decisions governing his working life unless he has an effective voice in the decisions of the union that represents him. There is more than a touch of irony in the fact that the United States, which has been less concerned with establishing industrial democracy than many European countries, has been far more concerned with guaranteeing by law democratic processes in unions. The so-called Landrum-Griffin Act of 1959 seeks to insure basic democratic rights for members in their union, reinforce democratic decision making, and require free and open elections. One of the explicit arguments for this legislation was, in the words of one of its chief proponents, that "the justification and certainly the desirability of unionization is that the individual worker in an industrial economy has little or no power when he stands alone. . . . It is through unionization and collective bargaining that he is able to make himself heard at the bargaining table. It becomes clear that this justification becomes meaningless when the individual worker is just as helpless within his union as he was within his industry."[41]

The Supreme Court has, in interpreting this statute, generally given effective protection to democratic processes in unions. It has voided union elections and required them to be rerun because qualifications for becoming a candidate were structured to exclude challenges and favor existing officers or candidates supported by the administration[42] or to exclude 90 percent of the members.[43] It has set aside elections because a small amount of union funds was used to support the campaign of the incumbent officers.[44] In these cases the Court recognized the advantages held by the incumbents and the dangers of abuse by entrenched leadership. It interpreted the statute to protect opposition groups and limit the disadvantage of challengers.

Perhaps the most important practical contribution of the Court to union democracy was its decision in *Hall v. Cole*,[45] which held that union members who were successful in suits enforcing their own democratic rights were entitled to recover their lawyer's fees from the union. Without this many of the statutory rights would have had little practical value for few union members could afford the legal fee to enforce their rights. The rationale of the Court, however, reached far beyond this practical consideration to the fundamental importance of democratic rights. The member, said

41. Statement by Senator McChellan on introducing his bill of rights amendment to S. 1555. 105 Cong. Rec. 6471–6 (1959).
42. *Wirtz v. Hotel, Motel And Club Employees Union, Local 6*, 391, U.S. 492 (1968).
43. *Local 3489, United Steelworkers of America v. Usery*, 429 U.S. 305 (1977).
44. *Hodgson v. Local 6799, United Steelworkers of America*, 403 U.S. 333 (1971).
45. 412 U.S. 1 (1973).

the Court, "by vindicating his own right of free speech . . . necessarily rendered a substantial service to the union as an institution and to all of its members. . . . By vindicating his own right, the successful litigant dispels the 'chill' cast upon the rights of others."

The Supreme Court's record, however, is not unmarred. In two recent cases the Court refused to protect challengers from the iron fist of the ruling oligarchy. In *Finnegan v. Leu*,[46] the Court upheld a union president's dismissal of a staff employee because the staff member had not supported the president in a union election. This tightens the officer's grip on the staff and insures him the solid support of those who are in a position to be politically influential, thereby increasing his advantage over challengers. In *Steelworkers v. Sadlowski*,[47] the Court upheld a union rule prohibiting candidates from accepting campaign funds from anyone but union members. Its effect is to cut off some of the important sources of funds of challengers, while leaving untouched the primary source of the incumbent, which is "voluntary" contributions from the staff and paid employees. The Court seemed to lose sight of the special need for achieving a measure of democratic responsiveness and meaningful elections in a one-party bureaucratic organization.

Conclusion

There is little need for summary or conclusions. They are painfully obvious. The role of the Supreme Court in industrial democracy has been to forget one of the central purposes of the National Labor Relations Act, to reach results that do not merely fail to foster, but frustrate, curtail, and ultimately deny industrial democracy as a statutory purpose or social value. The Supreme Court has contributed its share to the result that, in the United States today, there is less industrial democracy than there was forty years ago. We now have more democracy in unions and less democracy in the workplace.

46. 456 U.S. 431 (1982).
47. 457 U.S. 102 (1982).

17

The *Bundesverfassungsgericht* and Industrial Democracy after the Second World War

Ingwer Ebsen

Introduction

If one wishes to discuss the jurisdiction of the *Bundesverfassungsgericht* with respect to "industrial democracy" under the main heading "Constitution and Change in Industrial Societies," questions then arise as to what is meant by these terms.

The notion of "industrial democracy" can be differentiated from "economic democracy" (*Wirtschaftsdemokratie*), which is an older and more established term[1] in Germany, by excluding the macroeconomic level of decision.[2] Thus the notion includes the codetermination of the employees at the workplace, in the plant, and on the enterprise level.[3] In connection with this, industrial democracy can represent the entire field of collective industrial relations insofar as employee and employer representation is concerned and the labor contract relations are overlapped by regulations produced by the organizations of labor and capital.

The jurisdiction of the *Bundesverfassungsgericht* shall be examined with respect to these industrial relations. However, since the relevant constitutional and statutory provisions as well as the competencies

---

1. See the publication for the 1928 Hamburg conference of the *Allgemeiner Deutscher Gewerkschaftsbund*, by Fritz Naphtali, ed., *Wirtschaftsdemokratie: Ihr Wesen, Weg und Ziel* (Hamburg, 1966/68).
2. Meaning by exclusion of codetermination at the regional and national levels as it is contained in the union concept of economic and social councils (*Wirtschafts- und Sozialräte*); see, e.g., Gerhard Leminsky and Bernd Otto, *Politik und Programm des Deutschen Gewerkschaftsbundes* (Cologne, 1974), 147f.
3. See also Fritz Vilmar, "Wirtschaftsdemokratie: Theoretische und praktische Ansätze, entwickelt auf der Basis des gewerkschaftlichen Grundsatzprogrammes in der BRD," in Fritz Vilmar, ed., *Menschenwürde im Betrieb: Modelle der Humanisierung und Demokratisierung der industriellen Arbeitswelt*, 2 vols. (Reinbeck, 1973–75), 2: 26f.

and functions of the *Bundesverfassungsgericht* form the setting without which the role of the court in the field of industrial relations cannot be properly evaluated, they will be outlined beforehand.

In considering the impact of the *Bundesverfassungsgericht* upon industrial democracy (the enforcing or impeding of employee codetermination), the analysis of the court's jurisdiction will show that, in general, the court has exercised a specific judicial restraint in this field and has left the principal structuring to the legislature and to the labor courts. It has instead played an active role in maintaining and enforcing the strict equality of opportunity between competing labor associations. This tendency will finally be related to the general dispositions[4] of the *Bundesverfassungsgericht*.

The Legal Regulation of Industrial Relations in the Federal Republic of Germany

The Basic Law (Grundgesetz)

Particularly with respect to the subject of this paper, the basic law is the result of a political compromise. The fathers of the basic law (*Grundgesetz*) agreed upon precisely structuring liberal rights in opposition to state power as well as to the organization and process rules of political democracy. They did not agree, however, on the socioeconomic structure[5] of the society to be established. They chose rather to compromise and left the structuring of this to the decisions of the changing legislative majorities.[6] Thus, in the basic law, we have hardly any rules concerning the economic order as they were rudimentarily framed in the Weimar Constitution of 1919 (Articles 151–65) and in some constitutions of the states (*Länder*), for example, Articles 27–47 of the Constitution of the State of Hesse.

4. I.e., probable tendencies of action under certain conditions; cf. Ingwer Ebsen, *Das Bundesverfassungsgericht als Element gesellschaftlicher Selbstregulierung: Eine pluralistische Theorie der Verfassungsgerichtsbarkeit im demokratischen Verfassungsstaat* (Berlin, 1985), 215, 320.

5. Cf. Deputy Theodor Heuss, *Parlamentarischer Rat: Stenographischer Bericht über die 12. Sitzung der Vollversammlung des Parlamentarischen Rats*, 44, 45.

6. See, e.g., Werner Soergel, *Konsensus und Interessen: Eine Studie zur Entstehung des Grundgesetzes für die Bundesrepublik Deutschland*, Frankfurter Studien zur Wissenschaft von der Politik, 5 (Stuttgart, 1969), passim.

Nevertheless, the basic law contains some rules concerning economic life, in particular, industrial relations. Among the basic rights (*Grundrechte*) are: Article 9, section 1 (freedom of association); Article 9, section 3 (guarantee of the right to form associations for advancing the conditions of labor and the economy); Article 12 (freedom of vocation and a ban on forced labor); Article 14 (guarantee of private property combined with the expression of its social responsibility and the authorization of the legislature to define the content and limits of property); and Article 15 (which is not a basic right, but empowers the legislature to nationalize land, natural resources, and the means of production in exchange for compensation).

Moreover, the basic law establishes – this is the realization of the compromise to leave the socioeconomic structure to the simple legislative majorities on the federal level – far-reaching competencies for the federal legislature, namely, legislative power for the following:

- Economic law (Article 74, no. 11)
- Labor law including the works constitution and the law for social security (Article 74, no. 12)
- Nationalization of property in the sense of Article 15 (Article 74, no. 15)

Finally, the basic law guarantees the principle of the social state (*Sozialstaatsprinzip*) in a very prominent position in the Constitution: Article 20, section 1, which is particularly protected against change by Article 79, section 3. By using the term "social state," the basic law applies a word that, through its origin and original sense, is connected with the idea of the reformist branch of the labor movement to add social democracy to political democracy.[7]

7. The social-democratic member of the Parliamentary Council (Parlamentarischer Rat) Carlo Schmid spoke of the courage of drawing the social consequences from the postulates of democracy (Session of the plenary meeting on May 6, 1949, *Parlamentarischer Rat: Stenographischer Bericht*, 172); see also Werner Weber, *Spannungen und Kräfte im westdeutschen Verfassungssystem* (Berlin, 1970), 240. For historical background see Hermann Heller, "Rechtsstaat oder Diktatur?" (1929), in Hermann Heller, *Gesammelte Schriften*, 3 vols. (Leiden, 1971), 1: 443. The *Bundesverfassungsgericht* has also referred to this background and has spoken of the "ideal of social democracy in the forms of *Rechtsstaat*" (cf. BVerfGE 5, 85 [198]; references in BVerfGE 40, 121 [133]; 52, 303 [348]).

However, the term is so void of context that understanding it denotes nothing more than an option for constitutional development by means of constitutional decisions and jurisprudence.[8]

Thus, the basic law does not contain a program or even an applicable rule for industrial democracy or "parity of capital and labor" insofar as this goes beyond the "freedom of association of employees and employers" and the guarantee of an effective system of collective bargaining, including the right to strike. On the constitutional level, these concepts are political slogans but are not constitutional aims. On the other hand – this is the constitutional compromise – economic and industrial democracy are legitimate political aims, to be effected by simple legislation if the constitution (particularly the basic rights) is respected. Obviously this restriction can be a source of constitutional conflict if, by means of simple legislation, attempts are made to implement forms of economic or industrial democracy.

Federal Legislation

According to the broad notion of industrial democracy introduced above, one has to look for legislation that contains elements of codetermination of employees and the inclusion of unions in such codetermination. Above and beyond that, the elements of industrial autonomy and self-administration can be regarded as related to the idea of industrial democracy. Such elements are contained in the autonomy of collective bargaining and the equality of the bargaining parties. They are also included in the various provisions of participation of employee and employer representatives in public organizations and administrative bodies and even in the labor and social courts.

The most important federal statutes relating to the subject are the following:

8. According to the jurisdiction of the *Bundesverfassungsgericht* the social state principle has "relevance for the interpretation of basic rights and for the interpretation and constitutional estimation of statutes limiting basic rights according to a proviso (*Gesetzesvorbehalt*)" (BVerfGE 59, 231 [262f.]). But, according to the *Bundesverfassungsgericht*, "as a consequence of its vagueness [the principle] regularly [did] not contain an immediate direction" (BVerfGE 65, 182 [193]). It conferred a duty on the state, but said nothing about how to fulfill it in detail (BVerfGE 59, 231 [263]).

1. Collective agreement law of 1949 (*Tarifvertragsgesetz*):[9] Autonomy of collective bargaining is secured by empowering the parties to establish regulations that are immediately valid for their members; the possibility of extending the effect of the collective agreement to nonmembers ("outsiders") by a governmental declaration of general validity (*Allgemeinverbindlichkeitserklärung*); the limitation of this autonomy to labor unions, employers, and associations of employers.

2. Law concerning the codetermination of employees in the supervisory boards (*Aufsichtsräte*) and executive boards (*Vorstände*) of mining corporations and the iron and steel industry of 1951 (*Montanmitbestimmungsgesetz*):[10] Equal representation of employees on the supervisory board, with a union right of proposal for some employee seats and a neutral chairman of the board, is guaranteed. A member of the executive board, who cannot be elected without the assent of the workers' (employees') representative (*Arbeitsdirektor*), is guaranteed as well. The provisions of this statute were extended by a statute of 1956[11] to the departments of corporations that control corporations falling under the *Montanmitbestimmungsgesetz*, if the turnover is more than half that of the combined corporations.

3. Works-constitution law of 1952 (*Betriebsverfassungsgesetz*):[12] The works council (*Betriebsrat*) is to be elected by the staff, which consists of salaried and wage-earning employees. It has the right to be informed, to be heard, and to participate in the decision-making process for various subjects. The workers have the right to a one-third-parity representation in the supervisory board of corporations. This also empowers the establishment of regulations within the plant with the assent of both the works council and the employer (*Betriebsvereinbarung*).

4. Works-constitution law of 1972:[13] This replaces the works-constitution law of 1952, with the exception of the regulations regarding employee representation on the supervisory board. The codetermination rights of the works council are extended.

9. In the form of the publication of August 25, 1969 (BGBl. I, 1323).
10. BGBl. I, 347.
11. *Gesetz zur Ergänzung des Mitbestimmungsgesetzes* of August 7, 1956 (BGBl. I, 707).
12. BGBl. I, 681.
13. BGBl. I, 13.

Unions having members among the workers have a limited right of access.

5. Codetermination law of 1976 (*Mitbestimmungsgesetz*):[14] Numerical parity representation of workers on the supervisory boards of corporations with more than two thousand employees is guaranteed. But this has the effect of nonequal representation because at least one seat is guaranteed to a representative of the upper-level salaried employees and also because voting within the supervisory boards is controlled by means of regulations.

Besides these statutes, there are also regulations pertaining to this subject in other statutes which do not have industrial democracy as their focus (for example, for members of the works councils there is a specific protection against being given notice by the employer in the notice protection law [*Kündigungsschutzgesetz*][15]). The social self-administration of for the most part equal representation of employees and employers in branches of social security organizations is laid down in the fourth book of the Social Security Act of 1976.[16] Finally, it is to be pointed out that important parts of the body of law with respect to industrial relations – almost the entire body of the law with respect to labor conflict – is not regulated by statute, but is based for the most part on precedents set by the federal labor court (*Bundesarbeitsgericht*).[17]

Jurisdiction and Function of the *Bundesverfassungsgericht* as a Restriction to the Judication of Industrial Relations

There are three main reasons why the *Bundesverfassungsgericht* is prevented from giving meaningful and detailed shape to the system of industrial relations. First, it is not primarily the *Bundesverfassungsgericht*, but the labor courts and, to a degree, the social courts that have to apply, and thus shape in detail, the statutes concerning this subject. Therefore they have to develop precedents for cases for

14. BGBl. I, 1153.
15. See n. 9, 1317.
16. BGBl. I, 3845.
17. See, e.g., Hans Brox und Bernd Rüthers, *Arbeitskampfrecht: Ein Handbuch für die Praxis* (Stuttgart, 1982).

which there are no applicable statutes. The *Bundesverfassungsgericht* is confronted with the law of industrial relations only if:

1. A party who has lost before the labor or social courts in the last instance files a constitutional complaint (*Verfassungsbeschwerde*)
2. A court is convinced of the unconstitutionality of a statute rule and puts the question to the *Bundesverfassungsgericht* (Article 100 GG: concrete judicial review)

The third possibility, the abstract judicial review upon petition of the federal government, a state government, or one-third of the members of the *Bundestag*, can be neglected because – at least in the last thirty-five years – a petition regarding the subject discussed here has not been filed.[18] Already this restriction by competency of the *Bundesverfassungsgericht* has an effect in the field of industrial relations that is sporadic and more or less random.

Second, the *Bundesverfassungsgericht* decisions are limited to using the basic law as its standard (with the exception of examining state law on the basis of federal law). And this, as we have seen, does not contain many rules referring to industrial relations. Furthermore, the perspective in which the *Bundesverfassungsgericht* exercises its judication in this field is narrowed by the fact that constitutional complaints must be based upon the violation of basic rights and that, in cases of concrete judicial review, the constitutional question in the original case before the court that brought the question to the *Bundesverfassungsgericht* must be decisive.[19]

Third, there is a connection between legislation and the number of constitutional disputes likely to be brought before the *Bundesverfassungsgericht*. As the basic law does not contain explicit directives for the development of industrial relations in a particular direction, constitutional disputes derive primarily from legislatory activities, which have as their aim the changing of the status quo. Particularly with legislation enforcing employee and union codetermination, the question of its constitutionality will arise. In the past thirty-five years

18. The procedure for abstract law review in paragraph 116 of the employment promotion law (*Arbeitsförderungsgesetz*) in the form of the statute of May 15, 1986 (BGBl. I, 740) must, however, be pointed out.

19. Otherwise the petition will be rejected as unconstitutional, see Klaus Schlaich, *Das Bundesverfassungsgericht: Stellung, Verfahren, Entscheidungen* (Munich, 1985), 75.

there have not been many initiatives resulting in legislation that seriously raised the question of whether the limits of legislative discretion regarding the socioeconomic structure had been overstepped.

Considering these restrictions to constitutional jurisdiction in the field of industrial relations, it is not astonishing that, in relation to the more than two thousand panel decisions produced so far by the *Bundesverfassungsgericht*, there are only a small number dedicated to our subject. They shall be examined below.

But before these cases are discussed in detail, it must be pointed out that the reasons which may explain the small number of cases dedicated to industrial democracy cannot explain the relatively low range of constitutional law based upon precedents in this field. For the *Bundesverfassungsgericht* has the factual[20] choice, either to stick strictly to those constitutional questions which cannot be avoided for the decisions of the case or to utter more or less far-reaching obiter dicta which actually are respected in nearly the same way as those dicta that undoubtedly belong to the *ratio decidendi*.[21] And when, in several fields, the *Bundesverfassungsgericht* did use this elbowroom for an extensive development of law based upon precedents,[22] the question of more or less judicial restraint became an important aspect in the following survey of cases.

Decisions of the *Bundesverfassungsgericht* in the Field of Industrial Democracy

The seventy-two volumes of decisions of the *Bundesverfassungsgericht* were surveyed by means of the following criteria, insofar as

20. For the question of admissibility of obiter dicta see Wilfried Schlüter, *Das Obiter Dictum: Die Grenzen höchstrichterlicher Entscheidungsbegründung, dargestellt an Beispielen aus der Rechtsprechung des Bundesarbeitsgerichtes*, Schriften des Instituts für Arbeits- und Wirtschaftsrecht der Universität zu Köln, 29 (Munich, 1973), 57ff.; Brun-Otto Bryde, *Verfassungsentwicklung: Stabilität und Dynamik im Verfassungsrecht der Bundesrepublik Deutschland* (Baden-Baden, 1982), 373f.

21. For the correct interpretation of the grounds of *Bundesverfassungsgericht* decisions in the lawmaking process see Jürgen Jekewitz, "Bundesverfassungsgericht und Gesetzgeber: Zu den Vorwirkungen von Existenz und Rechtsprechung des Bundesverfassungsgerichts in dem Bereich der Gesetzgebung," *Der Staat* 19 (1980): 354ff.; Christine Landfried, *Bundesverfassungsgericht und Gesetzgeber: Wirkungen der Verfassungsrechtsprechung auf parlamentarischer Willensbildung und soziale Realität* (Baden-Baden, 1982), 51ff.

22. See Ebsen, *Das Bundesverfassungsgericht als Element gesellschaftlicher Selbstregulierung* (see n. 4), 103.

they were subjects of the court's argumentation:

- Collective industrial relations[23]
- Field of social self-government[24]
- Overlapping of politics and industrial relations
- Constitutional structures and regulating principles of the economy (*Wirtschaftsverfassung*) with reference to industrial democracy

This means that cases which derived from the sector of industrial relations, but were decided without any reference to it (for example, disallowance of a constitutional complaint or a submission by a court as inadmissible), were left out, whereas cases in which the court made obiter dicta relevant to the subject were included. Although industrial democracy and industrial relations usually do not refer to the sector of the civil service, cases concerning employee representation in the civil service are included because, on the constitutional level, most of the decisions of the *Bundesverfassungsgericht* on that matter have relevance to employee representation in the economic sector. The approximately thirty decisions fulfilling these criteria can be classified into four groups:

- Employee codetermination versus freedom of enterprise and comparable positions
- Statutes and relations of the parties in the collective bargaining system
- Union rights at the workplace
- Competition between labor associations[25]

Codetermination versus Freedom of Enterprise and Comparable Positions

The claims of the employees and their unions to codetermination in

23. I.e., excluding individual labor contract cases.
24. Meaning the field of public bodies with self-government on the basis of employee and employer representation.
25. The cases selected in this way are mainly the same as those commented upon in the reports on the jurisdiction of the *Bundesverfassungsgericht* by Wolfgang Zöllner, "Die Rechtsprechung des Bundesverfassungsgerichts zu Artikel 9 Abs. 3 Grundgesetz," *Archiv des öffentlichen Rechts* 98 (1973): 71ff.; and by Hugo Seiter, "Die Rechtsprechung des Bundesverfassungsgerichts zu Art. 9 Abs. 3 Grundgesetz,"

the enterprise and on the plant level is necessarily in direct conflict to the claims of the owners to undisturbed control of their property (as well as undisturbed business decisions). On the constitutional level, this conflict finds its expression in a tension between the guarantee of property and its social responsibility, which has to be established by means of legislation. The borderline of legislatory discretion in this field is the chief question of economic constitution as the epitome of constitutional rules with relevance to the structures of the economic system. In addition to this main point there are, in special sectors, particular constitutional positions effecting further limitations to employees' codetermination. This is the case with news-media enterprises, where in addition to the guarantee of private property the freedom of the press (Article 5, section 1 GG) must be considered, as well as with the establishment of churches or other religious societies, which are granted a particular status of autonomy by Article 140 GG, which incorporates into the basic law the articles of the Weimar Constitution referring to churches.[26]

Codetermination and Freedom of Enterprise

This basic problem was at the center of the spectacular case in connection with the *Mitbestimmungsgesetz* of 1976. Beside that, the *Bundesverfassungsgericht* made some obiter dicta on the subject and had, in two cases, to decide on issues that raised the question of whether the established status of employee influence had to be overturned for constitutional reasons.

Obiter Dicta on Industrial Democracy as a Constitutional Question

– BVerfGE 11, 310 – Guild Sickness Funds
In this case, which dealt with the constitutionality of the varied employee participation in the founding of works sickness funds (*Betriebskrankenkassen*) and guild sickness funds (*Innungskrankenkassen*), the *Bundesverfassungsgericht* pointed out the difference between

---

Archiv des öffentlichen Rechts 109 (1984): 88ff.
26. Particularly Art. 137, sec. 3 GG: "Jede Religionsgesellschaft ordnet und verwaltet ihre Angelegenheiten selbständig innerhalb der Schranken des für alle geltenden Gesetzes. Sie verleiht ihre Ämter ohne Mitwirkung des Staates oder der bürgerlichen Gemeinde." (Every religious organization is permitted to order and regulate their affairs without interference within the bounds of the law binding on everyone. They are allowed to confer religious offices without the intervention of the state or any civic communities.)

the legal situation under the Weimar Constitution and under the basic law. While Article 161 of the Weimar Constitution postulated an "overall social insurance system with the decisive influence of the insured,"[27] the basic law – according to the *Bundesverfassungsgericht* – neither explicitly demands self-government in social insurance nor can this be deduced from the principle of democracy. The social state principle is not mentioned by the Court. This decision, which is an example of relatively strict construction, has relevance for industrial codetermination, too, because the stated difference between the Weimar Constitution and the basic law is true for the other demands of the Weimar Constitution regarding the economic order as well. This is particularly the case for the program of codetermination on the plant, enterprise, and national level in Article 165 of the Weimar Constitution.[28]

– BVerfGE 12, 354 – Volkswagen Denationalization
In this decision, too, the *Bundesverfassungsgericht* refused to develop constitutional principles by means of broad interpretation. On the occasion of constitutional complaints against the criteria for the disposal of shares with the partial denationalization of the Volkswagen Company,[29] the *Bundesverfassungsgericht* made general remarks concerning the constitutionality of denationalization and came to the not surprising conclusion that this step was at the discretion of the legislature. Particularly, Article 15 GG was not

27. Art. 161: "Zur Erhaltung der Gesundheit und Arbeitsfähigkeit, zum Schutz der Mutterschaft und zur Vorsorge gegen die wirtschaftlichen Folgen von Alter, Schwäche und Wechselfällen des Lebens schafft das Reich ein umfassendes Versicherungswesen unter maßgebender Mitwirkung der Versicherten." (The government establishes a comprehensive insurance system which includes the active participation of the insured in order to preserve the health and working ability of its citizens, to protect motherhood, and to prevent the negative financial results of old age, infirmity, and the other vicissitudes of life.)

28. Art. 165, sec. 1: "Die Arbeiter und Angestellten sind dazu berufen, gleichberechtigt in Gemeinschaft mit den Unternehmern an der Regelung der Lohn- und Arbeitsbedingungen sowie an der gesamten wirtschaftlichen Entwicklung der produktiven Kräfte mitzuwirken." (Wage earning and salaried employees are called upon to participate equally and actively in the collective bargaining with the entrepreneur with respect to wages and working conditions as well as the economic development of their labor.) This program is then specified in more detail in the rest of the article.

29. The Volkswagen Company had been owned by the Deutsche Arbeitsfront, which had been dissolved by Allied order. Before the denationalization, the ownership produced a controversy between the Federal Republic and the state of Lower Saxony.

found to be impeding, as this regulation contained no constitutional principle with respect to nationalization, but instead, an authorization.

– BVerfGE 51, 43 – Participation of the Staff Committee
In a case of concrete judicial review of a regulation in the Bavarian staff representation law, in certain cases of notice by the public employer the staff council did not even have a right to be heard. The *Bundesverfassungsgericht* held this regulation to be constitutional and briefly stated that no right of staff participation in cases of notice by the public employers could be deduced from the basic law. Since this statement was not based on the particularities of the civil service, a generalization with respect to the private sector of the economy is also possible.

Altogether, these obiter dicta show that the *Bundesverfassungsgericht* has accepted the decision of the Parliamentary Council (Parlamentarischer Rat) not to determine the socioeconomic structure of the Federal Republic by constitutional means and has not been inclined to develop constitutional principles with regard to industrial democracy. Whether the court also upholds this openness of the Constitution in cases of legislatory reforms toward more industrial codetermination was the question which made the case of the codetermination law of 1976 the "cause célèbre" of the economic constitution.

The Codetermination Judgment – A Landmark Decision on the Economic System

– BVerfGE 50, 290 – Codetermination Law
In this case – presumably the most spectacular constitutional conflict with respect to industrial self-government – the *Bundesverfassungsgericht* had to decide on the constitutionality of the main provisions of the codetermination law (*Mitbestimmungsgesetz*) of 1976. The court had been barraged by a multitude of constitutional complaints and by a petition for concrete judicial review. The codetermination law had been politically controversial for a long time, with the issue of equal determination by labor and capital at the center of the controversy. The result was extended codetermination which, however, remained under the threshold of full equality.

On the one hand, for corporations with more than two thousand employees, the statute decrees a numerically equal employee representation on the supervisory board, which has to appoint the members of the executive board. On the other hand, the chairman of the supervisory board, who in the case of a stalemate, has the deciding vote, is either to be elected by a two-thirds majority or, if this majority is not reached, by the stockholders' representatives alone. Furthermore, among the employee representatives there must be at least one member of the board who is elected by the group of upper-level salaried employees and will usually have more affinity to the capital than to the labor side.[30] In spite of this unequal representation, which did not make it probable that the court would declare the statute void, the judgment was awaited with great interest because it was hoped and feared that dicta on the essentially crucial point, the real parity of labor and capital, would be made. The *Bundesverfassungsgericht* elegantly evaded that decision and declared the codetermination law constitutional without issuing a statement on the constitutionality of real parity.

In spite of this restraint, the judgment is of great general importance because the court refused to develop principles based upon the basic rights and other provisions of the basic law, which contained more restrictions to legislative reforms in the economic sector than could be deduced exclusively from the basic rights as guarantees of personal freedoms. Through this fundamental decision on the level of constitutional theory, the *Bundesverfassungsgericht* upheld the principle of openness of the Constitution to legislative changes of the socioeconomic status quo.

Acceptance of the Achieved Level of Codetermination

What the following two cases have in common is that in both the *Bundesverfassungsgericht* had to decide on matters relevant to the distribution of inner-enterprise and inner-plant power on the basis of constitutional provisions without reference to industrial relations. The court upheld the status quo of codetermination.

– BVerfGE 25, 371 – *lex Rheinstahl*
According to the *Montanmitbestimmungsgesetz* of 1951 the supervis-

---

30. On the question of leading employees see BVerfGE 59, 104.

ory board of corporations in the mining, iron, and steel industry is composed of equal numbers of labor and capital representatives, who have to elect a neutral chairman of the board. According to the statute of 1956, this real equal codetermination was extended to the holding corporations of combined corporations if the controlled corporations, which fall under the *Montanmitbestimmungsgesetz*, produce more than half of the total turnover. This extension would be nullified if in a period of two fiscal years the specific turnover fell short of this 50 percent limit. According to these provisions, the Rheinische Stahlwerke corporation was due to drop out of the equal codetermination regulations in 1967 but the two fiscal years' time was extended to five years in order to uphold the status quo. This statute – the so-called *lex Rheinstahl*[31] – was brought to the *Bundesverfassungsgericht* because it was seen as unconstitutionally retroactive and as an individual case statute that interfered with basic rights.[32] The case was prosecuted with great effort, which indicated its political significance. The *Bundestag* entered into the proceedings, which is relatively rare,[33] and several organizations were invited to give their opinions on the question. The court held the law to be constitutional, a decision that was not easy to make when one considers the question of retroactive effects. This can be viewed as a sign that the court was predisposed to uphold this law. It is interesting to note that the court explicitly left open the question of whether codetermination according to the *Montanmitbestimmungsgesetz* was in accordance with Article 14 GG (guarantee of private property).

– BVerfGE 59, 104 – Upper-Level Salaried Employees (Management)
In this case the relevance of the decision for the status quo of codetermination is not a surface issue. A district court submitted a concrete judicial review of the question of whether paragraph 5, section 3, no. 3 of the works constitution law of 1972 was unconstitutional because it was seen as a violation of the principle of rule clarity, which is an element of the *Rechtsstaat* principle. According

---

31. BGBl. I, 505.

32. This would have meant a violation of Art. 19, sec. 1 sentence 1.

33. See Ernst Benda, *Grundrechtswidrige Gesetze: Ein Beitrag zu den Ursachen verfassungsgerichtlicher Beanstandung*, Studien und Materialien zur Verfassungs-gerichtsbarkeit, 15 (Baden-Baden, 1979), 29f.

to that provision, the works constitution law is not applicable to upper-level salaried employees if "they for the most part independently perform tasks that are regularly entrusted to them because of their importance for the existence and the development of the enterprise with regard to their particular experiences and accomplishments."

The sociopolitical background of this seemingly rather theoretical question was that the federal labor court had developed a strict construction view of that provision which excluded only a small number of employees from the application of the works constitution law. Thus, on the one hand the number of employees, who are within the realm of participation rights of the works council, was kept large, and on the other hand the group of upper-level employees with particular representation according to the codetermination law of 1976 was kept small. The *Bundesverfassungsgericht* regarded the provision as sufficiently clear and capable of being carried out, characteristics which, in the eyes of the court, had been proven by the federal labor court's jurisdiction. In this way the *Bundesverfassungsgericht* supported that jurisdiction without, however, evaluating it in any respect.

Conclusion

When examining the general tendency of the *Bundesverfassungsgericht's* jurisdiction on the fundamentals of codetermination, it is obvious that the court has exercised judicial restraint toward legislation. This is true for the question of potential constitutional directives toward more industrial democracy, and it is true with regard to the construction of constitutional barriers to legislation. And it is an expression of restraint, too, that the court has not intervened in the given balance of power in the field of industrial relations.

The Special Position of the Press

In the press enterprises, we find on the one hand the same interest of the employed in codetermination that is found in the rest of the economy. On the other hand, the press enterprises exercise the freedom of the press, which is guaranteed by Article 5, section 1 GG. This fact has already been acknowledged by the legislature, who in paragraph 118, section 1, no. 2 of the works constitution law excluded press enterprises from the application of that statute in so far as the special position of the enterprise or the plant demands an exception. This extended enterprise autonomy of publishers against labor codetermination was supported by the *Bundesverfassungsgericht* with constitutional arguments.

– BVerfGE 52, 283 – Notice in Press Enterprise
While the position of the press according to simple legislation is no question to be put before the *Bundesverfassungsgericht*, the court, on the occasion of this case, took the opportunity to issue statements on the limitation of codetermination demanded by Article 5, section 1 GG. The federal labor court had declared void an employer's notice to a member of the editorial staff because the works council had not been able to review it. In respect to the constitutional complaint of the publisher, the *Bundesverfassungsgericht* stated that the freedom of the press contained the guarantee to determine and change the point of view of the newspaper without the influence of the works council because the basic right of freedom of the press was not applicable to the council. However, the actual constitutional complaint was rejected since the court did not regard the works council as influencing the point of view of the paper if the publisher had to consult the council before giving a member of the editorial staff notice. By this obiter dictum[34] the *Bundesverfassungsgericht* made clear that the special position of press enterprises is not only based on simple legislation, but is guaranteed by the Constitution. The court explicitly left open the question of whether codetermination of the editorial staff with reference to the tendency of the paper would be constitutional.

The Special Position of the Churches

The churches, too, have a special autonomy granted by the Constitution, which has been respected by legislation rendering the works constitution law not applicable to them and to their charitable and educational organizations at all (paragraph 118, section 2 of the works constitution law). In two decisions, the *Bundesverfas-*

34. Since in this case the *Bundesverfassungsgericht* denied any influence on the paper's tendency, the admissibility of such influence was not relevant to the decision.

sungsgericht decided for the special position of the churches and against claims to codetermination. In a third case concerning churches (BVerfGE 57, 220), the constitutional arguments are not limited only to this area. That case will be discussed later (under "Rights of Union Agents Not Belonging to the Plant").

– BVerfGE 46, 73 – Church Foundation
In the case of an old foundation established in the last century, what was controversial was whether the foundation, which ran a hospital, was a church establishment and therefore exempt from application of the works constitutional law. The federal labor court, in the last instance, had denied that qualification and had given the order to establish an electoral committee to arrange for the election of a works council. Due to constitutional complaint filed by the foundation, the *Bundesverfassungsgericht*, through interpretation of the wishes of the founder and consideration of the factual influence of the Catholic Church, qualified the hospital as a church establishment and overturned the decisions of the labor courts.

– BVerfGE 72, 278 – Vocational Training Committees
According to the vocational training law of 1969,[35] vocational training committees were to be installed as arms of the competent agency for the practice and supervision of vocational training. The members of the committee were to be appointed by the state; one-third were to be proposed by unions, one-third by the "competent agency," and one-third by the state. The churches are "competent agencies" for the vocation of a church administration clerk. In a case of concrete judicial review, the *Bundesverfassungsgericht* found it unconstitutional that the vocational training committee, as an arm of the church, was not installed by the decisive influence of the church itself. The legal provision in question was not a general law binding the churches as it would everyone else[36] because it did not consider sufficiently the autonomy of churches granted by the Constitution.

With both decisions, the *Bundesverfassungsgericht* enforced church autonomy in opposition to state interference and employee codetermination. On the one hand, the range of this autonomy was

35. BGBl. I, 1112.
36. This refers to Art. 137, sec. 3 of the Weimar Constitution.

extended to establishments with only mediate relations to a church (BVerfGE 46, 73). On the other hand, the legislatory competence to enact "laws, which are valid for everybody" (Article 137, section 3 of the Weimar Constitution), and are binding for churches too was interpreted in a rather restrictive way. This tendency of the *Bundesverfassungsgericht* to emphasize church autonomy is corroborated by a decision on individual labor contract law (BVerfGE 70, 138) in which the court confirmed the churches' right to demand very extensive loyalties from employees of their establishments, which would not be acceptable from a normal employer.

Status and Relations of the Parties of the Collective Bargaining System

The Bearers of Collective Bargaining Autonomy

One element of freedom of coalition (Article 9, section 3 GG) is collective bargaining autonomy authorizing the independent regulation of labor conditions.[37] Accordingly, which associations participate in this authority is important. The *Bundesverfassungsgericht* had to decide that question in several cases in which legislative and judicial forms (framings) of collective bargaining autonomy were attacked.

– BVerfGE 4, 96 – Economical Association
On the occasion of a marginal question, namely, the right to appear in labor lawsuits, the *Bundesverfassungsgericht* had its first opportunity to make fundamental statements on the freedom of coalition. The Bavarian state labor court refused an employee-member of the Economical Association, Bamberg Employers' Representation the right of representation before the labor court because of regulations that reserve this right for employee-members of associations capable of collective bargaining. This capacity was limited to branch associations of employers, whereas the "association of economy" was branch overlapping. In response to a constitutional complaint by this association, the *Bundesverfassungsgericht* first made clear that the freedom of coalition was a basic right not only of individuals, but also of industrial associations. It then deduced from Article 9,

37. See BVerfGE 20, 312 (317).

section 3 GG the guarantee that "a collective bargaining system in the sense of modern labor law has to be provided by the State and that collective agreements must be made by voluntarily organized associations."[38] Within the limits of that guarantee, the legislature was granted discretion, and it was found constitutional to reserve the capacity of collective bargaining for certain associations if the limitations of the capacity were appropriate. An exclusion of branch-overlapping associations was found to be acceptable.

– BVerfGE 18, 18 – Catholic Housemaids
While in BVerfGE 4, 96 exclusiveness with regard to branches was accepted as a condition of collective bargaining capacity, in this case the *Bundesverfassungsgericht* rejected the criterion of readiness to strike developed by the federal labor court as an element of the notion of "union" and as a condition of collective bargaining capacity of labor associations. All labor courts up to the federal labor court had declared void a collective agreement between the Bavarian section of a federal association of Catholic housemaids and lady housekeepers and the Bavarian section of a federal association of Catholic housewives because the housemaid association excluded strikes as an instrument of collective bargaining. In response to a constitutional complaint by the housemaid association, the *Bundesverfassungsgericht* overturned these decisions and stated that Article 9, section 3 GG was violated if the capacity of collective bargaining was made dependent upon the readiness of a housemaid association to strike. The court left open the question of whether willingness to engage in industrial conflict could be made a condition of the capacity of collective bargaining in other branches.

– BVerfGE 20, 312 – Trade Guilds
Once more, on the occasion of the question of the right to plead before labor courts, the *Bundesverfassungsgericht* had to decide on the constitutionality of a statute provision that gave collective bargaining capacity to trade guilds (voluntary associations of independent craftsmen of one trade in a certain district that are recognized under the law as a legal person having a legal monopoly for the district).[39] The provision was brought to the court in a case of concrete judicial

38. BVerfGE 4, 96 (106).
39. See paragraphs 52–85 of the *Handwerksordnung* in the form of the publication of December 28, 1965 (BGBl. 1966 I, 1).

review by the labor court of Hesse, which found that it violated the principle that industrial coalitions had to be free and voluntarily established. The *Bundesverfassungsgericht* upheld the provision without deciding whether or not trade guilds are coalitions in the sense of Article 9, section 3 GG. The freedom of coalition did not prevent the legislature from giving the collective bargaining capacity on the employer side to other institutions than associations in the sense of Article 9, section 3 GG, if such institutions essentially corresponded to free associations. This was the case with trade guilds and their federations.

– BVerfGE 58, 233 – Employee Association
The most important case in the field of collective bargaining capacity was a constitutional complaint against a decision of the federal labor court, which had refused the collective bargaining capacity of a labor association because it lacked sufficient power to exercise pressure on the employer. The *Bundesverfassungsgericht* rejected the complaint and thus affirmed the criterion of sufficient power. According to the court, those associations without sufficient power have the constitutional freedom of coalition but no bargaining power. This distinction was justified by an interesting parallel with political parties, the founding and activity of which is free, whereas their participation in parliaments can be made dependent upon limiting conditions (such as the 5 percent clause). This decision is remarkable, first of all, because it shows a certain contrast to the housemaid decision, second, because it strengthens the position of the established unions by raising the threshold for a break through of new unions, and third, because it extends to the labor side the consequence of BVerfGE 4, 96, that we have two sorts of coalitions in the sense of Article 9, section 3 GG: those with and those without participation in the autonomy of collective agreement.

Altogether, the *Bundesverfassungsgericht* has – with the exception of the housemaid case – accepted the legal and judicial forms of collective bargaining capacity. In view of the special situation of those employed as domestics, for whom strike is hardly possible anyway, there are nearly insurmountable factual difficulties. Thus the housemaid decision should not be regarded as a general case and the employee association decision cannot be regarded as a deviation.

Collective Bargaining Autonomy as Lawmaking Capacity

In three cases, the *Bundesverfassungsgericht* had the occasion to discuss the nature of collective agreement regulation and to relate it to state legislation.

– BVerfGE 34, 307 – Homework Committees

The first decision of the *Bundesverfassungsgericht* on lawmaking capacity as an element of collective bargaining autonomy does not concern the typical case of a collective agreement,[40] but the special case of settling work conditions by homework committees, based upon the homework law of 1951.[41] According to this statute, the competent labor agency installs homework committees for certain branches composed equally of representatives of the homeworkers and of the contractors. Under certain conditions these committees can conclude settlements of work conditions and of payments, which after the assent of the competent agency and after publication, have the effect of a collective agreement, having been declared generally valid. This provision was brought to the *Bundesverfassungsgericht* by means of a concrete judicial review on the grounds that it violated the principles of democracy and Rechtsstaat because the homework committees did not legitimately have the power to make laws. The *Bundesverfassungsgericht* rejected the petition. It argued that – by Article 9, section 3 GG – the state had granted autonomous lawmaking capacity to the collective bargaining parties and that for this reason it was constitutional too; because of the special situation in the homework sector, the legislature provided a system of lawmaking essentially similar to the collective agreement system.

– BVerfGE 44, 322 – Declaration of General Validity of Collective Agreements

The next decision, too, refers to a special case, the declaration of general validity of collective agreements by the government. Again upon a petition of concrete judicial review, the *Bundesverfassungsgericht* had to decide whether the provision of the collective agreement law, which allows the extension of the rules of a collective agreement to "outsiders" by declaration of general validity, is

---

40. According to paragraph 1 of the collective agreement law, see n. 9.
41. BGBl. I, 191.

unconstitutional because of noncompliance with the constitutional requirements of executive lawmaking. Again, the *Bundesverfassungsgericht* referred to the autonomous lawmaking capacity of industrial coalitions, which had to be regarded when evaluating the declaration of general validity as a specific act of lawmaking. The extension of the validity of collective agreements to outsiders was a means of lawmaking which came as near as possible to the intention of Article 9, section 3 GG. The combination of collective bargaining by the coalitions with the government declaration of validity for the outsiders was a constitutional means of balancing the principle of democracy and the freedom of coalition.

– BVerfGE 55, 7 – Joint Establishments
In this case, the *Bundesverfassungsgericht* applies and extends its pronouncements upon the constitutionality of declarations of general validity in BVerfGE 44, 322 to collective agreements in which joint establishments of the parties are installed. Joint establishments are private law corporations with immediate legal relations to the employers and employed for whom the collective agreement is applicable. The *Bundesverfassungsgericht* did not hesitate to accept as constitutional declarations of general validity for collective agreements on joint establishments.

The essential basis of this jurisdiction for lawmaking capacity is the interpretation of Article 9, section 3 GG, in the sense that the freedom of coalition contains lawmaking autonomy in the field of industrial relations. According to this interpretation, lawmaking by collective agreements becomes an independent model of regulation to which the constitutional provisions concerning state lawmaking are not applicable. Thus lawmaking by homework committees and by declaration of general validity of collective agreements can be regarded as mixed forms, which in so far as they do not comply with the rules for state lawmaking, can be justified by their closeness to the collective agreement model.

Industrial Conflict

– BVerfGE 38, 386 – Lockout of Works-Council Members
So far, only one decision of the *Bundesverfassungsgericht* deals with industrial conflict. This particular case concerns the problem of the admissibility of a lockout as a means of industrial conflict. In 1971

the federal labor court had overruled its former decision and decided that, in general, lockouts by a rescission of labor contracts were only admissible in exceptional situations and that members of the works council, in particular, could only be locked out by a limited suspension of their contract.[42] In a case where a constitutional complaint against a judgment of the federal labor court was based on this new jurisdiction, the *Bundesverfassungsgericht* had to decide whether the exclusion of contract dissolving lockouts of works-council members was constitutional. It was not surprising that the complaint was rejected, all the more because even the Federation of Employers' Associations, which like the unions had given its view on the question, held the restriction of lockout constitutional. The *Bundesverfassungsgericht* decided the case on grounds that are limited to its specific situation. So it did not make statements on the question of whether lockouts are guaranteed at all by the freedom of coalition. It only stated that the guaranteed core of the freedom of coalition was not infringed upon by only allowing a lockout of works-council members in the form of a contract suspension.

Since this single case on industrial conflict is so particular, generalizing conclusions can hardly be drawn; and because the court chose to abstain from obiter dicta, the field of industrial conflict is still without a basic ruling from the *Bundesverfassungsgericht*.

Chambers of Employees

– BVerfGE 38, 281 – Chambers of Employees
There is a certain link between the decision on the constitutionality of chambers of employees and the status of unions that is based on the question of whether such chambers violated the freedom of coalition. In the states of Bremen and Saarland the tradition of having chambers of employees goes back to the years just after the First World War. These chambers are public law corporations with compulsory membership, intended to further the interest of their members in economic, social, and cultural aspects and to support state agencies in various ways. They are financed by compulsory contributions from their members. In response to a constitutional complaint against compulsory membership and compulsory con-

42. BAG AP no. 43 to Art. 9 GG *Arbeitskampf*.

tributions, the *Bundesverfassungsgericht* decided that the freedom of coalition of unions and of individuals was not infringed upon and that the general freedom of the individual (Article 2, section 1 GG), which included the freedom not to be a compulsory member of any organization without good reason, was not violated because sufficient reasons could be found not to abolish the existing chambers. What was left open, however, was whether these reasons were sufficient to introduce such chambers, with their compulsory membership, in the other states of the Federal Republic. This argumentation reflects a certain skepticism toward the necessity for chambers of employees, and the decision shows that the court obviously aims not to intervene in the existing system of social self–government.

Union Rights of Access to the Plant

The possibility of union activities at the plant is essential for an effective organization of employees' interests. On the other hand, if such activities are not dependent upon the consent of the owners, it interferes with their property rights. With regard to this question, one must distinguish between the union activities of the employed and the access to and activities of union representatives, who do not belong to the plant staff. The *Bundesverfassungsgericht* has issued five decisions on the first subject and two decisions on the second subject.

Union Activities of the Employed

– BVerfGE 19, 303 – Union Publicity Prior to Staff Council Elections

This decision does not immediately concern industrial relations but involves the system of staff representation in the civil service. The case is also relevant for the private economic sector because of the parallel between public staff representation and works constitution, and particularly because of the corresponding position of the unions. A civil servant of the Federal Railways filed a constitutional complaint against a decision of the federal disciplinary court (*Bundesdisziplinargericht*), which had affirmed a disciplinary punishment for the distribution of handbills on the premises of the Federal

Railways; the leaflets contained promotions for the candidates of his union for a staff council election and also criticized a competing union. The *Bundesverfassungsgericht* overturned the judgment because of a violation of Article 9, section 3 GG. The essential argument is that a core of coalition–typical activities is an element of freedom of coalition, and at least prior to elections of employees' representatives, this includes a certain amount of union advertising at the plant.

– BVerfGE 28, 295 and BVerfGE 28, 310 – Union Membership
Promotions by Members of the Staff Council
In two parallel cases, the *Bundesverfassungsgericht* had to decide upon union membership information distributed by members of the staff council, who had been punished by the competent disciplinary and administrative courts with deprivation of membership on the staff council for violating their duty of neutrality. Referring to the jurisdiction over union rights at the plant, the *Bundesverfassungsgericht* included the right of union members to recruit at the plant. But the court found it constitutional to limit this right because staff council members have a duty to be neutral and for that reason they found that council members were not allowed to distribute advertisements at the plant. On these grounds the constitutional complaint was rejected.

– BVerfGE 42, 133 – Municipal Election Political
Advertisements Distributed by a Works-Council Member
While so far the *Bundesverfassungsgericht* had to decide upon union activities as forms of interunion competition, here we have a case of the overlapping of industrial and political democracy. Before a Bavarian municipal election, the chairman of a works council had distributed handbills at his plant which promoted the election of union members and contained the names of those electoral candidates who were members of the metal workers union. The candidates belonged to different parties. On petition of the employers, the Bavarian labor court had expelled him from the council for a violation of the prohibition against political activity at the plant. In response to his constitutional complaint, the *Bundesverfassungsgericht* overturned that decision on the grounds of a violation of the freedom of opinion (Article 5, section 1 GG). It did not find that this violated the freedom of coalition because this type of election

advertisement did not belong to coalition-typical activities. The question of whether the council member had acted illegally or not was left open. In any case, the court found that the expulsion was an inappropriate sanction.

– BVerfGE 47, 191 Expenses for the Training of Works-Council Members
The subject of this decision is the duty of employers to bear the cost of the activities of the works council, including paying for training courses for council members offered and organized by unions. An employer who found it unconstitutional that the members of the works council should be trained at his expense by the "industrial opponent" filed a constitutional complaint that appealed a labor court decision that had obliged him to do so. The *Bundesverfassungsgericht* rejected the complaint with the laconic statement that the duty of reimbursement did not impair the employer's capacity to conduct an effective labor struggle.

Even if the number of decisions is too small to draw general conclusions, it can be said that the *Bundesverfassungsgericht* has been rather liberal toward union activities of the employed and certainly more liberal than the courts engaged in four of the previous cases.

Rights of Union Agents Not Belonging to the Plant

The two decisions concerning access to the plant by union agents who were not plant employees did not confirm the liberal tendency just described.

– BVerfGE 17, 319 – Auxiliary Police in Bavaria
The first decision of the *Bundesverfassungsgericht* is dedicated to such a case so particular that no generalizations can be drawn from it. On the basis of a union's constitutional complaint against a Bavarian statute that forbade external union agents access to sessions of staff councils and to staff meetings of the auxiliary police, the *Bundesverfassungsgericht* explicitly left open the question of whether external union agents have a constitutional right to conduct activities at the plant at all. The court rejected the complaint on the grounds that, at least in the case of barracked police, it was a matter of legislative discretion whether or not to allow access to external union agents.

– BVerfGE 57, 220 – Union Access to Church Establishments
While the fundamental question of whether external union agents' rights to be active in plant activities is marginal in the previous case, it is the central point here. In the case of a church-related establishment for physically impaired persons, the federal labor court had judged, first, that the freedom of coalition (Article 9, section 3 GG) gave unions a right to send external agents to the establishment's premises for the purpose of distributing union advertisements and information. And second, it had decided that this right of access existed in relation to church establishments as well, if their staff was employed on the basis of labor contracts. The *Bundesverfassungsgericht* did not affirm this judicial extension of union rights, but found that it violated church autonomy. The significance of the case lies in the fact that the *Bundesverfassungsgericht* had already rejected the federal labor court's first step and had denied a union right to access by external union agents as an element of the freedom of coalition. The question of whether such a right could be granted by legislation was explicitly left open.

Not only the restrictive view of union rights is remarkable, but also the fact that the *Bundesverfassungsgericht* stopped the federal labor court in its law-developing activity. This, however, is probably not the expression of a general view of the role of the courts, which would have indicated a change in the jurisdiction of the *Bundesverfassungsgericht*.[43] However, it may be seen as deriving from the fact that in the works constitution law the legislature itself had decided under what conditions the unions had the right of access, so that the jurisdiction of the federal labor court was a deviation from the legislative decision.

Electoral Competition between Labor Associations

The competition between various labor associations has already been seen in connection with union advertisements at the plant. In addition, this subject has provoked a relatively large number of decisions dealing with the regulation of elections of employees' representatives in which the *Bundesverfassungsgericht* enforced the

43. Seiter, "Die Rechtsprechung des Bundesverfassungsgerichts" (see n. 25), 100, speaks of a "switch" in the jurisdiction of the court; this may be doubted for the reasons given in the text.

same principles of strict equality of chances and minority protection that it had developed for political elections.[44]

Principles of Strict Equality of Chances before the Election

– BVerfGE 30, 227 – Social Insurance Elections
In 1967, the legislature changed the statute provisions regulating the elections of the self-governing bodies of social insurance institutions in a way that contributed to deterioration in the position of associations of the employed, which were not unions but competed with unions. First, these associations were no longer allowed to bear the name of a social insurance institution in their names. This obliged some associations to change their established names. Second, the candidate lists of these associations had to be signed by a certain quorum of persons entitled to vote, whereas unions were free of such quorums. By means of constitutional complaints connected with a petition of concrete judicial review, the *Bundesverfassungsgericht* declared these provisions void. The restriction regarding the names was held unconstitutional because it violated the freedom of association (Article 9, section 1 GG) and the *Bundesverfassungsgericht* found no sufficient reason for it. And the unequal treatment regarding the signature quorum was deemed a violation of the principle of strict equality of electoral chances. This principle, which was developed for the competition of political parties, means that the legislature is not yet allowed to establish differences between competitors if there are just sensible reasons for doing so. But this is permissible if there is an urgent necessity for it, which can be justified on the basis of the constitution.[45] In this case, however, such necessities were not to be found.

– BVerfGE 60, 162 – Quorum of Signatures for Staff Council Elections I
In response to a petition of concrete judicial review by the Bremen administrative court, the *Bundesverfassungsgericht* again had to decide upon a signature quorum for candidate lists in the field of

44. See Hanns Rudolf Lipphardt, *Die Gleichheit der politischen Parteien vor der öffentlichen Gewalt: Eine kritische Studie zur Wahl- und Parteienrechtsjudikatur des Bundesverfassungsgerichts*, Schriften zum öffentlichen Recht, 271 (Berlin, 1975).

45. See Ingo von Münch, ed., *Grundgesetzkommentar*, 3 vols. (Munich, 1981–83), 2: Art. 21 no. 25ff.

industrial self-government. According to the Bremen staff representation law, candidate lists for the election of the staff council were only admissible if at least 10 percent of those entitled to vote in the representative groups had signed them. By this restriction even associations that would have received a seat on the council, had only signers voted for the list, were excluded from the election. Again, the *Bundesverfassungsgericht* stated that the rules developed for electoral equality in political democracy had to be applied here as well. According to these rules, a quorum of signatures for candidate lists is only admissible in so far as it is necessary to restrict the election to serious candidates who obviously do not have only a marginal chance of being elected.[46]

– BVerfGE 67, 369 – Quorum of Signatures for Staff Council Elections II

In this case a provision of the federal staff representation law was declared void for the same reason (10 percent signature quorum) and with the same arguments as in BVerfGE 60, 162. What is remarkable is not this result, but the fact that the federal legislature did not use the time from March 1982 until October 1984 to correct the statute.

– BVerfGE 71, 81 – Bremen Chamber of Employees

The last case on electoral equality concerns the Bremen chamber of employees. According to the statute provisions, which regulated the elections to the representative body of the chamber, election proposals could only be made by unions or their parent organizations and by employee associations with relevant weight in the industrial life of the state of Bremen. Referring to its jurisdiction on equality of electoral chances, the *Bundesverfassungsgericht* could declare this void because it was evidently unconstitutional.

What these four cases have in common is that the legislature had provided rules which obviously had the purpose of protecting the established unions from disagreeable competitors and which – perhaps with the exception of the name provision in BVerfGE 30, 227 – were very difficult to defend. These decisions may be regarded as examples of how the *Bundesverfassungsgericht* functions to

46. See Gerhard Leibholz and H.J. Rinck, *Grundgesetz für die Bundesrepublik Deutschland: Kommentar an Hand der Rechtsprechung des Bundesverfassungsgerichts* (Cologne, 1966), Art. 38 no. 7.

compensate for distortions in the political process caused by differences in pressure group power.[47]

Protection of Minorities after the Election

– BVerfGE 51, 77 – The Voting Out of Staff Council Members
The cases reported above contain the element of protection of minorities by means of constitutional requirements for election rules. Here – again a case of the Bremen staff representation law – the legislature had found a way of making it possible to change the results of the election at the cost of minorities. While the election system was proportional, a provision of the statute enabled the majority of those entitled to vote to vote out members of the staff council in a staff meeting. In this way the result of the proportional election, which allows minorities to elect their candidates as well, could be corrected afterward. The *Bundesverfassungsgericht* found this regulation to be unreconcilable with the system of proportional elections and representative mandates contained in the federal staff representation law and binding upon the Bremen legislature.[48]

Conclusion

This survey of the *Bundesverfassungsgericht* cases on industrial relations confirms the earlier statement that the subjects of the decisions are rather sporadic and more or less random. This is shown as well by the fact that some important questions have come to the court in untypical constellations. This was the case with the lawmaking capacity by collective agreement, the industrial conflict, and the access right of external union agents. In spite of the limitation caused by the cases brought to the court, the fragmentation of jurisdictional statements on constitutional questions in the field of industrial relations is based upon decisions of the court and not on legal necessities. The *Bundesverfassungsgericht* would have

47. Particularly for this function, see Hans Herbert von Arnim, *Gemeinwohl und Gruppeninteressen: Die Durchsetzungsschwäche allgemeiner Interessen in der pluralistischen Demokratie* (Frankfurt/Main, 1977), 212ff.
48. The federal legislature has the competence for framework legislation (*Rahmengesetzgebung*) according to Art. 75 no. 1.

been able – as it has done in the fields of individual basic rights[49] and public mass communication[50] or with the party system[51] – to develop the Constitution by obiter dicta. Obvious examples where this was possible but the court abstained from it are BVerfGE 50, 290 and 35, 386. Just as the *Bundesverfassungsgericht* has shown a tendency to accept legislatory structuring of industrial relations, it has left room for future developments by abstaining from constitutional pronouncements. Thus industrial relations is a sector in which the *Bundesverfassungsgericht* exercises particular judicial restraint. In this tendency the court has respected and implemented the decision of the framers of the Constitution to leave alteration of the socioeconomic structure to simple legislatory majorities.

There is a certain contrast between that restraint and the active awareness with which the protection of minorities and equality of chances between competing labor organizations has been controlled. On this point we find a parallel to the jurisdiction over the general political process, where the *Bundesverfassungsgericht* also exercises a clearly active role in order to assure an open and formally fair competition for power.[52]

The question of the motivation for these different tendencies in decisions leads to such unsafe ground that answers can only be attempted with utmost caution and only with due reservation. Even in leaving aside the differences in the individual cases, each of which actually ought to be explained in its full legal, social, and historical context, there are also insurmountable difficulties in obtaining the necessary information for a causal explanation of the *Bundesverfassungsgericht's* decisions, particularly because the inner-court decision making and the processes of recruitment of judges[53] are secret. Moreover, the question of to what degree a decision can be explained by the relevance of legal determination, independent of other factors, leads to basic problems in legal theory and an

---

49. E.g., BVerfGE 69, 315 on the freedom of assembly (Art. 8 GG).

50. BVerfGE 12, 205; 57, 295; 73, 118.

51. E.g., BVerfGE 20, 50; 20, 119; 20, 134; 24, 300; 28, 97; 53, 631; 73, 40 with detailed shapings of constitutional rules regarding party financing.

52. See on this Ebsen, *Das Bundesverfassungsgericht als Element gesellschaftlicher Selbstregulierung* (see n. 4), particularly chaps. 8–10.

53. For the recruitment of the *Bundesverfassungsgericht* judges see Landfried, *Bundesverfassungsgericht und Gesetzgeber* (see n. 21), 17ff.; Donald P. Kommers, *Judicial Politics in West Germany: A Study of the Federal Constitutional Court*, Sage Series on Politics and the Legal Order, 5 (Beverly Hills, CA, 1976), 113ff.

inseparable overlapping of the empirical question and of normative problems.[54] In this situation we must content ourselves with relating some founded assumptions about the dispositions of the *Bundesverfassungsgericht* to the case material described above, which for lack of space, can only be outlined.[55]

The former *Bundesverfassungsgericht* judge Konrad Zweigert once explained the particular judicial restraint of the *Bundesverfassungsgericht* to economic questions with "much more massive political will," which compared to other fields, here stood behind statutary provisions.[56] By this explanation Zweigert referred to the fact that the *Bundesverfassungsgericht* as an institution is not separated from the conflict of social interests as an element of the political process, but through the mode of its recruitment represents the spectrum of relevant political tendencies which, for their part, have particular affiliations to certain social interests.[57] In situations where social conflicts develop into constitutional questions, this mediated connection with social interests gives the court the chance to work as an integrating factor through the decision-making process and through the consequent acceptance of those decisions. On the other hand, there is the danger of failing acceptance and integration through the decision-making process (for example, majority decisions in factions, which can be politically explained) and through the decision itself (namely, infringing upon essential positions of relevant interests). This is true in so far as constitutional conflicts between relevant social interests are "hot potatoes" for the *Bundesverfassungsgericht*. That this is true, particularly for important questions in industrial relations, was shown by the constitutional conflict surrounding the codetermination law of 1976.

In this situation the stated disposition for judicial restraint, with respect to decisions taken in the political process as well as expansions of the decided issues by obiter dicta, is a plausible strategy for maintaining the court's integrative capacity. Abstention from

54. I.e., good reasons can regularly be found for different opinions on the question of whether the court was obliged by law to decide the way it did.

55. For a more detailed analysis see Ebsen, *Das Bundesverfassungsgericht als Element gesellschaftlicher Selbstregulierung* (see n. 4), particularly chaps. 8–10.

56. Konrad Zweigert "Duktus der Rechtsprechung des Ersten Senats des Bundesverfassungsgerichts und einige Erinnerungen an seine Anfangszeit" in *Das Bundesverfassungsgericht, 1951–1971* (Karlsruhe, [2]1971), 95f, 113f.

57. Ebsen, *Das Bundesverfassungsgericht als Element gesellschaftlicher Selbstregulierung* (see n. 4), 263ff.

actively influencing the relation of powers in the field of industrial democracy prevents charges of partiality and leaves conflicts in the legislature and labor courts' jurisdiction, where they are less fundamental than at the constitutional level because the decisions remain open to change from changing legislative majorities. Abstention from obiter dicta reduces matter for conflict and keeps the undecided constitutional questions up in the air. This too prevents "erosion" of the court's integrative capacity and facilitates inner-court consensus.

The opposite, rather active role of the *Bundesverfassungsgericht* with respect to elections and other forms of competition in industrial and social self-government can be explained by the fact that here the court's integrative function is not needed and its authority is not in danger. Insofar as the court sets up and enforces rules of protection for minorities and fair competition, it will – as in the field of the general political process[58] – find full acceptance, and those who are favored by unfair rules will hardly be able to mobilize a consensus for critique.

Thus, altogether, it can be said that the decisions of the *Bundesverfassungsgericht* in the sector of industrial democracy correspond to the patterns which were to be expected because of the means of its recruitment and its functions of integrating social interests and of playing the role of umpire in power conflicts.

58. Ibid., 340ff.

18.1
The Constitutional and Legal Situation of German Industrial Society and the Historical Development of Social Change

Ernst Benda

I believe that it is impossible to understand the present constitutional and legal situation without having a closer look at the historical background. I am going to mention only a few instances for there are many people present in this room, including the chairman of this meeting, who have written more about this period than I can pretend to know.

The subject of this session, broadly speaking, is "Constitutions and Change in Industrial Societies." The problem of change is not just that time passes but that people also change and this of course is a subject for the historian; at the same time it also poses important and difficult problems for a lawyer. How can constitutional law – which is supposed to remain unchanged for long periods, in ideal but not of course in real situations, even for eternity – interact with changing social situations? You cannot keep constitutional law for eternity for the simple reason that situations and in particular social and economic conditions change over time.

We have discussed this problem during the previous session: what are the tools, what are the methods to react properly to changing times – again this is a subject of importance for the lawyer as well as the historian. For the legal scholar the problem is that in principle a legal norm has, as any law does, mainly a conservative function. For it is the principal function of the law to maintain a situation for the present. How is the law able to adapt to social change, change which of course both countries, the United States and Germany, witnessed during the last years with ever increasing speed?

We have discussed this issue, for example, in the context of the

477

problem of "original intent," the problem of interpretation of law in general and of the Constitution in particular. These have been some of the major subjects in our discussions so far and it seems fitting for me to take them up again in the context of an industrial society in which there has been and continues to be the most dramatic change.

Using this background my principal question would be, do a written constitution and a method of judicial review both further or retard social change? What is the main function of a constitution and of a constitutional court or of a court which has constitutional functions in a changing society? To try to answer this question briefly we would have to look at the historical development of social change in our country. I will touch on this issue only very briefly.

We have to start by looking at the social situation in the middle of the nineteenth century when, and that holds true for both countries, industrialization began in earnest. Consider the times of Bismarck. A two-way approach to deal with the problem of the unruly working class evolved. This new class on the one hand was needed, yet on the other hand was regarded with suspicion by the then ruling classes, especially when the new class began to organize itself in trade unions and political parties that claimed to represent the interests of the industrial workers.

Now, the first key term that comes to everyone's mind in this context is the *Sozialistengesetz* of 1878 – the "Gesetz gegen die gemeingefährlichen Bestrebungen der Sozialdemokratie," a law designed to keep the new class from organizing and thus an effort to reverse the historical development. Yet this law has to be seen together with its twin brother, the legislation setting up the world's first comprehensive social insurance system under Bismarck.

Let us focus on the function of these laws in the 1880s: on the one hand law in this context was an instrument for oppression of the people but on the other hand it served as an instrument of social change. To give another example, the *Gewerbeordnung* of 1869 for the North German Confederation, which later was taken over by the empire, for the first time gave citizens the right to form coalitions of workers. With the revocation of the *Sozialistengesetz* freedom of assembly and convention was renewed. In the nine-teenth century the law both recognized and brought about social change.

I jump fifty years ahead to the end of the First World War, to the situation when William II was abdicating after the war had been lost. In this situation people and politicians faced – as one important alternative – the possibility of following the example of the new-born Soviet Union, now just one year old. Many people in Germany who had adopted the ideology of Lenin were firmly convinced that such a revolution had to start in an industrialized society; indeed it was anti-Leninist thinking to believe that it was possible to start a revolution in an agricultural state like Russia; Germany was the real place to begin a revolution. In particular the USPD, the Independent Social Democratic Party which had split from the Social Democratic Party, was firmly committed to the idea that Germany should go the revolutionary way.

Well, it took a couple of years and a good deal of internal strife to reject this revolutionary alternative as a model for Germany. And that of course was largely the work of the other social groups, who wanted to preserve as much of the old social and political order of the times before the First World War and who wanted no change at all if that was possible – except perhaps the substitution of the emperor, who as an option was no longer available, for a *Reichspräsident*. And indeed, if we look at least at Hindenburg, he was more or less the same even down to the uniform he wore: there was preciously little change!

Of course, neither alternative – revolutionary change on the one hand and no change at all on the other – could work. Thus the struggle during the Weimar Republic is the permanent attempt to chart a clear and new course, an effort too to adapt to rapid social change; the inability to find this new course is, in my opinion, one of the most important reasons why the Weimar Republic broke down.

What followed is too well known: Nazism and the Second World War, at the end total catastrophe, the whole country in ruins, everyone preoccupied with the simple problem of survival amidst ruins. Yet survival was only possible if everyone, blue-collar *and* white-collar workers alike, joined hands, worked together, and struggled to get out of the ruins, find a new beginning, start what later became known as the "economic miracle," the *Wirtschaftswunder*, of the 1950s. This was of course no miracle at all but, apart from a bit of good luck, mainly the result of hard work.

It is, however, important to mention the consequences stemming from this joint experience of all classes of society: it brought social reconciliation. Other factors were of equal importance. One of the luckiest coincidences in our recent history involved the personalities of Konrad Adenauer and Hans Böckler. Hans Böckler was the first president of the Confederation of Trade Unions and perhaps one of the greatest personalities in modern German history. These men's social backgrounds and their personal and educational experiences were completely different and yet due to some sort of chemistry they managed to work together in a partnership in which each represented the interests of social groups who, in the historical past, had looked in rather different directions.

Finally, one last historical force helped to shape our social past, Catholic social teachings (*Soziallehren*). Indeed, I sometimes wonder what the American constitutional principle of separation of church and state would have done in Europe; for the absence of this American constitutional principle in the latter part of the nineteenth century opened German social and political life to the strong workings of Catholic social thought, which in Europe was always the progressive side. Since at least the turn of the century no ruler – and that to some extent even included Hitler and the Nazis – could completely ignore the admonitions of the Catholic church, which much earlier than the Protestant church, realized the necessity and recognized the need to give the working people a fair share in society.

One of the key principles developed after the Second World War was that of codetermination. That principle of course had its origins in the Weimar Republic in the *Reichswirtschaftsrat*, an advisory body that was to represent trade unions and employers' associations and some other groups of society. This *Reichswirtschaftsrat* never really came to life, which was rather fortunate because I believe it to represent the wrong way to do things. Yet the idea of bringing the opposing social groups together was important and it was our good fortune that this idea survived.

Let me now turn to the final aspect of my comment, the constitutional consequences. As Mr. Ebsen rightly pointed out, the fundamental law of 1949 (*Grundgesetz*) did not establish a fixed economic order. This was only natural for at that time our thinking about the future was rather unclear. Indeed, for many it would have been a silly question to ask whether one wanted to be a socialist or a capitalist or anything else; what everyone wanted in

1949 was simply to survive. The important question concerning the shape and structure of the future economic order was thus left open and that indeed – although it was the result of an embarrassing inability to find the necessary answers – proved to be a very wise decision because in this important area it left the democratic process wide open and did not burden it with constitutional provisions that would have steered the development into a one-way street.

The constitutional court in one of its first decisions, the *German Lawyers and Investment Decision*, said that Parliament can make any law and decide on any form of economic policy as long as it respects the Constitution and in particular fundamental rights. This landmark decision is one of the most quoted sentences in the jurisdiction of the constitutional court. Strangely enough, the last part of the sentence, which ties parliamentary activities to the observance of fundamental rights, is omitted in most citations although it is of great importance because it plainly states that Parliament can initiate any social or economic policy it likes as long as it respects the fundamental rights of the people. In practice this means that it bars both the socialist and the communist models as well as the nineteenth-century capitalist model. Both are excluded; the true way is in the middle, between the two extreme concepts of social and economic order. Henceforth much of the political struggle focused on the shape and size of this "middle way."

This decision to refrain from including in the Constitution prescriptions for a particular economic order paved the way for politics and the constitutional court to try to achieve what may be the most important task in any society in the field of social and economic policy, to serve as a tool of reconciliation and to establish and keep social peace. In the context of social policy this is in my mind the most important function of legislation and of courts.

I have no objections to what Mr. Ebsen wrote in his paper – and restated during the discussion – but I do not object to the word "cautiousness" which he used in connection with the constitutional court. Having participated in and indeed presided at the time the *Mitbestimmung* decision was handed down in 1980, I can say with some authority that this was not an example of cautiousness; we knew what we wanted to do. We hope our decision was a successful attempt to carry out the most important function of the constitutional court in this context, to further the process of reconciliation, to establish social peace. This goal is at the center of the decision. In short, both the constitutional provisions and the work of the court are characterized by restraint. You can make policy by acting or by abstaining from action.

Mr. Summers very rightly pointed out the function of Article 9, §3 – "freedom of coalition." The meaning, and here I can only reinforce what you said for I completely agree with you, of Article 9, §3 is to enable and at the same time to force the employers' associations and the trade unions to cooperate, to keep pursuing the interests of the people they represent, and at the same time, to seek a consensus. This article addresses the central problem of society, that is, conflict, which is natural and unavoidable, while obliging both social groups to achieve consensus.

Finally and most important, I would like to stress more than Mr. Ebsen did, the *Sozialstaatsklausel* in the Constitution. Mr. Ebsen writes in this paper that this *Sozialstaatsklausel* is so empty of content that its function is unimportant. Of course this is right, but its meaning has been developed over time by both legal science and jurisdiction. The *Sozialstaatsklausel* is embodied in a very innocent-looking constitutional clause stating that the Federal Republic is a "democratic and social federal state" – one is tempted to overlook the word "social" for it does not seem to have any meaning in the first place. One of the first commentators on the Constitution, Grewe, referred to it as "substanzloser Blanketbegriff" (a term devoid of substance and meaning). People used to sneer about this little word "social" in the beginning. Now it is history.

I have written over six hundred pages about this question and at present everyone would love to have a copy of this bulky manuscript. Let me briefly summarize my major argument: the constitutional court ignored this little word "social" too, at first. One of the earliest dissenting opinions issued by the constitutional court – they first became part of the constitutional court's adjudication procedure in 1970 – pointed to the fact that the constitutional court had ignored the *Sozialstaatsklausel* for far too long; this dissent really achieved something. Indeed, it is a good example of how a dissenting opinion can get things moving.

Since then the Court has recognized the meaning of the *Sozialstaatsklausel*, which turned out to be one of the most important parts of the principal and fundamental section of the Constitution. I cannot explain this in detail but only focus on the gist of the problem. The main principle is, that according to constitutional jurisdiction and the thinking of jurisdictional scholars, the state is entitled and obliged to involve itself actively in the social and economic field. This means that we do not accept laissez-faire capitalism any more.

The underlying principle is that the common good does not just happen but that the state has to work actively for it. And this of course leads us back to some of the fundamental issues we have been arguing about over the last two days. In this general context the classical idea of the main function of fundamental rights to give independence to the state – important as it still is – no longer fulfills the needs of a changing modern society. It is not enough to understand fundamental rights in the context of just letting people alone with the prayer that they will be happy. On the contrary, the *Sozialstaatsklausel* entitles and obliges the state to become active.

This of course creates completely new dangers. Had we the time to look to the future, we could of course discern the danger of the individual's ever-increasing dependency on the state and thus the growing restriction of individual freedom. For we get our freedom from the state, which might give or deny it to us. To cope with this danger the Constitution should contain provisions helping to adapt it to rapidly changing social and economic circumstances.

18.2
The American Labor Movement and the Rule of Law

Laura Kalman

These two papers raise a question which has long troubled American historians.[1] Ninety percent of all German employees below the executive level are paid wages negotiated by collective agreements, while collective agreements cover 20 percent of American workers. German unions also have far more political strength than their American counterparts and are involved in the formation of economic policy. Why did the American labor movement never attain the strength of its European counterpart?

One theory, which both papers exemplify, lays the weakness of the American labor movement at the door of "the hostile state," a state willing to use courts and other instrumentalities to thwart labor. Clyde Summers suggests that since the enactment of the National Labor Relations Act, the U.S. Supreme Court has curtailed and denied the industrial democracy that the act was intended to promote. According to Summers, the Supreme Court has been reluctant to order or maintain collective bargaining. It has restricted the categories of employees eligible to bargain collectively so that even faculty members may no longer be "employees" within the meaning of the NLRA. It has limited the number of mandatory subjects covered by the collective bargaining agreement. It has denied employees access to information about their employers. And it has paid far greater attention to protecting the economic action of employers than employees. Thus Summers concludes that although the National Labor Relations Act was a charter for industrial democracy, the Supreme Court has impeded its achievement.

Conversely, in the Federal Republic, the state is not hostile and, when compared to the United States, the situation of German

1. I thank W. Randall Garr, Kermit Hall, and especially David Rabban for their thoughtful comments on this comment.

unions seems enviable. Unlike their American counterparts, German employers believe in collective bargaining. Summers has pointed out elsewhere that the Federal Republic's Codetermination Act potentially gives workers the voice to choose managing directors, declare dividends, and make investment decisions (although the fact that workers' councils, rather than unions, engage in codetermination leaves open the possibility of employer domination of the process).[2] In contradistinction to the United States, workers are permitted access to information about employer policy. Ingwer Ebsen's paper also shows that the Federal Republic's *Bundesverfassungsgericht* has generally exercised an unusual amount of restraint in the area of labor relations, thereby alllowing unions to strive for greater participation in the determination of employer and labor policy.

American exceptionalism is thus highlighted by the situation in Germany. Scholars interested in using these two papers to compare the lots of German and American workers might focus on several different areas. They might compare the concepts of codetermination and industrial democracy, point to the expectations German and American workers had with respect to socioeconomic arrangements when the Codetermination Act and the National Labor Relations Act became law, compare the cooperative approach to labor relations in the Federal Republic with the confrontational approach in the United States, indicate the role of law in both countries in encouraging parties to solve the problems that divide them, and determine whether workers are better off in the United States or Germany.

It is unclear, for example, how similar Summers's "industrial democracy" is to Ebsen's "codetermination." At times, Summers seems to assume that were it realized, industrial democracy in the United States would be the equivalent of codetermination in Germany. Yet his definition of industrial democracy as "giving workers an effective voice in determining the terms and conditions of their employment" makes it clear that industrial democracy falls far short of codetermination. Exactly what is industrial democracy and how does it compare to codetermination?

What roles do law and the state play in the attainment of

---

2. Clyde W. Summers, "Worker Participation in the U.S. and West Germany: A Comparative Study from an American Perspective," *American Journal of Comparative Law* 28 (1980): 370.

industrial democracy and in explaining the strength or weakness of a labor movement? In the United States, I would argue that the National Labor Relations Act was not as directed toward the promotion of industrial democracy as Summers implies and that the Supreme Court has not frustrated it as much as he suggests. To be sure, if I were a labor lawyer representing a union in a case requiring interpretation of the National Labor Relations Act, I would follow Summers in attempting to make the most out of the language in the act loosely referring to industrial democracy. As an historian, however, I can make a different, and I think, more historical argument.

In passing the National Labor Relations Act, Congress paid little attention to the concept of industrial democracy, except to assume that collective bargaining would lead to it. No proponent of the act thought that industrial democracy required the kind of joint determination that prevails in Germany. Wary of the act because it posed a threat to the tradition of labor voluntarism, the American Federation of Labor steered clear of industrial democracy and tried to limit the government's role to ensuring that employers dealt with independent unions. Thus the act did not aim at industrial democracy, unless industrial democracy is defined restrictively (and relatively meaninglessly) as the right to a collective bargaining process that will preclude unilateral action by employers with respect to certain subjects.

Rather, the major aims of the act were to promote industrial peace, to restrict employer interference with union activity, and to force employers to bargain collectively about wages, hours, and conditions of employment with unions chosen by the majority of employees. As Senator Wagner said and as the Communist party and the American Civil Liberties Union agreed, the act created no new substantive rights but sought to enforce the right to collective bargaining granted by previous legislation. In the context of the Depression, collective bargaining promised to be not only in labor's interest but in the broader interest of the economy as well.

Insofar as the National Labor Relations Act was novel, scholars such as Christopher Tomlins and David Montgomery have argued persuasively that it threatened labor. For it encouraged reliance on law and the state instead of labor voluntarism. Tomlins suggests that by giving the National Labor Relations Board the authority to determine the appropriate bargaining unit, the act destroyed the union's power to decide when and how to organize and reduced them to instruments of the state.[3]

Yet the National Labor Relations Act also proved a blessing for labor. Although declining union membership today might lead us to question its significance, at the time it seemed a radical departure. If it did not aim at industrial democracy or envision the fulfillment of the social goals associated with European unions, it nevertheless shifted the power of the state behind labor. For the first time in American history, the weight of the state was to be used to support labor rather than to oppress it. Labor, and the Congress of Industrial Organizations (CIO) in particular, relied on the enforcement of the NLRA as a way of organizing and maintaining union strength.

Has the Supreme Court maintained the balance of power the National Labor Relations Act envisioned? As Summers demonstrates, the Court could have, and sometimes should have, interpreted the act in a way more favorable to unions. But the Supreme Court has not consistently played the villain. In the 1960 *Insurance Agents'* case, for example, the Court required employers to bargain with unions even when their members were engaging in unprotected slowdowns.[4] As David Rabban has noted, "Surely this decision does not reveal an unbending adherence to the goal of industrial peace."[5] In this instance, the Court threw its weight behind labor.

To cite another example, we may have allowed the *Yeshiva* decision unduly to alarm us. There is indeed a danger that worker involvement in decision making will be used to exclude participating workers from coverage of the National Labor Relations Act under the *Yeshiva* rationale. Yet the majority in *Yeshiva* did not address the situation of industrial workers, stressed that other faculties might not possess managerial authority, and warned against an automatic identification of professional with managerial status. Courts may even confine the *Yeshiva* rationale principally to faculty. "After all," as Rabban observes in a speech based on his forthcoming study of the case, "college professors, even at institutions with relatively weak systems of faculty governance, have a

3. Christopher Tomlins, *The State and the Unions* (Cambridge, MA, 1985); David Montgomery, *Workers' Control in America* (Cambridge, MA, 1979), 165.

4. *NLRB v. Insurance Agents' International Union*, 361 U.S. 448 (1960).

5. David Rabban, "Has the NLRA Hurt Labor?" *University of Chicago Law Review* 54 (1987): 426.

greater role in formulating organizational policies than do most other professionals and virtually all nonprofessional employees.[6] More important, only one case has extended the *Yeshiva* reasoning to another profession – doctors – and this single precedent has never been followed. The wolf may be out there, but he may not yet be at the door.[7]

Further, notwithstanding some Supreme Court decisions hostile to labor, can organized labor's weakness be blamed on the Supreme Court? If the Court had decided every one of the cases that Summers criticizes in the way that he preferred, would the situation of American labor have become more comparable to its European counterpart and would American exceptionalism have ended? Perhaps not, but he may disagree.

If the Supreme Court is not responsible for the enervation of American labor, why is it so weak? The wolf may have reached the door long ago. The striking aspect of American labor in the 1920s, as opposed to the late 1890s, was its limited goals. The American Federation of Labor (AFL) abandoned republican ideology and European social democratic thought and became increasingly preoccupied with bread-and-butter goals or business unionism. By the 1920s, organized labor accepted corporate capitalism and essentially sought economic gains for its constituents through collective bargaining.

A significant exception ultimately proved the rule. In 1945 Walter Reuther sought a wage increase for the United Auto Workers (UAW). When General Motors countered that a wage increase would cause a price increase, he asked General Motors to open its books. German workers today could obtain the information Reuther sought, but General Motors refused and a four-month strike followed. Throughout the strike, GM steadfastly refused to let workers intrude into the realm of management. When it offered them a good raise while still refusing them access to its books, the UAW took the money. Neither Reuther nor any other union leader ever again attempted as significant an incursion into alleged managerial prerogatives. Certainly, at least until very recently, American unions have also never sought anything like codetermination.

6. David Rabban, Speech, Baruch Conference, May 4, 1987.
7. But see *U.S. Labor Law and the Future of Labor-Management Cooperation*, First Interim Report, U.S. Department of Labor (February 1987), 66–68 for a more pessimistic assessment.

For reasons of their own, not necessarily reasons of law, they have preferred to have the employer make the decision and then to challenge it.

We must pay greater attention to internal developments in the American labor movement in the early part of the century to discover why labor's goals became so limited. This does not suggest that all of the blame for labor's weakness should be laid at its own door. Doubtless we will find that the "hostile state" proved a significant constricting force. Judicial decisions, along with police and military action, may have convinced the AFL to seek less. Social and economic factors beyond labor's control also clearly played a role in crippling it, as did employer hostility. The answer to the riddle of the American labor movement's current weakness and its still exceptional position may lie in the past rather than in the present.

18.3
Discussion

CLYDE W. SUMMERS: It is perfectly clear that lawyers look to history to help demonstrate what they hope was true or wish to be true. And so they do selective readings. But I suppose that historians are not totally immune to that either. Now I acknowledge that industrial democracy was only a subsidiary goal of the National Labor Relations Act (NLRA), largely because the time the law passed was a time of depression in which arguments for industrial peace, for increased wages, etc., lacked contextual support. However I think that to look merely at the history of the 1930s would itself be somewhat limiting because the roots of the NLRA and the original principles go back to the turn of the century if not beyond.

I agree that the unions as well as the political climate are both in part responsible for later developments. However, a further factor has to be taken into account: I think there is no country in the Western world outside the United States of America in which employers behave with the kind of determined resistance to any recognition in dealing with the unions on the one hand and with the desire to destroy them on the other. That has been true since 1935 and the passage of the Wagner Act. Employers in the United States have never accepted collective bargaining; they have at best tolerated it where they felt it was inescapable.

My complaint with the U.S. Supreme Court is that essentially it has never acknowledged that the real problem in the United States was the curbing of employer anti-union managers so as to make collective bargaining a viable, effective, accepted part of the system. The refusal of the Supreme Court to recognize that problem has been the weakness in our system.

It is true that the union movement in the United States has a limited view of its goals. That limited view may have been true of Samuel Gompers and the American Federation of Labor (AFL) in the 1930s, but it was not true of many in the Congress of Industrial Organizations (CIO) unions. The American unions have bent with the times, have satisfied themselves with what was possible, have lost their ideology or most of what they had. But I think one has to recognize that a significant measure of the responsibility for this development lies with the courts, who failed to take what was applicable statute and handle it in a way that achieved its purported goals. They have defeated all of the goals of the statute, not just industrial democracy.

INGWER EBSEN: I would like to make two comments, one more legal, the other more historical or rather political. First to the legal aspects. I would admit that the social-state clause (*Sozialstaatsklausel*) is not "nothing." When I described the law relating to the social system I concentrated on applicable law. Of course the social-state clause can play an important role in juridical arguments if one – and that is the important point – decides to use it and to let it play an important role.

It is true that the framers of the *Grundgesetz* left the legislators free to decide which social and economic order they preferred as long as they did not infringe on basic rights, as Mr. Benda has pointed out; yet let me add that this meant of course not solving but formulating the problem. Where do acts of the legislature infringe on the basic law and where do they conform to it? Particularly in this context the *Sozialstaatsklausel* can be a counterweight to an individual approach to basic rights.

The second remark. When I characterized the constitutional court's decision on codetermination as "cautious" I did not use that word in the sense of "fearful." Of course I accept that the court was conscious of what it was doing and that it pursued a policy. Thus please read the word "cautious" rather as "prudent."

Now to the political aspect. When I read Mr. Summers' paper I asked myself, why are American and German social developments so different? We cannot explain this with reference only to the institutions in both countries; I believe that for an explanation we have to look to the nineteenth century. One of the important differences between the two countries is the class solidarity that the German labor movement developed; this class solidarity expressed itself not only in a special terminology and language but in a distinctive culture too. It evolved its own program. Based on these, the German labor movement formulated its own platform for bargaining even on the constitutional level.

It is not surprising that even the words "industrial democracy" have different meanings in America and in Germany. The Americans use the word "industrial democracy" for something which is distinctive less than codetermination; in Germany during the Weimar Republic the term "industrial democracy" was largely associated with the debate about the socialization of big enterprises and the question of how to organize socialized big enterprises. In this debate one school of thought advocated the concept of self-administration, which again was described as "industrial democracy." Thus the meaning of the term still has some relevance to the compromise between social interests in Germany.

RALPH KETCHAM: I want to shift the discussion for a moment to the problem of labor relations and productivity. It seems to me that there is an obvious relationship between the state of labor management relations and resulting efficiency and productivity. Of course we cannot talk about this question in 1987 without noticing industrial productivity in such leading nations as Japan, Germany, and the United States. How can we measure this? Is there some way in which the American confrontational system affects our industrial productivity?

CLYDE W. SUMMERS: I think there is a very direct relationship between the two. The confrontational character of collective bargaining in the United States makes it very difficult for workers to be concerned about the profitability of their enterprise especially when they are being told by the employer that profits and relating informations are none of their business. It is very difficult for workers to feel that they should help to make a firm more productive when they cannot even tell whether that will make any difference for themselves. Thus the confrontational system encourages the workers to feel that the employers treat them as strangers and not members of the firm. They are hired laborers – so they provide their labor.

The German system is much more collaborative; if you compare the attitudes for example, of the works' councils and those of American local unions you will find them to be totally different. In the works' councils there is concern about the productivity and effectiveness of the firm.

PAUL FINKELMAN: The problem of comparing American with

German labor transcends questions of law and goes directly to deeply rooted questions of culture and history. When Americans talk about American exceptionalism – a term used frequently on both sides of the Atlantic – one of the exceptionalist notions is that of upward mobility. This is on the one hand tied directly to notions of immigrants who come in and displace the last group of workers, pushing them up the ladder, and on the other hand to racism and the American understanding that if workers get too out of line and dare to strike there are always blacks in the South who can be brought in to displace those workers and break their strike.

Thus the working people in America have on the one hand been led to believe that they enjoy upward mobility. As long as immigrant workers – who made up the bulk of industrial workers in nineteenth-century America – believed this and as long as they were at the same time further divided by, first, their membership in different ethnic groups and, second, their inability to speak the same language, unlike their co-workers in a basically homogeneous Germany, to expect the kind of industrial democracy that developed in Europe to have developed in the United States may be to expect too much.

Let me add one further point. The experience of losing two wars in the twentieth century and of feeling the necessity in the post-Nazi period to build a new Germany generated a strong feeling of togetherness and joined all Germans in deeply felt common experiences. America has not experienced that. I wonder if German industrialists would be as open toward labor if Germany had not lost the Second World War.

JÖRG-DETLEF KÜHNE: Let me differentiate between the term "industrial democracy" and the German notion of *Sozialstaat*. In Germany we have two traditions: the strong guild tradition on the one hand, that of "fraternity" on the other. The former I cannot find in the United States. The guilds of course bound people together as well as protected them. Within the German context they can rightly claim an important role.

RALPH KETCHAM: Do you believe that this guild tradition is central to the whole German labor relations problem?

JÖRG-DETLEF KÜHNE: Yes, in the nineteenth century we have the term "constitutional manufactory," nowadays called "industrial democracy."

HERMANN WELLENREUTHER: I quite agree with you about the importance of guilds for nineteenth-century German developments. Yet by the end of the nineteenth century their importance is practically nil; thus I suspect that German and American employers' attitudes up to the Second World War did not differ much. The really big change came with the end of the Second World War. The cooperative efforts between labor and management at the beginning of the Weimar Republic broke down and that is one of the reasons why the republic failed. The fantastic break in worker-employer relations after 1945 was a real new beginning and partly so because the Allied powers insisted on it.

GERHARD A. RITTER: I partly agree and partly disagree with Mr. Wellenreuther. I disagree with your saying that this break only happened after 1945. The great break came in 1918–19 when the notion of the social state was included in the Weimar Constitution as the result of a collective agreement of November 15, 1918. All later legislation as well as most of the provisions in the Consitution were first laid down in this November agreement, which has been called the Magna Charta of the Weimar Republic.

On the other hand I have to agree with you that in the end this agreement failed. According to new research this failure was foreshadowed by events after 1926. In my opinion the initial phase of co-operation was the direct result of inflation pressures. As long as workers and employers could raise wages and supplementary wage benefits, which were higher than in any other country of the world, because they could be paid by inflation's thereby being handed on to consumers, this agreement worked. But when in 1923–24 inflation ended with the first stabilization and first rounds of unemployment, then this agreement broke down. In the final phase of the Weimar Republic the agreement of 1918 and thus labor relations collapsed.

In Germany the state is an important element in labor relations. In the German tradition since the time of the *Allgemeine Preußische Landrecht* (1794) and the Paulskirche (1848–49) it was always maintained that the state had a major role to play in social and economic affairs in order to prevent pauperism and thus social revolution. This explains Bismarck, with his social insurance legislation as well as other institutions, constantly referring social obligations onto the state. And here we meet a second notion – namely, that the major organizations and associations should cooperate with each other in reaching agreements. This was said in 1918. We already have *Tarifgemeinschaften*, collective bargaining, from the late nineteenth century in a number of industries. This became a stated principle in the order of December 23, 1918, which translated the 1918 November agreement into public law.

In my view the *Sozialstaatsklausel* in the *Grundgesetz* basically means two things and these two form a very sensitive balance. The one is that the state has an ultimate responsibility for social security – nobody should die because of hunger and poverty; this element may lead, as Mr. Benda has pointed out, to an extreme dependence on the state, which may not be desirable and which, from the point of view of an autonomous democratic society, may even be dangerous. Yet again, this has a long tradition and in its substance remained untouched even by the Nazis in the 1930s. This element has to be balanced and weighted against the second element, an element of the *Sozialstaat*, which provides for an autonomous regulation of labor relations by autonomous organizations within a framework guaranteed by the state but leaves as much as possible to the associations' concern. At the end of the Weimar Republic this precarious balance broke down, and it became impossible to reach wage agreements without direct interference by the state. One of the conclusions drawn from this is that it is preferable to have industrial strife and strikes but you do not want the state to take over the responsibility for fixing wages and hours of labor – this is the lesson of this last phase of the Weimar Republic. Thus I do think that these two elements are necessary and have to be kept in balance. They define a modern *Sozialstaat*.

Lastly, let me conclude with a remark about the German unions: the German unions were rightly very suspicious of the state during the *Kaiserreich*, but this is only part of the picture. They always presented demands that the state create laws to protect laborers and watch their interests. But let me remind you that not only Karl Marx but Ferdinand Lassalle, too, influenced German unions. Lassalle argued from a Hegelian position, maintaining that the state is the great instrument for the betterment of mankind. This line of reasoning, as well as the Marxian notion of the state being an instrument of the ruling classes, remained with the unions.

The first notion accounts for the fact that German unions are not as hostile to state interference as American unions were up to the end of the 1920s. For after all, until the beginning of the Great Depression, American unions simply did not want social insurance. They thought they could provide it by themselves. The only thing they wanted was *Schutzpflicht*.

ROBERT C. POST: Mr. Finkelman has pointed out that in America a deep ethnic diversity separated capital from labor. But there is another dimension to this problem, which is that in America there was a very strong ideological commitment to the prerogatives of property. Do any of the historians present see any continuity between the notion of freedom of contract, freedom of disposition of property, and the antislavery campaigns of the nineteenth century?

HAROLD MELVIN HYMAN: Let me suggest one possible answer: not all abolitionists died with abolition. A man such as Lewis Post, for example, who when very young was a lawyer in the Freedmen's Bureau, later became Woodrow Wilson's secretary of labor. The kind of ethic he brought to the question of American national public intervention in questions of the rights of labor to property, the fruits of their labor, and managing these certainly deserves further investigation. One of the factors important here is the linkage between generations. The abolitionist linkage seems to me to be worth very serious consideration.

WILLIAM M. WIECEK: Among the direct links between the abolitionist and labor movements, the most obvious one is Wendell Phillips, the leading Garrisonian, who after the abolition of slavery devoted the remainder of his extraordinary career to the late nineteenth-century labor movement and carried many ideas over into it. The indirect linkages, I think, tend to support the conservative character of American unions. Abolitionists were not socialists, they did not want to destroy property or derange contract relations except for one form of property relationship, slavery.

Mr. Ritter mentioned the concept of *Schutzpflicht*, the "duty of protection." The abolitionists, because of their personal experience, were deeply dedicated to this concept of the state's sole responsibility for freedom and for labor. Yet for them *Schutzpflicht* basically meant providing police services and guaranteeing that no one wantonly destroyed your personal opportunity; but the concept of *Schutzpflicht* does not mean that the state has any responsibility beyond that. I understand this as contributing to the unions' conservative body of thought.

ANDREAS FALKE: I think that it is no accident that there is no *Sozialstaatsgebot* in the American Constitution. For both societies have totally different attitudes to the welfare state and to social expenditure which have deep roots in American and German social history, respectively. Arnold Heidenheimer, a political scientist at Washington University, once analyzed the public expenditures on education and social services from 1910 to the present time. What he showed was that the share of social and educational expenditures in the United States and Germany were in almost exactly reverse proportions. For instance, during the German Empire and the Weimar Republic what Germany spent on social services was what, percentage wise, the United States spent on education. What we can learn from this is that in the United States you relieve social tension through individual upward mobility and in Germany you relieve social tension by rewarding people, through certain benefits and social safeguards, to stay in place. That study also shows that this pattern changed in the 1960s when the systems converged.

My other point focuses on the problem of "fragmentation." In the American collective bargaining system it is striking that you do not negotiate by district but by company or plant. In order to win a certification, a union has to get the workers of a company or plant on his side. In Germany everyone is automatically included in a *Tarifbezirk* as long as the employers are members of the employers' association. In the long run it might well turn out that this "fragmentation" will be one of the basic problems of the American working class, more important probably than the ethnic fragmentation mentioned earlier.

TIMOTHY H. BREEN: I think American labor history has created a fantasy. And the fantasy is the American working class and the analysis of a class we are not sure exists. But historians know that they want it to exist and thus they create it. And this class has ideology, is sometimes longing for republican roots, certainly has a corporate sense, and enjoys a mutual feeling for its fellow workers.

Unfortunately this fantasy, which does not of course exist, cooperates with the image so that workers in the workplace, especially in the South, act independently, competitively, nastily, and are perfectly capable of busting other workers' heads. When this occurs, it is seen by historians and others as an absence of ideology or as false consciousness which somehow has been brought to them because they have not seen the ideology in the labor history books.

In fact I would posit that there is ideology among American workers and that it is alive and well but that it is just different than the one we want to discover.

ROBERT C. POST: We are talking about problems of labor and law in a purely national context. But in fact, at the present time, labor and capital are becoming international. The distinctively national solutions that we have worked out for the relationship between labor and capital are even now facing the problem of mobility of capital, and this issue will have a deep impact on questions like the rights of unions.

GERHARD A. RITTER: We do not only have a mobility of capital on the European market but a mobility of labor too, which is amazing.

HERMANN WELLENREUTHER: May I just add that all the immigrants of the eighteenth and nineteenth centuries were workers shifting their place of abode from Europe to North or Latin America and elsewhere, there to seek and find new work. As regards capital flows, capital was internationally oriented from the sixteenth century as part of an international market system described by Immanuel Wallerstein. Certainly, for the eighteenth century we know that the farmer on the American frontier was part and parcel of an international market system that, for example, produced American grain which was sent to southern Europe after the Seven Years' War. Thus the international setting of capital and labor is not a new problem. The scale may be shifting but the fact as such has been affecting law, life, and economics since the eighteenth century at the latest.

CLYDE W. SUMMERS: Let me conclude with a personal observation. I have always considered the study of comparative labor law a most difficult, nearly impossible subject because one cannot study comparative labor law without studying the political and economic institutions, the unions, the social structure.

Now, speaking as an American lawyer who came here and is essentially on foreign ground when dealing with historians, I feel much more comfortable with German labor lawyers than with American historians. Let me say that I have come to the conclusion that there is something much more difficult than comparative labor law and that is comparative history. And indeed, at the moment I am nearly persuaded that it may well be nearly impossible to the human mind to deal with comparative history except in a very fragmentary way.

I can only say that I admire the boldness and courage of the historians who engage in this enterprise and I wish them well. I am not entirely convinced that they will not feel more frustrated than I am.

List of Contributors

ERICH ANGERMANN, Professor of History, is Director of the Abteilung für Anglo-Amerikanische Geschichte, University of Cologne, West Germany, a member of the Historical Commission of the Bavarian Academy of Sciences, Fellow of the Historisches Kolleg (1982/83), and chairman of the Board of Trustees of the German Historical Institute in Washington, DC. His publications include *Robert von Mohl (1799–1875) – Leben und Werk eines altliberalen Staatsgelehrten* (1962) and *Die Vereinigten Staaten von Amerika* (8th ed. 1987).

ERNST BENDA was Secretary of the Interior of the Federal Republic of Germany, 1968–69, and Chief Justice of the Federal Constitutional Court, 1971–84; as Professor of Public Law at Freiburg University, West Germany, his research interest is focused on constitutional law. His publications include *Notstandsverfassung und Arbeitskampf* (1963); *Industrielle Herrschaft und sozialer Staat. Wirtschaftsmacht von Großunternehmen als gesellschaftliches Problem* (1966); and *Sozialrechtliche Eigentumspositionen im Arbeitskampf. Ein Beitrag zur Diskussion um die Änderung des Paragraphen 116 des Arbeitsförderungsgesetzes* (1986).

HANS BOLDT holds the chair for political science and *Staatsrecht* at Düsseldorf University. He is particularly interested in nineteenth-century German constitutional history; his publications include *Rechtsstaat und Ausnahmezustand. Eine Studie über den Belagerungszustand als Ausnahmezustand des bürgerlichen Rechtsstaates im 19. Jahrhundert* (1967) and *Deutsche Staatslehre im Vormärz* (1975).

TIMOTHY H. BREEN, William Smith Mason Professor of American History at Northwestern University, is a specialist in early American intellectual and social history. His publications include *The Character of a Good Ruler* (1970); *Puritans & Adventurers: Change and Persistence in Early America* (1980); *Tobacco Culture: The Mentality of the Great Tidewater Planters on the Eve of Revolution* (1985).

MICHAEL DREYER is a specialist in nineteenth-century legal and political thought. As a fellow of the Deutsche Forschungsgemeinschaft he is working on *Leben und Werk von Hugo Preuß* and on the reciprocal influences of political theories in the United States of America and Germany. He is author of *Föderalismus als ordnungspolitisches und normatives Prinzip. Das föderative Denken der Deutschen im 19. Jahrhundert* (1987).

INGWER EBSEN, Professor of Law, is a member of the Institut für Öffentliches Recht und Politik at the Westfälische Wilhelms-Universität, Münster. He is author of *Gesetzgebung und "Richtigkeit" der Entscheidung. Eine Untersuchung zur juristischen Methodenlehre* (1974) and of *Das Bundesverfassungsgericht als Element gesellschaftlicher Selbstregulierung. Eine pluralistische Theorie der Verfassungsgerichtsbarkeit im demokratischen Verfassungsstaat* (1985).

ANDREAS FALKE is particularly interested in American urban politics; he is associated with the Cultural Affairs Section of the United States Information Service (USIS) of the Embassy of the United States in Bonn, West Germany. He is author of *Großstadtpolitik und Stadtteilbewegung in den USA. Die Wirksamkeit politischer Strategien gegen den Verfall* (1987).

PAUL FINKELMAN, Assistant Professor of History, is a specialist in American legal and constitutional history at the State University of New York at Binghamton. He is on the editorial boards of the *Journal of the Early Republic* (1985–88) and of the *Law and History Review*. His publications include *An Imperfect Union: Slavery, Federalism, and Comity* (1981); *Slavery in the Courtroom: An Annotated Bibliography of American Cases* (1985); and *The Law of Freedom and Bondage: A Casebook* (1986).

MARIE-LUISE FRINGS, currently coeditor of *American Book Prices Current*, was formerly associated with the University of Cologne; she is author of *Henry Clays American System und die sektionale Kontroverse in den Vereinigten Staaten von Amerika, 1815–1829* (1979) and has coedited, together with E. Angermann and H. Wellenreuther, *New Wine in Old Skins: A Comparative View of Socio-political Structures and Values Affecting the American Revolution* (1976) and with E. Angermann, *Comparing Germany and the United States: Studies in Commemoration of the 150th Anniversary of the Birth of Carl Schurz* (1981).

HANS R. GUGGISBERG, Professor of History at the Swiss University of Basel, is particularly interested in sixteenth-century European religious history and in early modern intellectual history. He is coeditor of the *Archiv für Reformationsgeschichte*; his publications include *Sebastian Castellio im Urteil seiner Nachwelt vom Späthumanismus bis zur Aufklärung* (1956); *Das europäische Mittelalter im amerikanischen Geschichtsdenken des 19. und des frühen 20. Jahrhunderts* (1964); *Alte und Neue Welt in historischer Perspektive* (1973); and *Geschichte der USA* (2d ed. 1988).

JAMES H. HUTSON, formerly assistant editor of the *Benjamin Franklin Papers* and Editor of Publications of the Institute of Early American History and Culture at Williamsburg, is now Director of the Manuscript Division, Library of Congress. He is particularly interested in the history of the American Revolution and the Early Republic. His publications include *Pennsylvania Politics, 1746–1770: The Movement for Royal Government and Its Consequences* (1972); *John Adams and the Diplomacy of the American Revolution* (1980); he is editor of a supplementary volume to *The Records of the Federal Convention of 1787* (1987).

HAROLD MELVIN HYMAN, William P. Hobby Professor of History at Rice University, is particularly interested in nineteenth-century American legal history. His many publications include *To Try Men's Souls: Loyalty Tests in American History* (1959); *Era of the Oath: Northern Loyalty Tests during the Civil War and Reconstruction* (1954); *Soldiers and Spruce: Origins of the Loyal Legion of Loggers and Lumbermen* (1963); *A More Perfect Union: The Impact of the Civil War and Reconstruction on the Constitution* (1973); *Union and Confidence: The 1860s* (1976); *American Singularity: The Seventeen Eighty-Seven Northwest Ordinance, the 1862 Homestead-Morrill Acts, & the 1944 GI Bill* (1986). Together with William M. Wiecek he is coauthor of *Equal Justice under Law: Constitutional Development, 1835–1875* (1981). He is presently working on a biography of Chief Justice Salmon Portland Chase.

LAURA KALMAN, Associate Professor of History at the University of California at Santa Barbara, is a specialist in twentieth-century American legal history. In 1986/87 she was a visiting scholar at the American Bar Foundation. She is author of *Legal Realism at Yale, 1927–1960* (1986).

STANLEY N. KATZ, currently President of the American Council of Learned Societies and former President of the Organization of American Historians, is a senior fellow of the Woodrow Wilson School at Princeton. His main field of research is eighteenth- and nineteenth-century legal and constitutional history. His publications include *Newscastle's New York: Anglo-American Politics, 1732–1753* (1968).

RALPH KETCHAM, Professor of History and Political Science at the Maxwell School of Citizenship and Public Affairs, Syracuse University, was in 1986/87 guest professor at the University of Leiden. He is particularly interested in eighteenth- and early nineteenth-century American intellectual and political history. He is author of *James Madison: A Biography* (1971); *From Colony to Country: The Revolution in American Thought, 1750–1820* (1974); *Presidents Above Party: The First American Presidency, 1789–1829* (1984); and *Individualism and Public Life: A Modern Dilemma* (1987).

GRETE KLINGENSTEIN, a specialist in eighteenth-century Austrian and European History, is professor of early modern history at Graz University, Austria. Since 1974 she has been coeditor of the *Wiener Beiträge zur Geschichte der Neuzeit*. Her publications include *Staatsverwaltung und kirchliche Autorität im 18. Jahrhundert. Das Problem der Zensur in der theresianischen Reform* (1970) and *Der Aufstieg des Hauses Kaunitz. Studien zur Herkunft und Bildung des Staatskanzlers Wenzel Anton* (1975).

DIETHELM KLIPPEL, Professor of German Legal History at the Justus-Liebig University at Gießen, is especially interested in eighteenth- and nineteenth-century legal and constitutional thought. He is author of *Politische Freiheit und Freiheitsrechte im deutschen Naturrecht des 18. Jahrhunderts* (1976) and of *Der zivilrechtliche Schutz des Namens. Eine historische und dogmatische Untersuchung* (1985).

KNUD KRAKAU, a specialist in German and American legal history as well as in twentieth-century international relations, is Professor of History at the John F. Kennedy Institut für Nordamerikastudien, Free University of Berlin. His publications include *Missionsbewußtsein und Völkerrechtsdoktrin in den Vereinigten Staaten von Amerika* (1967); *Die kubanische Revolution und die Monroe Doktrin. Eine Herausforderung der Außenpolitik der Vereinigten Staaten* (1968). He is coeditor (together with H. V. Wedel and A. Göhmann) of *UN-General Assembly Resolutions: A Selection of the Most Important Resolutions during the Period 1949 through 1974* (1975).

THOMAS KRUEGER is a doctoral candidate at the Georg-August University at Göttingen. He is interested in the dialogue between the English public and the House of Commons during the Restoration period.

JÖRG-DETLEF KÜHNE, Professor of German Public Law and Constitutional History at the University of Hanover, is especially interested in nineteenth-century constitutional history. He is author of *Die Abgeordnetenbestechung* (1971); *Grundrechtlicher Wohnungsschutz und Vollstreckungsdurchsuchungen. Ein Beitrag zum Verständnis des Artikels 13 GG* (1980); and *Die Reichsverfassung der Paulskirche. Vorbild und Verwirklichung im späteren deutschen Rechstleben* (1985).

HARTMUT LEHMANN, Professor of History at the University of Kiel (on leave) and presently Director of the German Historical Institute in Washington, DC, is especially interested in early modern religious history. His publications include *Pietismus und weltliche Ordnung in Württemberg vom 17. bis zum 20. Jahrhundert* (1969); *Das Zeitalter des Absolutismus* (1980); and *Martin Luther in the American Imagination* (1988). He is coeditor of the yearbook *Pietismus und Neuzeit*.

GERTRUDE LÜBBE-WOLFF is Director of the Environmental Protection Authority of the City of Bielefeld and teaches law and legal history at the University of Bielefeld. She has published *Rechtsfolgen und Realfolgen. Welche Rolle können Folgenerwägungen in der juristischen Regel- und Begriffsbildung spielen?* (1981) and *Die*

504

Grundrechte als Eingriffsabwehrrechte: Struktur und Reichweite der Eingriffsdogmatik im Bereich staatlicher Leistungen (1988).

FRED L. MORRISON, Professor of Law at the University of Minnesota Law School, is a specialist in international law. In 1982–83 he acted as Counselor on International Law to the U.S. Department of State and in 1984 he was Counselor for the United States in the International Court of Justice. He was visiting professor at the Universities of Bonn and Kiel in 1975/76 and 1986 respectively. He has published *Courts and the Political Process in England* (1973).

HELMUT NEUHAUS, Professor of History at the University Erlangen-Nürnberg, is a specialist in the history of the German Imperial Diet and the old German Empire. He is author of *Reichstag und Supplikationsausschuß. Ein Beitrag zur Reichsverfassungsgeschichte der ersten Hälfte des 16. Jahrhunderts* (1977) and *Reichsständische Repräsentationsformen im 16. Jahrhundert. Reichstag, Reichskreistag, Reichsdeputationstag* (1982). His study of the military constitution of the Old Empire will be published shortly.

PETER S. ONUF, Professor of History at University of Virginia, has worked on American religious, political, and legal problems of the second part of the eighteenth century. He is editor of *Maryland and the Empire, 1773* (1974), and author of *The Origins of the Federal Republic: Jurisdictional Controversies in the United States, 1775–1787* (1983); and of *Statehood and Union: A History of the Northwest Ordinance* (1987).

ROBERT C. POST, Acting Professor at the School of Law, University of California at Berkeley, is particularly interested in constitutional law. In 1978/79 he was law clerk to Justice William J. Brennan Jr. of the U.S. Supreme Court, and from 1980 until 1982 he was practicing as a lawyer. Among other publications he is author of "The Social Foundation of Defamation Law: Reputation and the Constitution," *California Law Review* (1986): 691–743.

GERHARD A. RITTER, Professor of History, University of Munich, is especially interested in English parliamentary history and in German social and political history of the nineteenth and twentieth century. He is a member of the Historical Commission of Westphalia and of the Historical Commission of the Bavarian Academy of Sciences. From 1976 to 1980 he was President of the Verband der Historiker Deutschlands. His many publications include *Die Arbeiterbewegung im Wilhelminischen Reich* (2d ed. 1963); *Deutscher und Britischer Parlamentarismus* (1962); *Parlament und Demokratie in Großbritannien* (1972); *Staat, Arbeiterschaft und Arbeiterbewegung in Deutschland* (1980); *Sozialversicherung in Deutschland und England* (1983); *Die deutschen Parteien, 1830–1914* (1985).

CLAUDIA SCHNURMANN, member of the Department of History of the Georg-August University, Göttingen, is interested in early modern English and American history; her doctoral thesis on special aspects of English-German trade relations in the sixteenth century will soon be published by the German Historical Institute, London.

GERALD STOURZH, Professor of History at the University of Vienna, Austria, is interested in American political thought and legal history as well as in English and Austrian constitutional and legal history. He is a corresponding member of the Austrian Academy of Sciences. He has authored among other works, *Benjamin Franklin and American Foreign Policy* (2d ed. 1969); *Alexander Hamilton and the Idea of Republican Government* (1970); *Vom Widerstandsrecht zur Verfassungsgerichtsbarkeit. Zum Problem der Verfassungswidrigkeit im 18. Jahrhundert* (1974); *Geschichte des Staatsvertrages, 1945–1955* (2d ed. 1980); *Die Gleichberechtigung der Nationalitäten in der Verfassung und Verwaltung Österreichs, 1858–1918* (1985).

CLYDE W. SUMMERS, Professor of Law at the Law School, University of Pennsylvania, is a specialist in American labor law. He is coauthor of *Cases and Materials on Labor Law* (2d ed. 1982) and, with Robert J. Rabin, authored *The Rights of Union Members* (1979).

HERMANN WELLENREUTHER, Professor of History, Georg-August University at Göttingen, Chairman of the Academic

Council of the City of Krefeld, Member of the Board of the German Historical Institute in London, Fellow of the Royal Historical Society, has been publishing on comparative aspects of the early modern Atlantic world, on American colonial history, and on eighteenth-century English parliamentary and German urban history. His publications include *Glaube und Politik in Pennsylvania, 1681–1776* (1972); *Repräsentation und Großgrundbesitz in England, 1730–1770* (1978); *Der Aufstieg des ersten britischen Weltreiches* (1987). He is coauthor and editor of *Göttingen, 1690–1755. Studien zur Sozialgeschichte einer Stadt* (1988). His current research focuses on public rhetoric in eighteenth-century England and on comparative aspects of English and North American parliamentary history.

WILLIAM M. WIECEK, Chester Adgate Congdon Professor of Public Law and Legislation, College of Law, Syracuse University, has been especially interested in nineteenth-century legal problems related to the history of American slavery. His publications include *The Guarantee Clause of the U.S. Constitution* (1972); *The Sources of Antislavery Constitutionalism in America, 1760–1848* (1977); *Equal Justice under Law: Constitutional Development, 1835–1875* (together with Harold M. Hyman, 1982); and *Nuclear America: Military and Civilian Nuclear Power in the United States, 1940–1980* (together with Gerard H. Clarfield, 1984).

Select Bibliography

This bibliography by no means covers the vast body of research on the six themes discussed during the conference. It is a selection designed to offer a fair idea of the body of research in both countries. The user should keep two things in mind. A title listed in one section will not be repeated even if pertinent to another section; thus it is always good policy to glance over the other lists of titles too. Second, since sections three and four focus essentially on the same period, the bibliographies for the German and American sides respectively have been merged.

1. Literature on the Constitution of the Holy Roman Empire and Federalism in the Late Eighteenth Century

Angermeier, Heinz. "Die Reichsregimenter und ihre Staatsidee." *Historische Zeitschrift* 211 (1970): 265–315.

Aretin, Karl Otmar Freiherr von. *Das Reich: Friedensgarantie und europäisches Gleichgewicht, 1648–1806.* Stuttgart, 1986.

———. *Heiliges Römisches Reich, 1776–1806: Reichsverfassung und Staatssouveränität.* Vol. 1. Veröffentlichungen des Instituts für europäische Geschichte Mainz, 38. Wiesbaden, 1967.

Binkley, Robert C. "The Holy Roman Empire versus the United States: Patterns for Constitution Making in Central Europe." In Conyers Read and Richard B. Morris, eds., *The Constitution Reconsidered.* New York, 1968, 271–84.

Böckenförde, Ernst-Wolfgang. "Der Westfälische Frieden und das Bündnisrecht der Reichsstände." *Der Staat* 8 (1969): 449–78.

Conrad, Hermann, ed. *Recht und Verfassung des Reiches in der Zeit Maria Theresias: Die Vorträge zum Unterricht des Erzherzogs Joseph in Natur- und Völkerrecht sowie im deutschen Staats- und Lehnrecht.* Wissenschaftliche Abhandlungen der Arbeitsgemeinschaft für Forschung des Landes Nordrhein-Westfalen, 28. Cologne, 1964.

Feine, Hans Erich. "Zur Verfassungsentwicklung des Heiligen Römischen Reiches seit dem Westfälischen Frieden." *Zeitschrift der Savigny-Stiftung für Rechtsgeschichte, Germanistische Abteilung* 52 (1932): 65–133.

Gagliardo, John G. *Reich and Nation: The Holy Roman Empire as Idea and Reality, 1763–1806.* Bloomington, IN, 1980.

Hartung, Fritz. *Deutsche Verfassungsgeschichte vom 15. Jahrhundert bis zur Gegenwart.* Stuttgart, ⁸1964.

——. *Geschichte des Fränkischen Kreises: Darstellung und Akten.* Vol. 1. Veröffentlichungen der Gesellschaft für fränkische Geschichte, 2, Reihe, 1. Leipzig, 1910.

Hofmann, Hanns Hubert. "Reichskreis und Kreisassoziation: Prolegomena zu einer Geschichte des Fränkischen Kreises, zugleich als Beitrag zur Phänomenologie des deutschen Föderalismus." *Zeitschrift für bayerische Landesgeschichte* 25 (1962): 377–413.

Kunisch, Johannes, ed. *Staatsverfassung und Heeresverfassung in der europäischen Geschichte der frühen Neuzeit.* Historische Forschungen, 28. Berlin, 1986.

Laufs, Adolf. *Der Schwäbische Kreis: Studien über Einungswesen und Reichsverfassung im deutschen Südwesten zu Beginn der Neuzeit.* Untersuchungen zur deutschen Staats- und Rechtsgeschichte, Neue Folge, 16. Aalen, 1971.

Mally, Anton Karl. *Der Österreichische Kreis in der Exekutionsordnung des Römisch-Deutschen Reiches.* Wiener Dissertationen aus dem Gebiete der Geschichte, 8. Vienna, 1967.

Mohnhaupt, Heinz. "Die verfassungsrechtliche Einordnung der Reichskreise in die Reichsorganisation." In Karl Otmar Freiherr von Aretin, ed., *Der Kurfürst von Mainz und die Kreisassoziationen, 1648–1746: Zur verfassungsmäßigen Stellung der Reichskreise nach dem Westfälischen Frieden.* Wiesbaden, 1975, 1–29.

Neuhaus, Helmut. *Reichsständische Repräsentationsformen im 16. Jahrhundert: Reichstag, Reichskreistag, Reichsdeputationstag.* Schriften zur Verfassungsgeschichte, 33. Berlin, 1982.

Schlie, Ulrich. *Johann Stephan Pütters Reichsbegriff.* Göttinger rechtswissenschaftliche Studien, 38. Göttingen, 1961, 33–55.

Schönberg, Rüdiger Freiherr von. *Das Recht der Reichslehen im 18. Jahrhundert: Zugleich ein Beitrag zu den Grundlagen der bundesstaatlichen Ordnung.* Studien und Quellen zur Geschichte des deutschen Verfassungsrechts, Reihe A: Studien, 10. Heidelberg, 1977.

Schubert, Friedrich Hermann. *Die deutschen Reichstage in der Staatslehre der frühen Neuzeit.* Schriftenreihe der Historischen Kommission bei der Bayerischen Akademie der Wissenschaften, 7. Göttingen, 1966.

Sheldon, William F. *The Intellectual Development of Justus Möser: The Growth of a German Patriot.* Osnabrücker Geschichtsquellen und Forschungen, 15. Osnabrück, 1970.

Sicken, Bernhard. *Der Fränkische Reichskreis. Seine Ämter und Einrichtungen im 18. Jahrhundert.* Veröffentlichungen der Gesellschaft für fränkische Geschichte, Fotodruckreihe, 1. Würzburg, 1970.

Vann, James Allen. *The Swabian Kreis: Institutional Growth in the Holy Roman Empire, 1648–1715.* Studies Presented to the International Commission for the History of Representative and Parliamentary Institutions, 53. Brussels, 1975.

Vierhaus, Rudolf. "Land, Staat und Reich in der politischen Vorstellungswelt deutscher Landstände im 18. Jahrhundert." *Historische Zeitschrift* 223 (1976): 40–60.

———. *Staaten und Stände: Vom Westfälischen Frieden bis zum Hubertusburger Frieden, 1648 bis 1763.* Propyläen Geschichte Deutschlands, 5. Berlin, 1984.

Wagner, Wolfgang, ed. *Das Staatsrecht des Heiligen Römischen Reiches Deutscher Nation: Eine Darstellung der Reichsverfassung gegen Ende des 18. Jahrhunderts nach einer Handschrift der Wiener Nationalbibliothek.* Studien und Quellen zur Geschichte des deutschen Verfassungsrechts, Reihe B: Quellen, 1. Karlsruhe, 1968.

Weber, Hermann, ed. *Politische Ordnungen und soziale Kräfte im Alten Reich.* Wiesbaden, 1980.

Wunder, Bernd. "Die Kreisassoziationen, 1672–1748." *Zeitschrift für die Geschichte des Oberrheins* 128 (1980): 167–266.

2. Literature on American Federalism during the American Revolution

Abernethy, Thomas Perkins. *Western Lands and the American Revolution.* New York, 1937.

Adair, Douglass. "'That politics May Be Reduced to a Science': David Hume, James Madison, and the Tenth Federalist." In H. Trevor Colbourn, ed., *Fame and the Founding Fathers: Essays by*

Douglass Adair. New York, 1974, 93–106.

Berkhofer, Robert F., Jr. "The Northwest Ordinance and the Principle of Territorial Evolution." In John Porter Bloom, ed., *The American Territorial System*. Athens, OH, 1973, 45–55.

Bestor, Arthur, "Constitutionalism and the Settlement of the West: The Attainment of Consensus, 1754–1784." In John Porter Bloom, ed., *The American Territorial System*. Athens, OH, 1973, 13–44.

Cooke, Jacob E., ed. *The Federalist*. Middletown, CT, 1961.

Davis, Joseph L. *Sectionalism in American Politics, 1774–1787*. Madison, WI, 1977.

Diamond, Martin, "What the Framers Meant by Federalism." In Robert A. Goldwin, ed., *A Nation of States*. Chicago, IL, 1961, 24–41.

Eblen, Jack Ericson. *The First and Second United States Empires: Governors and Territorial Government, 1784–1912*. Pittsburgh, PA, 1968.

Epstein, David F. *The Political Theory of the Federalist*. Chicago, IL, 1984.

Furtwangler, Albert. *The Authority of Publius*. Ithaca, NY, 1984.

Greene, Jack P. *Peripheries and Center: Constitutional Development in the Extended Polities of the British Empire and the United States, 1607–1788*. Athens, GA, 1986.

Jensen, Merrill. "The Cession of the Old Northwest." *Mississippi Valley Historical Review* 23 (1936): 27–48.

Jensen, Merrill et al., eds. *The Documentary History of the Ratification of the Constitution*. 6 vols. Madison, WI, 1976–.

Levy, Leonard, and Mahoney, Dennis, eds., *The Constitution: A History of Its Framing and Ratification*. New York, 1987.

McCoy, Drew R. *The Elusive Republic: Political Economy in Jeffersonian America*. Chapel Hill, NC, 1980.

———. "James Madison and Visions of American Nationality in the Confederation Period: A Regional Perspective." In Richard Beeman et al., eds., *Beyond Confederation: Origins of the Constitution and American National Identity*. Chapel Hill, NC, 1987, 226–58.

Onuf, Peter S. *The Origins of the Federal Republic: Jurisdictional Controversies in the United States, 1775–1787*. Philadelphia, PA, 1983.

———. *Statehood and Union: A History of the Northwest Ordinance.*

Bloomington, IN, 1987.

Rakove, Jack N. *The Beginnings of National Politics: An Interpretive History of the Continental Congress.* New York, 1979.

Wellenreuther, Hermann. "'First Principles of Freedom' und die Vereinigten Staaten als Kolonialmacht, 1787–1803: Die Northwest Ordinance von 1787 und ihre Verwirklichung im Northwest Territory." In Erich Angermann, ed., "Revolution und Bewahrung: Untersuchungen zum Spannungsgefüge von revolutionärem Selbstverständnis und politischer Praxis in den Vereinigten Staaten von Amerika." *Historische Zeitschrift,* Beiheft 5 (1979): 89–188.

Wiebe, Robert H. *The Opening of American Society.* New York, 1984.

Yarbrough, Jean. "Federalism in the Foundation and Preservation of the American Republic." *Publius* 6 (1976): 43–60.

———. "Representation and Republicanism: Two Views." *Publius* 9 (1979): 77–98.

3. Literature on the Concept of Rule and Government in North America during the American Revolution

Adams, Willi Paul. *Republikanische Verfassung und bürgerliche Freiheit: Die Verfassungen und politischen Ideen der amerikanischen Revolution.* Politica, 37. Darmstadt, 1973. In English: *The First American Constitutions.* Chapel Hill, NC, 1980.

Angermann, Erich. "Ständische Rechtstraditionen in der amerikanischen Unabhängigkeitserklärung." *Historische Zeitschrift* 200 (1965): 61–91.

Bailyn, Bernard. *The Ideological Origins of the American Revolution.* Cambridge, MA, 1967.

Breen, Timothy H. *The Character of a Good Ruler: A Study of Puritan Political Ideas in New England, 1630–1730.* Yale Historical Publications, Miscellany, 92. New Haven, CT, 1970.

Bushman, Richard L. *King and People in Provincial Massachusetts.* Chapel Hill, NC, 1985.

Corwin, Edward S. "The Progress of Constitutional Theory between the Declaration of Independence and the Philadelphia Convention." *American Historical Review* 30 (1925): 511–36.

Cunningham, Noble. *The Process of Government under Jefferson.*

Princeton, NJ, 1978.

Ermacora, Felix, ed. *Der Föderalist von Alexander Hamilton, James Madison und John Jay*. Vienna, 1958.

Greene, Jack P. *Pursuits of Happiness: The Social Development of Early Modern British Colonies and the Formation of American Culture*. Chapel Hill, NC, 1988.

Heideking, Jürgen. *Die Verfassung vor dem Richterstuhl: Vorgeschichte und Ratifizierung der amerikanischen Verfassung, 1787–1791*. Berlin, 1988.

Ketcham, Ralph. *Presidents above Party: The First American Presidency, 1789–1829*. Chapel Hill, NC, 1984.

——. ed. *The Political Thought of Benjamin Franklin*. Indianapolis, IN, 1965.

Lutz, Donald S. *The Origins of American Constitutionalism*. Baton Rouge, LA, 1988.

——. *Popular Consent and Popular Control: Whig Political Theory in the Early State Constitutions*. Baton Rouge, LA, 1980.

——. "The Relative Influence of European Writers on Late Eighteenth Century American Political Thought." *American Political Science Review* 78 (1984): 189–97.

Mcdonald, Forrest. *Novus Ordo Seclorum: The Intellectual Origins of the Constitution*. Lawrence, KS, 1985.

Meyer, Reinhold. *Classica Americana: The Greek and Roman Heritage in the United States*. Detroit, MI, 1984.

Morgan, Edmund S. *Governing Fictions: The Rise of Popular Sovereignty in England and America*. New York, 1988.

Stourzh, Gerald. *Alexander Hamilton and the Idea of Republican Government*. Stanford, CA, 1970.

White, Morton. *The Philosophy of the American Revolution*. New York, 1978.

Wood, Gordon S. *Creation of the American Republic, 1776–1787*. Chapel Hill, NC, 1969.

4. Literature on the Concept of Rule and the Image of the Ruler in Europe and Germany

Aretin, Karl Otmar Freiherr von, ed. *Der aufgeklärte Absolutismus*. Neue Wissenschaftliche Bibliothek. Cologne, 1974.

Bernard, Paul P. *Joseph II and Bavaria: Two Eighteenth Century*

Attempts at German Unification. The Hague, 1965.

Brunschwig, Henri. *Gesellschaft und Romantik in Preußen im 18. Jahrhundert: Die Krise des preußischen Staates am Ende des 18. Jahrhunderts und die Entstehung der romantischen Mentalität.* Frankfurt/Main, 1975. In French: *La crise de l'état prussien à la fin du XVIIIe siècle et la genèse de la mentalité romantique.* Paris, 1947.

Büsch, Otto. *Militärsystem und Sozialleben im alten Preußen, 1713–1807: Die Anfänge der sozialen Militarisierung der preußisch-deutschen Gesellschaft.* Veröffentlichungen der Historischen Kommission zu Berlin, 7. Berlin, 1962.

Conrad, Hermann. *Das allgemeine Landrecht von 1794 als Grundgesetz des friderizianischen Staates.* Schriftenreihe der Juristischen Gesellschaft Berlin, 22. Berlin, 1965.

——. "Reichsstaatliche Bestrebungen im Absolutismus Preußens und Österreichs am Ende des 18. Jahrhunderts." In Walther Hubatsch, ed., *Absolutismus.* Wege der Forschung, 314. Darmstadt, 1973, 310–60.

Gerhard, Dietrich, ed. *Ständische Vertretungen in Europa im 17. und 18. Jahrhundert.* Veröffentlichungen des Max-Planck-Instituts für Geschichte, 27. Göttingen, 1969.

Klingenstein, Grete. *Der Aufstieg des Hauses Kaunitz: Studien zur Herkunft und Bildung des Staatskanzlers Wenzel Anton.* Schriftenreihe der Historischen Kommission bei der Bayerischen Akademie der Wissenschaften, 12. Göttingen, 1975.

Klippel, Diethelm. *Politische Freiheit und Freiheitsrechte im deutschen Naturrecht des 18. Jahrhunderts.* Paderborn, 1976.

Klueting, Harm. *Die Lehre von der Macht der Staaten. Das außenpolitische Machtproblem in der politischen Wissenschaft und in der praktischen Politik im 18. Jahrhundert.* Historische Forschungen, 29. Berlin, 1986.

Koselleck, Reinhart. *Kritik und Krise: Eine Studie zur Pathogenese der bürgerlichen Welt.* Freiburg, 1959. New ed. Frankfurt/Main, 1979.

Link, Christoph. *Herrschaftsordnung und bürgerliche Freiheit: Grenzen der Staatsgewalt in der älteren deutschen Staatslehre.* Wiener Rechtsgeschichtliche Arbeiten, 12. Vienna, 1979.

Mehring, Franz. "Friedrichs aufgeklärter Despotismus." In Otto Büsch and Wolfgang Neugebauer, eds., *Moderne preußische Geschichte, 1648–1947: Eine Anthologie.* Veröffentlichungen der Historischen Kommission zu Berlin, 52. 3 vols. Berlin, 1981, 1:

152–53.

Raeff, Marc. *The Well-Ordered Police State: Social and Institutional Change through Law in the Germanies and Russia, 1600–1800.* New Haven, CT, 1983.

Schieder, Theodor. *Friedrich der Große: Ein Königtum der Widersprüche.* Frankfurt/Main, 1983.

——. "Friedrich der Große und Machiavelli: Das Dilemma von Machtpolitik und Aufklärung." *Historische Zeitschrift* 234 (1982): 265–94.

Stollberg-Rilinger, Barbara. *Der Staat als Maschine: Zur politischen Metaphorik des absoluten Fürstenstaats.* Historische Forschungen, 30. Berlin, 1986.

Stolleis, Michael. *Reichspublizistik und Policeywissenschaft, 1600–1800.* Geschichte des öffentlichen Rechts in Deutschland, 1. Munich, 1988.

Wagner, Wolfgang, ed. *Das Staatsrecht des Heiligen Römischen Reiches Deutscher Nation: Eine Darstellung der Reichsverfassung gegen Ende des 18. Jahrhunderts nach einer Handschrift der Wiener Nationalbibliothek.* Karlsruhe, 1968.

Wandruszka, Adam. *Leopold II: Erzherzog von Österreich, Großherzog von Toskana, König von Ungarn und Böhmen, Römischer Kaiser.* 2 vols. Vienna, 1963–65.

Willoweit, Dietmar. *Rechtsgrundlagen der Territorialgewalt: Landesobrigkeit, Herrschaftsrechte, und Territorium in der Rechtswissenschaft der Neuzeit.* Forschungen zur deutschen Rechtsgeschichte, 11. Cologne, 1975.

5. Literature on the Development of the American Constitution between 1830 and 1870

Angermann, Erich. "Abraham Lincoln und die Erneuerung der nationalen Identität der Vereinigten Staaten von Amerika." *Historische Zeitschrift* 239 (1984): 77–109.

Baer, Judith A. *Equality under the Constitution: Reclaiming the Fourteenth Amendment.* Ithaca, NY, 1983.

Berger, Raoul. *Government by Judiciary: The Transformation of the Fourteenth Amendment.* Cambridge, MA, 1977.

Bestor, Arthur. "State Sovereignty and Slavery: A Reinterpretation of Proslavery Constitutional Doctrine, 1846–1860." *Journal of the Illinois State Historical Society* 54 (1961): 117–80.

Bickel, Alexander M. "The Original Understanding and the Segregation Decision." *Harvard Law Review* 69 (1955): 1–65.

Fairman, Charles. "Does the Fourteenth Amendment Incorporate the Bill of Rights? Original Understanding." *Stanford Law Review* 2 (1949): 5–139. Also in Charles Fairman and Stanley Morrison. *The Fourteenth Amendment and the Bill of Rights: The Incorporation Theory.* New York, 1970.

——. *Reconstruction and Reunion, 1864–88.* History of the Supreme Court of the United States, 6. New York, 1971.

Fehrenbacher, Don E. *The Dred Scott Case: Its Significance in American Law and Politics.* New York, 1978.

Finkelman, Paul. "Antebellum States' Rights, North and South." In Kermit Hall and James Ely, eds., *An Uncertain Tradition: Constitutionalism and the History of the South.* Athens, GA, 1988.

——. *An Imperfect Union: Slavery, Federalism, and Comity.* Chapel Hill, NC, 1981.

——. "Prelude to the Fourteenth Amendment: Black Legal Rights in the Antebellum North." *Rutgers Law Journal* 17 (1986): 415–82.

——. ed. *Slavery, Race, and the American Legal System, 1700–1872.* New York, 1987.

Flack, Horace Edgar. *The Adoption of the Fourteenth Amendment.* Johns Hopkins University Studies in Historical and Political Science, 26. Baltimore, MD, 1908. Repr. Gloucester, MA, 1965.

Freehling, William W. *Prelude to Civil War: The Nullification Controversy in South Carolina, 1816–1836.* New York, 1967.

Gerteis, Louis. *Morality and Utility in American Antislavery Reform.* Chapel Hill, NC, 1987.

Gilmore, Grant. *The Ages of American Law.* Yale Law School, Storrs Lectures on Jurisprudence 1974. New Haven, CT, 1977.

Hyman, Harold Melvin. *American Singularity: The 1787 Northwest Ordinance, the 1862 Homestead-Morrill Acts, and the 1944 GI Bill.* The Richard B. Russel Lectures, 5. Athens, GA, 1986.

——. *Lincoln's Reconstruction: Neither Failure of Vision Nor Vision of Failure.* Fort Wayne, IN, 1980.

——. *A More Perfect Union: The Impact of the Civil War and Reconstruction on the Constitution.* New York, 1973.

——. *Quiet Past and Stormy Present? War Powers in American History: Bicentennial Essays on the Constitution.* Washington, DC, 1986.

Hyman, Harold Melvin, and Wiecek, William Michael. *Equal Justice under Law: Constitutional Development, 1835–1875.* New York, 1982.

Johnson, John. "Creativity and Adaptation: A Reassessment of American Jurisprudence, 1801–1857 and 1908–1940." *Rutgers-Camden Law Journal* 7 (1976): 625–47.

Kaczorowski, Robert. *The Politics of Judicial Interpretation: The Federal Courts, Department of Justice, and Civil Rights, 1866–76.* New York, 1985.

Kalman, Laura. *Legal Realism at Yale, 1927–1960.* Chapel Hill, NC, 1986.

Kammen, Michael G. *A Machine That Would Go of Itself.* New York, 1986.

Miller, Arthur Selwyn. *Social Change and Fundamental Law: America's Evolving Constitution.* Contributions in American Studies, 41. Westport, CT, 1979.

Morris, Thomas D. *Free Men All: The Personal Liberty Laws of the North, 1780–1861.* Baltimore, MD, 1974.

Palmer, Robert. "The Parameters of Constitutional Reconstruction: Slaughter-House (*Slaughter-House* Cases, 83 U.S. 36), Cruikshank (United States v. Cruikshank, 92 U.S. 542), and the Fourteenth Amendment." *University of Illinois Law Review* (1984): 739–70.

Phillips, Ulrich B. *Georgia and State Rights.* 1902. Repr. Yellow Spring, OH, 1968.

Scheiber, Harry N. "Federalism and Legal Process: Historical and Contemporary Analysis of the American System." *Law & Society Review* 14 (1980): 663–722.

Siegan, Bernard. *The Supreme Court's Constitution.* New Brunswick, NJ, 1987.

Smith, James Morton. *Freedom's Fetters: The Alien and Sedition Laws and American Civil Liberties.* Ithaca, NY, 1956.

Stampp, Kenneth. *And the War Came: The North and the Secession Crisis, 1860–1861.* Baton Rouge, LA, 1950. Repr. 1970.

Van Deusen, Glyndon G. *William Henry Seward.* New York, 1967.

Wiecek, William M. *The Sources of Antislavery Constitutionalism.* Ithaca, NY, 1978.

Wofford, John G. "The Blinding Light: The Uses of History in Constitutional Interpretation." *University of Chicago Law Review* 31 (1964): 502–33.

6. Literature on the Constitutional History of Germany, 1830–1875

Angermann, Erich. "Der deutsche Frühkonstitutionalismus und das amerikanische Vorbild." *Historische Zeitschrift* 219 (1974): 1–32.

——. *Robert von Mohl, 1799–1875: Leben und Werk eines altliberalen Staatsgelehrten.* Politica, 8. Neuwied, 1962.

Becker, Otto. *Bismarcks Ringen um Deutschlands Gestaltung.* Heidelberg, 1958.

Böckenförde, Ernst-Wolfgang. *Die verfassungstheoretische Unterscheidung von Staat und Gesellschaft als Bedingung der individuellen Freiheit.* Opladen, 1973.

Boldt, Hans. "Deutscher Konstitutionalismus und Bismarckreich." In Michael Stürmer, ed., *Das kaiserliche Deutschland.* Düsseldorf, 1970, 119–42.

Botzenhart, Manfred. *Deutscher Parlamentarismus, 1848–1850.* Düsseldorf, 1977.

Carol, Rose. "The Issue of Parliamentary Suffrage at the Frankfurt National Assembly." *Central European History* 5 (1972): 127–47.

Conze, Werner. "Das Spannungsfeld von Staat und Gesellschaft im Vormärz." In Werner Conze, ed., *Staat und Gesellschaft im deutschen Vormärz, 1815–1848.* Stuttgart, 1962, 207–69.

Deuerlein, Ernst. *Föderalismus.* Munich, 1972.

Dreyer, Michael. *Föderalismus als ordnungspolitisches und normatives Prinzip: Das föderative Denken der Deutschen im 19. Jahrhundert.* Frankfurt/Main, 1987.

Ellwein, Thomas. *Der Einfluß des nordamerikanischen Bundesverfassungsrechts auf die Verhandlungen der Frankfurter Nationalversammlung im Jahre 1848/49.* Erlanger juristische Dissertation, 1950, manuscript.

Eyck, Frank. *Deutschlands große Hoffnung: Die Frankfurter Nationalversammlung, 1848–49.* Munich, 1973. In English: *The Frankfurt Parliament, 1848–1849.* London, 1968.

——. *The Revolutions of 1848–49.* Edinburgh, 1972.

Fischer, Heinz, and Silvestri, Gerhard, eds. *Texte zur österreichischen Verfassungsgeschichte.* Vienna, 1970.

Franz, Eckart G. *Das Amerikabild der deutschen Revolution von 1848/49.* Heidelberg, 1958.

Gall, Lothar. *Bismarck: Der weiße Revolutionär.* Frankfurt/Main,

1980.

———. *Der Liberalismus als regierende Partei: Das Großherzogtum Baden zwischen Restauration und Reichsgründung.* Wiesbaden, 1968.

Gierke, Otto von. "German Constitutional Law in Its Relation to the American Constitution." *Harvard Law Review* 23 (1909/10): 273–90.

Hamerow, Theodore S. "History and the German Revolution of 1848." *American Historical Review* 60 (1954): 27–44.

———. *Restauration, Revolution, Reaction: Economics and Politics in Germany, 1815–1871.* Princeton, NJ, 1958.

Häusler, Wolfgang. "Vom Standrecht zum Rechsstaat: Politik und Justiz in Österreich (1848–1867)." In Erika Weinzierl and Karl R. Stadler, eds., *Justiz und Zeitgeschichte.* Vienna, 1977, 1–42.

Hawgood, John A. *Political and Economic Relations between the United States of America and the German Provisional Central Government in Frankfurt am Main in 1848–49.* Heidelberg, 1928.

Hespe, Klaus. *Die Entwicklung der Staatszwecklehre in der deutschen Staatsrechtswissenschaft des 19. Jahrhunderts.* Cologne, 1964.

Hoke, Rudolf. "Verfassungsgerichtsbarkeit in deutschen Ländern in der Tradition der deutschen Staatsgerichtsbarkeit." In Klaus Stern and Christian Starck, eds., *Landesverfassungsgerichtsbarkeit.* Vol. 1. Baden-Baden, 1983.

Huber, Ernst Rudolf. *Deutsche Verfassungsgeschichte seit 1789.* 3 vols. Stuttgart, ²1975–78.

———. "Grundrechte im Bismarckschen Reichssystem." In *Festschrift Ulrich Scheuner.* Berlin, 1973, 161–81.

———. ed. *Dokumente zur deutschen Verfassungsgeschichte.* 2 vols. Stuttgart, ³1978–86.

Hübner, Rudolf. "Der Verfassungsentwurf der 17 Vertrauensmänner: Ein Beitrag zur Vorgeschichte des Frankfurter Verfassungswerkes." In *Festschrift Eduard Rosenthal.* Jena, 1923, 109–68.

King-Hall, Stephen, and Ullmann, Richard K. *German Parliaments: A Study of the Development of Representative Institutions in Germany.* New York, 1954.

Klippel, Diethelm. "Persönlichkeit und Freiheit: Das 'Recht der Persönlichkeit' in der Entwicklung der Freiheitsrechte im 18. und 19. Jahrhundert." In Günter Birtsch, ed., *Grund- und Freiheitsrechte von der ständischen zur spätbürgerlichen Gesellschaft.* Göttingen, 1987, 269–90.

Koselleck, Reinhart. *Preußen zwischen Reform und Revolution.* Stuttgart, ³1981.

Kraehe, Enno E. *History of the German Confederation, 1850–1866.* Minneapolis, MN, 1948.

Krieger, Leonard. *The German Idea of Freedom.* Boston, MA, 1957. Repr. Chicago, IL, 1972.

Kühne, Jörg-Detlef. "Die Bedeutung der Genossenschaftslehre für die moderne Verfassung." *Zeitschrift für Parlamentsfragen* 15 (1984): 552–70.

———. *Die Reichsverfassung der Paulskirche.* Frankfurt/Main, 1985.

Langewiesche, Dieter. *Liberalismus und Demokratie in Württemberg zwischen Revolution und Reichsgründung.* Düsseldorf, 1974.

Lewis, John D. *The Genossenschafts-Theory of Otto von Gierke: A Study in Political Thought.* Madison, WI, 1935.

Moltmann, Günter. *Atlantische Blockpolitik im 19. Jahrhundert.* Düsseldorf, 1973.

Mosse, Werner E. *The European Powers and the German Question, 1848–1871.* New York, 1969.

Nipperdey, Thomas. *Deutsche Geschichte, 1800–1866.* Munich, 1983.

Noyes, Paul H. *Organization and Revolution: Working-Class Associations in the German Revolution of 1848/49.* Princeton, NJ, 1966.

Pflanze, Otto. *Bismarck and the Development of Germany: The Period of Unification, 1815–1871.* Princeton, NJ, 1963.

———. ed. *Innenpolitische Probleme des Bismarck-Reiches.* Schriften des Historischen Kollegs, 2. Munich, 1983.

Rauh, Manfred. *Föderalismus und Parlamentarismus im Wilhelminischen Reich.* Düsseldorf, 1973.

Rimscha, Wolfgang von. *Die Grundrechte im süddeutschen Konstitutionalismus.* Cologne, 1973.

Ritter, Gerhard A., ed. *Regierung, Bürokratie, und Parlament in Preußen und Deutschland 1848 bis zur Gegenwart.* Düsseldorf, 1983.

Robinson, James Harvey. *The German Bundesrath.* Philadelphia, PA, 1891.

Sheehan, James J. *German Liberalism in the Nineteenth Century.* Chicago, IL, 1978.

Siemann, Wolfram. *Die deutsche Revolution von 1848/49.* Frankfurt/Main, 1985.

Siemers, Bruno. "Die Vereinigten Staaten und die deutsche Einigung." In *Geschichtliche Kräfte und Entscheidungen: Festschrift Otto Becker*. Wiesbaden, 1954, 176–205.

Stourzh, Gerald. *Die Gleichberechtigung der Nationalstaaten in der Verfassung und Verwaltung Österreichs, 1848–1918*. Vienna, 1985.

Trefousse, Hans L. "The German-American Immigrants and the Newly Founded Reich." In Frank Trommler and Joseph McVeigh, eds., *America and the Germans*. 2 vols. Philadelphia, PA, 1985, 1: 160–75.

Ullner, Rudolf. *Die Idee des Föderalismus im Jahrzehnt der deutschen Einigungskriege*. Lübeck, 1965.

Valentin, Veit. *Geschichte der deutschen Revolution von 1848/49*. 2 vols. 1930/31. Repr. Cologne, 1970. A shorter English translation: *1848: Chapters of German History*. London, 1940.

Windell, Georg G. *The Catholics and German Unity, 1866–71*. Minneapolis, MN, 1954.

Wittke, Carl. *Refugees of the Revolution*. Philadelphia, PA, 1952.

Wollstein, Günter. *Deutsche Geschichte, 1848/49*. Stuttgart, 1986.

Zeydel, Edwin Hermann, ed. *Constitutions of the German Empire and German States*. Washington DC, 1919. Repr. Wilmington, DE, 1974.

7. Literature on the Protection of Fundamental and Constitutional Rights in Germany, 1870–1945

Adamovich, Ludwig. *Die Prüfung der Gesetze und Verordnungen durch den österreichischen Verfassungsgerichtshof*. Leipzig, 1923.

Anschütz, Gerhard. *Die Verfassung des Deutschen Reichs vom 11. August 1919: Ein Kommentar für Wissenschaft und Praxis*. Berlin, [14]1933. Repr. Darmstadt, 1965.

Apelt, Willibald. *Geschichte der Weimarer Verfassung*. Munich, [2]1964.

Buschmann, Arno. "100 Jahre Gründungstag des Reichsgerichts." *Neue Juristische Wochenschrift* (1979): 1966–73.

Fangmann, Helmut D. *Justiz gegen Demokratie*. Frankfurt/Main, 1979.

Fraenkel, Ernst. "Die Krise des Rechtsstaats und die Justiz" (1931). In *Zur Soziologie der Klassenjustiz und Aufsätze zur Verfassungskrise, 1931–1932*. Darmstadt, 1968, 42–56.

Gusy, Christoph. *Richterliches Prüfungsrecht*. Berlin, 1985.

Haller, Herbert. *Die Prüfung von Gesetzen.* Vienna, 1979.

Hempel, Norbert. *Richterleitbilder in der Weimarer Republik.* Frankfurt/Main, 1978.

Klein, Friedrich. "Verordnungsermächtigungen nach deutschem Verfassungsrecht." In W.E. Genzer and W. Einbeck, eds., *Die Übertragung rechtsetzender Gewalt im Rechtsstaat.* Frankfurt/Main, 1952, 7–78.

Lübbe-Wolff, Gertrude. "Über das Fehlen von Grundrechten in Hegels Rechtsphilosophie." In Hans-Christian Lucas and Otto Pöggeler, eds., *Hegels Rechtsphilosophie im Zusammenhang der europäischen Verfassungsgeschichte.* Stuttgart, 1986, 421–46.

———. "Das wohlerworbene Recht als Grenze der Gesetzgebung im neunzehnten Jahrhundert." *Zeitschrift der Savigny-Stiftung für Rechtsgeschichte, Germanistische Abteilung* 103 (1986): 104–39.

Maurer, Hartmut. "Das richterliche Prüfungsrecht zur Zeit der Weimarer Verfassung." *Die öffentliche Verwaltung* (1968): 683–88.

Neumann, Franz. *Die Herrschaft des Gesetzes.* 1936. Repr. Frankfurt/Main, 1980.

Perels, Joachim. *Kapitalismus und politische Demokratie: Privatrechtssystem und Gesellschaftsstruktur in der Weimarer Republik.* Frankfurt/Main, 1973.

Rittstieg, Helmut. *Eigentum als Verfassungsproblem.* Darmstadt, 1975.

Rümelin, Max. *Die Gleichheit vor dem Gesetz.* Tübingen, 1928.

Scheuner, Ulrich. "Die rechtliche Tragweite der Grundrechte in der deutschen Verfassungsentwicklung." In *Festschrift für Ernst Rudolf Huber.* Göttingen, 1973, 139–65.

Simons, Walter. "Das Reichsgericht." In Julius Magnus, ed., *Die höchsten Gerichte der Welt.* Leipzig, 1929, 1–28.

Unruh, Georg Christoph von. "Nordamerikanische Einflüsse auf die deutsche Verfassungsentwicklung." *Deutsches Verwaltungsblatt* (1976): 455–64.

Wahl, Rainer. "Rechtliche Wirkungen und Funktionen der Grundrechte im deutschen Konstitutionalismus." *Der Staat* 18 (1979): 321–48.

Wendenburg, Helge. *Die Debatte um die Verfassungsgerichtsbarkeit und der Methodenstreit der Staatsrechtslehre in der Weimarer Republik.* Göttingen, 1984.

8. Literature on the Protection of Fundamental and Constitutional Rights in the United States, 1870–1960

Berger, Raoul. *Government by Judiciary: The Transformation of the Fourteenth Amendment.* Cambridge, MA, 1977.

Berns, Walter. "The Constitution as Bill of Rights." In Robert A. Goldwin and William A. Schambra, eds., *How Does the Constitution Secure Rights?* Washington, DC, 1985, 50–73.

Brest, Paul. "The Fundamental Rights Controversy: The Essential Contradictions of Normative Constitutional Scholarship." *Yale Law Journal* 90 (1981): 1063–1109.

Corwin, Edward S. *The "Higher Law" Background of American Constitutional Law.* Ithaca, NY, 1963, reprint of the article in the *Harvard Law Review* (1928).

Dahl, Robert A. "Decision-Making in a Democracy: The Supreme Court as a National Policy-Maker." *Journal of Public Law* 6 (1957): 279–95.

Dennis, Everette E.; Gilmor, Donald; and Grey, David L., eds. *Justice Hugo Black and the First Amendment.* Ames, IA, 1978.

Ely, John Hart. *Democracy and Distrust: A Theory of Judicial Review.* Cambridge, MA, 1980.

Hutson, James H. "The Creation of the Constitution: The Integrity of the Documentary Record." *Texas Law Review* 65 (1986/87): 1–39.

Kammen, Michael. *Spheres of Liberty: Changing Perceptions of Liberty in American Culture.* Madison, WI, 1986.

Levy, Leonard W. *Against the Law: The Nixon Court and Criminal Justice.* New York, 1974.

Magee, James J. *Mr. Justice Black: Absolutist on the Court.* Charlottesville, VA, 1980.

Mason, Alpheus T. "The Burger Court in Historical Perspective." *Political Science Quarterly* 89 (1974): 27–45.

——. *Harlan Fiske Stone: Pillar of the Law.* New York, 1956.

Meiklejohn, Alexander. "The First Amendment Is an Absolute." In Philip B. Kurland, ed., *Free Speech and Association: The Supreme Court and the First Amendment.* Chicago, IL, 1975, 1–22.

Purcell, Edward A., Jr. *The Crisis of Democratic Theory: Scientific Naturalism and the Problem of Values.* New York, 1973.

Shapiro, Martin W. *Freedom of Choice: The Supreme Court and Judicial Review.* Englewood Cliffs, NJ, 1966.

Swindler, William F. "The Court, the Constitution, and Chief Justice Burger." *Vanderbilt Law Review* 27 (1974): 443–74.

Tribe, Laurence H. *American Constitutional Law*. Mineola, NY, 1988.

——. *Constitutional Choices*. Cambridge, MA, 1985.

Twining, William. *Karl Llewellyn and the Realist Movement*. London, 1973.

White, G. Edward. "The Evolution of Reasoned Elaboration: Jurisprudential Criticism and Social Change." *Virginia Law Review* 59 (1973): 279–302.

Wiecek, William M. "The Imperial Judiciary' in Historical Perspective." *Yearbook of the Supreme Court Historical Society* (1984): 61–89.

Witt, Elder. *A Different Justice: Reagan and the Supreme Court*. Washington, DC, 1986.

Wofford, John G. "The Blinding Light: The Uses of History in Constitutional Interpretation." *University of Chicago Law Review* 31 (1963/64): 502–33.

9. Literature on Constitutions and Change in Industrial Societies in Germany, 1900–1980

Arnim, Hans Herbert von. *Gemeinwohl und Gruppeninteressen: Die Durchsetzungsschwäche allgemeiner Interessen in der pluralistischen Demokratie*. Frankfurt/Main, 1977.

Benda, Ernst. *Grundrechtswidrige Gesetze: Ein Beitrag zu den Ursachen verfassungsgerichtlicher Beanstandung*. Studien und Materialen zur Verfassungsgerichtsbarkeit, 15. Baden-Baden, 1979.

Brox, Hans, and Rüthers, Bernd. *Arbeitskampfrecht: Ein Handbuch für die Praxis*. Stuttgart, ²1982.

Bryde, Brun-Otto von. *Verfassungsentwicklung: Stabilität und Dynamik im Verfassungsrecht der Bundesrepublik Deutschland*. Baden-Baden, 1982.

Ebsen, Ingwer. *Das Bundesverfassungsgericht als Element gesellschaftlicher Selbstregulierung: Eine pluralistische Theorie der Verfassungsgerichtsbarkeit im demokratischen Verfassungsstaat*. Berlin, 1985.

Kommers, Donald P. *Judicial Politics in West Germany: A Study of the Federal Constitutional Court*. Sage Series on Politics and the Legal Order, 5. Beverly Hills, CA, 1976.

Landfried, Christine. *Bundesverfassungsgericht und Gesetzgeber: Wirkungen der Verfassungsrechtsprechung auf parlamentarischer Willensbildung und soziale Realität.* Baden–Baden, 1982.

Leminsky, Gerhard, and Otto, Bernd. *Politik und Programm des Deutschen Gewerkschaftsbundes.* Cologne, 1974.

Lipphardt, Hanns Rudolf. *Die Gleichheit der politischen Parteien vor der öffentlichen Gewalt: Eine kritische Studie zur Wahl- und Parteienrechtsjudikatur des Bundesverfassungsgerichts.* Schriften zum öffentlichen Recht, 271. Berlin, 1975.

Mommsen, Wolfgang J., ed. *Die Entstehung des Wohlfahrtsstaates in Großbritannien und in Deutschland, 1850–1950.* Veröffentlichungen des Deutschen Historischen Instituts London, 11. Stuttgart, 1982.

Naphtali, Fritz, ed. *Wirtschaftsdemokratie: Ihr Wesen, Weg und Ziel.* Protokoll des Hamburger Kongresses des Allgemeinen Deutschen Gewerkschaftsbundes, 1928. Hamburg, 1966.

Ritter, Gerhard A., ed. *Geschichte der Arbeiter und der Arbeiterbewegung in Deutschland seit dem Ende des 18. Jahrhunderts.* Vol. 1–. Berlin, 1984–.

Schlaich, Klaus. *Das Bundesverfassungsgericht: Stellung, Verfahren, Entscheidungen.* Munich 1985.

Schlüter, Wilfried. *Das Obiter Dictum: Die Grenzen höchstrichterlicher Entscheidungsbegründung, dargestellt an Beispielen aus der Rechtsprechung des Bundesarbeitsgerichtes.* Schriften des Instituts für Arbeits- und Wirtschaftsrecht der Universität zu Köln, 29. Munich, 1973.

Soergel, Werner. *Konsensus und Interessen: Eine Studie zur Entstehung des Grundgesetzes für die Bundesrepublik Deutschland.* Frankfurter Studien zur Wissenschaft von der Politik, 5. Stuttgart, 1969.

Teuteberg, Hans-Jürgen. *Geschichte der industriellen Mitbestimmung.* Tübingen, 1961.

Vilmar, Fritz. "Wirtschaftsdemokratie: Theoretische und praktische Ansätze, entwickelt auf der Basis des gewerkschaftlichen Grundsatzprogrammes in der BRD." In Fritz Vilma, ed., *Menschenwürde im Betrieb: Modelle der Humanisierung und Demokratisierung der industriellen Arbeitswelt.* 2 vols. Reinbeck, 1973–75.

Weber, Werner. *Spannungen und Kräfte im westdeutschen Verfassungssystem.* Berlin, ³1970.

10. Literature on Constitutions and Change in Industrial Society in the United States, 1900–1980

Auerbach, Jerold S. *Labor and Liberty: The La Follete Committee and the New Deal*. Indianapolis, IN, 1966.

Baer, Judith A. *The Chains of Protection: The Judicial Response to Women's Labor Legislation*. Westport, CT, 1978.

Belush, Bernard. *The Failure of the NRA*. New York, 1975.

Berger, Monroe. *Equality by Statute: Legal Controls over Group Discrimination*. New York, 1952.

Black, Samuel Bruce. *Free Institutions and the Quest for Security: The Development of Workmen's Compensation in the U.S.A.* New York, 1951.

Cortner, Richard C. *The Wagner Act Cases*. Knoxville, TN, 1964.

Cox, Archibald. *The Warren Court: Constitutional Decisions as an Instrument of Reform*. Cambridge, MA, 1975.

Derber, M. *The American Idea of Industrial Democracy, 1865–1965*. N.p., 1970.

Groat, George Corham. *Attitude of American Courts in Labour Cases: A Study in Social Legislation*. Columbia University Studies, 42, no. 108. New York, 1911.

Hays, Paul Raymond. "Federalism and Labor Relations: A Case Study of Congressional Responsibility." In Arthur Whittier Macmahon, ed., *Federalism, Mature and Emergent*. Garden City, NY, 1955, 235–53.

Kutler, Stanley I. "Labor, the Clayton Act, and the Supreme Court." *Labor History* 3 (1962): 19–38.

Lubove, Roy. *The Struggle for Social Security, 1900–1935*. Cambridge, MA, 1968.

Montgomery, David. *Workers' Control in America*. Cambridge, MA, 1979.

Nelson, Daniel. *Unemployment Insurance: The American Experience, 1915–1935*. Madison, WI, 1969.

Rabban, David. "Has the NLRA Hurt Labor?" *University of Chicago Law Review* 54 (1987): 407–31.

Semonche, John E. *Charting the Future: The Supreme Court Responds to a Changing Society, 1890–1920*. Westport, CT, 1978.

Shapiro, Martin M. "The Court and Economic Rights." In M. Judd Harmon, ed., *Essays on the Constitution of the United States*. Port Washington, NY, 1978, 74–98.

Select Bibliography

Smith, Russell A. "The Evolution of the 'Duty to Bargain' Concept in American Law." *Michigan Law Review* 39 (1941): 1065–1108.

Summers, Clyde W. "Industrial Democracy: America's Unfulfilled Promise." *Cleveland State Law Review* 28 (1979): 29–49.

——. "Worker Participation in the U.S. and West Germany: A Comparative Study from an American Perspective." *American Journal of Comparative Law* 28 (1980): 367–92.

Swindler, William F. *Court and Constitution in the Twentieth Century.* 3 vols. Indianapolis, IN, 1969–74.

Tomlins, Christopher. *The State and the Unions.* Cambridge, MA, 1985.

"U.S. Labor Law and the Future of Labor-Management Cooperation." *First Interim Report, U.S. Department of Labor.* February 1987.

Vile, M.J.C. "Federalism and Labor Regulation in the United States." *Political Science Quarterly* 71 (1956): 223–41.